Farnham

ECONOMICS FOR MANAGERS

2010 Custom Edition

Taken from:
Economics for Managers, Second Edition
by Paul G. Farnham

STRAYER
U N I V E R S I T Y

Learning Solutions

New York   Boston   San Francisco
London   Toronto   Sydney   Tokyo   Singapore   Madrid
Mexico City   Munich   Paris   Cape Town   Hong Kong   Montreal

Cover Art: Courtesy of Glow Images/Getty Images.

Taken from:

Economics for Managers, Second Edition
by Paul G. Farnham
Copyright © 2010, 2005 by Pearson Education, Inc.
Published by Prentice Hall
Upper Saddle River, New Jersey 07458

Pearson Learning Solutions, 501 Boylston Street, Suite 900, Boston, MA 02116
A Pearson Education Company
www.pearsoned.com

Printed in the United States of America

5 6 7 8 9 10 V313 14 13 12 11 10

2009400154

DC

ISBN 10: 0-558-49627-X
ISBN 13: 978-0-558-49627-2

Dedication

To my friend and colleague, Dr. Jon Mansfield, who continues to excel at teaching economics for managers.

Brief Contents

Contents

Preface

The second edition of *Economics for Managers* builds on the strengths of the first edition while updating all examples and streamlining the macroeconomic analysis. *Economics for Managers*, Second Edition, does not attempt to cover all the topics in traditional principles of economics texts or in intermediate microeconomic and macroeconomic theory texts. As in the first edition, the goal of this text is to present the fundamental ideas of microeconomics and macroeconomics and then integrate them from a managerial decision-making perspective into a framework that can be used in a single-semester course for Master of Business Administration (MBA), Executive MBA (EMBA), and other business students.

Most micro/managerial economics and intermediate macroeconomics texts are written for economics students who will spend an entire semester using each text. The level of detail and style of writing in these texts are not appropriate for business students or for the time frame of a single-semester course. However, business students need more than a principles of economics treatment of these topics because they have often been exposed to that level of material already. The second edition of *Economics for Managers* will continue to present economic theory that goes beyond principles of economics, but the text is not as detailed or theoretical as a standard intermediate economics text given the coverage of both micro- and macroeconomics and the additional applications and examples included in this text. The compactness of the text and the style of writing are more appropriate for MBA students than what is typically found in large, comprehensive principles texts.

As in the first edition, each chapter of *Economics for Managers*, Second Edition, begins with a Case for Analysis section, which examines an article drawn from the current news media that illustrates the issues in the chapter. Thus, students begin the study of each chapter with a concrete, real-world example that highlights relevant economic concepts, which are then explained with the appropriate economic theory. Numerous real-world examples are used to illustrate the theoretical discussion. This approach appeals to MBA students who typically want to know the relevance and applicability of basic economic concepts and how these concepts can be used to analyze and explain events in the business environment.

Intended Audience

This text is designed to teach economics for business decision making to students in MBA and EMBA programs. It includes fundamental microeconomic and macroeconomic topics that can be covered in a single quarter or semester or that can be combined with other readers and case studies for an academic year course. The book is purposely titled *Economics for Managers* and not *Managerial Economics* to emphasize that this is *not* another applied microeconomics text with heavy emphasis on linear programming, multiple regression analysis, and other quantitative tools. This text is written for business students, most of whom will not take another course in economics, but who will work in firms and industries that are influenced by the economic forces discussed in the text.

A course using this text would ideally require principles of microeconomics and macroeconomics as prerequisites. However, the text is structured so that it can be used without these prerequisites. Coverage of the material in this text in one semester does require a substantial degree of motivation and maturity on the part of the students. However, the style of writing and coverage of topics in *Economics for Managers* will facilitate this process and are intended to generate student interest in these issues that lasts well beyond the end of the course.

Economics for Managers can be used with other industry case study books, such as *The Structure of American Industry* by James Brock. These books present extensive discussions of industry details from an economic perspective. Although they focus primarily on microeconomic and managerial topics, these texts can be used with *Economics for Managers* to integrate influences from the larger macroeconomic environment with the microeconomic analysis of different firms and industries.

Organization of the Text

The text is divided into three parts. Part 1, Microeconomic Analysis, focuses on how individual consumers and businesses interact with each other in a market economy. Part 2, Macroeconomic Analysis, looks at the aggregate behavior of different sectors of the economy to determine how changes in behavior in each of these sectors influence the overall level of economic activity. And finally, Part 3, Integration of the Frameworks, draws linkages between Parts 1 and 2.

Although many of the micro- and macroeconomic topics are treated similarly in other textbooks, this text emphasizes the connections between the frameworks, particularly in the first and last chapters. Changes in macroeconomic variables, such as interest rates, exchange rates, and the overall level of income, usually affect a firm through microeconomic variables such as consumer income, the price of the inputs of production, and the sales revenue the firm receives. Managers must be able to analyze factors relating to both market competition and changes in the overall economic environment so they can develop the best competitive strategies for their firms.

To cover all this material in one text, much of the detail and some topics found in other micro and macro texts have been omitted, most of which are not directly relevant for MBA students. There is no calculus in this text, only basic algebra and graphs. Algebraic examples are kept to a minimum and used only after the basic concepts are presented intuitively with examples. Statistical and econometric techniques are covered, particularly for demand estimation, at a very basic level, while references are provided to the standard sources on these topics. The text places greater emphasis than other texts on how managers use nonstatistical strategies to make decisions about the demand for their products and draws linkages between the statistical and nonstatistical approaches.

Economics for Managers, Second Edition, includes little formal analysis of input or resource markets, either from the viewpoint of standard marginal productivity theory or from the literature on the economics of organization, ownership and control, and human resource management. The latter are interesting topics that are covered in other texts with a focus quite different from this one. The macroeconomics portion of this text omits many of the details of alternative macro theories discussed elsewhere. Students are given the basic tools that will help them understand macroeconomics as presented in business sources, such as the *Wall Street Journal*, that emphasize how the national government and the Federal Reserve manage the economy to promote full employment, a stable price level, and economic growth.

Chapter-by-Chapter Breakdown: What's New in This Edition

Part 1: Microeconomic Analysis

The second edition of *Economics for Managers* includes updated news articles from 2006 to 2008 that serve as the cases for each chapter. In many chapters, the cases are on the same topic as in the first edition to facilitate the transition for current users of the text. An important exception is the opening case in Chapter 1 that focuses on Wal-Mart's successful expansion into Mexico. This case relates to the discussion of demand and consumer behavior in Chapters 2–4, the production and cost issues in Chapters 5 and 6, and the market strategies in Chapters 8 and 9. The Mexican currency crisis and economic collapse in 1994 and the 2007–2008 slowdown in the U.S. and Mexican economies are the major macroeconomic events that have influenced Wal-Mart's strategies in Mexico. The macroeconomic theory related to these developments is discussed in Chapters 14 and 15. The Wal-Mart case is then analyzed in Chapter 16, because students will now have all the relevant tools to examine the issues. The case that opens Chapter 16, McDonald's entry into the Chinese market, is also analyzed in that chapter. Thus, students and faculty will have two cases focusing on well-known companies that include microeconomic, macroeconomic, and globalization issues. These cases are presented in the opening and ending chapters to frame the entire analysis of the text. This innovation is a unique feature of *Economics for Managers*, Second Edition.

Chapter 2 uses a new introductory article on the copper industry, but it also discusses the original 1998 article for continuity. The current discussion highlights the issues of the global demand for copper, substitution with other metals, and the problem of copper thefts due to its high price, which have appeared extensively in the news media. New examples of the non-price factors influencing demand include: (1) Avian flu and the demand for chicken; (2) beer advertising aimed at Hispanics; (3) the demand for gourmet pet food; (4) the substitution of other electronic products for wrist watches; (5) the use of palladium as a substitute for platinum; (6) the relationship between printers and printer cartridges; and (7) the effect of expectations and increased population on world grain prices.

New examples of the non-price factors influencing supply include: (1) new technological processes to obtain nickel deposits; (2) the effect of increased fuel and raw materials prices on furniture production; (3) the effect of relative prices on the amount of land used for planting tobacco versus corn; (4) expectations and lumber supply; and (5) the effect of tariffs on furniture supply. The discussion of equilibrium now includes the example of excess demand for Notre Dame football stadium tickets and the resulting community spillovers. The effect of the termination of the tobacco subsidy program on equilibrium agricultural prices is also discussed. The extensive numerical example on the copper industry has been retained from the first edition.

Chapter 3 begins with an updated article on gasoline consumption and the price elasticity of demand for gasoline. I have also added examples of how airline demand elasticities vary by length of trip and more agricultural examples illustrating the (almost) perfectly elastic demand curve. The demand for "green" or environmentally friendly products and characteristics in the hotel industry is also discussed.

Chapter 4 on understanding consumer behavior uses a recent article on how General Motors is responding to consumer tastes by focusing its marketing on the Hispanic community and how past mistakes in this area contributed to the company's financial problems. There is added discussion of firms' use of census and survey data to develop marketing strategies for older consumers. I also discuss the development of whole grain white bread as managers tried to find the correct balance of taste and nutrition, and I show how some supermarkets in India had to cater to their consumer tastes by making their stores messier, noisier, and more cramped. I have retained the case study of automobile demand and the illustrations of the use of consumer market data in econometric demand studies from the first edition.

Chapter 5 begins with an updated article on the use of remote call centers to take drive-through orders in the fast-food industry. This article builds on the fast-food article that opened this chapter in the first edition, and I continue to discuss that article in the chapter. These issues tie in with the discussion of McDonald's entry into China in Chapter 16, given that the increased number of automobiles in China has made the drive-through a key component of McDonald's strategy in that country.

In the section on firm and industry productivity issues, I have added a discussion of productivity changes in hospitals and in the luxury handbag industry, and I update the discussion of improvements in the production of rice. For the automobile industry, I discuss the use of the Internet in supply chain management and Toyota's use of increased development time to offset quality problems in its new cars. I also discuss recent evidence on the impact of information technology on productivity growth across U.S. industries.

Chapter 6 uses a new opening article on the differences in productivity between an existing General Motors plant and a new Toyota plant in Texas to illustrate the issues of production and cost in the long run. I have also added the following examples of changes in production technology: (1) the airlines' use of radio frequency baggage ID tags; (2) the substitution of plastic for wood railroad ties; (3) the lack of input substitution by the Schantz Organ Company; and (4) the Fauxharmonic orchestra. I include new examples illustrating the role of input prices and incentives in a manager's choice of technology. These include the use of shaking machines in the fresh fruit industry and software to minimize fuel and overflight charges in the airline industry. I also discuss how unions may be taking a more cooperative approach in the automobile industry to keep those companies operating.

Chapter 7 begins with an updated article on the potato industry that focuses on the formation of farmers' cooperatives to help control production and keep prices high. This case shows how firms attempt to move outside the model of perfect competition, where they have no control over price, and the discussion relates to the cartel examples in Chapter 9. I also update the analysis of competitive strategies in the broiler chicken, milk, and trucking industries.

The opening article in Chapter 8 discusses the changes in market power facing Dell Computers in 2008. This is an example of the ongoing articles in the *Wall Street Journal* and other business publications outlining the shifting fortunes of the major players in the computer industry. I deleted some of the older examples in the chapter and added examples from the beer industry that tie in with the minimum efficient scale presentation in Chapter 6. I also discuss merger strategies in the mining industry that attracted much attention in the *Wall Street Journal* in 2007 and 2008.

For licensing and patents, I update the examples of the conflicts between psychiatrists and psychologists regarding the writing of prescriptions, and I discuss the latest strategies of the drug companies regarding patent infringement. I add a discussion of market power and switching costs on the Internet, and I include three new examples of changes in market power: the demand for Kleenex; Home Depot and customer service; and Borders bookstore's online strategy. The antitrust discussion now includes a presentation of the issues Microsoft has faced in Europe. In the section on monopolistic competition, I have added new discussions of independent drugstores, hardware stores, and bookstores, including the fact that Chapter 11 Bookstores in Atlanta had to file for Chapter 11 bankruptcy protection.

Chapter 9 includes a new introductory article that gives a striking example of price leadership in the airline industry. However, I have kept the example of the conflict between Frontier and United Airlines for continuity with the first edition and because it is an excellent example of oligopoly behavior. I present a new Table 9.1 on oligopolistic industries, and I have updated the discussion of Tim Hortons and Dunkin' Donuts and of DHL versus UPS and FedEx. For cartel behavior, I have added to the discussion of OPEC, and I have inserted a new section on DeBeers and the diamond cartel.

Chapter 10 presents a new opening industrial case that gives a clear distinction between markup pricing based simply on cost and pricing using customers' willingness to pay. The restaurant pricing example that opened this chapter in the first edition is now updated and included in the section that follows the derivation of the markup pricing formula. I have added a section on ticket pricing in professional sports that emphasizes both the possibility of goals other than profit maximization and the use of differential pricing with multiple products. I have updated the airline price discrimination examples and the discussion of personalized pricing. I have added more discussion of location-based price discrimination including examples of increased parking fees by local governments, variations in prices for ski resort tickets, and differential pricing for the Eurotunnel. At the end of the chapter I add to the discussion of the macro impacts on pricing in 2007–2008, and I present more recent data on the reasons for sticky prices.

Part 2: Macroeconomic Analysis

Part 2, Macroeconomic Analysis, is simplified by deleting the IS/LM model that was in the first edition. After introducing the macroeconomic variables in Chapter 11, the text discusses real spending by individuals, firms, and governments (C + I + G + X – M) in Chapter 12. This material draws on the analyses students see daily in the *Wall Street Journal* and other business publications. A discussion of money, money markets, and Federal Reserve policy is presented in Chapter 13. These elements are combined using the aggregate demand/aggregate supply (*AD/AS*) model in Chapter 14. Monetary and fiscal policy implementation issues are also presented in this chapter. Chapter 15 continues to focus on exchange rate and balance of payments issues and presents an updated discussion of controversies over the value of the euro and the Chinese yuan. The text continues to describe the impacts of policy changes in these areas on the U.S. and foreign economies. However, *as in the first edition, and unlike the presentation in other texts, Economics for Managers*, Second Edition, has an extensive discussion in both Chapters 14 and 15 of the impact of macro policy changes on the competitive strategies of both domestic and international firms. *This is a unique feature of this textbook*, which makes it most appropriate for MBA students who will probably never make macroeconomic policy but who will work in firms and industries influenced by these policy changes.

The macro section of the text was revised just as the U.S. economy was slipping into recession in 2008. Thus, the introductory macro articles in each chapter are all taken from the *Wall Street Journal* in 2008. Although the macro framework is the same as in the first edition, except for the removal of the IS/LM model, all examples have been updated with material from 2007 and 2008. The text discusses the crisis in the housing and credit markets, the economic stimulus package of 2008, the collapse of the financial sector of the U.S. economy in fall 2008, and the aggressive moves on the part of the Federal Reserve to stimulate the economy, including the lowering of the targeted federal funds rate to almost zero in December 2008. Certain examples from the first edition of *Economics for Managers* have also been retained. When the first edition was published, the United States had just come out of the recession of 2001. Now that the country is back in a recession, the contrast between the two cases is very instructive for students. They can see how the macro model works when the economy both speeds up and slows down.

Part 3: Integration of the Frameworks

As noted above, in Part 3 we return to the issues first discussed in Chapter 1, the relationship between microeconomic and macroeconomic influences on managerial decision making. Chapter 16 presents two cases illustrating these influences.

The first case discusses McDonald's entry and expansion in China. It shows how microeconomic factors, including consumer preferences and the increased use of automobiles, and macroeconomic factors influencing the growth of the Chinese economy have affected McDonald's competitive strategies. The second case returns to the discussion of Wal-Mart's entry into Mexico that opened Chapter 1. Students are now in a much better position to analyze these issues, having covered all of the micro and macro analysis in the earlier chapters.

The text ends by emphasizing its major theme: *Changes in the macro environment affect individual firms and industries through the microeconomic factors of demand, production, cost, and profitability.* Firms can either try to adapt to these changes or undertake policies to try to modify the environment itself. This theme is particularly important in this second edition of *Economics for Managers*, given the discussion of the impact of the 2007–2008 recession on the overall economy and on the strategies of different firms operating in this environment.

Unique Features of the Text

Chapter Opening Cases for Analysis

Each chapter begins with a Case for Analysis section, which examines an article drawn from the current news media that illustrates the issues in the chapter. Thus, students begin the study of each chapter with a concrete, real-world example that highlights relevant economic issues, which are then explained with the appropriate economic theory. For example, Chapter 2 begins with a *Wall Street Journal* article on the copper industry that illustrates forces on both the demand and supply sides of the market that influence the price of copper and have caused that price to change over time. This example leads directly to a discussion of demand and supply functions and curves, the concept of equilibrium price and quantity, and changes in those equilibria. Within this discussion, numerous real-world examples are included to illustrate demand and supply shifters. The chapter concludes by reviewing how formal demand and supply analysis relates to the introductory news article. Students thus go from concrete examples to the relevant economic theory and then back to real-world examples.

Interdisciplinary Focus

Economics for Managers, Second Edition, continues to have an interdisciplinary focus. For example, Chapter 3 presents demand price elasticity estimates drawn from both the economics and marketing literature. Empirical marketing and economic approaches to understanding consumer demand are both discussed in Chapter 4. The production and cost analysis in Chapters 5 and 6 relates to topics covered in management courses. This cross-discipline focus in the text reflects recent trends in MBA curricula as discussed in the *Wall Street Journal* ("M.B.A. Programs Blend Disciplines to Yield Big Picture," July 11, 2006). Thus, the second edition of *Economics for Managers* is uniquely positioned to serve the needs of instructors who are trying to integrate both micro- and macroeconomic topics and who want to relate this material to other parts of the business curriculum.

Focus on Global Issues

Global and international examples are included in both the microeconomic and macroeconomic sections of the text. For example, Chapter 2 discusses how the financial crisis in Southeast Asia in 1997 and the economic growth in China in 2007 and 2008 affected the copper industry. These international issues are revisited again in Chapters 15 and 16. Analyses of the impact of changing consumer demand, new production technologies, and rising input costs on both U.S. and international firms are included in many of the microeconomic chapters. Chapters 14 and 15 include discussions of the effects of U.S. and international macroeconomic policy changes on firms located around the world.

As noted above, *Economics for Managers*, Second Edition, takes the unique approach in Chapter 1 and the concluding Chapter 16 to discuss the impact of both microeconomic and macroeconomic factors on firms' competitive strategies in international markets. The cases of Wal-Mart's moves into Mexico and McDonald's entry into the Chinese market help students focus on the issues of GDP growth in potential foreign markets, the impact of macroeconomic policies in these countries, and the role of political stability, government incentives, and barriers to expansion. The cases allow students to analyze globalization issues using the micro- and macroeconomic frameworks developed in the text. This *integration of micro and macro tools* is a key feature of both editions of *Economics for Managers*.

Managerial Decision-Making Perspective

Economics for Managers is developed from a firm and industry decision-making perspective. Thus, the demand and elasticity chapters focus on the implications of elasticity for pricing policies, not on abstract models of consumer behavior. To illustrate the basic models of production and cost, the text presents examples of cost-cutting and productivity-improving strategies that firms actually use. It discusses the concept of input substitution intuitively with examples, but places the formal isoquant model in an appendix to Chapter 6. The text then compares and contrasts the various models of market behavior, incorporating discussions and examples of the measurement and use of market power, most of which are drawn from the current news media and the industrial organization literature.

Throughout the chapters you will find Managerial Rule of Thumb features, which are shortcuts for using specific concepts and brief descriptions of important issues for managers. For example, Chapter 3 contains several quick approaches for determining price and income elasticities of demand. Chapter 4 includes some key points for managers to consider when using different approaches to understanding consumer behavior.

Macroeconomics presents a particular challenge for managers because the subject matter is traditionally presented from the viewpoint of the decision makers, either the Federal Reserve or the U.S. Congress and presidential administration. Although *Economics for Managers*, Second Edition, covers the models that include this policy-making perspective, it also illustrates how the actions of these policy makers influence the decisions managers make in various firms and industries. This emphasis is important because most students taking an MBA economics course will never work or make policy decisions for the Federal Reserve or the U.S. government, but they are or will be employed by firms that are affected by these decisions and policies.

End-of-Chapter Exercises

As you will see, some of the end-of-chapter exercises are straightforward calculation problems that ask students to compute demand-supply equilibria, price elasticities, and profit-maximizing levels of output, for example. However, many exercises are broader analyses of cases and examples drawn from the news media. These exercises have a managerial perspective similar to the examples in the text. The goal is to make students realize that managerial decisions usually involve far more analysis than the calculation of a specific number or an "optimal" mathematical result. One of the exercises at the end of each chapter is related to the Case for Analysis discussed at the beginning of that chapter.

Instructor Resource Center

Economics for Managers is connected to the Instructor Resource Center available at **www.pearsonhighered.com/farnham.** Instructors can access a variety of print, digital, and presentation resources available with this text in downloadable format. Registration is simple and gives you immediate access to new titles and new editions. As a registered faculty member, you can download resource files and receive immediate access and instructions for installing course management content on your campus server. If you ever need assistance, our dedicated technical support team is ready to help with the media supplements that accompany this text. Visit **http://247.pearsoned.custhelp.com/** for answers to frequently asked questions and toll-free user support phone numbers. The following supplements are available to adopting instructors:

- Instructor's Manual
- Test Item File
- TestGen Test Generating Software
- PowerPoint Slides

Acknowledgments

As with any major project, I owe a debt of gratitude to the many individuals who assisted with this book.

I first want to thank my friend and colleague, Jon Mansfield, who worked with me in developing materials for the book. Jon and I have discussed the integration of microeconomics and macroeconomics for business students for many years as we both experimented with new ideas for teaching a combined course. We even team-taught one section of the course for EMBA students so that we could directly learn from each other. Jon is a great teacher, and his assistance in developing this approach has been invaluable.

I next want to thank the generations of students I have taught, not only in the MBA and EMBA programs, but also in the Master of Public Administration, Master of Health Administration, and Master of Public Health programs at Georgia State. They made it quite clear that students in professional master's degree programs are different from those in academic degree programs. Although these students are willing to learn theory, they have insisted, sometimes quite forcefully, that the theory must always be applicable to real-world managerial situations.

I also want to thank my colleagues Professors Harvey Brightman and Yezdi Bhada, now retired from Georgia State's Robinson College of Business, for their teaching seminars and for backing the approach I have taken in this book. I always knew that business and other professional students learned differently from economics students. Harvey and Yezdi provided the justification for these observations.

I want to acknowledge the contributions of several graduate research assistants supported by the Department of Economics, Georgia State University: Mercy Mvundura, Djesika Amendah, William Holmes, and Sarah Beth Link. They provided substantial assistance in finding the sources used in the text and in developing tables and figures for the book.

The Prentice Hall staff has, of course, been of immense help in developing the second edition of the text. I would especially like to thank Chris Rogers, my economics editor; Susie Abraham, assistant editor; Valerie Patruno, editorial assistant; and Clara Bartunek, production project manager. I also appreciate the assistance of Angela Williams Urquhart, editorial director at Thistle Hill Publishing Services, and Harry Ellis, accuracy checker.

I would also like to thank all those who assisted with supporting materials. Professor Leonie Stone of SUNY Geneseo contributed to the end-of-chapter questions in the micro section of the text. Professors James E. Payne and Jeffrey Lon Carlson of Illinois State University prepared the Test Bank. Professor Risa Kumazawa of Illinois Wesleyan University prepared the Instructor's Manual and Professor Kenneth Slaysman of York College of Pennsylvania created the PowerPoint Lecture Presentation to accompany the text.

I also want to acknowledge the assistance of all the reviewers of the various drafts of the text. These include:

Gerald Bialka, *University of North Florida*

John Boschen, *College of William and Mary*

Vera Brusentsev, *University of Delaware*

Chun Lee, *Loyola Marymount University*

Mikhail Melnik, *Niagara University*

Franklin E. Robeson, *College of William and Mary*

Dorothy R. Siden, *Salem State College*

Ira A. Silver, *Texas Christian University*

Donald L. Sparks, *The Citadel*

Kasaundra Tomlin, *Oakland University*

Doina Vlad, *Seton Hill University*

John E. Wagner, *SUNY-ESF*

E. Anne York, *Meredith College*

Finally, I want to thank my wife, Lynn, and daughters, Ali and Jen, for bearing with me during the writing of both the first and second editions of this text.

—*Paul G. Farnham*

About the Author

Paul G. Farnham is Associate Professor Emeritus of Economics at Georgia State University. He received his B.A. in economics from Union College, Schenectady, New York, and his M.A. and Ph.D. in economics from the University of California, Berkeley. For over 30 years, he specialized in teaching economics to students in professional master's degree programs including the Master of Business Administration and Executive MBA, Master of Public Administration, Master of Health Administration, and Master of Public Health. He has received both teaching awards and outstanding student evaluations at Georgia State. Dr. Farnham's research focused first on issues related to the economics of state and local governments and then on public health economic evaluation issues where he has published articles in a variety of journals. He co-authored two editions of *Cases in Public Policy Analysis* (1989, 2000), contributed to both editions of *Prevention Effectiveness: A Guide to Decision Analysis and Economic Evaluation* (1996, 2003), and wrote a chapter for the *Handbook of Economic Evaluation of HIV Prevention Programs* (1998). He is currently a Senior Service Fellow in the Division of HIV/AIDS Prevention at the Centers for Disease Control and Prevention in Atlanta. Dr. Farnham can be reached at pfarnham@gsu.edu.

Economics
for Managers

1 Managers and Economics

Why should managers study economics? Many of you are probably asking yourself this question as you open this text. Students in Master of Business Administration (MBA) and Executive MBA programs usually have some knowledge of the topics that will be covered in their accounting, marketing, finance, and management courses. You may have already used many of those skills on the job or have decided that you want to concentrate in one of those areas in your program of study.

But economics is different. Although you may have taken one or two introductory economics courses at some point in the past, most of you are not going to *become* economists. From these economics classes, you probably have vague memories of different graphs, algebraic equations, and terms such as *elasticity of demand* and *marginal propensity to consume*. However, you may have never really understood how economics is relevant to managerial decision making. As you'll learn in this chapter, managers need to understand the insights of both *microeconomics*, which focuses on the behavior of individual consumers, firms, and industries, and *macroeconomics*, which analyzes issues in the overall economic environment. Although these subjects are typically taught separately, this text presents the ideas from both approaches and then integrates them from a managerial decision-making perspective.

As in all chapters in this text, we begin our analysis with a specific case study derived from the *Wall Street Journal*. This article, "In Mexico, Wal-Mart Is Defying Its Critics," provides an overview of the issues we'll discuss throughout this text. In particular, it illustrates how U.S. firms may search for profitable opportunities in other countries and how developments in the overall economic and political environment in these countries influence these firms' strategies.

In Mexico, Wal-Mart Is Defying Its Critics

by John Lyons

Wall Street Journal, *March 5, 2007*

JUCHITAN, Mexico—For as long as anyone can remember, shopping for many items in this Zapotec Indian town meant lousy selection and high prices. Most families live on less than $4,000 a year. Little wonder that this provincial corner of Oaxaca, historically famous for keeping outsiders at bay, welcomed the arrival of Wal-Mart.

Back home in the U.S., Wal-Mart Stores Inc. is known not only for its relentless focus on low prices but also for its many critics, who assail it for everything from the wages it pays to its role in homogenizing American culture. But while its growth in the U.S. is slowing, Wal-Mart is striking gold south of the border, largely free from all the criticism. Like Wal-Mart fans in less affluent parts of America, most shoppers in developing countries are much more concerned about the cost of medicine and microwaves than the cultural incursions of a multinational corporation.

That fact is making Wal-Mart a dominant force in Latin America. Wal-Mart de Mexico SAB, a publicly traded subsidiary, is not only the biggest employer in Mexico—it's the biggest single retailer in Latin America. Sales at Wal-Mex, as the Mexican unit is called, are forecast to rise 16% to $21 billion this year, representing a quarter of Wal-Mart's foreign revenue. International revenue soared 30% to $77.1 billion, accounting for 22% of Wal-Mart's sales, in the fiscal year ended Jan. 31. Wal-Mex profits are forecast to grow 20% to $1.3 billion this year. . . .

Wal-Mart is now betting on the world's most populated developing nations as its engine for future growth. The retailer is acquiring a retail chain in China, for instance, and seeking to open in India, where it's been kept at bay, with new local partners. . . .

When Wal-Mart was building a store in Juchitan in 2005, local shopkeepers and leftist groups tried to rouse popular sentiment against the American invader. The efforts failed, and by the end of opening day sales were so strong "the place looked like it had been looted," says Max Jimenez, the store's 31-year-old manager. The store's sales nearly doubled Wal-Mart's initial projections last year, and it still attracts customers from hours away.

Wal-Mart bet on Mexico just as the country was opening to global trade. After Mexico's devastating currency crash and economic collapse in 1994, Sears Roebuck & Co. and former rival Kmart both pulled up stakes, but Wal-Mart stuck it out. Carrefour SA, a key global rival for Wal-Mart, pulled out in 2005 after failing to gain share in an increasingly competitive market.

In Mexico, Wal-Mart has been a counterweight to the powers that control commerce. One of the most closed economies in the world until the late 1980s, Mexico was dominated for decades by a handful of big grocers and retailers. All were members of a national retailing association called ANTAD, and cutthroat competition was taboo. At the local level, towns are still hostage to local bosses, known here as *caciques*, the Indian word for local strongmen who control politics and commerce. . . .

In a country where family connections often matter more than skill, Wal-Mart trains floor workers to rise to management. Plus, Wal-Mart lowered prices on thousands of staples from tomatoes to diapers, helping stretch low wages here for millions of middle-class and poor consumers.

The retailer entered Mexico in 1991, teaming up with local retailer Cifra SA. When Wal-Mart started to publish price comparisons showing how much cheaper its prices were, other retailers were outraged. In 2002, Wal-Mex was forced to resign from ANTAD. Then rivals were forced to improve service and keep up with price cuts to stay in business. In January alone, Wal-Mart cut prices on 7,500 items. . . .

Wal-Mart's success among the poor of Mexico has made it something of a hero with politicians here. Compare how Wal-Mart's applications to move into banking were received in the U.S. and in Mexico. North of the border, labor unions and banks have all but killed the plan. U.S. Federal Reserve Chairman Ben Bernanke raised concerns about regulating a combined lender and retailer.

In contrast, Mexico's central banker Guillermo Ortiz is a Wal-Mart fan, once crediting its price cutting with helping control inflation in the years after Mexico's 1994 currency collapse. Mr. Ortiz and other regulators hope Wal-Mart will change Mexican banking, which is dominated by a few foreign-owned financial firms that cater mainly to the wealthy. Wal-Mart got its Mexican banking license quickly, and branches of its Adelante bank (which means "forward" in Spanish) are set to open this year.

Wal-Mart's success in Mexico is on display in Juchitan, a sun-soaked desert village of 90,000 residents near southern Oaxaca state's Pacific coast. . . .

When Wal-Mart started to build one of its Bodega Aurrera stores—austere versions of the Super Center designed to meet small-town needs—a scattering of marchers gathered on a few days to protest that the new store would put local merchants out of business, and harm the local culture. But the protests died out because most people wanted the store, the first big national retailer to venture in.

In Juchitan, as in other small Mexican towns, consumer goods often cost far more than in cities, partly because of transport costs. But Wal-Mart's huge fleet of trucks and computerized logistics allow it to sell a microwave at the same price in Juchitan as in Mexico City. To do it, Wal-Mart squeezes out overhead even more aggressively in its small-town stores. The floors of the Bodega store are concrete, which requires a smaller cleaning staff.

In recent months, as rising prices for U.S. corn pushed up the price of Mexico's corn tortilla, a staple for millions of poor, Wal-Mart could keep its tortilla prices largely steady because of its long-term contracts with corn-flour suppliers. The crisis turned into free advertising for Wal-Mart, as new shoppers lined up for the cheaper tortillas. . . .

When Wal-Mart opened its doors here, it tried to fit in. It found Zapotec-speaking interviewers to put applicants at ease. At the morning sales meeting here, the obligatory Wal-Mart cheer is shouted in Zapotec. . . . Product announcements are broadcast in Zapotec by saleswomen in traditional flowing skirts and ornate blouses. . . .

In Mexican towns like Juchitan, shopping at a Wal-Mart is a high-end experience. The air conditioning and lights are on. Across town at an outdoor market, flies swarm on buckets of shrimp and fish piled on counters without ice, let alone refrigeration. . . .

Case for Analysis

Micro- and Macroeconomic Influences on Wal-Mart in Mexico

This article focuses on Wal-Mart's successful expansion into Mexico at a time when its growth in the U.S. is slowing and the company has been under criticism for its wage and benefit policies and its impact on American culture and business. Wal-Mart has been successful in Mexico due to its ability to charge lower prices than competitive stores and to provide a wider range of products and a more "high-end" shopping experience than is found in much of Mexico's informal retail sector. Given Wal-Mart's size, which helps lower its production costs, the store has been able to provide goods at lower prices than those found in local stores even in the town of Juchitan, the focus of the article. Wal-Mart's fleet of trucks and computerized logistical systems allow it to sell appliances at the same price in Juchitan as in Mexico City. Local merchants typically have to respond by lowering their own prices. Although there has been some resistance to the development of new Wal-Mart stores by Mexican merchants, these protests usually have been surpassed by consumer acceptance.

Most of the issues discussed in the article relate to microeconomic factors on either the demand or supply side of the market. These include the factors influencing consumer demand such as price, the income level of consumers, the quality of goods available from local producers in both formal and informal markets, and the strategies Wal-Mart adopted to fit in the Zapotec Indian town. Wal-Mart's ability to provide a wide range of consumer goods at low prices is derived from the company's size and the technology of its production and distribution systems.

The end result of these changes on both sides of the market was that Wal-Mart increased competition among all retailers in Mexico. Until the late 1980s, the economy had been closed to outside influences, and the retail sector was dominated by a small number of large firms who were members of a national retailing association called ANTAD that restricted intense competition. When Wal-Mart began publishing price comparisons showing its lower prices, the company was forced to resign from ANTAD. However, the increased competition caused rival companies to improve services and institute their own price cuts.

Several issues in the article also relate to developments in the overall macroeconomic environment. The article notes that Wal-Mart entered Mexico just as the country was opening to global trade. Mexico's currency devaluation and economic collapse in 1994 caused Sears Roebuck & Co. and Kmart to leave the country, but Wal-Mart continued to do business and became more successful as the economy improved. More recently in 2007 and 2008, Wal-Mart began to feel the effects of both the slowing U.S. and Mexican economies. Slow economic growth in the U.S. decreased the amount of money transfers Mexicans living in the U.S. sent back to their families. The Mexican central bank estimated that these transfers rose only 0.6 percent in the first half of 2007 compared with increases of 15 and 21 percent in the previous two years. This change resulted in a distinct slowing of growth in Wal-Mart sales in Mexico during this period.[1]

---

[1] Kris Hudson and Ana Campoy, "Hispanics' Hard Times Hit Wal-Mart; Results of U.S. Housing Slump Are Felt on Both Sides of Border with Mexico," *Wall Street Journal*, August 29, 2007.

The article also mentions how the Mexican central banker, Guillermo Ortiz, once credited Wal-Mart's price-cutting strategies with helping to control inflation in the years after Mexico's 1994 currency collapse. This may be an overstatement because Wal-Mart actually suspended construction on 13 Sam's Club Warehouses and 12 supercenters in 1995 in reaction to the currency devaluation. Wal-Mart managers at the time noted that concerns about both inflation and recession created great uncertainty for the economy and "if the consumer isn't there and doesn't have enough pesos in his pocket, it doesn't make much sense to open stores."[2] Others have also noted that Wal-Mart's *everyday low prices* strategy was not viable immediately following the currency crisis because the high inflation rates clouded price differences between companies. With inflation stabilized by the late 1990s, Wal-Mart rolled out this strategy in its Mexican stores and posted price comparisons with its competitors.[3] Thus, macroeconomic changes in the general price level as well as the level of overall economic growth have also influenced Wal-Mart's strategies in Mexico. ∎

[Handwritten margin note: Relative price of one good vs price of other goods. TV $1000 PC $2000   2000/1000 = (2)]

Two Perspectives: Microeconomics and Macroeconomics

As noted above, **microeconomics** is the branch of economics that analyzes the decisions that individual consumers and producers make as they operate in a market economy. When microeconomics is applied to business decision making, it is called **managerial economics**. The key element in any market system is pricing, because this type of system is based on the buying and selling of goods and services. As we'll discuss later in the chapter, **prices**—the amounts of money that are charged for different goods and services in a market economy—act as signals that influence the behavior of both consumers and producers of these goods and services. Managers must understand how prices are determined—for both the **outputs**, or products sold by a firm, and the **inputs**, or resources (such as land, labor, capital, raw materials, and entrepreneurship) that the firm must purchase in order to produce its output. Output prices influence the revenue a firm derives from the sale of its products, while input prices influence a firm's costs of production. As you'll learn throughout this text, many managerial actions and decisions are based on expected responses to changes in these prices and on the ability of a manager to influence these prices.

Managerial decisions are also influenced by events that occur in the larger economic environment in which businesses operate. Changes in the overall level of economic activity, interest rates, unemployment rates, and exchange rates both at home and abroad create new opportunities and challenges for a firm's competitive strategy. This is the subject matter of **macroeconomics**, which we'll cover in the second half of this text. Managers need to be familiar with the underlying macroeconomic models that economic forecasters use to predict changes in the macroeconomy and with how different firms and industries respond to these changes. Most of these changes affect individual firms via the pricing mechanism, so there is a strong connection between microeconomic and macroeconomic analysis.[4]

Microeconomics
The branch of economics that analyzes the decisions that individual consumers, firms, and industries make as they produce, buy, and sell goods and services.

Managerial economics
Microeconomics applied to business decision making.

Prices
The amounts of money that are charged for goods and services in a market economy. Prices act as signals that influence the behavior of both consumers and producers of these goods and services.

Outputs
The final goods and services produced and sold by firms in a market economy.

Inputs
The factors of production, such as land, labor, capital, raw materials, and entrepreneurship, that are used to produce the outputs, or final goods and services, that are bought and sold in a market economy.

Macroeconomics
The branch of economics that focuses on the overall level of economic activity, changes in the price level, and the amount of unemployment by analyzing group or aggregate behavior in different sectors of the economy.

---

[2] Bob Ortega, "Wal-Mart Suspends Mexican Expansion; Other Firms Stick to More-Modest Plans," *Wall Street Journal*, January 25, 1995.

[3] Chris Tilly, "Wal-Mart Goes South: Sizing Up the Chain's Mexican Success Story," in *Wal-Mart World*, Stanley D. Brunn, ed. (New York: Routledge Taylor & Francis Group, 2006), 357–68.

[4] Note that the terms *micro* and *macro* are used differently in various business disciplines. For example, in *Marketing Management, The Millennium Edition* (Prentice Hall, 2000), Philip Kotler describes the "macroenvironment" as dealing with *all* forces external to the firm. His examples include both (1) the gradual opening of new markets in many countries and the growth in global brands of various products (microeconomic factors for the economist) and (2) the debt problems of many countries and the fragility of the international financial system (macroeconomic problems from the economic perspective). In each business discipline, you need to learn how these terms and concepts are defined.

In essence, macroeconomic analysis can be thought of as viewing the economy from an airplane 30,000 feet in the air, whereas with microeconomics the observer is on the ground walking among the firms and consumers. While on the ground, an observer can see the interaction between individual firms and consumers and the competitive strategies that various firms develop. At 30,000 feet, however, an observer doesn't see the same level of detail. In macroeconomics, we analyze the behavior of individuals aggregated into different sectors in the economy to determine the impact of changes in this behavior on the overall level of economic activity. In turn, this overall level of activity combines with changes in various macro variables, such as interest rates and exchange rates, to affect the competitive strategies of individual firms and industries, the subject matter of microeconomics. Let's now look at these microeconomic influences on managers in more detail.

Microeconomic Influences on Managers

The discussion of Wal-Mart's strategies in Mexico in the *Wall Street Journal* article illustrates several of the microeconomic choices that firms must make. Given increasingly saturated home markets in the 1980s and 1990s and the reduced trade barriers from the North American Free Trade Agreement (NAFTA), Wal-Mart managers sought out new markets in Mexico where there would be a favorable consumer response to its low prices, the wide range of goods the company sells, and the clean, air-conditioned environment of its stores. The company adapted to the local Zapotec Indian environment in its employment and selling practices in certain stores. Wal-Mart's size and efficient production and distribution systems, reflecting past decisions on production technology and strategies to lower supplier costs, enabled it to not only compete in, but to dominate, the Mexican retail market. When Wal-Mart entered Mexico, it partnered with the local retailer, CIFRA. In 1997, it purchased a majority share of CIFRA, forming Wal-Mart de Mexico or Walmex, which then expanded aggressively. However, Wal-Mart was impacted by other competitors, such as the French grocery giants Carrefour (the world's second-largest retailer) and Auchan, J.C. Penney department stores, the Texas-based grocer HEB, and the Spanish apparel retailer Inditex, which also entered Mexico following the implementation of NAFTA.[5]

Relative prices
The price of one good in relation to the price of another, similar good, which is the way prices are defined in microeconomics.

Decisions about demand, supply, production, and market structure are all microeconomic choices that managers must make. Some decisions focus on the factors that affect consumer behavior and the willingness of consumers to buy one firm's product as opposed to that of a competitor. Thus, managers need to understand the variables influencing consumer demand for their products. Because consumers typically have a choice among competing products, these choices and the demand for each product are influenced by **relative prices**, the price of one good in relation to that of another, similar good. Relative prices are the focus of microeconomic analysis. At both home and abroad, Wal-Mart has used the everyday low prices strategy as a driver of its competitive strategy. However, this does not mean that the company charges lower prices on all of its goods in every store. Survey results of hundreds of items in Mexico's three largest cities in 2005 showed that Wal-Mart had the lowest price for between 3 and 18 percent of the items surveyed, but it had the highest price for between 4 and 7 percent of the items.[6] These differences were related to the company's assessment of the prices charged for these products by its competitors and their influence on consumer demand.

Much of the discussion in the *Wall Street Journal* article focused on Wal-Mart's production decisions in Mexico. The company built both Supercenters and

---

[5] Tilly, "Wal-Mart Goes South: Sizing Up the Chain's Mexican Success Story."
[6] Ibid.

smaller, more austere Bodega Aurrera stores better designed to meet small-town needs. Its scale of operation and its huge, automated distribution network allowed it to achieve lower costs of production than many of its competitors. The company inspired a local trucking company, Transportes EASO SA, to partner with a U.S. trucking firm to share a fleet of modern trucks and satellite systems to help plan delivery times. This strategy enabled EASO to cut costs by 25 percent, savings which it then passed on to Wal-Mart. Wal-Mart's size also allows it to obtain price discounts from its suppliers that are unavailable to its local competitors. Francisco Martinez, chief financial officer of Commercial Mexicana SA, Wal-Mart's biggest Mexican rival, has been quoted as saying, "I buy 20,000 plastic toys, and Wal-Mart buys 20 million. Who do you think gets them cheaper?"[7]

Production technology as well as the prices paid for the resources used in production influence a company's final costs of production. The relative prices of these resources or inputs of production will influence the choices that managers make among different production methods. Whether a production process uses large amounts of plant and equipment relative to the amount of workers and whether a business operates out of a small office or a giant factory are microeconomic production and cost decisions managers must make. Wal-Mart implemented the same highly automated inventory management system in Mexico that it used in the United States. It also took advantage of Mexico's cheap labor by replacing the robots used in U.S. distribution centers with Mexican workers earning $5 per day.[8]

Markets

As discussed in the *Wall Street Journal* article, Wal-Mart made strategic decisions in light of its knowledge of the market environment or structure. **Markets**, the institutions and mechanisms used for the buying and selling of goods and services, vary in structure from those with hundreds or thousands of buyers and sellers to those with very few participants. These different types of markets influence the strategic decisions that managers make because markets affect both the ability of a given firm to influence the price of its product and the amount of independent control the firm has over its actions.

There are four major types of markets in microeconomic analysis:

1. Perfect competition
2. Monopolistic competition
3. Oligopoly
4. Monopoly

These market structures can be located along a continuum, as shown in Figure 1.1. At the left end of the continuum, there are a large number of firms in the market, whereas at the right end of the continuum there is only one firm. (We'll discuss other characteristics that distinguish the markets later in the chapter.)

The two market structures at the ends of the continuum, perfect competition and monopoly, are essentially hypothetical models. No real-world firms meet all the assumptions of perfect competition, and few could be classified as monopolies.

Markets
The institutions and mechanisms used for the buying and selling of goods and services. The four major types of markets in microeconomic analysis are perfect competition, monopolistic competition, oligopoly, and monopoly.

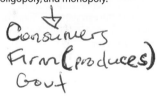

Large Number of Firms			Single Firm
Perfect Competition ----- Monopolistic Competition ----- Oligopoly ----- Monopoly			

FIGURE 1.1
Market Structure

---

[7] David Luhnow, "Crossover Success: How NAFTA Helped Wal-Mart Reshape the Mexican Market—Lower Tariffs, Retail Muscle Translate into Big Sales; Middlemen Are Squeezed—'Like Shopping in the U.S.,'" *Wall Street Journal*, August 31, 2001.

[8] Ibid.

However, these models serve as benchmarks for analysis. All real-world firms contain combinations of the characteristics of these two models. Managers need to know where their firm lies along this continuum because market structure will influence the strategic variables that a firm can use to face its competition.

The major characteristics that distinguish these market structures are

1. The number of firms competing with one another that influences the firm's control over its price
2. Whether the products sold in the markets are differentiated or undifferentiated
3. Whether entry into and exit from the market by other firms is easy or difficult
4. The amount of information available to market participants

The Perfect Competition Model   The model of **perfect competition**, which is on the left end of the continuum in Figure 1.1, is a market structure characterized by

1. A large number of firms in the market
2. An undifferentiated product
3. Ease of entry into the market
4. Complete information available to all market participants

Perfect competition
A market structure characterized by a large number of firms in an industry, an undifferentiated product, ease of entry into the market, and complete information available to participants.

In perfect competition, we distinguish between the behavior of an individual firm and the outcomes for the entire market or industry, which represents all firms producing the product. Economists make the assumption that there are so many firms in a perfectly competitive industry that no single firm has any influence on the price of the product. For example, in many agricultural industries, whether an individual farmer produces more or less product in a given season has no influence on the price of these products. The individual farmer's output is small relative to the entire market, so that the market price is determined by the actions of *all* farmers supplying the product and *all* consumers who purchase the goods. Because individual producers can sell any amount of output they bring to market at that price, we characterize the perfectly competitive firm as a **price-taker**. This firm does not have to lower its price to sell more output. In fact, it cannot influence the price of its product. However, if the price for the entire amount of output in the market increases, consumers will buy less, and if the market price of the product decreases, they will buy more.

Price-taker
A characteristic of a perfectly competitive firm in which the firm cannot influence the price of its product, but can sell any amount of its output at the price established by the market.

In the model of perfect competition, economists also assume that all firms in an industry produce the same homogeneous product, so there is no product differentiation. For example, within a given grade of an agricultural product, potatoes or peaches are undifferentiated. This market characteristic means that consumers do not care about the identity of the specific supplier of the product they purchase. They may not even know who supplies the product, and that knowledge would be irrelevant to their purchase decision, which will be based largely on the price of the product.

The third assumption of the perfectly competitive model is that entry into the industry by other firms is costless. This means that if a perfectly competitive firm is making a **profit** (earning revenues in excess of its costs), other firms will enter the industry in an attempt to earn profits also. However, these actions will compete away excess profits for all firms in a perfectly competitive industry.

Profit
The difference between the total revenue that a firm receives for selling its product and the total cost of producing that product.

The final assumption of the perfectly competitive model is that complete information is available to all market participants. This means that all participants know which firms are earning the greatest profits and how they are doing so. Thus, other firms can easily emulate the strategies and techniques of the profitable firms, which will result in greater competition and further pressure on any excess profits.

While the details of this process will be described in later chapters, these four assumptions mean that perfectly competitive firms have no **market power**—the ability to influence their prices and develop other competitive strategies that allow them to earn large profits over longer periods of time.

Market power
The ability of a firm to influence the prices of its products and develop other competitive strategies that enable it to earn large profits over longer periods of time.

All of the other market structures in Figure 1.1 represent **imperfect competition**, in which firms have some degree of market power. How much market power these firms have and how they are able to maintain it differ among the market structures.

The Monopoly Model   At the right end of the market structure continuum in Figure 1.1 is the **monopoly** model, in which a single firm produces a product for which there are no close substitutes. Thus, as we move rightward along the continuum, the number of firms producing the product keeps decreasing until we reach the monopoly model of one firm. A monopoly firm typically produces a product that has characteristics and qualities different from the products of its competitors. This product differentiation often means that consumers are willing to pay more for this product because similar products are not considered to be close substitutes.

In the monopoly model, there are also **barriers to entry**, which are structural, legal, or regulatory characteristics of the market that keep other firms from easily producing the same or similar products at the same cost and that give a firm market power. However, while market power allows a firm to influence the prices of its products and develop competitive strategies that enable it to earn larger profits, a firm with market power cannot sell any amount of output at a given market price, as in perfect competition. If a monopoly firm raises its price, it will sell less output, whereas if it lowers its price, it will sell more output.

The Monopolistic Competition and Oligopoly Models   The intermediate models of monopolistic competition and oligopoly in Figure 1.1 better characterize the behavior of real-world firms and industries because they represent a blend of competitive and monopolistic behavior. In **monopolistic competition**, firms produce differentiated products, so they have some degree of market power. However, because these firms are closer to the left end of the continuum in Figure 1.1, there are many firms competing with one another. Each firm has only limited ability to earn above-average profits before they are competed away over time. In **oligopoly** markets, a small number of large firms dominate the market, even if other producers are present. Mutual interdependence is the key characteristic of this market structure because firms need to take the actions of their rivals into account when developing their own competitive strategies. Oligopoly firms typically have market power, but how they use that power may be limited by the actions and reactions of their competitors.

The *Wall Street Journal* article opening this chapter does not discuss the specific market structure of Wal-Mart and its competitors in Mexico. However, because all of these firms are either large national or multinational companies, they obviously have substantial market power and are located far from the model of perfect competition on the continuum in Figure 1.1. The article notes that Wal-Mart's sales were estimated to be $21 billion and its profits were approximately $1.3 billion in 2007.

Large national or multinational companies typically find themselves operating in multiple markets, making the analysis of market structure more complicated as the market environment may differ substantially among these markets. For example, Wal-Mart sells a large line of products, effectively operating in a variety of markets and facing a different degree of competition in each of these markets. Wal-Mart stores compete against department stores, grocery chains, and even auto service centers. Each of these markets has its own characteristics in terms of the number and size of the competitors and product characteristics.

The Goal of Profit Maximization   In all of the market models we have just presented, we assume that the goal of firms is **profit maximization**, or earning the largest amount of profit possible. Because profit, as defined above, represents the difference between the revenues a firm receives for selling its output and its costs of production, firms may develop strategies to either increase revenues or reduce costs in an effort to increase profits. Profits act as a signal in a market economy. If firms in one sector of the economy earn above-average

---

Imperfect competition
Market structures of monopolistic competition, oligopoly, and monopoly, in which firms have some degree of market power.

Monopoly
A market structure characterized by a single firm producing a product with no close substitutes.

Barriers to entry
Structural, legal, or regulatory characteristics of a firm and its market that keep other firms from easily producing the same or similar products at the same cost.

Monopolistic competition
A market structure characterized by a large number of small firms that have some market power as a result of producing differentiated products. This market power can be competed away over time.

Oligopoly
A market structure characterized by competition among a small number of large firms that have market power, but that must take their rivals' actions into account when developing their own competitive strategies.

[handwritten notes:]
Profit

TR = P * Q

π = profit = TR - TC

Both or

Profit maximization
The assumed goal of firms, which is to develop strategies to earn the largest amount of profit possible. This can be accomplished by focusing on revenues, costs, or both.

profits, other firms will attempt to produce the same or similar products to increase their profitability. Thus, resources will flow from areas of low to high profitability. As we will see, however, the increased competition that results from this process will eventually lead to lower prices and revenues, thus eliminating most or all of these excess profits.

Profitability is the standard by which firms are judged in a market economy. Profitability affects stock prices and investor decisions. If firms are unprofitable, they will go out of business, be taken over by other more profitable companies, or have their management replaced. In subsequent chapters, we model a firm's profit-maximization decision largely in terms of static, single-period models where information on consumer behavior, revenues, and costs is known with certainty. Real-world managers must deal with uncertainty in all of these areas, which may lead to less-than-optimal decisions, and managers must be concerned with maximizing the firm's value over time. The models we present illustrate the basic forces influencing managerial decisions and the key role of profits as a motivating incentive.

Managerial Rule of Thumb

Microeconomic Influences on Managers

To develop a competitive advantage and increase their firm's profitability, managers need to understand:

- How consumer behavior affects their revenues
- How production technology and input prices affect their costs
- How the market and regulatory environment in which managers operate influences their ability to set prices and to respond to the strategies of their competitors ■

Macroeconomic Influences on Managers

The discussion of economic growth and collapse and concerns over increases in the general level of prices that influenced Wal-Mart's decisions in Mexico in the *Wall Street Journal* article that opened this chapter can be placed within the **circular flow model** of macroeconomics, shown in Figure 1.2. This model portrays the level of economic activity in a country as a flow of expenditures from the household sector to business firms as consumers purchase goods and services currently produced by these firms and sold in the country's output markets. This flow then returns to consumers as income received for supplying firms with the inputs or factors of production, including land, labor, capital, raw materials, and entrepreneurship, which are bought and sold in the resource markets. These payments, which include wages, rents, interest, and profits, become consumer income, which is again used to purchase goods and services—hence, the name *circular flow*. Figure 1.2 also shows spending by firms, by governments, and by the foreign sector of the economy. Corresponding to these total levels of expenditures and income are the amounts of output produced and resources employed.

The levels of expenditures, income, output, and employment in relation to the total capacity of the economy to produce goods and services will determine whether resources are fully employed in the economy or whether there is unemployed labor and excess plant capacity. This relationship will also determine whether and how much the absolute price level in the economy is increasing. The **absolute price level** is a measure of the *overall* price level in the economy as compared with the microeconomic concept of relative prices, which refers to the price of one particular good compared to that of another, as we discussed earlier.

Circular flow model
The macroeconomic model that portrays the level of economic activity as a flow of expenditures from consumers to firms, or producers, as consumers purchase goods and services produced by these firms. This flow then returns to consumers as income received from the production process.

Absolute price level
A measure of the overall level of prices in the economy.

$GDP_{(real)} = C + I + G + X - M$
70% 20% 10% (-)
$15T

$\dfrac{GDP}{Pop} = $ Per Capital GDP

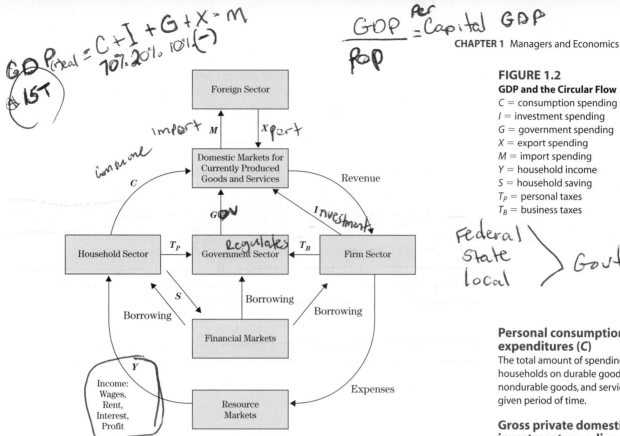

consume   import   *M*

C   *Xport*

Revenue

Investment

*G*ov   Regulates

Federal
State   } Govt
local

T_P   *T_B*

S

Borrowing   Borrowing   Borrowing

Y

Income:
Wages,
Rent,
Interest,
Profit

Expenses

FIGURE 1.2
GDP and the Circular Flow
C = consumption spending
I = investment spending
G = government spending
X = export spending
M = import spending
Y = household income
S = household saving
T_P = personal taxes
T_B = business taxes

Personal consumption expenditures (C)
The total amount of spending by households on durable goods, nondurable goods, and services in a given period of time.

Gross private domestic investment spending (I)
The total amount of spending on nonresidential structures, equipment, software, residential structures, and business inventories in a given period of time.

Government consumption expenditures and gross investment (G)
The total amount of spending by federal, state, and local governments on consumption outlays for goods and services, depreciation charges for existing structures and equipment, and investment capital outlays for newly acquired structures and equipment in a given period of time.

Net export spending (F)
The total amount of spending on exports (X) minus the total amount of spending on imports (M) or ($F = X - M$) in a given period of time.

Export spending (X)
The total amount of spending on goods and services currently produced in one country and sold abroad to residents of other countries in a given period of time.

Import spending (M)
The total amount of spending on goods and services currently produced in other countries and sold to residents of a given country in a given period of time.

Economists use the circular flow model in Figure 1.2 to define and analyze the spending behavior of different sectors of the economy, including

- **Personal consumption expenditures (C)** by all households on durable goods, nondurable goods, and services
- **Gross private domestic investment spending (I)** by households and firms on nonresidential structures, equipment, software, residential structures, and inventories
- Federal, state, and local **government consumption expenditures and gross investment (G)**
- **Net export spending (F)** or total **export spending (X)** minus total **import spending (M)**

Consumption spending (C) is largely determined by consumer income (Y), but it is also influenced by other factors such as consumer confidence, as noted below. Much business investment spending (I) is derived from borrowing in the financial markets and is, therefore, affected by prevailing interest rates. The availability of funds for borrowing is influenced by the amount of income that consumers save (S) or do not spend on goods and services.[9] Some consumer income (Y) is also used to pay personal taxes (T_P) to the government sector to finance the purchase of its goods and services. The government also imposes taxes on business (T_B). If government spending (G) exceeds the total amount of taxes collected ($T = T_P + T_B$), the resulting deficit must be financed by borrowing in the financial markets. This government borrowing may affect the amount of funds available for business investment, which in turn may cause interest rates to change, influencing firms' costs of production.

The foreign sector also plays a role in a country's circular flow of expenditures because some currently produced goods and services are purchased by residents

---

[9] Households also borrow from the financial markets, but they are net savers on balance.

of other countries, exports (X), while a given country's residents use some of their income to purchase goods and services produced in other countries, imports (M). Net export spending (F), or export spending (X) minus import spending (M), measures the net effect of the foreign sector on the domestic economy. Import spending is subtracted from export spending because it represents a flow of expenditures out of the domestic economy to the rest of the world.[10]

Spending by all these sectors equals **gross domestic product (GDP)**, the comprehensive measure of overall economic activity that is used to judge how an economy is performing. Gross domestic product measures the market value of all currently produced final goods and services within a country in a given period of time by domestic and foreign-supplied resources. GDP equals the sum of consumption spending (C), investment spending (I), government spending (G), and export spending (X) minus import spending (M).

Factors Affecting Macro Spending Behavior

In macroeconomics, we develop models that explain the behavior of these different sectors of the economy and how changes in this behavior influence the overall level of economic activity, or GDP. These behavior changes arise from

1. Changes in the consumption and investment behavior of individuals and firms in the private sector of the economy
2. New directions taken by a country's monetary or fiscal policy-making institutions (its central bank and national government)
3. Developments that occur in the rest of the world that influence the domestic economy

Changes in Private-Sector Behavior   Although there are many factors that influence consumption spending (C) and investment spending (I), credit availability, consumer wealth in the housing and stock markets, and confidence on the part of both consumers and businesspeople were extremely important factors influencing the U.S. economy in 2007 and 2008. The steep decline in housing prices combined with the decrease in the availability of credit caused a slowing of growth in the U.S. economy. This slowing of growth in the United States translated back to the Mexican economy with decreased income transfers from Mexicans living in the United States to their families in Mexico which caused a lower rate of growth of Wal-Mart sales in Mexico. In response to these macroeconomic changes, the company began cutting spending on advertising and marketing, eliminating jobs at its headquarters, and slashing prices on a new round of products.[11]

Monetary Policies   In response to the slowing U.S. economy in 2007, the Federal Reserve, the central bank in the United States, began lowering its target interest rate, which had been 5.25 percent since June 2006. By October 2008, this rate had decreased to 1.00 percent, the lowest rate since 2003 and 2004. These rate changes were reactions to slowing in consumer spending, employment, and manufacturing activity, continued turmoil in the housing and financial markets, and sharp drops in the stock market. Managers in any economy must be aware of the **monetary policies** of their country's central bank that influence interest rates and the amount of funds available for consumer and business loans.

Gross domestic product (GDP)
The comprehensive measure of the total market value of all currently produced final goods and services within a country in a given period of time by domestic and foreign-supplied resources.

Monetary policies
Policies adopted by a country's central bank that influence the money supply, interest rates, and the amount of funds available for loans, which, in turn, influence consumer and business spending.

[10] If a country's export spending and import spending do not balance, there will be a flow of financial capital among different countries. This flow will affect a country's currency exchange rate, the rate at which one country's currency can be exchanged for another. These issues will be discussed in detail in Chapter 15.
[11] Hudson and Campoy, "Hispanics' Hard Times Hit Wal-Mart."

Fiscal Policies   At this same time, Congress and the Bush administration were also proposing changes in **fiscal policy**—taxing and spending policies by a country's national government that can be used to either stimulate or restrain the economy ($T = T_P + T_B$ and G in the circular flow model in Figure 1.2). Fiscal policy decisions are made by a country's executive and legislative institutions, such as the president, his or her administration, and the Congress in the United States. As a result, fiscal policy actions may be undertaken to promote political as well as economic goals.

In February 2008, Congress passed a $168 billion tax cut bill to stimulate the U.S. economy. Under the final bill, most taxpayers received checks of up to $600 for individuals or $1,200 for married couples, amounts that phased out at higher incomes.[12] In October 2008, Congress passed a $700 billion package to help the financial sector and stem the slowing economic growth. Congressional leaders also began debating a second economic stimulus bill.[13]

Changes in the Foreign Sector   The opening discussion of Wal-Mart's strategies in Mexico noted that the country's currency devaluation and economic collapse in 1994 created obstacles for Wal-Mart and eventually caused several of its competitors to leave the country. The value at which a country's currency can be exchanged for another currency affects the flow of imports and exports to and from the country and the level of economic activity in the country. Policies to keep that exchange rate at a certain level can have negative effects on other economic goals and can be offset by the actions of currency traders in financial markets. Exchange rate policies need to be coordinated with monetary and fiscal policies to maintain the proper rate of economic growth.

Fiscal policy
Changes in taxing and spending by the executive and legislative branches of a country's national government that can be used to either stimulate or restrain the economy.

Managerial Rule of Thumb

Macroeconomic Influences on Managers

Changes in the macro environment affect individual firms and industries through the microeconomic factors of demand, production, cost, and profitability. Managers don't have control over these changes in the larger macroeconomic environment. However, managers must be aware of the developments that will have a direct impact on their businesses. Managers sometimes hire outside consultants for reports on the macroeconomic environment, or they ask in-house staff to prepare forecasts. In any case, they need to be able to interpret these forecasts and then project the impact of these macroeconomic changes on the competitive strategies of their firms. Although overall macroeconomic changes may be the same, their impact on various firms and industries is likely to be quite varied. ■

Summary

In this chapter, we discussed the reasons why both microeconomic and macroeconomic analyses are important for managerial decision making. *Microeconomics* focuses on the decisions that individual consumers and firms make as they produce, buy, and sell goods and services in a market economy, while *macroeconomics* analyzes the overall level of economic activity, changes in the price level and unemployment, and the rate of economic growth for the economy. All of these factors affect the decisions managers make in developing competitive strategies for their firms.

We illustrated these issues by analyzing a *Wall Street Journal* article on Wal-Mart's operations in Mexico. The company was able to use its size and production technology

---

[12] Sarah Lueck, "Congress Approves Economic-Stimulus Bill," *Wall Street Journal*, February 8, 2008.
[13] Deborah Solomon and David Enrich, "Devil Is in Bailout's Details," *Wall Street Journal*, October 15, 2008; Greg Hitt and Jonathan Weisman, "Pelosi Pushes Two-Part Stimulus," *Wall Street Journal*, November 7, 2008.

to become a major presence in the retail sector in Mexico and to put downward pressure on the prices charged by all its competitors. At the same time, when it first entered Mexico, Wal-Mart's strategies were influenced by the currency crisis and economic collapse in 1994. More recently, the company has been impacted by the slowing of the U.S. and Mexican economies in 2007 and 2008.

We then briefly introduced the concept of market structure and presented the four basic market models: *perfect competition, monopolistic competition, oligopoly,* and *monopoly.* We also showed how the economic activity between consumers and producers fits into the aggregate *circular flow model* of macroeconomics, and we defined the basic spending components of that model: *consumption, investment, government spending,* and *spending on exports and imports.* We illustrated the effects of changes in *monetary policy* by a country's central bank and changes in *fiscal policy* by the national administrative and legislative institutions on the overall level of economic activity.

In the following chapters, we'll analyze these issues in more detail. We first focus on the microeconomic concepts of demand and supply, pricing, production and cost, and market structures in Chapters 2 through 10. We'll then turn our attention to macroeconomic models and data in Chapters 11 through 15. We return to integrate these issues further in Chapter 16, where we'll look at more examples of the combined impact of both microeconomic and macroeconomic variables on managerial decision making.

Key Terms

absolute price level, p. 10

barriers to entry, p. 9

circular flow model, p. 10

export spending (*X*), p. 11

fiscal policy, p. 13

government consumption
   expenditures and gross
   investment (*G*), p. 11

gross domestic product
   (GDP), p. 12

gross private domestic investment spending (*I*), p. 11

imperfect competition, p. 9

import spending (*M*), p. 11

inputs, p. 5

macroeconomics, p. 5

managerial economics, p. 5

market power, p. 8

markets, p. 7

microeconomics, p. 5

monetary policies, p. 12

monopolistic competition, p. 9

monopoly, p. 9

net export spending (*F*), p. 11

oligopoly, p. 9

outputs, p. 5

perfect competition, p. 8

personal consumption
   expenditures (*C*), p. 11

prices, p. 5

price-taker, p. 8

profit, p. 8

profit maximization, p. 9

relative prices, p. 6

Exercises

Technical Questions

1. What are the differences between the microeconomic and macroeconomic perspectives on the economy?

2. Explain the differences between the inputs and outputs of a production process.

3. What are the four major types of markets in microeconomic analysis? What are the key characteristics that distinguish these markets?

4. Why do economists assume that firms are price-takers in the model of perfect competition? How does this pricing behavior differ from that in the other market models?

5. In macroeconomics, what are the five major categories of spending that make up GDP? Are all five categories added together to determine GDP?

6. Discuss the differences between fiscal and monetary policies.

Application Questions

1. Give illustrations from the opening news article in this chapter of how differences in political and cultural factors can influence a company's strategy when expanding internationally.

2. Drawing on the Internet and other media sources, discuss current developments in the Mexican economy and how they are influencing companies in the United States and the U.S. economy.

3. In each of the following examples, discuss which market model appears to best explain the behavior described:

   a. Dry weather unexpectedly cut the 2003 soybean harvest by 15 percent, making it the smallest harvest in seven years. China increased its demand for soybeans, acquiring a record 300 million U.S. bushels between September 2003 and April 2004. The Bush administration expected that U.S. farmers would respond to the high prices by planting more soybeans in the next cycle.[14]

   b. In spring 2004, General Motors launched another round of discounts, offering zero percent financing for five-year loans and $1,000 additional givebacks to customers. Following GM's move, Ford increased rebates on certain pickup models from $1,000 to $1,500, while DaimlerChrysler announced that 2005 minivans would come with a $1,000 rebate.[15]

   c. In spring 2004, the U.S. wireless telecommunications industry hoped that mergers among firms would decrease the number of rivals and eliminate cutthroat competition. However, the wireless carriers faced challenges from new technologies and a rush of new entrants into the market. Unlike their counterparts in the traditional phone industry, wireless companies never enjoyed a period of monopoly status.[16]

   d. Chinese cooking is the most popular food in America that isn't dominated by big national chains. Chinese food is typically cooked in a wok that requires high heat and a special stove. Specialized chefs are also required. Small mom-and-pop restaurants comprise nearly all of the nation's 36,000 Chinese restaurants, which have more locations than McDonald's, Burger King, and Wendy's combined.[17]

4. In current business publications, find examples of firms whose strategies to increase profits focus primarily on generating more revenue. Compare these cases with firms who are trying to cut costs to increase profits.

5. The downturn in economic activity or recession in 2007 and 2008 forced many firms to develop new competitive strategies to survive. Find examples of these strategies in various business publications.

On the Web

For updated information on the *Wall Street Journal* article at the beginning of the chapter, as well as other relevant links and information, visit the book's Web site at **www.pearsonhighered.com/farnham**

---

[14] Scott Kilman, "Soaring Soybean Prices Hit Home," *Wall Street Journal*, April 6, 2004.

[15] Joseph B. White, "Auto Makers' Price War to Widen," *Wall Street Journal*, April 1, 2004.

[16] Jesse Drucker, "Big-Name Mergers Won't Ease Crowding in Cellphone Industry," *Wall Street Journal*, February 13, 2004.

[17] Shirley Leung, "Big Chains Talk the Talk, But Can't Walk the Wok," Wall Street Journal, January 23, 2003.

2 Demand, Supply, and Equilibrium Prices

I n this chapter, we analyze demand and supply—probably the two most famous words in all of economics. *Demand*—the functional relationship between the price of a good or service and the quantity demanded by consumers in a given period of time, all else held constant—and *supply*—the functional relationship between the price of a good or service and the quantity supplied by producers in a given period of time, all else held constant—provide a framework for analyzing the behavior of consumers and producers in a market economy. Managers need to understand these terms to develop their own competitive strategies and to respond to the actions of their competitors. They also need to understand that the role of demand and supply depends on the environment or market structure in which a firm operates.

We begin our discussion of demand and supply by focusing on an analysis of the copper industry in the *Wall Street Journal* article "Copper Surplus Is Foreseen in '07." In our case analysis, we'll discuss how factors related to consumer behavior (demand) and producer behavior (supply) determine the price of copper and cause changes in that price. In the remainder of the chapter, we'll look at how the factors from the copper industry fit into the general demand and supply framework of economic theory. We'll develop a conceptual analysis of demand functions and demand curves; discuss the range of factors that influence consumer demand; analyze how demand can be described verbally, graphically, and symbolically using equations; and look at a specific mathematical example of demand. We'll then describe the supply side of the market and the factors influencing supply in the same manner. Finally, we'll discuss how demand- and supply-side factors determine prices and cause them to change.

Copper Surplus Is Foreseen in '07

by Allen Sykora

Wall Street Journal, *February 28, 2007*

A number of analysts are looking for the global copper market to have a surplus this year, citing an expectation for steadier production after a strike-filled 2006 and potential substitution for the mineral. . . .

Data for 2006 from the International Copper Study Group suggest the market already has moved into a small surplus. The group lists a surplus of 108,000 tons for the first 11 months of 2006, compared with a 263,000 deficit for the same period in 2005. . . .

Chuck Bradford, metals analyst with Soleil Securities, looks for a surplus in the 200,000-ton area.

"One of the interesting things in the International Copper Study Group piece [of Feb. 16] was a rebound in the operating rate at the mine level," Mr. Bradford said. "If you look at the operating rates in earlier '06, they were well below where they had been any time during the rest of the decade. . . .

Production was lost during much of 2006 due to a series of strikes, Mr. Bradford said.

The ICSG report said global mine output was up 3% in November compared with the same month in 2005. But production disruptions in the first part of the year left output for the first 11 months of 2006 essentially unchanged—up 0.1%—compared with the same period in 2005.

Mr. Bradford said he doesn't anticipate a "huge" copper surplus in 2007, "because I think we'll have strikes again." Also, he said, when prices are high, companies are willing to mine lower-grade material that they may have not otherwise. . . .

Michael Skinner, of base metals sales with Standard Bank, said his firm looks for a modest surplus this year, assuming there is a "constant stream of production" without as many labor disruptions as in 2006. . . .

"It mainly has to do with continuity of production this year," he said. "There is certainly incentive to do that at these prices. That will help take us into surplus."

Mr. Skinner cautioned there can be wide variations in the supply-and-demand estimates by various researchers. This is especially the case for copper due to the difficulty in obtaining data from China.

Mr. Skinner said while the ICSG put the surplus at 108,000 metric tons for the first 11 months of 2006, his firm estimated a surplus of 40,000 metric tons in all of 2006. . . .

Mr. Bradford said a measure of demand may be how much substitution for copper occurs due to historically strong prices.

"My biggest fear is substitution," he said. "I keep asking people about it, and I get very conflicting stories. The aluminum guys are all convinced they have benefited materially from substitution away from copper into aluminum.

"[Copper] has been losing markets because of the price. It just takes a long time for that to happen," Mr. Bradford said.

An example, he said, is the move toward plastic piping in home construction.

Mr. Skinner also said industry appears to be making some effort to find substitutions for copper.

He said his firm believes the economy won't slow as much as some have forecast. If demand in other parts of the world holds up, overall demand could increase "marginally" this year, he said.

The key may be the level of Chinese imports, he said.

"The market is looking at that very carefully. The scrap substitution is also a key," Mr. Skinner said.

While many analysts look for Chinese buying to pick up this year, some caution it may not be as aggressive as some expect. In particular, many suspect China has drawn down inventories that must now be rebuilt. . . .

Case for Analysis

Demand and Supply in the Copper Industry

This *Wall Street Journal* article focuses on changes in the copper industry that occurred in 2006 and 2007. Analysts were predicting an increase in the supply of copper in 2007 after many strikes limited production in 2006. This decreased production along with strong worldwide demand caused the price of copper to remain at historic highs during that year. Much of this demand was stimulated by the economic growth in China. A lack of new mining projects also limited supply, given that many large, known copper deposits were in areas with unstable governments or were difficult to reach.[1] Another impact of the high prices was the increased theft of copper coils in air-conditioning units, copper wires, and copper pipes used for plumbing in homes and businesses in many parts of the United States.[2]

Analysts in the article predicted that increased quantities of copper would be available in 2007 due to several factors. (1) The strikes that occurred in 2006 were not expected to continue the next year. (2) The higher copper prices encouraged companies to mine lower-grade copper that would not have been economically feasible with lower prices. However, the high copper prices also gave many copper users the incentive to find substitutes for the metal. The article discusses how aluminum producers may have benefited from the high copper prices, and how these prices stimulated the increased use of plastic piping in home construction.

The article also shows how forecasts of future prices and production can be very uncertain, given the variety of factors operating on both the demand and supply side of the market. One report estimated a surplus of 108,000 metric tons for the first 11 months of 2006, while another estimated a surplus of 40,000 metric tons for the entire year. The extent of substitution with other products was also difficult to estimate, as was the substitution with scrap metal. Moreover, when this article was written in February 2007, the first impacts of the slowing housing market on the U.S. economy were just beginning to appear. Thus, changes in the macro-economy also impacted this particular industry.

Copper prices continued to be influenced by the demand from China. This demand slowed in 2008 as the Chinese drew down their inventories when global prices were high and shut down some industrial activity preceding the Olympics in August 2008. The slowing Chinese economy in fall 2008 also impacted the world copper market where prices continued to fall.[3]

An analysis of a substantial decline in copper prices from November 1997 to February 1998 illustrated many of these same factors.[4] The 1997 financial crisis and recession in Southeast Asia had a significant impact on the copper industry as did uncertain demand from China and the increased use of copper in communications technology in North America. Expectations also played a role as many copper users were hesitant to buy because they thought prices might continue their downward trend.

On the supply side, the low price of copper forced mining companies to decide whether certain high-cost mines should be kept in operation. However, a new mining process called "solvent extraction" also allowed some companies to mine copper at a lower cost, which permitted more copper mines to stay in business.

We can see from this discussion that a variety of factors influence the price of copper and that these factors can be categorized as operating either on the demand (consumer) side or the supply (producer) side of the market. Sometimes the influence of one factor in lowering prices is partially or completely offset by the impacts of other factors that tend to increase prices. Thus, the resulting copper prices will be determined by the magnitude of the changes in all of these variables.

Note also that the article discusses *general* influences on the copper industry. There is no discussion of the strategic behavior of individual firms. This focus on the entire industry is a characteristic of a perfectly or highly competitive market, where there are many buyers and sellers and the product is

---

[1] Patrick Barta, "A Red-Hot Desire for Copper," *Wall Street Journal*, March 16, 2006.
[2] Sara Schaefer Munoz and Paul Glader, "Copper and Robbers: Homeowners' Latest Worry," *Wall Street Journal*, September 6, 2006.
[3] Allen Sykora, "China Copper Need Set to Rise," *Wall Street Journal*, August 25, 2008; James Campbell and Matthew Walls, "China Drags Down Metals; Slump in Real Estate; Export Industries May Keep Lid on Oil Prices,: *Wall Street Journal*, October 29, 2008; Allen Sykora, "Copper Is Vulnerable to Falling Further," *Wall Street Journal*, November 24, 2008.
[4] Aaron Lucchetti, "Copper Limbo: Just How Low Can It Go?" *Wall Street Journal*, February 23, 1998.

relatively homogeneous or undifferentiated (see Figure 1.1 in Chapter 1). Prices are determined through the overall forces of demand and supply in these markets. All firms, no matter where they are located on the market structure continuum in Figure 1.1, face a demand from consumers for their products. The factors influencing demand, which are discussed in this chapter, thus pertain to firms operating in every type of market. However, the demand/supply framework and the resulting determination of equilibrium prices apply only to perfectly or highly competitive markets. We'll now examine the concepts of demand and supply in more detail to see how managers can use this framework to analyze changes in prices and quantities of different products in various markets. ■

Demand

Although demand and supply are used in everyday language, these concepts have very precise meanings in economics.[5] It is important that you understand the difference between the economic terms and ordinary usage. We'll look at demand first and turn our attention to supply later in the chapter.

Demand is defined in economics as a functional relationship between the price of a good or service and the quantity demanded by consumers in a given period of time, *all else held constant*. (The Latin phrase *ceteris paribus* is often used in place of "all else held constant.") A **functional relationship** means that demand focuses not just on the current price of the good and the quantity demanded at that price, but also on the relationship between different prices and the quantities that would be demanded at those prices. Demand incorporates a consumer's willingness *and* ability to purchase a product.

Demand
The functional relationship between the price of a good or service and the quantity demanded by consumers in a given time period, *all else held constant*.

Functional relationship
A relationship between variables, usually expressed in an equation using symbols for the variables, where the value of one variable, the independent variable, determines the value of the other, the dependent variable.

Nonprice Factors Influencing Demand

The demand relationship is defined with "all else held constant" because many other variables in addition to price influence the quantity of a product that consumers demand. The following sections summarize these variables, many of which were discussed in the *Wall Street Journal* copper industry article.

Tastes and Preferences   Consumers must first desire or have tastes and preferences for a good. For example, in the aftermath of the September 11, 2001, terrorist attacks on New York and Washington, D.C., the tastes and preferences of U.S. consumers for airline travel changed dramatically. People were simply afraid to fly and did not purchase airline tickets regardless of the price charged. In October 2001, most of the major airlines began advertising campaigns to increase consumer confidence in the safety of air travel. United Airlines' advertisements featured firsthand employee accounts, while American Airlines encouraged people to spend time with family and friends over the upcoming holidays and beyond.[6]

Similarly, in spring 2006, the National Chicken Council waged a campaign to prevent fears of the avian flu in Asia from impacting the demand for chicken in the United States.[7] Maintaining and strengthening consumer tastes and preferences for

---

[5] Even basic terms such as *demand* may be defined differently in various business disciplines. For example, in *Marketing Management, The Millennium Edition* (Prentice Hall, 2000), Philip Kotler defines *market demand* as "the total volume that would be bought by a defined customer group in a defined geographical area in a defined time period in a defined marketing environment under a defined marketing program" (p. 120). Since advertising and marketing expenditures are the focus of this discipline, demand is defined to emphasize these issues rather than price.

[6] Melanie Trottman, "Airlines Launch New Ad Campaigns Using Emotion to Restore Confidence," *Wall Street Journal*, October 24, 2001.

[7] Jane Zhang, "'Merchant of Drumsticks' Aims to Allay Chicken-Flu Fears," *Wall Street Journal*, May 4, 2006.

chicken was crucial to the industry, which had $38 billion in annual retail sales at that time, particularly given a Harvard School of Public Health survey, which indicated that 46 percent of chicken eaters would stop eating chicken and 25 percent would eat less if avian flu entered the United States. The broiler chicken industry had benefited from increased consumer interest in healthy eating habits.[8] For the past 40 years, health associations have been warning about the dangers of a high-fat diet, which caused poultry consumption to increase, particularly at the expense of beef consumption.

Socioeconomic variables such as age, sex, race, marital status, and level of education are often good proxies for an individual's tastes and preferences for a particular good, because tastes and preferences may vary by these groupings and products are often targeted at one or more of these groups. In 2006, many of the largest beer brewers in the United States began aggressively courting Hispanics, the country's fastest growing and youngest population group. This strategy was developed in reaction to stagnating beer sales, an aging population who were drinking less beer, and the increased appeal of wines.[9]

Economic theory may also suggest that one or more of these socioeconomic variables influences the demand for a particular good or service. For example, persons with more education are believed to be more knowledgeable about using preventive services to improve their health. Marital status may influence the demand for acute care and hospital services because married individuals have spouses who may be able to help take care of them in the home.[10] Thus, tastes and preferences encompass all the individualistic variables that influence a person's willingness to purchase a good.

Normal good

A good for which consumers will have a greater demand as their incomes increase, all else held constant, and a smaller demand if their incomes decrease, other factors held constant.

Inferior good

A good for which consumers will have a smaller demand as their incomes increase, all else held constant, and a greater demand if their incomes decrease, other factors held constant.

Income   The level of a person's income also affects demand, because demand incorporates both willingness and ability to pay for the good. If the demand for a good varies directly with income, that good is called a **normal good**. This definition means that, all else held constant, an increase in an individual's income will increase the demand for a normal good, and a decrease in that income will decrease the demand for that good. If the demand varies inversely with income, the good is termed an **inferior good**. Thus, an increase in income will cause a consumer to purchase less of an inferior good, while a decrease in that income will actually cause the consumer to demand more of the inferior good. Note that the term *inferior* has nothing to do with the quality of the good—it refers only to how purchases of the good or service vary with changes in income.

Normal Goods   In many cases, the effect of income on particular goods and services is related to the general level of economic activity in the economy. Although jewelers used the transition from the year 1999 to 2000 to influence consumer tastes and preferences for jewelry, the strong economy and the booming stock market in 1999 also played a role in influencing demand.[11] On the other hand, the loss of both jobs and stock market wealth in fall 2008 caused retail spending to decline below already-weak forecasts.[12]

Both increases in income and changes in tastes and preferences have resulted in an increased demand for gourmet pet food, especially for dogs. The head of

---

[8] Richard T. Rogers, "Broilers: Differentiating a Commodity," in *Industry Studies*, 2nd ed., ed. Larry L. Duetsch (Armonk, N.Y.: Sharpe, 1998), 65–100.

[9] Miriam Jordan, "Cerveza, Si or No?" *Wall Street Journal*, March 29, 2006.

[10] The demand for health and medical services is discussed in Donald S. Kenkel, "The Demand for Preventive Medical Care," *Applied Economics* 26 (April 1994): 313–25, and in Rexford E. Santerre and Stephen P. Neun, *Health Economics: Theories, Insights, and Industry Studies*, 4th ed. (Mason, OH: Thomson South-Western, 2007).

[11] Rebecca Quick, "Jewelry Retailers Have Gem of a Holiday Season," *Wall Street Journal*, January 7, 2000.

[12] Ann Zimmerman, "Retailers Wallow and See Only More Gloom," *Wall Street Journal*, November 7, 2008.

Del Monte's food and pet division said in 2006 that "the humanization of pets is the single biggest trend driving our business."[13] Changes in tastes in human food spill over into the pet food market. However, the demand for gourmet pet food was also driven by the change in pet ownership from parents of small children, who had neither the time nor money to spend lavishly on their pets, to childless people ranging from gay couples to parents whose children have left home. These couples have larger incomes and treat their pets as they would their children.

Inferior Goods Firms producing inferior goods do not benefit from a booming economy. One such example is the pawnshop industry, which suffered during the economic prosperity of the late 1990s and 2000, as fewer people swapped jewelry and other items for cash to cover car payments and other debts.[14] Although pawnshops have always suffered from a somewhat disreputable image, the strong economy provided an income effect that further hurt the business and caused many chains to incur large losses.

In the health care area, it is argued that tooth extractions are an example of an inferior good. As individuals' incomes rise, they are able to afford more complex and expensive dental restorative procedures, such as caps and crowns, and they are able to purchase more regular preventive dental services. Thus, the need for extractions decreases as income increases.[15]

Prices of Related Goods There are two major categories of goods or products whose prices influence the demand for a particular good: substitute goods and complementary goods.

Substitute Goods Products or services are **substitute goods** for each other if one can be used in place of another. Consumers derive satisfaction from either good or service. If two goods, X and Y, are substitutes for each other, an increase in the price of good Y will cause consumers to decrease their consumption of good Y and increase their demand for good X. If the price of good Y decreases, the demand for substitute good X will decrease. Thus, changes in the price of good Y and the demand for good X move in the same direction for substitute goods. The amount of substitution depends on the consumer's tastes and preferences for the two goods and the size of the price change.

By 2006 the abundance and relatively low prices of cell phones, iPods, and laptop computers resulted in many teens and young adults no longer purchasing wristwatches. In 2005, sales of watches priced between $30 and $150, the type most often purchased by these age groups, declined more than 10 percent from 2004.[16] In response to this threat from substitute products, watchmakers developed new models that do much more than tell time, including watches with earbuds that play digital music files, watches with programmable channels, and models with compasses and thermometers.

In 2007, large increases in the price of platinum resulted in an increased demand for palladium, a lesser-known platinum-group metal. The price of an ounce of platinum was approximately $1,190 compared with $337 for an ounce of palladium. Because the two metals have a similar look and feel, many jewelers offered palladium to

Substitute goods

Two goods, X and Y, are substitutes if an increase in the price of good Y causes consumers to *increase* their demand for good X or if a decrease in the price of good Y causes consumers to *decrease* their demand for good X.

---

[13] Deborah Ball, "Nothing Says, 'I Love You, Fido' Like Food with Gourmet Flair," *Wall Street Journal*, March 18, 2006.

[14] Kortney Stringer, "Best of Times Is Worst of Times for Pawnshops in New Economy," *Wall Street Journal*, August 22, 2000.

[15] Rexford E. Santerre and Stephen P. Neun, *Health Economics: Theories, Insights, and Industry Studies*, rev. ed. (Orlando, FL: Dryden, 2000), p. 90.

[16] Jessica E. Vascellaro, "The Times They Are a-Changin'," *Wall Street Journal*, January 18, 2006.

customers as a less expensive alternative, particularly for wedding and engagement rings. World demand for palladium in jewelry was 1.12 million ounces in 2006 compared with 1.74 million ounces for platinum.[17]

Complementary goods

Two goods, *X* and *Y*, are complementary if an increase in the price of good *Y* causes consumers to *decrease* their demand for good *X* or if a decrease in the price of good *Y* causes consumers to *increase* their demand for good *X*.

Complementary Goods   **Complementary goods** are products or services that consumers use together. If products *X* and *Y* are complements, an increase in the price of good *Y* will cause consumers to decrease their consumption of good *Y* and their demand for good *X*, since *X* and *Y* are used together. Likewise, if the price of good *Y* decreases, the demand for good *X* will increase. Changes in the price of good *Y* and the demand for good *X* move in the opposite direction if *X* and *Y* are complementary goods.

As prices of personal computers have dropped over time, there has been an increased demand for printers and printer cartridges. This complementary relationship has allowed Hewlett-Packard Company to actually sell its printers at a loss that it recouped through its new ink and toner sales. Analysts estimated that in 2005 the company earned at least a 60 percent profit margin on both ink and toner cartridges and two-thirds of the company's profits were derived from these sales. In 2006, Walgreen Company, the drugstore chain, announced plans for an ink-refill service in 1,500 of its stores with a price at less than half the cost of buying new cartridges.[18] OfficeMax and Office Depot also offered these services. This example shows how a complementary relationship between two goods can create a profit opportunity for a firm, which then may still be competed away by the development of substitute goods.

Future Expectations   Expectations about future prices also play a role in influencing current demand for a product. If consumers expect prices to be lower in the future, they may have less current demand than if they did not have those expectations. In summer 2004, many consumers responded to high lumber prices by waiting to purchase until fall when a normal seasonal decline was expected to occur. One developer in Maryland bought only as much wood as he needed week-by-week because the high summer prices had increased the cost of wood for a typical apartment by 50 percent.[19]

Likewise, if prices are expected to increase, consumers may demand more of the good at present than they would without these expectations. In fall 2007, world grain prices were surging from major demand increases stimulated by U.S. government incentives encouraging businesses to turn corn and soybeans into motor fuel, increased incomes from the growing economies of Asia and Latin America, and a growing middle class in these areas that was eating more meat and milk, increasing the demand for grain to feed the livestock. Even though U.S. corn farmers expected a record harvest, which should have had a moderating effect on grain prices, traders in the futures markets for corn were already betting that the price of corn would increase from $3.25 per bushel to more than $4.00 in March 2008 and would stay above that level until 2010.[20]

Number of Consumers   Finally, the number of consumers in the marketplace influences the demand for a product. A firm's marketing strategy is typically based on finding new groups of consumers who will purchase the product. In many cases, a country's exports may be the source of this increased demand. In the broiler chicken industry, U.S. exports have grown from an insignificant amount in

---

[17] Elizabeth Holmes, "Palladium, Platinum's Cheaper Sister, Makes a Bid for Love," *Wall Street Journal*, February 13, 2007.
[18] Pui-Wing Tam, "A Cheaper Way to Refill Your Printer," *Wall Street Journal*, January 26. 2006.
[19] Avery Johnson, "Sticker Shock at the Lumberyard," *Wall Street Journal*, August 11, 2004.
[20] Scott Kilman, "Historic Surge in Grain Prices Roils Market," *Wall Street Journal*, September 28, 2007.

the 1950s and 1960s to over 4 billion pounds, or 16 percent of the market, in 1996 due to a larger consumer base. Russia changed from a nonimporter of U.S. broiler chickens in 1988 to the primary export destination in the mid-1990s, accounting, along with other members of the former Soviet Union, for 45 percent of all U.S. broiler exports. In addition to stimulating overall demand, this export increase helped U.S. producers because consumers in many of these other countries prefer dark meat, while U.S. customers prefer white meat. Thus, the U.S. producers could make more efficient use of the broiler chicken with these expanded markets.[21]

The effect of growing populations on demand and grain prices was discussed above in the future expectations section of the text. Both increases in the size of the population in Asian and Latin American economies and growth in the middle-class segments of these economies had a stimulating effect on the demand for many types of grain.

Demand Function

We can now summarize all the variables that influence the demand for a particular product in a generalized demand function represented as follows:

2.1 $Q_{XD} = f(P_X, T, I, P_Y, P_Z, EXC, NC, \ldots)$
where

Q_{XD} = quantity demanded of good X
P_X = price of good X
T = variables representing an individual's tastes and preferences
I = income
P_Y, P_Z = prices of goods Y and Z, which are related to the consumption of good X
EXC = consumer expectations about future prices
NC = number of consumers

Equation 2.1 is read as follows: The quantity demanded of good X is a function (f) of the variables inside the parentheses. An ellipsis is placed after the last variable to signify that many other variables may also influence the demand for a specific product. These may include variables under the control of a manager, such as the size of the advertising budget, and variables not under anyone's control, such as the weather.

Each consumer has his or her own **individual demand function** for different products. However, managers are usually more interested in the **market demand function**, which shows the quantity demanded of the good or service by *all* consumers in the market at any given price. The market demand function is influenced by the prices of related goods, as well as by the tastes and preferences, income, and future expectations of all consumers in the market. It can also change because more consumers enter the market.

Individual demand function
The function that shows, in symbolic or mathematical terms, the variables that influence the quantity demanded of a particular product by an individual consumer.

Market demand function
The function that shows, in symbolic or mathematical terms, the variables that influence the quantity demanded of a particular product by all consumers in the market and that is thus affected by the number of consumers in the market.

Demand Curves

Equation 2.1 shows the typical variables included in a demand function. To systematically analyze all of these variables, economists define demand as we did earlier in this chapter: the functional relationship between alternative prices and the quantities

---

[21] Rogers, "Broilers," p. 72.

FIGURE 2.1

The Demand Curve for a Product

A demand curve shows the relationship between the price of a good and the quantity demanded, all else held constant.

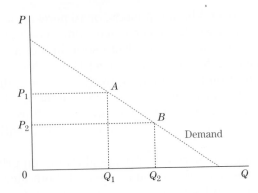

consumers demand at those prices, all else held constant. This relationship is portrayed graphically in Figure 2.1, which shows a **demand curve** for a given product. Price (P), measured in dollar terms, is the variable that is explicitly analyzed and shown on the vertical axis of the graph. Quantity demanded (Q) is shown on the horizontal axis. The other variables in the demand function are held constant with a given demand curve, but act as **demand shifters** if their values change.

As we just mentioned, demand curves are drawn with the price placed on the vertical axis and the quantity demanded on the horizontal axis. This may seem inconsistent because we usually think of the quantity demanded of a good (dependent variable) as a function of the price of the good (independent variable). The dependent variable in a mathematical relationship is usually placed on the vertical axis and the independent variable on the horizontal axis. The reverse is done for demand because we also want to show how revenues and costs vary with the level of output. These variables are placed on the vertical axis in subsequent analysis. In mathematical terms, an equation showing quantity as a function of price is equivalent to the inverse equation showing price as a function of quantity.

Demand curves are generally downward sloping, showing a **negative** or **inverse relationship** between the price of a good and the quantity demanded at that price, all else held constant. Thus, in Figure 2.1, when the price falls from P_1 to P_2, the quantity demanded is expected to increase from Q_1 to Q_2, if nothing else changes. This is represented by the movement from point A to point B in Figure 2.1. Likewise, an increase in the price of the good results in a decrease in quantity demanded, all else held constant. Most demand curves that show real-world behavior exhibit this inverse relationship between price and quantity demanded. (We'll discuss the economic model of consumer behavior that lies behind this demand relationship in the Appendix to Chapter 3.)

Change in Quantity Demanded and Change in Demand

The movement between points A and B along the demand curve in Figure 2.1 is called a **change in quantity demanded**. It results when consumers react to a change in the price of the good, all other factors held constant. This change in quantity demanded is pictured as a movement along a given demand curve.

It is also possible for the entire demand curve to shift. This shift results when the values of one or more of the other variables in Equation 2.1 change. For example, if consumers' incomes increase, the demand curve for the particular good generally shifts outward or to the right, assuming that the good is a normal good. This shift of the entire demand curve is called a **change in demand**. It occurs when one or more of the variables held constant in defining a given demand curve changes.

Demand curve

The graphical relationship between the price of a good and the quantity consumers demand, with all other factors influencing demand held constant.

Demand shifters

The variables in a demand function that are held constant when defining a given demand curve, but that would shift the demand curve if their values changed.

Negative (inverse) relationship

A relationship between two variables, graphed as a downward sloping line, where an increase in the value of one variable causes a decrease in the value of the other variable.

Change in quantity demanded

The change in quantity consumers purchase when the price of the good changes, all other factors held constant, pictured as a movement along a given demand curve.

Change in demand

The change in quantity purchased when one or more of the demand shifters change, pictured as a shift of the entire demand curve.

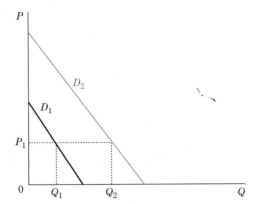

This distinction between a change in demand and a change in quantity demanded is very important in economic analysis. The two phrases mean something different and should not be used interchangeably. The distinction arises from the basic economic framework, in which we examine the relationship between two variables while holding all other factors constant.

An increase in demand, or a rightward or outward shift of the demand curve, is shown in Figure 2.2. We've drawn this shift as a parallel shift of the demand curve, although this doesn't have to be the case. Suppose this change in demand results from an increase in consumers' incomes. The important point in Figure 2.2 is that an increase in demand means that consumers will demand a larger quantity of the good *at the same price*—in this case, due to higher incomes. This outcome is contrasted with a movement along a demand curve or a change in quantity demanded, where a larger quantity of the good is demanded *only at a lower price*. This distinction can help you differentiate between the two cases.

Changes in any of the variables in a demand function, *other than the price of the product*, will cause a shift of the demand curve in one direction or the other. Thus, the relationship between quantity demanded and the first variable on the right side of Equation 2.1 (price) determines the slope of the curve (downward sloping), while the other right-hand variables cause the curve to shift. In Figure 2.2, we assumed that the good was a normal good so that an increase in income would result in an increase in demand, or a rightward shift of the demand curve. If the good was an inferior good, this increase in income would result in a decrease in demand, or a leftward shift of the curve. An increase in the price of a substitute good would cause the demand curve for the good in question to shift rightward, while an increase in the price of a complementary good would cause a leftward shift of the demand curve. A change in consumer expectations could also cause the curve to shift in either direction, depending on whether a price increase or decrease was expected. If future prices were expected to rise, the current demand curve would shift outward or to the right. The opposite would happen if future prices were expected to decrease. An increase in the number of consumers in the market would cause the demand curve to shift to the right, while the opposite would happen for a decrease in the number of consumers.

Individual Versus Market Demand Curves

The shift in the market demand curve as more individuals enter the market is illustrated in Figure 2.3, which shows how a market demand curve is derived from individual demand curves. In this figure, demand curve D_A represents the demand for individual A. If individual A is the only person in the market, this demand curve is also the market demand curve. However, if individual B enters the market with demand curve D_B, we then have to construct a new market

FIGURE 2.3
Individual Versus Market Demand Curve

A market demand curve is derived from the horizontal summation of individual demand curves; i.e., for every price, add the quantity each individual demands at that price to determine the market quantity demanded at that price.

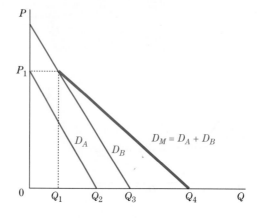

demand curve. As shown in Figure 2.3, individual B has a larger demand for the product than individual A. The demand curve for B lies to the right of the demand curve for A, indicating that individual B will demand a larger quantity of the product at every price level.

To derive the market demand curve for both individuals, we do a **horizontal summation of individual demand curves**. This means that for every price we add the quantity that each person demands at that price to determine the market quantity demanded at that price. At prices above P_1, only individual B is in the market, so demand curve B is the market demand curve in that price range. Below price P_1, we need to add together the quantities that each individual demands. For example, at a zero price, individual A demands quantity Q_2, and individual B demands quantity Q_3, so the quantity demanded by the market (both individuals) at the zero price is Q_4, which equals Q_2 plus Q_3. The market demand curve, D_M, is derived in the same manner by adding the quantities demanded at other prices.

Based on the information in Figure 2.3, we can infer that if another individual, C, came into the market, the market demand curve would shift further to the right. Thus, a market demand curve can shift as individuals enter or leave a market.

Horizontal summation of individual demand curves
The process of deriving a market demand curve by adding the quantity demanded by each individual at every price to determine the market demand at every price.

Linear Demand Functions and Curves

The demand curves in Figures 2.1, 2.2, and 2.3 have been drawn as straight lines, representing a **linear demand function**. A linear demand function is a specific mathematical relationship of the generalized demand function (Equation 2.1) in which all terms are either added or subtracted and there are no exponents in any terms that take a value other than 1. The graph of a linear demand function has a constant slope. This linear relationship is used both because it simplifies the analysis and because many economists believe that this form of demand function best represents individuals' behavior, at least within a given range of prices. However, not all demand functions are linear. We discuss the implications of a particular type of demand function for consumer behavior in greater detail in Chapter 3.

Linear demand function
A mathematical demand function graphed as a straight-line demand curve in which all the terms are either added or subtracted and no terms have exponents other than 1.

Mathematical Example of a Demand Function

Although we have been discussing demand functions and demand curves in verbal, symbolic, and graphical terms, these relationships can also be expressed as a mathematical equation. In this section, we begin a hypothetical numerical example based on the copper industry articles that we have used throughout the chapter. For simplicity, we assume that our demand and supply functions are both linear.

Suppose that the demand function for copper at the beginning of 1997 is represented by Equation 2.2:

2.2 $Q_D = 10 - 50P_C + 0.3I + 1.5TC + 0.5E$

where

Q_D = quantity demanded of copper (millions of pounds)

P_C = price of copper ($ per pound)

I = consumer income index

TC = telecom index showing uses or tastes for copper in the telecommunications industry

E = expectations index representing purchasers' expectations of a lower price over the following six months

We assume here that the quantity demanded of copper is a function only of P_C, the price of copper; I, consumer income; TC, the telecom index; and E, the expectations index. An economist or market analyst would develop this model of demand and derive the actual values of the constant term and coefficients of the variables in Equation 2.2 from real-world data using the empirical methods we'll discuss in Chapter 4.

The negative coefficient on the P_C variable shows the inverse relationship between price and quantity demanded of copper. If the price of copper increases, the quantity demanded decreases. This represents a typical downward sloping demand curve. We can see from this demand function that copper is a normal good because the income variable, I, in Equation 2.2 has a positive coefficient. Increases in income result in increases in the demand for copper. The positive coefficient on the TC variable means that as improved technology and higher demand for telecom services in North America and Europe create more uses for copper in the telecommunications industry, the overall demand for copper increases. The expectations index, E, represents consumers' expectations of a lower price over the following six months, where a lower index number implies that more purchasers expect a lower price. This expectation decreases the current demand for copper. Equation 2.2 is a mathematical representation of the conceptual relationships developed earlier in the chapter.

To define a specific demand curve for copper, we need to hold constant the level of consumer income, the telecom index, and the expectations index. Suppose that $I = \$100$, $TC = 10$, and $E = 10$. Substituting $100 for I, 10 for TC, and 10 for E in Equation 2.2 gives us Equation 2.3:

2.3 $Q_D = 10 - 50P_C + 0.3(100) + 1.5(10) + 0.5(10)$

or

$Q_D = 60 - 50P_C$ or $[P_C = 1.2 - 0.02Q_D]$

We can clearly see the meaning of the expression *all else held constant* in Equation 2.3. In that equation, the effects of consumer income, the telecom index, and the expectations index are embodied in the constant term 60. If we change the values of any of these three variables, the constant term in Equation 2.3 changes, and we have a change in demand or a new demand equation that graphs into a different demand curve. A change in quantity demanded in Equation 2.3 is represented by substituting different values for the price of copper and calculating the resulting quantity demanded at those prices. Equation 2.3 also shows the inverse demand function, with price as a function of quantity. These equations are equivalent mathematically.

Managerial Rule of Thumb

Demand Considerations

Managers need to understand the factors that influence consumer demand for their products. Although product price is usually important, other factors may play a significant role. In developing a competitive strategy, managers need to determine which factors they can influence and how to handle the factors that are beyond their control. ■

Supply

Supply
The functional relationship between the price of a good or service and the quantity supplied by producers in a given time period, *all else held constant.*

We now examine producer decisions to supply various goods and services and the factors influencing those decisions. **Supply** is the functional relationship between the price of a good or service and the quantity that producers are willing and able to supply in a given time period, *all else held constant.*

Nonprice Factors Influencing Supply

Although supply focuses on the influence of price on the quantity of a good or service supplied, many other factors influence producer supply decisions. These factors generally relate to the cost of production.

State of Technology   The state of technology, or the body of knowledge about how to combine the inputs of production, affects what output producers will supply because technology influences how the good or service is actually produced, which, in turn, affects the costs of production. For example, the discussion of the copper industry noted that a change in mining technology allowed companies to produce copper at a lower cost, keeping more of them in business. This change in technology contributed to a decrease in mining costs of 30 percent between the 1980s and the 1990s.[22]

In the nickel industry, most of the world's production has come from deposits that were relatively easy to exploit. However, these deposits comprise only about 40 percent or less of the world's remaining reserves. During the 1990s companies tried to develop a process called "high pressure acid leaching" to remove nickel from other rock deposits. The hope was that this new technology would open large new deposits of nickel. Although the initial equipment failed to stand up to the extreme heat and pressure of the process, more recent changes in the technology have increased its reliability and usefulness.[23]

Input Prices   Input prices are the prices of all the inputs or factors of production—labor, capital, land, and raw materials—used to produce the given product. These input prices affect the costs of production and, therefore, the prices at which producers are willing to supply different amounts of output. For broiler chickens, feed costs represent 70 percent to 75 percent of the costs of growing a chicken to a marketable size. Thus, changes in feed costs are so important that market analysts often use them as a proxy to forecast broiler prices and returns to broiler processors.[24]

---

[22] Lucchetti, "Copper Limbo: Just How Low Can It Go?"
[23] Patrick Barta, "With Easy Nickel Fading Fast, Miners Go After the Tough Stuff," *Wall Street Journal,* July 12, 2006.
[24] Rogers, "Broilers," p. 71.

In fall 2006, analysts predicted that consumers would face higher furniture prices, given the increased costs of fuel and other raw materials. Manufacturers Laneventure and Bradington-Young raised their furniture prices due to higher foam, spring, and metal costs.[25]

Prices of Goods Related in Production   The prices of other goods related in production can also affect the supply of a particular good. Two goods are substitutes in production if the same inputs can be used to produce either of the goods, such as land for different agricultural crops. Between 2005 and 2007, U.S. tobacco acreage increased 20 percent with tobacco being planted in areas such as southern Illinois that had not grown any substantial amount since the end of World War I. Even though corn prices were at near-record levels of $4.00 per bushel during this period, they were not high enough to compete with tobacco planting. Even with higher labor and other costs, one farmer in Illinois estimated that he netted $1,800 per acre from his 150 acres of tobacco compared with $250 per acre for corn and that planting tobacco had increased his annual income by 35 percent over the previous three years.[26]

There can also be a complementary production relationship, such as in the production of oil and natural gas or of light- and dark-meat chicken, as mentioned earlier. An increase in the demand for oil, which raised its price, would cause an increase in the supply of natural gas, because the two commodities are often produced together. As more oil and natural gas are produced, the supply of sulfur, which is removed from the products, also increases. Sixty-foot-high blocks of unwanted sulfur were reported in Alberta, Canada, and Kazakhstan in 2003.[27] Likewise, if the demand for and price of white-meat chicken increases, there will be an increase in the supply of dark-meat chicken.

Future Expectations   Future expectations can play a role on the supply side of the market as well. If producers expect prices to increase in the future, they may supply less output now than without those expectations. The opposite could happen if producers expect prices to decrease in the future. These expectations could become self-fulfilling prophecies. Smaller current supplies in the first case could drive prices up, while larger current supplies in the second case could result in lower prices. Expectations may not always be correct. Given the high demand and lumber prices in summer 2004 discussed previously, lumber manufacturers expected that demand would start to drop as interest rates rose. When this did not happen, prices continued to climb.[28]

Number of Producers   Finally, the number of producers influences the total supply of a product at any given price. The number of producers may increase because of perceived profitability in a given industry or because of changes in laws or regulations such as trade barriers. For example, the lumber market was reported to be exceedingly strong in January 1999, largely due to demand from the booming U.S. housing market. However, quotas on the amount of wood that Canada could ship into the United States also played a role in keeping the price of lumber high in the United States in January of that year.[29]

Similarly, in November 2004, tariffs on 115 Chinese producers of wooden bedroom furniture were lowered from 12.9 to 8.6 percent. Because these

---

[25] Christina S.N. Lewis, "What's Up in Furniture? The Prices," *Wall Street Journal*, October 19, 2006.
[26] Lauren Etter, "U.S. Farmers Rediscover the Allure of Tobacco," *Wall Street Journal*, September 18, 2007.
[27] Alexei Barrionuevo, "A Chip off the Block Is Going to Smell Like Rotten Eggs," *Wall Street Journal*, November 4, 2003.
[28] Johnson, "Sticker Shock at the Lumberyard."
[29] Terzah Ewing, "Lumber's Strength Defies Bearish Trend," *Wall Street Journal*, January 26, 1999.

companies accounted for 65 percent of the bedroom furniture imported to the United States from China, the resulting increased supply lowered prices for consumers and put more competitive pressure on U.S. furniture makers who had already closed dozens of factories in North Carolina and Virginia in the previous four years.[30]

Supply Function

A supply function for a product, which is defined in a manner similar to a demand function, is shown in Equation 2.4:

$$2.4 \quad Q_{XS} = f(P_X, TX, P_I, P_A, P_B, EXP, NP, \ldots)$$

where

Q_{XS} = quantity supplied of good X

P_X = price of good X

TX = state of technology

P_I = prices of the inputs of production

P_A, P_B = prices of goods A and B, which are related in production to good X

EXP = producer expectations about future prices

NP = number of producers

Individual supply function
The function that shows, in symbolic or mathematical terms, the variables that influence the quantity supplied of a particular product by an individual producer.

Equation 2.4 shows that the quantity supplied of good X depends on the price of good X, the other variables listed above, and possibly variables peculiar to the firm or industry that are not included in the list, as indicated by the ellipsis. As with the demand function, we can distinguish between an individual supply function and a market supply function. The **individual supply function** shows, in symbolic or mathematical terms, the variables that influence an individual producer's supply of a product. The **market supply function** shows the variables that influence the overall supply of a product by all producers and is thus affected by the number of producers in the market.

Market supply function
The function that shows, in symbolic or mathematical terms, the variables that influence the quantity supplied of a particular product by all producers in the market and that is thus affected by the number of producers in the market.

Supply curve
The graphical relationship between the price of a good and the quantity supplied, with all other factors influencing supply held constant.

Supply Curves

We graph a **supply curve** in Figure 2.4, showing price (P) on the vertical axis and quantity supplied (Q) on the horizontal axis. For simplicity, all supply curves in this

FIGURE 2.4

The Supply Curve for a Product
A supply curve shows the relationship between the price of a good and the quantity supplied, all else held constant.

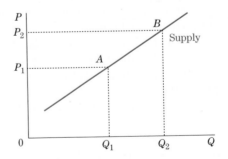

---

[30] Dan Morse, "U.S. Cuts Tariffs on Imports of China's Bedroom Furniture," *Wall Street Journal*, November 10, 2004.

chapter will represent market supply functions. The supply curve in Figure 2.4 shows the relationship between price and quantity supplied, holding constant all the other variables influencing the supply decision (all variables beside P_X on the right side of Equation 2.4). Changes in these variables, the **supply shifters**, will cause the supply curve to shift.

As you can see in Figure 2.4, a supply curve generally slopes upward, indicating a **positive** or **direct relationship** between the price of the product and the quantity producers are willing to supply. A higher price typically gives producers an incentive to increase the quantity supplied of a particular product because higher production is more profitable. The supply curve in Figure 2.4 represents a **linear supply function** and is graphed as a straight line. Not all supply functions are linear, but we will use this type of function for simplicity. Keep in mind that a supply curve does not show the actual price of the product, only a functional relationship between alternative prices and the quantities that producers want to supply at those prices.

Change in Quantity Supplied and Change in Supply

Figure 2.4 shows a given supply curve defined with all other factors held constant. If the price increases from P_1 to P_2, the quantity supplied increases from Q_1 to Q_2. This movement from point A to point B represents a movement along the given supply curve, or a **change in quantity supplied**. Some factor has caused the price of the product to increase, and suppliers respond by increasing the quantity supplied. This supply response is by the existing suppliers, since the number of suppliers is held constant when defining any given supply curve.

Figure 2.5 shows a shift of the entire supply curve. This represents a **change in supply**, not a change in quantity supplied. The supply curve shifts from S_1 to S_2 because one or more of the factors from Equation 2.4 held constant in supply curve S_1 changes. The increase in supply, or the rightward shift of the supply curve in Figure 2.5, shows that producers are willing to supply a larger quantity of output at any given price. Thus, the quantity supplied at price P_1 increases from Q_1 to Q_2. This differs from the movement along a supply curve, or a change in quantity supplied, shown in Figure 2.4, where the increase in quantity supplied is associated with a higher price for the product. This distinction between a change in quantity supplied and a change in supply is analogous to the distinction between a change in quantity demanded and a change in demand. We use the same framework—the relationship between two variables (price and quantity), all else held constant—on both the demand and the supply sides of the market.

Supply shifters
The other variables in a supply function that are held constant when defining a given supply curve, but that would cause that supply curve to shift if their values changed.

Positive (direct) relationship
A relationship between two variables, graphed as an upward sloping line, where an increase in the value of one variable causes an increase in the value of the other variable.

Linear supply function
A mathematical supply function, which graphs as a straight-line supply curve, in which all terms are either added or subtracted and no terms have exponents other than 1.

Change in quantity supplied
The change in amount of a good supplied when the price of the good changes, all other factors held constant, pictured as a movement along a given supply curve.

Change in supply
The change in the amount of a good supplied when one or more of the supply shifters change, pictured as a shift of the entire supply curve.

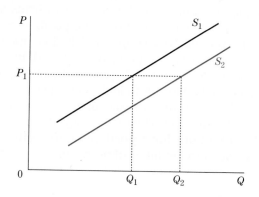

FIGURE 2.5
Change (Increase) in Supply
A change in supply occurs when one or more of the factors held constant in defining a given supply curve changes.

Developing new technology typically causes an increase in supply, or a rightward shift of the supply curve, because technology changes usually lower the costs of production. The same result holds for a decrease in the price of any of the inputs of production, which lowers the costs of production and causes the supply curve to shift to the right. Any increase in the price of inputs increases the costs of production and causes the supply curve of the product to shift to the left.

The effect of a change in the price of a related good on the supply of a given good depends on whether the related good is a substitute or complement in production. An increase in the price of a substitute good causes the supply curve for the given good to shift to the left. A decrease in the price of a substitute good causes an increase in the supply of the given good. The opposite set of relationships holds for goods that are complements in production. If the price of the complementary good increases, the supply of the given good increases.

Producer expectations of lower prices cause the supply curve of a good to shift to the right. The supply increases in anticipation of lower prices in the future. The opposite holds if producers expect prices to increase. There would be a smaller current supply than without those expectations.

Finally, an increase in the number of producers results in a rightward shift of the supply curve, while a decrease results in a leftward shift of the supply curve. A given supply curve shows how prices induce the current number of producers to change the quantity supplied. Any change in the number of producers in the market is represented by a shift of the entire curve.

Mathematical Example of a Supply Function

To continue the mathematical example we began in the demand section, we assume that the supply function for copper is represented by Equation 2.5. (Note that real-world supply functions are empirically estimated from data in different firms and industries.)

$$\textbf{2.5} \quad Q_S = -86 + 90P_C - 1.5W + 0.5T + 0.4N$$

where

Q_S = quantity supplied of copper (millions of pounds)
P_C = price of copper ($ per pound)
W = an index of wage rates in the copper industry
T = technology index
N = number of active mines in the copper industry

In Equation 2.5, we assume that the quantity supplied of copper is a function only of the price of copper, wage rates in the copper industry (the price of an input of production), the technology index, and the number of firms in the industry. The positive coefficient on the P_C variable shows the positive relationship between the price of copper and the quantity supplied. A higher price will elicit a larger quantity supplied. This relationship represents a normal, upward sloping supply curve. The other variables in Equation 2.5 cause the supply curve to shift. The wage rate index, *W*, has a negative coefficient. As wage rates increase, the supply of copper decreases because an increase in this input price represents an increase in the costs of production. The technology index (T) and the number of active mines variable (N) both have positive coefficients, indicating that an increase in technology or in the number of active mines will increase the supply of copper.

To define a specific supply curve, we need to hold constant the wage rate index, the technology index, and the number of firms in the copper industry. Suppose that $W = 10$, $T = 30$, and $N = 50$. Substituting these values into Equation 2.5 gives Equation 2.6.

2.6 $\quad Q_S = -86 + 90P_C - 1.5(10) + 0.5(30) + 0.4(50)$

or

$\quad Q_S = -66 + 90P_C$ or $[P_C = 0.73 + 0.011Q_S]$

As with the demand curve in Equation 2.3, the supply curve in Equation 2.6 shows the relationship between the price of copper and the quantity supplied, all else held constant. The constant term, -66, incorporates the effect of the wage and technology indices and the number of firms in the industry. Any changes in these variables change the size of the constant term, which results in a different supply curve.[31]

Summary of Demand and Supply Factors

Table 2.1 summarizes the factors influencing both the demand and the supply sides of the market. Notice the symmetry in that some of the factors—including the prices of related goods, future expectations, and the number of participants—influence both sides of the market.

Managerial Rule of Thumb

Supply Considerations

In developing a competitive strategy, managers must examine the technology and costs of production, factors that influence the supply of the product. Finding ways to increase productivity and lower production costs is particularly important in gaining a strategic advantage in a competitive market where managers have little control over price. ∎

TABLE 2.1 Factors Influencing Market Demand and Supply

DEMAND	SUPPLY
Price of the product	Price of the product
Consumer tastes and preferences	State of technology
Consumer income:	Input prices
Normal goods	
Inferior goods	
Price of goods related in consumption:	Prices of goods related in production:
Substitute goods	Substitute goods
Complementary goods	Complementary goods
Future expectations	Future expectations
Number of consumers	Number of producers

---

[31] If we rewrite the supply equation with price as a function of quantity supplied, we get $P = 0.73 + 0.011Q_S$, as shown in Equation 2.6. This equation implies that producers must receive a price of at least $0.73 per pound to induce them to supply any copper.

Demand, Supply, and Equilibrium

As we discussed earlier, demand and supply are both functional relationships between the price of a good and the quantity demanded or supplied. Neither function by itself tells us what price will actually exist in the market. That price will be determined when the market is in equilibrium.

Definition of Equilibrium Price and Equilibrium Quantity

Equilibrium price

The price that actually exists in the market or toward which the market is moving where the quantity demanded by consumers equals the quantity supplied by producers.

Equilibrium quantity (Q_E)

The quantity of a good, determined by the equilibrium price, where the amount of output that consumers demand is equal to the amount that producers want to supply.

In a competitive market, the interaction of demand and supply determines the **equilibrium price**, the price that will actually exist in the market or toward which the market is moving. Figure 2.6 shows the equilibrium price (P_E) for good X. The equilibrium price is the price at which the quantity demanded of good X by consumers equals the quantity that producers are willing to supply. This quantity is called the **equilibrium quantity (Q_E)**. At any other price, there will be an imbalance between quantity demanded and quantity supplied. Forces will be set in motion to push the price back toward equilibrium, assuming no market impediments or governmental policies exist that would prevent equilibrium from being reached.

Lower-Than-Equilibrium Prices

The best way to understand equilibrium is to consider what would happen if some price other than the equilibrium price actually existed in a market. Suppose P_1 is the actual market price in Figure 2.7. As you see in the figure, price P_1 is lower than the equilibrium price, P_E. You can also see that the quantity of the good demanded by consumers at price P_1 is greater than the quantity producers are willing to supply. This creates a shortage of the good, shown in Figure 2.7 as the amount of the good between Q_D and Q_S. At the lower-than-equilibrium price, P_1, consumers demand more of the good than producers are willing to supply at that price. Because there is an imbalance between quantity demanded and quantity supplied at this price, the situation is not stable. Some individuals are willing to pay more than price P_1, so they will start to bid the price up. A higher price will cause producers to supply a larger quantity. This adjustment process will continue until the equilibrium price has been reached and quantity demanded is equal to quantity supplied.

Price and rent controls are examples of the imbalances between demand and supply that result from lower-than-equilibrium prices. In New York City, which used rent controls for many years for certain apartments, the excess demand for these apartments meant that many of them never actually appeared on the market. They were either kept by the current occupants or transferred to those with connections to the occupants.[32] You can also observe lower-than-equilibrium

FIGURE 2.6

Market Equilibrium

Market equilibrium occurs at that price where the quantity demanded by consumers equals the quantity supplied by producers.

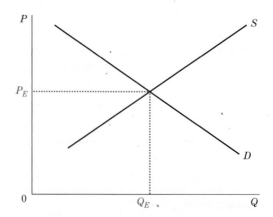

---

[32] Richard Arnott, "Time for Revisionism on Rent Control?" *Journal of Economic Perspectives* 9(1) (Winter 1995): 99–120.

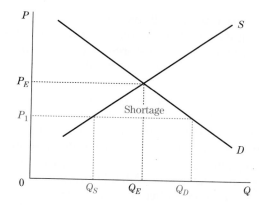

FIGURE 2.7
A Lower-Than-Equilibrium Price
A shortage of a good results when the market price, P₁, is below the equilibrium price, P_E.

prices being charged for tickets to the Super Bowl and many other sporting and entertainment events where scalpers sell tickets for prices far exceeding the stated price. The quantity demanded of tickets at the stated price is greater than the quantity supplied at that price, so people will pay much more than the stated price for these tickets. Recognizing this excess demand, the producers of the hit Broadway show *The Producers* began, in October 2001, setting aside at least 50 seats at every performance to sell at $480 per ticket, a price far exceeding the top regular charge of $100. This was a strategic move to tap into the excess demand and ensure that the creators of the play, and not the scalpers, received a bigger share of the royalties.[33]

   Notre Dame University conducts a lottery every year to parcel out the 30,000 seats available to contributors, former athletes, and parents for football games in its 80,000-seat stadium. In September 2006, the university had 66,670 ticket requests for the 30,000 seats for the Notre Dame–Penn State game. Individuals and businesses take advantage of the excess demand during game weekends. Houses for visitors rent for $3,000 or more, motel rooms normally renting for $129 per night sell out at $400, parking passes are sold on eBay for $500, and $59 tickets can fetch a price of $1,600.[34]

Higher-Than-Equilibrium Prices

Figure 2.8 shows the opposite case, a higher-than-equilibrium price. At price P_2, the quantity supplied, Q_S, is greater than the quantity demanded, Q_D, at that price. This above-equilibrium price creates a surplus of the good and sets into motion

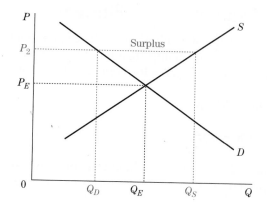

FIGURE 2.8
A Higher-Than-Equilibrium Price
A surplus of a good results when the market price, P₂, is above the equilibrium price, P_E.

---

[33] Jessie McKinley, "For the Asking, $480 a Seat for 'The Producers,'" *New York Times*, October 26, 2001.
[34] Ilan Brat, "Notre Dame Football Introduces Its Fans to Inflationary Spiral," *Wall Street Journal*, September 6, 2006.

forces that will cause the price to fall. As the price falls, the quantity demanded increases and the quantity supplied decreases until a balance between quantity demanded and quantity supplied is restored at the equilibrium price. Thus, the existence of either shortages or surpluses of goods is an indication that a market is not in equilibrium.

In this chapter, we have used several agricultural examples to illustrate the forces shifting demand and supply curves because agricultural markets exhibit many competitive characteristics. These markets also provide good examples of nonequilibrium prices and imbalances between demand and supply, given the extensive government agricultural subsidization programs that have been in operation over the years. These crop subsidy programs kept the price of many agricultural products above equilibrium, which resulted in an excess quantity supplied compared with quantity demanded. During the 1990s, the U.S. government began eliminating or cutting back many of these subsidy programs. As prices for their crops have fallen, many farmers have gone out of business.

The choices among crops to be planted are often influenced by the pattern of federal subsidies. The *Wall Street Journal* reported in April 1999 that U.S. farmers intended to plant a record 73.1 million acres of soybeans that spring, even in the face of declining prices for this product.[35] Although this move was likely to cause soybean prices to fall even further, farmers were responding to a soybean subsidy that was higher than those for other crops. This increased level of planting by U.S. farmers, combined with large harvests from other countries, was expected to push soybean prices to under $4 a bushel, the lowest level since the 1980s. However, under a U.S. Department of Agriculture marketing-loan program, U.S. farmers could expect a price of $5.26 per bushel of soybeans. In response, they were expected to produce 2.9 billion bushels of soybeans, up 5 percent from the previous year's harvest.

The tobacco subsidy program guaranteed farmers a minimum price for their crops and allocated quotas stating how many acres could be planted. Growers who did not own a quota had to purchase or rent one from current owners. This system increased prices and limited production to narrow geographic areas and to plots of land that were typically not larger than 10 acres. When the system was disbanded in 2004, thousands of farmers stopped growing tobacco. In 2005 acreage dropped 27 percent from the previous year, and tobacco prices fell from $1.98 to $1.64 per pound. However, over time tobacco production has increased again, given that farmers no longer have to purchase quotas and can plant much more acreage. Tobacco production has shifted to large tracts of land where the crop can be grown more efficiently.[36]

Mathematical Example of Equilibrium

We can illustrate the concept of equilibrium with the mathematical example of the copper industry we have been using throughout the chapter. So far, we have defined the demand and supply curves for copper in Equations 2.3 and 2.6:

2.3 $\quad Q_D = 60 - 50P_C$

2.6 $\quad Q_S = -66 + 90P_C$

Equilibrium in a competitive market occurs at the price where quantity demanded equals quantity supplied. Since Equation 2.3 represents quantity demanded as a

---

[35] Scott Kilman, "Farmers to Plant Record Soybean Acres Despite Price Drop, as a Result of a Subsidy," *Wall Street Journal*, April 4, 1999.

[36] Etter, "U.S. Farmers Rediscover the Allure of Tobacco."

function of price and Equation 2.6 represents quantity supplied as a function of price, we need an equilibrium condition to find the solution in the market. The equilibrium condition is shown in Equation 2.7 where we set the two equations equal to each other and solve for the equilibrium price and quantity.

2.7 $$Q_D = Q_S$$

$$60 - 50P_C = -66 + 90P_C$$

$$126 = 140P_C$$

$$P_C = P_E = \$0.90 \text{ and } Q_E = 15 \text{ (by substituting \$0.90}$$
$$\text{into either equation)}$$

Thus, the equilibrium price of copper in this example is $0.90 per pound, and the equilibrium quantity is 15 million pounds. This is the only price-quantity combination where quantity demanded equals quantity supplied. At a price lower than $0.90 per pound, the quantity demanded from Equation 2.3 will be greater than the quantity supplied from Equation 2.6, and a shortage of copper will result. At a price higher than $0.90 per pound, the quantity demanded will be less than the quantity supplied, and a surplus of copper will occur.

Changes in Equilibrium Prices and Quantities

Changes in equilibrium prices and quantities occur when market forces cause either the demand or the supply curve for a product to shift or both curves shift. These shifts occur when one or more of the factors held constant behind a given demand or supply curve change. Much economic analysis focuses on examining the changes in equilibrium prices and quantities that result from shifts in demand and supply.

Change in Demand   Figure 2.9 shows the effect of a change in demand in a competitive market. The original equilibrium price, P_0, and quantity, Q_0, arise from the intersection of demand curve D_0 and supply curve S_0. An increase in demand is shown by the rightward or outward shift of the demand curve from D_0 to D_1. This increase in demand could result from a change in one or more of the following nonprice variables: tastes and preferences, income, prices of related goods, expectations, or number of consumers in the market, as we discussed earlier. This increase in demand results in a new higher equilibrium price, P_1, and a new larger equilibrium quantity, Q_1, or in the movement from point A to point B in Figure 2.9. This change represents a movement along the supply curve or a change in quantity supplied. Thus, a change in demand (a shift of the curve on one side of the market) results in a change in quantity supplied (movement along the curve on the other side of the market).

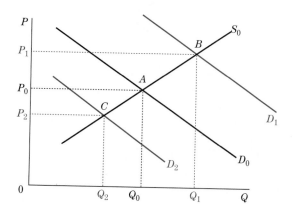

FIGURE 2.9
Change in Demand
A change in demand, represented by a shift of the demand curve, results in a movement along the supply curve.

FIGURE 2.10
Change in Supply
A change in supply, represented by a shift of the supply curve, results in a movement along the demand curve.

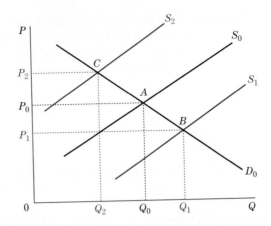

The opposite result occurs for a decrease in demand. In this case, the demand curve shifts from D_0 to D_2 in Figure 2.9, and the equilibrium price and quantity fall to P_2 and Q_2. This change in demand also causes a change in quantity supplied, or a movement along the supply curve from point A to point C.

Change in Supply   Figure 2.10 shows the effect of a change in supply on equilibrium price and quantity. Starting with the original demand and supply curves, D_0 and S_0, and the original equilibrium price and quantity, P_0 and Q_0, an increase in supply is represented by the rightward or outward shift of the supply curve from S_0 to S_1. As we discussed earlier, this shift could result from a change in technology, input prices, prices of goods related in production, expectations, or number of suppliers. The result of this increase in supply is a new lower equilibrium price, P_1, and a larger equilibrium quantity, Q_1. This change in supply results in a movement along the demand curve or a change in quantity demanded from point A to point B.

Figure 2.10 also shows the result of a decrease in supply. In this case, the supply curve shifts leftward or inward from S_0 to S_2. This results in a new higher equilibrium price, P_2, and a smaller equilibrium quantity, Q_2. This decrease in supply results in a decrease in quantity demanded or a movement along the demand curve from point A to point C.

Changes on Both Sides of the Market   As in the copper case discussed at the beginning of this chapter, most outcomes result from changes on *both* sides of the market. The trends in equilibrium prices and quantities will depend on the size of the shifts of the curves and the responsiveness of either quantity demanded or quantity supplied to changes in prices.

In some cases, we know the direction of the change in equilibrium price, but not the equilibrium quantity. This result is illustrated in Figures 2.11 and 2.12, which

FIGURE 2.11
Decrease in Supply and Increase in Demand: Increase in Equilibrium Quantity
These changes in demand and supply result in a higher equilibrium price and a larger equilibrium quantity.

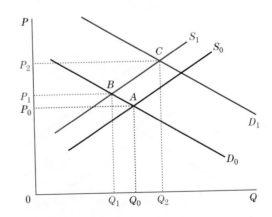

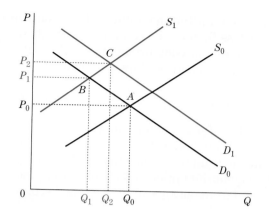

FIGURE 2.12
Decrease in Supply and Increase in Demand: Decrease in Equilibrium Quantity
These changes in demand and supply result in a higher equilibrium price and a smaller equilibrium quantity.

show a decrease in supply (the shift from point A to point B) combined with an increase in demand (the shift from point B to point C). Both shifts cause the equilibrium price to rise from P_0 to P_2. However, the direction of change for the equilibrium quantity (Q_0 to Q_2) depends on the magnitude of the shifts in the curves. If the decrease in supply is less than the increase in demand, the equilibrium quantity will rise, as shown in Figure 2.11. The equilibrium quantity will fall if the increase in demand is less than the decrease in supply, as shown in Figure 2.12.

In other cases, we know the direction of the change in the equilibrium quantity, but not the equilibrium price. Figures 2.13 and 2.14, which illustrate this situation, show an increase in supply (from point A to point B) combined with an increase in demand (from point B to point C). Both of these shifts in the curves result in a larger equilibrium quantity (an increase from Q_0 to Q_2). However, the direction of

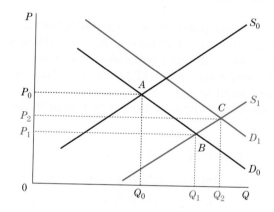

FIGURE 2.13
Increase in Supply and Increase in Demand: Lower Equilibrium Price
These changes in demand and supply result in a lower equilibrium price and a larger equilibrium quantity.

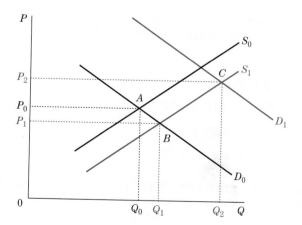

FIGURE 2.14
Increase in Supply and Increase in Demand: Higher Equilibrium Price
These changes in demand and supply result in a higher equilibrium price and a larger equilibrium quantity.

the price change depends on the magnitude of the shift in each curve. If the increase in demand is less than the increase in supply, the equilibrium price will fall, as shown in Figure 2.13. The equilibrium price will rise if the increase in supply is less than the increase in demand, as shown in Figure 2.14.

Mathematical Example of an Equilibrium Change

In Equation 2.7, we solved for the equilibrium price and quantity of copper with demand Equation 2.3 and supply Equation 2.6. This resulted in an equilibrium price of $0.90 per pound and an equilibrium quantity of 15 million pounds. We now show how a change in the equilibrium price and quantity from the beginning of 1997 to the end of 1998 resulted from changes in the factors discussed in the beginning of this chapter.

Suppose the recession in the Southeast Asian countries resulted in the cancellation of copper-using projects and there was no offsetting increase in the demand for copper from China. Assume that this change caused the income index (I) in demand Equation 2.3 to decrease from 100 to 80. The improved technology and higher demand for telecommunications services in North America and Europe caused the telecom index to increase from 10 to 28. The expectations index (E) decreased over the period from 10 to 8, given that a larger number of purchasers expected a lower price over the following six months. These changes give a new demand function, as shown in Equation 2.8.

$$2.8 \quad Q_{D2} = 10 - 50P_C + 0.3I + 1.5TC + 0.5E$$
$$= 10 - 50P_C + 0.3(80) + 1.5(28) + 0.5(8)$$
$$= 80 - 50P_C \text{ or } [P_C = 1.60 - 0.02Q_D]$$

Also suppose that the wage index, W, while important in the past, did not change from its value of 10 over this period. However, the use of the new solvent extraction mining process, combined with other technologies and improvements in physical capital, increased the technology index (T) from 30 to 102. Industry investment in the early 1990s also resulted in an increase in the number of active mines over the period from 50 to 80. These changes gave a new supply function, as shown in Equation 2.9.

$$2.9 \quad Q_{S2} = -86 + 90P_C - 1.5W + 0.5T + 0.4N$$
$$= -86 + 90P_C - 1.5(10) + 0.5(102) + 0.4(80)$$
$$= -18 + 90P_C \text{ or } [P_C = 0.20 + 0.011Q_S]$$

The new equilibrium price and quantity are derived in Equation 2.10 by setting the new demand function, Equation 2.8, equal to the new supply function, Equation 2.9.

$$2.10 \quad\quad Q_{D2} = Q_{S2}$$
$$80 - 50P_C = -18 + 90P_C$$
$$98 = 140P_C$$
$$P_C = P_E = \$0.70 \text{ and } Q_E = 45$$

The resulting equilibrium price is $0.70 per pound of copper, and the equilibrium quantity is 45 million pounds.

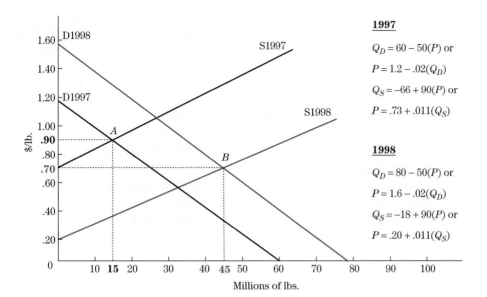

1997

$Q_D = 60 - 50(P)$ or

$P = 1.2 - .02(Q_D)$

$Q_S = -66 + 90(P)$ or

$P = .73 + .011(Q_S)$

1998

$Q_D = 80 - 50(P)$ or

$P = 1.6 - .02(Q_D)$

$Q_S = -18 + 90(P)$ or

$P = .20 + .011(Q_S)$

FIGURE 2.15
Copper Industry Example
This figure illustrates the changes in demand and supply in the copper industry discussed in the opening news article of the chapter. The supply shifts are greater than the demand shifts, resulting in a downward trend in copper prices.

Figure 2.15 shows the original and final equilibrium in the copper industry example (original P_E = \$0.90 per pound, Q_E = 15 million pounds; final P_E = \$0.70 per pound, Q_E = 45 million pounds, respectively). Both the demand and the supply curves are graphed from the equations showing price as a function of quantity. We can see that the supply curve shift is greater than the demand curve shift, illustrating the downward trend in copper prices discussed previously.

Summary

In this chapter, we discussed how the forces of demand and supply determine prices in competitive markets. In the case of the copper industry, we saw how both demand- and supply-side factors influenced copper prices. We also discussed how both microeconomic factors, such as a change in the technology of copper production, and macroeconomic factors, including changes in the Chinese economy, affected the prices charged, the profitability, and the competitive strategies of firms in the copper industry.

We examined these changes with the economic model of demand and supply. *Demand* is defined as the relationship between the price of the good and the quantity demanded by consumers in a given period of time, all other factors held constant. *Supply* is defined as the relationship between the price of the good and the quantity supplied by producers in a given period of time, all other factors held constant. The equilibrium price, or the price that actually exists in the market, is that price where quantity demanded equals quantity supplied and is represented by the intersection of given demand and supply curves. When the factors held constant behind a particular demand or supply curve change, equilibrium prices respond to these demand and supply shifters. We provided numerous examples of these shifters throughout the chapter and discussed the effect of these demand and supply changes on prices in the copper industry.

In the next chapter, we'll examine the quantitative concept of elasticity, which economists have developed to measure the amount of consumer response to changes in the variables in market demand functions. We'll also examine what impact elasticity has on a firm's revenues and pricing policies.

Key Terms

Exercises

Technical Questions

1. Consider the demand for computers. For each of the following, state the effect on demand:

   a. An increase in consumer incomes
   b. An increase in the price of computers
   c. A decrease in the price of Internet service providers
   d. A decrease in the price of semiconductors
   e. It is October, and consumers expect that computers will go on sale just before Christmas.

2. Consider the supply of computers. For each of the following, state the effect on supply:

   a. A change in technology that lowers production costs
   b. An increase in the price of semiconductors
   c. A decrease in the price of computers
   d. An increase in the wages of computer assembly workers
   e. An increase in consumer incomes

3. The demand curve is given by

   $$Q_D = 500 - 5P_X + 0.5I + 10P_Y - 2P_Z$$

   where

   Q_D = quantity demanded of good X

   P_X = price of good X

   I = consumer income, in thousands

   P_Y = price of good Y

   P_Z = price of good Z

   a. Based on the demand curve above, is X a normal or an inferior good?
   b. Based on the demand curve above, what is the relationship between good X and good Y?
   c. Based on the demand curve above, what is the relationship between good X and good Z?
   d. What is the equation of the demand curve if consumer incomes are $30,000, the price of good Y is $10, and the price of good Z is $20?
   e. Graph the demand curve that you found in (d), showing intercepts and slope.
   f. If the price of good X is $15, what is the quantity demanded? Show this point on your demand curve.
   g. Now suppose the price of good Y rises to $15. Graph the new demand curve.

4. The supply curve is given by

   $$Q_S = -200 + 20P_X - 5P_I + 0.5P_Z$$

   where

   Q_S = quantity supplied of good X

   P_X = price of good X

   P_I = price of inputs to good X

   P_Z = price of good Z

   a. Based on the supply curve above, what is the relationship between good X and good Z?
   b. What is the equation of the supply curve if input prices are $10 and the price of Z is $20?
   c. Graph the supply curve that you found in (b), showing intercepts and slope.

d. What is the minimum price at which the firm will supply any of good X at all?

e. If the price of good X is $25, what is the quantity supplied? Show this point on your supply curve.

f. Now suppose the price of inputs falls to $5. Graph the new supply curve.

5. Suppose the demand and supply curves for a product are given by

$$Q_D = 500 - 2P$$
$$Q_S = -100 + 3P$$

a. Graph the supply and demand curves.

b. Find the equilibrium price and quantity.

c. If the current price of the product is $100, what is the quantity supplied and the quantity demanded? How would you describe this situation, and what would you expect to happen in this market?

d. If the current price of the product is $150, what is the quantity supplied and the quantity demanded? How would you describe this situation, and what would you expect to happen in this market?

e. Suppose that demand changes to $Q_D = 600 - 2P$. Find the new equilibrium price and quantity, and show this on your graph.

6. Graph representative supply and demand curves for the breakfast cereal market, labeling the current equilibrium price and quantity. Then show the effect on equilibrium price and quantity of each of the following changes (consider each separately):

a. The price of muffins rises, assuming muffins and breakfast cereals are substitutes.

b. The price of wheat, an input to cereal production, rises.

c. Consumers expect that cereal prices will be higher in the future.

d. There is a change in technology that makes production less expensive.

e. New medical reports indicate that eating breakfast is less important than had previously been thought.

7. Consider the market for automobiles, and draw representative supply and demand curves.

a. Suppose that the price of gasoline rises, and at the same time, the price of steel (an input to automobile production) falls. Show this on your graph. If you have no other information, what can you say about the change in equilibrium price and quantity?

b. Now suppose that you have the additional information that the rise in gasoline prices has been relatively large, while the reduction in steel costs has been relatively small. How would this change your answer to (a)?

8. Consider the market for hamburger, and draw representative supply and demand curves.

a. Assume that hamburger is an inferior good. Suppose that consumer incomes fall, and at the same time, an improvement in technology lowers production costs. Show this on your graph. If you have no other information, what can you say about the change in equilibrium price and quantity?

b. Now suppose that you have the additional information that the change in consumer incomes has been relatively small, while the reduction in production costs has been relatively large. How would this change your answer to (a)?

Application Questions

1. Using the facts in the opening news article, the discussion in the chapter, and demand and supply curves, show the impacts of the events in the news article on the price and quantity of copper. Clearly distinguish between changes in demand and supply and changes in the quantity demanded and the quantity supplied.

2. Using data sources from business publications and the Internet, discuss significant trends in both demand and supply in the copper industry that have influenced the price of copper since

February 2007. What are the implications of these trends for managerial decision making in the copper industry?

3. The following discussion is drawn from "Prices of Wood Products Plunge, Indicating Volatility in Industry," *Wall Street Journal*, August 25, 1999.

Wood-product prices have plunged from their record and near-record levels of only a few weeks ago amid an unexpected supply glut. . . . Analysts cautioned that any slowdown in either the economy or housing market could cut short a resurgence in the timber industry that has been under way for much of the year . . . markets will stabilize and even rebound as housing and remodeling activity pick up—as long as the Federal Reserve doesn't move to raise interest rates too much. . . .

[T]he supply of wood products recently exceeded demand in part because of the unusually hot summer weather in many parts of the country. That led to construction delays that backed up timber products in the distribution pipeline. . . .

During the second quarter [of 1999], the industry pulled out of a two-year slump that was prompted by an oversupply of wood products and slackened demand from Asian markets. . . . Aside from being prone to the vagaries of economic cycles, . . . the industry suffers from being fragmented into thousands of producers who frequently manufacture excess quantities.

a. Using standard demand and supply curves, describe and illustrate the effect on the equilibrium price and quantity in the wood products market of (1) the unexpected supply glut, (2) a slowdown in the economy or the housing market, (3) the hot summer in many parts of the country, and (4) the impact of changes in the Asian markets.

b. What changes in the macroeconomic environment that impact the wood products industry are discussed in the excerpt?

c. What facts in the excerpt indicate that the wood products industry is highly competitive?

4. The following facts pertain to global food prices as discussed in Patrick Barta, "Crop Prices Soar, Pushing Up Cost of Food Globally," *Wall Street Journal*, April 9, 2007:

a. One of the chief causes of food-price inflation is new demand for ethanol and biodiesel, which can be made from corn, palm oil, sugar and other crops. That demand has driven up the price of those commodities, leading to higher

costs for producers of everything from beef to eggs to soft drinks.

b. Some economists think prices could come back down over time, especially if some countries that have more land that could be put under cultivation—particularly Brazil—can greatly increase production.

c. Technological advances, such as better seed varieties, could also help boost production to keep up with demand.

d. Changes in diets are also exacerbating the problem, as rising incomes allow the Chinese and consumers in many other places to eat more.

e. Some economists contend that China and India appear to be reaching a point where nothing short of a bumper crop of key commodities will be enough to meet local needs and prevent further surges in food prices.

Show the effects of each of these factors on equilibrium food prices using demand and supply analysis.

5. The following discussion is drawn from "Chicken Producers in Price Pinch," *Wall Street Journal*, May 21, 2008.

It has been a tough year in the poultry business, with supply outpacing demand and feed-grain prices rising substantially. But producers are hoping all that changes when the summer cook-out season starts.

The seasonal upswing in chicken consumption, along with the anticipated jump in spot-market poultry prices, could bring some relief to producers whose profit margins have been slashed by surging corn and soybean-meal costs.

Rising feed-grain prices, accelerated by the diversion of corn to make ethanol, have pushed up the cost of producing a live chicken by as much as 65% over the past two years.

Three factors make analysts more optimistic: Companies are cutting production, weekly egg-set numbers are declining (egg sets are fertile eggs placed in incubators), and prices are responding positively to the decreasing supply.

The production slowdown is a response to the surge in feed-grain prices last fall.

Profit margins at producers will not improve unless spot-market prices for chicken move up fast enough to cover costs paid for corn and soybean meal to feed chicken flocks.

Production cutbacks and seasonal demand have helped fuel a 20-cent increase in boneless, skinless breast-meat prices to $1.46 a pound. Prices are expected to reach at least $1.80 by summer 2008.

a. Use demand and supply analysis to illustrate the changes in chicken prices described in the above article.
b. Describe what has happened in the corn and soybean-meal markets and how that has influenced the chicken market.

On the Web

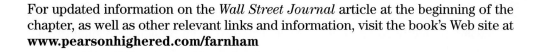

For updated information on the *Wall Street Journal* article at the beginning of the chapter, as well as other relevant links and information, visit the book's Web site at **www.pearsonhighered.com/farnham**

3 Demand Elasticities

I n this chapter, we explore the concept of demand in more detail. We focus on the downward sloping demand curve from Chapter 2, which shows an inverse relationship between the price of the good and the quantity demanded by consumers, all else held constant. As we discussed in the previous chapters, this demand curve applies to the entire market or industry in a perfectly competitive market structure, even though individual firms in this market are price-takers who cannot influence the product price.

All firms in the other market structures described in Chapter 1—monopolistic competition, oligopoly, and monopoly—face downward sloping demand curves because they have varying degrees of market power. These firms must lower the price at which they are willing to sell their product if they want to sell more units. If the product price is higher, consumers will buy fewer units. Thus, product price is a strategic variable that managers in all real-world firms must choose. Managers must also develop strategies regarding the other variables influencing demand, including tastes and preferences, consumer income, the price of related goods, and future expectations. This chapter focuses on the quantitative measure—demand elasticity—that shows how consumers respond to changes in the different variables influencing demand.

We begin the chapter with the *Wall Street Journal* article "Americans Start to Curb Their Thirst for Gasoline," which discusses the price of gasoline and motorists' sensitivity to changes in gasoline prices. We'll then formally present the concept of price elasticity of demand and develop a relationship among changes in prices, changes in revenues that a firm receives, and price elasticity. We then illustrate all elasticities with examples drawn from both the economics and the marketing literature.

The chapter appendix presents the formal economic model of consumer behavior, which shows how both consumer tastes and preferences and the constraints of income and product prices combine to influence the consumer's choice of different products.

Americans Start to Curb Their Thirst for Gasoline

by Ana Campoy

Wall Street Journal, March 3, 2008

As crude-oil prices climb to historic highs, steep gasoline prices and the weak economy are beginning to curb Americans' gas-guzzling ways.

In the past six weeks, the nation's gasoline consumption has fallen by an average 1.1% from year-earlier levels, according to weekly government data.

That's the most sustained drop in demand in at least 16 years, except for declines that followed Hurricane Katrina in 2005, which temporarily knocked out a big chunk of the U.S. gasoline supply system.

This time, however, there is evidence that Americans are changing their driving habits and lifestyles in ways that could lead to a long-term slowdown in their gasoline consumption. . . .

As refiners pay more for the oil they use, gasoline prices have gained sharply in recent weeks to an average of $3.13 a gallon in the week ended Feb. 25, up 40% from $2.24 a gallon in January 2007. That's stoking worries that prices will rise even more sharply as demand gets a boost from the approaching vacation season, when more Americans take to the road. . . .

If oil prices pull gasoline higher in the current economic climate, Americans are likely to pare back consumption even more, which should help at least damp the rise in prices as refiners build up a safety margin against fears of supply disruptions, experts say.

Of course, if the economy perks up, gasoline consumption could rise again. After softening between 1989 and 1991, as U.S. economic growth slowed, gasoline demand started to recover in 1992 and continued to expand until 2007, according to the U.S. Energy Information Administration. However, . . . demand would be likely to grow at a slower pace than in the past as Americans gradually become more fuel-efficient.

Economists and policy makers have puzzled for years over what it would take to curb Americans' ravenous appetite for fossil fuels. Now they appear to be getting an answer: sustained pain.

Over the past five years, the climb in gasoline prices, driven largely by the run-up in crude oil, hardly seemed to dent the nation's growing thirst for the fuel. Conventional thinking held that consumption would begin to taper off when gasoline hit $3 a gallon.

But $3 came and went in September 2005, and gasoline demand didn't flinch. Consumers complained about the cost of filling their tanks, pinched pennies by shopping at Wal-Mart, and kept driving.

Economists who study the effects of gasoline prices on demand say consumers tend to look at short-term price spikes as an anomaly, and don't do much to change their habits. They might spend less elsewhere to compensate, or take short-term conservation measures they can easily reverse, such as driving slower to taking public transportation, but the impact is minimal.

Regular gasoline prices jumped to $2.34 a gallon at the end of 2006, up 62% from 2003, according to the EIA. Yet demand continued to grow at an average 1.15 a year. Consumers were better able to absorb the increase because it was spread over four years, and the economy was doing fairly well.

Today a weakening economy is intensifying the effects of high gasoline prices, at the same time Americans are being pinched by broader inflation . . .

The longer gasoline prices remain high, the greater the potential consumer response. A 10% rise in gasoline prices reduces consumption by just 0.6% in the short term, but it can cut demand by about 4% if sustained over 15 years or so, according to studies compiled by the Congressional Budget Office.

As consumers make major spending decisions, such as where to live and what kind of vehicle to drive, they are beginning to factor in the costs of fuel. Some are choosing smaller cars or hybrids, or are moving closer to their jobs to cut down on driving. Those changes effectively lock in lower gasoline consumption rates for the future, regardless of the state of the economy or the level of gasoline prices. . . .

A weaker economy gets some of the credit for lessening demand. The EIA estimates that a 1% reduction in personal income cuts gasoline demand by 0.5% as consumers, along with truckers who deliver the goods, cut back on driving. . . .

The nation's slumping housing market has magnified that effect. In past years when the housing market was booming, consumers used home equity to finance spending, including the cost of filling their gas tanks. . . .

The housing boom encouraged the development of far-flung suburbs, contributing to longer commutes. Now developers are building more walkable neighborhoods close to city centers and public transit, and Americans are beginning to migrate back toward their workplaces. . . .

Pinched consumers also are speeding up their shift to more fuel-efficient cars. Sales of large cars dropped by 2.6% in 2006 and by 10.5% in 2007. In January, they plummeted 26.5% from a year earlier. . . .

Car dealers are selling fewer minivans and large sport-utility vehicles. In fact, only small cars and smaller, more fuel-efficient SUVs are showing a rise in sales. Small-car sales in January were up 6.5% from a year earlier, while sales of crossover vehicles grew 15.1%. . . .

Case for Analysis

Demand Elasticity and the American Gasoline Consumer

This article focuses on American motorists' reactions to the high price of gasoline and how, by spring 2008, there was finally some evidence of behavior change. The article noted that the increase in gasoline prices over the previous five years was driven by rising demand for oil as opposed to the reduced supplies that created the high prices during the 1970s. When gasoline prices hit $3.00 per gallon in 2005, consumers did not change their habits substantially because they perceived that this still might be a short-term price spike or an anomaly. These gasoline price increases were spread over four years, lessening their impact, and the overall economy was doing well so that consumer incomes were sustained. By 2008, the economy had weakened, impacting incomes and employment, and there were broader price increases, particularly in the food and energy sectors. Gasoline price increases appeared to be more long-term, so consumers started to change their behavior. A Congressional Budget Office study noted that a 10 percent rise in gasoline prices reduces consumption by just 0.6 percent in the short run, but by about 4 percent if sustained over 15 years or more. Consumer decisions on where to live and what type of car to drive were beginning to be influenced by the price of gasoline.

The article also discusses the impact of income on the demand for gasoline. The U.S. Energy Information Administration has estimated that a 1 percent reduction in personal income reduces gasoline demand by 0.5 percent as consumers and truckers cut back on driving. The slump in the housing market in 2007 and 2008 also made consumers cut back on the use of home equity loans to finance their consumption expenditures.

The article notes other long-term changes that appeared to be under way including the development of neighborhoods closer to city centers and public transit. City planners have observed that Americans were beginning to migrate back toward their workplaces.

There were other factors that also limited consumer responsiveness to gasoline price increases in the past.[1] First, although the nominal price of gasoline had increased, the real price in terms of spending power dropped since the 1970s and 1980s. In April 2006, the average price for a gallon of regular gas was $2.74, while the inflation-adjusted price for March 1981, was $3.18. Second, substantial changes in tastes and preferences occurred over this time period. Consumers became more concerned about other amenities of an automobile beside fuel efficiency. In particular, they focused on safety, which they perceived, perhaps inaccurately, to be associated with fuel-inefficient trucks and SUVs. Third, higher incomes meant that consumers were less affected by gasoline prices and that they used that income to buy fancier cars and to drive their existing cars more. Gasoline accounted for only 3 percent of personal consumption spending in 2006, down from 5 percent in 1981. Fourth, for many individuals, mass transit had not been a feasible substitute for driving, given that it was either not available or did not match existing commute patterns.

Thus, it appears from the above discussion that consumer responsiveness to price changes is related to

1. Tastes and preferences for various quality characteristics of a product as compared to the impact of price
2. Consumer income and the amount spent on a product in relation to that income
3. The availability of substitute goods and perceptions about what is an adequate substitute
4. The amount of time needed to adjust to change in prices

To examine these issues in more detail, we first define demand elasticity, which was mentioned in the article, and relate this discussion to the variables influencing demand presented in Chapter 2. ■

Demand elasticity
A quantitative measurement (coefficient) showing the percentage change in the quantity demanded of a particular product relative to the percentage change in any one of the variables included in the demand function for that product.

Demand Elasticity

A **demand elasticity** is a quantitative measurement (coefficient) showing the percentage change in the quantity demanded of a particular product relative to the percentage change in any one of the variables included in the demand function for

---

[1] Jeffrey Ball, "As Gasoline Prices Soar, Americans Resist Major Cuts in Consumption," *Wall Street Journal*, May 1, 2006.

that product. Thus, an elasticity can be calculated with regard to product price, consumer income, the prices of other goods and services, advertising budgets, education levels, or any of the variables included in the demand functions of Chapter 2.[2] The important point is that an elasticity measures this responsiveness in terms of *percentage changes in both variables*. Thus, an elasticity is a number, called a *coefficient*, that represents the *ratio* of two percentage changes: the percentage change in quantity demanded relative to the percentage change in the other variable.

Percentage changes are used so that managers and analysts can make comparisons among elasticities for different variables and products. If absolute changes were used instead of percentage changes and the quantities of products were measured in different units, elasticities could vary by choice of the unit of measurement. For example, using absolute values of quantities, managers would find it difficult to compare consumer responsiveness to demand variables if the quantity of one product is measured in pounds and another is measured in tons, because they would be comparing changes in pounds with changes in tons.

Price Elasticity of Demand

The **price elasticity of demand (e_P)** is defined as the percentage change in the quantity demanded of a given good, X, relative to a percentage change in its price, all other factors assumed constant, as shown in Equation 3.1.[3] A percentage change in a variable is the ratio of the absolute change ($Q_2 - Q_1$ or ΔQ; $P_2 - P_1$ or ΔP) in that variable to a base value of the variable, as shown in Equation 3.2.

> **Price elasticity of demand (e_P)**
> The percentage change in the quantity demanded of a given good, X, relative to a percentage change in its own price, all other factors assumed constant.

$$3.1 \quad e_P = \frac{\%\Delta Q_X}{\%\Delta P_X}$$

$$3.2 \quad e_P = \frac{\frac{\Delta Q_X}{Q_X}}{\frac{\Delta P_X}{P_X}} = \frac{\frac{Q_2 - Q_1}{Q_X}}{\frac{P_2 - P_1}{P_X}}$$

where

e_P = price elasticity of demand
Δ = the absolute change in the variable: ($Q_2 - Q_1$) or ($P_2 - P_1$)
Q_X = the quantity demanded of good X
P_X = the price of good X

Price elasticity of demand is illustrated by the change in quantity demanded from Q_1 to Q_2 as the price changes from P_1 to P_2, or the movement along the demand curve from point A to point B in Figure 3.1. Because we are moving along a demand curve, all other factors affecting demand *are assumed to be constant*, and we are examining only the effect of *price* on quantity demanded. All demand elasticities are defined with the other factors influencing demand assumed constant so that the effect of the given variable on demand can be measured independently.

---

[2] Although we can also calculate supply elasticities from a product supply function in a comparable manner, we will postpone our discussion of this issue until we present the model of perfect competition in Chapter 7.
[3] Price elasticity is sometimes called the "own price elasticity of demand" because it shows the ratio of the percentage change in the quantity demanded of a product to the percentage change in its *own* price.

FIGURE 3.1

Price Elasticity and the Movement Along a Demand Curve

Price elasticity is measured as a movement along a demand curve from point A to point B.

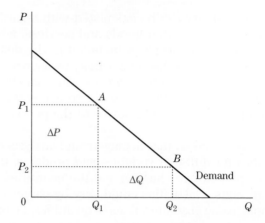

The Influence of Price Elasticity on Managerial Decision Making

Price elasticity of demand is an extremely important concept for a firm because it tells managers what will happen to revenues if the price of a product changes. It can also help firms develop a pricing strategy that will maximize their profits. Although we'll discuss the influence of price elasticity on pricing and profit maximization in more detail in Chapter 10, let's look at some examples here.

The price elasticity of demand for airline travel for pleasure travelers has been estimated at around −1.9, while that for business travelers is approximately −0.8.[4] Thus, a 10 percent change in airfares causes the number of trips to change by 19 percent for pleasure travelers, but only by 8 percent for business travelers. Airlines typically charge business travelers much higher fares because they know that these travelers are not very price sensitive. The number of trips businesspeople take will not decrease substantially if fares increase. However, pleasure travelers are much more likely to postpone a trip if they believe the airfare is too high. The airlines can collect higher revenue and earn greater profits if they charge different prices to these two groups than if they charge the same price to all travelers.

Information on the price elasticity of demand for gasoline will affect managerial decisions in the automobile industry, as discussed in the opening article of the chapter. Decisions on the size and fuel efficiency of different makes of automobiles are influenced by how consumers react to increases in the price of gasoline. As noted in the article, producers in the late 1990s and early in the next decade found that consumers valued quality features and size much more than fuel efficiency in their automobile purchasing decisions.

Elasticities are also important for management in the public sector. For example, a manager at a public transit agency needs to know how much decrease in ridership will result if the agency raises transit fares and the impact of this fare increase on the **total revenue** the agency receives from its passengers (the amount of money received by a producer for the sale of its product, calculated as the price per unit times the quantity sold).

Total revenue

The amount of money received by a producer for the sale of its product, calculated as the price per unit times the quantity sold.

Price Elasticity Values

The calculated value of *all* price elasticities for downward sloping demand curves is a negative number, given the inverse relationship between price and quantity demanded. If price increases, quantity demanded decreases and vice versa.

---

[4] Steven A. Morrison, "Airline Service: The Evolution of Competition Since Deregulation," in *Industry Studies*, ed. Larry L. Duetsch, 2nd ed. (Armonk, N.Y.: Sharpe, 1998), 147–75.

TABLE 3.1 Values of Price Elasticity of Demand Coefficients

VALUE OF ELASTICITY COEFFICIENT	ELASTICITY DEFINITION	RELATIONSHIP AMONG VARIABLES	IMPACT ON TOTAL REVENUE
$|e_P| > 1$	Elastic demand	$\% \Delta Q_X > \% \Delta P_X$	Price increase results in lower total revenue. Price decrease results in higher total revenue.
$|e_P| < 1$	Inelastic demand	$\% \Delta Q_X < \% \Delta P_X$	Price increase results in higher total revenue. Price decrease results in lower total revenue.
$|e_P| = 1$	Unit elastic or unitary elasticity	$\% \Delta Q_X = \% \Delta P_X$	Price increase or decrease has no impact on total revenue.

Therefore, it is easier to drop the negative sign and examine the absolute value ($|e_P|$) of the number to determine the size of the price elasticity. This procedure leads to the definitions shown in Table 3.1.

As shown in Table 3.1, demand is elastic if the coefficient's absolute value is greater than 1 and inelastic if the coefficient's absolute value is less than 1. For **elastic demand**, the percentage change in quantity demanded by consumers is greater than the percentage change in price. This implies a larger consumer responsiveness to changes in prices than does **inelastic demand**, in which the percentage change in quantity demanded by consumers is less than the percentage change in price. In the case of **unitary elasticity**, where $|e_P| = 1$, the percentage change in quantity demanded is exactly equal to the percentage change in price.

Elasticity and Total Revenue

The fourth column of Table 3.1 shows the relationship among price elasticity, changes in prices, and total revenue received by the firm, which, as noted above, is defined as price times quantity $[(P)(Q)]$. If demand is *elastic*, higher prices result in lower total revenue, while lower prices result in higher total revenue. This outcome arises because the percentage change in quantity is greater than the percentage change in price. If the price increases, enough fewer units are sold at the higher price that total revenue actually decreases. Likewise, with elastic demand, if price decreases, total revenue increases. Even though each unit is now sold at a lower price, there are enough more units sold that total revenue increases. Thus, for elastic demand, changes in price and the resulting total revenue move in the opposite direction. A higher price causes total revenue to decrease, while a lower price causes total revenue to increase.

These relationships for elastic demand are illustrated for the demand curve shown in Figure 3.2.[5] For this demand curve, at a price of $10, 2 units of the product are demanded, and the total revenue the firm receives is $10 × 2 units, or $20. If the price decreases to $9, the quantity demanded increases to 3 units, and the total revenue increases to $27. Demand is elastic in this range because total revenue increases as the price decreases.

This change in total revenue is illustrated graphically in Figure 3.2. If the price of $10 is labeled P_1 and the quantity of 2 units is labeled Q_1, the total revenue of $20 is represented by the area of the rectangle $0P_1AQ_1$. Likewise, if the price of $9 is labeled P_2 and the quantity of 3 units is labeled Q_2, the total revenue of $27 is represented by the area of the rectangle $0P_2BQ_2$. The change in revenue is represented by a comparison of the size of the rectangle P_1ACP_2 (rectangle Y) with that of the

Elastic demand
The percentage change in quantity demanded by consumers is greater than the percentage change in price and $|e_P| > 1$.

Inelastic demand
The percentage change in quantity demanded by consumers is less than the percentage change in price and $|e_P| < 1$.

Unitary elasticity (or unit elastic)
The percentage change in quantity demanded is exactly equal to the percentage change in price and $|e_P| = 1$.

---

[5] This demand curve is also the basis for the numerical example in the next section of the chapter.

FIGURE 3.2
Elastic Demand and Total Revenue
If demand is elastic, a decrease in price results in an increase in total revenue, and an increase in price results in a decrease in total revenue.

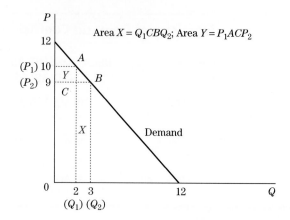

rectangle Q_1CBQ_2 (rectangle X). The first rectangle, Y, represents the loss in revenue from selling the original 2 units at the lower price of $9 instead of the original price of $10. This loss of revenue is 2 units times $1 per unit, or $2. The second rectangle, X, represents the gain in revenue from selling more units at the lower price of $9. This gain in revenue is 1 unit times $9 per unit, or $9. We can see both numerically and graphically that the gain in revenue (rectangle X) is greater than the loss in revenue (rectangle Y). Therefore, total revenue increases as the price is lowered when demand is elastic.

The opposite result holds for *inelastic* demand. In this case, if the price increases, total revenue also increases because the percentage decrease in quantity is less than the percentage increase in price. With a price increase, enough units are still sold at the higher price to cause total revenue to increase because each unit is sold at the higher price. Likewise, if price decreases, total revenue will decrease. All units are now being sold at a lower price, but the quantity demanded has not increased proportionately, so total revenue decreases. Thus, for inelastic demand, changes in price and the resulting total revenue move in the same direction. A higher price causes total revenue to increase, while a lower price causes total revenue to decrease.

Figure 3.3 illustrates this relationship for inelastic demand. For this demand curve, at a price of $4, 8 units are demanded, and the firm receives $32 in revenue. If the price falls to $3 per unit, the quantity demanded is 9 units, and the firm takes in $27 in revenue. Thus, as the price decreases, total revenue decreases, illustrating inelastic demand. In Figure 3.3, as in Figure 3.2, you can see the change in total revenue by comparing rectangle P_1ACP_2 (rectangle Y) with rectangle Q_1CBQ_2 (rectangle X). When the price is lowered from $4 to $3, the 8 units that were formerly sold at the price of $4 now are sold for $3 each. The associated revenue loss is $1 per

FIGURE 3.3
Inelastic Demand and Total Revenue
If demand is inelastic, a decrease in price results in a decrease in total revenue, and an increase in price results in a increase in total revenue.

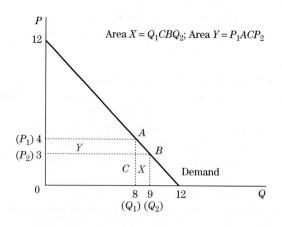

unit times 8 units, or $8. The revenue gain is the one additional unit that is now sold at a price of $3, or $3. It can be seen both graphically and numerically that the revenue gain (rectangle X) is less than the revenue loss (rectangle Y). Therefore, as the price decreases with inelastic demand, total revenue decreases.

If demand is *unit elastic*, changes in price have no impact on total revenue because the percentage change in price is exactly equal to the percentage change in quantity. The effects on price and quantity are equal and offsetting. Rectangles X and Y in Figures 3.2 and 3.3, representing the gain and loss of revenue, would be exactly the same size if demand were unit elastic.

Managerial Rule of Thumb

Estimating Price Elasticity

The examples of point elasticity and changes in revenue can be converted into managerial rules of thumb for estimating price elasticity.[6] Managers can get a ballpark estimate of price elasticity by asking their customers two questions:

1. What do you currently pay for my product? (Call this price P_1.)
2. At what price would you stop buying my product altogether? (Call this price P_2.)

Price elasticity can then be calculated as $P_1/(P_1 - P_2)$. The intuition behind this rule is that the higher the value of P_2, the higher the price the customer is willing to pay rather than do without the product, and the lower the price elasticity. This rule of thumb is based on an implicit linear demand function and the point price elasticity formula in Equation 3.5 below.

For the second rule, managers should ask themselves the following questions regarding a proposed 10 percent drop in the price of the firm's product:

1. By how much will the sales revenue increase as a result of the higher volume of sales? (Call this amount X.)
2. By how much will the sales revenue decrease as a result of a lower price on each unit sold? (Call this amount Y.)

The price elasticity of demand is the ratio of X/Y. This rule of thumb is based on the changes in revenue with elastic and inelastic demand illustrated in Figures 3.2 and 3.3. A large price elasticity coefficient means that X will be large relative to Y, whereas a small price elasticity coefficient means that Y will be large relative to X. ∎

Determinants of Price Elasticity of Demand

Three major factors influence the price elasticity of demand and cause it to differ among products:

1. The number of substitute goods
2. The percent of a consumer's income that is spent on the product
3. The time period under consideration

All else held constant, demand is generally more inelastic or less responsive to price

- The fewer the number of substitutes or perceived substitutes available
- The smaller the percent of the consumer's income that is spent on the product
- The shorter the time period under consideration

We'll look at each of these factors in turn.

---

[6] This discussion is drawn from Shlomo Maital, *Executive Economics* (New York: Free Press, 1994), pp. 186–88.

Number of Substitute Goods

If there are few substitute goods for a given product or, more important, if consumers *perceive* there are few substitute goods for the product, managers have more ability to raise prices without fear of losing sales than if a greater number of substitute goods are available. Coke and Pepsi engage in extensive advertising to convince their customers that the other product is not an adequate substitute. Each company wants to shift out the demand curve for its product and make it relatively more inelastic. This is a constant struggle, given the availability of a wide range of substitute drinks: other soft drinks, teas, fruit drinks, sports beverages, and even water. Coke and Pepsi have, of course, expanded into these other markets, so that each company owns a number of substitute products for the basic cola.

We noted earlier that the demand for airline travel by business passengers is relatively inelastic, with a coefficient equal to -0.8. Even though this elasticity is much smaller than for pleasure travelers, substitutes are still available, such as travel by car or van for shorter trips, video conferencing, faxes, and e-mail. Thus, while the airlines can charge higher prices for business than pleasure travelers, this ability to raise prices is not unlimited, given the availability of substitutes for airline travel. Even before the impact of the events of September 11, 2001, on the airline industry, business travelers had already begun to rebel against the high prices they were charged. During the first quarter of 2001, there was the largest drop recorded since 1992 in the percentage of full-fare coach and first-class tickets booked on a large sample of routes that American Express Travel Related Services tracked. In addition to scheduling videoconferences and using cars for shorter trips, businesses began buying restricted tickets and hunting for bargain fares even if they were less convenient. By 2002, some airlines were placing more restrictions on their low-cost fares to make them less attractive for business usage.[7]

Airline demand elasticities also depend on the length of the trip. Because cars, buses, and trains are substitutes for shorter airline flights, these flights should have a larger price elasticity of demand. Research studies have estimated the following price elasticities: long-haul international business, -0.26; long-haul international leisure, -0.99; long-haul domestic business, -1.15; long-haul domestic leisure, -1.52.[8] These estimates confirm expectations about the role of distance (international versus domestic flights) and the differing elasticities for business versus leisure travel.

The role of substitutes in influencing price elasticity of demand means that the price elasticity of demand for the product of a specific producer will be larger than the price elasticity for the product in general. All other producers of that same product are substitutes for the specific producer. We discuss several examples later in the chapter where the price elasticity of demand for the product is inelastic, whereas it is elastic for the output of a specific producer.

Percent of Consumer's Income Spent on the Product

Items that cost little tend to have more inelastic demands. If the price of your local newspaper doubles tomorrow, going from 50 cents to $1, you may not even notice the price increase, or perhaps you will choose to buy the paper four rather than five times per week. If the price of the European vacation you have planned for next summer doubles, you may consider traveling to a destination closer to home. In

---

[7] Martha Brannigan, Susan Carey, and Scott McCartney, "High Fares, Mediocre Service Cause Business Travelers to Mount Rebellion," *Wall Street Journal*, August 28, 2001; Scott McCartney, "Airlines Draw Flak over Disparity Between Business, Discount Fares," *Wall Street Journal*, December 13, 2001.

[8] D.W. Gillen, W.G. Morrison, and C. Stewart, *Air Travel Demand Elasticities: Concepts, Issues, and Measurement* (Ottawa: Department of Finance, 2002).

this case, your quantity demanded decreases to zero, whereas there was only a slight decrease for the newspaper case. As you would guess, consumers tend to be more sensitive to changes in the prices of goods that represent a large percent of their incomes.

Time Period

The shorter the time period, the less chance consumers have of finding acceptable substitutes for a product whose price has risen, and the more inelastic the demand. Over time, consumers can find a greater number of substitutes, and elasticities tend to be larger.

Numerical Example of Elasticity, Prices, and Revenues

We are now ready to explore the issues presented in Table 3.1 in more detail through the use of a numerical example that illustrates the relationships among elasticities, changes in prices, and changes in revenues to a firm. However, we first discuss a problem that arises in the calculation of price elasticities.

Calculating Price Elasticities

A problem occurs during the calculation of price elasticities because there are different sources of data available for these calculations. We may have data on actual quantities and prices, or we may have a demand equation that shows the functional relationship between price and quantity demanded.

Arc Price Elasticity   We first analyze the case with data on quantities and prices. In Figure 3.1, we illustrated a large price change that resulted in a large change in quantity demanded. If the price falls from P_1 to P_2, all else assumed constant, the quantity demanded increases from Q_1 to Q_2. Because points Q_1 and Q_2 may be significantly different from each other, a different value for the percentage change in quantity may result, depending on whether Q_1 or Q_2 is used for the base quantity in Equation 3.2. If we are measuring the effect of a price decrease from P_1 to P_2, which causes the quantity demanded to increase from Q_1 to Q_2, we will tend to use Q_1 as the base because that is our beginning quantity. If we are measuring the decrease in quantity demanded resulting from a price increase from P_2 to P_1, we will tend to use quantity Q_2 as the base quantity. The same problem occurs when we are measuring the percentage change in price. We will tend to use P_1 as the base for price decreases and P_2 as the base for price increases because these are the current prices of the product.

Because an elasticity coefficient is just a number, it is useful to have that coefficient be the same for an increase or a decrease in quantity demanded. However, that result might not occur with the example in Figure 3.1 because dividing the absolute change in quantity (ΔQ) by Q_1 could result in a quite different number than dividing it by Q_2. For example, if $Q_1 = 10$ and $Q_2 = 20$, $\Delta Q = 10$. $\Delta Q/Q_1 = 10/10 = 1.0$, or a 100 percent increase in quantity. However, $\Delta Q/Q_2 = 10/20 = 0.5$, or a 50 percent decrease in quantity. The percentage increase in quantity is substantially different from the percentage decrease in quantity.

This issue is *not* a problem with the definition of price elasticity; instead, it is a numerical or calculation problem that arises for elasticity of demand when the starting and ending quantities and prices are significantly different from each other, as in Figure 3.1. We are calculating elasticity over a region or arc on the demand curve (point *A* to point *B* in Figure 3.1). The calculation problem can also arise if a manager does not know the shape of the entire demand curve, but simply has data on several prices and quantities.[9]

Arc price elasticity of demand

A measurement of the price elasticity of demand where the base quantity or price is calculated as the average value of the starting and ending quantities or prices.

The conventional solution to this problem is to calculate an **arc price elasticity of demand**, where the base quantity (or price) is the average value of the starting and ending points, as shown in Equation 3.3.

$$3.3 \quad e_P = \frac{\dfrac{(Q_2 - Q_1)}{(Q_1 + Q_2)}}{2} \bigg/ \dfrac{\dfrac{(P_2 - P_1)}{(P_1 + P_2)}}{2}$$

Point Price Elasticity   A price elasticity is technically defined for very tiny or infinitesimal changes in prices and quantities. In Figure 3.1, if point B is moved very close to point A, the starting and ending prices and quantities are also very close to each other. We can then think of calculating an elasticity at a particular point on the demand curve (such as point A). This can be done in either of two ways: using calculus or using a noncalculus approach.

Point price elasticity of demand

A measurement of the price elasticity of demand calculated at a point on the demand curve using infinitesimal changes in prices and quantities.

Equation 3.4 shows the formula for **point price elasticity of demand** where d is the derivative from calculus showing an infinitesimal change in the variables.

$$3.4 \quad e_P = \frac{\dfrac{dQ_X}{Q_X}}{\dfrac{dP_X}{P_X}} = \frac{dQ_X P_X}{dP_X Q_X}$$

If you have a specific demand function, you can use calculus to compute the appropriate derivative (dQ_X/dP_X) for Equation 3.4.

However, because we're not requiring calculus in this text, we'll use a simpler approach for the linear demand function defined in Chapter 2. The point price elasticity of demand can be calculated for a linear demand function as shown in Equation 3.5.

$$3.5 \quad e_P = \frac{P}{(P - a)}$$

where

P = the price charged

a = the vertical intercept of the plotted demand curve (the P-axis)[10]

Thus, for any linear demand curve, a point price elasticity can be calculated for any price by knowing the vertical intercept of the demand curve (as plotted on the P-axis) and using the formula in Equation 3.5.

---

[9] If a manager has data only on prices and quantities, he or she needs to be certain that all other factors are constant as these prices and quantities change to be able to correctly estimate the price elasticity of demand. This is the major problem in estimating demand functions and elasticities, which we will discuss in Chapter 4.

[10] Following S. Charles Maurice and Christopher R. Thomas, *Managerial Economics*, 7th ed. (McGraw-Hill Irwin, 2002), p. 92, the derivation of this result is as follows. For a linear demand curve,

$P = a + bQ$ or $Q = [(P - a)/b]$

$b = (\Delta P/\Delta Q)$ and $1/b = (\Delta Q/\Delta P)$

$e_P = (\Delta Q/Q)/(\Delta P/P) = (\Delta Q/\Delta P)(P/Q) = (1/b)[P/(P - a)/b] = [P/(P - a)]$

Numerical Example

Table 3.2 presents a numerical example using a linear, or straight-line, downward sloping demand curve. Demand curves may be either straight or curved lines, depending on how people actually behave. (We'll discuss this issue in more detail in the next chapter on demand and elasticity estimation.) Throughout most of this text, we use *linear* downward sloping demand curves for our examples. These are the simplest types of curves to illustrate mathematically. They are also good representations of consumer behavior in different markets, as we show in Chapter 4.

The Demand Function

The demand function in Table 3.2 shows a relationship between quantity demanded (Q) and price (P), with all other factors held constant. The effect of all the other variables influencing demand is summarized in the constant term of 12.[11] Demand functions such as the one in Table 3.2 are estimated from data on real-world consumer behavior using the techniques we discuss in Chapter 4.

The first row in Table 3.2 shows that the demand function can be stated either as quantity as a function of price or as price as a function of quantity. Mathematically, the two forms of the relationship are equivalent. As noted in Chapter 2, in a behavioral sense, we usually think of quantity demanded as being a function of the price of the good. However, we use the inverse form of the relationship, price as a function of quantity, to plot a demand curve and to calculate the point price elasticity of demand, as shown in Equation 3.5.

Other Functions Related to Demand

Given the demand function in Table 3.2, we can derive a **total revenue function**, which shows the total revenue (price times quantity) received by the producer as a function of the level of output. To find total revenue, we can calculate the quantity demanded at different prices and multiply the terms together, or we can use the formal total revenue function given in Table 3.2.

Average revenue is defined as total revenue per unit of output. The **average revenue function** shows how average revenue is related to the level of output. Because total revenue equals $(P)(Q)$, average revenue equals the price of the product by definition. This is shown in the third line of Table 3.2. Thus, at any level of output, the average revenue received by the producer equals the price at which that output is sold.

Total revenue function
The functional relationship that shows the total revenue (price times quantity) received by a producer as a function of the level of output.

Average revenue
Total revenue per unit of output. Average revenue equals the price of the product by definition.

Average revenue function
The functional relationship that shows the revenue per unit of output received by the producer at different levels of output.

TABLE 3.2 Numerical Example of Demand, Total Revenue, Average Revenue, and Marginal Revenue Functions

Demand function	$Q = 12 - P$ or $P = 12 - Q$
Total revenue function	$TR = (P)(Q) = (12 - Q)(Q) = 12Q - Q^2$
Average revenue function	$AR = \dfrac{TR}{Q} = \dfrac{(P)(Q)}{Q} = P$
Marginal revenue function	$MR = \dfrac{\Delta TR}{\Delta Q} = \dfrac{TR_2 - TR_1}{Q_2 - Q_1}$
	$MR = \dfrac{dTR}{dQ} = 12 - 2Q$

---

[11] If we had a demand function that explicitly included another variable such as income, once we put in a specific value for income (to hold it constant), that number would become part of the constant term of the equation.

Marginal revenue
The additional revenue that a firm takes in from selling an additional unit of output or the change in total revenue divided by the change in output.

Marginal revenue function
The functional relationship that shows the additional revenue a producer receives by selling an additional unit of output at different levels of output.

Marginal revenue is defined as the additional revenue that a firm receives from selling an additional unit of output or the change in total revenue divided by the change in output. It can be calculated in discrete terms if you have data on the total revenue associated with different levels of output, as shown in the fourth line of Table 3.2. If you have a mathematical total revenue function, the **marginal revenue function** can be calculated by taking the derivative of the total revenue function with respect to output. (Because calculus is not required in this text, we will supply any marginal revenue functions that you need.)

The numerical values for the functional relationships in Table 3.2 are given in Table 3.3. The first two columns of Table 3.3 show the values of the demand function and the inverse relationship between price and quantity demanded. Column 3 presents total revenue for the different levels of output. Column 4 shows marginal revenue calculated in discrete terms, which represents the change in total revenue between one and two units of output, between two and three units of output, and so on. Column 5 shows marginal revenue calculated from the marginal revenue function presented in the last line of Table 3.2. In this case, marginal revenue is calculated for an infinitesimal change in output that occurs at a given level of output. Thus, Column 5 shows marginal revenue calculated precisely at a given level of output compared with the Column 4 calculations of marginal revenue between different levels of output. You will notice that the values in Columns 4 and 5 are very similar. The differences between Columns 4 and 5 are similar to the differences between the arc and point price elasticities of demand we discussed earlier. Remember that these are differences in the calculation of the numbers, not in the definition of the concepts.

Calculation of Arc and Point Price Elasticities

Table 3.4 illustrates arc and point price elasticity calculations from the demand functions in Tables 3.2 and 3.3. Table 3.4 illustrates both the differences in the calculation methods for arc and point price elasticities and the similarities in the

TABLE 3.3 Numerical Values for the Functional Relationships in Table 3.2

(1) Q	(2) P	(3) TR = (P)(Q)	(4) MR = ΔTR/ΔQ	(5) MR = dTR/dQ
0	12	0		12
1	11	11	11	10
2	10	20	9	8
3	9	27	7	6
4	8	32	5	4
5	7	35	3	2
6	6	36	1	0
7	5	35	−1	−2
8	4	32	−3	−4
9	3	27	−5	−6
10	2	20	−7	−8
11	1	11	−9	−10
12	0	0	−11	−12

TABLE 3.4 Arc Price Elasticity Versus Point Price Elasticity Calculations (Data from Tables 3.2 and 3.3)

ARC ELASTICITY: ELASTIC DEMAND

$P_1 = \$10; Q_1 = 2; TR_1 = \$20$

$P_2 = \$9; Q_2 = 3; TR_2 = \$27$

$$e_P = \frac{\dfrac{Q_2 - Q_1}{\dfrac{Q_1 + Q_2}{2}}}{\dfrac{P_2 - P_1}{\dfrac{P_1 + P_2}{2}}} = \frac{\dfrac{3 - 2}{\dfrac{2 + 3}{2}}}{\dfrac{9 - 10}{\dfrac{10 + 9}{2}}}$$

$$e_P = \frac{\dfrac{1}{\dfrac{5}{2}}}{\dfrac{-1}{\dfrac{19}{2}}} = \frac{\dfrac{2}{5}}{\dfrac{-2}{19}} = \frac{-19}{5} = -3.80$$

POINT ELASTICITY: ELASTIC DEMAND

$$e_P = \frac{P}{(P - a)}$$

where $a = 12$

$P = \$10$

$$e_P = \frac{10}{(10 - 12)} = \frac{10}{-2} = -5.00$$

POINT ELASTICITY: UNIT ELASTIC DEMAND

$$e_P = \frac{P}{(P - a)}$$

where $a = 12$

$P = \$6$

$$e_P = \frac{6}{(6 - 12)} = \frac{6}{-6} = -1.00$$

ARC ELASTICITY: INELASTIC DEMAND

$P_1 = \$4; Q_1 = 8; TR_1 = \$32$

$P_2 = \$3; Q_2 = 9; TR_2 = \$27$

$$e_P = \frac{\dfrac{Q_2 - Q_1}{\dfrac{Q_1 + Q_2}{2}}}{\dfrac{P_2 - P_1}{\dfrac{P_1 + P_2}{2}}} = \frac{\dfrac{9 - 8}{\dfrac{8 + 9}{2}}}{\dfrac{3 - 4}{\dfrac{4 + 3}{2}}}$$

$$e_P = \frac{\dfrac{1}{\dfrac{17}{2}}}{\dfrac{-1}{\dfrac{7}{2}}} = \frac{\dfrac{2}{17}}{\dfrac{-2}{7}} = \frac{-7}{17} = -0.41$$

POINT ELASTICITY: INELASTIC DEMAND

$$e_P = \frac{P}{(P - a)}$$

where $a = 12$

$P = \$4$

$$e_P = \frac{4}{(4 - 12)} = \frac{4}{-8} = -0.50$$

results. In this example, the arc price elasticity of demand between a price of $10 and a price of $9 is −3.80, while the point price elasticity calculated precisely at $10 is −5.00. The arc price elasticity calculated between a price of $4 and a price of $3 is −0.41, while the point price elasticity at $4 is −0.50.

Price Elasticity Versus Slope of the Demand Curve

We can see in Table 3.4 that the price elasticity of demand is not constant along this linear demand curve. At prices above $6, the demand is elastic, whereas the demand is inelastic at prices below $6. The demand is unit elastic at a price of $6. We'll explore these relationships in more detail in the next section of the chapter. However, this analysis does show us that elasticity and slope are *not* the same concepts. A linear demand curve, like any straight line, has a constant slope, but the price elasticity of demand varies along this demand curve. Thus, for a linear demand function, the price elasticity coefficient must be calculated for a specific price and quantity demanded on that curve because the coefficient is smaller at lower prices than at higher prices.[12]

Demand Elasticity, Marginal Revenue, and Total Revenue

The relationships among demand, total revenue, and marginal revenue in Tables 3.2 and 3.3 are summarized in Figures 3.4 and 3.5. The inverse demand curve, $P = 12 - Q$, is plotted in Figure 3.4 along with the corresponding marginal revenue curve. Values of the total revenue function are plotted in Figure 3.5.

A firm is always constrained by its demand curve. In the case of the linear demand curve in Figure 3.4, a price of $12 drives the quantity demanded to 0, and, at a price of $0, the quantity demanded is 12 units. Thus, total revenue (price times quantity) in Figure 3.5 begins and ends at zero at each end of the demand curve in Figure 3.4.

In the top half of the demand curve in Figure 3.4, when managers lower the price, total revenue in Figure 3.5 increases. This means that demand is elastic in this range of the demand curve, as a decrease in price results in an increase in total revenue. At a price of $6 and a quantity demanded of 6 units, total revenue is maximized at $36, as shown in Figure 3.5. Demand at this point is unit elastic. In the bottom half of the demand curve, below a price of $6, a decrease in price causes total revenue to fall as quantity demanded increases from 6 to 12 units of output. This means that demand is inelastic for this portion of the demand curve. The decrease in total revenue between 6 and 12 units of output is illustrated in Figure 3.5.

The marginal revenue curve is also plotted with the demand curve in Figure 3.4. The marginal revenue curve begins at the point where the demand curve intersects the

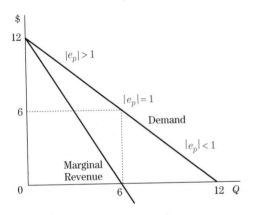

FIGURE 3.4
Demand and Marginal Revenue Functions
The demand, marginal revenue, and total revenue functions are interrelated, as shown in Figures 3.4 and 3.5.

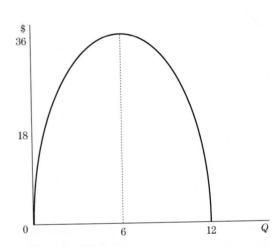

FIGURE 3.5
The Total Revenue Function

---

[12] Equation 3.2 can be simplified to show price elasticity as follows:

$$3.2 \quad e_P = \frac{\frac{\Delta Q_X}{Q_X}}{\frac{\Delta P_X}{P_X}} = \frac{(\Delta Q_X)(P_X)}{(\Delta P_X)(Q_X)}$$

The first ratio of variables in Equation 3.2 (Q_X/P_X) is a slope term. It shows the absolute change in quantity divided by the absolute change in price and is constant for a linear demand function. To calculate price elasticity, however, we must multiply this slope term by the ratio of a given price and quantity demanded, the second ratio of variables in Equation 3.2 (P_X/Q_X). While the slope term remains constant along the demand curve, the second term does not. As you move down the demand curve, price decreases and quantity demanded increases, so the ratio and, thus, the price elasticity of demand decrease.

TABLE 3.5 Relationships for a Linear Downward Sloping Demand Curve

ELASTICITY	IMPACT ON TOTAL REVENUE	MARGINAL REVENUE
Elastic $\|e_P\| > 1$ Upper half of demand curve	$\downarrow P \Rightarrow \uparrow TR$ $\uparrow P \Rightarrow \downarrow TR$	Positive (for increases in Q)
Inelastic $\|e_P\| < 1$ Lower half of demand curve	$\downarrow P \Rightarrow \downarrow TR$ $\uparrow P \Rightarrow \uparrow TR$	Negative (for increases in Q)
Unit Elastic $\|e_P\| = 1$ Midpoint of demand curve	$\downarrow P \Rightarrow$ No change in TR $\uparrow P \Rightarrow$ No change in TR TR is at its maximum value	Zero

price axis and then has a slope twice as steep as the demand curve. This can be seen in the equations in Table 3.2, where the demand function is expressed as $P = 12 - Q$ and the marginal revenue function is $MR = 12 - 2Q$. This relationship between the demand and the marginal revenue function holds for all linear downward sloping demand curves. Once you draw the demand curve, you can draw the corresponding marginal revenue curve, even if you do not have specific equations for the curves.

We can also see a relationship between marginal revenue and price elasticity in Figure 3.4. Marginal revenue is positive, but decreasing in value, between a price of $12 and a price of $6 (or between 0 and 6 units of output). This means that as price is lowered in that range, total revenue increases, but at a decreasing rate.[13] Figure 3.5 shows that total revenue increases from $0 to $36 as output increases from 0 to 6 units. However, the rate of increase lessens and the total revenue curve becomes flatter as output approaches 6 units. Because the top half of the demand curve is the elastic portion, marginal revenue must be a positive number when demand is elastic.

Decreases in the price below $6 cause the marginal revenue curve in Figure 3.4 to become negative. The additional revenue that the firm takes in from selling an additional unit of output is negative. The total revenue function in Figure 3.5 starts to decrease after 6 units of output are sold. We already established that the bottom half of the demand curve is the inelastic portion of that curve. Thus, when demand is inelastic, lowering the price decreases total revenue, so that marginal revenue must be negative.

At the exact midpoint of the demand curve, marginal revenue equals zero. This is also the point where total revenue reaches its maximum value. In Figure 3.5, total revenue is at a maximum of $36 at a quantity of 6 units of output and a price of $6. And as we established, demand is unit elastic at this price. Any small change in price at this point will have no impact on total revenue. Table 3.5 summarizes all of these relationships for a linear downward sloping demand curve.

Vertical and Horizontal Demand Curves

The previous discussion focused on *linear* downward sloping demand curves. We use these examples to represent all downward sloping demand curves that exhibit an inverse relationship between price and quantity demanded. These demand curves are important to managers because they reflect typical consumer behavior, with the price elasticity measuring how responsive quantity demanded is to

---

[13] This can be explained mathematically because marginal revenue is the slope of the total revenue function. The slope of the total revenue curve in Figure 3.5 decreases as output increases to 6 units.

changes in price. There are, however, two polar cases of demand curves that we should also consider: vertical and horizontal demand curves.

Vertical Demand Curves

Figure 3.6 presents a vertical demand curve. This curve shows that the quantity demanded of the good is the same regardless of the price—in other words, there is no consumer responsiveness to changes in the price of the good. This vertical demand curve represents **perfectly inelastic demand**, where the elasticity coefficient is zero ($e_P = 0$).

Perfectly inelastic demand
Zero elasticity of demand, illustrated by a vertical demand curve, where there is no change in quantity demanded for any change in price.

Can you guess what, if any, types of goods would have such a demand curve? Students often suggest products that are produced by only one supplier, such as the electricity supplied by a local power utility in a state where there has been no deregulation of electricity. Yet this answer is incorrect. Even if people can buy their electric power from only one source, and even if they usually will not be very responsive to price, they typically will not be totally *unresponsive* to changes in price. If the price of electricity increases, people may choose to run their air conditioners less in the summer or be more careful about how many lights they leave on in their houses. Thus, they are decreasing the quantity demanded of electricity in response to a higher price and therefore do not have a vertical demand curve for electricity.

A vertical demand curve would pertain to a product that is absolutely necessary for life and for which there are no substitutes. Insulin for a diabetic might be a reasonable example, although this answer relates to the product insulin in general and not to a particular type of insulin produced by a specific drug company. You would think that illegal, addictive drugs or other addictive substances would have very low elasticities of demand, even if they are not zero. However, the evidence is not clear even for these products. Researchers have estimated the price elasticity of demand for marijuana to lie between -1.0 and -1.5, while they estimated that for opium to be approximately -0.7 over shorter time periods and around -1.0 over longer periods. Cigarette smoking price elasticities have been estimated at -0.75 for adults, while teenage smoking elasticities may be greater than 1 in absolute value.[14] Thus, even for addictive substances, the price elasticities may

FIGURE 3.6
Vertical Demand Curve
A vertical demand curve represents perfectly inelastic demand.

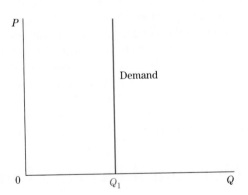

---

[14] Charles T. Nisbet and Firouz Vakil, "Some Estimates of Price and Expenditure Elasticities of Demand for Marijuana Among U.C.L.A. Students," *Review of Economics and Statistics* 54 (November 1972): 473–75; Jan C. Van Ours, "The Price Elasticity of Hard Drugs: The Case of Opium in the Dutch East Indies, 1923–1938," *Journal of Political Economy* 103 (1995): 261–79; Gary S. Becker, Michael Grossman, and Kevin M. Murphy, "An Empirical Analysis of Cigarette Addiction," *American Economic Review* 84 (June 1994): 396–418; Frank J. Chaloupka and Michael Grossman, *Price, Tobacco Control, and Youth Smoking*, NBER Working Paper Series, no. 5740 (Cambridge, Mass.: National Bureau of Economic Research, 1996); Frank J. Chaloupka and Henry Wechsler, "Price, Tobacco Control Policies, and Smoking Among Young Adults," *Journal of Health Economics* 16 (June 1997): 359–73.

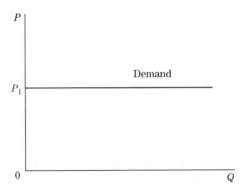

FIGURE 3.7
Horizontal Demand Curve
A horizontal demand curve represents perfectly or infinitely elastic demand.

not be close to zero. The key issues for perfectly inelastic demand are that the product is necessary for life and there are no substitutes.[15]

Horizontal Demand Curves

The other polar case, the horizontal demand curve, is shown in Figure 3.7. This is the example of **perfectly (or infinitely) elastic demand** ($e_P = \infty$). Any increases in price above P_1 in Figure 3.7 would cause the quantity demanded to decrease to zero, while any price decreases below P_1 would cause the quantity demanded to increase tremendously. This demand curve does not have any exact applications in reality, although estimates of the price elasticity of demand for the output of individual farmers are extremely large. Estimated absolute values of the demand elasticities for individual producers of common fruits and vegetables range from 800 to over 31,000, with most values greater than 2,000.[16] These values are not infinite in size, but they are extremely large compared with normal elasticity values.

The perfectly elastic demand curve plays a very important role in economic theory because it represents the demand curve facing an individual firm in the model of perfect competition, as we discussed in Chapter 1. In this model, the individual firm is one of a large number of firms producing a product such that no single firm can influence the price of the product. If such a firm tried to raise its price, its quantity demanded would fall to zero. Thus, each firm is a price-taker and faces a horizontal demand curve. Individual agricultural producers come close to fitting this definition. That is why the estimated demand elasticities presented above, while not infinite, are very large in size. We return to a discussion of the model of perfect competition in much greater detail in Chapter 7.

Perfectly (or infinitely) elastic demand
Infinite elasticity of demand, illustrated by a horizontal demand curve, where the quantity demanded would vary tremendously if there were any changes in price.

Income and Cross-Price Elasticities of Demand

Although price elasticity of demand is of great importance, managers also need to know the size of the other elasticities in the demand function for a given product. Two other common elasticities are the income elasticity and the cross-price elasticity of demand.

Income Elasticity of Demand

The **income elasticity of demand** shows how consumers change their demand for a particular product in response to changes in income. The elasticity coefficient

Income elasticity of demand
The percentage change in the quantity demanded of a given good, X, relative to a percentage change in consumer income, assuming all other factors constant.

---

[15] Although the individual demand curve for insulin might be perfectly inelastic, the market demand curve would have a nonzero elasticity coefficient. For every user of insulin, there is some maximum price they are willing and able to pay. When this price is exceeded, these users would drop out of the market, causing quantity demanded to vary with price.
[16] Dennis W. Carlton and Jeffrey M. Perloff, *Modern Industrial Organization*, 3rd ed. (New York: Addison-Wesley Longman, 2000).

is defined as the percentage change in the quantity demanded of the good relative to the percentage change in income, holding all other factors constant. This change in income could be a change for an individual consumer resulting from a raise or new job, or it could arise from a change in the general level of economic activity in the overall economy affecting all consumers.

If an increase in income results in an increase in the demand for the good or if declining income causes consumers to decrease their demand, the good has a *positive* income elasticity of demand and is called a *normal good*, which we discussed in Chapter 2. Thus, changes in income and the demand for normal goods move in the same direction. If an increase in income results in a decrease in demand or vice versa, the good has a *negative* income elasticity and is termed an *inferior good*, which you'll also recall from Chapter 2. As you've learned, this term has nothing to do with the quality of the product; it simply denotes a negative income elasticity of demand. Changes in income and the demand for inferior goods move in opposite directions. Thus, the *mathematical sign* of the income elasticity of demand coefficient (positive or negative) is as important as the *size* of the elasticity coefficient (magnitude of the number). The sign tells a manager whether the good is normal or inferior, while the size of the coefficient measures the responsiveness of the demand to changes in income.

For goods with positive income elasticities, we often make a distinction between necessities and luxuries. **Necessities** are defined as goods with an income elasticity between 0 and 1 ($0 < e_I < 1$), while **luxuries** are defined as goods with an income elasticity greater than 1 ($e_I > 1$). Consumer spending on necessities does not change substantially as income changes, whereas spending on luxury goods changes more than proportionately with changes in income.

Table 3.6 summarizes these concepts. For income elasticity of demand, the percentage change in quantity is the change between the two quantities demanded divided by

Necessity
A good with an income elasticity between 0 and 1, where the expenditure on the good increases less than proportionately with changes in income.

Luxury
A good with an income elasticity greater than 1, where the expenditure on the good increases more than proportionately with changes in income.

TABLE 3.6 Income Elasticity and Cross-Price Elasticity of Demand Coefficients

ELASTICITY NAME	ELASTICITY DEFINITION	VALUE OF ELASTICITY COEFFICIENT	IMPACT ON DEMAND
Income elasticity: e_I	$\dfrac{\%\Delta Q_X}{\%\Delta I} = \dfrac{\frac{\Delta Q_X}{Q_X}}{\frac{\Delta I}{I}}$	$e_I > 0$: Normal good	Increase in income results in increase in demand
		$0 < e_I < 1$: Necessity	
		$e_I > 1$: Luxury	Decrease in income results in decrease in demand
		$e_I < 0$: Inferior good	Increase in income results in decrease in demand
			Decrease in income results in increase in demand
Cross-price Elasticity: e_C	$\dfrac{\%\Delta Q_X}{\%\Delta P_Y} = \dfrac{\frac{\Delta Q_X}{Q_X}}{\frac{\Delta P_Y}{P_Y}}$	$e_C > 0$: Substitute good	Increase in the price of good Y results in increase in the demand for good X
			Decrease in the price of good Y results in decrease in the demand for good X
		$e_C < 0$: Complementary good	Increase in the price of good Y results in decrease in the demand for good X
			Decrease in the price of good Y results in increase in the demand for good X

the base quantity; the same is true for the percentage change in income. As with price elasticity, income elasticities can be calculated either for discrete changes in income and quantities (arc elasticity) or for infinitesimal changes (point elasticity).

In August 2006, several commentators noted that the higher gasoline prices were reducing consumers' discretionary income, which was then having an impact in other markets. Starbucks Corp. reported that sales in stores open at least 13 months rose just 4 percent in July 2006, the smallest increase in nearly five years.[17] Restaurant chains, such as Applebee's International, Inc., Cheesecake Factory, Inc, and KFC, noted that consumers were dining out less frequently. Consumers who had traded up to higher-end stores were cutting back as discretionary income declined.[18]

Managerial Rule of Thumb

Calculating Income Elasticity

The following is a simple rule of thumb for calculating the income elasticity of demand for a product based on two questions for a consumer:

1. What fraction of your total budget do you spend on Product X?
2. If you earned a bonus of an additional $1,000, what part of that bonus would you spend on Product X?

The ratio of the answer to question 2 to the answer to question 1 is the income elasticity of demand.[19] Applying this rule to different products will give managers a quick means of determining how changes in income will affect the demand for various products. ■

Cross-Price Elasticity of Demand

The **cross-price elasticity of demand** measures how the demand for one good, X, varies with changes in the price of another good, Y. The elasticity coefficient is defined as the percentage change in the quantity demanded of good X relative to the percentage change in the price of good Y, holding all other factors constant. Two goods with a *positive* cross-price elasticity of demand coefficient are said to be *substitute goods*, as we defined in Chapter 2. An increase in the price of good Y causes consumers to demand more of good X because they are substituting good X for good Y. Coffee and tea are substitute goods, as an increase in the price of coffee will cause some people to switch to drinking tea. If two goods have a *negative* cross-price elasticity of demand coefficient, they are called *complementary goods*, which you'll also recall from Chapter 2. An increase in the price of good Y results in a decrease in the demand for good X if the two goods are used together or are complements. Coffee and cream are complements because an increase in the price of coffee causes people to drink less coffee and, therefore, use less cream. Goods that have a zero cross-price elasticity of demand are unrelated in terms of consumption.

Thus, both the mathematical sign and the magnitude or size of the cross-price elasticity coefficient are important concepts for managers. The sign of the coefficient tells whether the goods are substitutes or complements, and the size of the

Cross-price elasticity of demand

The percentage change in the quantity demanded of a given good, X, relative to the percentage change in the price of good Y, all other factors held constant.

---

[17] Janet Adamy, "Are Frappuccino Woes or Frugality to Blame for Starbuck's Stumble?" *Wall Street Journal*, August 4, 2006.

[18] Justin Lahart and Amy Merrick, "Consumers Curb Upscale Buying as Gasoline Prices, Housing Bite," *Wall Street Journal*, August 21, 2006.

[19] This example is drawn from Shlomo Maital, *Executive Economics* (New York: Free Press, 1994), 195. The answer to question 1 is X/Y, where X is the amount of good X purchased and Y is income. The answer to question 2 is $(\Delta X)/(\Delta Y)$. The ratio of answer 2 to answer 1 is $(\Delta X/\Delta Y)/(X/Y)$, which can be converted to $(\Delta X/X)/(\Delta Y/Y)$, the definition for the income elasticity of demand.

cross-price elasticity measures the extent of the relationship between the goods. These relationships are summarized in the bottom part of Table 3.6.

The cross-price elasticity of demand plays a role in defining the relevant market in which different products compete. Although we will explore this issue further in subsequent chapters, we note here that cross-price elasticity figured prominently in the 1956 antitrust case brought by the U.S. Justice Department against DuPont for monopolizing cellophane production. In that case, the Justice Department argued that the relevant market, which DuPont clearly dominated, was cellophane sales only, given the unique properties of cellophane, the price differences that existed between cellophane and other packaging materials, the patents DuPont held, and the substantial profits the company earned. DuPont lawyers argued, based on large cross-price elasticities of demand, that the relevant market was all packaging material, in which DuPont had only an 18 percent market share. Both a Delaware district court and the U.S. Supreme Court accepted this broader market definition and acquitted DuPont of the monopolization charges.[20]

Similar issues have arisen in other antitrust cases. In 1986, the Federal Trade Commission (FTC) filed suit to block a merger between the Coca-Cola Company and the Dr. Pepper Company in order to maintain competition and, thus, lower prices in the carbonated soft drink market.[21] The size of the relevant market, the number of substitutes, and, therefore, the implied cross-price elasticities of demand between Coke and other beverages were key issues in these proceedings. The FTC's argument that the carbonated soft drink market was the relevant market was based on evidence that soft drink pricing and marketing strategies focused on the producers of other soft drinks, not fruit juices, milk, coffee, tea, or other beverages. Documents indicated that Coke officials gathered information on the prices and sales of other carbonated soft drink producers, not producers of other beverages. Although Coca-Cola argued that the company competed against all other beverages, which were, therefore, actual or potential substitutes for carbonated soft drinks, the judge in the case ruled for the FTC and accepted its argument regarding the narrower number of relevant substitutes.

Elasticity Estimates: Economics Literature

Table 3.7 presents estimates of elasticity of demand coefficients derived in the economics literature for various products. These estimates show how elasticities differ among products, groups of consumers, and over time. Remember that price elasticity coefficients are reported as negative numbers even though we look at their absolute values to determine the size of the coefficients.

Elasticity and Chicken and Agricultural Products

As shown in Table 3.7, broiler chickens have a low price elasticity of demand, as do many other agricultural products. This low demand elasticity accounts for the wide swings in the income of farmers, particularly in response to bumper crops, or large increases in supply. Farm production is subject to many factors outside producer control, such as the weather and attacks by insects. Crops are grown and then thrown on the market for whatever price they will bring. If there is a bumper crop, this increase in supply drives farm product prices down. Because quantity demanded does not increase proportionately, given the inelastic demand, total

---

[20] This example is drawn from F. M. Scherer and David Ross, *Industrial Market Structure and Economic Performance*, 3rd ed. (Boston: Houghton Mifflin, 1990), 457–58.

[21] This discussion is based on Lawrence J. White, "Application of the Merger Guidelines: The Proposed Merger of Coca-Cola and Dr. Pepper (1986)," in *The Antitrust Revolution: The Role of Economics*, eds. John E. Kwoka Jr. and Lawrence J. White, 2nd ed. (New York: HarperCollins, 1994), 76–95.

TABLE 3.7 Estimates of Demand Elasticities

PRODUCT	PRICE ELASTICITY COEFFICIENT	INCOME ELASTICITY COEFFICIENT	CROSS-PRICE ELASTICITY COEFFICIENT
CHICKEN AND AGRICULTURAL PRODUCTS			
Broiler chickens	−0.2 to −0.4	+1.0 (1950)	+0.20 (beef)
		+0.38 (1980s)	+0.28 (pork)
Cabbage	−0.25	N.A.	
Potatoes	−0.27	+0.15	
Eggs	−0.43	+0.57	
Oranges	−0.62	+0.83	
Cream	−0.69	+1.72	
Apples	−1.27	+1.32	
Fresh tomatoes	−2.22	+0.24	
Lettuce	−2.58	+0.88	
Fresh peas	−2.83	+1.05	
Individual producer	−800 to −31,000		
BEER			
Commodity	−0.7 to −0.9		
Individual brands	Reported as "quite elastic"		
THE AIRLINE INDUSTRY	−1.9 (pleasure)	+1.5	
	−0.8 (business)		
THE TOBACCO INDUSTRY (CIGARETTES)			
College students	−0.906 to −1.309		
Secondary school students	−0.846 to −1.450		
Adults, long-run, permanent change in price	−0.75		
Adults, short-run, permanent change in price	−0.40		
Adults, temporary change in price	−0.30		
HEALTH CARE			
Primary care	−0.1 to −0.7	$0.0 < e_I < +1.0$	
Total/elective surgery	−0.14 to −0.17		
Physician visits	−0.06		
Dental care	−0.5 to −0.7		
Nursing homes	−0.73 to −2.40		
Inpatient/outpatient hospital services	N.A.		+0.85 to +1.46
Individual physicians	−2.80 to −5.07		
HOTEL ROOM ATTRIBUTES	*Price/Attribute Elasticity*		
Economy hotel—standard room			
Price	−2.46		
Room quality	+1.13		
Check-in time	−0.06		
Guaranteed reservation	+2.21		
Free parking	+1.31		

(continued)

TABLE 3.7 *Continued*

PRODUCT	PRICE ELASTICITY COEFFICIENT	INCOME ELASTICITY COEFFICIENT	CROSS-PRICE ELASTICITY COEFFICIENT
Luxury hotel—standard room			
Price	−4.15		
Room quality	+1.45		
Check-in time	−0.17		
Guaranteed reservation	+2.27		
Free parking	+1.79		

Sources: Richard T. Rogers, "Broilers: Differentiating a Commodity," and Steven A. Morrison, "Airline Service: The Evolution of Competition Since Deregulation," in *Industry Studies*, ed. Larry L. Duetsch, 2nd ed. (Armonk, N.Y.: Sharpe, 1998). Daniel B. Suits, "Agriculture," and Kenneth G. Elzinga, "Beer," in *The Structure of American Industry*, eds. Walter Adams and James W. Brock, 10th ed. (Upper Saddle River, N.J.: Prentice Hall, 2001). Dennis W. Carlton and Jeffrey M. Perloff, *Modern Industrial Organization*, 3rd ed. (New York: Addison-Wesley Longman, 2000). Frank J. Chaloupka and Henry Wechsler, "Price, Tobacco Control Policies and Smoking Among Young Adults," *Journal of Health Economics* 16 (June 1997): 359–73. Frank J. Chaloupka and Michael Grossman, *Price, Tobacco Control, and Youth Smoking*, NBER Working Paper Series, no. 5740 (Cambridge, Mass.: National Bureau of Economic Research, 1996). Gary S. Becker, Michael Grossman, and Kevin M. Murphy, "An Empirical Analysis of Cigarette Addiction," *American Economic Review* 84 (June 1994): 396–418. Rexford E. Santerre and Stephen P. Neun, *Health Economics: Theories, Insights, and Industry Studies* (Orlando, Fla.: Dryden, 2000). Sherman Folland, Allen C. Goodman, and Miron Stano, *The Economics of Health and Health Care*, 3rd ed. (Upper Saddle River, N.J.: Prentice Hall, 2001). Raymond S. Hartman, "Hedonic Methods for Evaluating Product Design and Pricing Strategies," *Journal of Economics and Business* 41 (1989): 197–212. Raymond S. Hartman, "Price-Performance Competition and the Merger Guidelines," *Review of Industrial Organization* 18 (2001): 53–75.

revenue to the producers decreases. This is the essence of the "farm problem" that has confronted U.S. policy makers for many years.[22]

Table 3.7 shows that not all farm products have inelastic demands, however. Customers are much more responsive to the price of fresh tomatoes, lettuce, and fresh peas, with the elasticity of demand exceeding 2.00 in absolute value for these products. Table 3.7 also shows the difference between the elasticity of demand for the product as a whole and that for an individual producer of the product. While the elasticity of demand for many agricultural products is inelastic or less than 1 in absolute value, the elasticities of demand for individual producers are extremely large, ranging from −800 to −31,000. Farming can be considered a perfectly competitive industry, given the huge elasticities of demand for the individual producers of farm products. This is why we use the infinitely elastic or horizontal demand curve to portray the individual firm in perfect competition and the downward sloping demand curve for the output in the entire market.

Agricultural products are generally necessities, with income elasticities less than 1. However, the larger income elasticities for apples and cream mean that consumption will increase more than proportionately with increases in income. Broiler chickens have changed from a luxury good in the 1950s to a necessity today, as evidenced by the decrease in the size of their income elasticity. And, as expected, chicken is a substitute good with beef and pork, because chicken has a positive cross-price elasticity of demand with both of these products.

Elasticity and Beer

The price elasticities of demand for beer also differ for the overall commodity and individual brands. Price elasticity estimates for beer as a commodity are less than 1 in absolute value, whereas estimates for individual brands are reported to be quite elastic, as there are many more substitutes among brands of beer than for beer as a product.

---

[22] This discussion is drawn from Daniel B. Suits, "Agriculture," in *The Structure of American Industry*, eds. Walter Adams and James Brock, 10th ed. (Upper Saddle River, N.J.: Prentice Hall, Inc., 2001), 1–27.

Elasticity and the Airline Industry

We discussed the difference in price elasticities between business and pleasure airline travelers earlier. Table 3.7 also shows that airline travel is sensitive to changes in overall economic activity. The income elasticity of +1.5 means that spending on airline travel will change more than proportionately when income goes either up or down. This helps the airline industry in periods of strong economic activity, but can cause problems if the economy slows or moves toward a recession.

Elasticity and the Tobacco Industry

The price elasticity of demand for cigarettes is of interest to the tobacco industry, state and federal policy makers, and public health advocates. Legislators and public health advocates have long used cigarette taxation as a policy to attempt to limit smoking, particularly among teenagers. We noted earlier that cigarette price elasticity of demand for adults is inelastic, but not zero. The estimates in Table 3.7 also show that teenagers and college students have a larger price elasticity of demand for cigarettes than adults. This result is expected for several reasons. Teenagers are likely to spend a greater proportion of their disposable income on cigarettes than adults. There are also substantial peer pressure effects operating on young people. Increased cigarette taxes and prices have a direct negative effect on consumption, as shown by the elasticity estimates. Using taxes to reduce teenage smoking is an effective policy overall because few people begin smoking after the age of 20. The tobacco industry has long been aware of these price effects on smoking behavior and has lobbied to limit cigarette tax increases.[23]

The cigarette data also illustrate the differences between behavior in the near future versus behavior over longer periods of time and between temporary and permanent price changes. Consumers are more price sensitive if they believe a price change is going to be permanent. As noted earlier, consumers also have larger price elasticities over longer periods of time because they are able to search out more substitutes for the product in question.

Elasticity and Health Care

The price elasticity estimates for health care are important because arguments are often made that the demand for these services is medically driven (people "need" health care). Table 3.7 shows that consumers are price sensitive to medical care goods and services. Although the demand is relatively inelastic, it is not perfectly inelastic, as the "needs" argument suggests. As the table shows, the demand for primary care is more inelastic than the demand for more discretionary services, such as dental care and nursing homes. The income elasticity of demand for health care services is generally less than +1.00, indicating that most consumers consider these services to be necessities. Inpatient and outpatient hospital services are generally thought to be substitute goods, as shown by the positive cross-price elasticities in Table 3.7, particularly because there has been a trend to perform many services on an outpatient basis that previously had been done in the hospital. However, some studies have derived negative cross-price elasticity estimates, indicating that these services might be complements in certain cases because some procedures done in the hospital may require follow-up

---

[23] This discussion is based on George M. Guess and Paul G. Farnham, *Cases in Public Policy Analysis*, 2nd ed. (Washington, D.C.: Georgetown University Press, 2000).

outpatient visits. This example shows that economic theory alone may not be able to predict the sign of an elasticity and that elasticity coefficients need to be estimated from data on consumer behavior.

The differences in health care elasticities for overall primary care (-0.1 to -0.7) and for services provided by individual physicians (-2.80 to -5.07) again illustrate the principle that demand can be much more elastic for the individual producer of a product than for the product in general. Although these differences between product and individual producer elasticities are not as large as those between agricultural products and their producers, they still indicate that individual physicians are considered substitutes for one another.

Elasticity and Hotel Room Attributes

The last category of elasticity results in Table 3.7 is drawn from a study of competition among different types of hotels offering a variety of prices and room attributes. Hotels compete on the basis of product lines—standard, medium, and deluxe rooms—and on numerous product attributes, including price, room quality, the amount of check-in time, the availability of guaranteed reservations, and the provision of free parking. The elasticity estimates in the table show the percentage change in quantity demanded relative to a percentage change in each of the characteristics, all else held constant.

Customers are likely to have different elasticities or degrees of sensitivity to these characteristics, which may also differ by type of hotel. The results for business travelers presented in Table 3.7 show that the demand for all hotel rooms is price elastic, with customers of luxury hotels being more price sensitive than those of economy hotels. Room quality, the availability of guaranteed reservations, and the provision of free parking are all important attributes, with elasticities greater than 1 in absolute value. Room quality and the availability of free parking appear to be more important factors for customers of luxury hotels than those of economy hotels. Customers of all hotels are much less sensitive to other product attributes, such as the amount of time spent for hotel check-in.

A more recent development in the hotel industry is the consumer demand for "green" or environmentally friendly products and characteristics.[24] Although there appears to be a demand for hotels to use recycled materials and limit their water and energy consumption, managers have yet to determine the importance of these factors. Some hotels have sought certification from the U.S. Green Building Council, a nonprofit group that grades commercial buildings on issues such as water efficiency, energy use, building materials, and indoor air quality, as a response to this change in consumer behavior.

Managerial Rule of Thumb

Price Elasticity Decision Making

Which demand elasticity, the one for the entire product or the one for the individual producer, is appropriate for decision making by the firm? In markets where firms have some degree of market power, that answer depends on the assumption made about the reaction of other firms to the price change of a given firm. If all firms change prices together, the product demand elasticity is relevant. However, if one firm changes price without the other firms following, the larger elasticities for individual producers shown in Table 3.7 are appropriate. ∎

---

[24] Tamara Audi, "Hotel Chains Grapple with Meaning of Green," *Wall Street Journal*, September 11, 2007.

Elasticity Issues: Marketing Literature

Marketing brings greater detail to the basic economic analysis of price elasticity by examining such issues as the demand for specific brands of products and the demand at the level of individual stores. Marketers are also concerned about the size of the price elasticity of demand compared with the **advertising elasticity of demand**, as both price and advertising are strategic variables under the control of managers. Changes in product price cause a movement along a given demand curve, while increases in advertising can cause changes in consumer preferences and bring new consumers into the market, thus shifting the entire demand curve. A key issue for managers is which strategy has the greatest impact on product sales. Table 3.8 presents the results of three major marketing studies, all of which we'll look at in more detail in the remainder of this section.

Advertising elasticity of demand
The percentage change in the quantity demanded of a good relative to the percentage change in advertising dollars spent on that good, all other factors held constant.

Marketing Study I: Tellis (1988)

The first group of elasticities, analyzed by Tellis, is from a meta-analysis or survey of other econometric studies of selective demand. Selective demand is defined by Tellis as "demand for a particular firm's branded product, measured as its sales or market share."[25] It differs from the demand for the overall product category, which is the focus of most of the economic studies of price elasticity in Table 3.7. The term *brand* is used generically by Tellis "to cover the individual brand, business unit, or firm whose sales or market share is under investigation."[26]

Tellis's study included 367 elasticities from 220 different brands or markets for the period 1961 to 1985. For all products in his study, Tellis found a mean price elasticity of −1.76. Therefore, on average for these firms and products, a 1 percent change in price results in a 1.76 percent change in sales in the opposite direction. The mean price elasticities for all product groups were also greater than 1 in absolute value. Tellis found that the demand for pharmaceutical products is relatively more inelastic than those for the other categories, given that safety, effectiveness, and timing considerations may be more important than price in influencing consumer demand. Pharmaceuticals requiring prescriptions are likely to be covered by health insurance for many consumers, which would make these individuals less price sensitive because part of that price is paid by a third party. The results of the Tellis analysis are important because they are based on numerous empirical studies of the price elasticity of demand of many different brands of products.

Marketing Study II: Sethuraman and Tellis (1991)

The second group of elasticities in Table 3.8 is derived from a meta-analysis of 16 studies conducted from 1960 to 1988 that estimated both price and advertising elasticities. This sample is different from the first meta-analysis described in the table because the studies surveyed in this analysis were required to have estimated both price and advertising elasticities. There were 262 elasticity estimates representing more than 130 brands or markets in this survey.

For this sample, Sethuraman and Tellis found a mean price elasticity of −1.609 (rounded to −1.61) and a mean short-term advertising elasticity of +0.109 (rounded to +0.11). Thus, the ratio of the two elasticities is 14.76, which means that the size of the average price elasticity is about 15 times the size of the average advertising elasticity. Pricing is obviously a powerful tool influencing consumer demand.

---

[25] Gerard J. Tellis, "The Price Elasticity of Selective Demand: A Meta-Analysis of Econometric Models of Sales," *Journal of Marketing Research* 25 (November 1988): 331.

[26] Ibid.

TABLE 3.8 Elasticity Coefficients from Marketing Literature

STUDY	PRODUCT	PRICE ELASTICITY COEFFICIENT	ADVERTISING ELASTICITY COEFFICIENT
Tellis (1988)	Detergents	−2.77	
	Durable goods	−2.03	
	Food	−1.65	
	Toiletries	−1.38	
	Others	−2.26	
	Pharmaceutical	−1.12	
Sethuraman and Tellis (1991)	All products	−1.61	0.11
	Durables	−2.01	0.23
	Nondurables	−1.54	0.09
	Product life cycle—early	−1.10	0.11
	Product life cycle—mature	−1.72	0.11
Hoch et al. (1995)	Soft drinks	−3.18	
	Canned seafood	−1.79	
	Canned soup	−1.62	
	Cookies	−1.60	
	Grahams/saltines	−1.01	
	Snack crackers	−0.86	
	Frozen entrees	−0.77	
	Refrigerated juice	−0.74	
	Dairy cheese	−0.72	
	Frozen juice	−0.55	
	Cereal	−0.20	
	Bottled juice	−0.09	
	Bath tissue	−2.42	
	Laundry detergent	−1.58	
	Fabric softener	−0.79	
	Liquid dish detergent	−0.74	
	Toothpaste	−0.45	
	Paper towels	−0.05	

Sources: Gerard J. Tellis, "The Price Elasticity of Selective Demand: A Meta-Analysis of Econometric Models of Sales," *Journal of Marketing Research* 25 (November 1988): 331–41; Raj Sethuraman and Gerald J. Tellis, "An Analysis of the Tradeoff Between Advertising and Price Discounting," *Journal of Marketing Research* 28 (May 1991): 160–74; Stephen J. Hoch, Byung-Do Kim, Alan L. Montgomery, and Peter E. Rossi, "Determinants of Store-Level Price Elasticity," *Journal of Marketing Research* 32 (February 1995): 17–29.

In Table 3.8, the price elasticity for durable goods is greater than that for nondurables. However, Sethuraman and Tellis argue that these estimates are not significantly different, while the differences in advertising elasticity estimates between durable and nondurable goods (0.23 versus 0.09) are significant. These researchers also argue that durable goods may have a lower price elasticity than nondurables because consumers will pay a higher price for the higher perceived quality associated with known brands of durable goods, while customers will be more likely to shop around for a low price on nondurable goods. Advertising elasticities are likely to be higher for durable goods because consumers generally seek much information before the purchase of these goods.

Marketers have also focused on the stages in a product's life cycle—Introduction, Growth, Maturity, and Decline.[27] When a new product is introduced, there is usually a period of slow growth with low or nonexistent profits, given the large fixed costs often associated with product introduction. In the Growth period, the product is more widely accepted, and profits increase. When the product reaches Maturity, sales slow because the product has been accepted by most potential customers, and profits slow or decline because competition has increased. Finally, in the period of Decline, both sales and profits decrease. Marketers have hypothesized that the price elasticity of demand increases over the product life cycle. Consumers are likely to be better informed and more price conscious about mature products, and there is likely to be more competition at this stage. Those who adopt a product early, during the Introduction and Growth stages, are likely to focus more on the newness of the product rather than its price. These expected differences in elasticities are shown in the estimates in Table 3.8.

Tellis also found that the ratio of the median price elasticity to advertising elasticity is three times higher for the United States than for Europe (19.5 versus 6.2).[28] Thus, consumers may be more price sensitive than advertising sensitive in the United States. compared with Europe. This difference could mean that the level of advertising is too high in the United States or that there is less opportunity for price discounting in Europe than in the United States.

Analysis of Pricing Versus Advertising Strategies   Sethuraman and Tellis also developed a conceptual analysis of the role of pricing and advertising strategies for a firm to show which strategy or combination of strategies might be most beneficial for the firm. The analysis included the following variables:

- The proportion of a price cut that retailers pass through to consumers
- The fraction of the original quantity demanded that is now purchased at the lower price
- The contribution-price ratio, which shows the relationship between the firm's profit margin or contribution and the prices of various products

Using reasonable assumptions for all these values, the authors developed the following analysis, reproduced in Figure 3.8, showing alternative pricing and marketing strategies.

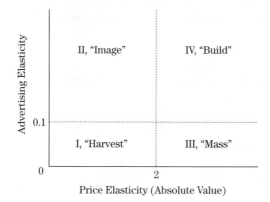

FIGURE 3.8
Price-Advertising Elasticities and Relevant Strategies (from Sethuraman and Tellis, 1991)

[27] This discussion is based on Philip Kotler, *Marketing Management: The Millennium Edition* (Upper Saddle River, N.J.: Prentice-Hall, 2000), 303–16.
[28] Gerald J. Tellis, *Effective Advertising: Understanding When, How, and Why Advertising Works* (Thousand Oaks, CA: Sage Publications, Inc., 2004).

In Region I, "Harvest," of Figure 3.8, products are neither price nor advertising elastic. This would be the case for well-established niche markets, such as Cutex nail polish or Gillette razor blades, where consumer preferences are set. Neither price cuts nor major advertising campaigns would have a substantial effect for these products. Consumers for products in Region II, "Image," respond more to advertising that creates a distinct image than to price discounts. Producers in this region, which includes products such as cosmetics, new products, and luxury goods, should concentrate their strategies on advertising policies. Region III, "Mass," includes mass-produced and generic products, where there is little real product differentiation and consumers react more to price changes than to increased advertising expenditures. Region IV, "Build," includes differentiable goods, such as cereals and home furniture, and goods with seasonal sales, such as winter clothes and toys, where both price and advertising information influence consumer behavior.

Marketing Study III: Hoch et al. (1995)

The third set of elasticities in Table 3.8 comprises store-level price elasticities estimated from scanner data from Dominick's Finer Foods, a major chain in the Chicago metropolitan area. Table 3.8 shows large differences in price elasticities among product categories. Hoch et al. also found that the elasticities differed by store location. They analyzed how the elasticities were related to both the characteristics of the consumers in the market area and the overall competitive environment. Their results are summarized as follows:[29]

- More-educated consumers have higher opportunity costs, so they devote less attention to shopping and, therefore, are less price sensitive.
- Large families spend more of their disposable income on grocery products, and, therefore, they spend more time shopping to garner their increased returns to search; they are also more price sensitive.
- Households with larger, more expensive homes have fewer income constraints, so they are less price sensitive.
- Black and Hispanic consumers are more price sensitive.
- Store volume relative to the competition is important, suggesting that consumers self-select for location and convenience or price and assortment.
- Distance from the competition also matters. Isolated stores display less price sensitivity than stores located close to their competitors. Distance increases shopping costs.

Managerial Rule of Thumb

Elasticities in Marketing and Decision Making

You will most likely pursue these issues raised by the marketing literature in more depth in your marketing courses. The major point for business students is to recognize the importance of price elasticity of demand and the linkages between economics and marketing. Managers must be familiar with the fundamentals of demand and consumer responsiveness to all variables in a demand function because their marketing departments will build on these concepts to design optimal promotion and pricing strategies. ∎

---

[29] Stephen J. Hoch, Byung-Do Kim, Alan L. Montgomery, and Peter E. Rossi, "Determinants of Store-Level Price Elasticity," *Journal of Marketing Research* 32 (February 1995): 28.

Summary

In this chapter, we explored the concept of elasticity of demand, noting that an elasticity coefficient can be calculated with regard to any variable in a demand function to determine how consumer demand responds to that variable. We focused most of our attention on the price elasticity of demand because this concept shows the relationship between price and revenue changes for the firm. We illustrated the elasticity concepts in the opening case on consumer responses to higher gasoline prices and with numerous examples throughout the chapter. We also showed how elasticity is a fundamental concept in marketing and serves as the basis for most pricing and promotion strategies.

In the following appendix, we present the standard economic model of consumer choice. This model incorporates the concepts of consumer tastes and preferences, income, and the market prices of goods and services to show how consumer decisions change in the face of changing economic variables. The end products of this model are the consumer demand curve and its relevant elasticities that we have been studying in this chapter.

In Chapter 4, we discuss the methods that both managers and economists use to gather empirical information about consumer demand and elasticity.

Appendix 3A Economic Model of Consumer Choice

Economists have developed a formal model of consumer choice that focuses on the major factors discussed in this chapter that influence consumer demand: tastes and preferences, consumer income, and the prices of the goods and services. We briefly review this model to show how it can be used to derive a consumer demand curve and to illustrate reactions to changes in income and prices.

Consumer Tastes and Preferences

In this model, we assume that consumers are faced with the choice of different amounts of two goods, X and Y (although the model can be extended mathematically to incorporate any number of goods or services). We need to develop a theoretical construct that reflects consumers' preferences between these goods. Consumers derive *utility*, or satisfaction, from consuming different amounts of these goods. We use an *ordinal measurement of utility* in which consumers indicate whether they prefer one bundle of goods to another, but there is no precise measurement of the change in utility level or how much they prefer one bundle to another. Ordinal measurement allows our utility levels to be defined as one "being greater than another," but not one "being twice as great as another."

We also make the following assumptions about consumer preference orderings over different amounts of the goods:

1. Preference orderings are complete. Consumers are able to make comparisons between any combinations or bundles of the two goods and to indicate whether they prefer one bundle to another or whether they are indifferent between the bundles.
2. More of the goods are preferred to less of the goods (i.e., commodities are "goods" and not "bads"). Preferences are transitive. If bundle A is preferred to bundle B, and bundle B is preferred to bundle C, then bundle A is preferred to bundle C.

3. Consumers are selfish. Their preferences depend only on the amount of the goods they directly consume.
4. The goods are continuously divisible so that consumers can always purchase one more or one less unit of the goods.

From these assumptions, we develop a consumer's *indifference curve* that shows alternative combinations of the two goods that provide the same level of satisfaction or utility. We show in Figure 3.A1 that such an indifference curve must be downward sloping if the above assumptions about preferences hold.

In Figure 3.A1, point A represents an initial bundle of goods X and Y, with X_1 amount of good X and Y_1 amount of good Y. All combinations of the two goods are represented as points in Figure 3.A1. According to the above preference assumptions, the bundle of goods represented by point A must be preferred to any bundle of goods in the shaded rectangle to the southwest of point A because point A contains either more of both goods or more of one good and no less of the other. Likewise, any bundle of goods in the shaded area northeast of point A must be preferred to the bundle of goods at point A. We can, therefore, conclude that the indifference curve through point A must lie in the nonshaded areas of Figure 3.A1. Only in these areas of the figure will there be other combinations of goods X and Y that provide the consumer with the same satisfaction or utility as that provided at point A.

Figure 3.A2 illustrates such an indifference curve through point A. This indifference curve must be downward sloping, given the above discussion. Facing a choice between the bundle of goods represented by point A (X_1, Y_1) and point B (X_2, Y_2), the consumer is indifferent between these bundles because they both provide the same level of utility (U_1). Other bundles of goods, such as point C (X_3, Y_3), provide greater levels of utility because they lie on indifference curves farther from the origin. Thus, utility levels increase as we move in the direction of the arrow (northeast from the origin).

Looking at points B and A on indifference curve U_1, we can see that if the consumer gives up a certain amount of good Y, he needs an additional amount of good X to keep the utility level constant. If he gives up the amount of good Y represented by $Y_2 - Y_1$ or ΔY, he needs $X_1 - X_2$ or ΔX to keep his utility level constant. The ratio $\Delta Y/\Delta X$, which shows the rate at which the consumer is willing to trade off one good for

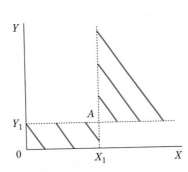

FIGURE 3.A1
Derivation of a Consumer Indifference Curve
The indifference curve through point A must lie in the nonshaded areas of the quadrant.

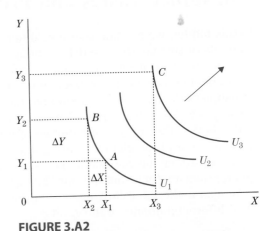

FIGURE 3.A2
Illustration of Consumer Indifference Curves
The consumer is indifferent between the bundles of goods, X and Y, represented by points A and B. These points lie on the same indifference curve, U_1. Point C represents a bundle of goods with a greater level of utility, U_3. Consumer preferences are represented by the marginal rate of substitution ($\Delta Y/\Delta X$) or the rate at which the consumer is willing to trade off one good for the other.

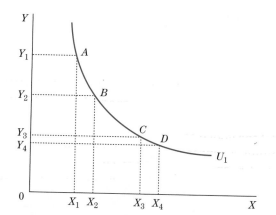

FIGURE 3.A3
A Convex Indifference Curve
An indifference curve is typically drawn convex to the origin, representing a diminishing marginal rate of substitution.

another and still maintain a constant utility level, is called the *marginal rate of substitution* (MRS_{XY}). Mathematically, it is the slope of the indifference curve.

An indifference curve is typically drawn convex to the origin or as shown in Figures 3.A2 and 3.A3.

The slope of the convex indifference curve in Figure 3.A3 decreases as you move down the curve. This result implies that an individual has a diminishing marginal rate of substitution. When the individual is at point A (X_1, Y_1), with only a small amount of good X, he is willing to trade off a large amount of good Y, or $Y_1 - Y_2$, to gain an additional amount of X and move to point B (X_2, Y_2). However, starting at point C (X_3, Y_3), the individual is willing to give up a much smaller amount of good Y, or $Y_3 - Y_4$, to obtain the additional amount of good X and move to point D (X_4, Y_4). This diminishing marginal rate of substitution reflects the principle of *diminishing marginal utility*. The additional or marginal utility that an individual derives from another unit of a good decreases as the number of units the individual already has obtained increases. When an individual has only X_1 units of good X, he is willing to trade off more units of good Y to obtain an additional unit of good X than when he has a large amount of good X (X_3) already.

The behavioral assumption behind the consumer choice model is that the consumer wants to maximize the utility derived from the goods and services consumed (goods X and Y, in this case). However, the consumer is constrained by his level of income and by the prices he faces for the goods. We need to illustrate the effect of this constraint and then show how the consumer solves this *constrained maximization problem.*

The Budget Constraint

The consumer's budget constraint is represented by Equation 3.A1:

3.A1　$I = P_X X + P_Y Y$

　　　　where

　　　　　　I = level of consumer's income
　　　　　P_X = price of good X
　　　　　　X = quantity of good X
　　　　　P_Y = price of good Y
　　　　　　Y = quantity of good Y

Equation 3.A1 shows that a consumer's income (I) can be spent either on good X [(P_X)(X)] or on good Y [(P_Y)(Y)]. For simplicity, we assume that all income is spent on the two goods.

FIGURE 3.A4
The Budget Line
The budget line shows alternative combinations of the two goods, X and Y, that can be purchased with a given income and with given prices of the goods.

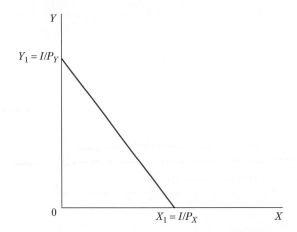

With given values of I, P_X, and P_Y, we can graph a budget line, as shown in Figure 3.A4. The budget line shows alternative combinations of the two goods that can be purchased with a given income and with given prices of the two goods.

The budget line intersects the X-axis at the level of good X that can be purchased (X_1) if the consumer spends all his income on good X. The level of income (I) divided by the price of good X (P_X) gives this maximum amount of good X. Likewise, the budget line intersects the Y-axis at the level of good Y that can be purchased (Y_1) if all income is spent on good Y. This amount of good Y is determined by dividing the level of income (I) by the price of good Y (P_Y). The slope of the budget line is distance $0Y_1/0X_1 = (I/P_Y)/(I/P_X) = P_X/P_Y$. Thus, the slope of the budget line is the ratio of the relative prices of the two goods.

We illustrate a change in income, holding prices constant, in Figure 3.A5. Because the slope of the budget line is the ratio of the prices of the two goods and because prices are being held constant, a change in income is represented by a parallel shift of the budget line. If income increases from level I_1 to I_2, the budget line shifts out from B_1 to B_2, as shown in Figure 3.A5. This increase in income allows the consumer to purchase more of both goods, more of one good and the same amount of the other, or more of one good and less of the other.

We illustrate a decrease in the price of good X, holding both income and the price of good Y constant, in Figure 3.A6. The budget line swivels out, pivoting on the Y-axis. Because the price of good Y has not changed, the maximum quantity of

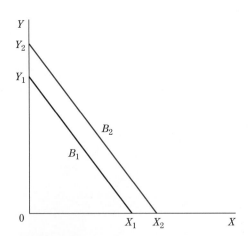

FIGURE 3.A5
Change (Increase) in Income (Prices Constant)
A change in income, assuming prices are constant, is represented by a parallel shift of the budget line.

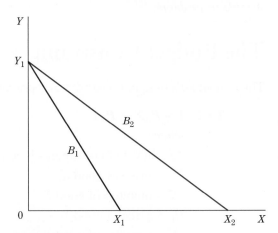

FIGURE 3.A6
Change (Decrease) in the Price of Good X (All Else Constant)
A decrease in the price of good X is represented by a swiveling of the budget line around the intercept on the Y-axis.

Y that can be purchased does not change either. However, the price of good X has decreased, so good X has become cheaper relative to good Y. Budget line B_2 has a flatter slope because the slope of the line is the ratio of the prices of the two goods, which has changed.

The Consumer Maximization Problem

We illustrate the solution to the consumer problem of maximizing utility subject to the budget constraint in Figure 3.A7. Point A, with X_1 amount of good X and Y_1 amount of good Y, is the solution to the consumer maximization problem. This point gives the consumer the highest level of utility (the indifference curve farthest from the origin), while still allowing the consumer to purchase the bundle of goods with the current level of income and relative prices shown in the budget line. Compare point A with point B (X_2 amount of good X and Y_2 amount of good Y). Point B lies on the budget line, so it represents a bundle of goods that the consumer could purchase. However, it would lie on an indifference curve closer to the origin (not pictured). This curve would represent a lower level of utility, so the consumer would not be maximizing the level of utility. Point C, corresponding to X_3 amount of good X and Y_3 amount of good Y, lies on the same indifference curve as point A and, therefore, provides the same level of utility as the goods represented by point A. However, point C lies outside the current budget line. It is not possible for the consumer to purchase this bundle of goods with the given income and prices of the goods.

Point A is characterized by the tangency of the indifference curve farthest from the origin with the budget line. The slopes of two lines are equal at a point of tangency. The slope of the indifference curve is the marginal rate of substitution between goods X and Y, while the slope of the budget line is the ratio of the prices of the two goods. Thus, point A, or *consumer equilibrium*, occurs where $MRS_{XY} = (P_X/P_Y)$.

Changes in Income

We can now use the concept of consumer equilibrium to illustrate changes in consumer behavior in response to changes in economic variables. Figure 3.A8 shows an increase in income, all else held constant. The original point of consumer equilibrium is point A, with X_1 amount of good X and Y_1 of good Y. The increase in

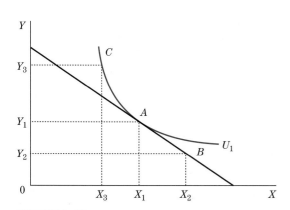

FIGURE 3.A7
The Consumer Maximization Problem
Point A represents the combination of goods where the consumer maximizes utility subject to the budget constraint.

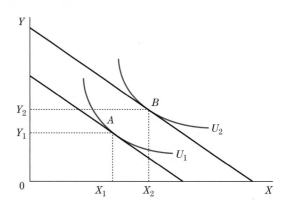

FIGURE 3.A8
Consumer Equilibrium with a Change in Income (Two Normal Goods)
To maximize utility, the consumer moves from point A to point B as income increases, consuming more of both goods.

FIGURE 3.A9

Consumer Equilibrium with a Change in Income (One Normal and One Inferior Good)

To maximize utility, the consumer moves from point A to point B as income increases, consuming more of good Y and less of good X.

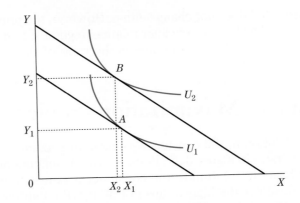

income is represented by an outward parallel shift of the budget line. To maximize utility with the new budget line, the consumer now moves to point B and consumes X_2 of good X and Y_2 of good Y. In this case, we can see that both X and Y are normal goods because the consumer increases the quantity demanded of each good in response to an increase in income, all else held constant.

Figure 3.A9 is a similar example showing an increase in income. However, we can see in this example that good X is an inferior good. In Figure 3.A9, the original equilibrium occurs at point A (X_1, Y_1), while the new equilibrium after the income increase occurs at point B (X_2, Y_2). As income increases, the quantity demanded of good Y increases, but the quantity demanded of good X decreases. Thus, Y is a normal good in this example, while X is an inferior good.

Changes in Price

Figure 3.A10 shows a decrease in the price of good X, all else held constant. The original consumer equilibrium in Figure 3.A10 occurs at point A, with X_1 of good X and Y_1 of good Y. The decrease in the price of good X, all else held constant, is represented by the swiveling of the budget line with a new consumer equilibrium at point B (X_2, Y_2). Thus, the movement from point A to point B represents a movement along the consumer's demand curve for good X because a decrease in the price of good X results in an increase in the quantity demanded.

If we think of good Y as a *composite good* representing all other goods and services, we can see in Figure 3.A10 that the decrease in the price of good X caused expenditure on good X to decrease because spending on the composite

FIGURE 3.A10

Consumer Equilibrium with a Decrease in the Price of Good X (Inelastic Demand for X)

A decrease in the price of good X results in an increase in the quantity demanded but a decrease in the total revenue for good X, so that the demand for good X must be inelastic.

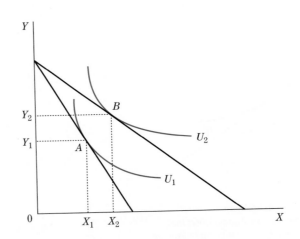

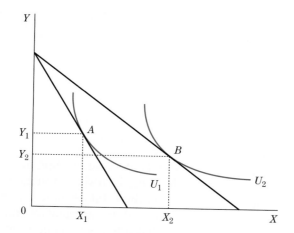

FIGURE 3.A11
Consumer Equilibrium with a Decrease in the Price of Good X (Elastic Demand for X)
A decrease in the price of good X results in an increase in the quantity demanded and in the total revenue from good X, so that the demand for good X must be elastic.

good Y increased. Decreased expenditure on good X is equivalent to decreased total revenue for the producers of good X. Thus, in Figure 3.A10, a decrease in the price of good X results in a decrease in the total revenue for good X, so that the demand for good X must be inelastic. We illustrate the opposite case of elastic demand for good X in Figure 3.A11.

In Figure 3.A11, the original consumer equilibrium occurs at point A (X_1, Y_1), and the equilibrium after the decrease in the price of good X occurs at point B (X_2, Y_2). In this case, the quantity demanded of good X has increased so much that total spending on the composite good, Y, has decreased, so spending on good X has increased. A decrease in the price of good X has resulted in an increase in expenditure on X and, therefore, in the total revenue to the firm producing X. When a decrease in price results in an increase in total revenue, demand is elastic.

If we think of good Y as simply another good and not a composite good, Figures 3.A10 and 3.A11 illustrate the cross-price elasticity of demand. In Figure 3.A10, a decrease in the price of good X results in an increase in the quantity demanded of good Y. Thus, the two goods in this figure must be complements in consumption because the cross-price elasticity of demand is negative. The opposite case holds in Figure 3.A11, where a decrease in the price of good X results in a decrease in the quantity demanded of good Y. Here goods X and Y are substitute goods with a positive cross-price elasticity of demand.

Key Terms

Exercises

Technical Questions

1. For each of the following cases, calculate the *arc* price elasticity of demand, and state whether demand is elastic, inelastic, or unit elastic.

   a. When the price of milk increases from $2.25 to $2.50 per gallon, the quantity demanded falls from 100 gallons to 90 gallons.

   b. When the price of paperback books falls from $7.00 to $6.50, the quantity demanded rises from 100 to 150.

   c. When the rent on apartments rises from $500 to $550, the quantity demanded decreases from 1,000 to 950.

2. For each of the following cases, calculate the *point* price elasticity of demand, and state whether demand is elastic, inelastic, or unit elastic. The demand curve is given by

   $$Q_D = 5{,}000 - 50P_X$$

   a. The price of the product is $50.

   b. The price of the product is $75.

   c. The price of the product is $25.

3. For each of the following cases, what is the expected impact on the total revenue of the firm? Explain your reasoning.

   a. Price elasticity of demand is known to be -0.5, and the firm raises price by 10 percent.

   b. Price elasticity of demand is known to be -2.5, and the firm lowers price by 5 percent.

   c. Price elasticity of demand is known to be -1.0, and the firm raises price by 1 percent.

   d. Price elasticity of demand is known to be 0, and the firm raises price by 50 percent.

4. The demand curve is given by

   $$Q_D = 500 - 2P_X$$

   a. What is the total revenue function?

   b. The marginal revenue function is $MR = 250 - Q$. Graph the total revenue function, the demand curve, and the marginal revenue function.

   c. At what price is revenue maximized, and what is revenue at that point?

   d. Identify the elastic and inelastic regions of the demand curve.

5. You have the following information for your product:
   - The price elasticity of demand is -2.0.
   - The income elasticity of demand is 1.5.
   - The cross-price elasticity of demand between your good and a related good is -3.5.

   What can you determine about consumer demand for your product from this information?

6. You have the following information for your product:
   - The price elasticity of demand is -0.9.
   - The income elasticity of demand is 0.5.
   - The cross-price elasticity of demand between your good and a related good is 2.0.

   What can you determine about consumer demand for your product from this information?

Application Questions

1. The following questions are based on the *Wall Street Journal* article that opened this chapter.

   a. Using the data in the article, calculate the short-run price elasticity of demand for gasoline, the long-run price elasticity, and the income elasticity of demand. What is the relationship between the short-run and long-run price elasticity? Is gasoline a normal good? Explain.

   b. The article cited a study of gasoline pricing by the Congressional Budget Office: *Effects of Gasoline Prices on Driving Behavior and Vehicle Markets*, January 2008. Find this study on the CBO Web site. How have high gasoline prices affected driving behavior and the market share of different types of vehicles? How is this information useful for managerial decisions in the automobile industry? Can you find any additional, more recent studies that update the CBO results?

   c. Discuss how the macroeconomic issues raised in Chapter 1 relate to the pricing and elasticity of demand issues presented in this chapter. How do current macroeconomic conditions influence the price of gasoline and consumer behavior?

2. In the second half of 2002, several major U.S. airlines began running market tests to determine if they

could cut walk-up or unrestricted business fares and maintain or increase revenues. Continental Airlines offered an unrestricted fare between Cleveland and Los Angeles of $716, compared with its usual $2,000 fare, and found that it earned about the same revenue as it would have collected with the higher fare. Making similar changes on its routes from Cleveland to Houston, Continental found that the new fare structure yielded less revenue, but greater market share. On the Houston–Oakland route, the new fare structure resulted in higher revenue. (Scott McCartney, "Airlines Try Business-Fare Cuts, Find They Don't Lose Revenue," *Wall Street Journal*, November 22, 2002.)

   a. What did these test results imply about business traveler price elasticity of demand on the Cleveland–Los Angeles, Cleveland–Houston, and Houston–Oakland routes for Continental Airlines?

   b. How did these results differ from the discussion of airline elasticity in this chapter?

   c. What factors caused these differences?

3. Based on the elasticity data in Table 3.7, discuss why public health officials generally advocate the use of cigarette taxes to reduce teenage smoking, while state and local governments often use these taxes to raise revenue to fund their services.

4. The price elasticity of demand for urban transit fares has been estimated to lie between −0.1 and −0.6. Based on these results, what is the economic argument for raising transit fares? What political arguments might local governments and transit authorities encounter in opposition to these economic arguments?

5. Develop a case study of a retailer that uses rewards or loyalty programs to influence demand and price elasticity of demand for their products. How do these programs influence both current and future demand?

6. Why would we expect that the price elasticity of demand for the product of an individual firm would typically be greater than the price elasticity of demand for the product overall? Illustrate your answer with examples from this chapter.

7. Find examples in the current business news media of how eBay and other online sellers obtain information about the price elasticity of demand by making unannounced temporary adjustments to their prices and fee structures.

8. Priority Mail has been one of the most profitable products for the U.S. Postal Service, growing six times faster than first-class deliveries over the period from 1995 to 1999 and accounting for almost 8 percent of the Postal Service's mail revenue. Because the Postal Service lost $480 million in the fiscal year ending September 30, 2000, it adopted the strategy of raising Priority Mail rates by 16 percent to help offset this loss. Bear Creek Corporation planned to ship 15 to 20 percent fewer Priority Mail packages in response to the rate increase. If this corporation's response is typical for Priority Mail customers, will the Postal Service meet its goal of reducing its deficit with this policy? (Rick Brooks, "Priority Mail Is Prey for Rivals after Raising Rates a Steep 16%," *Wall Street Journal*, January 24, 2001.)

On the Web

For updated information on the *Wall Street Journal* article at the beginning of the chapter, as well as other relevant links and information, visit the book's Web site at **www.pearsonhighered.com/farnham**

Techniques for Understanding Consumer Demand and Behavior

I n this chapter, we explore how both managers and economists use marketing and other consumer data to analyze the factors influencing demand for different products. Many firms, particularly large corporations, hire economists who employ sophisticated statistical or econometric techniques to estimate demand functions or to forecast future demand. Most managers, however, will *not* be involved with forecasting and undertaking the complex statistical analyses performed by business economists. Managers are more likely to work with marketing and consumer research departments to profile and understand a company's customers and to try to anticipate changes in consumer behavior.

We begin this chapter with the *Wall Street Journal* article "Behind GM's Slide: Bosses Misjudged New Urban Tastes," which focuses on the importance of information about consumer tastes and preferences regarding product characteristics in the auto industry. We then illustrate and evaluate the techniques managers and marketing departments typically use to obtain this information. Next we look briefly at how economists use the econometric technique of multiple regression analysis to empirically estimate demand functions. The goal of this discussion is not to train you as business economists who produce these statistical analyses, but to help you become better consumers of this type of work and to see its usefulness for *managerial* decision making. We end the chapter by illustrating the interrelationships between the marketing/consumer research approach to analyzing consumer demand, which managers favor, and the formal econometric approach used by economists.

Behind GM's Slide: Bosses Misjudged New Urban Tastes

by Lee Hawkins Jr.

Wall Street Journal, *March 8, 2006*

Copyright © 2008 Dow Jones & Co. Reprinted by permission of Dow Jones & Co. via Copyright Clearance Center.

In December, General Motors Corp. ran a series of ads across the U.S. showing Cadillacs being driven in snow. The decision to do so was made by the giant car maker's executives in Detroit, where on Christmas Day, temperatures hovered just above freezing.

The ads also ran in Miami, a vibrant car market where GM has bombed for the past 15 years. As Christmas dawned, temperatures there started climbing into the high 70s.

GM is struggling under a financial burden created by monumental pension and health-care obligations. But it's also having a hard time persuading Americans to buy its cars. One reason: GM's cumbersome and unresponsive bureaucracy, the one that ran the snow ads in Miami, has for years failed to connect with the tastes and expectations of consumers outside the company's Midwestern base.

In Miami, where no GM car is a top seller, GM started bilingual advertising much later than its rivals. Some of the ads it did run were duds. One wooed Miami's mostly Cuban-Hispanic population by showing a woman in a Mexican dress standing in front of the Alamo as GM Saturns raced around her. Another was built on the theme "Breakthrough"—a word that doesn't have a direct Spanish translation.

In the late 1990s, years before GM's Cadillac Escalade became a hit, dealers in Miami suggested GM build such a luxury sport-utility vehicle. They were shot down by executives in Detroit who said it would never work. GM later went on to sell more than 400,000 of the luxury SUVs.

As a result, GM has a paltry 13.8% of the retail market in South Florida, a slide it is now trying to reverse. The problem is repeated in the U.S.'s rich, coastal metropolises where Japanese and European auto makers first set up dealerships in the 1970s and 1980s. There, overseas car makers exploited consumers' memories of GM's unreliable and unattractive mass-market vehicles. . . .

GM employs 325,000 people, almost as many as the population of Miami itself. At various times there have been as many as six layers of management between top executives in Detroit and those in the field. GM's general manager for the Southeast has 38 teams reporting to him, overseeing relations with the region's 1,400 dealers, among other things.

In addition to these geographic units, the company is divided along functional lines, with global groups overseeing areas such as marketing, product development, and human resources. . . .

Since the mid-1980s, GM's overall U.S. market share has fallen by about 15 percentage points. Last year, the company reported a loss of $8.6 billion, the bulk of which stems from its U.S. auto business. The company has said it plans to slash costs, including cutting 30,000 jobs in the next couple of years, and has sliced benefits for both union and nonunion employees.

In Miami, GM is in third place behind Toyota Motor Corp. and Ford Motor Co. Toyota began tailoring marketing to Hispanics in the 1980s. Ford started similar efforts in Florida and California about 15 years ago. None of GM's vehicles are among the top 15 vehicles registered in the greater Miami area. . . .

It wasn't until 1995 that any of GM's divisions thought about advertising directly to Hispanics. Their early efforts were clumsy—such as the Saturn ad set at the Alamo. The ad missed the mark because Mexicans comprise only about 4% of Miami's Hispanic population. . . .

Feeling shut off from the GM executives in Detroit, some Miami dealers started pooling their advertising dollars to buy bilingual ads tailored to the Miami market. But a 1999 reorganization designed to centralize the company's sales and marketing operations killed this local dealer spending and provoked a firestorm. GM executives in Detroit quickly recognized the mistake, but it took two years for them to reinstate the groups. . . .

GM has charged Ms. Green, the marketing executive, with rebuilding the company's image and sales among South Florida's Hispanic population. . . .

At GM, one of Ms. Green's first jobs was persuading the company to use in Miami something trendier than Cadillac's advertising theme song, Led Zeppelin's "Rock and Roll," which was a hit in the early 1970s. . . .

Instead, Ms. Green lined up Daddy Yankee, a Puerto Rican recording artist known as "The King of Reggaeton," to do a series of bilingual commercials for the launch of the Chevrolet Cobalt, a trendy compact. Reggaeton, a hot phenomenon, is a fusion of Caribbean and dance music. . . .

GM encourages dealers to attend seminars designed to make them more effective selling to Hispanic and black consumers. Because many immigrant Hispanic families like to bring their entire family to the showroom, dealers are urged to keep multiple chairs in offices that are used to finalize vehicle sales. . . .

David Borchelt, general manager of the Southeast region, says GM's retail sales volume in South Florida rose 8.4% in 2005, compared with the year earlier, mostly due to newly launched GM vehicles.

Case for Analysis

Consumer Behavior and GM Vehicles

This article illustrates the importance of understanding consumer behavior as managers consider new products and different market demographics. The article focuses on the mistakes that General Motors' executives made in selling cars in Miami, "a vibrant market where GM has bombed for the past 15 years." Given its Midwestern location, the company failed to understand the tastes and expectations of consumers in other areas, particularly in the large cities on the east and west coasts of the country.

The article discusses both the development of a new luxury SUV and the approaches needed to sell automobiles to the Hispanic community in South Florida. Although it is not clear from the article what market research was undertaken before the development of the Cadillac Escalade, GM executives in the late 1990s did not correctly anticipate the demand for this type of vehicle. They also did not recognize the need to advertise directly to the Hispanic community, and they initially used inappropriate methods for communicating with these potential customers. These mistakes contributed to a decrease in GM's share of the U.S. market since the mid-1980s and the loss of $8.6 billion in 2005.

The success of any new vehicle, therefore, depends on whether GM correctly analyzes consumer tastes and preferences for vehicle characteristics, how customers react to advertising expenditures and the price of the vehicles, and the differences between the GM vehicles and their Ford, Toyota, and Honda competitors. Incorrect decisions on any of these factors can have a substantial financial impact on the company. ■

Understanding Consumer Demand and Behavior: Marketing Approaches

The GM case shows that strategic managerial decisions can be made on the basis of consumer sensitivity to any of the variables in the demand function for a product. To obtain this information on consumer behavior, firms typically rely on

1. Expert opinion
2. Consumer surveys
3. Test marketing and price experiments
4. Analyses of census and other historical data
5. Unconventional methods

Much of the discussion of these nonstatistical approaches to learning about demand and consumer behavior is found in the marketing literature.[1] We briefly summarize this literature—which is usually covered more extensively in marketing courses—and then relate these approaches to statistical or econometric demand estimation, the approach used most often by economists.

Analyzing demand and consumer behavior involves the study of what people say, what they do, or what they have done.[2] Surveys of consumers, panels of experts, or the sales force working in the field can provide information on how people say they

---

[1] Kent B. Monroe, *Pricing: Making Profitable Decisions*, 2nd ed. (New York: McGraw-Hill, 1990); Gary L. Lilien, Philip Kotler, and K. Srindhar Moorthy, *Marketing Models* (Englewood Cliffs, N.J.: Prentice Hall, 1992); Philip Kotler, *Marketing Management: Analysis, Planning, Implementation, and Control*, 8th ed. (Englewood Cliffs, N.J.: Prentice Hall, 1994); Robert J. Dolan and Hermann Simon, *Power Pricing: How Managing Price Transforms the Bottom Line* (New York: Free Press, 1996); Philip Kotler, Swee Hoon Ang, Siew Meng Leong, and Chin Tiong Tan, *Marketing Management: An Asian Perspective* (Singapore: Prentice Hall, 1996); Financial Times, *Mastering Marketing: The Complete MBA Companion in Marketing* (London: Pearson Education, 1999); Philip Kotler, *Marketing Management: The Millennium Edition* (Upper Saddle River, N.J.: Prentice Hall, 2000).

[2] The following discussion of the marketing approaches used to understand consumer behavior is based largely on Philip Kotler, *Marketing Management: The Millennium Edition* (Upper Saddle River, N.J.: Prentice Hall, 2000); and Robert J. Dolan and Hermann Simon, *Power Pricing: How Managing Price Transforms the Bottom Line* (New York: Free Press, 1996).

behave. Test marketing and price experiments focus on what people actually do in a market situation. Analyses of census and other historical data and statistical or econometric demand estimation are based on data showing how consumers behaved in the past. These studies then use that behavior as the basis for predicting future demand. Let's start by looking at the role of expert opinion.

Expert Opinion

Sales personnel or other experts, such as dealers, distributors, suppliers, marketing consultants, and members of trade associations, may be interviewed for their **expert opinion** on consumer behavior. At least 10 experts from different functions and hierarchical levels in the organization should be involved with making an expert judgment on a particular product. For example, large appliance companies and automobile producers often survey their dealers for estimates of short-term demand for their products. This approach is especially useful in multiproduct situations, where other strategies may be prohibitively expensive.

The inherent biases of this approach are obvious, as sales personnel and others closely related to the industry may have strong incentives to overstate consumer interest in a product. These individuals may also have a limited view of the entire set of factors influencing product demand, particularly factors related to the overall level of activity in the economy. Therefore, this approach works better in business-to-business markets, where there are fewer customers and where experts are likely to know the markets well.

Expert opinion
An approach to analyzing consumer behavior that relies on developing a consensus of opinion among sales personnel, dealers, distributors, marketing consultants, and trade association members.

Consumer Surveys

Consumer surveys include both direct surveys of consumer reactions to prices and price changes and conjoint analyses of product characteristics and prices.

In **direct consumer surveys**, consumers are asked how they would respond to certain prices, price changes, or price differentials. Questions may include the following:

Direct consumer surveys
An approach to analyzing consumer behavior that relies on directly asking consumers questions about their response to prices, price changes, or price differentials.

- At what price would you definitely purchase this product?
- How much are you willing to pay for the product?
- How likely are you to purchase this product at a price of $XX?
- What price difference would cause you to switch from Product X to Product Y?

These surveys are easily understood and less costly to implement than other approaches to analyzing consumer behavior. Surveys have the greatest value when there are a relatively small number of buyers who have well-defined preferences that they are willing to disclose in a survey format. Surveys are most useful for new products, industrial products, and consumer durables that have a long life, as well as for products whose purchase requires advanced planning. In these surveys, market researchers may also collect information on consumer personal finances and consumer expectations about the economy.

Limitations to this approach include the issue of whether consumer responses to the questions reflect their actual behavior in the marketplace. This problem is particularly important regarding reactions to changes in prices. Can consumers know and accurately respond to questions on how they *would* behave when facing different prices for various products? Surveys also tend to focus on the issue of price in isolation from other factors that influence behavior. There may be response biases with this approach because interviewees may be reluctant to admit that they will not pay a certain price or that they would rather purchase a cheaper product. Surveys also typically ask for a person's response at a time when they are not actually making the purchase, so they may not give much thought to their answer.

Consumer surveys are not always successful in obtaining accurate information. In one survey conducted by a major hotel chain that covered all aspects of the hotel's operations, including the prices, guests were asked what price was considered too high, as well as what was the highest acceptable price.[3] The results of this survey indicated that the hotel chain's prices in various cities were about as high as business guests would pay. Managers realized there was a bias in the survey because respondents were also asked what price they were currently paying for the hotel rooms. Respondents were unwilling to tell the hotel management that they would have paid more than the rates they were currently being charged. Thus, the survey biased the results on willingness to pay toward the current hotel rates.

A more sophisticated form of consumer survey is **conjoint analysis**, which has been used in the pricing and design of products ranging from computer hardware and software to hotels, clothing, automobiles, and information services. In this approach, a consumer is faced with an array of products that have different attributes and prices and is asked to rank and choose among them. The analysis allows the marketer to determine the relative importance of each attribute to the consumer. Computer interviewing has become a standard procedure for conjoint analysis.

The advantage of conjoint analysis is that it presents the consumer with a realistic set of choices among both product characteristics and prices. For example, in the case of a new automobile, managers might develop an analysis that focuses on attributes such as brand, engine power, fuel consumption, environmental performance, and price. Different levels of each of the attributes are presented to the consumer. Comparisons are set up where the consumer has to make a trade-off between different characteristics. Thus, his or her choices reveal information about consumer preferences for the product characteristics.[4] Note that conjoint analysis employs an approach to consumer behavior that is similar to the economic indifference curve model described in the appendix to Chapter 3 of this text.

Test Marketing and Price Experiments

Test marketing and price experiments are particularly important for analyzing consumer reaction to new products. **Test marketing** allows companies to study how consumers handle, use, and repurchase a product, and it provides information on the potential size of the market. In *sales-wave research*, consumers who are initially offered the product at no cost are then reoffered the product at different prices to determine their responses. Simulated test marketing involves selecting shoppers who are questioned about brand familiarity, invited to screen commercials about well-known and new products, and then given money to purchase both the new and the existing products. Full-scale test marketing usually occurs over a period of a few months to a year in a number of cities and is accompanied by a complete advertising and promotion campaign. Marketers must determine the number and types of cities for the testing and the type of information to be collected. Information on consumer behavior in the test cities is gathered from store audits, consumer panels, and buyer surveys.

Price experiments to determine the effect of changes in prices may be conducted in test market cities or in a laboratory setting. Direct mail catalogs can also be used for these experiments, as prices can be varied in the catalogs shipped to

---

Conjoint analysis
An approach to analyzing consumer behavior that asks consumers to rank and choose among different product attributes, including price, to reveal their valuation of these characteristics.

Test marketing
An approach to analyzing consumer behavior that involves analyzing consumer response to products in real or simulated markets.

Price experiments
An approach to analyzing consumer behavior in which consumer reaction to different prices is analyzed in a laboratory situation or a test market environment.

---

[3] This example is drawn from Kent B. Monroe, *Pricing: Making Profitable Decisions*, 2nd ed. (New York: McGraw-Hill, 1990), 107–8.
[4] More details of this approach to analyzing consumer behavior are presented in Philip Kotler, *Marketing Management: The Millennium Edition* (Upper Saddle River, N.J.: Prentice Hall, 2000), 339–40; and Robert J. Dolan and Hermann Simon, *Power Pricing: How Managing Price Transforms the Bottom Line* (New York: Free Press, 1996), 55–69.

different regions of the country without a high level of consumer awareness. Although testing in a laboratory situation helps to control for other factors influencing consumer behavior, the disadvantage of this approach is that it is not a natural shopping environment, so consumers may behave differently in the experimental environment. Doing an experiment in an actual test market may be more realistic, but it raises problems about controlling the influence on consumer behavior of variables other than price.

Analysis of Census and Other Historical Data

The most recent U.S. census is always a vital marketing tool, given the development of **targeted marketing**, which defines various market segments or groups of buyers for particular products based on the demographic, psychological, and behavioral characteristics of these individuals. For example, Sodexho Marriott Services, a provider of food services to universities and other institutions, analyzed 1990 census data to develop menu programs specifically designed for students on particular campuses. Starbucks Corporation has used complex software algorithms to analyze both census and historical sales data in order to obtain a positive or negative response to every address considered as a potential store site, while Blockbuster managers have studied household census data to determine how many copies of particular video games and movies to stock in a given store.[5]

Companies such as Claritas of San Diego provide consulting services on how to use census data to develop marketing plans and analyze consumer behavior. Using census data on age, race, and median income and other survey lifestyle information, such as magazine and sports preferences, Claritas has developed 62 clusters or consumer types for targeted marketing. Hyundai Corporation has used these data and buyer profiles to determine which of its models will appeal to consumers in different parts of a community and to plan the locations of new dealerships. Hyundai has also used cluster data to send test-drive offers to certain neighborhoods, instead of entire cities, and has reported that it cut its cost per vehicle sold in half as a result of this targeting strategy.[6]

Many companies have used census and survey data to develop new marketing strategies focused on older customers, a population segment that has often been overlooked in the past.[7] A study by AARP, the advocacy group for people over 50, found that, for many products, the majority of people over 45 were not loyal to a single brand. Companies have begun to realize that this segment of the population is increasing in size, may have more discretionary income than younger groups, and may respond to appropriate advertising.

Targeted marketing
Selling that centers on defining different market segments or groups of buyers for particular products based on the demographic, psychological, and behavioral characteristics of the individuals.

Unconventional Methods

Companies may also use more unconventional methods to assess consumer demand and develop appropriate advertising strategies. For example, in designing its "Whassup?" campaign for Budweiser, Anheuser-Busch executives had employees attend underground film festivals and examine new art forms to determine what factors would appeal to the company's target audience, composed primarily of 20- to 30-year-old men. The resulting information on current language, styles, and attitudes was then incorporated into new advertising campaigns.[8]

---

[5] Amy Merrick, "New Population Data Will Help Marketers Pitch Their Products," *Wall Street Journal*, February 14, 2001.

[6] Ibid.

[7] Kelly Greene, "Marketing Surprise: Older Consumers Buy Stuff, Too," *Wall Street Journal*, April 6, 2004.

[8] Patricia Winters Lauro, "Advertising: America's Asking Whassup?" *Wall Street Journal*, February 16, 2001.

In May 2001, Procter & Gamble announced plans to send video crews with cameras into 80 households around the world to record the daily routines of the occupants.[9] The company anticipated that this approach would yield better and more useful data than the consumer research methods discussed above because consumer behavior would be directly observed in a household setting rather than in an experimental environment. This approach would also avoid the response bias that can be present in a consumer survey. More recently, Procter & Gamble began partnering with Google Inc. to develop strategies appealing to online customers. The company invited "mommy bloggers"—women who run popular Web sites about child rearing—to tour the baby division to increase awareness and obtain feedback on Procter & Gamble products.[10]

To try to halt a 30-year decline in the sales of white bread, Sara Lee Corp. used taste testers to try to determine the optimum amount of whole grains that could be introduced into white bread to provide additional health benefits without discouraging users of traditional white bread who preferred that taste and consistency to darker and grainier whole grain breads.[11] The result, a bread called Soft & Smooth with 70 calories and 2 grams of fiber per slice, became one of the best selling brands in 2006 and encouraged other companies to produce similar breads.

Retailers have found that Western-style supermarkets with clean, wide aisles and well-stocked shelves do not work well in India, particularly for lower middle-class shoppers who are more comfortable in tiny, cramped stores.[12] One retailer, Pantaloon Retail (India) Ltd., spent $50,000 in a store to replace long, wide aisles with narrow, crooked ones to make the store messier, noisier, and more cramped. Products were clustered on low shelves and in bins because customers were used to shopping from stalls and finding products such as wheat, rice, and lentils in open containers that they could handle and inspect. Pantaloon Retail (India) Ltd., eventually became India's largest retailer in 2007 with annual sales of $875 million.

Evaluating the Methods

All research on consumer behavior involves extrapolating from a sample of data to a larger population. When designing surveys and forming focus groups for interviews, marketers must be careful that participating individuals are representative of the larger population. For example, Procter & Gamble does 40 percent of its early exploratory studies of new products in its hometown of Cincinnati. Given the number of P&G employees and retirees in the area, the company needs to make certain that its focus group members do not have an undue positive bias toward the products or are not influenced by family connections with the company.[13]

As mentioned earlier, responses given in an experimental format may not reflect actual consumer behavior. Although economists have recently used more experimental techniques, for many years these researchers preferred to rely on market data that showed how consumers actually *behaved*, not how they *said* they would behave. Surveys and focus groups must also be designed to determine the independent effect of each of the demand function variables on product sales or quantity

---

[9] Emily Nelson, "P & G Plans to Visit People's Homes to Record (Almost) All Their Habits," *Wall Street Journal*, May 17, 2001.

[10] Ellen Byron, "A New Odd Couple: Google, P&G Swap Workers to Spur Innovation," *Wall Street Journal*, November 19, 2008.

[11] Steven Gray, "How Sara Lee Spun White, Grain into Gold," *Wall Street Journal*, April 25, 2006.

[12] Eric Bellman, "In India, a Retailer Finds Key to Success Is Clutter," August 8, 2007.

[13] Emily Nelson, "P & G Keeps Focus Groupies of Cincinnati Busy as Guinea Pigs in Product Studies," *Wall Street Journal*, January 24, 2002.

demanded. Finding simple correlations between market variables and product sales does not mean that these variables have the same effect with other variables held constant.

Managerial Rule of Thumb

Marketing Methods for Analyzing Consumer Behavior

When using expert opinion, consumer surveys, test marketing, and price experiments to analyze consumer behavior, managers must consider

1. Whether the participating groups are truly representative of the larger population
2. Whether the answers given in these formats represent actual market behavior
3. How to isolate the effects of different variables that influence demand ■

Consumer Demand and Behavior: Economic Approaches

As we mentioned in the introduction to this chapter, many companies hire business economists to develop quantitative estimates of the relationships among the variables influencing the demand for their products. Results of a survey of 538 companies employing 4 to over 380,000 employees published in the mid-1990s indicated that 37.4 percent of the companies had economics departments.[14]

Economists typically use the statistical technique of **multiple regression analysis** to estimate the effect of each relevant independent variable on the quantity demanded of a product, *while statistically holding constant the effects of all other independent variables.* This approach involves the analysis of historical data to develop relationships among the variables and to predict how changes in these variables will affect consumer demand.

In the physical sciences, many of these types of relationships can be tested experimentally in the laboratory. However, experiments in the social and policy sciences are often very expensive, time-consuming, and complex to perform. Although the use of experimental approaches has been increasing, most research still relies on statistical or econometric techniques, such as multiple regression analysis, to examine the relationship between two variables, while statistically holding constant the effects of all other variables.

In the remainder of this section, we present an introduction to the use of multiple regression analysis and references for further study of the topic. We begin by focusing on a case involving one dependent and one independent variable, which we illustrate with a Microsoft Excel spreadsheet. We then move to an Excel case involving two independent variables to show how additional variables can modify the results of an analysis. Although both Excel examples are too simplistic for real-world market analysis, they illustrate the basic principles of the econometric approach to demand estimation. We next present a discussion of how regression analysis has been used to examine the factors influencing the demand for automobiles, the central issue in the opening news article of this chapter. In the last section

Multiple regression analysis
A statistical technique used to estimate the relationship between a dependent variable and an independent variable, *holding constant the effects of all other independent variables.*

---

[14] John J. Casson, "The Role of Business Economists in Business Planning," *Business Economics* 31 (July 1996): 45–50.

of the chapter, we discuss the relationship between the consumer research data that managers and marketers use and the statistical analysis of consumer behavior that economists undertake.[15]

Relationship Between One Dependent and One Independent Variable: Simple Regression Analysis

Let's begin with a very simple hypothetical example of a demand function similar to those we discussed in Chapters 2 and 3. Suppose that a manager has a sample of data on price and quantity demanded for oranges, shown in Figure 4.1 and in the bottom part of Table 4.1 [Actual Q (lbs.), Actual P (cents/lb.)].[16] These data could be either **cross-sectional data** or **time-series data**. If the data are cross-sectional data, they represent the behavior of different individuals facing different prices for oranges at a specific point in time. If the data are time-series data, they represent a set of observations on the same observational unit at a number of points in time, usually measured annually, quarterly, or monthly. Many recent studies use **panel data** sets, which are based on the same cross-section data observed at several points in time.[17]

If we want to estimate the relationship between quantity demanded and price, we can first just examine the data points in Figure 4.1 and Table 4.1. These data points show what appears to be a negative relationship between the variables—that is, as price decreases, quantity demanded increases, or as price increases, quantity demanded decreases.

Cross-sectional data
Data collected on a sample of individuals with different characteristics at a specific point in time.

Time-series data
Data collected on the same observational unit at a number of points in time.

Panel data
Cross-sectional data observed at several points in time.

Quantitative Measure Most managers need more information about this relationship than can be inferred just by examining the raw data in Figure 4.1 and Table 4.1. Managers want a quantitative measure of the size of this relationship that shows how much quantity demanded will change as price either increases or decreases. One quantitative measure would be to draw the line that best reflects the relationship shown by the data points in Figure 4.1 and Table 4.1. We would like to draw a straight line indicating a linear relationship between the variables because a linear relationship is the easiest case to analyze, as we noted in our discussion of demand in Chapters 2 and 3. However, we can see in Figure 4.1 that all the data points will not fall on a single straight line. For example, at a price of 70 cents per pound, four individuals demand different quantities. Thus, there is variation in the data, which means that some data points will deviate from any line fitted to the data. We want to find the line that "best fits" the data.

FIGURE 4.1
Hypothetical Demand for Oranges
This figure plots the sample data of the demand for oranges showing price (cents per lb.) and quantity demanded (lbs.).

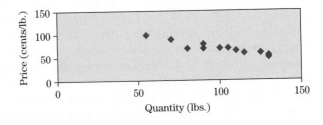

[15] Economists also use models to forecast the future values of economic variables based on trends in these values over time. We do not include these techniques in this book.
[16] This example is drawn from Jan Kmenta, *Elements of Econometrics* (New York: Macmillan, 1971). See that text for a complete derivation and discussion of the statistical procedures and results.
[17] William H. Greene, *Econometric Analysis*, 6th ed. (Upper Saddle River, N.J.: Prentice Hall, 2008).

TABLE 4.1 Simple Regression Analysis Results

REGRESSION STATISTICS

Multiple R	0.943
R *square*	0.889
Adjusted R *square*	0.878
Standard error	8.360
Observations	12.000

ANALYSIS OF VARIANCE (ANOVA)

	Degrees of Freedom	Sum of Squares	Mean Square	F-statistic	Significance of F-statistic
Regression	1.000	5601.111	5601.111	80.143	0.000
Residual	10.000	698.889	69.889		
Total	11.000	6300.000			

	Coefficients	Standard Error	t-statistic	P-value	Lower 95%	Upper 95%
Intercept	210.444	12.571	16.741	0.00000001	182.435	238.454
Price	−1.578	0.176	−8.952	0.00000434	−1.970	−1.185

RESIDUAL OUTPUT

Observation	Predicted Q	Residuals	Actual Q (lbs.)	Actual P (cents/lb.)
1	52.667	2.333	55	100
2	68.444	1.556	70	90
3	84.222	5.778	90	80
4	100.000	0.000	100	70
5	100.000	−10.000	90	70
6	100.000	5.000	105	70
7	100.000	−20.000	80	70
8	107.889	2.111	110	65
9	115.778	9.222	125	60
10	115.778	−0.778	115	60
11	123.667	6.333	130	55
12	131.556	−1.556	130	50

As with any straight line, a linear demand relationship can be expressed in an equation, as shown in Equation 4.1.

4.1 $Q = a - bP$

where

Q = quantity demanded
a = vertical intercept
b = slope of the line = $\Delta Q / \Delta P$
P = price

The vertical intercept, a, represents the quantity demanded of the product as a result of other variables that influence behavior that are not analyzed in Equation 4.1. For example, the quantity demanded may be influenced by an individual's income or by the size of the firm's advertising budget. The slope parameter, b, shows the change in quantity demanded that results from a unit change in price. We have assumed that b is a negative number, given the usual inverse relationship between price and quantity demanded. Once we know the parameters, a and b, we know the specific relationship between price and quantity demanded shown in Table 4.1, and we know how quantity demanded changes as price changes.

Simple regression analysis
A form of regression analysis that analyzes the relationship between one dependent and one independent variable.

Simple Regression Analysis   The relationship between price and quantity demanded can be estimated in this hypothetical example using **simple regression analysis**, as there is only one independent variable (P) and one dependent variable (Q). Regression analysis, as noted above, is a statistical technique that provides an equation for the line that "best fits" the data. "Best fit" means minimizing the sum of the squared deviations of the sample data points from their mean or average value.[18] Most of the actual data points will not lie on the estimated regression line due to the variation in consumer behavior and the influence of variables *not* included in Equation 4.1. However, the estimated line captures the relationship between the variables expressed in the sample data.

To estimate Equation 4.1, a manager needs to collect data on price and quantity demanded for a sample of individuals, as represented by the data points in Figure 4.1 and Table 4.1. The manager can then use any standard statistical software package to estimate the regression parameters, coefficients a and b in Equation 4.1, for that sample of data.[19] The computer program estimates the parameters of the equation and provides various summary statistics.

The results of such an estimation process, using the Excel regression feature, are shown in the middle rows of Table 4.1. The estimated value of the intercept term is 210.444, while the estimated value of the price coefficient is −1.578. The demand relationship is shown in Equation 4.2:

$$\textbf{4.2} \quad Q = 210.444 - 1.578P$$

The price coefficient, −1.578, shows that the quantity demanded of oranges decreases by 1.578 pounds for every one cent increase in price. However, as we discussed in Chapter 3, both economists and managers are usually more interested in the price elasticity of demand than in the absolute changes in quantity and price. Because this is a linear demand curve, the price elasticity varies along the demand curve. Equation 4.3 shows the calculation of price elasticity at the average price (70 cents per pound) and average quantity demanded at that price (100 pounds), based on Equation 3.2 and footnote 12 from Chapter 3.

$$\textbf{4.3} \quad e_P = \frac{(\Delta Q)(P)}{(\Delta P)(Q)} = \frac{(-1.578)(70)}{(100)} = -1.105$$

Equation 4.3 shows that the demand for oranges is slightly price elastic using the average values of the data in this sample. The percentage change in the quantity demanded of oranges is slightly greater than the percentage change in price.

---

[18] The technical details of this process can be found in any standard econometrics textbook. See, for example, Robert S. Pindyck and Daniel L. Rubinfeld, *Econometric Models and Economic Forecasts*, 4th ed. (New York: McGraw-Hill, 1998), and the books by Greene and Kmenta noted above.
[19] Standard statistical packages include SAS, SPSS, and STATA. Spreadsheet software packages such as Excel also include regression analysis.

Significance of the Coefficients and Goodness of Fit

There are numerous questions involving how well the regression line fits the sample data points in any regression analysis. Two important issues are

1. Hypothesis testing for the significance of the estimated coefficients
2. The goodness of fit of the entire estimating equation

Because the estimated coefficients in Equation 4.2 are derived from a sample of data, there is always a chance that the sizes of the estimated coefficients are dependent on that particular sample of data and might differ if another sample was used. The coefficients might also not be different from zero in the larger population. This issue would be of particular concern with the small data sample in Table 4.1. Table 4.1 includes the predicted value of quantity demanded and the residual, or the difference between the actual and predicted values, for each observation. Figure 4.2 plots the predicted quantity demanded at each price with the actual quantity demanded. Although the actual and predicted values appear to be relatively similar, we need a quantitative measure of how well the data fit the estimated equation.

Regression analysis packages provide an estimate of the **standard error** of each estimated coefficient, a measure of how much the coefficient would vary in regressions based on different samples. A small standard error means that the coefficient would not vary substantially among these regressions. In Table 4.1, the standard error of the price coefficient is 0.176, while that of the constant term is 12.571. Managers can use a ***t*-test**, based on the ratio of the size of the coefficient to its standard error, to test for the significance of the coefficients of the independent variables in a regression analysis. The *t*-test is used to test the hypothesis that a coefficient is significantly different from zero (that is, whether there is a high probability that, in repeated drawings of samples from the population, the coefficient will be a number different than zero or $H_1: B \neq 0$) versus the hypothesis that the coefficient is equal to zero ($H_0: B = 0$). This result is typically indicated by a *t*-statistic greater than 2.0, which means that a manager can be 95 percent certain that the coefficient is not zero in the larger population.

Large values of the *t*-statistic show statistically significant results because the standard error is small relative to the size of the estimated coefficient. In Table 4.1, the *t*-statistic for the price coefficient is −8.952, while that for the constant term is 16.741. Because both of these numbers are greater than 2 in absolute value, a manager can be at least 95 percent certain that the estimated coefficients are statistically significant and that the data support the hypothesis $H_1: B \neq 0$. The Excel program shows the actual degree of significance associated with the *t*-statistics. There is a 434 in 100,000,000 chance that the price coefficient is not statistically significant, while there is a 1 in 100,000,000 chance that the constant term is not statistically significant.

The Excel program also calculates **confidence intervals** around the estimated coefficients. These statistics show the range of values in which we can be confident that the true coefficient actually lies with a given degree of probability, usually 95 percent. Given the results in Table 4.1, a manager can be 95 percent confident

---

Standard error
A measure of the precision of an estimated regression analysis coefficient that shows how much the coefficient would vary in regressions from different samples.

t-test
A test based on the size of the ratio of the estimated regression coefficient to its standard error that is used to determine the statistical significance of the coefficient.

Confidence interval
The range of values in which we can be confident that the true coefficient actually lies with a given degree of probability, usually 95 percent.

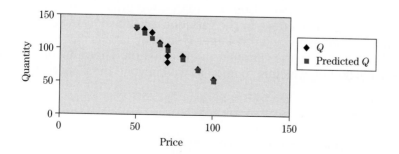

FIGURE 4.2
Simple Regression Analysis Actual Versus Predicted Results
This figure plots the actual and predicted quantity demanded relative to price in the simple regression analysis of quantity and price.

that the true value of the price coefficient lies between -1.185 and -1.970 and that the constant term lies between 182.435 and 238.454.

Coefficient of determination (R^2)
A measure of how the overall estimating equation fits the data, which shows the fraction of the variation in the dependent variable that is explained statistically by the variables included in the equation.

The goodness of fit of the entire estimating equation to the data set is shown by the **coefficient of determination (R^2)**. The value of this coefficient ranges from 0 to 1, with the size of the coefficient indicating the fraction of the variation in the dependent variable that is explained statistically by the variables included in the estimating equation. In Table 4.1, the variation in quantity demanded is due partly to the variation in price (the regression effect) and partly to the effect of a random disturbance (the residual or error effect). The coefficient of determination tests how well the overall model fits the data by decomposing the overall variation into the variation resulting from each of these effects.

The coefficient of determination is defined as the ratio of the sum of squared errors from the regression effect to the total sum of squared errors (regression plus residual effect). In Table 4.1, this ratio is $5,601/6,300 = 0.889$ (shown as the value of the R^2 statistic at the top of the table). There is no absolute cutoff point for the value of the R^2 statistic. The values of the coefficient of determination are typically higher for time-series data than for cross-section data, as many variables move together over time, which can explain the variation in the dependent variable. R^2 statistics for time-series analyses can exceed 0.9 in value, while those for cross-section studies are often in the range of 0.3 to 0.4.

When more variables are added to a regression equation, the R^2 statistic can never decrease in size. Thus, one method for obtaining a higher value of this statistic is to keep adding independent variables to the estimating equation. Because this procedure could give misleading results, managers can also use the **adjusted R^2 statistic**, which is defined in Equation 4.4.

Adjusted R^2 statistic
The coefficient of determination adjusted for the number of degrees of freedom in the estimating equation.

$$4.4 \quad \bar{R}^2 = 1 - (1 - R^2)\frac{(n-1)}{(n-k)}$$

where
$\bar{R}^2$ = adjusted R^2
R^2 = coefficient of determination
n = number of observations
k = number of estimated coefficients

Degrees of freedom
The number of observations (n) minus the number of estimated coefficients (k) in a regression equation.

The number of observations (n) minus the number of estimated coefficients (k) is called the **degrees of freedom** in the estimating equation. You cannot have more estimated coefficients than observations in an equation. The estimated equation in Table 4.1 has 10 degrees of freedom because there are 12 observations and 2 estimated coefficients. The adjusted R^2 statistic is typically lower than the coefficient of determination because it adjusts for the number of degrees of freedom in the estimating equation, and the statistic could actually be negative. In Table 4.1, the value of the adjusted R^2 statistic is 0.878 compared to 0.889 for the coefficient of determination. There is only a small difference between the two statistics, given the 10 degrees of freedom in the equation.

F-statistic
An alternative measure of goodness of fit of an estimating equation that can be used to test for the joint influence of all the independent variables in the equation.

An alternative measure of goodness of fit is the **F-statistic**, which is the ratio of the sum of squared errors from the regression effect to the sum of squared errors from the residual effect, or the variation explained by the equation relative to the variation not explained.[20] A larger F-statistic means that more variation in the data is explained by the variables in the equation. The value of the F-statistic in Table 4.1 is 80.143, which is significant well beyond the 95 percent probability level.

---

[20] These terms are adjusted for their degrees of freedom.

The *F*-statistic can be used to test the significance of all coefficients jointly in equations that have multiple independent variables. It is similar in concept to the *t*-statistic for testing the significance of individual regression coefficients. It is possible that the *t*-statistics might indicate that the individual coefficients are not statistically significant, while the *F*-statistic is statistically significant. This result could occur if the independent variables in the equation are highly correlated with each other. Their individual influences on the dependent variable may be weak, while the joint effect is much stronger.

Relationship Between One Dependent and Multiple Independent Variables: Multiple Regression Analysis

We now extend the Excel example of simple regression analysis showing the relationship between price and quantity demanded of oranges in Table 4.1 to a multiple regression analysis, which adds advertising expenditure to the estimating equation in Table 4.2. Although we know from Chapters 2 and 3 that many other variables should also influence the demand for oranges, we can illustrate multiple regression analysis by simply adding one more variable to the equation.

We use multiple regression analysis to estimate the demand function in Equation 4.5.

4.5 $Q = a - bP + cADV$

 where

   Q = quantity demanded

   a = constant term

   b = coefficient of price variable = $\Delta Q/\Delta P$, all else held constant

   P = price

   c = coefficient of advertising variable = $\Delta Q/\Delta ADV$, all else held constant

   ADV = advertising expenditure

As with the simple regression analysis example, we are estimating a linear relationship between the dependent variable, quantity demanded, and the two independent variables, price and advertising expenditure. The constant term, a, shows the effect on quantity demanded of other variables not included in the equation. The coefficients, b and c, show the effect on quantity demanded of a unit change in each of the independent variables. Each coefficient shows this effect while statistically holding constant the effect of the other variable. Thus, using multiple regression analysis to estimate demand relationships from behavioral data solves the "all else held constant" problem by statistically holding constant the effects of the other variables included in the estimating equation.

The demand relationship estimated in Table 4.2 is shown in Equation 4.6, using the variables defined in Equation 4.5.

4.6 $Q = 116.157 - 1.308P + 11.246ADV$

We can see that the coefficient of the price variable in Equation 4.6 is different from that in Equation 4.2 even though we use the same data in both equations. The difference arises from the fact that Equation 4.6 includes advertising expenditure, so that this equation shows the effect of price on quantity demanded, holding constant the level of advertising. Because no other variables are held constant in Equation 4.2, the price variable coefficient in that equation may pick up the effects of other variables not included in the equation that also influence the quantity demanded of oranges. This result is likely to occur if there are

TABLE 4.2 Multiple Regression Analysis Results

REGRESSION STATISTICS

Multiple R	0.980
R *square*	0.961
Adjusted R *square*	0.952
Standard error	5.255
Observations	12.000

ANOVA

	Degrees of Freedom	Sum of Squares	Mean Square	F-statistic	Significance of F-statistic
Regression	2.000	6051.510	3025.755	109.589	0.000000481
Residual	9.000	248.490	27.610		
Total	11.000	6300.000			

	Coefficients	Standard Error	t-statistic	P-value	Lower 95%	Upper 95%
Intercept	116.157	24.646	4.713	0.001	60.404	171.909
Price	−1.308	0.129	−10.110	0.000	−1.601	−1.015
Advertising	11.246	2.784	4.039	0.003	4.947	17.545

RESIDUAL OUTPUT

Observation	Predicted Q	Residuals	Quantity (lbs.)	Price (cents/lb.)	Advertising Expenditure ($)
1	47.222	7.778	55	100	5.50
2	69.297	0.703	70	90	6.30
3	92.497	−2.497	90	80	7.20
4	103.327	−3.327	100	70	7.00
5	95.455	−5.455	90	70	6.30
6	107.263	−2.263	105	70	7.35
7	87.583	−7.583	80	70	5.60
8	111.553	−1.553	110	65	7.15
9	122.029	2.971	125	60	7.50
10	115.281	−0.281	115	60	6.90
11	124.632	5.368	130	55	7.15
12	123.861	6.139	130	50	6.50
Average			100	70	6.70

other excluded variables that are highly correlated with price. Thus, it is important to have a well-specified estimating equation based on the relevant economic theory.

The coefficients of the price and advertising variables in Equation 4.6 show the change in quantity demanded resulting from a unit change in each of these variables, all else held constant. As with the simple regression analysis example, these coefficients can be used to calculate the relevant elasticities. Using the average values of price, quantity demanded, and advertising expenditure, we calculate the price elasticity of demand in Equation 4.7 and the advertising elasticity in Equation 4.8.

$$4.7 \quad e_P = \frac{(\Delta Q)(P)}{(\Delta P)(Q)} = \frac{(-1.308)(70)}{(100)} = -0.9156$$

$$4.8 \quad e_{ADV} = \frac{(\Delta Q)(ADV)}{(\Delta ADV)(Q)} = \frac{(11.246)(6.70)}{(100)} = 0.7535$$

The price elasticity calculated in Equation 4.7 is smaller than that calculated in Equation 4.3. In fact, the estimated elasticity coefficient in Equation 4.7—derived from Equation 4.6, with the level of advertising expenditure held constant—indicates that demand is price inelastic, while the coefficient in Equation 4.3—derived from Equation 4.2, which does not include the level of advertising expenditure—indicates elastic demand. It appears that the price variable in Equation 4.2 is picking up some of the effect of advertising on demand because the latter variable is not included in that equation. Managers must realize that econometric results can vary with the specification of the demand equation. All relevant variables need to be included in these equations to derive the most accurate empirical results.

Table 4.2 also presents the summary statistics for the multiple regression analysis. We can see that the standard errors of the two independent variables and the constant term are all small relative to the size of the estimated coefficients, so that the t-statistics are larger than 2 in absolute value. The two independent variables and the constant term are statistically significant well beyond the 95 percent level of confidence. Table 4.2 also shows the confidence intervals for all of the terms.

Figure 4.3 shows the actual and predicted values of quantity demanded relative to price, while Figure 4.4 shows the same values relative to advertising expenditure. Regarding the goodness of fit measures, the value of the coefficient of determination (R^2) is 0.961, while that of the adjusted R^2 statistic is 0.952. Although the latter is smaller than the former as expected, both statistics increased in value from the simple regression analysis in Table 4.1, indicating the greater explanatory power of the multiple regression model. The F-statistic is also highly significant in Table 4.2.

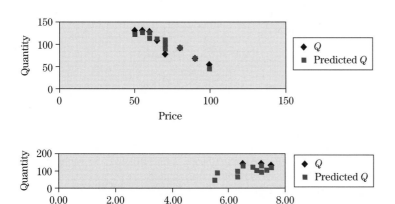

FIGURE 4.3
Multiple Regression Analysis, Fit of Price Variable
This figure plots the actual and predicted quantity demanded relative to price in the multiple regression analysis of quantity, price, and advertising expenditure.

FIGURE 4.4
Multiple Regression Analysis, Fit of Advertising Variable
This figure plots the actual and predicted quantity demanded relative to advertising expenditure in the multiple regression analysis of quantity, price, and advertising expenditure.

Other Functional Forms

The linear demand functions, estimated in Equations 4.2 and 4.6, imply both that there is some maximum price that drives consumers' quantity demanded of the product back to zero and that there is some maximum quantity that people demand at a zero price. As we have seen, the price elasticity of demand also changes at different prices along a linear demand curve. These characteristics of a linear demand function may not always adequately represent the behavior of different groups of individuals or the demand for various products, particularly at the end points of the demand curve.

It is often hypothesized that a multiplicative nonlinear demand function of the form shown in Equation 4.9 (where the variables are defined as in Equation 4.5) better represents individuals' behavior:

$$\textbf{4.9} \quad Q_X = (a)(P_X{}^b)(ADV^c)$$

This function, illustrated in general in Figure 4.5, is called a log-linear demand function because it can be transformed into a linear function by taking the logarithms of all the variables in the equation. This function is also called a *constant-elasticity demand function* because the elasticities are constant for all values of the demand variables and are represented by the exponents, b and c, in Equation 4.9.[21] Thus, the price and advertising elasticities can be read directly from the statistical results if this type of function is used in the estimation process. No further calculations are needed to determine the elasticities. This function may also better represent consumer behavior in certain cases because it implies that as price increases, quantity demanded decreases, but does not go to zero.

Demand Estimation Issues

Demand functions estimated for actual products are obviously much more complex than the simple examples presented in Equations 4.2 and 4.6. Managers could not use the results of such simple equations for decision making. However, these examples provide a starting point for understanding the more complex analyses discussed

FIGURE 4.5
Log-Linear Demand Curve
A log-linear demand curve has a constant price elasticity everywhere along the curve.

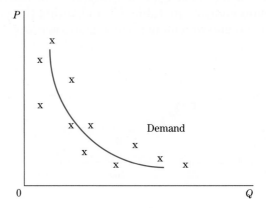

---

[21] Using calculus and the elasticity formula from Chapter 3, the price elasticity can be calculated as follows for a simple constant elasticity demand function:

$e_P = (dQ_X/dP_X)(P_X/Q_X)$

$Q_X = (a)(P_X{}^b)$

$e_P = [(a)(b)P_X{}^{b-1}][P_X/Q_X] = [(b)(a)P_X{}^b]/[(a)(P_X{}^b)] = b$

Similar calculations follow for other terms in such a function.

below. The estimation process and the choice of functional form in real-world demand equations are based on the issues presented in these simple examples.

The variables included in a multiple regression analysis may be influenced by data availability, as well as by the underlying economic theory. Data for demand estimation are often drawn from large-scale surveys undertaken by the federal government, universities, nonprofit groups, industry or trade associations, and company consumer research departments. In many cases, analysts would like to include certain variables, but a consistent set of observations for all individuals in the analysis may not be available. Some data sources may have better information on economic variables, while others may have more data on personal characteristics of the individuals included in the analysis. Analysts may also have to use other variables as proxies for the variables of greatest interest.

Every multiple regression analysis is influenced by the sample of data—time-series, cross-sectional, or panel—that is used. The analyst wants to estimate behavioral relationships that can be generalized beyond the sample of observations included in the analysis. Yet large-scale data collection can be very expensive and time-consuming. Thus, the analyst must be concerned that the estimated relationships may hold only for the sample of data analyzed, and not the larger population. As we discussed above, the analyst engages in hypothesis testing to determine how much confidence can be placed in the results of a particular analysis and whether these outcomes can be generalized to a larger population.

Managerial Rule of Thumb

Using Multiple Regression Analysis

In using multiple regression analysis to estimate consumer demand, a manager must decide which variables to include in the analysis. Various types of statistical problems can arise if relevant variables are excluded from the analysis or if irrelevant variables are included. The choice of variables is derived from economic theory, real-world experience, the problem under consideration, and common sense. ■

Case Study of Statistical Estimation of Automobile Demand

We began this chapter with a *Wall Street Journal* article discussing General Motors' failure to initially determine the correct consumer demand for a new luxury SUV and its problems in marketing to the Hispanic community in South Florida. We also discussed other cases where managers used surveys and other traditional consumer research methods to try to determine consumer preferences for product characteristics and price. We now discuss issues arising with the use of multiple regression analysis to estimate the demand for automobiles and the associated elasticities.[22] This discussion illustrates many of the methodological problems just presented.

Automobile demand studies have used both cross-sectional and time-series analysis with aggregate and disaggregated data. Studies have been undertaken for the entire market, market segments (domestic versus foreign), and particular brands of automobiles. Thus, given the differences in data sets, the functional forms of the estimating equations, and the variables included, we would expect to find a range of elasticity estimates in these studies. Aggregate time-series studies generally estimate market automobile price elasticities to be less than 1 in absolute value and income elasticities to be greater than +2.00, indicating a lack of sensitivity to price

---

[22] This discussion is based on Patrick S. McCarthy, "Market Price and Income Elasticities of New Vehicle Demands," *Review of Economics and Statistics* 78 (August 1996): 543–47.

for automobiles as a commodity, but a strong sensitivity in the demand for automobiles to changes in income. The disaggregated cross-sectional studies found price elasticities for particular vehicle types ranging from -0.51 to -6.13. The large elasticities at the upper end of the range should not be surprising, given the degree of substitution between different brands of cars.

Price elasticities have been found to be smaller for subcompact and compact vehicles compared to larger models and for two-vehicle households compared to one-vehicle households. The cross-section literature also found income elasticities greater than $+1.00$ and, in some cases, greater than $+5.00$. A 1985 study estimated an income elasticity of $+1.96$ for a Chevy Chevette and $+7.49$ for a Mercedes 280S, indicating a substantial consumer response for these models to changes in income. Automobile demand by households owning one vehicle tended to be less sensitive to changes in income than by two-vehicle households.

Automobile demand studies typically include price, income, credit availability, and automobile stocks as independent variables. One issue that has been debated in the literature is whether to include variables measuring automobile quality, which are typically derived from *Consumer Reports* and surveys by J.D. Power and Associates, a major marketing research firm. Thus, complex research studies often use data from sources that both managers and consumers read. Excluding quality variables from demand estimation studies could create econometric problems. The estimated price elasticity of demand coefficient would be biased downward if a model is estimated without including quality variables and if quality is positively associated with price and demand. Statistical and econometric problems can also arise if the independent variables in the model are highly correlated with each other. It may be difficult to separate out the effect of price from the other variables in this case. These issues again illustrate the problem of estimating the relationship between price and quantity demanded, "all else held constant," which we have been discussing in Chapters 2, 3, and 4.

In a 1996 study, Patrick S. McCarthy[23] estimated automobile demand based on data from the J.D. Power and Associates 1989 New Car Buyer Competitive Dynamics Survey of 33,284 households. This survey contained information on the vehicle purchased, household socioeconomic and demographic characteristics, and various activities associated with purchasing the vehicle. McCarthy's sample of 1,564 households, which was approximately 5 percent of the usable survey records, was randomly drawn from the larger survey to enable generalizations to be made to the larger population. The author supplemented the data from the J.D. Power survey with data on price, warranty, exterior and interior size, fuel economy, reliability, and safety from the *1989 Automotive News Market Data Book*, *Consumer Reports*, and the *1989 Car Book*. He obtained gasoline prices from the *Oil and Gas Journal* and population estimates from the U.S. Bureau of the Census.

Table 4.3 shows the independent variables, estimated coefficients, and summary statistics for McCarthy's study. The independent variables included measures of automobile costs (price and operating cost per mile), physical characteristics and vehicle style (horsepower, length, government crash test results, and vehicle type), quality (results of a consumer satisfaction index), manufacturer, consumer search activities (the number of first and second visits to different dealers and whether the consumer repurchased the same brand as previously), and household socioeconomic data. The study used multinomial logit analysis, a special form of regression analysis in which the dependent variable is a discrete variable (to purchase or not purchase a specific vehicle) rather than a continuous variable (the number of vehicles purchased).

McCarthy was satisfied with the precision of the estimating model in terms of the estimated signs of the variables, the *t*-statistics, and the coefficient of determination.

---

[23] Ibid.

TABLE 4.3 The Demand for Automobiles

	INDEPENDENT VARIABLES	COEFFICIENT (*T*-STATISTIC)
Cost-related attributes	Vehicle price/annual income	−2.452 (−9.1)
	Operating cost per mile (cents)	−0.4498 (−5.8)
	Metropolitan population if > 50,000	0.0000173 (1.4)
Vehicle style and physical attributes	Crash test variable	0.2409 (3.0)
	Net horsepower	0.00949 (6.0)
	Overall length (inches)	0.0166 (5.4)
	SUV, van, pickup truck	1.445 (4.8)
	Sports car segment	−1.277 (−4.7)
	Luxury segment—domestic	−0.4944 (−3.7)
Perceived quality	Consumer satisfaction index	0.0085 (3.5)
Vehicle search costs	1st dealer visit—domestic	3.034 (11.1)
	1st dealer visit—European	4.274 (15.2)
	1st dealer visit—Asian	3.726 (11.6)
	Subsequent dealer visits—Domestic	0.3136 (5.6)
	Subsequent dealer visits—European	0.7290 (5.7)
	Subsequent dealer visits—Asian	0.3337 (5.9)
	Repurchase same brand	2.320 (2.0)
Socioeconomic variables	Resident of Pacific Coast	−1.269 (−5.0)
	Age > 45 years old	0.9511 (4.8)
Manufacturing brand variables	Chrysler	1.007 (4.7)
	Ford, General Motors	1.721 (8.5)
	Honda, Nissan, Toyota	1.267 (9.1)
	Mazda	1.005 (5.5)
Summary statistics	R^2	0.26
	Number of observations	1564

Source: Patrick S. McCarthy, "Market Price and Income Elasticities of New Vehicle Demands," *Review of Economics and Statistics* 78 (August 1996): 543–47. © 1996 by the President and Fellows of Harvard College and the Massachusetts Institute of Technology.

Most of the signs of the variables were estimated as predicted, and the *t*-statistics indicated that the variables were statistically significant. The value of the coefficient of determination (0.26) was low, but comparable to those of other cross-section studies.[24]

The results in Table 4.3 show that both higher vehicle prices, relative to annual income, and higher vehicle operating costs lowered the quantity demanded of automobiles (the negative sign on those coefficients). Thus, the estimated demand curve is downward sloping. Vehicle safety, net horsepower, and overall vehicle length all

---

[24] The coefficient of determination and other measures of goodness of fit are slightly different in this model than in the standard linear regression model, given the discrete nature of the dependent variable.

had a significantly positive effect on automobile demand (as evidenced by the positive coefficients for these variables). Increased values of these variables would shift the demand curve to the right. Consumers in this sample exhibited a greater demand for vans, SUVs, and pickup trucks relative to automobiles and station wagons and a smaller demand for sports cars and domestic cars in the luxury segment.

We can also see that demand was positively related to increases in perceived quality (the positive coefficient on the consumer satisfaction index variable) and that search costs influenced vehicle demands. McCarthy argued that the positive coefficients on the dealer-visits variables indicated that the information benefits from an additional visit more than offset the additional search costs, but that the additional benefits declined with subsequent visits. The variable showing whether a consumer repurchased the same vehicle brand also had a positive coefficient, indicating a positive effect on demand. Because repurchasing the same brand lowers search and transactions costs, this variable had the expected positive sign. These results indicate that consumers react not just to the monetary price of an automobile, but also to the full purchasing costs, including the costs of obtaining information and searching for the vehicle. The study also determined that younger consumers and those residing on the Pacific Coast had smaller demands for domestic vehicles than other age and geographic groups.

Table 4.4 shows McCarthy's estimated price and income elasticities for both the entire market and the domestic, European, and Asian segments. The estimated demand for automobiles in this study was generally price inelastic, although the elasticity estimate for European models was slightly greater than 1 in absolute value. The cross-price elasticities were estimated to be positive numbers, indicating substitute goods, as economic theory suggests. Sales of European and Asian automobiles responded more to changes in the prices of substitute brands than did sales of U.S. automobiles. All income elasticities were found to be greater than $+1.00$, indicating substantial sensitivity to income changes.

The McCarthy study is particularly useful for managers because it is short and well written, and it focuses on the issues relevant to managerial decision making. Although academic consumer demand studies do not always meet these criteria, they can be useful starting points for managers. While the results of academic research studies may sometimes be too general for managerial decision making, they can be suggestive of strategies that managers should pursue. For example, McCarthy found that vehicle characteristics, quality, and consumer search variables were important influences on automobile demand.

One other problem with academic studies is the time lag often involved in their publication. The McCarthy article was published in 1996, using data from 1989. This type of lag is typical for academic research because articles are peer-reviewed

TABLE 4.4 Automobile Demand Elasticities

	OWN-PRICE ELASTICITY	CROSS-PRICE ELASTICITY	INCOME ELASTICITY
Entire market	−0.87	0.82	1.70
Market segment			
Domestic	−0.78	0.28	1.62
European	−1.09	0.76	1.93
Asian	−0.81	0.61	1.65

Source: Patrick S. McCarthy, "Market Price and Income Elasticities of New Vehicle Demands," *Review of Economics and Statistics* 78 (August 1996): 543–47. © 1996 by the President and Fellows of Harvard College and the Massachusetts Institute of Technology.

and revised several times.[25] While this time lag may limit the usefulness of academic research for managerial decision making, it does not make these studies worthless. The peer review process increases the reliability of the research results. In many cases, these results are available online or in the form of working papers long before they are officially published. Studies of past market behavior can also give managers insights into future trends.

Many of these issues regarding the estimation of price and advertising elasticities have been raised in the marketing literature that we discussed in Chapter 3.[26] Elasticity studies, particularly of specific product brands, may produce biased estimates if they do not include variables measuring product quality, the distribution of the product, advertising expenditures, other promotion activities such as coupons and rebates, and lagged prices and sales. Thus, one of the major problems in statistical demand studies is to correctly specify the model being estimated and to locate data on all the variables that should be included in the model.

Managerial Rule of Thumb

Using Empirical Consumer Demand Studies

Empirical consumer demand studies are important to managers because they show the types of data available for analyzing the demand for different products. Many data sources, such as industry and consumer surveys that researchers discover, may not have been widely publicized. Demand studies also discuss previous analyses, and they indicate how researchers conceptualize the problem of estimating the demand for a particular product. ▪

Relationships Between Consumer Market Data and Econometric Demand Studies

In the 1998 book *Studies in Consumer Demand: Econometric Methods Applied to Market Data*, Jeffrey A. Dubin illustrates the relationships between consumer market data, which managers typically use, and formal econometric demand studies based on these data.[27] In many cases, researchers analyze market data to obtain insights on what variables to include in their econometric models of demand. Although Dubin employs advanced econometric methods to estimate the demand for various products, we focus on two selected cases—Carnation Coffee-mate and Carnation Evaporated Milk—to illustrate the relationships between consumer market data and econometric models of demand. We also discuss the empirical research on the demand for hotel rooms that we first presented in Chapter 3.

Case Study I: Carnation Coffee-mate

To estimate the value of intangible assets, such as brand names, Dubin used Carnation Coffee-mate as one of his examples. He began with consumer surveys drawn from Carnation's marketing files and interviews with key individuals who

---

[25] The use of electronic communication has considerably reduced the time lags in the academic review process.

[26] Gerard J. Tellis, "The Price Elasticity of Selective Demand: A Meta-Analysis of Econometric Models of Sales," *Journal of Marketing Research* 25 (November 1988): 331–41; Raj Sethuraman and Gerard J. Tellis, "An Analysis of the Tradeoff Between Advertising and Price Discounting," *Journal of Marketing Research* 28 (May 1991): 160–74.

[27] Jeffrey A. Dubin. *Studies in Consumer Demand: Econometric Methods Applied to Market Data* (Boston: Kluwer Academic Publishers, 1998).

were marketing the products during the 1980s. Dubin used a Carnation Consumer Research Department survey to help define the market for the product. According to this survey, 37 percent of all cups of coffee were whitened, with milk used in half of these cases and a nondairy powdered creamer in another 20 percent. Coffee-mate was the best selling nondairy powdered creamer, with Cremora by Borden a major competitor. In addition to milk, other substitutes for Coffee-mate included cream, evaporated milk, and powdered milk.

Trends in coffee consumption also affected the demand for whiteners, given the complementary relationship between the two goods. A beverage industry survey showed that there had been a long-term decline in the per-capita daily consumption of coffee in the United States between 1962 and 1985. Although the average number of cups consumed by adults and the proportion of the population drinking coffee declined, these trends were offset by increases in the total U.S. population, so that the total amount of coffee consumed actually increased.

Marketing studies showed that coffee consumption differed by season, region, gender, and age. Socioeconomic status also played a role in consumption. A Carnation marketing study showed that Coffee-mate consumption was highest among coffee drinkers who had incomes under $10,000, had no more than a high school education, were employed in blue-collar occupations, lived in smaller cities or rural areas, and were African American. Studies also indicated that Coffee-mate had higher brand loyalty than did its competitors and that Coffee-mate users were less likely to use coupons to purchase the product.

Carnation Coffee-mate Demand Model Variables and Elasticities

Dubin based his demand model for Coffee-mate on these survey results. He used a constant elasticity model, as illustrated in Equation 4.9 and Figure 4.5, so that his estimated coefficients were the various elasticities of demand. Dubin included the following variables in his analysis:

- The price of Coffee-mate
- The prices of substitute goods
- Variables accounting for trends over time and seasonality effects
- Real income (adjusted for price changes) per capita
- Frequency of coffee consumption
- The total volume of all commodity sales in the region
- Real advertising expenditure of branded creamers
- Retail support measures, including in-aisle displays, in-ad coupons, and special pricing

He focused on the 16-ounce size of Coffee-mate, which had the highest sales volume in the product line and was marketed primarily in the retail distribution channel.

Dubin estimated a price elasticity coefficient of -2.01 for the 16-ounce Coffee-mate, as well as positive cross-price elasticities with its competitor brands. In addition to the role of price, he found seasonal effects on the demand for Coffee-mate (increased consumption in February and March), resulting from the patterns of coffee consumption. Although the real income and coffee consumption variables were not significantly different from zero, the all-commodity sales variable was highly significant, indicating the impact of activity in larger markets on the demand for nondairy creamer. Of the retail support variables, only in-ad coupons and special prices showed positive effects on the demand for Coffee-mate. Displays of the product within the stores did not have an impact on consumer demand, according to the study results. Increased advertising for Coffee-mate also did not increase the demand for the product. However, increased advertising for

Cremora actually increased the demand for Coffee-mate. Dubin attributed this result to the increased consumer awareness of creamers from advertising even if that advertising was not directed specifically to Coffee-mate. Thus, the study of Coffee-mate both confirmed the predictions of economic theory about price and cross-price elasticities and tested for the influence of other variables suggested by consumer research.

Case Study II: Carnation Evaporated Milk

Dubin also examined the market for evaporated milk, focusing on the leading brand, which was produced by Carnation. Marketing studies had shown that there were two distinct market segments—those individuals who used evaporated milk in coffee and everyday foods, such as soups, potatoes, and sauces, and those who used it for holidays and seasonal foods. These groups had different purchasing patterns, brand preferences, and demographic characteristics. A 1987 Carnation marketing study found that while only 13 percent of all evaporated milk consumers made five or more purchases per year, they represented 61 percent of the total category sales volume. In addition, 60 percent of evaporated milk consumers made only one purchase per year (representing 15 percent of sales volume). Compared to its competitors, Carnation sales were more concentrated among light users of evaporated milk. Much consumer research also indicated that Hispanics and African Americans tended to be heavy users of evaporated milk for both everyday and holiday foods unique to their cultures. This demographic characteristic created a geographic pattern of demand, with increased consumption in the South and Southwest, where many members of these groups live. Evaporated milk consumption was found to be greater in the fall and winter months, given the use of this product in coffee, baked goods, and soups, products more likely to be consumed during those months. Consumer research also indicated that younger, less affluent, and less educated households were more likely to purchase store label or generic evaporated milk than brand names.

Carnation Evaporated Milk Demand Model Variables and Elasticities
Given this background, Dubin estimated the demand for Carnation evaporated milk as a function of the following variables:

- The price of the Carnation product
- The price of substitute goods
- Variables accounting for trends over time, seasonality effects, and regional differences
- Real income level
- The percent of the population that is Hispanic
- Real advertising expenditures
- Retail support measures, including in-aisle displays, local advertising, and special pricing

Dubin found that Carnation evaporated milk had a price elasticity of -2.03, while its competitors had smaller elasticities of -0.88 (PET Evaporated Milk) and -1.22 (all other brands). He estimated the expected positive cross-price elasticities between these products. Dubin found a positive effect of retail support, particularly through displays and local advertising. He found that Carnation's advertising increased the overall demand for evaporated milk, while PET's advertising was not significant in influencing demand. Although real income was positively related to the demand for evaporated milk, the Hispanic population variable was not significant in the analysis. The latter result was surprising, given the emphasis placed on this subgroup in the consumer marketing studies. Either this variable was not important by itself, or it was correlated with other variables, and the statistical analysis was unable to determine its independent effect.

Case Study III: The Demand for Hotel Rooms

The hotel price and characteristic elasticities that we discussed in Table 3.7 in Chapter 3 were derived from a study of business travelers' demand for hotel rooms.[28] A conjoint analysis was used to determine business traveler preferences for three product lines—standard, medium, and deluxe rooms—and nine product characteristics, including the price and quality of the room, the quality of the public areas, the check-in and check-out times, the general performance of the staff, and the availability of guaranteed reservations, frequent guest programs, nonsmoking floors, and free parking. This conjoint analysis was based on a set of hypothetical products and attributes reflecting the entire range of attributes and products actually on the market. An experimental approach was employed instead of a consumer survey because it was far less expensive and more likely to reflect actual consumer behavior. To obtain consumer information about choices among hotels, it would have been necessary to undertake a large regional or national telephone survey or to interview individuals at airports, train stations, or other ports of entry to the hotel market in a given city.

This study also used a logit demand estimation model to estimate the weights that business travelers placed on hotel room price and the other characteristics noted above. The model estimated the probability that a traveler selected a room with a given set of characteristics. The results of the study indicated that the most important hotel room attributes for business travelers were price, room quality, a guaranteed reservation, the availability of a nonsmoking floor, and the availability of convenient free parking. Travelers were willing to pay the most for room quality, a guaranteed reservation, and parking.

Managerial Rule of Thumb

Using Consumer Market Data

Business economists and researchers use the consumer market data familiar to managers and marketers to estimate statistical/econometric models of demand and consumer behavior. These demand studies, in turn, can assist managers in developing competitive strategies by indicating the importance of the characteristics influencing the demand for different products and by showing what trade-offs consumers may be willing to make among those characteristics. ■

Summary

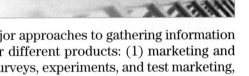

In this chapter, we have illustrated two major approaches to gathering information about consumer behavior and demand for different products: (1) marketing and consumer research methods that include surveys, experiments, and test marketing, among others; and (2) statistical and econometric approaches to formally estimating demand relationships. Managers tend to favor the former approach, while economists in business and academia use the latter. Most of the data for econometric analyses, however, are derived from consumer research studies. We have

[28]Raymond S. Hartman, "Hedonic Methods for Evaluating Product Design and Pricing Strategies," *Journal of Economics and Business* 41 (1989): 197–212; Raymond S. Hartman, "Price-Performance Competition and the Merger Guidelines," *Review of Industrial Organization* 18 (2001): 53–75.

suggested that managers be familiar with both approaches because each provides useful information on consumer behavior.

Managers need to realize that marketing analysis builds on the fundamental economic concepts of demand and elasticity. Marketers take these basic economic concepts and develop analyses of brand differentiation, market segmentation, and new product pricing. While some of the formal statistical approaches used by economists to estimate demand relationships may appear abstract and academic to managers and marketers, these approaches may do a better job of determining the effects of different variables on demand, while holding all else constant. This information is useful to both academic researchers attempting to improve the methods of demand estimation and managers needing to make decisions about advertising spending or how to counter the strategic moves of a competitor.

In the next chapter, we begin our discussion of production and cost. We then integrate these issues with our demand and consumer analysis to examine the competitive strategies and pricing policies of firms operating in different market environments.

Key Terms

adjusted R^2 statistic, p. 96

coefficient of determination
(R^2), p. 96

confidence interval, p. 95

conjoint analysis, p. 88

cross-sectional data, p. 92

degrees of freedom, p. 96

direct consumer surveys, p. 87

expert opinion, p. 87

F-statistic, p. 96

multiple regression
analysis, p. 91

panel data, p. 92

price experiments, p. 88

simple regression analysis, p. 94

standard error, p. 95

targeted marketing, p. 89

test marketing, p. 88

time-series data, p. 92

t-test, p. 95

Exercises

Technical Questions

1. In each of the following examples, describe how the information given about consumer demand helped managers develop the appropriate strategies to increase profitability and how this information was obtained:

   a. For nearly four decades, Wendy's International Inc. served only one kind of Frosty: a vanilla-and-chocolate hybrid thicker than a milk shake yet creamier than most fast-food ice cream. To connect with younger diners, Wendy's is now revamping the Frosty, along with the rest of its menu by adding new flavors that come with wide straws and bubble-shaped tops. Research has shown that the Frosty is the No. 4 reason people go out of their way to visit Wendy's. The company polled customers to ask which new flavors, including vanilla, cherry and strawberry, they liked best. Although Wendy's settled on vanilla, picking the exact type of vanilla flavor took months. Suppliers brought Wendy's 100 different varieties of vanilla flavoring with some tasting like cotton candy or bourbon and others having hints of smokiness or a slight taste of wet cardboard. Wendy's narrowed the vanillas to two varieties and brought more than 100 consumer testers into stark white tasting booths at its headquarters. The testers were told to take at least three bites of each sample before deciding which they preferred. They picked the sample with the stronger cotton candy flavoring. But a few said they didn't like the idea at all. "Vanilla is just not Wendy's," one tester wrote after sampling it. Since Wendy's launched the vanilla Frosty in July, Frosty sales have increased 25%. (*Based on:* Janet Adamy, "Why No. 3 Wendy's Finds Vanilla So Exciting," *Wall Street Journal*, April 6, 2007.)

   b. The Oreo has long been the top-selling cookie in the U.S. market. But Kraft Foods Inc. had to reinvent the Oreo to make it sell well in China given that the Chinese were not big cookie eaters. Kraft learned that traditional Oreos were too sweet for Chinese tastes and that the packages of 14 Oreos priced at 72 cents were too expensive. The company developed 20 prototypes of reduced-sugar Oreos and tested them with Chinese consumers before arriving at a formula that tasted right. The new Chinese Oreo consisted of four layers of crispy wafers filled with vanilla and chocolate cream, coated in chocolate. Kraft developed a proprietary handling process to ensure that the chocolate product could be shipped across the country, withstanding the cold climate in the north and the hot, humid weather in the south, yet still be ready to melt in the mouth. Kraft also noticed China's growing thirst for milk and began a grassroots marketing campaign to educate Chinese consumers about the American tradition of pairing milk with cookies. The company created an Oreo apprentice program at 30 Chinese universities that drew 6,000 applicants (*Based on:* Julie Jargon, "Kraft Reformulates Oreo, Scores in China," *Wall Street Journal*, May 1, 2008.)

c. In developing a line of talking toys aimed at children in China, engineers at Fisher-Price had to struggle to perfect the Mandarin "Sh" sound, which involves a soft hiss that was difficult to encode on sound-data chips embedded in the toys. Developers finally solved the problem of recording the phrase "It's learning time!" in Mandarin, but the company will soon be examining the LCD screens on learning toys to determine whether Chinese characters can be displayed clearly. These challenges arise as Fisher-Price is pursuing new markets in Brazil, Russia, and Poland, where brand-name American toys for toddlers are just beginning to appear and are perceived as novelties. Creating products for these markets has presented some unexpected hurdles such as the problem of recording Mandarin. Previously, Fisher-Price encountered problems with a reading toy called "Storybook Rhymes" that featured a traditional Turkish poem paired with an illustration of a pig. Fisher-Price officials realized this was not appropriate for a Muslim country and replaced the pig with pictures of cats. Market researchers have been traveling around the world searching for the next big market for preschoolers such as India. Many Indian mothers weren't willing to make an investment in the company's educational toys because research showed they didn't perceive the playthings as potential learning tools. But a shift in attitude began about two years ago, along with an increasing middle class able to purchase the toys. (*Based on:* Nicholas Casey, "Fisher-Price Game Plan: Pursue Toy Sales in Developing Markets," *Wall Street Journal*, May 29, 2008.)

2. The following figure plots the average farm prices of potatoes in the United States for the years 1989 to 1998 versus the annual per capita consumption. Each point represents the price and quantity data for a given year. Explain whether simply drawing the line that approximates the data points would give the demand curve for potatoes.

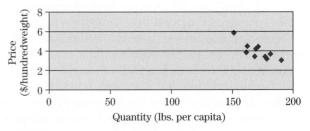

FIGURE 4.E1
Demand for Potatoes, 1989–1998
Source: Daniel B. Suits, "Agriculture," in *The Structure of American Industry*, ed. Walter Adams and James Brock, 10th ed. (Upper Saddle River, N.J.: Prentice-Hall, 2001).

3. The following table shows the regression coefficients (B) and the t-statistics (t) for the variables influencing business traveler demand for hotel rooms (including hotel prices and attributes) from the study that was discussed in this chapter and in Chapter 3.

BUSINESS TRAVELER DEMAND FOR HOTEL ROOMS

Attribute	B	(t)
Price ($/night)	−0.0346	(8.83)
Room quality 1 = average 2 = finest	1.258	(5.92)
Quality of public areas 1 = average 2 = finest	0.227	(0.88)
Check-in time (minutes)	−0.036	(−1.50)
Guaranteed reservation 1 = no 2 = yes	1.227	(4.88)
General staff performance 1 = average 2 = excellent	0.169	(0.74)
Frequent guest program 1 = no 2 = yes	0.37	(1.52)
Availability of nonsmoking floors 1 = no 2 = yes	0.359	(2.29)
Availability of free parking 1 = no 2 = yes	0.969	(4.61)

Source: Raymond S. Hartman, "Hedonic Methods for Evaluating Product Design and Pricing Strategies," *Journal of Economics and Business* 41 (1989): 197–212. Reprinted by permission.

Which characteristics are most and least important in influencing business traveler demand for hotel rooms?

4. In multiple regression analysis, explain why the typical hypothesis that analysts want to test is whether a particular regression coefficient (B) is equal to zero (H_0: $B = 0$) versus whether that coefficient is not equal to zero (H_1: $B \neq 0$).

Application Questions

1. Find evidence on how changes in the macroeconomic environment and the financial crises in 2007 and 2008 impacted General Motors' operations. Discuss the role of these factors versus the consumer demand issues described in the opening news article of this chapter.

2. "All else held constant" is the major problem facing all methods of estimating the demand for business products. Compare and contrast how the marketing and economic approaches deal with this problem.

3. Explain what types of biases arise in the different approaches to understanding consumer demand and behavior.

4. How does the empirical analysis of automobile demand presented in this chapter illustrate the fact that not only do consumers consider the monetary price of purchasing an automobile, but also they are sensitive to other costs (or the "full price") of the purchase?

5. The following table shows the results of a multiple regression study of the demand for ethical or prescription drugs, using panel data across seven countries (France, West Germany, Italy, Japan, Spain, the United Kingdom, and the United States) from 1980 to 1987. (The United States variable is omitted from the results because it is the country used for comparison.)

   The authors hypothesized that

   a. Price would be inversely related to quantity demanded.

   b. Income differences across countries would affect the demand for these drugs, which are hypothesized to be normal goods.

THE DEMAND FOR ETHICAL (PRESCRIPTION) DRUGS, 7 COUNTRIES, 1980–1987

Variable	B	(t)
Price	−3.25	(−4.39)
Income	1.55	(8.35)
France	−4.11	(−3.12)
Germany	−1.53	(−2.53)
Italy	−3.32	(−3.88)
Japan	−1.78	(−12.02)
Spain	−6.41	(−3.39)
United Kingdom	−7.54	(−4.65)
Number of doctors	1.55	(2.14)
Time trend variable	0.20	(6.00)
R^2	0.99	

Source: Donald L. Alexander, Joseph E. Flynn, and Linda A. Linkins, "Estimates of the Demand for Ethical Pharmaceutical Drugs Across Countries and Time," *Applied Economics* 26 (1994): 821–26. Reprinted by permission.

c. An increase in the number of doctors across countries would increase the demand for prescription drugs because doctors are required to write prescriptions and a larger number of doctors in a country reduces wait times for prescriptions.

d. A time trend variable is needed to control for factors, such as country demographics, that change over time.

e. The demand differs by country, given varying political and health care institutions, so that dummy variables that take on the value of zero or one are included to control for the effects of each country on drug demand.

Given the above results, did the data support the research hypotheses? How useful are these study results for managerial decision making?

On the Web

For updated information on the *Wall Street Journal* article at the beginning of the chapter, as well as other relevant links and information, visit the book's Web site at **www.pearsonhighered.com/farnham**

5

Production and Cost Analysis in the Short Run

I n this chapter, we analyze production and cost, the fundamental building blocks on the supply side of the market. Just as consumer behavior forms the basis for the demand curves we have studied in previous chapters, producer behavior lies behind the supply curve. As we learned in Chapter 2, the prices of the inputs of production and the state of technology are two factors held constant when defining a market supply curve. Production processes (or "production functions," as economists call them) and the corresponding cost functions, which show how costs vary with the level of output produced, are also very important when we analyze the behavior and strategy of individual firms and industries.

We begin this chapter with a *New York Times* article, "The Long-Distance Journey of a Fast-Food Order," which discusses efficiency and costs in the fast-food industry. Next we discuss short-run versus long-run production and cost and present a model of a short-run production function. We also examine economic data on the differences in productivity among firms and industries. We then present a model of short-run cost functions and discuss evidence on the shapes of these cost functions. We also distinguish between the types of costs measured by accountants and the cost concepts used by economists.

The Long-Distance Journey of a Fast-Food Order

by Matt Richtel

New York Times, *April 11, 2006*

Copyright © 2006 The New York Times Co. Reprinted by permission.

Like many American teenagers, Julissa Vargas, 17, has a minimum-wage job in the fast-food industry—but hers has an unusual geographic reach.

"Would you like your Coke and orange juice medium or large?" Ms. Vargas said into her headset to an unseen woman who was ordering breakfast from a drive-through line. . . .

What made the $12.08 transaction remarkable was that the customer was not just outside Ms. Vargas's workplace here on California's central coast. She was at a McDonald's in Honolulu. And within a two-minute span Ms. Vargas had also taken orders from drive-through windows in Gulfport, Miss., and Gillette, Wyo.

Ms. Vargas works not in a restaurant but in a busy call center in this town, 150 miles from Los Angeles. She and as many as 35 others take orders remotely from 40 McDonald's outlets around the country. The orders are then sent back to the restaurants by Internet, to be filled a few yards from where they were placed.

The people behind this setup expect it to save just a few seconds on each order. But that can add up to extra sales over the course of a busy day at the drive-through.

While the call-center idea has received some attention since a scattered sampling of McDonald's franchises began testing it 18 months ago, most customers are still in the dark. . . .

And the order-taking is not seamless. Often customers' voices are faint, forcing the workers to ask for things to be repeated. During recent rainstorms in Hawaii, it was particularly hard to hear orders from there over the din.

Ms. Vargas seems unfazed by her job, even though it involves being subjected to constant electronic scrutiny. Software tracks her productivity and speed, and every so often a red box pops up on her screen to test whether she is paying attention. She is expected to click on it within 1.75 seconds. In the break room, a computer screen lets employees know just how many minutes have elapsed since they left their workstations. . . .

McDonald's is joined by the owner of Hardee's and Carl's Jr., CKE Restaurants, which plans to develop a similar system later this year in restaurants in California.

Not everyone is sold on the idea. Denny Lynch, a spokesman for Wendy's Restaurants, said that the approach had not yet proved itself to be cost-effective. "Speed is incredibly important," he said, but "we haven't given this solution any serious thought. . . ."

But the backers of the technology are looking to expand into new industries. The operator of one of the McDonald's centers is developing a related system that would allow big stores like Home Depot to equip carts with speakers that customers could use to contact a call center wirelessly for shopping advice. . . .

Efficiency is certainly the mantra at the Bronco call center, which has grown from 15 workers six months ago to 125 today. Its workers are experts on the McDonald's menu; they are trained to be polite, to urge customers to add items to their order and, above all, to be fast. Each worker takes up to 95 orders an hour during peak times.

Customers pulling up to the drive-through menu are connected to the computer of a call-center employee using Internet calling technology. The first thing the McDonald's customer hears is a prerecorded greeting in the voice of the employee. The order-taker's screens include the menu and an indication of whether it is time for breakfast or lunch at the local restaurant. A "notes" section shows if that restaurant has called in to say that it is out of a particular item.

When the customer pulls away from the menu to pay for the food and pick it up, it takes around 10 seconds for another car to pull forward. During that time, Mr. King said, his order-takers can be answering a call from a different McDonald's where someone has already pulled up.

The remote order-takers at Bronco earn the minimum wage ($6.75 an hour in California), do not get health benefits and do not wear uniforms. . . .

Some 50 McDonald's franchises are testing remote order-taking, some using Bronco Communications. Others are using Verety, a company based in Oak Brook, Ill. (also the home of McDonald's), that has taken the concept further by contracting workers in rural North Dakota to take drive-through orders from their homes.

A spokesman for McDonald's, Bill Whitman, said that the results of the test runs had been positive so far, but that it had not yet decided whether to expand its use of the technology.

The system does sometimes lead to mix-ups and customer confusion. The surprised customer will say to the cashier, "You didn't take my order," said Bertha Aleman, manager of the McDonald's in Pleasant Hill. . . .

Ms. Aleman said that, over all, the system had improved accuracy and helped her cut costs. She said that now she did not need an employee dedicated to taking orders or, during the lunch rush, an assistant for the order-taker to handle cash when things backed up. "We've cut labor," she said.

Case for Analysis

Production and Cost Analysis in the Fast-Food Industry

This article focuses on the latest developments in how fast-food outlets use drive-through windows to increase their profitability: outsourcing the drive-through calls to call centers located hundreds or thousands of miles from the outlet. With 65 percent of fast-food revenue being derived from drive-through windows, these windows have become the focal point for market share competition among fast-food outlets such as Wendy's, McDonald's, Burger King, Arby's, and Taco Bell. Even chains that did not use drive-through windows in the past, such as Starbucks and Dunkin' Donuts, have added them to their stores.[1]

Production technology changes have included the use of separate kitchens for the drive-through window, timers to monitor the seconds it takes a customer to move from the menu board to the pickup window, kitchen redesign to minimize unnecessary movement, and scanners that send customers a monthly bill rather than having them pay at each visit. Now, in an attempt to cut costs and increase speed even further, approximately 50 McDonald's franchises have been testing remote order-taking. It takes an average of 10 seconds for a new car to pull up to a drive-through menu after one car has moved forward. With a remote call center, an order-taker can answer a call from a different McDonald's where another customer has already pulled up. This means that during peak periods, a worker can take up to 95 orders per hour. The trade-offs with this increased speed at the drive-through window are employee dissatisfaction with constant monitoring and the stress of the process, decreases in accuracy in filling orders, and possible break-downs in communication over long distances. However, this technology may be expanded to allow stores, such as Home Depot, to equip carts with speakers that customers could use to wirelessly contact a call center for shopping assistance.

This case illustrates how firms can use production technology to influence their costs, revenues, and profits. Because firms in more competitive markets may not have much ability to influence the prices of their products, they may depend more on strategies to increase the number of customers and lower the costs of production. These strategies may involve changing the underlying production technology, lowering the prices paid for the inputs used, and changing the scale of operation.

To analyze these issues, we'll first discuss the nature of a firm's production process and the types of decisions that managers make regarding production. We'll then show how a firm's costs of production are related to the underlying production technology. Because the time frame affects a manager's decisions about production and cost, we distinguish between the short run and the long run and discuss the implications of these time frames for managerial decision making. This chapter focuses on short-run production and cost decisions, while Chapter 6 analyzes production and cost in the long run. ■

Defining the Production Function

To analyze a firm's production process, we first define a production function and distinguish between fixed and variable inputs and the short run versus the long run.

The Production Function

Production function
The relationship between a flow of inputs and the resulting flow of outputs in a production process during a given period of time.

A **production function** describes the relationship between a flow of inputs and the resulting flow of outputs in a production process during a given period of time. The production function describes the *physical relationship* between the inputs or factors of production and the resulting outputs of the production process. It is essentially an engineering concept, as it incorporates all of the technology or knowledge involved with the production process. The production function illustrates how inputs are combined to produce different levels of output and how different combinations of inputs may be used to produce any given level of output. It shows the maximum amount of output that can be produced

---

[1] Jennifer Ordonez, "An Efficiency Drive: Fast-Food Lanes, Equipped with Timers, Get Even Faster," *Wall Street Journal*, May 18, 2000.

with different combinations of inputs. This concept rules out any situations where inputs are redundant or wasted in production. The production function forms the basis for the economic decisions facing a firm regarding the choice of inputs and the level of outputs to produce.[2]

A production function can be expressed with the notation in Equation 5.1:

5.1 $Q = f(L, K, M \ldots)$

> *where*
>
> Q = quantity of output
> L = quantity of labor input
> K = quantity of capital input
> M = quantity of materials input

As with the demand relationships we looked at in earlier chapters, Equation 5.1 is read "quantity of output is a function of the inputs listed inside the parentheses." The ellipsis in Equation 5.1 indicates that more inputs may be involved with a given production function. There may also be different types of labor and capital inputs, which we could denote by L_A, L_B, L_C and K_A, K_B, and K_C, respectively. Note that in a production function, capital (K) refers to *physical* capital, such as machines and buildings, not financial capital. The monetary or cost side of the production process (that is, the financial capital needed to pay for workers and machines) is reflected in the functions that show how costs of production vary with different levels of output, which we'll derive later in the chapter.

A production function is defined in a very general sense and can apply to large-scale production processes, such as the fast-food outlets in this chapter's opening case analysis, or to small firms comprising only a few employees. The production function also can be applied to different sectors of the economy, including both goods and services. In this chapter, we use very simple production functions to illustrate the underlying theoretical concepts, while the examples focus on more complex, real-world production processes.

Fixed Inputs Versus Variable Inputs

Managers use both fixed inputs and variable inputs in a production function. A **fixed input** is one whose quantity a manager cannot change during a given time period, while a **variable input** is one whose quantity a manager can change during a given time period. A factory, a given amount of office space, and a plot of land are fixed inputs in a production function. Automobiles or CD players can be produced in the factory, accounting services can be undertaken in the office, and crops can be grown on the land. However, once a manager decides on the size of the factory, the amount of office space, or the acreage of land, it is difficult, if not impossible, to change these inputs in a relatively short time period. The amount of automobiles, CD players, accounting services, or crops produced is a function of the manager's use of the variable inputs in combination with these fixed inputs. Automobile workers, steel and plastic, accountants, farm workers, seed, and fertilizer are all variable inputs in these production processes. The amount of output produced varies as managers make decisions regarding the quantities of these variable inputs to use, while holding constant the underlying size of the factory, office space, or plot of land.

Fixed input
An input whose quantity a manager cannot change during a given period of time.

Variable input
An input whose quantity a manager can change during a given period of time.

---

[2] The production function incorporates *engineering* knowledge about production technology and how inputs can be combined to produce the firm's output. Managers must make *economic* decisions about what combination of inputs and level of output are best for the firm.

Short-Run Versus Long-Run Production Functions

Two dimensions of time are used to describe production functions: the short run and the long run. These categories do not refer to specific calendar periods of time, such as a month or a year; they are defined in terms of the use of fixed and variable inputs.

Short-run production function

A production process that uses at least one fixed input.

A **short-run production function** involves the use of at least one fixed input. At any given point in time, managers operate in the short run because there is always at least one fixed input in the production process. Managers and administrators decide to produce beer in a brewery of a given size or educate students in a school with a certain number of square feet. The size of the factory or school is fixed in the short run either because the managers have entered into a contractual obligation, such as a rental agreement, or because it would be extremely costly to change the amount of that input during the time period.

Long-run production function

A production process in which all inputs are variable.

In a **long-run production function**, all inputs are variable. There are no fixed inputs because the quantity of all inputs can be changed. In the long run, managers can choose to produce cars in larger automobile plants, and administrators can construct new schools and abandon existing buildings. Farmers can increase or decrease their acreage in another planting season, depending on this year's crop conditions and forecasts for the future. Thus, the calendar lengths of the short run and the long run depend on the particular production process, contractual agreements, and the time needed for input adjustment.

Managerial Rule of Thumb

Short-Run Production and Long-Run Planning

Managers always operate in the short run, but they must also have a long-run planning horizon. Managers need to be aware that the current amount of fixed inputs, such as the size of a factory or amount of office space, may not be appropriate as market conditions change. Thus, there are more economic decisions for managers in the long run because all inputs can be changed in that time frame and inputs can be substituted for each other. ∎

Productivity and the Fast-Food Industry

The fast-food articles that opened this chapter gave a good illustration of the differences between short- and long-run production functions. With a given technology and fixed inputs, as employees at the drive-through windows work faster to reduce turnaround time for a drive-through customer, the quality of the service begins to decline, and worker frustration and dissatisfaction increase. This situation represents the increased use of variable inputs relative to the fixed inputs in the short run. The management response to these problems has been to implement new technologies for the production process: placing an intercom at the end of the drive-through line to correct mistakes in orders; finding better ways for employees to perform multiple tasks in terms of kitchen arrangement; and, most recently, outsourcing the drive-through calls to remote call centers. This situation represents the long run, in which all inputs can be changed.

Model of a Short-Run Production Function

In this section, we discuss the basic economic principles inherent in a short-run production function, illustrated in the fast-food example. To do so, we need to define three measures of productivity, or the relationship between inputs and output: total product, average product, and marginal product. We then examine how each measure changes as the level of the variable input changes.

Total Product

Total product is the total quantity of output produced with given quantities of fixed and variable inputs.[3] To illustrate this concept, we use a very simple production function with one fixed input, capital ($\bar{K}$), and one variable input, labor (L). This production function is illustrated in Equation 5.2.

5.2 TP or $Q = f(L, \bar{K})$

  where

  TP or Q = total product or total quantity of output produced
    L = quantity of labor input (variable)
    $\bar{K}$ = quantity of capital input (fixed)

Equation 5.2 presents the simplest type of short-run production function. It has only two inputs: one fixed ($\bar{K}$) and one variable (L). The bar over the K denotes the fixed input. In this production function, the amount of output (Q) or total product (TP) is directly related to the amount of the variable input (L), while holding constant the level of the fixed input ($\bar{K}$) and the technology embodied in the production function.

Average Product and Marginal Product

To analyze the production process, we need to define two other productivity measures, average product and marginal product. The **average product** is the amount of output per unit of variable input, and the **marginal product** is the additional output produced with an additional unit of variable input. These relationships are shown in Equations 5.3 and 5.4.

5.3 $AP = TP/L$ or Q/L

  where

  AP = average product of labor

5.4 $MP = \Delta TP/\Delta L = \Delta Q/\Delta L$

  where

  MP = marginal product of labor

Table 5.1 presents a numerical example of a simple production function based on the underlying equations shown in the table. As with marginal revenue in Table 3.3 in Chapter 3, marginal product in Table 5.1 can be calculated either for discrete changes in labor input (Column 5) or for infinitesimal changes in labor input using the specific marginal product equation in the table (Column 6). Column 5 shows the marginal product between units of input (Column 2), whereas Column 6 shows the marginal product calculated precisely at a given unit of input. Column 6 gives the exact mathematical relationships discussed below.

Relationships Among Total, Average, and Marginal Product

Let's examine how the total, average, and marginal product change as we increase the amount of the variable input, labor, in this short-run production function, holding constant the amount of capital and the level of technology. We can see in Table 5.1 that the

---

[3] This variable is sometimes called total physical product to emphasize the fact that the production function shows the physical relationship between inputs and outputs. We use total product for simplicity.

TABLE 5.1 A Simple Production Function[a]

QUANTITY OF CAPITAL (K) (1)	QUANTITY OF LABOR (L) (2)	TOTAL PRODUCT (TP) (3)	AVERAGE PRODUCT (AP) (4)	MARGINAL PRODUCT (MP) ($\Delta TP/\Delta L$) (5)	MARGINAL PRODUCT (MP) (dTP/dL) (6)
10	1	14	14.0	14	18
10	2	35	17.5	21	24
10	3	62	20.7	27	28
10	4	91	22.8	29	30
10	4.5	106	23.6	30	30.25
10	5	121	24.2	30	30
10	6	150	25.0	29	28
10	6.75	170	25.1875	26.67	25.1875
10	7	175	25.0	25	24
10	8	197	24.6	22	18
10	9	212	23.6	15	10
10	10	217	21.7	5	0
10	11	211	19.2	−6	−12

[a]In this example, the underlying equations showing total, average, and marginal products as a function of the amount of labor, L (with the level of capital assumed constant), are

$$TP = 10L + 4.5L^2 - 0.3333L^3$$
$$AP = 10 + 4.5L - 0.3333L^2$$
$$MP = dTP/dL = 10 + 9L - 1.0L^2$$

total product or total amount of output (Column 3) increases rapidly up to 4.5 units of labor. This result means that the marginal product, or the additional output produced with an additional unit of labor (Column 6), is increasing over this range of production. Between 4.5 and 10 units of labor, the total product (Column 3) is increasing, but the rate of increase, or the marginal product, is becoming smaller (Columns 5 and 6). Total product reaches its maximum amount of 217 units when 10 units of labor are used, but total product decreases if 11 units of labor are employed. The marginal product of labor is 5 as labor is increased from 9 to 10 units and −6 as labor is increased from 10 to 11 units (Column 5). Therefore, the marginal product is zero when the total product is precisely at its maximum value of 217 units (Column 6).

The average product of labor, or output per unit of input (Column 4), also increases in value as more units of labor are employed. It reaches a maximum value with 6.75 units of labor and then decreases as more labor is used in the production process. As you can see in Table 5.1, when the marginal product of labor is greater than the average product of labor (up to 6.75 units of labor), the average product value increases from 14 to 25.1875 units of output per input. When more units of labor are employed, the marginal product becomes less than the average product, and the average product decreases in value. Therefore, the marginal product must equal the average product when the average product is at its maximum value.[4]

---

[4] The maximum point of average product in Table 5.1 occurs at 6.75 units of labor, where both the average and the marginal products have the value of 25.1875 units of output per input. This relationship holds for any average and marginal variables. Suppose your average grade on two exams is 80. Your third exam is your marginal grade. If you receive a 90 on the third exam, your average grade increases to 83.3. However, if you receive a grade of 60 on your third exam, your average drops to 73.3. If the marginal variable is greater than the average variable, the average variable increases. If the marginal variable is less than the average variable, the average variable decreases.

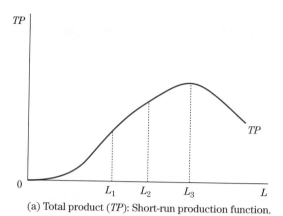

(a) Total product (*TP*): Short-run production function.

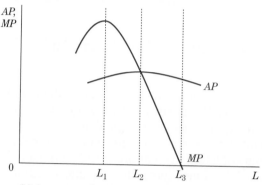

(b) Average product (*AP*) and marginal product (*MP*):
Short-run production function.

FIGURE 5.1

The Short-Run Production Function

The short-run production function illustrates the law of diminishing returns where the marginal product, or the additional output produced with an additional unit of variable input, eventually decreases.

Figures 5.1a and 5.1b show the typical shapes for graphs of the total, average, and marginal product curves. These graphs illustrate the relationships in Table 5.1, but are drawn more generally to move beyond this specific numerical example. Labor input is measured on the horizontal axis of both Figures 5.1a and 5.1b, with different quantities shown as L_1, L_2, and L_3. The total product is measured on the vertical axis of Figure 5.1a, while the average and marginal products are measured on the vertical axis of Figure 5.1b. The variables are measured on separate graphs because the sizes of the numbers are quite different, as was shown in Table 5.1.

As in Table 5.1, Figure 5.1a shows the total product (or level of output) first increasing very rapidly up to labor input level L_1 and then increasing at a slower rate as more labor input is added. The total product curve becomes flatter and flatter until it reaches a maximum output level at labor input level L_3. If more labor is added beyond level L_3, the total amount of output, or the total product, decreases. This total product curve implies that the marginal product of labor first increases rapidly, then decreases in size, and eventually becomes zero or even negative in value, as illustrated in Figure 5.1b.

We can also see in Figure 5.1b the typical relationship between the marginal product and average product curves. Between zero and L_2 units of labor, the marginal product curve lies above the average product curve, which causes the average product curve to increase. Beyond L_2 units of input, the marginal product curve lies below the average product curve, which causes the average product curve to decrease. Therefore, the marginal product curve must intersect the average product curve at the maximum point of the average product curve. Table 5.2 summarizes these relationships.

TABLE 5.2   Relationships Among Total Product (*TP*), Average Product (*AP*), and Marginal Product (*MP*) in Figures 5.1a and 5.1b

INPUT RANGE	EFFECT ON TOTAL AND/OR AVERAGE PRODUCT	EFFECT ON MARGINAL PRODUCT
Input values: zero to L_1	TP increases at increasing rate	MP is positive and increasing
Input values: L_1 to L_3	TP increases at decreasing rate	MP is positive and decreasing
Input values: beyond L_3	TP decreases	MP is negative and decreasing
Input values: L_3	TP is at a maximum	MP equals zero
Input values: zero to L_2	AP increases	MP is greater than AP
Input values: beyond L_2	AP decreases	MP is less than AP
Input values: L_2	AP is at a maximum	MP equals AP

Economic Explanation of the Short-Run Production Function

Why do the graphs of total, average, and marginal products in Figures 5.1a and 5.1b typically have these shapes? To answer this question, we need to focus on the marginal product curve. In Figure 5.1b, the marginal product curve increases up to labor input level L_1. We call this the region of **increasing marginal returns**. Once we have employed L_1 units of labor, the marginal product of labor begins to decline and keeps decreasing until it becomes zero, when L_3 units of labor are utilized. This portion of the marginal product curve illustrates what is known as the **law of diminishing marginal returns** (or the **law of the diminishing marginal product**). All short-run marginal product curves will eventually have a downward sloping portion and exhibit this law. Beyond L_3 units of labor, the marginal product of labor is negative. This is the region of **negative marginal returns**.

The law of diminishing marginal returns occurs because the capital input and the state of technology are held constant when defining a short-run production function. As more units of labor input are added to the fixed capital input, the marginal product may increase at first (zero to L_1 units of labor in Figure 5.1b), but the curve will eventually decline and possibly reach zero or negative values (beyond L_3 units of labor in Figure 5.1b). The additional output generated by the additional units of the variable input (the marginal product) must decrease at some point because there are too many units of the variable input combined with the fixed input. (For example, there are too many automobile workers in the factory, too many accountants in the office space, or too many farmhands on the plot of land.) The production process becomes constrained by the amount of the fixed input, so that additional units of the variable input become redundant.

Although a firm is constrained by its scale of production (the amount of its fixed inputs) and by the state of technology embodied in the production function, the entire set of curves in Figures 5.1a and 5.1b can shift if the firm either changes the scale of production or adopts new technology. As we saw in the fast-food example, this was the managerial response to diminishing returns in the drive-through window.

Increasing marginal returns
The results in that region of the marginal product curve where the curve is positive and increasing, so that total product increases at an increasing rate.

Law of diminishing marginal returns or law of the diminishing marginal product
The phenomenon illustrated by that region of the marginal product curve where the curve is positive, but decreasing, so that total product is increasing at a decreasing rate.

Negative marginal returns
The results in that region of the marginal product curve where the curve is negative and decreasing, so that total product is decreasing.

Real-World Firm and Industry Productivity Issues

The model of a short-run production function is very important for the development of the theory of cost and profit maximization and for the analysis of firms in different market environments. Before proceeding with short-run cost theory, we'll discuss several other examples of productivity differences among firms and industries.

Other Examples of Diminishing Returns

The poultry industry has always faced the problem that chickens, unlike pigs and cattle, cannot be herded.[5] Chickens raised for meat are allowed to roam freely inside huge chicken houses, so that poultry farmers have traditionally had to rely on human catchers to run around inside the barns grabbing chickens by hand. Adding increased amounts of catchers to a chicken house would easily result in diminishing returns. Human catchers are typically expected to grab as many as 1,000 birds an hour. As with the drive-through fast-food windows, output quality deteriorates as birds are injured through the speed of the process. Bruised chickens cannot be sold at grocery meat counters.

After years of failure, manufacturers finally produced machines capable of catching and caging chickens, up to 150 birds per minute. A five-man crew with this mechanical harvester can do the work of eight men alone, with chicken injuries reduced by as much as 50 percent. This technological change would shift the previous set of marginal and average product curves upward, representing increased productivity.

Surgical instruments called broaches, which are used to grind bones during hip-replacement surgery, used to be so complex that they could be made only by hand.[6] It is clear that diminishing returns would set into this process as employees worked longer hours or additional workers were added to the production process. These devices are now made more quickly and more cheaply, given advances in computer controls and new materials. One producer can make a broach in 11 minutes, down from 222 minutes in 1994. The increased quality of these tools has also allowed surgeons to decrease a typical one-hour procedure by at least 10 minutes.

As hospitals treat increasing numbers of patients, concerns have arisen about how to reduce the number of medical errors and improve patient safety. Errors and accidents are examples of diminishing returns in this production process. Although procedures related to human error, such as encouraging nurses to wash their hands more often and improving physicians' handwriting on prescriptions, have been instituted, changes in the nature of the capital inputs, the hospital buildings themselves, are now being undertaken. Technological innovations include the design of identical rooms so that doctors and nurses can find equipment easily, placing nurses' stations so that all patients are visible, and using filters and ultraviolet devices to trap and kill germs and improve the hospital airflow. These changes have reduced infection rates, injuries from falls, and medication errors, thus lowering patient length of stay, which, in turn, frees up beds and allows hospitals to serve more patients.[7]

In the luxury handbag industry, Louis Vuitton incurred diminishing returns and production shortages from the organization of its production process. Traditionally each factory had approximately 250 employees with each worker specializing in one skill such as cutting leather and canvas, gluing and sewing, or making pockets. Specialists worked on only one batch of bags at a time, while half-completed purses waited on carts until someone wheeled them to the next section of the assembly line. Using techniques from the Japanese auto industry, Vuitton has now organized groups of 6 to 12 workers arranged in clusters of U-shaped workstations containing sewing machines on one side and assembly tables on the other. Workers pass their work around the cluster and are able to make more types of bags because each worker is less specialized.[8]

---

[5] Scott Kilman, "Poultry in Motion: With Invention, Chicken Catching Goes High-Tech," *Wall Street Journal*, June 4, 2003.

[6] Steve Liesman, "U.S. Productivity Gains Driven by Changes in Machine Tools," *Wall Street Journal*, September 28, 2001.

[7] Gautam Naik, "To Reduce Errors, Hospitals Prescribe Innovative Designs," *Wall Street Journal*, May 8, 2006.

[8] Christina Passariello, "Louis Vuitton Tries Modern Methods on Factory Lines," *Wall Street Journal*, October 9, 2006.

Productivity and the Agriculture Industry

New production methods for agricultural crops have led to large increases in productivity in this sector over time. A significant example is an experiment in China that resulted in a doubling of rice crop yields without the use of expensive chemical fungicides.[9] Instead of continuing the practice of planting a single type of rice, farmers planted a mixture of two different types of rice. This change greatly reduced the incidence of rice blast, the major disease of this crop, and, in turn, increased productivity and allowed farmers to abandon expensive chemical treatments of their crops.

Concerns still exist about diminishing returns in rice production as the increased demand for this food staple has caused farmers to increase fertilizer and water use, exhausting the soil and draining the water table. Many rice farmers have also begun planting two crops a year, which places further demands on the soil. Recent technological innovations that have attempted to offset these diminishing returns include developing seed varieties that can withstand droughts or floods, planting rice in dry soil rather than flooded paddies, altering the way rice plants perform photosynthesis, and developing hybrid varieties than can increase yields by as much as 20 percent.[10]

Productivity and the Automobile Industry

The automobile industry is an obvious example of an industry in which huge productivity increases have occurred over time, beginning with Henry Ford's use of the assembly line at the beginning of the twentieth century. However, Japan's use of improved production techniques in the 1970s and 1980s created major problems for the U.S. auto industry. The number of vehicles per worker had ranged between 8 and 15 for both domestic and foreign producers in 1960. Although productivity for General Motors, Ford, and Chrysler remained in that range in 1983, the number of vehicles per worker increased to 42 for Nissan and 58 for Honda in that year.[11]

The Japanese productivity advantage in the early 1980s did not result primarily from differences in technology or labor.[12] Approximately two-thirds of the cost advantage resulted from changes in management focusing on inventory systems, relations with suppliers, and plant layout. Japanese production was organized around a lean and coordinated system, with inventories delivered from nearby suppliers every few hours. Workers could stop the assembly line as soon as problems arose, which improved quality and eliminated the need for repair stations. The organization of the Japanese workforce with far fewer job classifications also gave Japanese plants greater flexibility and less downtime than U.S. plants.

In response to these productivity differences, the U.S. automobile industry has initiated drastic productivity and management changes over the past 20 years, including redesigned production operations, reorganized management procedures, and the closing of outdated plants. Between 1979 and 1998, assembly productivity increased 45 percent at Chrysler and 38 percent at General Motors and Ford. In fact, over the past two decades, these companies narrowed the productivity gap with the Japanese by about one-half. However, while some Ford and Chrysler plants now meet (or exceed) Japanese labor productivity, General Motors is the least efficient firm in the industry—half as productive in its use of labor as Nissan, Toyota, and Honda.

---

[9] Carol Kaesuk Yoon, "Simple Method Found to Vastly Increase Crop Yields," *New York Times*, August 22, 2000.
[10] Patrick Barta, "Feeding Billions, a Grain at a Time," *Wall Street Journal*, July 28, 2007.
[11] Michael A. Cusumano, *The Japanese Automobile Industry* (Cambridge: Harvard University Press, 1985), 187–88.
[12] The discussion of productivity in the automobile industry is based on John E. Kwoka Jr., "Automobiles: Overtaking an Oligopoly," in *Industry Studies*, ed. Larry L. Duetsch, 2nd ed. (Armonk, N.Y.: Sharpe, 1998), 3–27; and James W. Brock, "Automobiles," in *The Structure of American Industry*, eds. Walter Adams and James W. Brock, 10th ed. (Upper Saddle River, N.J.: Prentice Hall, 2001), 114–36.

A recent technological innovation is the use of the Internet to link companies with their auto parts suppliers to facilitate bidding on and executing contracts.[13] Traditionally the supply process involved periodic contracts with thousands of supplier for a variety of parts, components, and general supplies. Bids were evaluated through phone calls and exchange of paper. Ford and GM introduced online supply exchanges in 1999 for price quotes, bidding, and monitoring the physical movement of supplies. Separate exchanges have been replaced by Covisint, which served DaimlerChrysler, Renault S.A., and Nissan Motor Co., in addition to Ford and GM. In early 2007, General Motors announced that it was using Covisint to connect and integrate more than 18,000 production and nonproduction suppliers including firms in Europe, Asia, and Latin America. Cost savings of up to 15 percent of annual purchasing costs have been estimated from the use of this new technology.

Even with more advanced technologies, diminishing returns can still occur in the auto production process. Toyota Motor Corp. has been accelerating its worldwide growth to try to overtake General Motors as the world's No. 1 auto maker. This fast-paced expansion resulted in an increasing number of quality problems in North America, Japan, and elsewhere that threatened Toyota's image. Toyota began to rely more heavily on computer-aided design tools that shorten vehicle-development times by skipping steps such as making physical prototypes to test components. Computer-aided engineering tools also allow potential design flaws to slip through the production process. To overcome these problems, Toyota began adding as much as 3 to 6 more months to projects with a normal development lead time of 2–3 years.[14]

Productivity Changes Across Industries

Productivity changes differ substantially across industries in the United States. While productivity for the overall economy increased 0.45 percent per year from 1958 to 1996, annual growth ranges varied from 1.98 percent in electronic and electric equipment to –0.52 percent in government enterprises.[15]

Data released in 2000 showed accelerating labor productivity in a range of industries, including the service sector and durable goods manufacturing. Many of these productivity gains can be attributed to the increased use of information technology (IT) in these industries.[16]

More recent analyses indicate that information technology accounted for almost 80 percent of the increase in productivity growth in the late 1990s. Each generation of new computer equipment greatly outperformed prior generations. Given large price declines for information technology investment, firms made massive investments in IT equipment and software and substituted IT assets for other productive inputs. The impact of IT on productivity growth declined in both a relative and absolute sense in the post-2000 period with IT investment accounting for about one-third of the productivity growth in this period. This was still a substantial impact, given that IT investment was less than 5 percent of aggregate output.[17]

---

[13] This discussion is based on: John E. Kwoka, Jr., "Automobiles: The Old Economy Collides with the New," *Review of Industrial Organization* 19 (2001): 55–69; and John Larkin, "Global Collaboration Easier, More Productive and Safer," *Automotive Industries* 186 (2) (Second Quarter 2007): 60–61.

[14] Norihiko Shirouzu, "Toyota May Delay New Models to Address Rising Quality Issues," *Wall Street Journal*, August 25, 2006.

[15] Dale W. Jorgenson and Kevin W. Stiroh, "U.S. Economic Growth at the Industry Level," *American Economic Review* 90 (2) (May 2000): 161–67.

[16] Martin Neil Bailey, "The New Economy: Post Mortem or Second Wind?" *Journal of Economic Perspectives* 16 (2) (Spring 2002): 3–22.

[17] Dale W. Jorgensen, Mun S. Ho, and Kevin J. Stiroh, "A Retrospective Look at the U.S. Productivity Growth Resurgence," *Federal Reserve Bank of New York Staff Reports*, no. 277, February 2007.

Model of Short-Run Cost Functions

We now analyze how a firm's costs of production vary in the short run, where at least one input of production is fixed. We first discuss the economic definition of cost and then develop **cost functions** that show the relationship between the cost of production and the level of output, all other factors held constant.

Measuring Opportunity Cost: Explicit Versus Implicit Costs

Cost function
A mathematical or graphic expression that shows the relationship between the cost of production and the level of output, all other factors held constant.

Opportunity cost
The economic measure of cost that reflects the use of resources in one activity, such as a production process by one firm, in terms of the opportunities forgone in undertaking the next best alternative activity.

Explicit cost
A cost that is reflected in a payment to another individual, such as a wage paid to a worker, that is recorded in a firm's bookkeeping or accounting system.

Implicit cost
A cost that represents the value of using a resource that is not explicitly paid out and is often difficult to measure because it is typically not recorded in a firm's accounting system.

Economists have a very specific way of defining the costs of production that managers should, but do not always, consider. To correctly measure all the relevant costs of production, managers need to make certain they are measuring the opportunity costs of the resources they are using. **Opportunity costs** reflect the cost of using resources in one activity (production by one firm) in terms of the opportunities forgone in undertaking the next best alternative activity. In most cases, these costs are **explicit costs** because they are paid to other individuals and are found in a firm's bookkeeping or accounting system. However, even these bookkeeping costs may reflect an accounting definition rather than a true economic definition of opportunity cost. In other cases, these costs are **implicit costs**. This means that although they represent the opportunity cost of using a resource or input to produce a given product, they are not included in a firm's accounting system and may be difficult to measure.

In many cases, the prices that a firm actually pays for its inputs reflect the opportunity cost of using those inputs. For example, if the wages of construction workers are determined by the forces of demand and supply and if all workers who want to work are able to do so, the monetary or explicit cost paid to those workers accurately reflects their opportunity cost or their value in the next best alternative. If the workers are currently employed by Firm A, managers at Firm B must pay a wage at least equal to that paid by Firm A if they want to hire the workers away from Firm A. If a firm leases office space in a building or a farmer rents a plot of land, the explicit rental payments to the owners of these inputs reflect the opportunity cost of using those resources.

What happens if the firm already owns the building or the plot of land? In these cases, there may not be any budgetary or accounting cost recorded. Does this zero accounting cost mean that the opportunity cost of using those resources is also zero? The answer to this question is usually no, because the firm could rent or lease those resources to another producer. If Firm A could rent the office space it owns to Firm B for $100,000 per year, then the opportunity cost to Firm A of using that space in its own production is $100,000 per year. This is an implicit cost if it is not actually included in the firm's accounting system.

If managers do not recognize the concept of opportunity cost, they may have too much investment tied up in the ownership of buildings, given the implicit rate of return on these assets compared with the return on other uses of these resources. For example, Reebok made the strategic decision to contract with other manufacturers around the world to produce its shoes rather than invest in plants and equipment itself. Its managers estimated that there was a greater rate of return from these activities than from investment in buildings.[18]

Another example of an implicit cost is the valuation of the owner's or family member's time in a family-operated business. In such businesses, family members may not explicitly be paid a salary, so the costs of their time may not be included as a cost of production. However, this practice overstates the firm's profitability. If

---

[18] This example is drawn from S. lomo Maital, *Executive Economics* (New York: Free Press, 1994), 30.

the owner or family member could earn $40,000 per year by working in some other activity, that figure represents the opportunity cost of the individual's time in the family business, but this cost may be implicit and not be reflected in any existing financial statement. It does reflect a real cost of using those resources in a production process.

In certain cases, accounting costs may not accurately represent the true opportunity cost of using the resource, given the distinction between historical and opportunity cost. **Historical costs** reflect what the firm paid for an input when it was purchased. For machines and other capital equipment, this cost could have been incurred many years in the past. Firms have their own accounting systems to write off or depreciate this historical cost over the life of the capital equipment. In many cases, these depreciation guidelines are influenced by Internal Revenue Service regulations and other tax considerations. From an opportunity cost perspective, the issue is what that capital equipment could earn in its next best alternative use at the current time. This rate of return may bear little relationship to historical cost or an annual depreciation figure.

Historical cost
The amount of money a firm paid for an input when it was purchased, which for machines and capital equipment could have occurred many years in the past.

Accounting Profit Measures Versus Economic Profit Measures

The other important example of opportunity cost relates to the return on financial capital invested in a firm. If investors can earn 10 percent in an alternative investment of similar risk, this 10 percent return is an implicit cost of production. A firm must pay at least 10 percent on its invested capital to reflect the true opportunity cost of this resource and to prevent investors from placing their money elsewhere. A firm's **profit** is defined as the difference between its total revenue from sales and its total cost of production. Given the different approaches used by accountants and economists, we now distinguish between accounting and economic profit. **Accounting profit** measures typically focus only on the explicit costs of production, whereas **economic profit** measures include both the explicit and the implicit costs of production.

There are numerous problems involved in correctly calculating a firm's economic profit, many of which relate to the value of the capital costs of plant and equipment.[19] The appropriate capital cost measure is an annual rental fee or the price of renting the capital per time period, not the cost of the machine when it was purchased. The rental cost should be based on the replacement cost of the equipment or the long-run cost of purchasing an asset of comparable quality. This rental rate should be calculated after economic depreciation is deducted on the equipment. Economic depreciation reflects the decline in economic value of the equipment, not just an accounting measure, such as straight-line depreciation. Advertising and research and development expenditures also create problems for the calculation of economic profit because, as with capital equipment, the benefits of these expenditures typically extend over a number of years. Economic profit should also be calculated on an after-tax basis and adjusted for different degrees of risk because investors generally dislike risk and must be compensated for it.

This distinction between accounting and economic profit has played an important role at the Coca-Cola Company.[20] Coca-Cola had long followed a strategy of obtaining its resources through equity financing—selling stock to shareholders—rather than debt financing—borrowing from banks. Thus, the company had very low explicit interest payments on its books. Realizing that shareholders could also invest elsewhere, former CEO Roberto Goizueta calculated that the opportunity

Profit
The difference between the total revenue a firm receives from the sale of its output and the total cost of producing that output.

Accounting profit
The difference between total revenue and total cost where cost includes only the explicit costs of production.

Economic profit
The difference between total revenue and total cost where cost includes both the explicit and any implicit costs of production.

---

[19] This discussion is based on Dennis W. Carlton and Jeffrey M. Perloff, *Modern Industrial Organization*, 4th ed. (Boston: Pearson Addison Wesley, 2005), 247–53.
[20] This example is drawn from Maital, *Executive Economics*, 23–25.

cost of the shareholders' equity capital was a 16 percent rate of return. He then learned that all Coke's business activities except soft drinks and juices returned only 8 to 10 percent per year. Coca-Cola was essentially borrowing money from shareholders at 16 percent per year and paying them only an 8 percent return. These opportunity costs are difficult to detect because Coke's treasurer did not write an annual check for 16 percent of the company's equity capital. The cost was reflected in Coke's capital stock growing less rapidly than it could have grown.

Goizueta's response to this management problem was to turn an implicit cost into an explicit cost:[21]

> His solution was first, to sell off those businesses whose capital made a lower return—i.e., less than 16 percent—than it cost, and second, introduce a system of accounting in which every operating division of Coca Cola knew precisely its *economic profit*. What he meant by economic profit was sales revenue minus operating costs, including an opportunity-cost charge for capital. Those divisions earning a 16 percent return on their shareholder's capital were told that their *economic* profit was zero. And each division's operations were judged solely on the basis of the *economic* profit it earned. The results of doing so at Coca Cola were not slow in coming. "When you start charging people for their capital," Goizueta said, "all sorts of things happen. All of a sudden, inventories get under control. You don't have three months' concentrate sitting around for an emergency. Or you figure out that you can save a lot of money by replacing stainless-steel containers with cardboard and plastic."

Managerial Rule of Thumb

The Importance of Opportunity Costs

Measuring true opportunity costs can be difficult for managers because accountants are trained to examine and measure costs explicitly paid out. Valuing implicit costs may seem like an imaginary exercise to accountants. However, as in the Coca-Cola example, managers must recognize the importance of these costs and devise strategies for turning implicit costs into explicit costs that can be used for strategic decision making. ■

Definition of Short-Run Cost Functions

Short-run cost function
A cost function for a short-run production process in which there is at least one fixed input of production.

A **short-run cost function** shows the relationship between output and cost for a firm based on the underlying short-run production function we looked at earlier in the chapter. Thus, the shapes of the marginal and average product curves in Figure 5.1b influence the shapes of the short-run cost curves, or how costs change as production is increased or decreased. Given that the production function shows only the technology of how inputs are combined to produce outputs, we must introduce an additional piece of information, the prices of the inputs of production, to define cost functions. To continue with the example presented in Table 5.1, Equation 5.2, and Figures 5.1a and 5.1b, we define P_L as the price per unit of labor (the variable input) and P_K as the price per unit of capital (the fixed input). The former can be thought of as the wage rate per worker, while the latter can be considered the price per square foot of office space or the price per acre of land.

We use this information on production and input prices to define the family of short-run cost functions in Table 5.3. Even though we define some of the cost functions in Table 5.3 in terms of the inputs of production (labor and capital), we show numerical and graphical relationships between costs and the level of output (costs as

---

[21] Ibid., 24–25.

TABLE 5.3 Short-Run Cost Functions (Based on the production function in Equation 5.2 and input prices P_L and P_K)

COST FUNCTION	DEFINITION
Total fixed cost	$TFC = (P_K)\,(\bar{K})$
Total variable cost	$TVC = (P_L)\,(L)$
Total cost	$TC = TFC + TVC$
Average fixed cost	$AFC = TFC/Q$
Average variable cost	$AVC = TVC/Q$
Average total cost	$ATC = TC/Q = AFC + AVC$
Marginal cost	$MC = \Delta TC/\Delta Q = \Delta TVC/\Delta Q$

a function of output). The underlying production function gives us the relationship between the level of labor input (L) and the resulting level of output (Q).

Fixed Costs Versus Variable Costs

Three categories of costs—total, average, and marginal, with further subdivisions between fixed and variable costs—are shown in Table 5.3. **Total fixed cost** is the cost of using the fixed input, $\bar{K}$. It is defined as the price per unit of capital times the quantity of capital (i.e., price per square foot of office space times the number of square feet). Because the quantity of capital does not change, total fixed cost remains constant regardless of the amount of output produced. **Total variable cost** is defined as the price per unit of labor (or wage rate) times the quantity of labor input. This cost does change when different levels of output are produced because it reflects the use of the variable input. **Total cost** is the sum of total fixed and total variable costs.

Each of the average costs listed in Table 5.3 is the respective total cost variable divided by the amount of output produced. **Average fixed cost** is the total fixed cost per unit of output, while **average variable cost** is the total variable cost per unit of output. As you can see in Table 5.3, **average total cost** is defined as total cost per unit of output, but it also equals average fixed cost plus average variable cost. This equivalence results from the fact that $TC = TFC + TVC$. Dividing each one of these terms by Q gives the relationship $ATC = AFC + AVC$.

Marginal cost is the additional cost of producing an additional unit of output. As you can see in Table 5.3, $MC = \Delta TC/\Delta Q = \Delta TVC/\Delta Q$. This equivalence results from the fact that marginal cost shows the changes in costs as output changes. Total variable costs change as the level of output varies, but total fixed costs are constant regardless of the level of output. Therefore, total fixed costs do *not* influence the marginal costs of production, and the above definition holds.

Table 5.4 presents short-run cost functions that are based on the production function from Table 5.1, a price per unit of capital of $50, and a price per unit of labor of $100.

Relationships Among Total, Average, and Marginal Costs

The first three columns of Table 5.4 show the production function drawn from Table 5.1. Total fixed cost (Column 4) shows the total cost of using the fixed input, which remains constant at $500 ($50 per unit times 10 units), regardless of the amount of output produced. Total variable cost in Column 5 ($100 times the number of units of labor used) increases as more output is produced. Total cost (Column 6) is the sum of total fixed and total variable costs.

Total fixed cost
The total cost of using the fixed input, which remains constant regardless of the amount of output produced.

Total variable cost
The total cost of using the variable input, which increases as more output is produced.

Total cost
The sum of the total fixed cost plus the total variable cost.

Average fixed cost
The total fixed cost per unit of output.

Average variable cost
The total variable cost per unit of output.

Average total cost
The total cost per unit of output, which also equals average fixed cost plus average variable cost.

Marginal cost
The additional cost of producing an additional unit of output, which equals the change in total cost or the change in total variable cost as output changes.

TABLE 5.4 Short-Run Cost Functions (Based on the production function from Table 5.1 and input prices P_K = $50 and P_L = $100)

K (1)	L (2)	TP = Q (3)	TFC (4)	TVC (5)	TC (6)	AFC (7)	AVC (8)	ATC (9)	MC (10)
10	0	0	$500	$0	$500				
10	1	14	$500	$100	$600	$35.71	$7.14	$42.85	$7.14
10	2	35	$500	$200	$700	$14.29	$5.71	$20.00	$4.76
10	3	62	$500	$300	$800	$8.06	$4.84	$12.90	$3.70
10	4	91	$500	$400	$900	$5.49	$4.40	$9.89	$3.45
10	5	121	$500	$500	$1,000	$4.13	$4.13	$8.26	$3.33
10	6	150	$500	$600	$1,100	$3.33	$4.00	$7.33	$3.45
10	7	175	$500	$700	$1,200	$2.86	$4.00	$6.86	$4.00
10	8	197	$500	$800	$1,300	$2.54	$4.06	$6.60	$4.55
10	9	212	$500	$900	$1,400	$2.36	$4.25	$6.61	$6.67
10	10	217	$500	$1,000	$1,500	$2.30	$4.61	$6.91	$20.00

Average fixed cost (Column 7) decreases continuously as more output is produced. This relationship follows from the definition of average fixed cost, which is total fixed cost per unit of output. Because total fixed cost is constant, average fixed cost must decline as output increases and spreads the total fixed cost over a larger number of units of output. Both average variable cost (Column 8) and average total cost (Column 9) first decrease and then increase. We can see that average total cost always equals average fixed cost plus average variable cost. Marginal cost (Column 10) also first decreases and then increases much more rapidly than either average variable cost or average total cost.

Figures 5.2a and 5.2b show the typical shapes for graphs of the total, average, and marginal cost curves. Although these graphs illustrate the relationships in Table 5.5, they are drawn to present the general case of these functions.

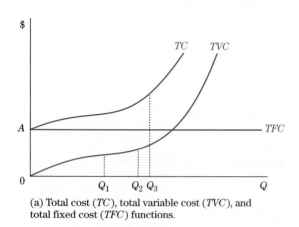

(a) Total cost (*TC*), total variable cost (*TVC*), and total fixed cost (*TFC*) functions.

(b) Marginal cost (*MC*), average total cost (*ATC*), average variable cost (*AVC*), and average fixed cost (*AFC*) functions.

FIGURE 5.2

Short-Run Cost Functions

The short-run total cost functions in Figure 5.2a are related to the average and marginal cost functions in Figure 5.2b.

In Figure 5.2a, total fixed costs (*TFC*) are represented by a horizontal line, as these costs are constant regardless of the level of output produced. Notice that these fixed costs are incurred *even at a zero level of output*. If land is rented or office space is leased, these costs must be covered even if no output is produced with those fixed inputs. Total variable costs, on the other hand, are zero when no output is produced because the variable input is used only when there is a positive amount of output. Total variable costs are shown as increasing slowly at first and then more rapidly as output increases. The total cost curve has the same general shape as the total variable cost curve because the distance between the two curves is total fixed cost, which is constant ($TC = TFC + TVC \Rightarrow TFC = TC - TVC$). The total cost of producing zero units of output is represented by the distance $0A$, or the amount of the fixed costs. The total fixed cost is the vertical distance between the total cost and total variable cost curves at any level of output.[22]

In Figure 5.2b, the average fixed cost curve is declining throughout the range of production for the reasons discussed above. Both average variable cost and average total cost are drawn as U-shaped curves, showing that these average costs first decrease, reach a minimum point, and then increase. Average total cost lies above average variable cost at every unit of output, but the distance between the two curves decreases as output increases, as that distance represents average fixed cost, which is declining ($ATC = AFC + AVC \Rightarrow AFC = ATC - AVC$).

Marginal cost in Figure 5.2b is also a U-shaped curve, showing that marginal cost first decreases, reaches a minimum level, and then increases very rapidly as output increases. Why would a marginal cost curve typically have this shape? Look back at Figure 5.1b, which shows the short-run production function that underlies these cost functions. Notice the range of diminishing returns or declining marginal product in Figure 5.1b. If the additional output obtained from using an additional unit of labor input is decreasing, then marginal cost, or the additional cost of producing another unit of output, must be increasing. Thus, the explanation for the upward sloping short-run marginal cost curve is the existence of diminishing returns in the short-run production function.

Likewise, the shape of the average variable cost curve in Figure 5.2b is determined by the shape of the underlying average product curve in Figure 5.1b. When average product increases, average variable cost decreases. If average product decreases, average variable cost increases.

Also observe in Figure 5.2b that the marginal cost curve intersects the average variable cost curve at its minimum point and the average total cost curve at its minimum point. This is the same average-marginal relationship that we discussed when describing the short-run production function. If marginal cost is less than average variable cost, as shown between zero and Q_2 units of output in Figure 5.2b, average variable cost is decreasing. Beyond Q_2 units of output, marginal cost is greater than average variable cost, so average variable cost is increasing. Thus, the marginal cost curve must intersect the average variable cost curve at its minimum point, or Q_2 units of output.

The same relationships hold between marginal cost and average total cost. Marginal cost is less than average total cost up to Q_3 units of output. This causes average total cost to decrease in this range. Beyond Q_3 units of output, marginal cost is greater than average total cost, so average total cost increases.

---

[22] In Table 5.4 total variable cost and total cost may look as if they are increasing at a constant rate. When these costs are plotted against the level of output, not the level of input, they exhibit the shapes of the curves in Figure 5.2a.

TABLE 5.5 Short-Run Production and Cost Functions

COST/PRODUCTION RELATIONSHIP	DERIVATION
Relationship between marginal cost (MC) and marginal product of labor (MP_L)	$MC = \dfrac{\Delta TVC}{\Delta Q} = \dfrac{(P_L)(\Delta L)}{\Delta Q}$ $MC = \dfrac{P_L}{(\Delta Q / \Delta L)} = \dfrac{P_L}{MP_L}$
Relationship between average variable cost (AVC) and average product of labor (AP_L)	$AVC = \dfrac{TVC}{Q} = \dfrac{(P_L)(L)}{Q}$ $AVC = \dfrac{P_L}{(Q/L)} = \dfrac{P_L}{AP_L}$

Thus, the marginal cost curve must cut the average total cost curve at its minimum point, or Q_3 units of output. The only difference in this marginal-average relationship between the production and cost functions is that the marginal cost curve intersects the average cost curves at their minimum points, whereas the marginal product curve intersects the average product curve at its maximum point. This intersection occurs at either a maximum or a minimum point of the average curves.

Relationship Between Short-Run Production and Cost

The relationships we've described in this chapter show the influence of the underlying production technology on the costs of production. These relationships, based on the production function defined in Equation 5.2 and graphed in Figures 5.1a and 5.1b, are explored further in Table 5.5. This table shows that marginal cost and marginal product are inversely related to each other, as are average variable cost and average product. The derivation in the right column of Table 5.5 uses the definitions of marginal cost and average variable cost to show the inverse relationship between these costs and marginal product and average product, respectively. These relationships are shown graphically in Figures 5.3a and 5.3b.

Figures 5.3a and 5.3b show the relationship between short-run production and cost functions. In these figures, labor input level L_1 is used to produce output level Q_1, while labor input level L_2 is used to produce output level Q_2. The graphs

FIGURE 5.3
The Relationship Between Short-Run Production and Cost
The shape of the short-run production function in Figure 5.3a determines the shape of the short-run cost function in Figure 5.3b.

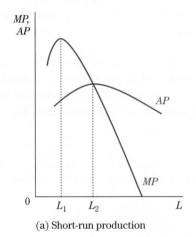

(a) Short-run production

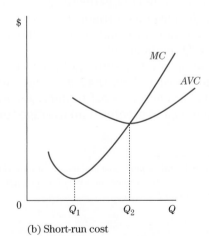

(b) Short-run cost

clearly show the inverse relationship between the product and cost variables. The marginal product of labor increases up to L_1 input level, so the marginal cost of production decreases up to Q_1 units of output. The decreasing marginal product beyond L_1 units of labor (diminishing returns) causes the marginal cost curve to rise beyond Q_1 units of output. The average product curve increases, reaches its maximum at L_2 units of input, and then decreases. This causes the average variable cost curve to decrease, reach a minimum value at Q_2 units of output, and then increase.

Other Short-Run Production and Cost Functions

We have argued that the underlying production function determines the shapes of the short-run cost curves, and we have illustrated the standard case with a marginal product curve that first increases and then decreases, resulting in decreasing and then increasing marginal cost. These traditional-shaped curves result from diminishing returns in the production function as increased variable inputs are used relative to the amount of the fixed inputs.

Consider an alternative set of production and cost curves shown in Figures 5.4a, 5.4b, 5.4c, and 5.4d. Figure 5.4a shows a linear total product curve that results in the constant marginal product curve in Figure 5.4b. This production function exhibits constant, and not diminishing, returns to the variable input, labor. Because the marginal product of labor is constant, the average product is also constant and equal to the marginal product. Although diminishing returns will eventually set in for this production process as the firm approaches the maximum capacity of its fixed inputs, the production relationships shown in Figures 5.4a and 5.4b may be valid over a wide range of input and output.

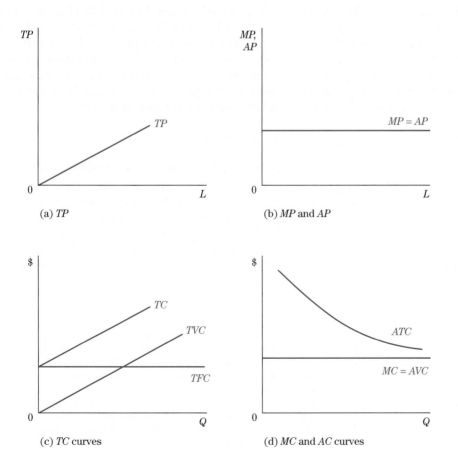

(a) *TP*   (b) *MP* and *AP*

(c) *TC* curves   (d) *MC* and *AC* curves

FIGURE 5.4
Alternative Short-Run Production and Cost Functions
The underlying production function influences the costs of production.

The implications of this production function for the costs of production are shown in Figures 5.4c and 5.4d. If marginal product is constant over this range of output, marginal cost must be constant also. There are no diminishing returns in the production function that would cause the marginal cost of further production to increase. Because marginal cost is constant, average variable cost is also constant and equal to marginal cost. Average total cost decreases throughout because it is being pulled down by the declining average fixed cost. Marginal cost must be less than average total cost because average total cost is decreasing. Because marginal cost is constant, the total cost and total variable cost functions must be linear, with the difference between the two curves equal to total fixed cost.

Managerial Rule of Thumb

Understanding Your Costs

Managers need to understand how their firm's technology and prices paid for the inputs of production affect the firm's costs. They need to know the difference between costs that change with output (variable costs) and those that are unrelated to the output level (fixed costs). They also need to understand the difference between average cost (cost per unit of output) and marginal cost (the additional cost of producing an additional unit of output). ∎

Empirical Evidence on the Shapes of Short-Run Cost Functions

Although we use the standard U-shaped cost curves (Figure 5.2b) for most of our theoretical analysis, much empirical evidence on the behavior of costs for real-world firms and industries indicates that total cost functions are linear and, therefore, marginal and average variable costs are constant for a wide range of output (Figure 5.4d). There is even some evidence that firms may produce where marginal cost is decreasing. Researchers have based their conclusions on both the econometric estimation of cost functions and surveys of firms' behavior.[23]

Econometric Estimation of Cost Functions

Much of the empirical estimation of cost functions was undertaken in the 1940s, 1950s, and 1960s.[24] Joel Dean's classic studies of a furniture factory, a leather belt shop, and a hosiery mill all showed that a linear total cost function best fit the data. These studies examined data sets where the plant, equipment, and technology were relatively constant over the data period analyzed. Jack Johnston estimated cost functions for British electric generating plants, road passenger transport, and a multiproduct food processing firm. From both his own estimation work and a

---

[23] A focus on the average total cost of production may predate modern economic theory. Between 1800 and 1805, German sheet music publisher Gottfried Christoph Hartel calculated the average total cost of printing sheet music using two different technologies: engraving and printing with movable type. His calculations for engraved music implied a linear total cost function with a fixed setup cost of 900 Pfennigs per sheet and a constant marginal cost of 5 Pfennigs per sheet. These calculations influenced his decision not to publish Ludwig van Beethoven's early works, for which sales volumes were uncertain and average total costs were high, but to publish a number of the composer's later works. See F. M. Scherer, "An Early Application of the Average Total Cost Concept," *Journal of Economic Literature* 39 (September 2001): 897–901.

[24] J. Johnston, *Statistical Cost Analysis* (New York: McGraw-Hill, 1960); Joel Dean, *Statistical Cost Estimation* (Bloomington: Indiana University Press, 1976).

comprehensive survey of existing studies, Johnston concluded that a constant marginal cost and declining average total cost best characterized the cost-output data for a wide variety of firms.

Recent studies have used much more sophisticated econometric techniques and have estimated cost structures in the context of larger decisions such as inventory management. Analyzing the food, tobacco, apparel, chemical, petroleum, and rubber industries from 1959 to 1984 and the automobile industry from 1966 to 1979, one researcher found evidence for declining marginal costs of production.[25] To determine whether these results were related to the use of industry-level data, this researcher reestimated cost equations for 10 divisions of the automobile industry and still found evidence of declining marginal costs. Other researchers[26] developed elaborate models of firm pricing behavior that are consistent with a constant marginal cost of production.

Survey Results on Cost Functions

Although some early work used a survey or questionnaire approach to make inferences about firms' cost functions, most of the more recent research studies have been econometric analyses. One notable exception is the survey by Alan Blinder and his colleagues at Princeton University in the early 1990s.[27] Blinder and his colleagues drew a sample of 333 firms in the private, unregulated, nonfarm, for-profit sector of the economy, 200 of which participated in the survey.

The researchers asked officials in these companies a series of structured questions designed to test alternative theories about why firms do not change prices regularly in response to changing economic conditions. Although the main goal of the survey was to test hypotheses about price stickiness, the researchers included a number of questions about the firms' cost structures.

Officials in firms responding to the survey reported on average that 44 percent of their costs were fixed and 56 percent were variable. If these results can be generalized to the entire economy, fixed costs appear to be more important to firms than is shown in the standard cost curves of economic theory (see Figure 5.2b). Fixed costs were less important in wholesale and retail trade (mean of 33 percent) and construction and mining (mean of 29 percent) and more important in transportation, communications, and utilities (mean of 53 percent) and services (mean of 56 percent). The researchers found that many executives did not think in terms of fixed versus variable costs. Eighteen executives, or 9 percent of the sample, did not answer the question.

The researchers also had difficulty asking whether marginal cost varied with production because many executives were not familiar with this concept. The researchers had to frame the question in terms of the "variable costs of producing additional units." The researchers often had to repeat, rephrase, or explain the question to executives who did not understand the concept. Even with this effort, 10 interviewees were unable to provide an answer. The responses to this question were quite surprising in light of standard economic theory.

Forty-eight percent of the respondents indicated that their marginal costs were constant, 41 percent said they were decreasing, and only 11 percent responded that their marginal costs were increasing. Although some, if not many, respondents may

---

[25] Valerie A. Ramey, "Nonconvex Costs and the Behavior of Inventories," *Journal of Political Economy* 99 (1991): 306–34.

[26] Robert E. Hall, "Market Structure and Macroeconomic Fluctuations," *Brookings Papers on Economic Activity* 2 (1986): 285–322; Robert E. Hall, "The Relation Between Price and Marginal Cost in U.S. Industry," *Journal of Political Economy* 96 (1988): 921–47.

[27] Alan S. Blinder, Elie R. D. Canetti, David E. Lebow, and Jeremy B. Rudd, *Asking About Prices: A New Approach to Understanding Price Stickiness* (New York: Sage, 1998).

have confused marginal and average costs and may really have been reporting that their average costs were decreasing, this survey response indicates that business executives do not perceive the textbook U-shaped marginal cost curve to be relevant in many situations.

Constant Versus Rising Marginal Cost Curves

Some of this discrepancy between textbook U-shaped cost curves and real-world constant or declining marginal cost curves can be explained by the fact that economic theory shows the range of possibilities for the cost relationships, not what actually exists in different firms and industries. Econometric estimation based on real-world data and surveys of executives may show constant or declining marginal cost for the range of output that the firm is actually producing. Even if firms are currently producing with constant marginal cost, they will, at some point, reach the capacity of their fixed inputs, which will cause marginal cost to increase.

Another explanation for the discrepancy regarding the shapes of the cost curves relates to the differences between agricultural and manufacturing production.[28] The concept of diminishing returns and rising short-run marginal cost—with its emphasis on the fixed, indivisible factors of production, such as land, and on the variable, divisible factors, such as labor, which change in proportion to the use of the fixed factors—was derived from agricultural settings. That producers experience diminishing returns is very plausible when adding additional amounts of labor, capital equipment, seed, and fertilizer to a fixed amount of land. There is no need to distinguish between the *stock* of the fixed input, land, and the *flow* of services derived from it. The land provides services continuously and is not turned off at night.

However, this model may be less appropriate in manufacturing and industrial settings. Much research has indicated that inputs in these settings are likely to be used in fixed proportions up to the capacity of the plant. Although the stock of a fixed input is fixed, the flow of services from that stock may be varied and combined with the services of a variable input in fixed proportions. The size of a machine may be fixed, but the number of hours it is put in operation can be varied. Both capital and labor *services* are variable in the short run and can be changed together in fixed proportions, thus preventing diminishing returns and rising marginal costs from occurring in many manufacturing operations.

In manufacturing assembly operations, the normal work period of the plant is used to adjust the level of output in the short run. For example, automobile assembly plants use a relatively fixed number of employees per shift and a pre-set speed for the flow of materials and components through the line. Output can be adjusted by changing the length of existing shifts or adding additional shifts in the face of changing demand. Other assembly operations, such as a collection of sewing machines in clothing manufacturing, are organized around workstations rather than a rigid assembly line. Output is varied in these operations by changing the duration and intensity of the work period at the individual workstations. In continuous processing operations, such as oil refineries, steel mills, cement plants, and paper mills, plants operate nearly 24 hours per day, 7 days

---

[28] This discussion is based on C. Corrado and J. Mattey, "Capacity Utilization," *Journal of Economic Perspectives* 11 (1997): 151–67; Richard A. Miller, "Ten Cheaper Spades: Production Theory and Cost Curves in the Short Run," *Journal of Economic Education* 31 (Spring 2000): 119–30; and Richard A. Miller, "Firms' Cost Functions: A Reconstruction," *Review of Industrial Organization* 18 (2001): 183–200.

per week, given the large shutdown and start-up costs. Output is typically varied by shutting down part or all of the plant. In all of these cases, output is adjusted by increasing or decreasing the amount of capital and labor services in constant proportion so that diminishing returns do not occur and a constant marginal cost can be maintained.

There may be areas other than manufacturing where this type of production technology is applicable. For example, even though the size of a restaurant is fixed, managers may shut down part of the table space, given a lack of demand. Once again, the services of the fixed input are varied even though the stock is constant. These services can then be used in a fixed proportion with other variable inputs, such as labor, to avoid the problem of rising marginal cost.

Implications for Managers

Costs play an important role in determining an effective competitive strategy, particularly if a firm does not have much control over the price of its product. The distinction between fixed and variable costs is important, as is the concept of marginal cost. However, as noted in the survey by Blinder and his colleagues, many executives and managers are not familiar with these concepts. Cost accounting systems often focus more on management, control, and Internal Revenue Service considerations than on concepts useful for decision making. It may also be more difficult for managers to cut costs when firms are profitable than when they are not because it may be less obvious that competitors are catching up.[29]

Lack of knowledge about costs is not a recent phenomenon. Even though Henry Ford pioneered the use of mass production and the assembly line as a cost-cutting measure, he disliked bookkeepers and accountants. Shlomo Maital tells the following story:

> Once, walking into a room, Henry Ford asked an aide what the white-collar workers in the room do. Told they were accountants, he ordered, "I want them all fired. They're not productive, they don't do any real work." The result was chaos, as Arjay Miller (who later became president) discovered. Miller was asked to obtain a monthly estimate of Ford company profits. Doing so required estimates of revenues and costs. Sales projections were fairly straightforward. But Miller was amazed to learn that the Ford Motor Co. estimated its costs by dividing its bills into four piles (small, medium, large, extra-large), guessing at the average sum of the bills in each pile, *then measuring the height of each pile* and multiplying the height in inches by average bill size. The system was not unlike that used 20 years earlier; when piles of bills were not quite so unwieldy, the understaffed accountants had weighed them.[30]

Maital also relates how Akio Morita, the founder of Sony Corp., made a better strategic decision for his company based on his knowledge of the costs of production. In 1955, Morita was trying to market a small, cheap, practical transistor radio in the United States. Several buyers asked for price quotes on 5,000, 10,000, 30,000, 50,000, and 100,000 units. Because Sony's current capacity was less than 1,000 radios per month, Morita knew that the entire production process would have to be expanded to fill these large orders and that this would impact the costs of

---

[29] This insight is drawn from Maital, *Executive Economics*, 76.
[30] Ibid., 69.

production. Morita essentially drew the economist's U-shaped average cost curve showing that he would charge the regular price for 5,000 units and a discount for 10,000 units, but successively higher prices for 30,000, 50,000, and 100,000 units. These higher prices reflected increased short-run average and marginal costs of production.[31]

Summary

We have discussed and illustrated short-run production and cost in this chapter. The discussion has focused on production functions where there is at least one fixed input. These production functions all eventually incur diminishing returns when increased units of the variable inputs are used relative to the amount of the fixed inputs and the additional amount of output produced begins to decline. Diminishing returns are fundamental to all short-run production processes.

We then illustrated the impact of the production function on the costs of production. Diminishing returns in production cause short-run marginal cost to increase for a producer. We saw how the U-shaped cost curves of economic theory show the full range of outcomes in a production process, but that real-world cost curves may have different shapes. Marginal cost may be constant over a wide range of output as managers take steps to prevent diminishing returns from occurring immediately. We also discussed the concept of opportunity cost, which measures the value of any resource in terms of its next best alternative use. Economists use this concept when discussing cost, and managers should use it for correct decision making. The latter do not always do so, given the problems in correctly measuring opportunity costs.

In the next chapter, we examine long-run production and cost, where all inputs in a production function are variable. This discussion focuses on input substitution and the shape of the long-run average cost curve. The issues in both of these chapters are fundamental to the discussion of pricing and other competitive strategies in Chapters 7 through 10.

Key Terms

accounting profit, p. 125	increasing marginal returns, p. 120	opportunity cost, p. 124
average fixed cost, p. 127	law of diminishing marginal returns or law of the diminishing marginal product, p. 120	production function, p. 114
average product, p. 117		profit, p. 125
average total cost, p. 127		short-run cost function, p. 126
averaged variable cost, p. 127	long-run production function, p. 116	short-run production function, p. 116
cost function, p. 124	marginal cost, p. 127	total cost, p. 127
economic profit, p. 125	marginal product, p. 117	total fixed cost, p. 127
explicit cost, p. 124	negative marginal returns, p. 120	total product, p. 117
fixed input, p. 115		total variable cost, p. 127
historical cost, p. 125		variable input, p. 115
implicit cost, p. 124		

---

[31] Ibid., 66–68.

Exercises

Technical Questions

1. The following table shows data for a simple production function.

Capital (K)	Labor (L)	Total Product (TP)	Average Product (AP)	Marginal Product (MP)
10	0	0	—	—
10	1	5		
10	2	15		
10	3	30		
10	4	50		
10	5	75		
10	6	85		
10	7	90		
10	8	92		
10	9	92		
10	10	90		

a. From the information in the table, calculate marginal and average products.
b. Graph the three functions (put total product on one graph and marginal and average products on another).
c. For what range of output does this function have diminishing marginal returns?
d. At what output is average product maximized?

2. The following table shows data for a simple production function.

Capital (K)	Labor (L)	Total Product (TP)	Average Product (AP)	Marginal Product (MP)
10	0		—	—
10	1			25
10	2			75
10	3			120
10	4			83
10	5			54
10	6			35
10	7			22
10	8			10
10	9			4
10	10			1

a. From the information in the table, calculate total and average products.
b. Graph the three functions (put total product on one graph and marginal and average products on another).
c. For what range of output does this function have diminishing marginal returns?
d. At what output is average product maximized?

3. Jim is considering quitting his job and using his savings to start a small business. He expects that his costs will consist of a lease on the building, inventory, wages for two workers, electricity, and insurance.
   a. Identify which costs are explicit and which are opportunity (implicit) costs.
   b. Identify which costs are fixed and which are variable.

4. Jill resigns from her job, at which she was earning $50,000 per year, and uses her $100,000 savings, on which she was earning 5 percent interest, to start a business. In the first year, she earns revenue of $150,000, and her costs are as follows:

Rent	$25,000
Utilities	$12,000
Wages	$30,000
Materials	$20,000

a. Calculate Jill's accounting profit.
b. Calculate Jill's economic profit.

5. The following table shows data for the simple production function used in Question 1. Capital costs this firm $20 per unit, and labor costs $10 per worker.

K	L	TP	TFC	TVC	TC	AFC	AVC	ATC	MC
10	0	0							
10	1	5							
10	2	15							
10	3	30							
10	4	50							
10	5	75							
10	6	85							
10	7	90							
10	8	92							

a. From the information in the table, calculate total fixed cost (TFC), total variable cost (TVC), total cost (TC), average fixed cost (AFC), average variable cost (AVC), average total cost (ATC), and marginal cost (MC).
b. Graph your results, putting TFC, TVC, and TC on one graph and AFC, AVC, ATC, and MC on another.
c. At what point is average total cost minimized? At what point is average variable cost minimized?

6. The following table shows data for the simple production function used in Question 2. Capital costs this firm $50 per unit, and labor costs $20 per worker.
   a. From the information in the table, calculate total fixed cost (TFC), total variable cost

(TVC), total cost (TC), average fixed cost (AFC), average variable cost (AVC), average total cost (ATC), and marginal cost (MC). (Note that in this case, you are starting from MP, not TP, and, thus, you should calculate TP first if you didn't already do that in Question 2.)

K	L	MP	TFC	TVC	TC	AFC	AVC	ATC	MC
10	0	—			—				—
10	1	25							
10	2	75							
10	3	120							
10	4	83							
10	5	54							
10	6	35							
10	7	22							
10	8	10							
10	9	4							
10	10	1							

b. Graph your results, putting TFC, TVC, and TC on one graph and AVC, ATC, and MC on another.

c. At what point is average total cost minimized? At what point is average variable cost minimized?

7. Consider the shape of the production and cost functions for two different firms.

a. For Firm 1, workers have constant marginal product. That is, each worker produces exactly the same amount as the previous worker. Use this information to graph the approximate shape of the firm's short-run product and cost curves.

b. For Firm 2, workers have diminishing marginal returns everywhere. That is, each worker always produces less than the previous worker. Use this information to graph the approximate shape of the firm's short-run product and cost curves.

8. How would an improvement in technology that increased the marginal productivity of labor change the firm's cost curves?

9. Suppose that a firm's only variable input is labor. When 50 workers are used, the average product of labor is 50, and the marginal product of the 50th worker is 75. The wage rate is $80, and the total cost of the fixed input is $500.

a. What is average variable cost? Show your calculations.

b. What is marginal cost? Show your calculations.

c. What is average total cost? Show your calculations.

d. Is each of the following statements true or false? Explain your answer.

1. Marginal cost is increasing.
2. Average variable cost is increasing.
3. Average total cost is decreasing.

Application Questions

1. In the fast-food industry article that opened this chapter, describe how diminishing returns set in for the production process and how management responded to this situation.

2. The following information about pharmaceutical manufacturing was reported in Leila Abboud and Scott Hensley, "New Prescription for Drug Makers: Update the Plants," *Wall Street Journal*, September 3, 2003:

> The Food and Drug Administration (FDA) has concluded that the pharmaceutical industry needs to adopt manufacturing innovations, partly to raise quality standards. In other industries, manufacturers constantly change their production lines to find improvements. But FDA regulations leave drug-manufacturing processes virtually frozen in time. As part of the drug-approval process, a company's detailed manufacturing plan—and even the factory itself—must obtain FDA approval. After approval, even a tiny change in how a drug is produced requires another round of FDA review and authorization that involves time and paperwork.
>
> Quality testing is done by hand. Computerized equipment and robots are not used as commonly as in other high-tech industries. Most pharmaceuticals are made according to recipes that involve many separate steps. Each step produces an intermediate batch of chemicals that must be stored, sometimes for long periods. Only then can the process move on to the next step. Gauging the dryness of a batch requires a technician to stop a dryer, break a vacuum seal, and pluck a sample by hand for testing in a specialized laboratory. Before the concoction can move on, a worker might have to wait hours for test results.
>
> Under the old system for testing for bacterial contamination, a scientist looked for contamination by peering through a microscope to count colonies of organisms in a petri dish.

a. Describe how diminishing returns are likely to set in for the pharmaceutical production process.

b. Why do you think the FDA allowed firms to maintain these types of production processes?

3. The following discussion based on Gabriel Kahn, "Made to Measure: Invisible Supplier Has Penney's Shirts All Buttoned Up," *Wall Street Journal*, September 11, 2003, describes a new inventory system used by J.C. Penney:

> In an industry where the goal is rapid turnaround of merchandise, J.C. Penney stores now hold almost no extra inventory of house-brand shirts. Less than a decade ago, Penney would have stored thousands of them in warehouses across the U.S., tying up capital and slowly going out of style.

> The entire program is designed and operated by TAL Apparel Ltd., a closely held Hong Kong shirt maker. TAL collects point-of-sale data for Penney's shirts directly from its stores in North America for analysis through a computer model it designed. The Hong Kong company then decides how many shirts to make, and in what styles, colors, and sizes. The manufacturer sends the shirts directly to each Penney store, bypassing the retailer's warehouses and corporate decision makers.

a. Discuss how this case illustrates the concept of the opportunity cost of capital.

b. How does this innovation also help in demand management?

4. Explain why a change in a firm's total fixed cost of production will shift its average total cost curve, but not its marginal cost curve.

5. Is it true that in a short-run production process, the marginal cost curve eventually slopes upward because firms have to pay workers a higher wage rate as they produce more output? Explain your answer.

On the Web

For updated information on the *New York Times* article at the beginning of the chapter, as well as other relevant links and information, visit the book's Web site at **www.pearsonhighered.com/farnham**

Production and Cost Analysis in the Long Run

I
n this chapter, we examine production and cost issues in the long run, where all inputs in a production process are variable. In doing so, we'll build on the short-run production and cost issues we discussed in the previous chapter. As you'll learn in this chapter, a manager faces more decisions in the long run because it is possible to change the combination of all inputs used in the production process.

We begin this chapter with the *Wall Street Journal* article "A Tale of Two Auto Plants," which illustrates the differences between an existing General Motors automobile plant and a newly designed Toyota plant incorporating cost-saving technology and organization. This case is an example of a long-run production function, in which all inputs can be varied and possibly substituted for each other. We discuss both the feasibility of input substitution in technological terms and the possible incentives for input substitution in various sectors of the economy. We present an intuitive analysis of these issues in the chapter and include the formal model of long-run production, the isoquant model, in the chapter appendix.

We then define and examine long-run cost functions, focusing on a firm's long-run average cost. We show how this concept is derived in economic theory, and we then provide numerous illustrations of the shapes of long-run average cost curves for different firms and industries. We end the chapter by discussing implications of a firm's long-run average cost for a manager's competitive strategy, a topic we pursue in greater detail in Chapters 8 and 9.

A Tale of Two Auto Plants

by Lee Hawkins Jr. and Norihiko Shirouzu

Wall Street Journal, *May 24, 2006*

ARLINGTON, Texas—For more than 50 years, General Motors Corp. has built cars and trucks here at Texas' only auto assembly plant. . . .

The sprawling factory, one of GM's best, employs 3,000 people and buys myriad parts and services from local suppliers to build the big sport utility vehicles that have been among the company's most profitable—including "the national car of Texas," the Chevrolet Suburban.

Now, though, a rival has come deep into the heart of Texas to battle GM. At a 2,000-acre site in San Antonio, Toyota Motor Corp. is getting ready to start production later this year of the newest generation of Tundra pickup trucks in a plant that will use the Japanese car maker's most advanced machinery and methods.

Separated by 280 miles, these two factories bring into stark relief the competitive problems plaguing GM at home at a time when car-building in the U.S. is thriving, even though American car companies are faltering. In no small part, the world's largest auto maker's difficulties stem from the fact that its challengers can start fresh, unencumbered by old plants and old obligations that limit innovation and add hundreds of dollars to the cost of each vehicle. . . .

In Texas, Toyota appears to be working aggressively to make the most of its advantages. The company has been able to deploy the latest know-how to fit various manufacturing processes—from stamping to welding to painting to final assembly—into a relatively compact space and make the plant more efficient.

On the other hand, even though Arlington is the country's most efficient large-SUV plant, GM can't maximize its success by adopting its newest, best methods there. . . .

For example, GM's body shop is housed in a separate building, which was built in 2000 to introduce new technology. The bodies are transported on an elaborate, enclosed conveyor to the final assembly area, where they are painted and stored before being bolted onto frames. GM managers say they would use a more modern layout that would help boost the plant's productivity even more, but GM can't afford to shut down operations and completely rebuild the plant. . . .

In Arlington, GM pays union-scale wages of $26.50 to $30.50 an hour to its 2,800 hourly workers there. On average, GM pays $81.18 an hour in wages and benefits to U.S. hourly workers, including pension and retiree medical costs. At that rate, labor costs per vehicle at Arlington are about $1,800. . . .

In San Antonio, Toyota will use non-union labor and will start its 1,600 hourly workers at $15.50 to $20.33 per hour, which will grow after three years to $21 to $25. Harbour Consulting President Ron Harbour estimates Toyota's total hourly U.S. labor costs, with benefits, at about $35 an hour—less than half of GM's rates. The brand-new plant won't have any direct retiree costs for many years. So if the San Antonio factory does no better than match the Arlington plant in productivity, it could still enjoy a labor cost advantage of about $1,000 per vehicle, a substantial sum in industry terms. . . .

The San Antonio plant is installing smaller, lighter machinery with a simpler design that takes up less space than previous generations of equipment. . . . Smaller machines mean Toyota can spend less on the building that houses them, while simpler design means those machines are cheaper to install, easier to maintain, much less likely to break down and simpler to fix if they do. The plant covers about 2.2 million square feet, including some metal-stamping operations, which are not done in Arlington. Still, the Toyota plant is roughly a third smaller than the 3.75 million-square-foot GM plant.

Further, Toyota has arranged for 21 key Tundra suppliers to set up factories right on the same site. . . . Engines still come from a Toyota plant in Alabama and axles from a supplier in Arkansas, but most other major parts, from instrument panels to seats to exhaust systems, are assembled at those on-site suppliers. That cuts the cost of transporting parts and storing large inventories on site as insurance against missed shipments. It also eliminates risks of having too many components on route to San Antonio—a potential logistical nightmare that could cost Toyota dearly if a defect suddenly appears . . .

GM, in contrast, is restricted by space, existing deals with suppliers who are located elsewhere and its agreements with the United Auto Workers that prohibit it from using lower-wage, non-union workers on the same site. Of the total 3,330 different kinds of parts that are supplied to the Arlington facility, about 1,075 come from Michigan suppliers, while 739 come from Texas and the rest from Canada and Mexico.

Having suppliers located far away has a price tag. Shipping costs have increased in the wake of rising gas prices, GM says, but it is difficult to estimate how much compared with previous years, when Arlington was building older generations of SUVs that required fewer parts because they were available with fewer options.

Moreover, because the Tundra plant brings new jobs to San Antonio, Toyota, which chose the city over a rival site in Arkansas, has been able to bargain for a generous package of subsidies from various levels of government. The state gave a total of $13.25 million in direct incentives, including a reprieve from utility bills and a discount on property taxes, along with road improvements worth $57 million. . . .

The direct incentives alone, averaged over roughly one year's production, amount to more than $600 per vehicle savings for Toyota.

Even though it has made significant investments in Arlington in recent years, GM no longer gets the same pampering. Since 1996, GM has spent about $910 million on the plant and converted it from building cars to making SUVs. In 2000, GM installed more than 600 robots in an overhaul of the plant's body shop, where the frames and underbodies of trucks are fabricated.

Much of this new investment, however, is deemed by the state and other government agencies as job-retention rather than job-creation, meaning GM doesn't qualify for incentives similar to those offered Toyota. . . .

Arlington's SUVs and San Antonio's Tundras won't directly compete, although both are designed to appeal to American consumers who like quintessentially American vehicles: Big V-8-powered, body-on-frame trucks. But Toyota is clearly sensitive about appeals to economic patriotism by GM, which calls itself the "global car company that's proud to be American." The Japanese auto maker has mounted an aggressive campaign to win over public opinion in Texas and elsewhere, by highlighting its U.S. investments. . . .

Case for Analysis

Production and Cost Analysis in the Automobile Industry

This article discusses how managers' ability to make changes in the size of their plants and the use of technology in the long run have become a crucial part of firms' overall competitive strategies. In this case, Toyota Motor Corp. has a distinct advantage over General Motors Corp. in its ability to increase productivity and minimize costs because it has not been locked into existing plants and old labor contracts. This enables Toyota to lower its labor costs by approximately $1,000 per vehicle.

In Texas, Toyota was able to build a more efficient-sized plant with the latest stamping, welding, and painting technologies. The Toyota plant used lighter machinery, which was easier to install and maintain and that took up less space, thus requiring a plant of only 2.2 million square feet compared with the 3.75 million-square-foot GM plant. Toyota was able to lower its labor costs by hiring nonunion labor compared with General Motors, which was locked into unionized labor contracts. Toyota also arranged for 21 auto parts suppliers to establish factories on the same site, thus minimizing transportation costs, while General Motors had existing contracts with suppliers in Michigan, Canada, and Mexico. Because it established a new plant, Toyota was even able to negotiate a package of subsidies and incentives from various levels of government that were not available to GM. The Toyota plant site also had room for expansion in the event that it was needed in the future. ∎

Model of a Long-Run Production Function

Long-run production function
A production function showing the relationship between a flow of inputs and the resulting flow of output, where all inputs are variable.

This case study illustrates **long-run production functions**, where all inputs in the production process are variable and inputs may be substituted for each other. The case also shows that the long run is a planning horizon. Before building the plant, Toyota was able to consider new technologies and changes in all of the inputs of production.

A simplified long-run production function is presented in Equation 6.1:

6.1 $Q = f(L, K)$

where

Q = quantity of output

L = quantity of labor input (variable)

K = quantity of capital input (variable)

Unlike the production function in Equation 5.2 in the previous chapter, both inputs in this production function can be varied. Thus, the amount of output that can be produced is related to the amount of both capital and labor used. In this section, we'll discuss how changes in the scale of production impact costs in the long run.

But first let's look at the concept of input substitution, another important issue that arises when more than one input is variable.

Input Substitution

Suppose that a firm has already decided that it wants to produce quantity Q_1 in the production function in Equation 6.1. With this production function, firms have still another economic choice to make. Because both inputs are variable, the firm must decide what combination of inputs to use in producing output level Q_1. The firm might use either a labor-intensive or a capital-intensive method of production. With a **labor-intensive method of production**, managers use large amounts of labor relative to other inputs to produce the firm's product. However, it might also be possible to use a production method that relies on large quantities of capital equipment and smaller amounts of labor; this is called a **capital-intensive method of production**. The number of methods that can be used depends on the degree of **input substitution**, or the feasibility of substituting one input for another in the production process.

A manager's choice of inputs will be influenced by

- The technology of the production process
- The prices of the inputs of production
- The set of incentives facing the given producer[1]

The Technology of the Production Process　Production functions vary widely in the technological feasibility of input substitution. The development of the assembly line in the automobile industry is one of the best examples of changes in production technology and the substitution of capital for labor.[2] Before Henry Ford introduced the assembly line, it took 728 hours to assemble an automobile from a pile of parts located in one place. Initially, Ford installed a system in which a winch moved the auto-body frame 250 feet along the factory floor and workers picked up parts spaced along that distance and fitted them to the car. Longer assembly lines, more specialized workers, and automatic conveyer belts eventually resulted in tremendous reductions in the time necessary to make one automobile.

The fast-food industry is another example of a production process built around a capital-intensive assembly line in each franchise that includes conveyer belts and ovens resembling commercial laundry presses. High-technology capital-intensive production methods have also been developed to supply the inputs to these franchises. The Lamb Weston plant in American Falls, Idaho, one of the biggest french-fry factories in the world, was founded in 1950 by F. Gilbert Lamb, inventor of the Lamb Water Gun Knife, a device that uses a high-pressure hose to shoot

> **Labor-intensive method of production**
> A production process that uses large amounts of labor relative to the other inputs to produce the firm's output.
>
> **Capital-intensive method of production**
> A production process that uses large amounts of capital equipment relative to the other inputs to produce the firm's output.
>
> **Input substitution**
> The degree to which a firm can substitute one input for another in a production process.

---

[1] The formal rule to minimize the cost of using two variable inputs, labor (L) and capital (K), to produce a given level of output in a production process is to use quantities of each input such that $(MP_L/P_L) = (MP_K/P_K)$, where MP is the marginal product showing the additional output generated by an additional unit of each input, P_L is the price per unit of labor, and P_K is the price per unit of capital. The intuition of this rule is shown as follows. Assume that there is diminishing marginal productivity (diminishing returns) for both inputs and that the above ratio is 10/1 for labor and 5/1 for capital. If 1 more unit of labor and 1 less unit of capital are used in the production process, there is a gain of 10 units of output and a loss of 5 units, so it makes sense to reallocate the inputs. However, as more labor is used, its marginal product decreases, while the marginal product of capital increases as less of this input is used. Thus, eventually the ratios will equalize—say, at 8/1. No further reallocation of inputs will increase output for a given input cost or reduce cost for a given level of output. This rule, which is formally derived in Appendix 6A, *shows that managers minimize costs by considering both the technology of the production process, which influences productivity, and the prices of the inputs.*

[2] This discussion is drawn from Shlomo Maital, *Executive Economics* (New York: Free Press, 1994), 94–95.

potatoes at a speed of 117 feet per second through a grid of sharpened steel blades to create perfect french fries. In *Fast Food Nation*, Eric Schlosser describes this production process as follows:

> [In one plant, there was] a mound of potatoes that was twenty feet deep and a hundred feet wide and almost as long as two football fields. . . . The trucks dumped their loads onto spinning rods that brought the larger potatoes into the building and let the small potatoes, dirt, and rocks fall to the ground. The rods led to a rock trap, a tank of water in which the potatoes floated and the rocks sank to the ground. . . .
>
> Conveyer belts took the wet, clean potatoes into a machine that blasted them with steam for twelve seconds, boiled the water under their skins, and exploded their skins off. Then the potatoes were pumped into a preheat tank and shot through a Lamb Water Gun Knife. They emerged as shoestring fries. Four video cameras scrutinized them from different angles, looking for flaws. When a french fry with a blemish was detected, an optical sorting machine time-sequenced a single burst of compressed air that knocked the bad fry off the production line and onto a separate conveyer belt, which carried it to a machine with tiny automated knives that precisely removed the blemish. And then the fry was returned to the main production line.
>
> Sprays of hot water blanched the fries, gusts of hot air dried them, and 25,000 pounds of boiling oil fried them to a slight crisp. Air cooled by compressed ammonia gas quickly froze them, a computerized sorter divided them into six-pound batches, and a device that spun like an out-of-control lazy Susan used centrifugal force to align the french fries so that they all pointed in the same direction. The fries were sealed in brown bags, then the bags were loaded by robots into cardboard boxes, and the boxes were stacked by robots onto wooden pallets. Forklifts driven by human beings took the pallets to a freezer for storage. Inside the freezer [there were] 20 million pounds of french fries, most of them destined for McDonald's, the boxes of fries stacked thirty feet high, the stacks extending for roughly forty yards. And the freezer was half empty.[3]

In 2007, airlines and airports considered adopting radio-frequency ID (RFID) baggage tags to replace existing bar-code printed tags. Industry studies had shown that the RFIDs, which transmit a bag's identifying number in a manner similar to a toll-road pass, could reduce lost luggage by 20 percent. The system was estimated to be 99 percent accurate in reading baggage tags, a significant improvement over the 80–90 percent accuracy of optical scanners reading bar-coded tags. U.S. airlines spent approximately $400 million on lost luggage in 2006 to reimburse passengers and deliver late bags to hotels and homes. This decision to change technology had been limited in the past by the cost of the RFIDs of approximately $1.00 per tag compared with 4 cents for a bar-code printed tag. However, the price of the RFID tags had begun to decrease to as low as 15 cents per tag.[4]

In the railroad industry, managers have begun to consider the use of plastic railroad ties made from old tires, grocery bags, milk cartons, and Styrofoam coffee cups as a replacement for wooden ties, which are vulnerable to rot, fungus, and termite infestation. Quality is a crucial issue in this decision because railroad ties, which are spaced 18 or 24 inches apart, must be stiff enough to support heavy-laden freight trains but flexible enough to bounce back from their tremendous impact. Plastic tie manufacturers claim their ties can last for at least 50 years, but these ties typically cost twice as much as wood ties.[5]

---

[3] Eric Schlosser, *Fast Food Nation* (Boston: Houghton Mifflin, 2001), 130–31.

[4] Scott McCartney, "A New Way to Prevent Lost Luggage," *Wall Street Journal*, February 27, 2007.

[5] Daniel Machalaba, "New Recyclables Market Emerges: Plastic Railroad Ties," *Wall Street Journal*, October 19, 2004.

Input substitution can also occur in smaller-scale businesses. The Union Tool Company, a Japanese manufacturer of precision tool bits that cut holes in printed circuit boards, developed a technique to build the bits with a stainless steel shank and a tip made of tungsten carbide, a strategy that gave the company a cost advantage of as much as 30 percent over competitors who used all-tungsten tips.[6] Rhode Island–based Evans Findings Company, which makes metal parts for various products, developed a production process in which only machines and no employees worked the 3:00 P.M. to 10:30 P.M. shift. Using this "lights-out" process, the owner expected to double his output within two years without adding to his 49 workers.[7]

Other production processes may not be as conducive to substitution between inputs, particularly if they involve a series of complex processes and a highly trained labor force such as found in the pipe organ industry. At the Schantz Organ Co., the largest maker of pipe organs in the United States, each worker takes an average of 30 to 40 hours of hand labor to bend specially made sheets of soft metal into the 61 pipes comprising one of the shorter "ranks" or rows of pipes with the seam of each pipe hand-dabbed with solder. The number of ranks can range from 3 to 150 or more. It takes four to five years for a worker to become a good pipe maker, while the "voicers" who tune the pipes spend up to seven years as apprentices. Although some new technologies, such as computer-controlled routers, have been adopted, labor costs represent 57 percent of the $8 million sales revenue at Schantz. The average labor cost relative to shipments for all U.S. manufacturing is 17 percent, while it is as low as 2 percent in some highly automated sectors such as soybean processing.[8]

Economists have traditionally argued that input substitution may be less feasible in the provision of services, particularly in the public sector, than in the production of goods, a factor that has become increasingly important as the U.S. economy has become more service-oriented.[9] In some service areas, this argument is being questioned as more input substitution occurs than might be expected. For example, research indicates a significant degree of substitution between physicians and nurses in hospitals is possible.[10] This development has caused growing tension between these groups as nurses have taken over tasks previously performed by physicians, sometimes even obtaining the authority to write prescriptions.

The process of syndicating corporate loans among banks has undergone rapid technological change. Until the late 1990s, syndicating a large corporate loan meant that a bank had to distribute an offering document, often totaling 200 pages, to 50 to 100 banks using overnight mail, fax machines, and hordes of messengers. That process, now largely handled through banking Web sites, may reduce the time to close a deal by 25 percent.[11]

Input substitution is occurring even in the fine arts. In November 2003, the Opera Company of Brooklyn announced that it would stage *The Marriage of Figaro* with only 12 musicians and a technician overseeing a computer program that would play all the other parts.[12] The conductor, Paul Henry Smith, has developed the Fauxharmonic Orchestra, a computer program composed of over a million recorded notes played by top musicians. The latest software lets users choose from

---

[6] Robert A. Guth, "Scrappy Tokyo Company Drills into Costs," *Wall Street Journal*, December 14, 1999.

[7] Timothy Aeppel, "Workers Aren't Included in Lights-Out Factories," *Wall Street Journal*, November 19, 2002.

[8] Timothy Aeppel, "Few Hands, Many Hours," *Wall Street Journal*, October 27, 2006.

[9] William Baumol, "Macroeconomics of Unbalanced Growth: The Anatomy of the Urban Crisis," *American Economic Review* 62 (June 1967): 415–26.

[10] Gale A. Jensen and Michael A. Morrisey, "The Role of Physicians in Hospital Production," *Review of Economics and Statistics* 68 (1986): 432–43.

[11] Steve Lohr, "Computer Age Gains Respect of Economists," *New York Times*, April 14, 1999.

[12] Jon E. Hilsenrath, "Behind Surging Productivity: The Service Sector Delivers," *Wall Street Journal*, November 7, 2003.

a large library of digitally stored sounds, adjust for texture and nuance, and assemble them into a complete symphony. A conductor's jacket, a cyclist's jersey embedded with a dozen sensors, has been developed to map conductors' movements and physiology and translate them to control a piece of music.[13]

Empirical studies have found that labor productivity growth in the service industries has proceeded at about the economy-wide rate since 1995. These increases are broad-based and not just found among a small number of large industries. Much of this growth is related to the increased use of information technology.[14]

The Prices of the Inputs of Production   As mentioned above in the case of the adoption of radio-frequency ID baggage tags and plastic railroad ties, the prices of the inputs of production also influence the degree of input substitution. To minimize their costs of production, firms want to substitute cheaper inputs for more expensive ones. How much substitution can occur in the face of high input prices depends on the technology of the production process and institutional factors.

As the movement toward electricity deregulation intensified in southern California and other parts of the country in the late 1990s and at the turn of the century, electricity prices fluctuated and in some cases increased dramatically as market forces swept into the formerly regulated industry. Companies responded to increased electricity prices through both input substitution and implementation of innovative contracts with their service providers. Because Intel Corporation used huge amounts of electricity to keep its automated, temperature- and humidity-sensitive semiconductor-fabrication operations running 24 hours a day, the company could not enter into interruptible supply contracts with electricity generators that would provide lower prices, but a nonconstant supply. Instead, Intel negotiated voluntary consumption restrictions through reduced lighting and air-conditioning levels, and it designed factory equipment that was less energy-intensive.[15]

Increased costs of gas, oil, and electricity continue to influence managerial decisions about input use. Arla Foods, a farmer-owned cooperative based in Denmark and the world's fifth-largest dairy producer by revenue, cut energy use in response to Denmark's high taxes on energy consumption. Arla undertook about a dozen projects to save energy including changing the water chiller, replacing the absorption dryer in the cheese-aging room, and repairing leaks in compressed-air pipes.[16]

Managers have attempted to replace workers with machinery even in the fresh fruit industry where many products have traditionally been picked by hand to maintain quality. One company in the Florida citrus industry turned to canopy shakers to harvest half of the 40.5 million pounds of oranges grown annually from its 10,000 acres in southwestern Florida. In less than 15 minutes, these machines can shake loose 36,000 pounds of oranges from 100 trees, catch the fruit, and drop it into a storage car, a job that would have taken four pickers an entire day.[17]

The ability to change all inputs in the face of changing input prices has affected the development of numerous industries over time.[18] Supermarkets have become the dominant form of grocery store in the United States. Because these stores are a land-intensive form of organization—given their size and the need for parking lots around them—their development depends on the availability of large accessible plots of land

---

[13] Jacob Hale Russell and John Jurgensen, "Fugue for Man & Machine," *Wall Street Journal*, May 5, 2007.

[14] Jack E. Triplett and Barry P. Bosworth, "'Baumol's Disease has Been Cured: IT and Multifactor Productivity in U.S. Services Industries," in Dennis W. Jansen (ed.), *The New Economy and Beyond: Past, Present, and Future* (Northampton, MA: Edward Elgar, 2006), pp. 34–71.

[15] Jonathan Friedland, "Volatile Electricity Market Forces Firms to Find Ways to Cut Energy Expenses," *Wall Street Journal*, August 14, 2000.

[16] Leila Abboud and John Biers, "Business Goes on an Energy Diet," *Wall Street Journal*, August 27, 2007.

[17] Eduardo Porter, "In Florida Groves, Cheap Labor Means Machines," *New York Times*, March 22, 2004.

[18] This discussion is based on Martin Neil Bailey and Robert M. Solow, "International Productivity Comparisons Built from the Firm Level," *Journal of Economic Perspectives* 15 (Summer 2001): 151–72.

at relatively low prices. In Germany, where less land is available and the population is more concentrated in central cities, small supermarkets or minimarkets have increased productivity by making bulk purchases at the firm level and by providing only a small variety of goods.

The ability to manufacture goods with cheaper labor abroad led to the decline of U.S. manufacturing from 20 percent of GDP in 1980 to 12 percent in 2006. However, even some types of manufacturing are better done closer to the customer. These include appliances and electronic equipment that are high-end, locally customized, delicate, very large, or have manufacturing processes that involve almost no labor, such as medical testing or automated electric-component, chemical, or metal-fabricating plants.[19]

The Incentives Facing a Given Producer   The third factor influencing input substitution is the set of incentives facing a given producer. Firms will substitute cheaper inputs of production for more expensive ones if they face major incentives to minimize their costs of production.

The Role of Competitive Environments   Input substitution will occur most often in a competitive market environment where firms are trying to maximize their profits or are operating under extreme conditions.

The substitution of machinery for labor in the fresh fruit industry discussed above was a response to increased global competition facing American farmers. In the early 1990s, Florida orange farmers had overplanted, and there were large bumper crops in Brazil where harvesting costs were about one-third as high as in Florida. These changes gave Florida growers the incentive to invest over $1 million per year into research in mechanical harvesting to reduce their costs. By the 1999–2000 harvest, this investment resulted in four different types of harvesting machines working commercially.[20]

U.S. airlines, operating under extreme competition and facing huge increases in the cost of fuel, are trying to gain control over the costs of plane parts either by searching for less expensive suppliers or by determining how to make the parts themselves at significantly lower costs. Continental Airlines estimates that it has saved almost $2 million per year by making its own parts such as tray tables and window shades.[21]

The airlines are also using new aviation software to help minimize their fuel costs and the overflight fees charged by countries for using their airspace. These fees, which cost the world's air carriers $20 billion per year, are usually based on takeoff weight and distance travelled. The software, which calculates multiple scenarios, balances the overflight fees with additional fuel costs if an alternative route is less direct. United Airlines expects that once the software system is fully installed for its 1,600 daily mainline flights, the company will save more than $20 million per year.[22]

Firms that have some degree of market power may have fewer incentives to constantly search for the cost-minimizing combination of inputs. Economists have called this concept **X-inefficiency**.[23] There is both statistical and case study evidence that some degree of X-inefficiency exists in less-competitive industries where firms have greater market power.[24] Studies of manufacturing sector productivity indicate that firms increase productivity when they are exposed to the

X-inefficiency
Inefficiency that may result in firms with market power that have fewer incentives to minimize the costs of production than more competitive firms.

---

[19] Mark Whitehouse, "For Some Manufacturers, There Are Benefits to Keeping Production at Home," *Wall Street Journal*, January 22, 2007.

[20] Porter, "In Florida Groves, Cheap Labor Means Machines."

[21] Melanie Trottman, "Nuts-and-Bolts Savings," *Wall Street Journal*, May 3, 2005.

[22] Susan Carey, "Calculating Costs in the Clouds," *Wall Street Journal*, March 6, 2007.

[23] Harvey Leibenstein, "Allocative Inefficiency vs. X-Inefficiency," *American Economic Review* 56 (1966): 392–415.

[24] F. M. Scherer and David Ross, *Industrial Market Structure and Economic Performance*, 3rd ed. (Boston: Houghton Mifflin, 1990), 668–72.

Best practices
The production techniques adopted by the firms with the highest levels of productivity.

Lean production
An approach to production pioneered by Toyota Motor Corporation, in which firms streamline the production process through strategies such as strict scheduling and small-batch production with low-cost flexible machines.

world's **best practices**—the production techniques adopted by the firms with the highest levels of productivity.[25] A study of nine manufacturing industries in the United States, Germany, and Japan concluded that industries with the greatest exposure to the best practices used by the world's high-labor-productivity industries had relatively higher productivity themselves.[26]

In retail trade, Wal-Mart has played a central role in increasing overall productivity, given its large size and highly productive methods of operation related to logistics, distribution, and inventory control. By the late 1970s, all stores, distribution centers, and the company's headquarters were connected to a computer network. Wal-Mart installed bar code readers in all its distribution centers by the late 1980s, which reduced the labor cost of processing shipments by one-half. The company is currently one of the leaders in the use of radio-frequency identification to track shipments of its products.[27]

Labor Issues Proponents of cost-cutting strategies may run into resistance from individuals and organizations that feel threatened by these strategies. United States auto workers have in the past opposed **lean production**, a strategy U.S. automobile manufacturers adopted from Toyota Motor Corporation that includes strict scheduling and small-batch production with low-cost flexible machines, a major change from previous auto production methods.[28]

Worker and union attitudes at Ford have changed more recently as the company's future became more tenuous. In 2007, the company, which lost $12.7 billion the previous year, persuaded the United Auto Workers locals at 33 of its 41 plants to accept "competitive operating agreements" that loosened various complex and often costly work rules. Union members have agreed that some non-Ford workers earning half their pay could take certain jobs in a plant.[29]

On the U.S. west coast, the International Longshore and Warehouse Union (ILWU) has had a major influence on what wages dockworkers are paid and on how the production process is structured. In 2002, there was a dispute between the Pacific Maritime Association, which represents the operators of the terminals, and the ILWU over the introduction of electronic technology to automatically collect cargo information that union clerks had been entering manually into computers.[30] This issue reached an impasse in October 2002, when management locked out the dockworkers.[31] Later that fall an agreement was reached in which the union agreed to allow the installation and use of new information technology, such as software for designing how containers are filled and global-positioning-satellite-system technology for tracking cargo, in return for the protection of the jobs (until they retired) of registered dockworkers whose work was displaced by the technology.[32] Although the ILWU has great power to influence productivity and costs on the docks, this power is not unlimited, given increased competition from nonunion ports in certain U.S. states and other countries and pressure from large retailers, such as Wal-Mart, to cut costs in their supply systems.[33]

---

[25] Bailey and Solow, "International Productivity Comparisons."

[26] Many companies have also adopted the Six Sigma management strategies to improve manufacturing processes and reduce costs. See Motorola University—What is Six Sigma? (http://www.motorola.com).

[27] Emek Basker, "The Causes and Consequences of Wal-Mart's Growth," *Journal of Economic Perspectives* 21 (3) (Summer, 2007): 177-198.

[28] Norihiko Shirouzu, "Beyond the Tire Mess, Ford Has a Problem with Quality," *Wall Street Journal*, May 25, 2001.

[29] Jeffrey McCracken, "Desperate to Cut Costs, Ford Gets Union's Help," *Wall Street Journal*, March 2, 2007.

[30] Daniel Machalaba and Queena Sook Kim, "West Coast Docks Face a Duel with Union About Technology," *Wall Street Journal*, May 17, 2002.

[31] Jeanne Cummings and Carlos Tejada, "U.S. Judge Swiftly Orders End to Lockout at West Coast Ports," *Wall Street Journal*, October 19, 2002.

[32] Daniel Machalaba and Queena Sook Kim, "West Coast Ports, Dockworkers Set Tentative Deal on Key Issue," *Wall Street Journal*, November 4, 2002.

[33] Anne Marie Squeo, "How Longshoremen Keep Global Wind at Their Backs," *Wall Street Journal*, July 26, 2006.

Nonprofit Organizations   Organizations that do not face strict profit-maximizing constraints may also have fewer incentives to minimize the costs of production. There is continuing controversy over whether nonprofit hospitals, whose typical goals are to serve the community and provide services that may not be profitable, achieve these goals or use their revenue to build expensive facilities and pay high executive salaries.[34] Past evidence indicated that hospital administrators engaged in "medical arms races," competing with each other on the purchase of costly high technology equipment and driving up overall health care costs.[35] These outcomes occurred before the widespread utilization of prospective payment systems by Medicare and other managed care organizations, whose goals are to cut costs and impose the discipline of the competitive market in the health care sector. Recent studies have shown that for-profit and nonprofit hospitals tend to act more similar when they are located in the same metropolitan areas and compete with each other.[36]

Political and Legislative Influences   Political and legislative factors can also influence input combinations. In 1999, California became the first state to require hospitals to meet fixed nurse-to-patient ratios.[37] This legislation was a reaction to concerns about the quality of health care in light of the cost-cutting efforts of managed care systems.

Legislating input combinations can have unforeseen consequences.[38] In the nursing example, it is not clear what nurse-patient threshold is necessary for improved outcomes. Minimum nurse-to-patient ratios may also cause hospitals to focus too narrowly on staffing instead of other factors that might contribute to the quality of care. As an alternative to mandated ratios, some hospitals have begun redesigning medical-surgical units so that nurses can spend more time on direct patient care and using sophisticated computer software to help analyze staffing needs and nurse allocation.[39]

Model of a Long-Run Cost Function

Let's now discuss how costs vary in the long run by focusing on the concept of **long-run average cost (*LRAC*)**. This is defined as the minimum average or unit cost of producing any level of output *when all inputs are variable*. In this section, we'll derive the long-run average cost curve and show the range of possibilities for its shape. We'll then discuss the actual shapes of the *LRAC* curve for different firms and define the minimum efficient scale (*MES*) of operation. We'll conclude this section by discussing the implications of the shape of the *LRAC* curve for competitive strategy.

Long-run average cost (*LRAC*)
The minimum average or unit cost of producing any level of output *when all inputs are variable.*

Derivation of the Long-Run Average Cost Curve

Figure 6.1 shows several **short-run average total cost (*SATC*)** curves drawn for different scales of operation. These curves represent the average total cost of production for firms with different-sized manufacturing plants or different amounts of

Short-run average total cost (*SATC*)
The cost per unit of output for a firm of a given size or scale of operation.

---

[34] John Carreyrou and Barbara Martinez, "Nonprofit Hospitals, Once for the Poor, Strike It Rich," *Wall Street Journal*, April 4, 2008.

[35] Rexford E. Santerre and Stephen P. Neun, *Health Economics: Theories, Insights, and Industry Studies*, rev. ed. (Orlando, Fla.: Dryden, 2000), 475–77.

[36] Mark Schlesinger and Bradford H. Gray, "How Nonprofits Matter in American Medicine, and What to Do About It," *Health Affairs* (June 20, 2006): W287–W303.

[37] Todd S. Purdum, "California to Set Level of Staffing for Nursing Care," *New York Times*, October 12, 1999.

[38] Janet M. Coffman, Jean Ann Seago, and Joanne Spetz, "Minimum Nurse-to-Patient Ratios in Acute Care Hospitals in California," *Health Affairs* 21 (5) (September–October 2002): 53–64.

[39] Laura Landro, "Why Quota for Nurses Isn't Cure-All," *Wall Street Journal*, December 13, 2006.

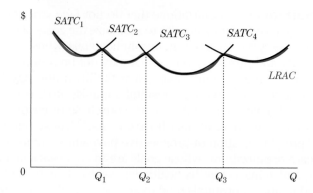

the fixed input, buildings. For simplicity, the curves are labeled $SATC_1$, $SATC_2$, $SATC_3$, and $SATC_4$ to show the short-run average total cost associated with the first scale of operation, the second scale of operation, and so on. These are the same short-run average total cost curves that you saw in Chapter 5, except that we are now showing curves representing different scales of production.

You can see in Figure 6.1 that the cheapest method of producing up to Q_1 units of output is to use the plant represented by $SATC_1$. The short-run average total cost for this plant size would first decrease and then begin to increase as diminishing returns set into the production function. If the firm decided that it wanted to produce a level of output greater than Q_1, it would minimize its cost by building a larger plant and switching to cost curve $SATC_2$, associated with that larger plant. Between Q_1 and Q_2 units of output, $SATC_2$ represents the optimal plant size with the lowest average cost of production. The firm would not want to use this $SATC_2$ plant to produce fewer than Q_1 units of output because the $SATC_2$ curve lies above the $SATC_1$ curve in that range of production. The plant with the $SATC_2$ curve has larger fixed costs of production than the $SATC_1$ plant, so its average total costs of production do not become lower until the fixed costs are spread over greater output.

The same arguments hold for still larger levels of output. The $SATC_3$ curve represents the lowest cost of production for output levels between Q_2 and Q_3, while $SATC_4$ minimizes cost for output levels larger than Q_3. The shaded long-run average cost ($LRAC$) curve in Figure 6.1 traces out the locus of points of minimum average cost. It is derived as an envelope curve of the respective short-run average cost curves and shows the minimum average cost of production *when all inputs are variable.*

Economies and Diseconomies of Scale

Economies of scale
Achieving lower unit costs of production by adopting a larger scale of production, represented by the downward sloping portion of a long-run average cost curve.

Diseconomies of scale
Incurring higher unit costs of production by adopting a larger scale of production, represented by the upward sloping portion of a long-run average cost curve.

If we assume that plant size can be varied continuously, the $LRAC$ curve in Figure 6.1 becomes the smooth, U-shaped curve in Figure 6.2. The downward sloping portion of this curve, up to output level Q_1 in Figure 6.2, is defined as the range of **economies of scale**. This means that the average costs of production are lowered as the firm produces larger output levels with an increased scale of production. Large-scale production is cheaper than small-scale production up to output level Q_1. Beyond output level Q_1, larger-sized plants result in a higher average cost of production, or **diseconomies of scale**. With a U-shaped $LRAC$ curve, as shown in Figure 6.2, the size of plant represented by the $SATC_2$ curve represents the optimal scale of production. This plant size minimizes the overall average costs of production, assuming that the firm wants to produce output at or near level Q_1. The standard U-shaped $LRAC$ in Figure 6.2 shows that larger-scale production first lowers and then increases the average cost of production. It also shows there is an optimal plant size in terms of minimizing the average costs of production. Note there is no distinction between fixed and variable costs when defining the long-run average cost curve because all costs are variable in the long run.

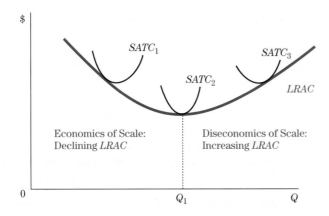

FIGURE 6.2
The Standard Long-Run Average Cost Curve (*LRAC*)
A firm can experience both economies of scale (decreasing LRAC) or diseconomies of scale (increasing LRAC) as it expands plant size. The size of the plant represented by the SATC$_2$ curve minimizes the overall average cost of production, assuming the firm wants to produce output at or near level Q$_1$.

Factors Creating Economies and Diseconomies of Scale

Figure 6.2 shows a possible shape for an *LRAC* curve that encompasses both economies and diseconomies of scale. What factors would cause economies of scale to exist, and why might diseconomies of scale set in at large levels of output?

Factors Creating Economies of Scale   The major factors creating economies of scale are

- Specialization and division of labor
- Technological factors
- The use of automation devices
- Quantity discounts
- The spreading of advertising costs
- Financial factors

As Adam Smith noted over two hundred years ago in *The Wealth of Nations*, large-scale production allows for increased specialization and the division of labor among different tasks.[40] In the case of ball-bearing production, a skilled operator on a general-purpose lathe can customize a few bearings in five minutes to one hour. If a sizeable batch of bearings is needed, operators will use a more specialized automatic screw machine. However, it is not cost-effective to use this machine until at least 100 bearings are needed, and the costs decrease even more with 1,000 or 10,000 bearings. For very large quantities, such as 1,000,000 bearings per year, an automated, computer-guided production approach will be adopted. With this scale of production, unit costs may be 30 to 50 percent lower than with a medium-volume batch. However, the production line must be kept running two shifts per day without a changeover to realize these cost reductions.

Economies of scale can arise from expanding the size of individual processing units in chemical and metallurgical processing industries such as petroleum refining, iron ore reduction, and chemical synthesis. Due to the physical relationships between processing unit size and level of output, increases in capacity occur with a less-than-proportionate increase in equipment cost. The number of workers needed to operate a larger processing unit may barely exceed what is needed for a smaller unit.

"Economies of massed reserves" may also play a role in various types of industrial production. Plants may keep specialized machines in reserve to sustain

---

[40] The following examples of economies and diseconomies of scale are based on Scherer and Ross, 97–106.

production in case the machine currently operating breaks down. In a large plant with several machines, holding a single extra machine in reserve does not add proportionately to costs and, therefore, can create economies of scale.

Specialization and the division of labor, technological factors, and the use of automation devices are technical economies of scale relating to the combination of inputs and the technology of the production process. Quantity discounts, the spreading of advertising costs, and financial factors are pecuniary gains, as they represent financial issues associated with large-scale production. Firms may receive discounts when they place large orders for their inputs. Advertising costs per unit decrease as more output is produced. Large-scale firms may also be able to obtain loans and other financial support on more generous terms than smaller firms.

Factors Creating Diseconomies of Scale   Diseconomies of scale are associated with

- The inefficiencies of managing large-scale operations
- The increased transportation costs that result from concentrating production in a small number of very large plants

If the specialization and division of labor that create economies of scale are pushed too far, workers can become alienated by dull, routine jobs. Inefficiencies will set into the production process that will begin to raise costs. The long-run average cost curve will then slope upward, reflecting the higher costs of larger plants. Managers have responded to these types of problems with quality circles and job enrichment programs to try to limit the impact on costs.

Other factors also contribute to diseconomies of scale. If greater numbers of workers are needed for large-scale production, they may have to be drawn from a greater distance away or from other labor markets by paying higher wages, which increases the costs of production. Physical laws, such as the bursting point of large pipes, will eventually limit the size of the capital equipment in a production process. Perhaps the most important limitation to large-scale production is the management function. Plants can become too large to manage efficiently. Chief executive officers and other upper-level management can become too far removed from the day-to-day production and marketing operations, so that their ability to make sound decisions decreases.

General Motors (GM) is the classic example of a firm that tried to avoid the inefficiencies of managing a large enterprise through decentralization. Beginning in the 1920s, GM delegated much authority to operating divisions and established a set of managerial incentives related to performance objectives of these divisions. Tendencies toward centralization reappeared in the 1950s and continued through the 1970s. By the mid-1980s, GM found that it was not able to respond to the increased foreign competition and changing consumer preferences as easily as many of its smaller rivals.

Current evidence shows that there are definite limits to economies of scale in the automobile industry. The average capacity of GM, Ford, and Chrysler plants is around 230,000 vehicles per year, which suggests this may be the optimum-sized plant. The Big Three auto makers have also reduced their size by divesting large portions of their parts- and components-making operations. They are also increasingly outsourcing the production of entire modules—parts preassembled into complete units to other suppliers. Industry experts estimate that these reductions may cut production costs by as much as 30 percent. Small, more flexible assembly plants also allow the auto makers to more quickly adapt to changing consumer fashions and preferences.[41]

[41] James W. Brock, "Automobiles," in *The Structure of American Industry*, eds. Walter Adams and James Brock, 11th ed. (Upper Saddle River, NJ: Prentice-Hall, 2005), 96–118.

Other Factors Influencing the Long-Run Average Cost Curve

Two other factors that can affect the shape or position of the long-run average cost curve are learning by doing and transportation costs.[42]

Learning by doing reflects the drop in unit costs as total cumulative production increases because workers become more efficient as they repeat their assigned tasks. This process was first observed in defense production during World War II. For the B-29 bomber, unit costs declined by 29.5 percent on average with each doubling of cumulative output. Large-scale integrated circuit production also exhibits the efficiencies of learning by doing, given the difficulty of learning to deposit the correct amount of material into various parts of the circuits. It has been estimated that costs can decrease by 25 to 30 percent with each doubling of cumulative output due to the learning process. The cost advantages from learning by doing affect the position, not the shape, of the long-run average cost curve because they are associated with the cumulative output produced by the firm, not the level of output at different scales of operation. Substantial cost savings from learning by doing would cause the *LRAC* curve to shift down.

Transportation costs can affect the shape of the long-run average cost curve for a firm, particularly the point of minimum average cost. If production is centralized in a small number of large plants, then the product has to be delivered over greater distances to the customers. Transportation costs are particularly important for heavy, bulky products such as bricks and ready-made concrete. If these transportation costs increase with large-scale production, the long-run average cost curve that includes these costs will have a lower optimum scale of operation than a curve without these costs. These levels of output could differ substantially depending on the shapes of, and relationship between, the transportation cost curve and the *LRAC* curve.

> **Learning by doing**
> The drop in unit costs as total cumulative production increases because workers become more efficient as they repeat their assigned tasks.

The Minimum Efficient Scale of Operation

An important concept that affects the structure of an industry and the resulting competitive strategy is the **minimum efficient scale (*MES*)** of operation in that industry. The *MES* is that scale of operation at which the long-run average cost curve stops declining or at which economies of scale are exhausted. At this scale, there are no further advantages to larger-scale production in terms of lowering production costs. The important point is the location of this minimum efficient scale relative to the total size of the market. Figure 6.3 shows the minimum efficient scales associated with four different *LRAC* curves and a market demand curve.

> **Minimum efficient scale (*MES*)**
> That scale of operation at which the long-run average cost curve stops declining or at which economies of scale are exhausted.

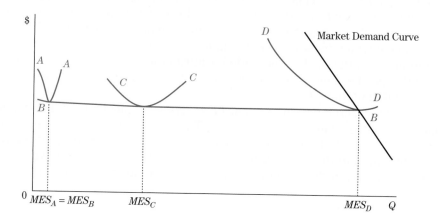

> **FIGURE 6.3**
> **Minimum Efficient Scale (*MES*) with Different *LRAC* Curves**
> *For various firms, the minimum efficient scale (MES), where the LRAC stops decreasing, is reached at different points relative to total market demand.*
> *Source:* Adapted from Shepherd, William G., *The Economics of Industrial Organization,* 4th ed., Upper Saddle River, NJ: Prentice Hall, 1997.

---

[42] This discussion is based on Scherer and Ross, 98–108.

The four *LRAC* curves differ in terms of the location of their minimum efficient scales of operation and the gradient or slope of their cost curves—that is, how quickly costs change as output varies.[43] Firm A represents a firm that could operate in a competitive market with a large number of producers. It has a relatively small *MES* compared to the size of the market. Any scale economies are exhausted quickly. The cost curve also has a relatively steep gradient, indicating that producing output at a level much greater or less than MES_A will result in a rapid increase in costs. Thus, a competitive market could support a large number of these small A-type firms.

Firm B has the same minimum efficient scale of operation as Firm A. Unlike Firm A, its *LRAC* curve is relatively flat over a large range of output. This means that there is no optimal scale of operation for Firm B. Firms of many different sizes are consistent with this *LRAC* curve. Competition is viable because the *MES* is relatively small, but larger firms may exist because diseconomies of scale do not set in over the relevant range of the market. These larger firms may have enough market power to give them a competitive advantage even though their costs are not reduced by the larger-scale production.

Firm C has a cost structure that is more consistent with an oligopoly market structure. The minimum efficient scale is one-third of the market, so it is likely that only a few firms will emerge in the market. The gradient of the curve is relatively steep, so this scale of operation is optimal. Firm D represents a natural monopoly, where one large-scale firm will dominate the market. The minimum efficient scale of production comprises the entire market. Any smaller firms will have greatly increased costs of production.

Methods for Determining the Minimum Efficient Scale   What is the shape of the *LRAC* curve for different firms and industries, and what is the minimum efficient scale of operation? Researchers have obtained empirical estimates of long-run costs through

- Surveys of expert opinion (engineering estimates)
- Statistical cost estimation
- The survivor approach

Surveying expert opinion is a time-consuming process that relies on the judgments of those individuals closely connected with different industries. Reporting biases may obviously occur with this approach. With statistical cost estimation, researchers attempt to estimate the relationship between unit costs and output levels of firms of varying sizes *while holding constant all other factors influencing cost in addition to size.* This is usually done with multiple regression analysis in a manner similar to that described for demand estimation in Chapter 4. With the survivor approach, the size distribution of firms is examined to determine the scale of operation at which most firms in the industry are concentrated. The underlying assumption is that this scale of operation is most efficient and has the lowest costs because this is where most firms have survived. Each of these approaches has its strengths and limitations.[44]

Most of this research has shown that *LRAC* curves typically look like the curve in Figure 6.4 rather than that in Figure 6.2. The curve in Figure 6.4 resembles the B curve in Figure 6.3. Economies of scale for many firms occur over a modest range of output, and then the *LRAC* curve becomes essentially flat, with neither further economies nor diseconomies in the relevant range of the market.

[43] This discussion is drawn from William G. Shepherd, *The Economics of Industrial Organization*, 4th ed. (Upper Saddle River, N.J.: Prentice Hall, 1997), 169–71.

[44] Scherer and Ross, 111–18; Shepherd, 179–85.

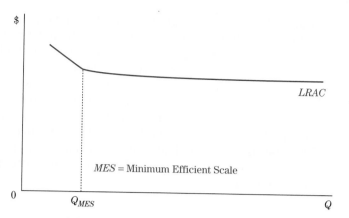

FIGURE 6.4
**Empirical Long-Run Average Cost
(*LRAC*) Curve**
*This figure shows the typical shape
for a firm's LRAC curve based on
empirical data.*

Empirical Estimates of the Minimum Efficient Scale   In general, research evidence shows that the minimum efficient scale for most industries is small relative to entire demand in the U.S. market and that the gradient of the *LRAC* curve—how quickly costs change as output increases—is not steep. When transportation costs are taken into account, these results are modified somewhat, as these costs lead to geographic markets that are considerably smaller than the national measures.[45]

For the beer industry, there is a fairly large decrease in the long-run average cost curve up to a plant with a capacity of 4.0 million barrels per year, with smaller cost decreases up to a plant with an annual capacity of 12 million barrels. Survivor analysis has shown a decline in breweries with a capacity of less than 2 million barrels and a large increase in plants with a capacity of more than 5 million barrels. The 18 plants of Anheuser-Busch and Miller in 1998 had an average capacity slightly exceeding 8.6 million barrels.[46] In the 1970s, technological change occurred in the beer industry that favored large-scale firms and drove many small firms from the market. The *MES* was 1 million barrels during most of the 1960s, but this increased to 8 million in 1970, 16 million in 1980 and 1990, and 18 million in 2000. Between 1950 and 1991, no firms entered the industry, while 344 of 369 firms exited.[47] Even as this trend was occurring, there was a concurrent development of small microbreweries serving local markets. The number of breweries with 10,000- to 15,000-barrel capacity increased from around 50 in 1986 to more than 175 in 1998. However, the share of the market of all microbreweries was estimated to be only 0.16 percent in 1990.[48]

Widely cited empirical evidence on multiplant economies of scale that pertain to the entire firm, although dated, suggests that scale factors alone do not explain the large-scale production that exists in many sectors of the economy.[49] The cost gradient for multiplant economies is only slight to moderate for most industries. In beer brewing, petroleum refining, and refrigerators, the actual scale of operation appears to be driven by economies of scale. However, in fabric weaving, steel, and storage batteries, the average market share far exceeds the minimum necessary to achieve multiplant economies of scale.

---

[45] Scherer and Ross, 117.

[46] Kenneth G. Elzinga, "Beer," in *The Structure of American Industry*, eds. Walter Adams and James Brock, 11th ed. (Upper Saddle River, N.J.: Prentice Hall, 2005), 72–95.

[47] Joe R. Kerkvliet, William Nebesky, Carol Horton Tremblay, and Victor J. Tremblay, "Efficiency and Technological Change in the U.S. Brewing Industry," *Journal of Productivity Analysis* 10 (1998): 271–88; Victor J. Tremblay and Carol Horton Tremblay, *The U.S. Brewing Industry* (Cambridge: The MIT Press, 2005), pp. 30–34.

[48] Elzinga, 81–83; Kerkvliet et al., 271–88.

[49] Scherer and Ross, 140.

Recent research indicates that aggregate concentration, or the share of private-sector economic activity attributed to the largest 100, 500, and 1,000 companies, declined during the 1980s and early 1990s, but increased again in the late 1990s.[50] Moderately large firms appear to have increased in relative importance, given the greater influence of sunk costs, such as advertising and promotion, to be spread over the output produced. Firm size also tended to increase due to the rising importance of exports for the U.S. economy and the scale needed to compete abroad. Improved monitoring and managing technologies may have stimulated the growth of middle-range firms, but these technologies also allowed firms to monitor their partners in alliances and joint ventures more effectively, eliminating the need for extremely large-scale companies.

Long-Run Average Cost and Managerial Decision Making

In June 1999, Toyota Motor Corporation announced that it was planning to expand its North American capacity through either a new production line or a new factory in response to strong demand in the U.S. market for sport-utility vehicles.[51] This decision was driven by the strength of the American economy and the demand for Toyota automobiles at that time, which was much stronger than expected. The company, which had an annual production capacity in North America of approximately 1.2 million vehicles, sold 1.37 million vehicles in the United States and 130,000 vehicles in Canada in 1998. The company president stated, "We can't sit around and wait another five years to build new facilities." Industry analysts argued that it would be cheaper for Toyota to build a second line at an existing plant than to build an entirely new plant. They also noted that if the automobile demand driven by the strong economy was not sustained, the expansion decision could result in an excess supply of sport-utility vehicles. This example shows that cost factors are part of a manager's long-run strategic decision to expand capacity. Overall strategy depends on how well a manager relates production and cost decisions to changes in consumer demand.

Economies of scale can influence the production of services as well as goods. There has been much controversy over this issue in the hospital industry, particularly given the changes in the health care system over the past two decades. Early statistical studies found that economies of scale existed up to a hospital size of around 500 beds.[52] However, these studies may not have adequately controlled for the multiproduct nature of hospitals and for the possible lack of incentives for cost minimization discussed previously. Survivor analysis has indicated that from 1970 to 1996, the percentage of hospitals with under 100 beds decreased, while the percentage with 100 to 400 beds increased. It now appears that the minimum point of the long-run average cost curve for short-term community hospitals is reached at around 200 beds and that the cost curve is probably shallow. This means that hospitals of many different sizes can compete with each other. Some hospital administrators may be able to develop positions in niche or specialized markets that allow them to remain profitable even if they are not of optimal size.

---

[50] This discussion is based on Lawrence J. White, "Trends in Aggregate Concentration in the United States," *Journal of Economic Perspectives* 16 (Fall 2002): 137–60.

[51] Norihiko Shirouzu, "Toyota Plans an Expansion of Capacity Due to Demand," *Wall Street Journal*, June 29, 1999.

[52] This discussion is based on Santerre and Neun, 464–66.

Summary

In this chapter, we discussed the long-run decisions that managers must make regarding strategies to minimize the costs of production. We saw how issues were more complex in the long run than in the short run, given that the scale of operation is also variable in this time frame. Managers need to consider whether the current scale of operation is optimal, given estimates of long-run demand and market size. Costs may be decreased by changing the combination of inputs used in the production process or by changing the entire scale of operation.

The empirical evidence on economies of scale showed that the long-run average cost curve tends to be relatively flat for many firms when looking at both single-plant and multiplant operations. This means that there is no single optimal size firm in these industries in terms of minimizing the unit costs of production. We may expect to see firms of many different sizes in these industries. A manager's choice of firm size may be influenced by cost considerations, but it also depends on many other factors. We pull these factors together in our discussion of the four basic types of market structure—perfect competition, monopolistic competition, oligopoly, and monopoly—in Chapters 7, 8, and 9.

Appendix 6A Isoquant Analysis

Economists have developed a model of long-run production decisions that incorporates output, the technology of production, and the prices and quantities of the inputs. We will use this model to illustrate input substitution, cost minimization, the derivation of short- and long-run cost curves, and technological change.[53]

Production Technology and Input Substitution

We begin our analysis with the long-run production function shown in Equation 6.A1:[54]

6.A1 $Q = f(L, K)$

where

Q = quantity of output

L = amount of the labor input (variable)

K = amount of the capital input (variable)

Both inputs are variable in this production function and can be changed when different levels of output are produced or substituted for each other in the production of a given level of output. We illustrate this input substitution with an *isoquant*, a theoretical construct based on the technology of production that shows alternative combinations of inputs a manager can use to produce a given level of output. *Isoquant* means equal quantity because any point on the curve

---

[53] You will notice many similarities between the isoquant model in this appendix and the economic model of consumer choice in Appendix 3A in Chapter 3.

[54] This is the same function as Equation 6.1 in the text.

FIGURE 6.A1

A Production Isoquant

An isoquant represents production technology by showing the marginal rate of technical substitution or the rate at which one input can be substituted for another while maintaining the same level of output.

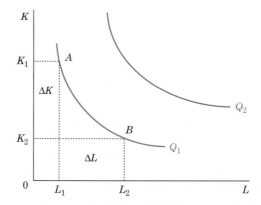

represents the same amount of output. There are a whole series of isoquants for a given production process, with isoquants farther from the origin representing larger amounts of output.

Figure 6.A1 shows two typical production isoquants. Isoquant Q_1 shows the various combinations of labor and capital that can be used to produce output level Q_1. This level of output could be produced with a capital-intensive process at point A (L_1 amount of labor and K_1 amount of capital) or with a more labor-intensive process at point B (L_2 amount of labor and K_2 amount of capital). Based on the technology embodied in the production function, either combination of inputs is feasible to use to produce output level Q_1. Point A involves more capital and less labor, while point B uses more labor and less capital. Thus, the two points illustrate input substitution in the production process.

Isoquant Q_2 shows alternative combinations of labor and capital that can be used to produce output level Q_2, where Q_2 is greater than Q_1. There are other isoquants (not pictured) farther from the origin that show even larger levels of output.

The shape of the isoquants shows the degree of input substitution that is possible in any production process. Comparing point B with point A on isoquant Q_1 in Figure 6.A1, we see that if the amount of capital is reduced from K_1 to K_2, or ΔK, the amount of labor must be increased from L_1 to L_2, or ΔL, to produce the same level of output, Q_1. The ratio, $\Delta K/\Delta L$, is called the *marginal rate of technical substitution* of labor for capital ($MRTS_{KL}$). It shows the rate at which one input can be substituted for another while still producing the same amount of output.

If this ratio is shown for very small changes in labor and capital, it is represented by the slope of a line tangent to the isoquant at different points on the curve. The isoquant in Figure 6.A1 exhibits a diminishing marginal rate of technical substitution, as the slope of a tangent to the isoquant at point B is flatter than the slope of the tangent at point A. Figure 6.A1 shows a production process in which the inputs are imperfect substitutes for each other because the marginal rate of technical substitution depends on the amounts of the inputs used.

There are two polar cases for the shapes of isoquants, shown in Figures 6.A2 and 6.A3. Figure 6.A2 illustrates the case where the two inputs are perfect substitutes for each other. There is a given marginal rate of technical substitution between the inputs that does not depend on the combination of inputs used. Thus, the isoquant is a straight line with a constant slope. In Figure 6.A3, the two inputs are perfect complements with each other. This isoquant is often called a fixed-proportions production function. It implies that there is only one combination of inputs (L_1, K_1, at point A) that can be used to produce output level Q_1 and that the inputs have to be used in this proportion. No input substitution is possible because moving along the isoquant in either direction (from point A to point B or from point A to point C) involves the greater use of one input and no smaller amount of the other input.

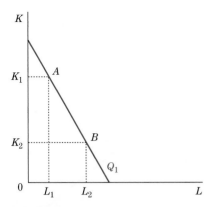

FIGURE 6.A2
Perfect Substitutes
The inputs in this production function are perfect substitutes for one another.

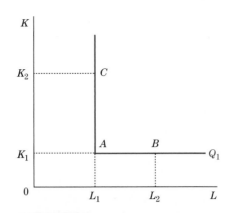

FIGURE 6.A3
Perfect Complements (Fixed Proportions)
The inputs in this production function can be used only in fixed proportions.

The Isocost Line

To show how a firm would minimize the costs of producing a given output level, we need the *isocost line,* which presents alternative combinations of inputs that result in a given total cost of production with a given set of input prices. Equation 6.A2 represents a given isocost (equal cost) line:

6.A2 $TC = P_L L + P_K K$

> *where*
> TC = total cost of production
> P_L = price per unit of labor
> L = quantity of labor input
> P_K = price per unit of capital
> K = quantity of capital input

Equation 6.A2 shows that the expenditure on the labor input (price per unit times quantity of labor) and on the capital input (price per unit times quantity of capital) equals a given expenditure on inputs, or the total cost of production. Thus, an isocost line shows alternative combinations of inputs that can be purchased with a given total cost of production.

With a given value of TC, P_L, and P_K, we can graph an isocost line, as shown in Figure 6.A4. The isocost line intersects the horizontal axis at the maximum level of

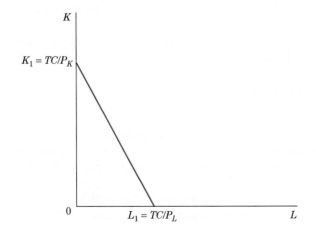

FIGURE 6.A4
The Isocost Line
The isocost line shows alternative combinations of the inputs (L, K) that can be purchased for a given total cost (TC) and with given input prices (P_L, P_K).

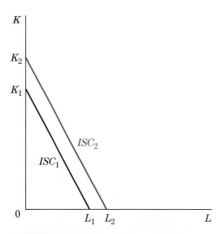

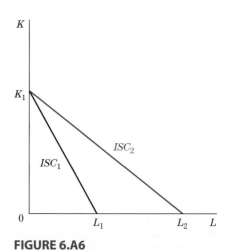

FIGURE 6.A5

Change (Increase) in the Total Cost of Production (Input Prices Constant)

An increase in the total cost of production, with input prices constant, is represented by a parallel outward shift of the isocost line.

FIGURE 6.A6

Change (Decrease) in the Price of Labor (All Else Constant)

A decrease in the price of labor, all else constant, is represented by an outward swiveling of the isocost line.

labor input (L_1) that can be purchased if all the expenditure representing the given total cost of production is used to purchase labor. The total cost of production (TC) divided by the price per unit of labor (P_L) gives this maximum amount of labor input. Likewise, the isocost line intersects the K-axis at the maximum level of capital (K_1) that can be purchased if all the expenditure is on capital. This amount of capital is determined by dividing the total cost (TC) by the price per unit of capital (P_K). The slope of the isocost line is distance $0K_1/0L_1 = (TC/P_K)/(TC/P_L) = P_L/P_K$. Thus, the slope of the isocost line is the ratio of the prices of the two inputs of production.

We illustrate a change in the total cost of production, holding input prices constant, in Figure 6.A5. Because the slope of the isocost line is the ratio of the prices of the two inputs of production and because prices are being held constant, a change in the total cost of production is represented by a parallel shift of the isocost line. If the total cost of production increases from TC_1 to TC_2, the isocost line shifts out from ISC_1 to ISC_2, as shown in Figure 6.A5. For a higher total cost of production, the firm can purchase more of both inputs, more of one input and no less of the other, or less of one input and a great amount more of the other.

We illustrate a decrease in the price of labor, holding constant the price of capital and the total cost of production, in Figure 6.A6. The isocost line swivels out, pivoting on the K-axis. Because the price of capital has not changed, the maximum quantity of K that can be purchased does not change either. However, the price of labor has decreased, so labor has become cheaper relative to capital. Isocost line ISC_2 has a flatter slope because the slope of the isocost line is the ratio of the prices of the two inputs, which has changed.

Cost Minimization

We now use isoquants and isocost lines to illustrate in Figure 6.A7 the combination of inputs that minimizes the cost of producing a given level of output. In Figure 6.A7, if managers have decided to produce output level Q_1, they must still determine what combination of inputs to use, as any point on Q_1 represents a feasible combination of inputs. Given the prices of the inputs of production whose ratio is reflected in the slope of the isocost line, the solution to this problem is to find the isocost line closest to the origin that is just tangent to the given isoquant, Q_1. This point of

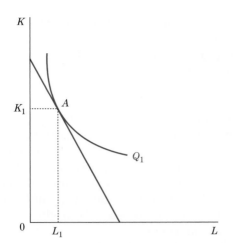

FIGURE 6.A7
Cost Minimization
The cost-minimizing combination of inputs (L₁, K₁) is represented by point A, the tangency between the isoquant and the isocost line where the marginal rate of technical substitution equals the ratio of the input prices.

tangency occurs in Figure 6.A7 at point A, representing L_1 amount of labor input and K_1 amount of capital. Any other point on the isoquant represents a higher total cost of production, as these points lie on isocost lines farther from the origin. Any other point on the given isocost line represents a combination of labor and capital that is not sufficient to product output level Q_1. Thus, the combination of labor and capital at point A, L_1, and K_1, represents the cost-minimizing combination of inputs that can be used to produce output level Q_1.[55]

At this point of tangency (point A), the slope of the isoquant is equal to the slope of the isocost line. The slope of the isoquant is the marginal rate of technical substitution between labor and capital, while the slope of the isocost line is the ratio of the prices of the two inputs of production. Thus, the *cost-minimizing combination of inputs* occurs where $MRTS_{LK} = (P_L/P_K)$.[56]

Input Substitution

If the price ratio of the inputs of production changes, firms will substitute the cheaper input for the more expensive input if the production technology allows them to do so. We illustrate input substitution in Figure 6.A8. The original point of

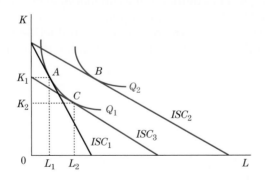

FIGURE 6.A8
Input Substitution
To minimize the costs of production, firms will substitute a cheaper input, labor, for a more expensive input, capital, when the price of labor decreases.

---

[55] Point A in Figure 6.A7 is also the solution to the problem of maximizing the level of output produced for a given total cost of production.

[56] We now can show that this expression is the same rule that we presented in footnote 1 of this chapter. As we move along isoquant Q_1 in Figure 6.A1, the change in output is represented by the following equation: $\Delta Q = (MP_L)(\Delta L) + (MP_K)(\Delta K)$, where MP is the marginal product of each input. The change in the amount of output is a function of changes in the quantities of both inputs and their respective marginal productivity. Because the change in output along a given isoquant is zero by definition, the expression becomes $0 = (MP_L)(\Delta L) + (MP_K)(\Delta K)$. Rearranging terms, $-(MP_L)(\Delta L) = (MP_K)(\Delta K)$ and $(MP_L)/(MP_K) = -(\Delta K)/(\Delta L)$. The right side of the last equation is the $MRTS_{LK}$. Therefore, the cost-minimizing equation above in the text shows that $MRTS_{LK} = (MP_L)/(MP_K) = (P_L/P_K)$. Rearranging terms again gives the expression in footnote 1: $(MP_L/P_L) = (MP_K/P_K)$.

cost minimization to produce output level Q_1 is point A, with L_1 amount of labor and K_1 amount of capital. This point results from the tangency of isoquant Q_1 and isocost line ISC_1. If the price of labor decreases, the isocost line swivels from ISC_1 to ISC_2. This change means that, for the same total cost of production, the firm is now able to produce output level Q_2 with the combination of inputs represented by point B.

Suppose the firm only wants to produce output level Q_1. Even in this case, it will use more of the cheaper input, labor, and less of the relatively more expensive input, capital. This outcome is shown by point C in Figure 6.A8, the tangency between isocost line ISC_3 and isoquant Q_1. Isocost line ISC_3 is drawn parallel to isocost line ISC_2, so it represents the new lower price of labor inherent in the ISC_2 line. However, line ISC_3 is tangent to isoquant Q_1 and closer to the origin than isocost line ISC_2. Therefore, it now costs less to produce output level Q_1, given the lower price of labor. The firm will produce at point C, using L_2 amount of labor and K_2 amount of capital, instead of point A, with L_1 amount of labor and K_1 amount of capital. Thus, the firm substitutes labor for capital when the price of labor decreases relative to the price of capital.[57]

Changes in the Costs of Production

We now use the isoquant model to illustrate both short- and long-run costs of production, as shown in Figure 6.A9. In this figure, the original level of production is output level Q_1, with the input combination at point A (L_1, K_1). This point represents the tangency between isoquant Q_1 and isocost line ISC_1, which incorporates total cost of production TC_1. If the firm wants to produce output level Q_2 in the long run, it will use L_2 amount of labor and K_2 amount of capital (point B), as both inputs are variable. The total cost of production at point B is TC_2, which is incorporated in isocost curve ISC_2. Likewise, to produce output level Q_3, the firm in the long run should move to point C, with L_3 amount of labor, K_3 amount of capital, and TC_3 total cost of production (isocost line ISC_3). Points A, B, and C represent the least-cost combination of inputs to produce the three levels of output when all inputs are variable (the long run). The long-run total cost is shown in Figure 6.A9 with each of the isocost lines. Long-run average cost is long-run total cost divided by the corresponding level of output. Long-run marginal cost is the change in long-run total cost divided by the change in output.

Figure 6.A9 also shows the short-run costs of production if the capital input is fixed at level K_1. In the short run with fixed capital, the firm would move from

FIGURE 6.A9

Short- and Long-Run Costs of Production

To minimize the costs of production, firms choose a different combination of inputs in the long run, when all inputs are variable (points B and C), than in the short run, when the capital input is fixed (points B' and C').

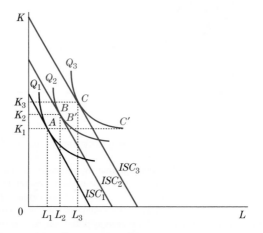

___

[57] For the fixed-proportions production function of Figure 6.A3, the firm would not be able to substitute labor for capital. The total cost of production would still be reduced, given the decrease in the price of labor, but not as much as it would if input substitution were possible.

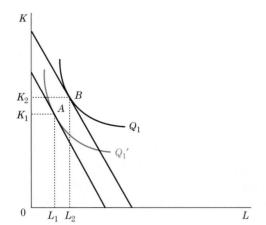

FIGURE 6.A10
Change in Technology
A change in technology is represented by a shifting of an isoquant showing the same level of output.

point A to point B' in order to produce output level Q_2 and to point C' in order to produce output level Q_3. Point B' lies on an isocost line farther from the origin than point B (not shown), and point C' lies on an isocost line farther from the origin than point C (not shown). Thus, the cost of production rises faster in the short run when the level of capital is fixed at K_1 than when all inputs are allowed to vary (the long run). We saw earlier in this chapter that short-run average total cost rises more quickly for a given firm than does long-run average cost. This result occurs because the firm is unable to change to the cost-minimizing combination of inputs in the short run, given that some inputs (capital, in this case) are fixed.

Technological Change

Technological change in the production function is illustrated by a shift in the isoquants as in Figure 6.A10. The original point of production of output level Q_1 is at B, with L_2 amount of labor and K_2 amount of capital. Technological change typically increases productivity and decreases the costs of production. In Figure 6.A10, we represent this type of technological change by a shift of the Q_1 isoquant from Q_1 to Q_1'. The Q_1' isoquant is now tangent to an isocost line closer to the origin at point A, representing a lower total cost of production. Thus, productivity has now increased, as the firm is able to produce output level Q_1' using only L_1 amount of labor input and K_1 amount of capital input.

Key Terms

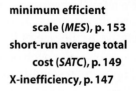

best practices, p. 148

capital-intensive method of
    production, p. 143

diseconomies of
    scale, p. 150

economies of
    scale, p. 150

input substitution, p. 143

labor-intensive method
    of production, p. 143

lean production, p. 148

learning by doing, p. 153

long-run average
    cost (*LRAC*), p. 149

long-run production
    function, p. 142

minimum efficient
    scale (*MES*), p. 153

short-run average total
    cost (*SATC*), p. 149

X-inefficiency, p. 147

Exercises

Technical Questions

1. A company operates plants in both the United States (where capital is relatively cheap and labor is relatively expensive) and Mexico (where labor is relatively cheap and capital is relatively expensive).

   a. Why is it unlikely that the cost-minimizing factor choice will be identical between the two plants? Explain.

   b. Under what circumstances will the input choice be relatively similar?

2. The following graph shows short-run average total cost (*SATC*) curves for three different scales of production. If these are the only plant sizes possible for this firm, what will the firm's long-run average cost curve be?

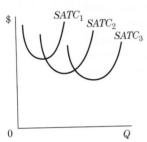

3. Industry studies often suggest that firms may have long-run average cost curves that show some output range over which there are economies of scale and a wide range of output over which long-run average cost is constant; finally, at very high output, there are diseconomies of scale.

   a. Draw a representative long-run average cost curve, and indicate the minimum efficient scale.

   b. Would you expect that firms in an industry like this would all produce about the same level of output? Why?

4. Each of the following statements describes a market structure. What would you expect the long-run average cost curve to look like for a representative firm in each industry? Graph the curve, and indicate the minimum efficient scale (*MES*).

   a. There are a few large firms in the industry.

   b. There are many firms in the industry, each small relative to the size of the market.

5. [Appendix Exercise] For each of the following technologies, graph a representative set of isoquants:

   a. Every worker requires exactly one machine to work with; no substitution is possible.

   b. Capital and labor are perfect substitutes.

   c. The firm is able to substitute capital for labor, but they are not perfect substitutes.

6. [Appendix Exercise] A firm pays $10 per unit of labor and $5 per unit of capital.

   a. Graph the isocost curves for $TC = \$100$, $TC = \$200$, and $TC = \$500$.

   b. Suppose that the cost of capital increases to $10. Graph the new isocost curves.

7. [Appendix Exercise] The following graph shows the firm's cost-minimizing input choice at current factor prices.

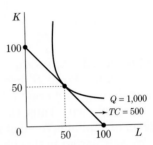

   a. What are the current prices of capital and labor, based on the graph?

   b. Suppose that the price of labor increases. If the firm wishes to continue to produce the current level of output, how will the firm's optimal input choice change (relative to its current choice)? Support your answer with a graph.

8. [Appendix Exercise] The following graph shows the firm's cost-minimizing input choice at current factor prices. The firm is currently employing 100 units of capital and 100 units of labor. The wage rate is $20, and the price per unit of capital is $10.

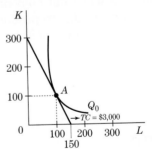

   a. In the short run, the firm cannot change its level of capital. The price of labor rises to $25. If the firm wishes to continue to produce the current level of output, show the firm's short-run cost-minimizing input choice.

   b. What will happen to the firm's short-run cost curves?

   c. How will the firm's cost-minimizing input choice be different in the long run, when all factors of production are variable? Support your answer with a graph.

Application Questions

1. Discuss how the "tale of two auto plants" in the opening article shows how the choices facing a firm making a long-run decision on plant location are much greater than those for a firm with a plant already in operation. Why is the long run considered to be a planning horizon?

2. In the current business news media, find and discuss two other examples of input substitution.

3. The following graph shows economies of scale in the beer brewing industry.[58]

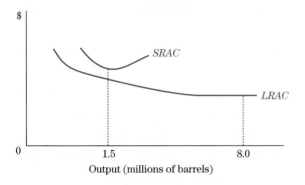

a. What does this graph tell us about the nature of economies of scale in the beer brewing industry?

b. What are the particular problems associated with the firm represented by the *SATC* curve shown in the graph? Does it represent a firm that would be able to survive over time?

4. The following quotation appeared in a *Wall Street Journal* article on the battle for market share in the automobile industry in 2000: "The huge fixed costs involved in developing new vehicles and running big auto factories means auto makers feel compelled to maintain—or expand—market share. Losing share long term could mean shutting down factories, or running factories at unprofitable rates." Do these statements support economic theory and show that economies of scale do not benefit a firm if the output level is small? Explain.

5. A 1964 study of the broiler chicken processing industry showed that "processing costs decreased continually with output size, but after 10 million birds per year the decrease was small." Researchers concluded from the study that "an output of 10 million birds per year, representing 0.33 percent of 1969 broiler production, captured most of the efficiencies." A more recent study "concluded that a technically efficient and cost-effective processing plant should process 8,400 birds per hour. Expanding this processing rate to an annual production volume results in an estimated *MES* [minimum efficient scale] value of 0.4 percent of the market."[59] Do these results show that competition among a large number of plants and firms in the broiler chicken industry is possible? Explain.

---

[58] Elzinga, 95.

[59] Richard T. Rogers, "Broilers," in *Industry Studies*, ed. Larry L. Duetsch, 2nd ed. (Armonk, N.Y.: Sharpe, 1998), 83.

On the Web

For updated information on the *Wall Street Journal* article at the beginning of the chapter, as well as other relevant links and information, visit the book's Web site at **www.pearsonhighered.com/farnham**

7 Market Structure: Perfect Competition

I n this chapter, we begin our discussion of market structure, or the environment in which firms operate. This discussion integrates the demand and pricing material in Chapters 3 and 4 with the production and cost issues of Chapters 5 and 6.

You may recall from Figure 1.1 and our discussion in Chapter 1 that there are four major forms of market structure: perfect competition, monopolistic competition, oligopoly, and monopoly. The perfectly competitive firm has no market power because it cannot influence the price of the product. On the other end of the spectrum is the monopoly firm that has market power because it can use price and other strategies to earn larger profits that typically persist over longer periods of time. Between these two benchmarks are the market structures of monopolistic competition and oligopoly. Firms have varying degrees of market power in these market structures that combine elements of both competitive and monopoly behavior.

Managers are always trying to devise strategies that will help their firms gain and maintain market power. If, and how, they can do this depends on the type of market structure in which their firms operate.

We begin this chapter with the *Wall Street Journal* article "This Spud's Not for You," which describes the operation of the potato industry, the reactions of different potato farmers to changes in industry prices, and the attempts by potato farmers to coordinate the amount of potatoes they produce. We relate the discussion in the article to earlier, similar changes in the potato industry and show how this industry contains the essential elements of the model of perfect competition. We then discuss the model of perfect competition in depth, drawing on the issues we first raised in Chapter 1. We end the chapter with a discussion of managerial strategies in several additional highly competitive industries that shows how firms in all of these industries attempt to shield themselves from the volatility of the competitive market.

This Spud's Not for You

by Timothy W. Martin

Wall Street Journal, *September 26, 2006*

Shelley, Idaho—It took farmer Merrill Hanny three days to bury $100,000 worth of his perfectly good potatoes. He remembers how they crunched beneath his tractor as he plowed over his muddy field in the spring of last year.

Mr. Hanny destroyed part of his crop at the behest of the United Potato Growers of America, a fledgling group of regional farming cooperatives. The group aspires to be to potatoes what OPEC is to oil by carefully managing to keep demand high and constant, resulting in a more stable return for farmers.

The new organization has been a boon to Mr. Hanny, 53 years old, and other farmers who for years have watched potato overproduction push down prices and mash profits. . . .

From the french-fry farms of Washington state to the spud fields of Texas, potato farmers are joining the new movement. Formed in March 2005, United Potato says it has recruited farmers and regional cooperatives who till more than 60% of the potato acreage in the U.S. Some Canadian growers have also enlisted.

In the past year, United Potato helped erase 6.8 million hundred-pound potato sacks from the U.S. and Canadian markets—the equivalent of about 1.3 billion medium orders of french fries at McDonald's. For farmers, their open-market returns surged to $10.04 per hundred pounds, up 48.5% from last year.

So far, for competitive reasons, supermarkets have absorbed the increased payments to farmers so potato prices for consumers have risen only slightly. In general, restaurants that serve french fries haven't pumped up prices either, but if open-market prices remain high, farmers under contract to restaurants may have more leverage to ask for higher prices. . . .

United Potato says it is trying to preserve the North American potato farm. There are fewer than 10,000 potato farmers today, down from more than 50,000 three decades ago, says the U.S. Agriculture Department. That's partly because, as with other crops, big growers are gobbling up small ones. Also, demand for potatoes has tapered off due to dietary trends. Potatoes remain the most popular individual accompaniment to a main dish, but people are cooking fewer at home.

In a sign of the uncertainty that today's farmers face, even Idaho is reexamining its identity as a potato-producing region, with lawmakers recently debating a measure that would remove the phrase "Famous Potatoes" from state license plates. The proposal fizzled, but the anxiety over the future of potato growing remains.

United Potato's annual campaign to support potato farming begins a few months before the spring potato planting season.

That's when United Potato's 20-member board of directors decides, with the approval of the membership, whether farmers are on track to overproduce and, if they are, sets a target for acreage reduction. The decision is based on reports from the field and input from analysts. Then the directors meet with the regional co-ops to determine how to execute cutbacks locally. That could mean, for instance, slashing more acres of one particular variety of potato over another. United Potato also might pay a farmer to keep excess crops off the market.

In years past, potato farmers were all too willing to take a loss on sales if it meant increasing their market share. The result was that prices became so low, the industry was unprofitable. By destroying some of their crop, many farmers believe they are helping to create a seller's market. Mr. Hanny says he willingly destroyed part of his crop to prove his loyalty to the group. . . .

The spud cartel's manipulation of supply is perfectly legal. Orange, dairy and other farmers have employed similar co-ops as market stabilizers since 1922, when the Capper-Volstead Act exempted farmers from federal antitrust laws, permitting them to share prices and orchestrate supply. Over the years, though, farmers of fresh vegetables have tended to avoid co-ops due to market volatility, varying regional tastes and quality-control concerns stemming from climate differences.

Potato farmers have proven especially resistant to joining national groups, partly because different growers serve different customers. Most french-fry potato farmers have contracts with food companies that set production levels and prices. Others sell their potatoes without fixed contracts on the open market, where they're more vulnerable to shifting supply and demand. Historically, growers have responded to thin profit margins by planting extra acres—which helped depress prices further.

"It's one good year, then four or five bad years," says Albert Wada, one of Idaho's biggest growers. In recent years, price wars cropped up as farmers tried to steal market share from one another. "It has become a last-man-standing mentality," says Doug Hanks, a third-generation potato farmer in St. Anthony, Idaho.

In September of 2004, Mr. Wada and another grower, Keith Cornelison, summoned nearly two dozen of the state's growers to a crammed office in Blackfoot, Idaho, which calls itself the "Potato Capital of the World." They talked about how to curb production and boost prices. After more meetings, phone calls and emails, they agreed to form the United Potato Growers of Idaho.

That November, Mr. Wada presented the plan to 650 state farmers in Idaho Falls, prompting a standing ovation. Many farmers signed up on the spot, agreeing to pay annual dues ranging from about $10,000 to $500,000, depending on how much a farmer grows.

Mr. Hanny was one. The third-generation farmer had lost about $500,000 in the previous few years and wouldn't have planted potatoes at all—but then he found out about the co-op. After hearing Mr. Wada, he wrote to fellow growers praising United Potato and urging them to think of their children's college education driving away with the truckloads of potatoes they grew.

The Idaho group next hired Jerry Fields, a former H.J. Heinz Co. and ConAgra Foods Inc. executive, to handle business decisions. He pushed the group to go national. Although Idaho produces around 30% of U.S. potatoes, Mr. Fields believed the co-op couldn't influence prices without members from other big potato states.

The Idaho group became the national group. Messrs. Fields and Wada crisscrossed the country, recruiting farmers from California, Oregon, Wisconsin, Colorado, Washington, Texas, and elsewhere. . . .

Past regional co-ops crumbled after initial successes as growers slowed production to take advantage of higher prices. United Potato members say this group will last because many large growers across the country have joined, recognizing that food-industry consolidation makes it imperative that growers unite.

Some skeptical nonmembers think the co-op is merely a way to help large Idaho farmers who typically have overproduced. . . .

A big test for United Potato will come this spring, when higher prices could tempt members to plant more than they're allotted. Keeping them in line is "not going to be easy," says Tim O'Connor, CEO of the U.S. Potato Board, the industry's marketing arm. United Potato says it will monitor farmers with the aid of satellite photography and global-positioning-system technology. Violators can be fined up to $100 an acre; so far, no fines have been levied.

Mr. Hanny recently replaced one entire potato field with wheat to comply with United Potato's acreage reduction.

Case for Analysis

Competition and Co-operative Behavior in the Potato Industry

This article discusses the movement by potato farmers in September 2004 to form a cooperative, United Potato Farmers of America, to help manage supply in the potato industry to keep prices high and increase profits. The group began in Idaho, but then expanded nationally. Traditionally, high prices for potatoes caused famers to overproduce, which drove prices down below costs of production for many farmers, making the industry unprofitable. The article notes that potato farmers have been especially reluctant to join national groups. Each farmer has typically tried to gain market share under the assumption that other farmers will have a small crop due to weather, frosts, pests, or some other natural disaster. If growing conditions turn out favorable, the increased supply of potatoes pushes prices down and causes financial hardship.

This situation has occurred many times in the past. In 1996 there was a major increase in the supply of fresh potatoes, which drove the price of fresh potatoes from $8 per 100 pounds in 1995 to between $1.50 and $2 per 100 pounds in 1996, a price that was one-third the cost of production. Based on the substantial profits they had earned with their 1995 crops, farmers increased production in 1996, resulting in a 48.8-billion-pound crop, the largest in U.S. history.[1]

Until 2004, individual potato farmers let the market determine the price they obtained for their crops. Idaho farmers did have some competitive advantage in the markets for bagged potatoes in supermarkets and for baked potatoes in restaurants. Their potatoes often sold for a premium price of $2 or more per 100 pounds as a result of brand name recognition. Thus, Idaho producers gained some market power in these segments by turning an undifferentiated product into an identifiable brand.[2]

The United Potato cooperative has been successful for farmers at least in its first year of operation. However, some growers have expressed concern about whether the cooperative can maintain its control over supply and whether most of the benefits of the organization flow only to Idaho producers.

There have also been changes in the demand for potatoes that have caused problems for potato farmers. The U.S. Agriculture Department reported that, after a decade of phenomenal growth, U.S. consumption of french fries was expected to decrease 1 percent in the fiscal year ending June 30, 2002.[3] Most of this decrease was anticipated to result from slower expansion of the fast-food industry due to market saturation and increased numbers of outlets, such as Subway restaurants, that do not sell french fries.

[1] Stephen Stuebner, "Anxious Days in Potatoland: Competitive Forces Threaten to Knock Idaho from Top," *New York Times*, April 12, 1997.

[2] Stuebner, "Anxious Days in Potatoland."

[3] This discussion is based on Jill Carroll and Shirley Leung, "U.S. Consumption of French Fries Is Sliding As Diners Opt for Healthy," *Wall Street Journal*, February 20, 2002.

U.S. exports of fries have also slowed, given a saturated Japanese market and the difficulties U.S. firms face in entering the Chinese market. The U.S. Department of Agriculture has also developed a fry made from a rice flour mixture that absorbs 30 percent less oil when cooked and could become a substantial competitor to the traditional french fry in the future. Although the french-fry industry has fought back by introducing new products, including blue, chocolate, and cinnamon-and-sugar french fries, there are still severe consequences for potato producers from the decreased fry consumption.

Potato farmers and potato prices have also been affected by changes in consumers' eating habits, including the popularity of the low-carbohydrate Atkins diet. It has been estimated that consumption of fresh potatoes per head is 40 percent below the level of 40 years ago because Americans do less cooking at home.[4] ∎

The Model of Perfect Competition

The description of the potato industry in the chapter's opening article shows that this industry closely approximates a perfectly competitive industry. The actual model of perfect competition is hypothetical. Although no industry meets all the characteristics described here, the industries discussed in this chapter come close on many of them.

Characteristics of the Model of Perfect Competition

As shown in Table 7.1, **perfect competition** is a market structure characterized by

1. A large number of firms in the market
2. An undifferentiated product
3. Ease of entry into the market or no barriers to entry
4. Complete information available to all market participants

In perfect competition, we distinguish between the behavior of an individual firm and the outcomes for the entire market or industry. The *Wall Street Journal* article discussed both the production decisions of individual farmers and the outcomes for

Perfect competition
A market structure characterized by a large number of firms in the market, an undifferentiated product, ease of entry into the market, and complete information available to all market participants.

TABLE 7.1 Market Structure

CHARACTERISTIC	PERFECT COMPETITION	MONOPOLISTIC COMPETITION	OLIGOPOLY	MONOPOLY
Number of firms competing with each other	Large number	Large number	Small number	Single firm
Nature of the product	Undifferentiated	Differentiated	Undifferentiated or differentiated	Unique differentiated product with no close substitutes
Entry into the market	No barriers to entry	Few barriers to entry	Many barriers to entry	Many barriers to entry, often including legal restrictions
Availability of information to market participants	Complete information available	Relatively good information available	Information likely to be protected by patents, copyrights, and trade secrets	Information likely to be protected by patents, copyrights, and trade secrets
Firm's control over price	None	Some	Some, but limited by interdependent behavior	Substantial

---

[4] "United States: Pass the Spuds; The Potato Industry," *The Economist* 378 (March 25, 2006): 62.

the entire potato industry. The model of perfect competition is characterized by having so many firms in the industry that no single firm has any influence on the price of the product. Farmers make their own independent planting decisions and take the price that is established in the market by the overall forces of demand and supply. Because each farmer's individual output is small relative to the entire market, individual producers are **price-takers** who cannot influence the price of the product.

In a perfectly competitive market, products are undifferentiated. This market characteristic means that consumers do not care about the identity of the specific supplier of the product they purchase. Their purchase decision is based on price. In the potato industry, this characteristic holds in the french-fry market, where processors do not differentiate among the suppliers of potatoes except in terms of transportation costs. The article notes that this characteristic does not hold in the markets for restaurant baked potatoes and bagged potatoes, where the Idaho brand name carries a premium price.

The third characteristic of the perfectly competitive model is that entry into the industry by other firms is costless or that there are no barriers to entry. This characteristic is reasonably accurate in the potato industry, as the number of producers has increased around the world to satisfy the demands of french-fry processing plants in different countries.

The final characteristic of the perfectly competitive model is that complete information is available to all market participants. This means that all participants know which firms are earning the greatest profits and how they are doing so. Although this issue is not explicitly discussed in the *Wall Street Journal* article, it appears that information on the technology of growing potatoes is widespread and can be easily transferred around the world. The quotes from the individual farmers in the article indicate that they have a good understanding of the typical costs of production and the relationship between prices and costs in the industry.

Model of the Industry or Market and the Firm

Let's examine the impact of these characteristics in the model of the perfectly competitive industry or market in Figure 7.1a and the individual firm in Figure 7.1b. Figure 7.1a presents the model of demand and supply that we introduced in Chapter 2. The industry or market demand curve is the downward sloping demand curve from Chapter 2 showing the relationship between price and quantity demanded by the consumers in the market, holding all other factors constant. The industry supply curve, which we also discussed in Chapter 2, shows the relationship between the price of the good and the quantity producers are willing to supply, all else held constant.

We now add a description of the individual firm in perfect competition to this model (see Figure 7.1b). Note first that the demand curve facing the individual firm is horizontal. The individual firm in perfect competition is a price-taker. It takes the price established in the market and must then decide what quantity of output to

Price-taker

A characteristic of a perfectly competitive market in which the firm cannot influence the price of its product, but can sell any amount of its output at the price established by the market.

FIGURE 7.1

The Model of Perfect Competition

The perfectly competitive firm takes the equilibrium price set by the market and maximizes profit by producing where price, which also equals marginal revenue, is equal to marginal cost. The level of profit earned depends on the relationship between price and average total cost.

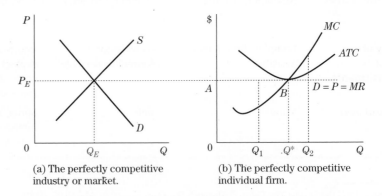

(a) The perfectly competitive industry or market.

(b) The perfectly competitive individual firm.

produce. Because the firm cannot affect the price of the product, it faces a perfectly or infinitely elastic demand curve for its product.[5]

Determining the Profit-Maximizing Level of Output

How much output will this individual firm want to produce? The answer to that question depends on the goal of the firm, which we assume is **profit maximization**, or earning the largest amount of profit possible. Our definition of profit, first presented in Chapter 1, is given again in Equation 7.1.

7.1 $\pi = TR - TC$

> *where*
>
> π = profit
> TR = total revenue
> TC = total cost

Profit maximization
The assumed goal of firms, which is to develop strategies to earn the largest amount of profit possible. This can be accomplished by focusing on revenues or costs or both factors.

Profit is the difference between the total revenue the firm receives from selling its output and the total cost of production. Because both total revenue and total cost vary with the level of output produced, profit also varies with output. Given the goal of profit maximization, the firm will find and produce that level of output at which profit is the greatest.[6]

To do so, the firm should follow the **profit-maximizing rule**, given in Equation 7.2.

7.2   Produce that level of output where $MR = MC$

> *where*
>
> MR = marginal revenue = $\Delta TR/\Delta Q$
> MC = marginal cost = $\Delta TC/\Delta Q$

Profit-maximizing rule
To maximize profits, a firm should produce the level of output where marginal revenue equals marginal cost.

We introduced and defined marginal revenue in Chapter 3 and marginal cost in Chapter 5. If a firm produces the level of output at which marginal revenue equals marginal cost, it will earn a larger profit than by producing any other amount of output.[7]

Although we can derive this rule mathematically,[8] Figure 7.1b presents an intuitive explanation for why output level Q^*, where marginal revenue equals

---

[5] Refer to Chapter 3 for a discussion of the perfectly elastic demand curve.

[6] Various organizations may pursue other goals. Niskanen (1971) proposed the goal of budget maximization for government bureaucracies. In this environment, managers receive rewards for the size of the bureaucracies they control, even if some employees are redundant. Newhouse (1970) and Weisbrod (1988) also proposed alternative goals for nonprofit organizations. We will see in Chapter 9 that even profit-maximizing firms may not always choose the levels of inputs and output that maximize profits in the short run. There may also be the principal-agent problem where profit maximization might be the goal of a firm's shareholders but not necessarily of the managers or agents they hire to run the firm. See William A. Niskanen, *Bureaucracy and Representative Government* (Chicago: Aldine-Atherton, 1971); Joseph Newhouse, "Toward a Theory of Nonprofit Institutions: An Economic Model of a Hospital," *American Economic Review* 60 (March 1970): 64–74; Burton A. Weisbrod, *The Nonprofit Economy* (Cambridge: Harvard University Press, 1988); and Paul Milgrom and John Roberts, *Economics, Organization, and Management* (Englewood Cliffs, NJ: Prentice-Hall, 1992).

[7] In some cases, the profit-maximizing rule will lead to the loss-minimizing level of output. If market conditions are so unfavorable that a firm is not able to earn a positive profit at any level of output, the level of output where marginal revenue equals marginal cost will be the level where the firm minimizes its losses. If it produced any other level of output, it would suffer greater losses.

[8] Given $TR(Q)$ and $TC(Q)$,

$$\pi = TR(Q) - TC(Q)$$
$$d\pi/dQ = dTR/dQ - dTC/dQ = 0$$
$$dTR/dQ = dTC/dQ \text{ or } MR = MC$$

Differentiating the profit function with respect to output and setting the result equal to zero give maximum profit, which occurs where marginal revenue equals marginal cost.

marginal cost, maximizes profit for the perfectly competitive firm. In Figure 7.1b, we have drawn a short-run marginal cost curve similar to the one we discussed in Chapter 5. It has a long upward sloping portion due to the law of diminishing returns in production.

In Chapter 3, we discussed the relationship between demand and marginal revenue for a firm facing a downward sloping demand curve. The demand curve showing price was always greater than marginal revenue for all positive levels of output. However, the perfectly competitive firm faces a horizontal or perfectly elastic demand curve. In this case, *and only in this case*, the demand curve, which shows the price of the product, is also the firm's marginal revenue curve.

Marginal revenue for the perfectly competitive firm
The marginal revenue curve for the perfectly competitive firm is horizontal because the firm can sell all units of output at the market price, given the assumption of a perfectly elastic demand curve. Price equals marginal revenue for the perfectly competitive firm.

Price equals **marginal revenue for the perfectly competitive firm** because the firm cannot lower the price to sell more units of output, given that it cannot influence price in the market. If the price of the product is $20, the firm can sell the first unit of output at $20. The marginal revenue, or the additional revenue that the firm takes in from selling this first unit of output, is $20. The firm can then sell the next unit of output at $20, given the price-taking characteristic of perfect competition. Total revenue from selling two units of output is $40. The marginal revenue from selling the second unit of output is $40 − $20 or $20. Therefore, the marginal revenue the firm receives from selling the second unit is the same as that received from selling the first unit and is equal to the product price. This relationship holds for all units of output.

An intuitive argument for why the firm's profit-maximizing level of output (Q^* in Figure 7.1b) occurs where marginal revenue equals marginal cost is that producing any other level of output will result in a smaller profit. To understand this argument, let's examine output levels both larger and smaller than Q^*. Consider output level Q_2 in Figure 7.1b, where $MR < MC$. At this level of output, the additional revenue that the firm takes in is less than the additional cost of producing that unit. Thus, the firm could not be maximizing profits if it produced that unit of output. This same argument holds not only for output Q_2, but also for all units of output greater than Q^*. Now look at output Q_1. At this level of output, $MR > MC$. The firm makes a profit by producing and selling this unit because the additional revenue it receives is greater than the additional cost of producing the unit. However, if the firm stopped producing at output Q_1, it would forgo all the profit it could earn on the units of output between Q_1 and Q^*. Thus, stopping production at Q_1 or at any unit of output to the left of Q^* would not maximize the firm's profits. Therefore, Q^* has to be the profit-maximizing unit of output where the firm earns the greatest amount of profit possible.[9]

Determining the Amount of Profit Earned   The next question we examine is what amount of profit the firm in Figure 7.1b will earn if it produces output level Q^*. Although producing where marginal revenue equals marginal cost tells us that the firm is maximizing its profits, this equality does not tell us the amount of profit earned. To know whether profits are positive, negative, or zero, we need to examine the relationship either between total revenue and total cost or between price and average total cost. This relationship is shown in Table 7.2.

If you know total revenue and total cost at the current level of output, you can quickly calculate the amount of profit earned. If you have total revenue and total cost function graphs showing how these variables change with the level of output

---

[9] A graph of profit versus output would resemble a hill where profit starts low, increases and reaches a maximum, and then decreases. The equality of marginal revenue and marginal cost gives the level of output (Q^* in Figure 7.1b) at which the top of the hill is located. One qualification is that the equality of marginal revenue and marginal cost must be achieved where marginal cost is upward sloping. Profit would be minimized if marginal revenue equaled marginal cost on the downward sloping portion of the marginal cost curve. As noted previously, in certain situations the profit-maximizing level of output may be the loss-minimizing level of output.

TABLE 7.2 Calculation of Profit

$$\pi = TR - TC$$
$$\pi = (P)(Q) - (ATC)(Q)$$
$$\pi = (P - ATC)(Q)$$
If $P > ATC, \pi > 0$

If $P < ATC, \pi < 0$

If $P = ATC, \pi = 0$

Profit formula
$\pi = (P\text{-}AC) * Q$

produced, you can find the profit-maximizing level of output, where there is the greatest distance between the two curves, and calculate the profit at that point.[10]

Table 7.2 shows an alternative method of calculating profit that will be very useful in our market models. As we discussed in Chapters 3 and 5, we can substitute $(P)(Q)$ for total revenue and $(ATC)(Q)$ for total cost in Table 7.2. Rearranging terms gives the expression $(P - ATC)(Q)$ for profit. Therefore, if we know, either numerically or graphically, the relationship between product price and the average total cost of production, we know whether profit is positive, negative, or zero.

We can see that the firm in Figure 7.1b is earning zero profit because it is producing the level of output Q^*, where the product price just equals the average total cost of production. Graphically, the product price is distance $0A$ and the product quantity is distance $0Q^*$, so total revenue (which equals price times quantity) is the area $0ABQ^*$. Average total cost is the distance Q^*B (which equals $0A$) and quantity is the distance $0Q^*$, so total cost (which equals average total cost times quantity) is also the area $0ABQ^*$. Therefore, total revenue equals total cost, and profits are zero.

The Shutdown Point for the Perfectly Competitive Firm We show the zero profit point for the perfectly competitive firm again in Figure 7.2 as output level Q_2, where price P_2 equals average total cost. Suppose the price in the market falls to P_1. The goal of profit maximization means that the firm will now produce output Q_1 because that is the output level where the new price (P_1), which is equivalent to marginal revenue (MR_1), equals marginal cost. However, price P_1 is below the average total cost at output level Q_1. Although the firm is earning negative economic profits or suffering losses by producing output level Q_1, it

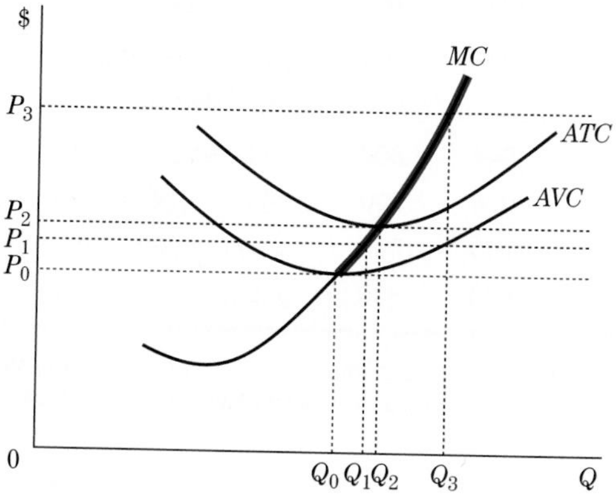

FIGURE 7.2
The Supply Curve for the Perfectly Competitive Firm
The perfectly competitive firm will shut down if the market price falls below average variable cost. The supply curve for the perfectly competitive firm is that portion of its marginal cost curve above minimum average variable cost.

[10] In mathematical terms, profit is maximized at the output level where the slope of the total revenue curve (marginal revenue) equals the slope of the total cost curve (marginal cost). This is the level of output where there is the greatest distance between the two curves. Examining the values of total revenue and total cost gives you the amount of profit at that output level.

should continue to produce at this price because it is covering all of its variable costs ($P_1 > AVC$) and some of its fixed costs. Remember that fixed costs are shown as the vertical distance between AVC and ATC. The firm could not continue forever in this situation, as it needs to cover the costs of its fixed input at some point. However, it is rational in this case for managers of the firm to wait and see if the product price will increase.

If the price should fall still further to P_0 ($= MR_0$) and the firm produces output Q_0 (where $MR_0 = MC$), the firm is just covering its average variable cost ($P_0 = AVC$), but it is not covering any of its fixed costs. If the price falls below P_0 and is expected to remain there, managers would be better off shutting the firm down. By shutting down, the firm would lose only its fixed costs. If it continued to operate at a price below P_0, the firm would lose both its fixed costs and some of its variable costs, as price would be less than average variable cost. Thus, P_0, the price that equals the firm's minimum average variable cost, is the **shutdown point for the perfectly competitive firm**.

We illustrate these relationships among prices, costs, and profits for a specific set of cost and revenue functions in Table 7.3, Columns 1–8, where the alternative methods for calculating profit are shown in Columns 9 and 10. Columns 4 and 5 show that the firm is always following the profit-maximizing rule because it is producing where marginal revenue equals marginal cost. For the perfectly competitive firm, marginal revenue also equals price. The zero-profit level of output for the firm is 10 units, where total revenue equals total cost ($1,200) or price equals average total cost ($120). At a price of $204, the firm produces 12 units of output and earns a positive profit of $928.

If the price falls to $60, the firm produces 8 units of output and earns −$544 in profit. This price is less than average total cost ($128), but greater than average variable cost ($28). Thus, the firm is covering some of its fixed costs at this level of output. Total revenue of $480 exceeds total variable cost of $224 ($TC - TFC$), so that $256 is applied to the fixed costs. If the price falls to $24, the firm produces 6 units of output and suffers a loss of $800. This price is exactly equal to the minimum average variable cost, so the firm covers all of its variable costs, but loses the

Shutdown point for the perfectly competitive firm
The price, which equals a firm's minimum average variable cost, below which it is more profitable for the perfectly competitive firm to shut down than to continue to produce.

TABLE 7.3 Numerical Example Illustrating the Perfectly Competitive Firm (Q measured in units; all costs, revenues, and profits measured in dollars)

Q (1)	AVC (2)	ATC (3)	MC (4)	P = MR (5)	TR = PQ (6)	TC (7)	TFC (8)	$\Pi = TR - TC$ (9)	$\Pi = (P - ATC)Q$ (10)
5	25	185	15	15	75	925	800	75 − 925 = −850 (Shutdown)	(15 − 185)5 = −850 (Shutdown)
6	24	157.33	24	24	144	944	800	144 − 944 = −800	(24 − 157.33)6 = −800
8	28	128	60	60	480	1,024	800	480 − 1,024 = −544	(60 − 128)8 = −544
10	40	120	120	120	1,200	1,200	800	1,200 − 1,200 = 0	(120 − 120)10 = 0
12	60	126.67	204	204	2,448	1,520	800	2,448 − 1,520 = 928	(204 − 126.67)12 = 928

Source: This example is based on the following cost functions derived and modified from Alpha C. Chiang, *Fundamental Methods of Mathematical Economics*, 3rd ed. (New York: McGraw-Hill, 1984). We have not analyzed specific mathematical cost functions in this text, but we have discussed general cost and revenue functions.

Total fixed cost: $TFC = 800$

Total variable cost: $TVC = Q^3 - 12Q^2 + 60Q$

Total cost: $TC = TFC + TVC = 800 + Q^3 - 12Q^2 + 60Q$

Average fixed cost: $AFC = 800/Q$

Average variable cost: $AVC = Q^2 - 12Q + 60$

Average total cost: $ATC = TC/Q = AFC + AVC = (800/Q) + Q^2 - 12Q + 60$

Marginal cost: $MC = dTC/dQ = 3Q^2 - 24Q + 60$

entire fixed cost of $800. If the price falls to $15 and the firm continues to produce, the best it could do would be to produce 5 units of output and suffer a loss of $850. Because this price is below the average variable cost, the firm would be better off shutting down and losing only the $800 of fixed costs. Thus, the actual level of output at a price of $15 would be zero, with a profit equal to −$800.

Supply Curve for the Perfectly Competitive Firm Figure 7.2 shows that if the price determined in the market is P_0, the firm will produce output level Q_0 because that is the profit-maximizing level of output where $P = MR = MC$ and $P = AVC$. If the price increases to P_1, the firm will increase its output to Q_1. Similarly, if the price is P_2, the firm will produce output level Q_2, and it will increase output to level Q_3 if the price rises to P_3. This procedure traces the **supply curve for the perfectly competitive firm**. This supply curve, which shows a one-to-one relationship between the product price and the quantity of output the firm is willing to supply, is that portion of the firm's marginal cost curve above the minimum average variable cost. The firm will stop producing if the price falls below the average variable cost. This supply curve is upward sloping because the firm's marginal costs are increasing as the firm reaches the capacity of its fixed inputs.

Supply curve for the perfectly competitive firm
The portion of a firm's marginal cost curve that lies above the minimum average variable cost.

Supply Curve for the Perfectly Competitive Industry In Chapter 2 on demand and supply and in Figure 7.1a in this chapter, we drew the **supply curve for the perfectly competitive industry** as upward sloping. We can now see the rationale for the shape of this industry curve, given the shape of the firm's supply curve. The industry supply curve shows the quantity of output produced by all firms in the perfectly competitive industry at different prices. Because individual firms produce more output at higher prices, the industry supply curve will also be upward sloping.[11]

Supply curve for the perfectly competitive industry
The curve that shows the output produced by all perfectly competitive firms in the industry at different prices.

The industry supply curve would typically be flatter than the firm's supply curve because it reflects the output produced by all firms in the industry at each price. However, the slope of the industry supply curve could become steeper if the prices of any inputs in production increase as firms produce more output. If any inputs are in limited supply, firms might bid up their prices as they increase output. We typically assume that input prices are constant even with changes in production. Appendix 7A discusses industry supply in more detail and presents several agricultural examples.

The Short Run in Perfect Competition

Figure 7.2 presents the possible short-run outcomes for a firm in a perfectly competitive industry. The short run is a period of time in which the existing firms in the industry cannot change their scale of operation because at least one input is fixed for each firm. Firms also cannot enter or exit the industry during the short run.

The different prices facing the firm in Figure 7.2 are determined by the industry demand and supply curves (Figure 7.1a). Because the firm cannot influence these prices, it produces the profit-maximizing level of output (where $P = MR = MC$) and can earn positive, zero, or negative profit, depending on the relationship between the existing market price and the firm's average total cost. At price P_3, the firm earns positive profit; at price P_2, zero profit; and at prices P_1 and P_0, negative profit. If the price falls below P_0, the firm will consider shutting down.

---

[11] This is the short-run supply curve for the perfectly competitive industry, as it assumes that the number of firms in the industry is constant.

Long-Run Adjustment in Perfect Competition: Entry and Exit

Both entry and exit by new and existing firms and changes in the scale of operation by all firms can occur in the long run. We analyze each of these factors in turn to illustrate the characteristics of the long-run equilibrium that occurs in perfect competition. Although we describe these two adjustments sequentially, they could also occur simultaneously.

Returning to Figure 7.2, we now argue that the zero-profit point at output level Q_2 and price P_2 represents an equilibrium situation for the firm in perfect competition. This outcome results from the method that economists use (and managers should use) to define costs. As you may recall from Chapter 5, costs in economics are defined from the perspective of opportunity cost, which includes both explicit and implicit costs. The costs measured by the ATC curve in Figure 7.2 include both the explicit costs and any implicit costs of production. Suppose that investors have a choice between investing in this firm and buying a government security paying 8 percent. Managers of the firm would have to pay at least 8 percent to attract financial investors to the firm. This 8 percent rate of return is included in the average total cost curve in Figure 7.2.[12] Thus, the firm in Figure 7.2 is earning a zero economic profit that includes a normal rate of return on the investment in the firm. Resources in this activity are doing as well as if they were invested elsewhere. Therefore, the zero-profit point is an **equilibrium point for the perfectly competitive firm**.

We illustrate this concept by showing what happens if an equilibrium situation is disturbed in Figures 7.3a and 7.3b. Suppose that some factor causes the industry demand curve to shift out from D_1 to D_2 in Figure 7.3a. This shift could result from a change in any of the factors held constant in demand curve D_1, including consumer tastes and preferences, consumer income, and the price of goods related in consumption (substitutes and complements). This increase in demand causes the equilibrium price in the market to rise from P_{E1} to P_{E2} and the equilibrium quantity to increase from Q_{E1} to Q_{E2}.

How does the perfectly competitive firm respond to this change in the market? The firm's reaction is shown in Figure 7.3b. Because the firm is a price-taker, it must accept the new equilibrium price and determine the level of output that maximizes profit at this new price. The firm faces a new horizontal demand curve, D_2, where the new price, P_2, equals the new marginal revenue, MR_2. To maximize profits, the firm must produce where MR_2 equals MC, or at output level Q_2. However, at this level of output, the firm is now earning positive economic profits because the price

Equilibrium point for the perfectly competitive firm
The point where price equals average total cost because the firm earns zero economic profit at this point. Economic profit incorporates all implicit costs of production, including a normal rate of return on the firm's investment.

FIGURE 7.3

Long-Run Adjustment in Perfect Competition: Entry and Exit
An increase in industry demand will result in a positive economic profit for a perfectly competitive firm. However, this profit will be competed away by the entry of other firms into the market in the long run. The zero economic profit point or the point where price equals average total cost is the equilibrium point for the perfectly competitive firm.

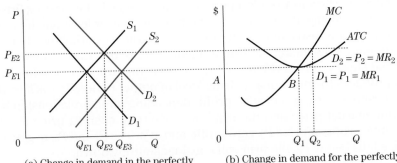

(a) Change in demand in the perfectly competitive industry or market.

(b) Change in demand for the perfectly competitive individual firm.

---

[12] Remember the example in Chapter 5 where Coca-Cola CEO Robert Goizueta judged his managers in each operating division on the basis of their economic profit earned.

of the product, P_2, is greater than the average total cost of production at output Q_2. Firms in this industry are now doing better than firms in other areas of the economy. Given this situation, firms in other sectors of the economy will enter this industry in pursuit of these positive economic profits. All firms know of the existence of these positive economic profits, given the characteristic of perfect information in the model of perfect competition. Other firms are able to enter the industry, given the characteristic of perfect mobility or no barriers to entry.

Entry by new firms into the industry is shown by a rightward shift of the industry supply curve in Figure 7.3a from S_1 to S_2. As the supply curve shifts along demand curve D_2, the equilibrium price begins to fall. Thus, the price, marginal revenue, and demand line D_2 in Figure 7.3b start to shift down. The profit-maximizing level of output for the firm moves back toward Q_1, and the level of positive economic profit decreases because the price of the product is closer to the average total cost of production.

Entry continues until the industry supply curve has shifted to S_2. At this point, the firm is once again producing Q_1 level of output and earning zero economic profit (Figure 7.3b). Industry output is larger (Q_{E3}) because there are more firms in the industry (Figure 7.3a). However, because firms in the industry are once again earning zero economic profit, there is no incentive for further entry into the industry. Thus, the zero-economic-profit point is an equilibrium position for firms in a perfectly competitive industry.[13]

If, starting at the equilibrium position in Figure 7.3a, there was a decrease in industry demand, the return to equilibrium would occur, but in the opposite direction. The decrease in demand would result in a lower equilibrium price. A lower equilibrium price in the market would cause some firms to exit from the industry because they were earning negative economic profits or suffering losses. As firms exited the industry, the industry supply curve would shift to the left, driving the equilibrium price back up. This adjustment process would continue until all the losses had been competed away and firms in the industry were once again earning zero economic profit.

Adjustment in the Potato Industry

The process we have just described is illustrated for the potato industry in the opening discussion of this chapter. Figure 7.4a shows the demand and supply conditions for the potato industry in 1995 and 1996, while Figure 7.4b shows the profitability of individual farmers. The high price of $8.00 per 100-pound sack and the profits earned by individual farmers are shown at point A in both of the figures. In response to these prices and profits, farmers planted more potatoes in 1996, shifting the supply curve from S_{95} to S_{96}. Favorable weather and insect conditions helped increase this supply, which drove the price of potatoes down to $2.00 per 100-pound sack (point B in Figure 7.4a). This price was below the average total cost for many farmers, leaving them with significant debts (point B in Figure 7.4b).

Although not discussed, it is likely that many farmers produced fewer potatoes in 1997, shifting the supply curve to the left and driving price back up toward the zero-economic profit equilibrium, as the competitive model predicts. Further changes in the potato market would result from the subsequent decreased demand for french fries discussed following the news article.

---

[13] Figure 7.3 illustrates the case of a constant-cost industry where the entry of other firms does not affect the cost curves of firms in the industry. If entry increased the demand for inputs, which increased their prices and caused firms' cost curves to shift up, the equality of price and average total cost would occur at a higher level of cost and this would be an increasing-cost industry. If the opposite should happen and costs were lower after entry, this would be a decreasing-cost industry.

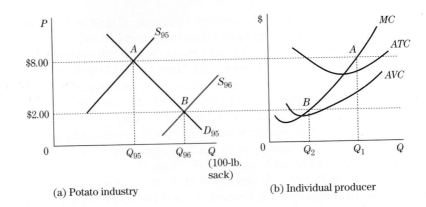

(a) Potato industry   (b) Individual producer

Long-Run Adjustment in Perfect Competition: The Optimal Scale of Production

We have just seen how entry and exit in a perfectly competitive industry result in the zero-economic profit equilibrium ($P = ATC$). That discussion focused on the role of entry and exit in response to positive or negative economic profits in achieving equilibrium. However, we illustrated the discussion in terms of a given scale of operation or a given set of short-run cost curves. As we noted in Chapter 6, firms also must choose their optimal scale of operation. Let's now look at how a competitive market forces managers to choose the most profitable scale of operation for the firm and how entry and exit again result in a zero-economic profit equilibrium.

Figure 7.5 shows a U-shaped long-run average cost curve ($LRAC$) similar to those we discussed in Chapter 6. This curve incorporates both **economies of scale** (decreasing long-run average cost) and **diseconomies of scale** (increasing long-run average cost) for the firm. Suppose that the perfectly competitive firm is originally producing at the scale of operation represented by the short-run marginal and average total cost curves SMC_1 and $SATC_1$. The firm is in equilibrium at price P_1 because the firm is producing output Q_1, where $P_1 = MR_1 = MC$ and $P_1 = SATC_1$. In the short run, this represents the most profitable strategy for the firm, as the firm is locked into this scale of production.

If managers of the firm know that the long-run average cost curve is as pictured in Figure 7.5, they can decrease their costs of production by moving to larger-scale production. Perfectly competitive firms cannot influence the price of the product, but they can find means of lowering production costs. Managers of the firm in Figure 7.5 should switch to the scale of production represented by the short-run marginal and average total cost curves SMC_2 and $SATC_2$. Price P_1 is significantly above the short-run average total cost represented by $SATC_2$, so that a firm of this size would earn positive economic profits.

Positive economic profits, however, will attract other firms to the industry, and entry will shift the industry supply curve (not pictured in Figure 7.5) to the right,

Economies of scale

Achieving lower unit costs of production by adopting a larger scale of production, represented by the downward sloping portion of a long-run average cost curve.

Diseconomies of scale

Incurring higher unit costs of production by adopting a larger scale of production, represented by the upward sloping portion of a long-run average cost curve.

FIGURE 7.5

Long-Run Adjustment in Perfect Competition: The Optimal Scale of Operation

In the long run, the perfectly competitive firm has to choose the optimal scale of operation. This decision, combined with entry and exit, will force price to equal long-run average cost.

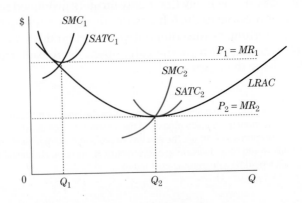

lowering price. These new firms entering the industry will also build plants at the SMC_2 and $SATC_2$ scale of operation, as that size represents the scale of operation that minimizes a firm's costs. This process will continue until all economic profits have been competed away and price equals long-run average cost. Firms will produce at the scale of operation represented by SMC_2 and $SATC_2$ and will earn zero economic profit. This scale is at the minimum point of the long-run average cost curve, so that production costs are minimized. Figure 7.5 combines the two types of adjustments that are made to reach equilibrium ($P = LRAC$) in the long run:

1. The choice of the scale of operation that minimizes costs in the long run
2. Entry by firms, which lowers product price and competes away any positive economic profits

Managerial Rule of Thumb

Competition Means Little Control over Price

Managers in highly or perfectly competitive markets have little or no control over the price of their product. They typically compete on the basis of lowering the costs of production. Perfectly competitive firms will end up earning zero economic profit because entry by other firms will rapidly compete away any excess profit. ■

Other Illustrations of Competitive Markets

Most markets that people encounter on a day-to-day basis are not perfectly or even highly competitive because these markets do not meet the four characteristics discussed above. We examine the agricultural sector in more detail to show how farming is one of the best examples of a perfectly competitive industry. Using the cases of broiler chickens, red meat, and milk, we then show how industries or sections of industries can become less competitive over time through mergers among producers and increased product differentiation. These factors represent violations of the first two characteristics in the competitive model:

1. A large number of price-taking firms in each industry
2. Production of an undifferentiated product

We then discuss how the trucking industry, although not perfectly competitive, illustrates many of the behaviors and outcomes of an extremely competitive industry.

In this discussion, we introduce the concept of **industry concentration**, which is a measure of how many firms produce the total output of an industry. The more concentrated the industry, the fewer the firms operating in the industry. By definition, a perfectly competitive industry is so unconcentrated that individual firms are price-takers and do not have any market power. We will discuss different measures of industry concentration when we describe the strategies and behaviors of managers in firms with market power.

Industry concentration
A measure of how many firms produce the total output of an industry. The more concentrated the industry, the fewer the firms operating in that industry.

Competition and the Agricultural Industry

Although the number of farms has decreased significantly over the past 70 years, there are still approximately 2 million farms in the United States today.[14] The average

---

[14] This discussion is based on Daniel B. Suits, "Agriculture," in *The Structure of American Industry*, eds. Walter Adams and James W. Brock, 11th ed. (Upper Saddle River, N.J.: Prentice Hall, 2005), 1–22; Bruce W. Marion and James M. MacDonald, "The Agriculture Industry," in *The Structure of American Industry*, ed. James W. Brock, 12th ed. (Upper Saddle River, NJ: Prentice-Hall, 2009), 1–29.

farm contains less than 440 acres, but large-scale farms dominate much of the market due to economies of scale. While only 5 percent of all farms contain 1,000 acres or more, these farms cover more than 40 percent of total farm acreage. Today corporate farms operate 12 percent of all U.S. farmland and sell 22 percent of the total value of farm crops.

Although farming has become an increasingly concentrated industry, the perfectly competitive model can still be used to characterize it. The largest 2 or 3 percent of the growers of any particular product are characterized by a large number of independent producers. For example, 2 percent of the largest farms grow half of all the grain in the United States. However, this 2 percent consists of 27,000 farms. In contrast, highly competitive manufacturing industries, such as men's work clothing and cotton-weaving mills, have 300 and 200 firms, respectively. There are nearly 100 times as many independent producers in farming as in most competitive manufacturing industries.

Demand for most farm crops is highly inelastic. People can only eat so much food, most commodities have few good substitutes, and these commodities constitute small shares of the total costs of the processed products to which they are converted. Products are typically grown and brought to market without individual farmers knowing exactly what price they will receive. If, as we discussed in the opening article of this chapter, farmers have responded to previously high prices and there are unusually good growing conditions, there may be large increases in supply, which drive down prices. As we learned in our discussion of price elasticity in Chapter 3, a decrease in product price with inelastic demand results in a decrease in total revenue for producers because consumers do not increase quantity demanded in proportion to the price decrease.

This outcome results in what has been called the "farm problem" in the United States and most industrialized countries. Prices for farm products are extremely volatile. For example, from 1970 to 2006 the mean annual corn price received by Iowa farmers was $2.23 per bushel, but prices ranged from a low of $1.04 to a high of $3.20. Because farm incomes are subject to extreme changes not under the control of farmers, governments have often implemented farm price support programs and other methods to control production. These programs have caused imbalances between supply and demand in otherwise competitive markets, as support prices are higher than the equilibrium prices in these markets. The lack of control over prices has also led farmers to organize cooperatives, as discussed in the opening article.

Competition and the Broiler Chicken Industry

Broiler chickens present an interesting example of an industry that traditionally was unconcentrated and produced a relatively undifferentiated product, but that has changed significantly over time.[15] Broiler processing is a vertically integrated industry with the processors either owning or contracting each stage of the system from the breeder farms through the processing plants to the final products for market. Concentration in the broiler processing industry remained relatively low from 1954 until the mid-1970s. The four largest firms in the industry accounted for only 18 percent of the market over this period. Although this concentration increased throughout the 1980s, so that the four largest firms produced 40 percent of industry output by 1989, concentration in the broiler industry is still less than that found in other food manufacturing industries. Most of the increase in industry concentration during the 1980s resulted from mergers among the leading firms in the industry. Tyson Foods is the leading broiler processor, with a 22 percent

---

[15] This discussion is based primarily on Richard T. Rogers, "Broilers: Differentiating a Commodity," in *Industry Studies*, ed. Larry L. Duetsch, 2nd ed. (Armonk, N.Y.: Sharpe, 1998), 65–100.

market share, followed by Gold Kist and Perdue Farms, each with 8 percent, and ConAgra Poultry, with 6 percent. Many of the smaller broiler processors specialize in various regions of the country.

Integration reduced costs by coordinating production at each stage to avoid over-production and shortages and by achieving economies of scale to purchase feed, medicine, and equipment at lower prices. In the 1930s, there were approximately 11,000 independent facilities hatching broiler chicks, each with an average capacity of 24,000 eggs. By 2001, the number of hatcheries had declined by 97 percent to only 323, each with an average incubator capacity of 2.7 million eggs. Integration increased quality control and allowed firms to complete the entire production process in one localized area. This change had an important effect on costs, given the high rate of bird death and weight loss during transport. Integration also helped in the diffusion of new technology given that off-farm firms had greater access to capital and credit opportunities that could be used for new investments in genetic research and feed development.[16]

Both real and subjective product differentiation exists among the different broiler processors. Early differentiation focused on differences in product quality, product form, and the level of services provided to the retailer. In the 1970s, Holly Farms was the first processor to develop tray-packed chicken ready for the meat case. Processors today often apply the retailer's own scanner pricing labels before shipment. Skin color became a differentiating characteristic, with Perdue Farms making its yellow color the first theme in its advertising campaign. This was followed by an emphasis on the fat content of the chickens. The amount of advertising in relation to product sales is a measure of product differentiation, as there is no need for individual suppliers to advertise an undifferentiated product in the perfectly competitive model. Broiler chicken advertising gained momentum with Frank Perdue of Perdue Farms, who was used in ads for his own product because he looked and sounded like a chicken. By 1990, the broiler industry was spending over $30 million on advertising, with Perdue Farms accounting for 41.6 percent of the total expenditure. Even with these increases, the advertising–sales ratio for broiler producers was just 0.2 percent in 1992 compared to an average for all food and tobacco industries of 2.0 percent.[17]

Competition among broiler processors depends on the marketing channel used and the extent of value-added processing involved. Food service and retail food stores are the two major marketing channels. Value-added processing ranges from unbranded fresh whole chickens to breaded nuggets and marinated prime parts. Firms tend to compete within these subcategories and to create barriers to entry in these submarkets. Other market niches are kosher chickens and free-range chickens, grown with fewer antibiotics and hormones. Consumer prices vary by these different subcategories.

We noted above that, for competitive firms, price = marginal revenue = marginal cost for profit maximization and price = average total cost in equilibrium. Analysts often use the **price-cost margin (*PCM*)** from the Census of Manufactures as a proxy for these relationships. As would be expected for a competitive industry, broiler processing has one of the lowest PCMs in the food system. In 1992, the PCM for broilers was 11.9 percent compared with an average of 30 percent for all food and tobacco product classes. For more concentrated and differentiated food industries, the PCM ranged as high as 67.2 percent for breakfast cereals, 56.7 percent for chewing gum, and 49.6 percent for beer.

Price-cost margin (PCM)
The relationship between price and costs for an industry, calculated by subtracting the total payroll and the cost of materials from the value of shipments and then dividing the results by the value of the shipments. The approach ignores taxes, corporate overhead, advertising and marketing, research, and interest expenses.

---

[16] Elanor Starmer, Aimee Witteman, and Timothy Wise, "Feeding the Factory Farm: Implicit Subsidies to the Broiler Chicken Industry." Medford, MA: Tufts University Global Development and Environmental Institute Working Paper No. 06-03, June 2006.

[17] Food industries with the highest ratios in 1992 included chewing gum (16 percent), breakfast cereals (11 percent), chocolate candy (13 percent), and instant coffee (10 percent). See Rogers, "Broilers," 79–88.

Thus, although the broiler processing industry exhibits many characteristics of a highly competitive industry, there are forces leading toward increased industry concentration and less-competitive behavior. This is to be expected, as most managers want to gain control over their market environment and insulate themselves from the overall supply and demand changes of a competitive market.

Competition and the Red-Meat Industry

Managers in the red-meat packing industry have recently followed the same strategies as those in the broiler chicken industry by introducing a campaign to turn what had been an undifferentiated product into one with brand names.[18] Hormel Foods, IBP, and Farmland Industries, along with the meatpacking divisions of Cargill and ConAgra Foods, now sell prepackaged meat, including steaks, chops, and roasts, under their brand names. According to the National Cattlemen's Beef Association, 474 of these new beef products were introduced in 2001 compared with 70 in 1997. This is an important trend in an industry with $60 billion in annual sales.

Branding represents a major shift in the red-meat industry, which traditionally labeled only its low-end products such as Spam. It also represents a strategy to combat the long-term decline in red-meat consumption in the United States, including the 41 percent decline in beef demand over the past 25 years. Much of this decline is related to health concerns regarding red-meat consumption. With both spouses working in many families, the time needed to cook roast beef is also a factor that has decreased beef demand. Managers in the red-meat industry were forced to develop and invest in new technology to produce roasts and chops that could be microwaved in less than 10 minutes. This involved cooking the beef at low temperatures for up to 12 hours and designing a plastic tough enough to hold the beef and its spices during this cooking process, consumer refrigeration, and microwaving.

Managers also faced the problem of acceptance of this new product by both consumers and retail stores. Hormel targeted women in their twenties, who were the first generation to grow up with microwave ovens and who might have less reluctance than older women to put red meat in the microwave. All producers focused their marketing campaigns on the convenience of the new products, which they contend allow women to prepare a home-cooked meal for a family dinner while having time to relax. The goal of IBP's marketing director, Jack Dunn, has been to "create an irrational loyalty to our product."[19]

While many grocery stores welcomed the Hormel and IBP products, Kroger, the largest chain in the country, developed its own brand of fresh beef, the Cattleman's Collection. Kroger managers followed the product differentiation strategy, but created a brand that consumers could not find elsewhere, which was more profitable for them than selling brands from other companies. All producers used coupons, product demonstrations, and extensive advertising budgets to promote the new products. As we discuss in Chapter 8, these actions represent the behavior of managers in firms with market power. Thus, the strategy of managers in competitive industries is to develop market power by creating brand identities for previously undifferentiated products. This process involves analyzing and changing consumer behavior and developing new technology and production processes.

---

[18] This section is based on Scott Kilman, "Meat Industry Launches Campaign to Turn Products into Brand Names," *Wall Street Journal*, February 20, 2002.

[19] Ibid.

Competition and the Milk Industry

Another strategy managers in competitive industries can use is to form industry or trade associations to promote the overall product, even if the identity of specific producers is not enhanced. This is a strategy to increase industry demand, as illustrated in Figure 7.3a. The milk industry has followed this strategy with its "Got milk?" and milk mustache campaigns.[20] Milk consumption had been decreasing in the early 1990s before the initial "Got milk?" campaign was launched by Dairy Management Inc., representing dairy farmers, and the Milk Processor Education Program, sponsored by commercial milk producers. These organizations, with marketing budgets of $24 million in California and $180 million nationwide, are financed largely by industry members.

A study by the California Milk Processor Board in early 2001 indicated that milk consumption in California had stabilized at the precampaign levels instead of continuing to decrease at 3 percent per year. Nationwide annual milk consumption also increased from 6.35 billion gallons to 6.48 billion gallons from 1995 to 2000. Although this campaign has increased the overall demand for milk, major national brands have yet to develop because milk production and pricing vary and are regulated by geographic region. The milk industry has also had to confront changes in lifestyles that work against it. Fewer people in all age groups are eating dry cereal with milk, and more are purchasing breakfast bars in the morning. In an attempt to stop the declining consumption in the teenage market, milk producers are developing single-serve packages and introducing an increasing variety of milk flavors.

To enter Asian markets, New Zealand's Fonterra, one of the world's largest milk producers, has experimented with exotic flavors such as wheatgrass and the pandan leaf. Asia's $35 billion overall dairy market has been expanding at a rate of 4 percent annually compared with a 2 percent annual increase in the United States. Fonterra also arranged for teaching hospitals in Hong Kong and Malaysia to conduct clinical trials to demonstrate the effect of milk on bone density, and it placed two dozen bone scanners in supermarkets across Asia to show consumers that their bones were not as dense as recommended by health experts.[21] These moves represent the combined strategies of differentiating products and increasing overall demand in an industry that is still highly competitive.

In 2004 the federal Dietary Guidelines Advisory Committee suggested that adults increase their milk consumption from two to three servings per day to "reduce the risk of low bone mass and contribute important amounts of many nutrients." The dairy industry campaigned intensely for this change, launching a "3-A-Day" advertising campaign supported by companies such as Kraft Foods Inc. and warning of a "calcium crisis." The National Dairy Council, funded by the country's dairy farmers, spent $4 to $5 million in 2003 on research concluding that calcium and other nutrients in dairy products had significant health benefits.[22] Political action is, therefore, another way to influence demand for a product.

Competition and the Trucking Industry

The trucking industry is another example of a highly, if not perfectly, competitive industry. There are more than 150,000 companies in the truckload segment of the industry, which delivers full trailer loads of freight.[23] Most of these companies operate six or fewer trucks, and many are family-run businesses that make just

---

[20] Bernard Stamler, "Got Sticking Power?" *New York Times*, July 30, 2001.

[21] Cris Prystay, "Milk Industry's Pitch in Asia: Try the Ginger or Rose Flavor," *Wall Street Journal*, August 9, 2005.

[22] Nicholas Zamiska, "How Milk Got a Major Boost by Food Panel," *Wall Street Journal*, August 30, 2004.

[23] Daniel Machalaba, "Trucking Firms Seek Rate Increase as Demand Rises, Fuel Costs Jump," *Wall Street Journal*, December 9, 1999.

enough money to cover truck payments and living costs. Bob White, global services transportation director at Emerson Electric, characterized the trucking industry as follows: "There are enough truckload carriers out there that if one wants to increase rates there are others that will be willing to take on new business at the old or lower rates."[24] This quote describes the price-taking behavior and the horizontal demand curve facing firms in the model of perfect competition.

As expected in a competitive industry, the changing forces of demand and supply can alter the profitability of trucking companies very quickly. In December 1999, trucking companies increased rates by 5 to 6 percent, given higher fuel prices and a shortage of truck drivers. Demand during this period was strong due to continued economic growth and greater reliance on trucking for freight transportation. However, the push from the cost side, combined with the limited ability to raise prices, meant that profits were still low for many trucking companies.

By the fourth quarter of 2000, trucking companies faced not only continued higher costs, but also adverse weather and an overall slowing in the economy.[25] Snowstorms in the Midwest forced many companies' trucks to sit idle during the winter of 2000–2001. The slowing of consumer spending lowered sales of products that truckers haul. Business inventories began to increase, which made companies reluctant to ship more merchandise. Close to 4,000 trucking companies went out of business in 2000, and approximately 1,100 failed in the first quarter of 2001. As failed trucking companies left the industry, the remaining companies saw prices rise and became somewhat more profitable. Sale prices for used trucks decreased substantially due to the large number of trucking company bankruptcies. These bargains encouraged some truckers to reenter the business. One trucker stated, "You can find some great deals on trucks from companies like mine that went bankrupt. Who knows? I started out with one truck before. This business still fascinates me."[26]

Excess capacity continued to put downward competitive pressure on trucking rates, and rising costs for labor, fuel, and equipment continued to impact the trucking industry in 2006 and 2007. Increasing retirements among the nation's drivers combined with the stressful nature of the job reduced the supply of drivers, causing wages to increase. Diesel fuel costs represent 25 percent of operating costs in the industry resulting in truckers spending $103 billion on 53 billion gallons of fuel in 2006. Demand for hauling services was negatively influenced by the defaults in the subprime mortgage markets. In response, some companies reduced the number of company-owned trucks in their fleets and shifted business to other freight services.[27]

This discussion of the trucking industry illustrates the forces in the perfectly competitive model discussed in this chapter. Trucking firms have little power over price and are subject to the forces that change industry demand and supply. When demand declines and prices begin to decrease, some firms go out of business as price falls below their average variable costs. After firms exit the industry, prices begin to rise again, and the profitability of the remaining firms improves. Those firms still in the industry move back toward the zero-profit equilibrium point. As in the quotation above, some individuals and companies may even see opportunities to earn greater than normal profits, which would cause new entry into the industry. Thus, there is a constant push toward the zero-economic profit equilibrium in a perfectly or highly competitive industry.

---

[24] Ibid.

[25] This section is based on the following articles: Sonoko Setaishi, "Truckers See Lackluster Results, Hurt by Higher Costs, Flat Rates," *Wall Street Journal*, January 15, 2001; Sonoko Setaishi, "Truckers Face Dismal 1Q amid Softer Demand, Higher Costs," *Wall Street Journal*, April 5, 2001; Robert Johnson, "Small Trucking Firms Are Folding in Record Numbers Amid Slowdown," *Wall Street Journal*, June 25, 2001.

[26] Johnson, "Small Trucking Firms Are Folding."

[27] Ian Urbina, "Short on Drivers, Truckers Offer Perks," *New York Times*, February 28, 2006; Daniel P. Bearth, "Trucking Faced Economic, Regulatory Challenges," *Transport Topics*, December 24–31, 2007; Joan Garrett, "The Burden of Diesel Costs," *McClatchy-Tribune Business News*, January 11, 2008.

Managerial Rule of Thumb

Adopting Strategies to Gain Market Power in Competitive Industries

Managers in highly competitive industries can gain market power by merging with other competitive firms, differentiating products that consumers previously considered to be undifferentiated commodities, and forming producer associations that attempt to change consumer preferences and increase demand for output of the entire industry. ■

Summary

Perfect competition is a form of market structure in which individual firms have no control over product price, which is established by industry or market demand and supply. In the short run, perfectly competitive firms take the market price and produce the amount of output that maximizes their profits. Profits earned in the short run can be positive, zero, or negative. Perfectly competitive firms are not able to earn positive economic profits in the long run because these profits will be eroded by entry of other firms. Likewise, any losses will be removed by firms leaving the industry. To lower their costs, firms also seek to produce at the optimal scale of operation. However, this scale will be adopted by all firms in the long run, and entry will force prices to equal long-run average cost, the zero-economic profit equilibrium.

Managers of firms in perfectly or highly competitive environments often attempt to gain market power by merging with other firms, differentiating their products, and forming associations to increase the demand for the overall industry output. We discuss these strategies in more detail when we examine firms with market power in the next chapter.

Appendix 7A Industry Supply

Elasticity of Supply

The shape of the industry supply curve reflects the *elasticity of supply* within that industry. The elasticity of supply is a number showing the percentage change in the quantity of output supplied relative to the percentage change in product price. Because the quantity supplied usually increases with price, a supply elasticity is a positive number. As with demand elasticity, a supply elasticity number greater than 1 indicates *elastic supply*. The percentage change in quantity of output supplied is greater than the percentage change in price. *Inelastic supply* occurs when the percentage change in quantity supplied is less than the percentage change in price.[28]

A vertical supply curve represents *perfectly inelastic supply*, where there is a fixed quantity of the product supplied that is not influenced by the product price. In this case, the product price is determined entirely by changes in demand for the product as the demand curve moves up and down along a vertical supply curve. The best example of perfectly inelastic supply would be a painting, such as the Mona Lisa, by a deceased artist. There is only one of these paintings, and the supply will never be increased. The other polar case is *perfectly elastic supply*, illustrated

[28] William G. Tomek and Kenneth L. Robinson, *Agricultural Product Prices*, 3rd ed. (Ithaca, N.Y.: Cornell University Press, 1990), 59–75.

by a horizontal supply curve. In this case, the industry is willing to supply any amount of product at the market price. Supply curves that are approaching being vertical are relatively more inelastic and show a smaller response of quantity supplied to changes in price, while flatter curves indicate a much larger (more elastic) supply response.

Agricultural Supply Elasticities

Supply curves for various agricultural products are illustrated by an S-shaped curve, as shown in Figure 7.A1.[29] Changes in supply elasticity for a particular farm product are likely to occur at a price that just covers average variable costs or at a price at which the returns from alternative uses of resources are approximately equal. As we discussed earlier, a price below the average variable cost means that a farmer will not offer any output for sale. At a price exceeding the average variable cost, supply may be elastic if more land is brought into production. Intermediate-level prices may cause supply elasticity to decrease if no additional land is available for cultivation or if equipment and labor are fully employed, whereas even higher prices may bring these resources into production and increase supply elasticity.

Supply elasticities are typically lower for major crops grown in areas where there are few alternative uses of land, such as dry-land wheat, than for minor crops and poultry products. Supply elasticities can also differ by the stage of production. For broiler chickens, for example, the supply price response is greater for the breeding flock that supplies chicks for the broiler industry than for the production of broilers.

The aggregate supply relationship for all farm output in most countries is very price inelastic in the short run. Resources committed to agriculture tend to remain in use, especially if alternative uses of these resources are limited. The land, labor, and equipment employed in agriculture often have few alternative uses elsewhere. And even with low product prices, farmers may produce other crops rather than seek employment off the farm. From 1929 to 1932, when farm prices fell by 50 percent, the aggregate amount of farm output remained relatively constant. The short-run price elasticity of aggregate farm output in the United States has been estimated to be no larger than 0.15.

The increased specialization in farm equipment and skills has made short-run supply response even more difficult over time. For livestock products, supply changes are limited by the availability of the female stock and the time required to produce a new generation. Time periods up to eight years or more are required for a complete quantity adjustment to changing prices for some tree crops. Crop yields are influenced by the availability of irrigation water, the amount of fertilizer applied, and the pest control programs employed. Irrigation water is, in turn, influenced by

FIGURE 7.A1

Representative Supply Curve for a Farm Product

The elasticity of supply for a farm product will vary with the price of the product.

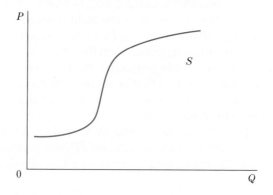

[29] The following discussion is based on ibid., 59–61.

pumping costs and water allotment rights. The weather, of course, also has a major influence on agricultural supply. If the weather is unusually wet, farmers may not be able to plant the desired acreage of their most profitable crop and may be forced to plant an alternative crop with a shorter growing season.

Key Terms

diseconomies of scale, p. 178

economies of scale, p. 178

equilibrium point for the perfectly
    competitive firm, p. 176

industry concentration, p. 179

marginal revenue for the perfectly
    competitive firm, p. 172

perfect competition, p. 169

price-cost margin (PCM), p. 181

price-taker, p. 170

profit maximization, p. 171

profit-maximizing rule, p. 171

shutdown point for the perfectly
    competitive firm, p. 174

supply curve for the perfectly
    competitive firm, p. 175

supply curve for the perfectly
    competitive industry, p. 175

Exercises

Technical Questions

1. For each of the following graphs, identify the firm's profit-maximizing (or loss-minimizing) output. Is each firm making a profit? If not, should the firm continue to produce in the short run?

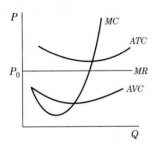

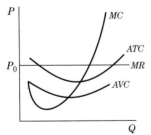

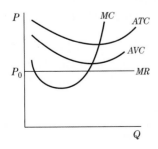

2. Consider a firm in a perfectly competitive industry. The firm has just built a plant that cost $15,000. Each unit of output requires $5 worth of materials. Each worker costs $3 per hour.

a. Based on the information above, fill in the table on the following page.

b. If the market price is $12.50, how many units of output will the firm produce?

c. At that price, what is the firm's profit or loss? Will the firm continue to produce in the short run? Carefully explain your answer.

d. Graph your results.

3. The following graph shows the cost curves for a perfectly competitive firm. Identify the shutdown point, the breakeven point, and the firm's short-run supply curve.

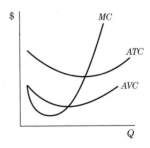

4. Consider the following graph, which shows a demand curve and two supply curves. Suppose that there is an increase in demand. Compare the equilibrium price and quantity change in both cases, and use those results to explain what you can infer about the elasticity of supply.

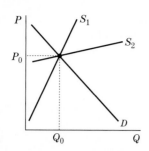

5. Draw graphs showing a perfectly competitive firm and industry in long-run equilibrium.

   a. How do you know that the industry is in long-run equilibrium?

   b. Suppose that there is an increase in demand for this product. Show and explain the short-run adjustment process for both the firm and the industry.

   c. Show and explain the long-run adjustment process for both the firm and the industry. What will happen to the number of firms in the new long-run equilibrium?

6. Draw graphs showing a perfectly competitive firm and industry in long-run equilibrium.

   a. Suppose that there is a decrease in demand for this product. Show and explain the short-run adjustment process for both the firm and the industry.

   b. Show and explain the long-run adjustment process for both the firm and the industry. What will happen to the number of firms in the new long-run equilibrium?

7. The following graph shows the long-run average cost curve for a firm in a perfectly competitive industry. Draw a set of *short-run* cost curves consistent with output Q_E and use them to explain

   a. Why the only output that a competitive firm will produce in the long run is Q_E

   b. Why it will be a profit-maximizing decision to produce more than Q_E in the short run if the price exceeds P_E

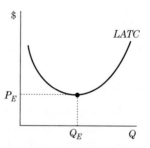

Number of Worker Hours	Output (Q)	Total Fixed Cost (TFC)	Total Variable Cost (TVC)	Total Cost (TC)	Marginal Cost (MC)	Average Variable Cost (AVC)	Average Total Cost (ATC)
0	0				—	—	—
25	100						
50	150						
75	175						
100	195						
125	205						
150	210						
175	212						

Application Questions

1. Discuss how the facts in the opening article and subsequent discussion of the potato industry illustrate the lack of control over prices by individual potato producers in a competitive market, the response to high prices predicted by the model of perfect competition, and the attempts by producers in a competitive market to gain control over price. Check recent business publications to find out how successful the United Potato Growers of America cooperative has been since the time of this chapter's article.

2. Discuss the shifts in demand and supply and the impact on prices and the profitability of individual

producers that occurred in the cranberry industry in 2006 and 2007 resulting from the following facts:[30]

   a. Cranberries are no longer relegated to a Thanksgiving side dish. They can now be found in more than 2,000 products from muffin mix to soap.

   b. Cranberries prefer cold winters and plenty of rain. So last year's unusually warm winter and a summer drought in many parts of the United

---

[30] Joseph Pereira and Betsy McKay, "Bounty of the Bog Gets Pricier," *Wall Street Journal*, November 21, 2007.

States and Canada hurt the crop now being harvested. However, one producer says that although his crop is down 30 percent this year, the higher prices will result in a profit decline of only 10–15 percent.

c. Research has shown that cranberries help prevent urinary tract infections. More studies are underway to help determine whether cranberries can prevent dental plaque and tooth decay and help blood move more effectively through blood vessels.

d. Ocean Spray and other growers have unleashed a steady flow of new products, including new low-calorie drinks such as Diet Ocean Spray. The company has also introduced a line of "Grower's Reserve" 100 percent natural juices, including a "Super Antioxidant" variety with blueberry, pomegranate, and cranberry juices.

3. The following facts characterize the furniture industry in the United States:[31]

a. The industry has been very fragmented, so that few companies have the financial backing to make heavy investments in new technology and equipment.

b. In 1998, only three U.S. furniture manufacturers had annual sales exceeding $1 billion. These firms accounted for only 20 percent of the market share, with the remainder split among 1,000 other manufacturers.

c. Capital spending at one manufacturer, Furniture Brands, was only 2.2 percent of sales compared with 6.6 percent at Ford Motor Company. Outdated, labor-intensive production techniques were still being used by many firms.

d. Furniture manufacturing involves a huge number of options to satisfy consumer preferences, but this extensive set of choices slows production and raises costs.

e. Small competitors can enter the industry because large manufacturers have not built up any overwhelming advantage in efficiency.

f. The American Furniture Manufacturers Association has prepared a public relations campaign to "encourage consumers to part with more of their disposable income on furniture."

g. In fall 2003, a group of 28 U.S. furniture manufacturers asked the U.S. government to impose antidumping trade duties on Chinese-made bedroom furniture, alleging unfair pricing.

h. The globalization of the furniture industry since the 1980s has resulted from technological innovations, governmental implementation of economic development strategies and regulatory regimes that favor global investment and trade, and the emergence of furniture manufacturers and retailers with a capacity to develop global production and distribution networks. The development of global production networks using Chinese subcontractors has accelerated globalization in recent years.

Discuss how these facts are consistent with the model of perfect competition.

4. Evaluate the following statement:
In the short run, information about a perfectly competitive firm's fixed costs is needed to determine *both* the profit-maximizing level of output and the amount of profit earned when producing that level of output.

5. In a perfectly competitive industry, the market price is $25. A firm is currently producing 10,000 units of output, its average total cost is $28, its marginal cost is $20, and its average variable cost is $20. Given these facts, explain whether the following statements are true or false:

a. The firm is currently producing at the minimum average variable cost.

b. The firm should produce more output to maximize its profit.

c. Average total cost will be less than $28 at the level of output that maximizes the firm's profit.

Hint: You should assume normal U-shaped cost curves for this problem.

[31] James R. Hagerty and Robert Berner, "Ever Wondered Why Furniture Shopping Can Be Such a Pain?" *Wall Street Journal*, November 2, 1998; Dan Morse, "U.S. Furniture Makers Seek Tariffs on Chinese Imports," *Wall Street Journal*, November 3, 2003; and Mark H. Drayse, "Globalization and Regional Change in the U.S. Furniture Industry," *Growth and Change* 39 (June 2008): 252–282.

On the Web

For updated information on the *Wall Street Journal* article at the beginning of the chapter, as well as other relevant links and information, visit the book's Web site at **www.pearsonhighered.com/farnham**

Market Structure: Monopoly and Monopolistic Competition

I n this chapter, we contrast the perfectly and highly competitive markets that we discussed in Chapter 7 with the market structures of monopoly and monopolistic competition. These markets, along with the oligopoly markets we'll discuss in Chapter 9, are called *imperfectly competitive markets* or *imperfect competition*. We show how managers of firms in these markets have varying degrees of *market power*, or the ability to influence product prices and develop other competitive strategies that enable their firms to earn positive economic profits. The degree of a firm's market power is related to the *barriers to entry* in a given market—the structural, legal, or regulatory characteristics of a firm and its market that keep other firms from producing the same or similar products at the same cost.

We begin this chapter with the *Wall Street Journal* article "Dell's Revival Strategy Runs into Trouble." This article describes the changing nature of the personal computer market and how those changes eroded Dell Inc.'s market power. After discussing this article, we present the monopoly model and illustrate the differences between this model and the perfectly competitive model. We then describe the major sources and measures of market power, illustrating the strategies that managers use to maintain and increase market power in several different industries. We also discuss basic antitrust policies that the federal government employs to control market power and promote competition, and we illustrate how market power tends to disappear in the monopolistically competitive market structure.

Dell's Revival Strategy Runs into Trouble

by Justin Scheck

Wall Street Journal, *November 28, 2008*

Michael Dell's plan to fix the company he founded, Dell Inc.—once the biggest personal-computer maker in the world—is stalling.

Dell reported falling revenue and shrinking profits last week for its most recent quarter. And while profit margins grew, the gains resulted from painful cost cuts, including massive layoffs and decisions not to invest in launching products like portable music players and cellphones—the kinds of gadgets Mr. Dell had described previously as building "brand lust."

By contrast, Dell's main rival, Hewlett-Packard Co., on Monday announced increased quarterly sales and a 10% jump in PC revenue from last year.

Mr. Dell, who famously founded his company in a University of Texas dorm room, once ruled the PC market with a simple strategy: Build reliable desktop PCs, and sell directly to customers over the phone or online, cutting out the middleman.

When he left Dell in 2004, it sold more PCs in the U.S. than its four closest rivals combined, according to the analysis firm Gartner. Back then, H-P was struggling in second place.

Now the tables are turned. Dell's core business of selling desktop PCs directly to companies keeps slowing, and it has lagged behind H-P and others in adapting to the growing popularity of consumer laptops—which people would rather buy in stores, where they can try them out.

Dell's challenges are testament to the rapidly changing global gadget business. The rise of notebooks, tiny "netbooks" and smartphones such as Apple's iPhone is forcing PC makers to rethink the very definition of a "personal computer."

At the same time, Dell has lost its low-cost edge as its rivals shifted to using Asian factories-for-hire to build their wares. Today, many of Dell's own factories, such as one in North Carolina that's only three years old, can no longer compete on cost.

Dell is trying to sell off some plants. But in October, tech-industry analysis firm iSuppli suggested that Dell may actually have to pay other companies to take them. . . .

Mr. Dell has made some significant progress. Despite recent weak sales, the company's operating profit is up thanks to a nearly two-year cost-cutting effort. That resulted in higher profit margins than last year, beating analysts' earnings predictions. Dell has almost 10,000 fewer employees than a year ago.

Dell has also released more new products this year than in past years, and has boosted sales and profits in its consumer division—the fastest-growing segment of the PC market, and historically a Dell weak spot. . . .

Mr. Dell, 43, returned to the company as chief executive in early 2007 with a two-pronged rescue plan: Cut costs in the thin-profit PC business, and invest in new areas, including not only music players and new portable devices, but also "business services" such as running corporate in-house networks.

Now Mr. Dell's dual aims—cutting at the low end, while pushing new high-end gear and services—are in conflict. Dell's slim profit margins make it tough to invest heavily in R&D even in good times. . . .

The impact of the downturn is particularly clear in corporate sales, Dell's single biggest business, which generated about 80% of revenue the past year. After posting annual unit increases of 12% or more each quarter for the past year, commercial shipments dropped 5% in the most recent quarter, and revenue declined 6%. For years, commercial PCs had been a reliable growth source for the industry. . . .

In its heyday, Dell boasted industry-leading profit margins and an assembly system so efficient that it was the subject of scholarly papers. Dell today is in a "squeeze play." . . . On one side are low-cost Asian PC makers, while at the other is Apple, which commands premium prices that help fund R&D. . . .

H-P has a significant advantage over Dell. Its highly profitable printer business and business-services division are far bigger than Dell's. This has helped insulate H-P from PC-market weakness. PCs are about 35% of H-P's revenue; they're about 60% of Dell's.

H-P has continued to beat Dell in PC sales. Last month, analysis firm IDC reported that H-P remained the world's largest PC maker in this year's third quarter. Its shipments increased 14.9% compared to the year-earlier period. Dell increased shipments only 11.4%. . . .

Dell's fortunes looked much better four years ago, when Mr. Dell left the CEO post. The low-cost business model of selling PCs directly to customers had propelled 2004 sales above $40 million. But growth stalled in 2006.

A big factor: H-P found Dell's weak spot by focusing sales on retail stores, where Dell had no presence.

Mr. Dell took back the reins from then-CEO Kevin Rollins early in 2007, pronouncing his old business model dead. After his return, he announced the company would start selling in stores.

Today Dell needs to worry about retail sales cannibalizing its higher-profit direct sales. . . .

Mr. Dell also focused on the consumer-laptop business, which by that time suffered from a troubled reputation. For instance, tech blogs had a field day after Dell and a few other manufacturers' notebooks caught fire due to battery problems. Dell recalled the faulty batteries, which it hadn't manufactured.

Mr. Dell hired top executives from outside the company to push into new markets and cut costs. Mobile technology was also to be a promising new foray, since smartphones have recently been a sweet spot of computer growth. . . .

Early this year, Dell executives discussed entering the phone market in 2009. . . . But it has held back due to cost and the uncertain market. . . .

Dell has pushed into the hot market for netbooks—small, low-power laptops designed mainly for Internet access. However, netbooks have thin profit margins and sell for as little as $350.

Meanwhile, H-P this year introduced a line of two consumer-oriented smartphones in Europe. It also beat Dell into the netbook market.

Dell's biggest transformation may be in manufacturing, which was narrowly tailored to its original direct-sales strategy. The company eschewed inventory, and its famously efficient factories quickly assembled build-to-order PCs. Plants were often located in local markets to speed up delivery times.

But Dell stuck to that approach too long, opening new plants in the U.S. while rivals like Apple and H-P shifted to Asia. . . .

Case for Analysis

Changing Market Power in the PC Industry

The opening article describes how market power can change relatively quickly even for one of the leaders in the personal computer industry. In 2004 Dell sold more PCs that its four closest rivals, while Hewlett-Packard was struggling in second place. However, given changes in consumer tastes, the development of new products, and changes in production technology, Dell is now struggling to compete. It kept its direct sales model even as consumers were shifting to purchasing PCs in retail stores, and it lagged behind in the development of the popular notebooks and netbooks. Dell lost its low-cost advantage because it did not shift production to Asia as quickly as did rivals Apple and Hewlett-Packard. In the face of these negative factors, Dell has had to incur massive layoffs and delay decisions on investing in popular new products. All of these changes occurred over a period of just a few years. ■

Firms with Market Power

✳Market power

The ability of a firm to influence the prices of its products and develop other competitive strategies that enable it to earn large profits over longer periods of time.

The *Wall Street Journal* article illustrates several strategies used by firms with **market power**, including pricing, cost reduction, new product development, and the method of reaching the consumer. These strategies should enable firms to earn larger profits over longer periods of time. However, as we note for Dell computers, market power can often change as market conditions and the strategies of competitor firms evolve. We discuss additional strategies after we present the monopoly model and contrast it with the model of perfect competition.

The Monopoly Model

Monopoly

A market structure characterized by a single firm producing a product with no close substitutes.

Price-setter

A firm in imperfect competition that faces a downward sloping demand curve and must set the profit-maximizing price to charge for its product.

In Chapter 7, we argued that the *industry* or market demand curve in perfect competition is the standard downward sloping demand curve even though the perfectly competitive *firm* faces a horizontal demand curve. If we begin with our definition of a **monopoly** as a market structure characterized by a single firm producing a product with no close substitutes, we can see that a monopolist faces a downward sloping demand curve because the single firm produces the entire output of the industry. More generally, we argue that any firm in imperfect competition faces a downward sloping demand curve for its product. Firms in imperfect competition are therefore *not* price-takers; if managers want to sell more output, they must lower the price of their product. Raising the price means they will sell less output. Thus, firms in imperfect competition are **price-setters**. Managers of these firms must set the optimal price, which we define as the price that maximizes the firm's profits. This price depends on the firm's demand, marginal revenue, and

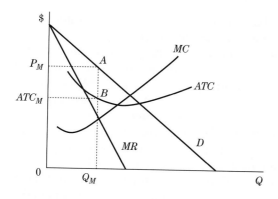

FIGURE 8.1A
The Monopoly Model with
Positive Economic Profit
The monopolist maximizes profits by producing where marginal revenue equals marginal cost and typically earns positive economic profit due to barriers to entry.

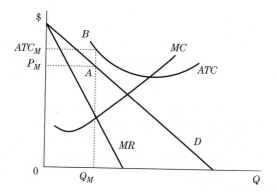

FIGURE 8.1B
The Monopoly Model with
Negative Economic Profit
or Losses
The monopolist could suffer losses if average total cost is greater than price at the profit-maximizing level of output.

marginal cost curves, but may also be determined through the markup pricing methods we discuss in Chapter 10.

Figures 8.1a and 8.1b present the monopoly model. In these figures, the monopolist faces a downward sloping demand curve. You will remember from Chapter 3 that a linear downward sloping demand curve has a marginal revenue (MR) curve that intersects the vertical axis at the same point as the demand curve and has a slope that is twice as steep as the demand curve. In Figures 8.1a and 8.1b, we have also included a marginal cost (MC) and average total cost (ATC) curve similar to those we developed in Chapter 5.

Given that the goal of the firm is to maximize profit, the firm in Figures 8.1a and 8.1b will produce output level Q_M where marginal revenue equals marginal cost. This is the standard rule for profit maximization that we used in our discussion of the perfectly competitive model of Chapter 7. The difference here is that the marginal revenue curve is downward sloping and separate from the demand curve. The price (P_M) that the monopolist can charge for output Q_M is read directly off the demand curve above that output level. As you may recall, a demand curve shows the price at which a given quantity is demanded, as well as the quantity demanded at any given price. We can see in Figures 8.1a and 8.1b that this price-quantity combination is the optimal combination for the firm, as there is no other price at which marginal revenue equals marginal cost.

We next examine whether the firm in Figure 8.1a is earning positive, negative, or zero economic profit. To do so, we look at the relationship between price and average total cost. As shown in Figure 8.1a, this firm is earning positive economic profit because price is greater than average total cost at output level Q_M. Total revenue is represented by the area $0P_MAQ_M$, while total cost equals the area $0(ATC_M)BQ_M$. Thus, economic profit is the area of the rectangle $P_MAB(ATC_M)$.

In the competitive model of Chapter 7, we argued that positive economic profits would disappear through the entry of other firms into the industry, which would lower the product price until it was again equal to average total cost. This outcome is less likely to happen in the monopoly model or for firms with market power due to the existence of barriers to entry that prevent other firms from producing the same or similar products at the same cost.

A monopolist does not necessarily earn an economic profit. If the average total cost curve is located above the demand curve, the firm earns negative economic profit or suffers losses, as in Figure 8.1b. Total revenue (area $0P_MAQ_M$) is now less than total cost (area $0(ATC_M)BQ_M$), so the loss to the firm is measured by the area $((ATC_M)BAP_M)$. If price is less than average variable cost, this firm can minimize its losses by shutting down for the same reasons as in the case of perfect competition. Given the existence of barriers to entry, these outcomes are less likely for the monopoly firm, but can still occur, as we discuss below.

The monopoly firm in Figures 8.1a and 8.1b does not have a supply curve. We argued in Chapters 2 and 7 that a supply curve is associated with the price-taking behavior of a firm in perfect competition. For a firm with market power, a demand shift will cause the profit-maximizing output and price to change because the marginal revenue curve shifts. If the costs of production change such that the marginal cost curve shifts, there will also be a different profit-maximizing level of output and price. Thus, unlike the perfectly competitive market, there is no one-to-one relationship between price and quantity supplied for any firm with market power.

We can also see in Figures 8.1a and 8.1b that product price P_M is greater than the marginal cost of production at the profit-maximizing level of output for the monopoly (Q_M). This outcome represents another difference with the perfectly competitive firm that produces where product price equals marginal cost. This inequality of price and marginal cost forms the basis for one of the measures of market power we'll discuss later in the chapter.

Comparing Monopoly and Perfect Competition

Figures 8.2a and 8.2b summarize the differences between the outcomes for the perfectly competitive *firm* and the monopoly *firm* with market power.[1] The perfectly competitive firm in Figure 8.2a produces the profit-maximizing level of output where marginal revenue equals marginal cost. The competitive firm is a price-taker

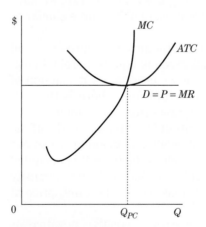

FIGURE 8.2A
The Perfectly Competitive Firm
At Q_{PC}:
MR = MC
  P = ATC
  P = MC
Minimum Point of ATC Curve
Price-Taker
Firm Has Supply Curve

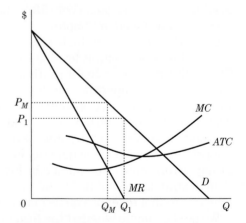

FIGURE 8.2B
The Monopoly Firm
At Q_M:
MR = MC
  P > ATC
  P > MC
Not at Minimum Point of ATC
Price-Searcher
Firm Has No Supply Curve

---

[1] The industry or market demand and supply curves are not illustrated here for the perfectly competitive firm.

that responds to the price set by the forces of demand and supply in the overall market. This price-taking assumption means that the demand curve facing the perfectly competitive firm is infinitely elastic or horizontal and that the price equals the firm's marginal revenue. This behavior, combined with the goal of profit maximization, also implies that the firm produces the level of output where price equals marginal cost and that the firm's supply curve is the upward sloping portion of its marginal cost curve above minimum average variable cost.

In long-run equilibrium, perfectly competitive firms produce where price equals average total cost and earn zero economic profit, given that any positive or negative profits will be competed away by entry into and exit from the market. In perfect competition, the equality of price and average total cost also occurs at the minimum point of the average total cost curve. Thus, firms are producing at the lowest point on their average total cost curve and, due to the forces of entry and exit, are charging consumers a price just equal to that average total cost. Managers of perfectly competitive firms would like to earn positive economic profits, but they are unable to do so in this market environment.

The monopoly firm in Figure 8.2b also produces where marginal revenue equals marginal cost, given the goal of profit maximization. However, this firm must set the optimal price, which depends on its demand and cost conditions. The firm with market power will produce a level of output at which price is greater than marginal cost, given the downward sloping demand and marginal revenue curves. Firms with market power typically produce where price is greater than average total cost and earn positive economic profit. However, the amount of this profit and how long it exists depend on the strength of the barriers to entry in this market.

Firms with market power might also pursue other goals in the short run, such as sales or revenue maximization, to gain market share and increase profits over future periods. This outcome would occur in Figure 8.2b at output level Q_1, where marginal revenue equals zero.[2] The corresponding price, P_1, would be lower than the profit-maximizing price, P_M. We discuss other non-profit-maximizing strategies in Chapter 9.

The differences in outcomes between *industries* in monopoly and perfect competition are shown in Figure 8.3, which presents the downward sloping demand and marginal revenue curves facing a monopolist. For simplicity, we assume that the monopolist's average cost is constant and, therefore, equal to its marginal cost. The monopolist produces output Q_M, where marginal revenue equals marginal cost, and charges price P_M. The output that is produced by a competitive industry with comparable demand and cost curves is Q_C. This is the level of output where price P_C equals marginal cost, the rule for profit maximization in the perfectly competitive model.[3] Because price P_C equals average cost, this outcome represents the zero-economic profit equilibrium in perfect competition.

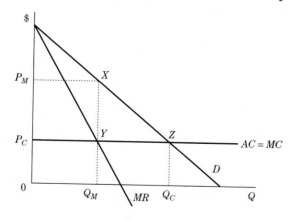

FIGURE 8.3
Comparing a Perfectly Competitive and a Monopolistic Industry
A monopolistic industry will produce a smaller amount of output and charge a higher price than a competitive industry with the same demand and cost conditions.

---

[2] Remember from Chapter 3 that total revenue is maximized where marginal revenue equals zero.
[3] Remember from Chapter 7 that price equals marginal revenue in perfect competition, so that producing where marginal revenue equals marginal cost is equivalent to producing where price equals marginal cost.

We can see in Figure 8.3 that, with the same demand and cost conditions, the price will be higher and the output lower under monopoly than under perfect competition. The higher price results in the monopolist earning an economic profit represented by the area $P_M X Y P_C$, compared with the zero-economic profit equilibrium of competition. Consumers value the units of output between Q_M and Q_C by the prices measured along segment XZ of the demand curve. Because these prices are higher than the corresponding marginal cost, consumers would have purchased these units of output if they had been produced by the monopolist. Therefore, monopoly results in a misallocation of resources compared with perfect competition. These conclusions are derived from the static model of perfect competition and monopoly presented in Figure 8.3. In the following sections, we will see that there are other factors to consider in comparing competitive firms and firms with market power.

Sources of Market Power: Barriers to Entry

Barriers to entry
The structural, legal, or regulatory characteristics of a firm and its market that keep other firms from producing the same or similar products at the same cost.

The following are the major **barriers to entry** that help firms maintain market power and earn positive economic profits:

1. Economies of scale
2. Barriers created by government
3. Input barriers
4. Brand loyalties
5. Consumer lock-in and switching costs
6. Network externalities

These factors apply to all imperfectly competitive firms, including the oligopoly firms we discuss in Chapter 9. We'll now describe each of these factors and provide examples of their effects.

Economies of Scale   Economies of scale exist when a firm's long-run average cost curve ($LRAC$) slopes downward or when lower costs of production are associated with a larger scale of operation at either the plant or the firm level. We described the reasons for the existence of economies of scale in Chapter 6. Economies of scale can act as a barrier to entry in different industries because only large-scale firms can achieve the cost-reduction benefits of these economies. Industries with significant economies of scale tend to be dominated by a small number of large firms. Even though these large-scale firms may have lower costs of production, there is no guarantee they will pass these low costs on to consumers in the form of lower prices, given the lack of entry into the industry. Therefore, managers may simply use economies of scale as part of their competitive strategy to earn positive economic profits. As we discuss later in this chapter, this trade-off between lower costs from large-scale production and the market power of these firms is one of the dilemmas of U.S. antitrust policy.

Mergers are one means of achieving the necessary size to realize economies of scale. Mergers are particularly important in the areas of technology, media, and telecommunications, where fixed costs are large and marginal costs are very low.[4] For example:

- Two-thirds of the cable television market is dominated by three companies, compared with the thousands of small, family-operated companies that existed two decades ago.
- The three big textbook companies—Pearson, Thomson, and McGraw-Hill—account for 62 percent of college textbook sales compared with 35 percent in 1990.
- Five large defense contractors dominate that industry.

---

[4] This discussion is based on Yochi J. Dreazan, Greg Ip, and Nicholas Kulish, "Oligopolies Are on the Rise As the Urge to Merge Grows," *Wall Street Journal*, February 25, 2002.

Illustrating even more rapid change, more than 10 firms offered job recruitment Web sites in 1999, while only three firms (CareerBuilder, Inc.; Monster.com; and HotJobs, Inc.)—dominated in 2002.

Economies of scale have been one of the factors behind many of these mergers. In the textbook industry, large-scale production means that sales representatives can become more specialized. Because many texts are offered with Web site support, sales need to be large to cover the increased costs of production. Online job recruiting Web sites must incur large marketing costs to attract a critical number of employers and potential employees. In other areas, such as the manufacturing of semiconductors, new plants now cost between $2 and $3 billion compared with only $1 billion five years earlier. Drug companies spent $30 billion on research in 2001, more than three times the amount a decade earlier. A 2001 study estimated that it cost $802 million to discover and develop a new drug, a figure two and one-half times larger than in 1987.[5] Small-scale firms could not finance these expenditures.

The increasing minimum efficient scale (MES) of production in the beer industry has been one of the factors leading to the large number of mergers in the industry. In 1950 there were 350 firms in the beer industry that could efficiently support 829 firms. By 1960, 175 brewers were forced to compete in a market that could efficiently support only 88 firms, and by 2000 there were 24 brewers in an industry that could support only 11. The large-scale production in the beer industry was also influenced by successful marketing campaigns and the use of television to market and advertise nationally. There is strong evidence suggesting that television advertising caused national brewers to increase their overall advertising, which then generated growth relative to regional and local brewers.[6]

These trends continued in late 2007 when London's SABMiller PLC announced its plans to combine its U.S. unit, Miller Brewing Co., with the U.S. division of Molson Coors Brewing Co., creating a joint venture called MillerCoors. A week later European brewers Heineken NV and Carlsberg AS announced they had formed a consortium to bid for the United Kingdom's best-selling brewer, Scottish & Newcastle PLC. These mergers were a reaction to sluggish beer sales growth in Western Europe and the U.S., increasing competition from wine and spirits, and the rising cost of key commodities such as grain, glass, and aluminum. Miller and Coors sought to become a stronger competitor to the long-dominant Anheuser-Busch Co.[7]

Consolidation has also been proposed in the mining industry. In November 2007, Anglo-Australian miner BHP Billiton announced a $125 billion proposal to merge with Anglo-Australian rival Rio Tinto. This merger would combine the world's No. 1 and No. 3 miners into a company worth at least $320 billion, bigger than every global oil company except ExxonMobil and Russia's OAO Gazprom. The merged mining company would be the world's largest producer of copper and aluminum, the second largest iron ore provider, and potentially the largest source of uranium.[8] However, in November 2008, BHP Billiton abruptly stopped its pursuit of Rio Tinto, given the inherent risk in the $68 billion deal from falling commodity prices and the slowing world economy. BHP feared that its debt would increase too much if the merger occurred.[9]

---

[5] Gardiner Harris, "Why Drug Makers Are Failing in Quest for New Blockbusters," *Wall Street Journal*, April 18, 2002. See also Ernst R. Berndt, "Pharmaceuticals in U.S. Health Care: Determinants of Quantity and Price," *Journal of Economic Perspectives* 16 (Fall 2002): 45–66.

[6] Victor J. Tremblay and Carol Horton Tremblay, *The U.S. Brewing Industry* (Cambridge, MA: The MIT Press, 2005), 45–48.

[7] Jason Singer and David Kesmodel, "Why Consolidation Storm Is Brewing in Beer Industry," *Wall Street Journal*, October 18, 2007.

[8] Patrick Barta and Robert Guy Matthews, "Mining Firms Bulk Up, Echoing Big Oil Mergers," *Wall Street Journal*, December 18, 2007; Dennis K. Berman, "Proposed Mining Megadeal Could Make the Earth Move," *Wall Street Journal*, February 12, 2008.

[9] Robert Guy Matthews, Dana Cimilluca, and Patrick Barta, "Death of a Megadeal: BHP Ends Its Pursuit of Rio," *Wall Street Journal*, November 26, 2008.

Delta Air Lines and Northwest Airlines did announce their merger in October 2008.[10] Managers argued that the combined company would be better able to withstand the rapidly changing fuel prices and the continued worldwide economic slowdown, given the $2 billion in projected cost savings and additional revenue expected from the merger. The combined airline would have more than $35 billion in revenue, a fleet of nearly 800 planes, and 75,000 employees.

Barriers Created by Government   Barriers to entry created by government include licenses, patents, and copyrights. Each of these regulations was created for various public policy purposes, but all have the potential to act as barriers to entry.

Licenses   The licensing of physicians and other professionals is usually justified on the basis of maintaining the quality of the individuals in these professions. However, because the licensure of physicians also restricts their numbers, it acts as a barrier to entry and can generate higher profits for those in the profession. Physicians have raised the quality argument in disputes over the range of medical services that other medical professionals, such as physicians' assistants and nurses' aides, can perform. Critics have charged that physicians are simply trying to maintain their incomes in the face of increased competition among medical service providers. The debate has also surfaced between psychiatrists and psychologists. For many years, the American Psychological Association lobbied for legislation that would allow psychologists to write prescriptions for their patients, a privilege that was given only to psychiatrists.[11] Psychiatrists argued that patients often have other medical problems that psychologists would not understand and, therefore, psychologists should not be able to write prescriptions. Yet there is also a potential loss of income for psychiatrists should this restriction be lifted. Proponents have also argued that this change would increase the availability of mental health services in underserved areas. In March 2002, New Mexico became the first state to grant limited prescribing privileges to psychologists. Louisiana and the U.S. territory of Guam also passed similar laws, while lobbying groups urged a similar change in Missouri's laws in 2008.[12]

Patents and Copyrights   Patents and copyrights give the producer of a new invention or printed work the right to the profits from that work for a number of years in order to encourage research, innovation, and the development of new products. These issues of research and new product development go beyond the static competitive and monopoly comparisons in Figure 8.3 that do not focus on dynamic changes in industries over time. Patents can help firms gain market power through innovation and then act as a barrier to entry, protecting that information and innovation for a given period of time. Economist Joseph Schumpeter first presented the argument that a market structure with monopoly power through patents might be more conducive to innovation than a more competitive market.[13] The public policy concern is that highly competitive markets may result in too few innovations if any positive economic profits from competitive firms are competed away too rapidly. Public policy makers believe

[10] Susan Carey and Paulo Prada, "Delta Air Lines, Northwest Complete Merger," *Wall Street Journal*, October 30, 2008.

[11] Erica Goode, "Psychologists Get Prescription Pads and Furor Erupts," *New York Times*, March 26, 2002; Ellen Barry, "Psychiatrists Fight Blurring Line with Psychologists," *Boston Globe*, June 1, 2002.

[12] Rosemary Frei, "The Prescribing Psychologist," *Medical Post*, November 2, 2004; Anonymous, "Prescription Privileges Law for Missouri Psychologists Improves Patient Access to Quality Mental Health Care," *PR Newswire*, January 9, 2008.

[13] Joseph Schumpeter, *Capitalism, Socialism, and Democracy*, 3rd ed. (New York: Harper and Row, 1950). Evidence on this issue is mixed, particularly for the U.S. economy. See Dennis W. Carlton and Jeffrey M. Perloff, *Modern Industrial Organization*, 3rd ed. (Reading, Mass.: Addison-Wesley Longman, 2000), chap. 16. Much of the discussion of patents in this text is drawn from the Carlton and Perloff book.

that competitive markets will produce too few innovations and too little new information and are, therefore, willing to grant firms some degree of market power to stimulate innovation.

In some industries, patents may not be as important in maintaining a competitive advantage as factors such as secrecy, lead time, the lowering of costs through greater experience in production, and increased sales and service efforts. However, patents play an extremely important role in achieving and maintaining market power in the pharmaceutical industry. The role of patents in protecting the profits of pharmaceutical producers is illustrated by the steps these manufacturers are willing to take to prevent competition from generic drugs when their patents expire or are about to expire.[14] A generic drug has the same chemical content as the corresponding branded drug, but it cannot be sold until the patent on the branded drug expires. On average, a generic drug can decrease U.S. sales of a branded drug by approximately 50 percent during the first six months of competition. To prevent competition from generics, the major drug companies have often filed suits raising concerns about the safety of generic drugs and the procedures used to make these pharmaceuticals. In some instances, the drug companies have changed the dosage of medications to prevent generic substitution because the new drugs are no longer exactly equivalent to the branded drugs. Even if these strategies do not prevent the generics from being introduced, the strategies may delay the introduction of generics, which increases the sales of the branded drug during the delay period.

Competition from generics has been of particular importance to the drug companies since 2000, when patents on many of their major revenue-generating drugs began to expire.[15] The market power of the pharmaceutical industry has also been reduced because it has become much more difficult for these companies to develop new drugs that are significantly different from existing drugs and to raise prices on their existing drugs, given increased competition among the drug manufacturers and managed care's role in containing the costs of health care. Thus, protection of market power through patent disputes has been the major competitive strategy of the pharmaceutical industry.[16]

More recently pharmaceutical companies have often been capitulating in patent dispute cases by agreeing to shorten the patent life of a drug, foregoing hundreds of millions of dollars in potential revenue, in return for the assurance that they can market the drug for a few years free from the threat of litigation by their generic rivals. For example, Cephalon Inc. settled with three of the four generic makers of its sleep-disorder drug, Provigil, by allowing the generic manufacturers to sell the medicine in 2011, three years before the disputed patent expires.[17] However, in 2008 Cephalon also sharply increased the price of Provigil in anticipation of launching a longer-acting version of the drug called Nuvigil, which will have a lower price. The company anticipated that users would switch to Nuvigil by the time the Provigil patent expires.[18]

Similar issues regarding patent infringement have arisen in the market for computer printer ink. Ink cartridges are a major source of revenue for Hewlett-Packard Co., which has a market share of 50 percent in the U.S. and more than 4,000 patents on its ink formulations and cartridge design. Because the company made more

---

[14] Gardiner Harris and Chris Adams, "Drug Manufacturers Are Intensifying Courtroom Attacks That Slow Generics," *Wall Street Journal*, July 12, 2001; Gardiner Harris, "Why Drug Makers Are Failing in Quest for New Blockbusters," *Wall Street Journal*, April 18, 2002; Laurie McGinley and Scott Hensley, "Drug Industry Exhorts Companies to Avoid Coalition Pushing Generics," *Wall Street Journal*, May 3, 2002. See also Ernst E. Berndt, "Pharmaceuticals in U.S. Health Care: Determinants of Quantity and Price," *Journal of Economic Perspectives* 16 (Fall 2002): 45–66.

[15] Eli Lilly & Company's patent on the antidepressant Prozac and Merck & Company's patent on the ulcer drug Pepcid both expired in 2001.

[16] Harris and Adams, "Drug Manufacturers Are Intensifying."

[17] Leila Abboud, "Branded Drugs Settling More Generic Suits," *Wall Street Journal*, January 17, 2006.

[18] Jonathan D. Rockoff, "How a Drug Maker Tries to Outwit Generics," *Wall Street Journal*, November 17, 2008.

than 80 percent of its 2005 operating profit of $5.6 billion from ink and toner supplies, it sued other ink and cartridge manufacturers and stores with ink-cartridge refilling stations for patent infringements. The company employs chemists who analyze competitors' inks to determine whether H-P patents have been violated.[19]

Input Barriers. Other barriers to entry include control over raw materials or other key inputs in a production process and barriers in financial capital markets. For example, the De Beers diamond cartel traditionally controlled the major sources of diamonds and, therefore, had a monopoly on diamond production.[20] Formed during the 1930s, De Beers and the companies with whom it contracted controlled 70 to 80 percent of the world's supply of rough diamonds and influenced almost every stage of diamond production from extraction to the distribution of rough diamonds. However, even this market power is constantly threatened by the development of new sources of diamonds, changing consumer preferences for less-than-perfect gems, and the increased competition by Internet sellers and retail chains such as Wal-Mart and Costco.

In the airlines industry, the major companies control the crucial inputs of airport gates and time slots for flying.[21] Dominant airlines effectively own their hub airports because they have long-term leases on the gates, which they can even leave unused. These airlines have veto rights over airport expansion that could increase competition, and they may even control ground-handling and baggage services.

In 1999, the *Wall Street Journal* reported on a particularly vivid example of this barrier to entry, the case of Spirit Airlines.[22] After seven years of operation, Spirit Airlines had been unable to acquire or sublease any gates at the Detroit airport, the major hub for Northwest Airlines. Thus, Spirit flew at the convenience of the major airlines because it had to negotiate the rental of gates for the specific departures and arrivals of its planes on a daily basis, often when planes were en route to Detroit. Spirit had to pay $250 to $400 per turn to rent spare gates for a total of $1.3 million per year, which the company claimed was more than twice the amortized cost of owning two gates with jetways.

Barriers to purchasing the inputs of production can also arise from lack of access to financial capital by small firms compared with larger firms. Research studies have shown that larger firms can enjoy up to a percentage point difference in terms of the interest cost of financing new investment. Small firms tend to have smaller security offerings, so that the fixed transactions costs are spread over fewer securities. Investors often perceive the offerings of small corporations as being more risky and, therefore, demand higher interest payments.[23]

Brand Loyalties The creation of brand loyalties through advertising and other marketing efforts is a strategy that many managers use to create and maintain market power. The beer industry presents one of the best examples of this strategy.[24] Many blind taste tests have shown that consumers cannot distinguish between

[19] Christopher Lawton, "H-P Chemists Hunt Violators of Ink Patents," *Wall Street Journal*, August 29, 2006.
[20] Donald G. McNeil, Jr., "A Diamond Cartel May Be Forever: The Hereditary Leader of De Beers Pursues Post-Apartheid Growth," *New York Times*, January 12, 1999; Anthony DePalma, "Diamonds in the Cold: New Canadian Mine Seeks Its Place in a De Beers World," *New York Times*, April 13, 1999; Leslie Kaufman, "Once a Luxury, Diamond Rings Now Overflow Bargain Tables," *New York Times*, February 13, 2002; Tracie Rozhon, "Competition Is Forever," *New York Times*, February 9, 2005.
[21] William G. Shepherd, "Airlines," in *The Structure of American Industry*, eds. Walter Adams and James Brock, 10th ed. (Upper Saddle River, N.J.: Prentice Hall, 2001), 199–223.
[22] Bruce Ingersoll, "Gateless in Detroit, Low-Fare Spirit Docks at Rivals' Convenience," *Wall Street Journal*, July 12, 1999.
[23] F. M. Scherer and David Ross, *Industrial Market Structure and Economic Performance*, 3rd ed. (Boston: Houghton Mifflin, 1990), 126–30.
[24] This discussion is drawn from Douglas F. Greer, "Beer: Causes of Structural Change," in *Industry Studies*, ed. Larry L. Duetsch, 2nd ed. (Armonk, N.Y.: Sharpe, 1998), 28–64. Individual brands of beer are not cited in this article.

brands of beer. In one taste test sponsored by *Consumer Reports*, a panel of 17 knowledgeable tasters, ranging from brewmasters to brewing students, was asked to assess the qualities and defects of dozens of brands of beer.[25] The two top-ranked brands were among the least expensive, while the brands that were ranked the lowest were among the most expensive brands. The correlation coefficient between the prices of 16 beers and their taste-test quality ratings was .018, which was not significantly different from zero.

Because there are few real differences among many brands of beer, the major beer companies have focused their advertising and marketing efforts on creating perceived differences, many of which are associated with different prices—popular, premium, and super premium. Beer advertising also focuses on images of pleasure, belonging, and other psychological benefits of the product. Persuasive advertising is dominant in the beer industry because the product is a relatively inexpensive perishable good. Thus, consumers have few incentives to spend time and energy trying to collect objective information about the product. Beer companies have also used advertising to segment their brand images along white-collar and blue-collar lines.[26]

Brand loyalty is created in other industries by determining the proper amount to spend on customer service. In 2003, Starbucks Corp. made the decision to invest $40 million systemwide to add 20 hours of labor per week in each store to speed up service. Studies had shown that speed of service was critical to customers' satisfaction and that highly satisfied customers spent 9 percent more than those who were simply satisfied.[27]

Consumer Lock-In and Switching Costs   Barriers to entry can also result if consumers become locked into certain types or brands of products and would incur substantial switching costs if they changed. Table 8.1 shows the major types of **lock-in and switching costs**.[28] Although these types of lock-in are

Lock-in and switching costs
A form of market power for a firm in which consumers become locked into purchasing certain types or brands of products because they would incur substantial costs if they switched to other products.

TABLE 8.1 Consumer Lock-In and Associated Switching Costs

LOCK-IN CATEGORY	SWITCHING COSTS
Contractual commitments	Compensatory or liquidated damages.
Durable purchases	Replacement of equipment; tend to decline as the durable ages.
Brand-specific training	Learning a new system, both direct costs and lost productivity; tend to rise over time.
Information and databases	Converting data to a new format; tend to rise over time as collection grows.
Specialized suppliers	Funding of new supplier; may rise over time if capabilities are difficult to find/maintain.
Search costs	Combined buyer and seller search costs; includes learning about quality of alternatives.
Loyalty programs	Any lost benefits from current supplier, plus possible need to rebuild cumulative use.

Source: Carl Shapiro and Hal R. Varian, *Information Rules: A Strategic Guide to the Network Economy* (Boston: Harvard Business School Press, 1999), 117. Copyright © 1999 by the Harvard Business School Publishing Corporation; all rights reserved.

---

[25] *Consumer Reports*, June 1996, 10–17, as reported in Greer, 42.

[26] Victor J. Tremblay and Carol Horton Tremblay, *The U.S. Brewing Industry* (Cambridge, MA: The MIT Press, 2005).

[27] Ryan Chittum, "Price Points," *Wall Street Journal*, October 30, 2006.

[28] The discussion of lock-in, switching costs, and network externalities is based on Carl Shapiro and Hal R. Varian, *Information Rules: A Strategic Guide to the Network Economy* (Boston: Harvard Business School Press, 1999), 103–225.

dominant in the information industries, they represent managerial strategies that can be used elsewhere in the economy to gain and maintain market power.

Contractual Commitment   A contractual commitment to purchase from a specific supplier is the most explicit type of lock-in because it is a legal document. Some contracts force the buyer to purchase all requirements from a specific seller for a period of time, whereas others specify only a minimum order requirement.

Durable Purchases   In the 1980s, Bell Atlantic selected AT&T over Northern Telecom and Siemens for the purchase of its 5ESS digital switches to operate its telephone network, given the quality of the AT&T product. However, the company also submitted itself to extensive lock-in, as the switches utilized a proprietary operating system controlled by AT&T. AT&T also remained in control of a wide range of enhancements and upgrades to its switches. The market power to AT&T from this lock-in was particularly important because the switches had a useful life of 15 or more years and were costly to remove or reinstall. Customers may be able to circumvent some of this lock-in if they can lease rather than purchase the equipment.

Brand-Specific Training   Closely related to the durable equipment lock-in is the brand-specific training that may be required for the personnel who use the equipment. If employees become accustomed to a particular brand of software, switching will be much more difficult unless competing software is also easy to learn and use. For example, Microsoft Word provides technical assistance screens to former WordPerfect users to lower the switching costs to the Microsoft product.

Information and Databases   The costs of transferring information from one database to another or of switching from one technology to another can be substantial, particularly if the original database or technology has unique characteristics. There were typically large switching costs when consumers changed from phonograph records to CDs to DVDs. Tax preparation software, on the other hand, is often designed so that later versions are compatible with earlier versions and the company can attract and lock in a new group of consumers.

Specialized Suppliers   Sellers of specialized equipment also use lock-in to gain market power. This specialization becomes a more powerful strategy for the seller if alternative firms are no longer in business after an initial purchase is made. The Department of Defense has long faced this problem, given the limited number of defense contractors supplying the Department.

Search Costs   Large search costs for alternative suppliers give existing firms a competitive advantage. Search costs involve the time and effort both for consumers to gather information about alternative products and for new suppliers to search out and attract new customers.

Loyalty Programs   Loyalty programs are another explicit strategy for increasing consumer lock-in. The best examples are the airlines' frequent-flyer programs. These programs create customer loyalty because frequent-flyer points may be forfeited if they are not used within a certain time period and many benefits, such as preferential service, are based on cumulative usage of the airline. Hotels, grocery stores, and local retailers have also implemented similar loyalty programs. The number of such programs is expected to increase as businesses gain better access to databases on consumer buying habits.

Switching Costs Example   Direct deposits of paychecks, Social Security, and pension checks and automatic payments of utility, phone, and insurance bills have increased the switching costs among bank checking account customers in recent years. These innovations have caused the 15 percent of customers who leave their bank every year to decline as more customers are locked in by the automated transactions to their accounts. In response, many banks have made increased efforts to lure customers from their competitors by offering to contact companies and employers for their customers to help change the automatic transactions from their old to their new accounts. These switching services may be used strategically as certain services may be available only to customers who purchase premium and more profitable services from the bank.[29]

Switching Costs and the Internet   In the late 1990s and early 2000s, many believed that e-commerce and the use of the Internet would lead to more intense price competition due to less product differentiation, lower search costs, and lower fixed costs.[30] The geographical dimension of product differentiation would be eliminated, price searches would be facilitated online, and Internet firms would likely have lower fixed costs leading to greater entry and more competition. However, research has shown that there is price dispersion online, and that online prices may not be much lower than offline prices. The amount of price dispersion in markets with "branded" Web sites is substantial, and price dispersion has been found in markets where consumers use price search engines.

These results mean that firms can develop market power even on the Internet. Amazon.com and Barnes & Noble online do not have the geographic differentiation that occurs in the offline world, but they compete on the basis of consumer preferences for service, atmosphere, and reputation. Search costs also may not be lower on the Internet because retailers can engage in strategies such as offering complicated menus of prices, bundling products, personalizing prices, or making the process of comparing prices complex. Because Internet firms such as Amazon.com offer multiple products, they may set prices lower today so that customers will not incur the real or psychic costs of trying out another bookstore and will continue to purchase from Amazon in the future. As in the offline world, Internet firms can also set low prices for low quality items on Pricewatch and then design their Web sites to persuade consumers who visit to purchase additional items or higher quality items at higher prices.[31]

Managerial Rule of Thumb

Using Lock-In as a Competitive Strategy

To best use lock-in as a competitive strategy, managers should be prepared to invest in a given base of customers by offering concessions and attractive terms to initially gain these customers. Being first to market is one of the best ways to obtain the initial advantage. Selling to influential buyers and attracting buyers with high switching costs are other strategies for building a consumer base. After attracting new customers, managers need to make them entrenched to increase their commitment to the products and technology. Loyalty programs and cumulative discounts are part of these entrenchment strategies. Leveraging a firm's installed base of customers also involves selling complementary products to the customers and selling access to the customer base to other producers. ■

---

[29] Jane J. Kim, "Banks Push Harder to Get You to Switch," _Wall Street Journal_, October 12, 2006.

[30] This discussion is based on Glenn Ellison and Sara Fisher Ellison, "Lessons About Markets from the Internet," _Journal of Economic Perspectives_ 19 (Spring 2005): 139–58.

[31] Researchers have shown that the costs of switching from eBay, the largest single online marketplace, to an alternative Web site for an established seller with a strong reputation on eBay averages around 3 percent of the item's value. See Mikhail Melnik and James Alm, "Seller Reputation, Information Signals, and Prices for Heterogeneous Coins on eBay," _Southern Economic Journal_ 72 (2005): 305-327; Mikhail Melnik and James Alm, "Does a Seller's eCommerce Reputation Matter? Evidence from eBay Auctions," _Journal of Industrial Economics_ 50 (2002): 337–349.

Network externalities
A barrier to entry that exists because the value of a product to consumers depends on the number of consumers using the product.

Network Externalities **Network externalities** act as a barrier to entry because the value of a product to consumers depends on the number of customers using the product. Examples of such products include software networks, compatible fax machines and modems, e-mail software, ATMs, and particular computer brands such as Macintosh. Often one brand of a product becomes the industry standard, and its value increases when it does so.

Network externalities can be considered demand-side economies of scale, in contrast to the supply-side economies that we discussed earlier in this chapter and in Chapter 6. Microsoft's dominance in software results from these demand-side economies of scale. These economies are prominent in the information industry, and their power increases as the size of the network grows.

Changes in Market Power

Market power can be a very fluid and elusive concept. In this section, we look at several examples that illustrate how managers had to change their strategies to keep up with the dynamics of the marketplace and to avoid losing market power.

Shifting Demand for Kleenex Kimberly-Clark Corp., maker of Kleenex, an 83-year-old brand, has been faced both with increased competition from cheap generic tissue and with pressure to add high-tech ingredients to basic paper products.[32] Kleenex, which has $1.6 billion in global sales, is part of the company's consumer tissue division, which produces more than a third of the company's annual sales. However, consumer tissue has the smallest profit margin of the company's three divisions, given the high prices of energy and wood pulp. Furthermore, the facial tissue category has been shrinking since 2001, with tissue sales suffering their largest decline in the past five years. Lower-priced private brands have gained market share, and consumers have often used substitute products, such as paper towels, toilet paper, and free napkins from fast-food restaurants. Advances in cold therapies, both prescription and over-the-counter, may also have decreased the demand for tissues.

Kimberly-Clark's response in 2004 was to develop Anti-Viral, a Kleenex laced with a mild pesticide to fight cold and flu viruses. In developing this new product, Kimberly-Clark needed to obtain approval from the Environmental Protection Agency to use a pesticide in the tissue. It had to re-think its marketing because it had always presented Kleenex with a soft touch, not as a killer of viruses. The company had tried a similar germ-fighting tissue in 1984 but had to pull the product after just a few months in five test markets. Consumers were resistant to the idea of a chemical-laced tissue in this period before widespread use of antibacterial soaps, fabrics, and hand wipes. The product also cost more than regular tissues.

By 1987 Procter & Gamble had launched Puffs Plus With Lotion, the first tissue treated with lotion. Kimberly-Clark developed its own similar product and found that customers would pay extra for these characteristics. These changes encouraged the company to develop the anti-virus tissue even though some health experts remain skeptical of Anti-Viral's health benefits. Kimberly-Clark did not want to promote the health benefits too aggressively so that the product did not become "the sick box." The Environmental Protection Agency required that Kleenex state on its label that the product had not been tested against bacteria, fungi, or other viruses, and it made certain that the box design did not appeal to children. By 2007, Anti-Viral held 4 percent of the U.S. market and had generated more than $140 million in global sales since it was launched in 2004.

---

[32] This discussion is based on Ellen Byron, "Can a Re-Engineered Kleenex Cure a Brand's Sniffles?" *Wall Street Journal*, January 22, 2007.

Home Depot and Customer Service   Home Depot became the world's largest home-improvement chain largely due to its customer service, much of which was provided by its skilled employees who were often former plumbers, electricians, and carpenters. However, service began to deteriorate in 2001 as the company hired more part-time workers and added a salary cap that drove off many more experienced workers. The company also moved about 40 percent of its workers to overnight stocking positions, often leaving customers searching for an employee to answer their questions. These cost-cutting changes, combined with increased competition from Lowe's, had already hindered the company's sales.

In early 2007 Home Depot began to try to reverse its reputation for poor service. Managers began efforts to improve store displays, add new workers, and reward stores for improved customer service.[33]

In 2007 Home Depot also announced the opening of two test stores called Home Depot Design Centers, which were fashioned as a hybrid of the typical Home Depot store and its Expo stores and developed to appeal to women shoppers. These stores carry more bath and kitchen showrooms as opposed to professional construction products such as lumber and building materials.[34]

All of these changes were designed to not only influence customer perceptions and meet the competition from Lowe's, but also to counter the fallout from the decline in the housing sector in 2007 and 2008. In November 2008, Home Depot reported a 31 percent decline in its third quarter net income and reduced its full-year revenue projection in response to continued tight credit and consumer fears about the economy.[35]

Borders Bookstores' Online Strategy   Borders Group Inc. had traditionally focused on opening more stores rather than emphasizing online book sales.[36] It increased the number of its U.S. superstores from 290 in 2000 to 499 in 2007, and the number of its overseas superstores from 22 in 2001 to 73 in 2007. Borders transferred its online business to Amazon.com in 2001. Amazon was to operate the Web site, keeping all revenue generated except for a commission paid to Borders. This strategy proved incorrect as sales at U.S. bookstores dropped 2.9 percent in 2006 while online book sales soared.

In March 2007 Borders announced that it would reopen its own branded Web site in early 2008, ending the alliance with Amazon.com, and that it would sell or franchise most of its 73 overseas Borders stores. The company also planned to close nearly half of its Waldenbooks outlets in the U.S. These changes reflect the increased competition that book retailers face from the sluggish book market and from Web-based and other discount booksellers such as Amazon.com and Costco Wholesale Corp. These outlets sell a variety of goods in addition to books, so they can offer the books at substantially reduced prices and make up the revenue on the other goods. Borders also designed new superstores that would include a digital center where customers could purchase a variety of digital products.

In March 2008 Borders put itself up for sale after surprising investors by disclosing a potential liquidity problem. The turmoil in the credit markets had closed off some of its usual sources of financing. At that time Barnes & Noble announced that it would look at the option of purchasing Borders. No sale occurred by fall 2008,

---

[33] Ann Zimmerman, "Home Depot Tries to Make Nice to Customers," *Wall Street Journal*, February 20, 2007.

[34] Jennifer Waters, "Home Depot Set to Test Stores Geared to Women," *Wall Street Journal*, October 10, 2007.

[35] Mary Ellen Lloyd, "Home Depot Net Falls, but Tops Estimates," *Wall Street Journal*, November 19, 2008.

[36] This discussion is based on Jeffrey A. Trachtenberg, "Borders Business Plan Gets a Rewrite," *Wall Street Journal*, March 22, 2007; and Greta Guest, "Bookseller Will Innovate Beyond Online in Stores: New Solutions on Way for Retail Puzzle," *McClatchy-Tribune Business News*, October 14, 2007.

and Borders was still experiencing credit and financial problems. In November 2008, the company posted a net loss of $175.4 million.[37]

Measures of Market Power

Economists have developed several measures of market power, some of which are based on the models of market structure we discussed earlier in this chapter. Managers can use these measures to gain a better understanding of their markets and to anticipate any antitrust actions in their industry, as the Justice Department uses a number of these measures to determine whether antitrust actions are warranted in merger cases.

Lerner Index
A measure of market power that focuses on the difference between a firm's product price and its marginal cost of production.

The Lerner Index   The **Lerner Index** focuses on the difference between a firm's product price and its marginal cost of production, which, as we discussed previously, exists for a firm with market power, but does not exist for a perfectly competitive firm. The Lerner Index is defined in Equation 8.1:

$$8.1 \quad L = \frac{(P - MC)}{P}$$

where

L = value of the Lerner Index

P = product price

MC = marginal cost of production

Because profit-maximizing perfectly competitive firms produce where price equals marginal cost, the value of the Lerner Index is zero under perfect competition and increases as market power increases. The value of the index and market power vary inversely with the price elasticity of demand.

Although this measure of market power is derived directly from economic theory, it is often difficult to use in practice because data on marginal cost are scarce. You may remember from the survey data presented in Chapter 5 that many managers were unable to answer questions about their firm's marginal cost because the concept was foreign to them. Given these data problems, this ratio is often calculated as the difference between price and average variable cost or as sales revenue minus payroll and materials costs divided by sales. This approach typically ignores capital, research and development, and advertising costs. It may also be biased if average and marginal costs are not constant and equal to each other. In Chapter 7, we contrasted the price-cost margin of 11.9 percent for the highly competitive broiler chicken industry with the much higher margins in the more concentrated, differentiated food industries.[38]

Marginal costs have been estimated for the airline industry, so that price/marginal cost ratios can be calculated for different market structures on various routes within the industry.[39]

Table 8.2 shows the price/marginal cost calculations by the number of carriers on different routes and the share of all airline routes in these different market structures. A dominant firm is defined as one that has at least 60 percent of ticket

---

[37] Jeffrey A. Trachtenberg and Karen Richardson, "At Borders Group, The Next Best Seller Might Be Itself," *Wall Street Journal*, March 21, 2008; Jeffrey A. Trachtenberg, "Barnes & Noble Studies Bid for Borders," *Wall Street Journal*, May 21, 2008; Jeffrey A. Trachtenberg and Sara Silver, "Borders's Loss Deepens," *Wall Street Journal*, November 26, 2008.

[38] Richard T. Rogers, "Broilers: Differentiating a Commodity," in *Industry Studies*, ed. Larry L. Duetsch, 2nd ed. (Armonk, N.Y.: Sharpe, 1998), pp. 65–100.

[39] Jeffrey M. Perloff, Larry S. Karp, and Amos Golan, *Estimating Market Power and Strategies* (New York: Cambridge University Press, 2007), 28–30; Jesse C. Weiher, Robin C. Sickles, and Jeffrey M. Perloff, "Market Power in the U.S. Airline Industry," in *Measuring Market Power, Contributions to Economic Analysis*, vol. 255, ed. Daniel J. Slottje (Amsterdam: Elsevier, 2002), 309–23.

TABLE 8.2 Airline Price-Cost Margins and Market Structure

TYPE OF MARKET	P/MC	SHARE OF ALL ROUTES (%)
All markets	2.1	100
Dominant firm	3.1	40
Dominant pair	1.2	42
One firm (monopoly)	3.3	18
Two firms	2.2	19
Dominant firm	2.3	14
No dominant firm	1.5	5
Three firms	1.8	16
Dominant firm	1.9	9
No dominant firm	1.3	7
Four firms	1.8	13
Dominant firm	2.2	6
Dominant pair	1.3	7
No dominant firm or pair	2.1	~0
Five or more firms	1.3	35
Dominant firm	3.5	11
Dominant pair	1.4	23
No dominant firm or pair	1.1	0.1

Sources: Jeffrey M. Perloff, Larry S. Karp, and Amos Golan, *Estimating Market Power and Strategies* (New York: Cambridge University Press, 2007), 28–30; Jesse C. Weiher, Robin C. Sickles, and Jeffrey M. Perloff, "Market Power in the U.S. Airline Industry," in *Measuring Market Power, Contributions to Economic Analysis*, vol. 255, ed. Daniel J. Slottje (Amsterdam: Elsevier, 2002), 309–23.

sales by value but is not a monopoly. Two carriers are a dominant pair if they collectively have at least 60 percent of the market but neither firm is a dominant firm and three or more firms fly this route. All but 0.1 percent of the routes have either a monopoly (18 percent), a dominant firm (40 percent), or a dominant pair (42 percent).

On average, price is slightly more than double marginal cost on all U.S. routes and market structures. However, price is 3.3 times marginal cost when one firm monopolizes a route and 3.1 times marginal cost when there is a dominant firm. This research shows that the amount by which price exceeds marginal cost depends more on whether there is a dominant firm or dominant pair than on the total number of firms in the market. Market power is clearly shown in cases where a single firm dominates a route. Even if two firms dominate, the excess of price over marginal cost is substantially lower than if a single firm dominates.

Cross-Price Elasticity of Demand   The cross-price elasticity of demand, or the percentage change in the quantity demanded of good X relative to the percentage change in the price of good Y, which we introduced in Chapter 3, is another measure of market power. If two goods have a positive cross-price elasticity of demand, they are substitute goods. The higher the cross-price elasticity, the greater the potential substitution between the goods, and the smaller the market power possessed by the firms producing the two goods.

Concentration Ratios   **Concentration ratios** measure market power by focusing on the share of the market held by the X largest firms, where X typically

Concentration ratios
A measure of market power that focuses on the share of the market held by the X largest firms, where X typically equals four, six, or eight.

equals four, six, or eight.[40] The assumption is that the larger the share of the market held by a small number of firms, the more market power those firms have.[41] One problem with concentration ratios is that they describe only one point on the size distribution of firms in an industry. One industry could have four firms that each hold 20 percent of the market share, while another could have four firms that hold 60, 10, 5, and 5 percent shares. The four-firm concentration ratios would be equal for both industries, but most researchers and managers would argue that the degree of competition would be quite different in the industries.

Another problem with concentration ratios is that the market definitions used in their construction may be arbitrary. The economic definition of a market focuses on those goods that are close substitutes in both consumption and production. Substitutes in consumption would imply a high cross-price elasticity of demand, as noted above. Substitution in production would imply that a high price for good A would cause some firms to switch production in their facilities from good B to good A.[42] The concentration ratios published by the U.S. Bureau of the Census do not generally conform to the economic definition of a market because the Census definitions were developed "to serve the general purposes of the census and other government statistics" and were "not designed to establish categories necessarily denoting coherent or relevant markets in the true competitive sense, or to provide a basis for measuring market power."[43] Thus, the Census definitions often include products that are not close substitutes in the same industry, and they may omit products that are close substitutes. If consumer demand indicates that plastic bottles compete with glass bottles, the concentration ratio for the glass bottle industry may not provide much information about the competitive nature of that industry.

Concentration ratios also are often based on national statistics and may not reflect differences in transportation costs among local markets that could result in substantial concentration at that level. In addition, concentration ratios ignore imports and exports, which for industries such as the domestic automobile producers could lead to a very biased view of market competition.

Herfindahl-Hirschman Index (*HHI*)

A measure of market power that is defined as the sum of the squares of the market share of each firm in an industry.

The Herfindahl-Hirschman Index   The **Herfindahl-Hirschman Index (*HHI*)** is a measure of market power that makes use of more information about the relative market shares of firms in the industry. The *HHI* is defined as the sum of the squares of the market share of each firm in the industry. The values of the *HHI* range from near zero for competitive firms to 10,000 if one firm monopolizes the entire market ($HHI = 100^2$). The *HHI* is also sensitive to unequal market shares of different firms. For example, if an industry has two firms with equal market shares, the *HHI* equals $(50)^2 + (50)^2 = 2,500 + 2,500 = 5,000$. If the market shares of the two firms are 90 percent and 10 percent, the value of the *HHI* equals $(90)^2 + (10)^2 = 8,100 + 100 = 8,200$.

The *HHI* is important because the Antitrust Guidelines of the Justice Department use the index to evaluate the competitive effects of mergers between firms in order to determine whether any antitrust action is appropriate. If the postmerger *HHI* is less than 1,000, the Justice Department will rarely challenge the merger. If the postmerger *HHI* is greater than 1,800 and the merger itself causes the *HHI* to increase by 100 points or more, the Justice Department presumes the merger is

---

[40] The discussion of concentration ratios, the Herfindahl-Hirschman Index (*HHI*), and antitrust issues is based on the following sources: Dennis W. Carlton and Jeffrey M. Perloff, *Modern Industrial Organization*, 3rd ed. (Reading, Mass.: Addison-Wesley Longman, 2000); W. Kip Viscusi, John M. Vernon, and Joseph E. Harrington, Jr., *Economics of Regulation and Antitrust*, 2nd ed. (Cambridge, Mass.: MIT Press, 1995); John E. Kwoka, Jr., and Lawrence J. White, *The Antitrust Revolution: Economics, Competition, and Policy*, 3rd ed. (New York: Oxford University Press, 1999).

[41] We first introduced this concept when discussing the agricultural industry in Chapter 7.

[42] We first discussed substitution in both consumption (demand) and production (supply) in Chapter 2.

[43] Quoted in Viscusi, Vernon, and Harrington, 148.

anticompetitive and should be challenged unless the companies' lawyers and economists can present offsetting evidence. Mergers with *HHI* values between these limits are less likely to be challenged by the Justice Department. In practice, the Justice Department often tends to be more lenient in interpreting the values of the *HHI* than the guidelines would suggest.

An *HHI* of 1,000 would result from a market with 10 equal-sized firms, each with a 10 percent market share, while an *HHI* of 1,800 would result from a market with five to six equal-sized firms. The two *HHI* decision points correspond roughly to four-firm concentration ratios of 50 and 70 percent, respectively.

Another way to use the *HHI* is to calculate the number of "effective competitors" by examining the inverse of the *HHI* when market shares are expressed as fractions rather than percentages.[44] This procedure may give a more intuitive meaning to values of the *HHI*. For example, in the above case of two firms with equal market shares, the number of effective competitors is $1/0.5 = 2.00$. In the case of two firms with market shares of 90 and 10 percent, the number of effective competitors is $1/0.82 = 1.22$. Thus, in the second case there is only slightly more than one effective competitor in the market.

Table 8.3 shows the four- and eight-firm concentration ratios and the *HHI* for several major manufacturing industries in the United States for 1997. For the four-firm concentration ratios of the 470 manufacturing industries in the *1997 Census of Manufactures*, the ratio is below 40 percent for more than half of the industries, between 41 and 70 percent in about a third of the industries, and over 70 percent in approximately 10 percent of the industries.[45]

Antitrust Issues

As we mentioned earlier, the U.S. government has developed **antitrust laws** to limit the market power of firms and to regulate how firms use market power to compete with each other. In this section, we present some of the basic issues of

Antitrust laws
Legislation, beginning with the Sherman Act of 1890, that attempts to limit the market power of firms and to regulate how firms use their market power to compete with each other.

TABLE 8.3 Measures of Market Power, Selected Manufacturing Industries (1997)

INDUSTRY	CR4	CR8	*HHI* (50 LARGEST COMPANIES)
Meat products	35	48	393
Breakfast cereal	83	94	2,446
Cigarettes	99	N/A	N/A
Sawmills	15	20	87
Book printing	32	45	364
Household refrigerators/freezers	82	97	2,025
Motor vehicles/car bodies	87	94	N/A
Computers	40	68	658

Source: U.S. Department of Commerce, *1997 Economic Census: Concentration Ratios in Manufacturing* (2001, Table 2), http://www.census.gov/prod/ec97/m31s-cr.pdf.

---

[44] Steven A. Morrison, "Airline Service: The Evaluation of Competition Since Deregulation," in *Industry Studies*, ed. Larry L. Duetsch, 2nd ed. (Armonk, N.Y.: Sharpe, 1998), 147–75.

[45] Dennis W. Carlton and Jeffrey M. Perloff, *Modern Industrial Organization*, 4th ed. (Boston: Pearson Addison Wesley, 2005).

antitrust legislation that managers should know, and we relate these issues to the previous discussion of market power.[46] We focus on mergers and market power here and discuss the legal aspects of oligopoly strategies in Chapter 9.

Three major pieces of legislation have shaped U.S. antitrust policy:

- The Sherman Act of 1890
- The Clayton Act of 1914
- The Federal Trade Commission Act of 1914

Section 1 of the Sherman Act prohibits contracts, combinations, and conspiracies in restraint of trade, while Section 2 prohibits monopolization, attempts to monopolize, and combinations or conspiracies to monopolize "any part of the trade or commerce among the several states, or with foreign nations." Section 1 targets price-fixing arrangements and prohibits explicit cartels. As interpreted, Section 2 does not prohibit monopoly, but focuses on the behavior of firms with market power.

The Sherman Act was amended in 1914 by the Clayton Act and the Federal Trade Commission Act. The Clayton Act focused on four specific practices:

1. Price discrimination that lessens competition (amended in 1936 by the Robinson-Patman Act)
2. The use of tie-in sales, in which a consumer can purchase one good only if he or she purchases another as well; and exclusive dealings, where a manufacturer prohibits its distributors from selling competing brands that lessen competition
3. Mergers between firms that reduce competition (as amended by the Celler-Kefauver Act of 1950)
4. The creation of interlocking directorates (interrelated boards of directors) among competing firms

The Federal Trade Commission Act created the Federal Trade Commission (FTC) to enforce antitrust laws and resolve disputes under the laws. Section 5 of the FTC Act prohibits "unfair" competition.

These antitrust laws were written in very general terms, so their intent has been interpreted through court cases and litigation over the years. Although some cases of monopolization have been attacked directly, greater attention has been paid to anticompetitive practices that facilitate coordination among sellers, vertical structures and arrangements that increase market power where a firm participates in more than one successive stage of production and distribution, and mergers that increase concentration and the likelihood of coordinated behavior among firms.

Regarding mergers, the Justice Department and the FTC currently operate under the Horizontal Merger Guidelines, which were established in 1982 and revised in 1992 and 1997. The goal of the guidelines is to prevent harm to consumers enabled by the use of increased market power that might result from a merger. To do so, the guidelines focus on six major issues:

1. The definition of the relevant market
2. The level of seller competition in that market
3. The possibility that a merging firm might be able to unilaterally affect price and output
4. The nature and extent of entry into the market
5. Other characteristics of the market structure that would influence coordination among sellers
6. The extent to which any cost savings and efficiencies could offset any increase in market power

---

[46] See the sources in footnote 40 for a more complete discussion of these issues.

Almost every merger case centers on the definition of the relevant market. Regarding the merger of Whirlpool and Maytag, the issue was whether front-loading washing machines were in the same market as top-loading machines. In the telecommunications industry, the question is whether cell phones are in the same market as landline phones. For movie theaters, the issue is how close together two movie theaters need to be in order to be considered in the same market.[47]

We illustrate these issues in the case of the proposed merger of Staples and Office Depot in 1997. This case shows the managerial strategies used to defend the firms' actions and how the litigation focused on the microeconomic issues developed in this text. We then briefly discuss the celebrated Microsoft antitrust case in both the United States and Europe to analyze the trade-offs between market power and the continued innovation and development of new products.

The Proposed Merger of Staples and Office Depot   In September 1996, Office Depot and Staples, the two largest office superstores in the United States, announced an agreement to merge.[48] Staples, which introduced the superstore concept in 1986, operated 550 stores in 1997, while Office Depot owned approximately 500 stores. Although there had been 23 office superstores competing earlier in the 1990s, by the time of the proposed merger, only Office Max was a close rival to Staples and Office Depot. Over this time period, the superstore chains had driven thousands of small, independent office supply companies out of business because these smaller companies could not compete with the economies of scale and the market power of the 23,000- to 30,000-square-foot superstores stocking 5,000 to 6,000 items. Consumers had benefited from the low prices and the one-stop shopping for office supplies.

Seven months after the merger was proposed, the FTC voted to oppose the merger on the grounds that it would harm competition and lead to higher prices in the office superstore market. The FTC argued that the relevant market was the "sale of consumable office supplies through office superstores," not the entire market for office supplies. The FTC made this distinction because the superstores carry a broad range of office supplies and maintain a huge inventory that lets consumers do one-stop shopping at these stores. Neither small retailers nor mail-order suppliers could provide this range of services and, thus, the FTC claimed that the superstores operate in a separate market. The FTC presented company documents that showed that the superstores considered only other superstores as their main competitors and that the presence of nonsuperstore competitors had little effect on the prices charged by the superstores. Staples' documents also showed that the company anticipated having to lower prices or raise quality if the merger did not take place and that its retail margins would decline by 1.5 percentage points by 2000 if the merger was not approved.

The FTC thus claimed that the superstores were their own effective competition and that a merger between Staples and Office Depot would allow the new store to raise prices until it was eventually constrained by the nonsuperstore competition. Both Staples and Office Depot had significantly lower prices when they competed with each other in local markets. When all three superstores (Staples, Office Depot, and Office Max) were located in the same geographic area, their prices were virtually the same, but they were lower than those of the nonsuperstores. The FTC developed

---

[47] Dennis W. Carlton, "Does Antitrust Need to Be Modernized?" *Journal of Economic Perspectives* 21 (Spring 2007): 155–76. A related issue is whether markets are contestable with ease of entry and exit. Industries with only a few firms can be competitive if there is the threat of entry by other firms and if firms can also exit readily. See Carlton and Perloff, *Modern Industrial Organization*, 4th ed.

[48] This discussion is based on Serdar Dalkir and Frederick R. Warren-Boulton, "Prices, Market Definition, and the Effects of Merger: Staples–Office Depot (1997)," in *The Antitrust Revolution: Economics, Competition, and Policy*, eds. John E. Kwoka, Jr., and Lawrence J. White, 3rd ed. (New York: Oxford University Press, 1999), 143–64.

a large-scale econometric analysis similar to those discussed in Chapter 4 that predicted that a merger between Staples and Office Depot would raise prices in markets where all three stores were present by 8.49 percent, exceeding the 5 percent rule in the guidelines.

The FTC also argued that the threat of entry by another superstore, such as Office Max, would not prevent the merged store from raising prices until the new entry actually occurred. The FTC claimed that economies of scale at both the store level and the chain level could act as a significant barrier to entry. Staples' strategy had already been to build a critical mass of stores in a given geographic region so that it would be cost-effective to advertise in the regional media.

Staples' and Office Depot's defense in this case was based on

1. A claim that the FTC's definition of the relevant product market was incorrect
2. An argument that efficiencies from the merger, combined with ease of entry into the market and a history of a low pricing policy, made it unlikely that the merger would raise prices

Staples and Office Depot claimed that they were in competition with all other office suppliers, not just the superstores, and that the FTC had taken statements from their documents out of context. This argument meant that the two stores were part of a larger market and had only small market shares. They also claimed that there would be substantial economies of scale from the merger in terms of production, administrative, marketing, advertising, and distribution costs and that the merged firm would pass two-thirds of these cost reductions on to consumers. Staples and Office Depot claimed that entry into the office supply business was relatively easy because stores could be constructed within several months. They cited data on planned store openings by Office Max to justify this contention.

The judge in this case accepted the arguments by the FTC and granted a preliminary injunction blocking the merger, which was then dropped by the companies. He accepted the FTC's definition of the relevant market and found that a merger would have had anticompetitive effects. The premerger *HHI* in the least concentrated market was 3,600, while it was approximately 7,000 in the most concentrated market. The judge accepted the pricing evidence that showed that an office superstore was likely to raise prices when it faced less competition from similar firms. He also found that economies of scale were a significant barrier to entry, particularly because many markets were already saturated by existing office supply superstores.

United States Versus Microsoft   In the widely publicized Microsoft antitrust case, the U.S. Department of Justice, 18 state attorneys general, and the attorney general of the District of Columbia brought suit in 1998 against Microsoft for engaging in anticompetitive practices designed to maintain its computer operating system monopoly.[49] Key issues in the suit were the origin and nature of Microsoft's market power, the effects of its strategy on market competition, and the degree to which consumers were harmed by this behavior. The government's case alleged that Microsoft forced computer manufacturers to license and install its own Internet Explorer browser, entered into contracts that excluded rivals, and engaged in other conduct that was damaging to competitors.

The dispute between the government and Microsoft focused on alternative Internet browsers, such as Netscape, and the Java programming language as vehicles for competition with Microsoft's Windows operating system. The Java language was a "middleware" software that occupied a position between applications packages and the underlying operating system, meaning that applications could be designed for Java independent of the Windows operating system. Netscape was a

---

[49] This discussion is based on Richard J. Gilbert and Michael L. Katz, "An Economist's Guide to U.S. vs. Microsoft," *Journal of Economic Perspectives* 15 (Spring 2001): 25–44.

threat to Microsoft because its Netscape browser was a distribution vehicle for Java. Netscape could also grow into a substitute for Windows or serve applications that made minimal use of Windows. The government asserted that Microsoft sought to eliminate Netscape as a viable competitor and to undermine the independence of the Java operating system by promoting a Windows-specific version of Java.

The government claimed that Microsoft was a monopolist in what it defined as the relevant market—Intel-compatible personal computer operating systems—because purchasers of these computers had no substitutes for the operating systems and any other operating system would have great difficulty competing with Windows due to network externalities. Microsoft officials contended that competition in the personal computer software market was among platforms, software interfaces to which programmers write applications, not operating systems, and that Microsoft faced significant competition in this arena. Debate also focused on whether Microsoft charged monopoly prices consistent with the theory developed in this chapter and the differences between the elasticity of demand for the market as a whole and that for a specific firm, as we discussed in Chapter 3. Other observers concluded that Microsoft did have significant market power, given the network effects and the applications barriers to entry, but the more important question for antitrust policy was the use of that market power.

The government charged that Microsoft used its market power to develop several strategies that harmed consumers. These strategies included contracts with Internet service providers, such as America Online and AT&T Worldnet, in which Microsoft made it easy for consumers to connect with these service providers in return for the providers' agreement to deny most or all of their subscribers a choice of Internet browser. Other contracts stipulated that computer manufacturers could not remove the Internet Explorer icon and that Internet content providers were given preferential, no-cost placement on the Internet Explorer's channel bar in return for promotion of the Internet Explorer browser. Microsoft contended that these were simply basic elements of its competitive strategy against Netscape.

In April 2000, Microsoft was found guilty of violating the Sherman Antitrust Act. The judge found that Microsoft's barriers to the entry of operating system competitors were illegal. Various remedies were proposed, including dividing the company into two parts. Litigation continued in this case.[50] In June 2001, the U.S. Court of Appeals for the District of Columbia reversed the decision to break up the company. The appeals court agreed that Microsoft's actions had been anticompetitive and that it had tried illegally to maintain its monopoly with the Windows operating system, but the court asked the lower court to revisit the issue of whether Microsoft had illegally bundled the Internet Explorer Web browser with Windows. In fall 2001, the Justice Department announced that it would drop the claim over the bundling of the Internet Explorer, but would ask the court to impose restrictions on the business practices that Microsoft could use in the future. These restrictions would include prohibiting the company from punishing computer makers that distributed rival software, requiring Microsoft to license Windows to all computer manufacturers at the same price, and giving manufacturers greater flexibility to change how Windows is installed.

Nine of the 18 states that were coplaintiffs with the federal government refused to join in the settlement, so litigation continued into 2002.[51] These states argued that the

[50] John R. Wilke and Ted Bridis, "Justice Department Says It Won't Seek Court-Ordered Breakup of Microsoft," *Wall Street Journal*, September 7, 2001; Kara Swisher, "Truth About Microsoft Deal Is in Facts Behind the Bluster," *Wall Street Journal*, December 3, 2001.

[51] John R. Wilke, Rebecca Buckman, and Don Clark, "Microsoft Antitrust Pact Draws Criticism from Competitors But Delights Investors," *Wall Street Journal*, November 2, 2001; Don Clark, Mark Wigfield, Nick Wingfield, and Rebecca Buckman, "Judge Approves Most of Pact, in Legal Victory for Microsoft," *Wall Street Journal*, November 1, 2002; Daniel L. Rubinfeld, "Case 19: Maintenance of Monopoly: U.S. v. Microsoft (2001)," in *The Antitrust Revolution: Economics, Competition, and Policy*, eds. John E. Kwoka, Jr., and Lawrence J. White, 4th ed. (New York: Oxford University Press, 2004), 476–501.

proposed remedies were likely to be ineffective in prohibiting retaliatory conduct and restrictive licensing practices and that the settlement would allow Microsoft to withhold vital technical information from developers of rival middleware. In November 2002, a federal judge approved nearly all the elements of the 2001 proposed settlement with the Justice Department and the nine consenting states. The judge also rejected the efforts by the nine other states to seek tougher remedies. Many observers considered the final outcome to be a victory for Microsoft.

Microsoft in Europe   Six years after the Microsoft case in the U.S. was settled, the company was still battling the European Union (EU) over similar issues.[52] Prompted by a complaint from Sun Microsystems Inc. that Microsoft was damaging its business by concealing technical information regarding the interface between its software and Microsoft Windows, the EU investigation began in December 1998. The EU started a separate investigation in 2001 on whether Microsoft was illegally injuring makers of music and video-playing software by embedding the company's own Windows Media Player software free of charge in its Windows programs. The EU issued its antitrust ruling in March 2004, which carried a $613 million fine and ordered Microsoft to stop building the free copy of its media player into Windows and to produce an instruction manual to help rivals write Windows-compatible software for connecting complex office computer networks. Microsoft paid more than $3 billion to Sun, Novell Inc., and RealNetworks to drop their related complaints in both the U.S. and Europe. From 2004 to 2007, there was a continuing battle between Microsoft and the EU as to whether Microsoft was complying in a timely manner with the EU ruling, particularly with regard to the development of the instruction manual. The EU charged that Microsoft was dragging its feet and producing unintelligible instructions. The company did eventually remove its Media Player from Windows in one version. However, this product did not sell well because it was priced the same as the version with the Media Player.

In September 2007, the Luxembourg-based Court of First Instance announced that the European Commission had acted properly in 2004 in finding that Microsoft had abused its market power. Microsoft's total fines and penalties could reach $2.77 billion. The company also announced that it would hand over the information to its rivals that the commission demanded. European regulators hailed the decision as a victory for consumers who are "suffering at the hands of Microsoft," while Microsoft argued that the ruling would stifle innovation by making it more difficult to design products with new features. In October 2007, the company decided not to appeal the ruling of the Luxembourg court, and it agreed to license information that its competitors needed to make their software work better with Windows. Competitors would pay a one-time fee of 10,000 Euros for the license rather than royalties. If competitors wanted to license patents from Microsoft, the latter was required to give a license at the rate of 0.4 percent of the competitors' revenue from the product rather than the 5.95 percent rate that Microsoft had once wanted.

In January 2008, the EU opened two new investigations of Microsoft. One questioned whether the company illegally bundled its Internet Explorer Web browser with Windows and the other investigated whether Microsoft's control of file formats and other technical specifications improperly harmed software vendors competing with Microsoft to write programs for Windows.[53]

---

[52] This discussion is based on Mary Jacoby, "Why Microsoft Battles Europe Years After Settling with U.S." *Wall Street Journal*, May 5, 2006; Charles Forelle, "Microsoft Loss in Europe Raises American Fears," *Wall Street Journal*, September 18, 2007; Charles Forelle, "Microsoft Yields to EU in Antitrust Battle," *Wall Street Journal*, October 23, 2007.

[53] Charles Forelle, "Europe's Antitrust Chief Defies Critics, and Microsoft," *Wall Street Journal*, February 25, 2008.

Managerial Rule of Thumb

Understanding Antitrust Laws

Managers of firms with market power are in a constant struggle to preserve and increase this power. Their ability to do so is constrained by antitrust legislation and other regulations. Many of these laws were written in terms of general principles, so managers may not know whether their actions are illegal unless the government initiates litigation. ■

Monopolistic Competition

We now turn to the model of **monopolistic competition**, a market structure characterized by a large number of small firms that have some market power from producing differentiated products. Because this model incorporates many of the concepts we developed in the first part of this chapter, this section presents only a brief discussion of monopolistic competition.

Characteristics of Monopolistic Competition

You may remember from Figure 1.1 in Chapter 1 and Table 7.1 in Chapter 7 that monopolistic competition lies on one end of the competitive spectrum, close to the model of perfect competition. However, as the name implies, the model incorporates elements of both the perfectly competitive and the monopoly models.

The following are the major characteristics of the model of monopolistic competition:

1. Product differentiation exists among firms
2. There are a large number of firms in the product group
3. No interdependence exists among firms
4. Entry and exit by new firms is relatively easy

Monopolistic competition describes the operation of the small retail stores, restaurants, barber shops, beauty salons, and repair shops that most people encounter in their daily lives. These establishments offer differentiated products, so they do not fit under the model of perfect competition. All Chinese restaurants serve Chinese food, but the range and types of offerings differ among establishments. The location of these businesses also serves as another aspect of product differentiation. Customers may choose a restaurant or repair shop with higher prices that is close to home, even if cheaper products and services are available elsewhere. In monopolistic competition, there are a large number of firms producing the same or similar products. The term *product group* is often used to characterize monopolistically competitive firms in contrast to the industry of perfect competition, which includes all firms producing the same homogeneous product. Given the large number of firms in a product group, there is no interdependence in their behavior. Finally, entry and exit are relatively easy in a product group. There are no substantial barriers to entry, such as economies of scale, which would make firms unlikely to enter the product group if positive economic profits were being earned.

Short-Run and Long-Run Models of Monopolistic Competition

The short-run and long-run models of monopolistic competition are presented in Figures 8.4a and 8.4b. The short-run model in Figure 8.4a is the same as the monopoly model in Figure 8.1. The monopolistically competitive firm faces a

Monopolistic competition
A market structure characterized by a large number of small firms that have some market power from producing differentiated products. This market power can be competed away over time.

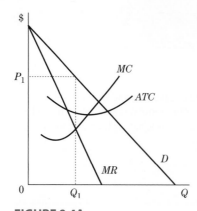

FIGURE 8.4A
Monopolistic Competition, Short Run
At Q$_1$:
MR = MC
  P > ATC
  P > MC
ATC *Not at Minimum Point*

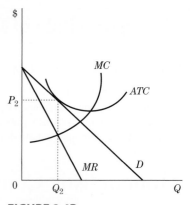

FIGURE 8.4B
Monopolistic Competition, Long Run
At Q$_2$:
MR = MC
  P = ATC
  P > MC
ATC *Not at Minimum Point*

downward sloping demand curve, as do all firms in imperfect competition. At any given price, the demand curve for the monopolistically competitive firm may be more elastic than that for the monopolist, given the larger number of substitutes. The monopolistically competitive firm produces the profit-maximizing level of output, where marginal revenue equals marginal cost, and charges the price read off the demand curve. The firm typically earns positive economic profits $(P > ATC)$ in the short run because factors such as product differentiation and geographic location give the firm market power. This is the monopolistic aspect of this model.

Given that entry is relatively easy in the long run, the short-run positive economic profits in Figure 8.4a cannot be sustained. Other firms will begin to produce the same or similar products. This will cause the demand curve in Figure 8.4a to shift back in toward the origin and become more elastic as other firms absorb some of the demand previously faced by this firm. The demand curve will shift back until it is tangent to the average total cost curve, resulting in zero economic profit. This position of long-run equilibrium is shown in Figure 8.4b. The firm earns zero economic profit $(P = ATC)$ at the profit-maximizing level of output $(MR = MC)$. Although this result is a "competitive" type of outcome due to entry into the product group, the equality of price and average total cost does not occur at the minimum point of the average total cost curve, as it does in the model of perfect competition. Monopolistically competitive firms do not have an incentive to produce at the lowest point of their average total cost curve. Because the monopolistically competitive firm has market power and faces a downward sloping demand curve, it also produces where price is greater than marginal cost. This result is different from the perfectly competitive outcome, where price equals marginal cost.

Any positive economic profits tend to disappear relatively quickly for a monopolistically competitive firm, given the lack of substantial barriers to entry. Managers in these firms must continually search for strategies, including product differentiation, market niches, geographic location, and advertising, that can give them at least temporary market power. The monopolistically competitive firm, unlike the perfectly competitive firm, does have an incentive to advertise.

Examples of Monopolistically Competitive Behavior

To illustrate how monopolistically competitive firms attempt to keep market power in the face of intense competition, we discuss the strategies that many of these firms have developed.

Drugstores   Small independent drugstores have been able to compete against the large chains by cutting prices down to cost on at least some of their drugs in order to match the lower prices chains have achieved through economies of scale. The independents have also developed innovative strategies such as providing more consultation time with the pharmacists, filling special orders on the same day, accepting IOUs from patients unable to pay, and finding products not carried by the chains, including homeopathic remedies. Even so, the number of independent drugstore outlets fell 24 percent to 20,641 between 1992 and 1998 as the number of chain sites increased 16 percent. The chains have responded to the strategies of these monopolistically competitive firms by offering a friendlier atmosphere and more individualized service in some of their outlets.[54]

These trends have continued in recent years.[55] The National Community Pharmacists Association reported that the number of community pharmacies dropped 5 percent in 2006 and net operating income fell by 30 percent. Independent pharmacies face increased pressure on their costs and prices from pharmacy benefit managers employed by the major private health insurance companies and from the Medicare and Medicaid programs. For customers with health insurance who may pay the same price for a prescription wherever they have it filled, customer service and convenience are critical to the success of individual pharmacies. Approximately half of the 23,000 independent pharmacies in the United States are in communities with fewer than 20,000 people, thus filling a niche that the large corporate chains may avoid. Independent pharmacies can also purchase services from other firms, such as Cardinal Health, that offers a claim management program, or PharmAccount that developed a set of calculators providing detailed reports on true dispensing costs, the costs of providing services such as medication therapy management, and a calculator focused on a pharmacy's financial data. Community pharmacies are also increasing their emphasis on specialty drugs—those that are high-cost, injectable, infused, oral, or inhaled, and that generally require close supervision and monitoring.

Hardware Stores   Small independent hardware stores have followed similar strategies to compete with chains such as Home Depot and Lowe's by offering personal service and convenience and by selling items that require instructions and advice from knowledgeable salespersons.[56] Small hardware stores are usually located in neighborhoods close to their customers, which

---

[54] Laura Johannes, "Feisty Mom-and-Pops of Gotham Take Aim at Drugstore Chains," *Wall Street Journal*, March 20, 2000.

[55] This discussion is based on Reid Paul, "Besieged? Here's a Helping Hand for Independents," *Drug Topics*, 151 (17), September 3, 2007, 14; Jack Minch, "Competing with the Giants Pepperell's Tracie Ezzio Bucks Industry Trend with Independent Pharmacy," *Knight Ridder Tribune Business News*, September 26, 2007; Brian C. Rittmeyer, "Independent Pharmacies Face More Competition from Chains," *McClatchy–Tribune Business News*, December 13, 2007; Leah Perry, "Specialty Pharmacy: Don't Miss the Boat," *Drug Topics*, 152 (1), January 14, 2008, 22.

[56] Barnaby J. Feder, "In Hardware War, Cooperation May Mean Survival," *New York Times*, June 11, 1997; James R. Hagerty, "Home Depot Raises the Ante, Targeting Mom-and-Pop Rivals," *Wall Street Journal*, January 25, 1998.

gives them geographic market power because the 112,000-square-foot chain warehouse stores are typically built in locations requiring customers to drive to the stores.

Many small hardware stores are also able to obtain some economies of scale because they are part of cooperatives such as Ace Hardware Corp. and TruServe Corp., which owns the True Value, ServiStar, and Coast to Coast trading names. The cooperatives buy goods in bulk on behalf of their members, who then can obtain merchandise 10 to 20 percent cheaper than if they purchased it on their own. The cooperatives also undertake research on store design and promotion, which the individual stores would not be able to afford, and they may manufacture exclusive lines of paint, tools, or other products.

In 2003 Ace Hardware began developing an increasing number of larger format stores with a wide selection of national brands while trying to maintain the personalized service of the small independent stores. In 2006 the cooperative had more than 4,600 members who earned an estimated $13 billion in retail sales in 2005. The cooperative has been experimenting with non-traditional marketing strategies as well as two national community outreach programs.[57]

Independent hardware stores have developed new operations such as full-service paint departments and formed small cooperatives to create their own brand of paint. They may also develop specialty services such as marine goods, or stock a much more extensive inventory of seasonal items than Home Depot. In many cases these independent hardware stores are family-owned businesses that are not burdened with rent or mortgage payments because the stores have been owned by the families for years.[58]

Bookstores   Small independent bookstores, such as Chapter 11 the Discount Bookstore in Atlanta, developed market power through steep discounts on books, aggressive marketing, and accessible locations in strip malls.[59] Although Chapter 11 could not match the amenities and selection of Barnes & Noble and Borders superstores, it could offer low prices because its stores were small (3,000 to 6,000 square feet compared with 20,000 for the chains). Chapter 11 stores had special events such as book signings, and each store was allowed to tailor its selections to the characteristics of its neighborhood. Overall selections were focused on mass-market titles as opposed to specialty markets.

Other independent booksellers have followed similar strategies. An owner in Peoria Heights, Illinois, learned each of her patrons' reading preferences to sell books one-on-one while encouraging the customers to post their favorite authors and books on a chalk board in the store. In Indiana, 97 of its 142 bookstores are independent and are located in rural communities outside the greater Indianapolis area, which are not served by the national chains. Alaska, with many towns too small to attract a chain store, has half the population but a third more independent bookstores than Hawaii, where Borders is the dominant bookseller. These independent stores innovate by hosting workshops, book clubs, and book signings and by specializing in areas such as pop culture titles or New Age topics.[60]

---

[57] Lisa Girard, "Ace Drafts Blueprint for Growth," *Home Channel News*, 32 (13), October 2, 2006, 13.

[58] Tom Meade, "Hardware Survivors," *Knight Ridder Tribune Business News*, February 27, 2007; Marc D. Allan, "Retailer Battles Big Boxes," *Indianapolis Business Journal*, 28 (25), August 27, 2007, A29.

[59] Jeffrey A. Tannenbaum, "Small Bookseller Beats the Giants at Their Own Game," *Wall Street Journal*, November 4, 1997.

[60] Claire Kirch, "Indies Find a Niche," *Publishers Weekly*, 254 (13), March 26, 2007, 28; Karen Holt, "All Bookselling Is Local," *Publishers Weekly*, 254 (52), December 31, 2007, 12.

However, as the model of monopolistic competition would suggest, not all of these stores survive. The independent stores' share of book sales dropped from about 30 percent to 10 percent between 1990 and 2002, while the roster of the American Booksellers Association, the trade association for independent stores, decreased from 4,000 members in the early 1990s to 1,800 in 2007. In some cases loyal customers have banded together to put up the financial backing to keep the stores open. However, even the Atlanta-based Chapter 11 bookstore filed for Chapter 11 bankruptcy protection in 2006.[61]

Managerial Rule of Thumb

Maintaining Market Power in Monopolistic Competition

Managers of monopolistically competitive firms must develop a variety of strategies to maintain their market power in the face of intense competition. These strategies include exploiting geographic advantages, offering improved customer service, becoming part of larger cooperatives to lower costs, and developing specialized niches in the market. ■

Summary

In this chapter, we discussed the strategies of firms with market power using the models of monopoly and monopolistic competition. We first showed how the outcomes of the models differed from those of perfect competition. We then discussed the sources and measurement of market power, how market power is used by firms, and why market power can change over time. We also discussed how firms' strategies are constrained by government antitrust legislation and other regulations as well as market demand.

In Chapter 9, we will examine the final model of imperfect competition—oligopoly. This model incorporates the concepts of market power discussed in this chapter, but adds the issue of interdependent behavior among rival firms.

Key Terms

antitrust laws, p. 209

barriers to entry, p. 196

concentration ratios, p. 207

Herfindahl-Hirschman
  Index (*HHI*), p. 208

Lerner Index, p. 206

lock-in and switching
  costs, p. 201

market power, p. 192

monopolistic competition, p. 215

monopoly, p. 192

network externalities,
  p. 204

price-setter, p. 192

---

[61] Carolyn Shapiro, "Small Local Stores Bank on Personal Service and Unique Offerings," *McClatchy–Tribune Business News*, December 6, 2007; Nathaniel Popper, "Weekend Journal; Taste: Who's Buying the Bookstore?" *Wall Street Journal*, January 18, 2008; Judith Rosen, "Next Chapter for Chapter 11," *Publishers Weekly*, 253 (18), March 1, 2006, 12.

Exercises

Technical Questions

1. Given the demand curve in the following graph, find (and label) the monopolist's profit-maximizing output and price.

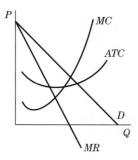

2. Show graphically an example of a monopolist that is producing the profit-maximizing output, but is *not* making a profit.

3. Suppose the demand curve for a monopolist is $Q_D = 500 - P$, and the marginal revenue function is $MR = 500 - 2Q$. The monopolist has a constant marginal and average total cost of $50 per unit.

   a. Find the monopolist's profit-maximizing output and price.
   b. Calculate the monopolist's profit.
   c. What is the Lerner Index for this industry?

4. Demonstrate graphically why persuasive advertising, which makes consumers more loyal to the advertised brand, is likely to increase a firm's market power (its ability to raise price above marginal cost). Will it necessarily increase profit as well?

5. The top four firms in Industry A have market shares of 30, 25, 10, and 5 percent, respectively. The top four firms in Industry B have market shares of 15, 12, 8, and 4 percent, respectively. Calculate the four-firm concentration ratios for the two industries. Which industry is more concentrated?

6. In both Industry C and Industry D, there are only four firms. Each of the four firms in Industry C has a 25 percent market share. The four firms in Industry B have market shares of 80, 10, 5, and 5 percent, respectively.

   a. Calculate the three- and four-firm concentration ratios for each industry.
   b. Calculate the Herfindahl-Hirschman Index for each industry.
   c. Are these industries equally concentrated? Explain your answer.

7. The following graph shows a firm in a monopolistically competitive industry.

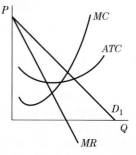

   a. Show the firm's short-run profit-maximizing quantity and price. Is the firm making a profit?
   b. Carefully explain what will happen in the industry over time, and draw a graph of a monopolistically competitive firm in long-run equilibrium.

8. Because products are typically differentiated in some way, there tends to be significant advertising in monopolistically competitive industries. How will advertising affect a typical firm in a monopolistically competitive industry? Explain, using a graph to support your answer.

Application Questions

1. Drawing on current business publications, discuss ongoing changes in market power among the firms in the personal computer industry. What new strategies have Dell and its competitors developed to protect, maintain, or increase market power?

2. The following discussion describes a takeover attempt in the beer industry in 2008:[62]

In June 2008, InBev NV, a Belgian-Brazilian giant, launched an unsolicited bid to acquire Anheuser-Busch Cos. for $46.4 billion, a move that would create the world's largest brewer with annual sales of approximately $36 billion. InBev, the maker of Stella Artois and Labatt Blue, has long considered acquiring Anheuser-Busch, which controls nearly half the U.S. beer market. The two companies market about 300 brands on six continents and are the second- and third-largest brewers in the world in terms of volume.

---

[62] David Kesmodel and Matthew Karnitschnig, "InBev Uncorks Anheuser Takeover Bid," *Wall Street Journal*, June 12, 2008.

Anheuser has struggled with slow growth of its mass-market beers in recent years. U.S. sales have suffered from greater competition from a wide range of beers, including small-batch "craft" beers and imports, as well as from wine and spirits. There is increasing consolidation in the global beer industry as brewers try to balance slow growth in mature markets, such as the United States and Western Europe, with rapid growth in emerging markets such as China and Eastern Europe. There are also increasing expenses for commodities, such as barley, aluminum, and glass, making it important to gain economies of scale.

InBev has only a tiny presence in the United States and would like to acquire Anheuser, which has led the U.S. industry since 1957. InBev, which is intensely budget-conscious, sees an opportunity to wring significant cost-savings out of Anheuser. The two companies have relatively little geographic overlap. By merging, they could gain a stronger position in China, where they both have been expanding recently. China is the world's largest beer market by volume.

InBev has secured commitments from banks to provide at least $40 billion in debt financing for the merger. Its success in raising the financial capital is an indication that banks are willing to lend substantial sums to companies with investment-grade credit ratings despite the continued turmoil in the financial markets and the efforts of a number of institutions to raise capital.

InBev also has the U.S. public to consider because many U.S. citizens believe that Budweiser remains a powerful symbol of Americana. A Florida couple recently started a Web site called SaveBudweiser.com to rally support against a sale to InBev.

a. Based on the concepts in this chapter, discuss the factors leading to this proposed takeover merger in the beer industry.

b. What factors might create problems for the merger?

3. The following discussion describes a patent dispute in the pharmaceutical industry:[63]

State and federal authorities are examining whether Abbott Laboratories violated antitrust laws in its efforts to prevent an Israeli company from successfully selling a generic version of its cholesterol medicine, TriCor. Drug companies usually have three to 10 years of exclusive patent rights remaining when their products hit the market. However, they can often find ways to extend their monopolies by patenting slight improvements to those drugs. Twenty-five states and the District of Columbia filed suit in federal court alleging that in addition to filing new patents on questionable improvements to TriCor, Abbott engaged in a practice known as "product switching." This involves retiring an existing drug and replacing it with a modified version that is marketed as "new and improved," preventing pharmacists from substituting a generic for the branded drug when they fill prescriptions for it. Although this strategy is not illegal, the plaintiffs argue that Abbott employed it and other strategies solely to preserve its monopoly on TriCor.

One year after TriCor hit the market in 1999, Israeli Teva Pharmaceuticals Industries applied to the Food and Drug Administration (FDA) to market a similar version of the drug. Abbott sued Teva for patent infringement, which triggered a 30-month waiting period during which the generic drug could not be launched while patent challenges were being debated. During the waiting period, Abbott altered its product, lowering the dosage and changing it to a tablet from a capsule. It filed for a patent on this modified form of TriCor, bought back the remaining supplies of the capsules and replaced them with the lower-dose tablet. When the 30 months had elapsed, Teva could no longer launch its generic drug because it was no longer strictly bioequivalent to the modified TriCor.

This process was repeated again from 2002 to 2005. Teva filed a counter-suit alleging anti-trust law violation. The company argued that Abbott's strategy would allow pharmaceutical companies to protect their monopolies indefinitely. Abbott said it has the right to protect its innovations and denies switching formulations for the sole purpose of warding off generic competition. It said the two switches brought improvements for patients. Teva argued that the drug's active ingredient stayed the same and that the supposed improvements were smoke screens.

Describe the role of patents as barriers to entry in the pharmaceutical industry. In the current business media, follow up on this and other similar cases involving drug patents to determine the strategies that

---

[63] Shirley S. Wang, "TriCor Case May Illuminate Patent Limits," *Wall Street Journal*, June 2, 2008.

drug firms are currently employing to maintain their market power.

4. The following discussion describes Walgreen Co.'s new strategies in early 2008:[64]

> Walgreen Co. thrived for decades by opening stores faster than its competitors and by filling more prescriptions per year than any other chain. But facing pressure from rivals, a weak economy and changes in the healthcare system, the company is refashioning itself into a broad healthcare provider. In March 2008, Walgreen announced its plans to buy I-trax Inc. and Whole Health Management, two companies that run a total of 350 health centers at corporate offices and that offer services from treating simple illnesses to counseling patients on managing diabetes. Walgreen expects to open more pharmacies at worksites and to attract employees, their family members, and retirees to its stores. The acquired companies will form part of Walgreen's new health and wellness division and will include Take Care Clinics, which operate 136 clinics inside Walgreens stores.

> Walgreen has dropped its longtime aversion to acquisitions by purchasing specialty pharmacies that are experts in infertility, cancer, AIDS, and other conditions that are expensive to treat, and by opening pharmacies in hospitals and assisted-living facilities.

> Investors are uncertain about this new approach. In October 2007, Walgreen reported its first quarterly earnings decline in nearly a decade, hurt by lower generic-drug reimbursements and higher store and advertising expenses. Meanwhile, two of Walgreen's big rivals, Wal-Mart Stores Inc. and CVS Caremark Corp., are expanding in what they consider a big growth area: the business of managing employer drug-benefit programs. CVS has staked its business on the future success of pharmacy-benefit managers (PBMs) by purchasing Caremark in 2007. PBMs provide prescription-drug coverage to workers at most

> U.S. companies, negotiate lower prices at retail pharmacies, and collect rebates from drug manufacturers. Walgreen executives say their chain does not plan to purchase a major PBM.

> Pharmacy profits are under pressure because fewer generic-drug launches are planned for the first half of 2008 compared with the same period in 2007. U.S. prescription sales grew only 3.8% in 2007, the slowest growth rate since 1961. Walgreen has responded to this changing environment in part by expanding into the specialty pharmacy sector where drug sales are growing much faster than the overall prescription market.

> Walgreen executives plan to bring together its Take Care Clinics, specialty operations, and workplace centers using electronic prescriptions and medical records to cover a range of needs.

Describe how this case study illustrates the concepts of shifting market power described in the chapter.

5. Indicate whether each of the following statements is true or false, and explain your answer.

   a. If a monopolist is producing a level of output at which demand is inelastic, the firm is not maximizing profits, and increasing output will decrease total revenue.

   b. When a monopolist maximizes profits, the price is greater than the marginal cost of producing the output. This means that consumers are willing to pay more for additional units of the product than these additional units cost to produce. Thus, the monopolist should produce and sell additional units of output.

   c. A monopolistically competitive firm produces a level of output at which price equals $80, marginal revenue equals $40, average total cost equals $100, marginal cost equals $40, and average fixed cost equals $10. To maximize profit, the firm should produce a smaller output and sell it at a higher price.

   d. In a monopolistically competitive market, a firm has market power because it produces a differentiated product. This means that the firm earns positive economic profit in the long run.

---

[64] Amy Merrick, "How Walgreen Changed Its Prescription for Growth," *Wall Street Journal*, March 19, 2008.

On the Web

For updated information on the *Wall Street Journal* article at the beginning of the chapter, as well as other relevant links and information, visit the book's Web site at **www.pearsonhighered.com/farnham**

Market Structure: Oligopoly

I n this chapter, we examine the fourth market model, *oligopoly*. This model is close to the monopoly model in Figure 1.1 of Chapter 1 and at the other end of the market structure spectrum from the model of perfect competition.

Oligopoly firms typically have market power derived from barriers to entry. Thus, all the barriers to entry we discussed in Chapter 8 are relevant for oligopoly firms. However, the key characteristic of oligopoly is that there are a small number of firms competing with each other, so their behavior is mutually interdependent. This interdependence distinguishes oligopoly from all other market structures. In perfect competition and monopolistic competition, there are so many firms that each firm doesn't have to consider the actions of other firms. If a monopolist truly is a single firm producing a product with no close substitutes, it can also form its own independent strategies. However, when 4, 6, or 10 major firms compete with each other, behavior is interdependent. The strategies and decisions by managers of one firm affect managers of other firms, whose subsequent decisions then affect the first firm.

This chapter begins with the article "The Anatomy of an Airline Fare Increase," which describes the interdependent behavior in airline pricing. We'll then examine additional cases of oligopoly behavior drawn from the news media. Next we'll look at several models of oligopoly to see how economists have modeled both noncooperative and cooperative interdependent behavior. The goal is not to cover the huge number of oligopoly models that have been developed over the years, all of which attempt to illustrate different aspects of interdependent behavior. Instead, we'll present the insights of a few models and then illustrate these principles with descriptions of real-world oligopolistic behavior. We'll conclude by describing how government antitrust legislation and enforcement influence oligopoly behavior.

The Anatomy of an Airline Fare Increase

by Trebor Banstetter

Knight Ridder Tribune Business News, *September 11, 2007*
Reprinted by permission of TMS Reprints.

The major airlines played an intricate chess game with airfares over the weekend, raising and lowering prices on routes nationwide as they responded to Friday's price increase by Delta Air Lines.

Rick Seaney, chief executive of FareCompare.com, an Internet travel site based near Plano [Texas] that monitors ticket prices, said the maneuvering typifies how airlines react to competitors' price changes.

"There's almost never a case where it's clear cut," he said. "Has a fare increase stuck? It depends on how you look at it."

Seaney said a clear picture won't emerge until today. But "it is safe to say right now that a significant number of passengers are paying $10 round trip more than they did on Thursday last week.

He broke down several days' worth of price tactics:

Thursday, 9 p.m.
Delta raises fares $5 each way nationwide.
Friday, 12:30 p.m.
No other airlines have matched.
Friday, 8 p.m.
American and US Airways match 50 percent of the increases, while United matches all of it. Northwest and Continental are still up in the air.

Saturday, 11:20 a.m.
Northwest fully matches the increase. Continental raises fares on 33 percent of flights. United rolls back its increase on 20 percent of flights.
Sunday, 5 p.m.
American has rolled back the increase on 8 percent of flights, Continental and Delta on 10 percent, Northwest on 12 percent, US Airways on 15 percent.
Monday, 1:21 p.m.
Delta restores all of its increases. Northwest terminates the increase on 20 percent of flights, United on 6 percent.

Here are the percentages of flights that, as of late Monday, had experienced a fare increase:

45% American
23% Continental
75% Delta
68% Northwest
74% United
 5% US Airways

Case for Analysis

Oligopoly Behavior in the Airline Industry

This article describes airline pricing behavior that has taken place for many years. There are a small number of players in the airline industry, so that price changes by one airline affect the demand for flights of its competitors. As discussed later in this chapter, overt price fixing is illegal in this country and even tacit collusion can be dangerous for firms in terms of antitrust enforcement. Thus, the airlines often try to coordinate their strategies with one company taking a leadership role and then watching for the reactions of its competitors. Price changes are usually implemented on Thursdays or Fridays, so that the lead airline can watch the reaction over the weekend and then make adjustments by Monday. These reactions typically vary by the size and market power of the airline and may differ by the route flown. Referring to these strategies as an "intricate chess game" is an extremely appropriate way to characterize this behavior.

In March 2002, American Airlines increased its three-day advanced purchase requirement on low-priced business tickets to seven days with the hope that competitors would follow this implicit price increase.[1] When the competitors refused to do so, American retaliated by offering deep discounts on business fares in several of the competitors' markets. In response, Northwest Airlines began offering $198 round-trip fares with connections on three-day advanced purchase tickets in 160 of American's nonstop markets, where the average unrestricted business fare was $1,600. American then offered $99 one-way fares in 10 markets each flown by Northwest, United, Delta, and US Airways. Only Continental Airlines' markets were excluded from these low fares, an outcome that probably resulted because Continental had matched American's original change in all markets.

In March 2004, Continental Airlines tried to raise its fares across the board to cover the rising cost of fuel. Low-cost rivals Southwest and JetBlue refused to follow because they had protected themselves against rising fuel costs with hedging agreements. Continental had hedged fuel for 2003 but stopped buying the contracts when they became more expensive due to the rising oil prices. For an entire month, one airline or another had tried to impose network-wide fare increases but had to back off because all of their rivals would not follow the increases except on certain routes.[2]

By spring 2005, the airlines had some greater pricing power, having achieved seven fare increases in the first five months of the year. Demand for airline seats had been increasing, particularly with the approach of summer. In May 2005, the price increase was led by American Airlines and was imposed even in markets where it competed with Southwest. As of the Friday afternoon when it was announced, Delta, Continental, Northwest, United, and US Airways had all matched the increase in varying combinations.[3] ■

Case Studies of Oligopoly Behavior

Oligopoly
A market structure characterized by competition among a small number of large firms that have market power, but that must take their rivals' actions into account when developing their own competitive strategies.

The behavior just described represents the interdependence of firms operating in an **oligopoly** market. This behavior has become more pervasive as oligopolies have come to dominate many industries in the United States, as shown in Table 9.1. We next discuss oligopoly behavior in several key industries.

The Airline Industry

In addition to the pricing strategies discussed in the opening article, there are numerous other examples of oligopoly behavior in the airline industry. In the late 1990s, Frontier Airlines was the small upstart carrier trying to compete with United Airlines, particularly at the Denver airport. Frontier developed strategies to compete

---

[1] Scott McCartney, "Airfare Wars Show Why Deals Arrive and Depart," *Wall Street Journal*, March 19, 2002.
[2] Elizabeth Souder, "Continental Attempts Fare Hike, But Rivals Won't Budge," *Wall Street Journal*, March 26, 2004.
[3] Melanie Trottman, "U.S. Airlines Attempt New Round of Fare Increases," *Wall Street Journal*, May 16, 2005.

TABLE 9.1 Oligopolistic Industries in the United States

INDUSTRY	NUMBER OF FIRMS	MARKET SHARE (%)
Carbonated soft drinks	3	80
Beer	3	80
Cigarettes	3	80
Recorded music	4	80
Railroad operations	4	100
Movies	6	85
Razors and razor blades	3	95
Cookies and crackers	2	80
Carpets	2	75
Breakfast cereals	4	80
Light bulbs	2	85
Consumer batteries	3	90

Source: Stephen G. Hannaford, *Market Domination! The Impact of Industry Consolidation on Competition, Innovation, and Consumer Choice* (Westport, CT: Praeger, 2007), 5. Reprinted by permission.

with its rival by "getting inside United's corporate head, anticipating its moves and countermoves, and chipping away as much business as it can get away with."[4] Frontier officials developed aggressive strategies on pricing and flight scheduling, but restrained these strategies enough to avoid provoking a substantial competitive response from United, which would have had a detrimental impact on Frontier.

Frontier learned from experience that United was likely to tolerate not more than two flights a day to one of its competitive cities and that timing Frontier's flights outside United's windows of connecting flights would make United unlikely to establish a new head-to-head competing flight. Frontier's managers also waited to announce the company's new flights from United's hub at Denver International Airport to Portland, Oregon, until United had loaded its summer schedule into the computer system. This tactic made it difficult for United to rearrange its published schedule of flights to compete against Frontier. Frontier's pricing strategy was to raise ticket prices enough to avoid a price-cutting response from United, but to keep prices low enough to appeal to customers and attract new business. Setting prices far below those of United would have resulted in United not only lowering prices, but also scheduling many more flights to compete with Frontier. However, United's managers needed to make certain that their competitive strategies did not violate U.S. antitrust laws. The U.S. Justice Department had previously accused American Airlines of cutting prices and increasing capacity to stifle new competition in its Dallas–Fort Worth hub airport.

By summer 2003, there was a three-way struggle among United, which was now reorganizing its business in bankruptcy court; Frontier, the growing low-cost airline; and the city of Denver, which operated the city's airport, the hub for this competition.[5] Frontier claimed that while United's market share at the Denver airport had declined from 74 percent to 64 percent, the airport had increased the number of United's gates from 43 to 51. Frontier's market share had more than doubled, increasing from 5.6 to 13.3 percent, while the number of its gates increased

---

[4] Scott McCartney, "Upstart's Tactics Allow It to Fly in Friendly Skies of a Big Rival," *Wall Street Journal*, June 23, 1999.

[5] Edward Wong, "Denver's Idle Gates Draw Covetous Eyes," *New York Times*, August 5, 2003.

from only 6 to 10. United also demanded that the city build a new $65 million regional jet terminal with an additional 38 gates. United wanted to hold its existing gates for future expansion, while Frontier argued that it could put many of those gates to more productive use. The city was caught between the demands of its dominant airline, which had less market power than before 1999, and those of the aggressive low-cost competitor.

Competition for amenities has been another aspect of oligopolistic strategies, particularly among international airlines. Lufthansa Airlines opened a first-class terminal in Frankfurt in 2005 where passengers could have a bubble bath, rest in a cigar room, and be driven to the plane in a Mercedes or Porsche. Middle Eastern carriers have installed lavish closed-door suites in the front of planes, while Virgin Atlantic opened a Clubhouse at London's Heathrow Airport with a beauty salon, cinema, and Jacuzzi.[6] In fall 2007, Singapore Airlines began the first commercial flight of the Airbus A380, the biggest passenger jet ever built, with twelve first-class passengers housed in fully enclosed cabins with expandable beds, while 60 seats in business class were 34 inches wide—twice the width of a typical economy seat.[7]

By spring 2008, with the slow economy and oil prices exceeding $130 per barrel, all of the major U.S. airlines were adopting similar strategies to cut costs and raise prices. In June 2008, United Airlines followed the lead of American Airlines in charging passengers for the first checked bag. United had been the first airline to charge for the second checked bag in February 2008, and rivals soon followed. The airlines grounded planes and removed flights from schedules to limit the supply of seats and raise prices. They also searched for new ways to reduce costs, including installing winglets on jets to improve performance, eliminating magazines in cabins to reduce weight, carrying less fuel above required reserve levels, and washing jet engines with new machines that could deep clean while collecting and purifying the runoff.[8]

The Soft Drink Industry

Although Coca-Cola Company and PepsiCo Inc. have long battled each other in the cola wars, their interdependent behavior has moved into the bottled water market with Coke's Dasani and Pepsi's Aquafina brands.[9] Although bottled water comprised less than 10 percent of each company's beverage sales in 2002, bottled water sales in the United States grew 30 percent in 2001 compared with 0.6 percent growth for soft drinks. The bottled water market in 2001 was dominated by a few large firms: Nestle's Perrier Group (37.4 percent market share), Pepsi (13.8 percent), Coca-Cola (12.0 percent), and Danone (11.8 percent). Coke and Pepsi tried to avoid the pricing wars in grocery stores that occurred with the colas, so they concentrated on selling single, cold bottles in convenience stores or vending machines. However, price discounting was already occurring in some grocery stores as more consumers bought water to take home. The rivals also focused on making the product readily available and packaging the water in convenient and attractive bottles. Pepsi launched its Aquafina in a new bottle with a transparent label, while Coke developed a Dasani bottle with a thin, easy-to-grip cap for sports enthusiasts.

---

[6] Scott McCartney, "A Bubble Bath and a Glass of Bubbly—at the Airport," *Wall Street Journal*, July 10, 2007.

[7] Bruce Stanley and Daniel Michaels, "Taking a Flier on Bedroom Suites," *Wall Street Journal*, October 24, 2007.

[8] Scott McCartney, "As Airlines Cut Back, Who Gets Grounded?" *Wall Street Journal*, June 6, 2008; Scott McCartney, "Flying Stinks—Especially for the Airlines," *Wall Street Journal*, June 10, 2008; J. Lynn Lunsford, "Airlines Dip into Hot Water to Save Fuel," *Wall Street Journal*, June 11, 2008; Mike Barris, "United Matches American Airlines in Charging for First Checked Bag," *Wall Street Journal*, June 13, 2008.

[9] Betsy McKay, "Pepsi, Coke Take Opposite Tacks in Bottled Water Marketing Battle," *Wall Street Journal*, April 18, 2002; Scott Leith, "Beverage Titans Battle to Grow Water Business," *Atlanta Journal-Constitution*, October 31, 2002.

The rivals have used different strategies to market goods that are virtually identical. Coke developed a combination of minerals to give Dasani a clean, fresh taste. The formula for this mix is kept as secret as the original Coke formula. Managers also paid much attention to developing the Dasani name, which was intended to convey crispness and freshness with a foreign ring. Pepsi claimed that Aquafina was purer because nothing was added to its exhaustively filtered water and focused its marketing activities around customers "wanting nothing." Both companies developed enhanced versions of their waters. Coke launched Dasani Nutriwater, with added nutrients and essences of pear and cucumber, in late 2002, while Pepsi introduced Aquafina Essentials, with vitamins, minerals, and fruit flavors, in summer 2002. In a joint venture with Group Danone, Coke also took over distribution of Dannon bottled water, which gave the company a low-priced brand that would complement the mid-priced Dasani.

By 2008 the two rivals were both managing a complex portfolio of drinks, given that U.S. consumers were buying fewer soft drinks and more beverages such as teas, waters, and energy drinks. From 2003 to 2008 noncarbonated beverages grew from one-quarter to one-third of the nonalcoholic beverage market. Pepsi diversified first by signing joint ventures with Lipton in 1991 and Starbucks in 1994 and acquiring SoBe in 2000 and Gatorade in 2001. These moves gave it the lead in teas, ready-to-drink coffees, and sports drinks. Coca-Cola countered by buying Glaceau enhanced waters and Fuze juice drinks and reaching agreements for Campbell's juice drinks and Caribou and Godiva bottled coffees. Coke and Pepsi continue to try to gain an advantage even in small markets by searching for nuances or trends to determine the best product mix.[10]

The Doughnut Industry

In the summer of 2001, Krispy Kreme Doughnuts of Winston-Salem, North Carolina, announced its plans to open 39 outlets in Canada over the following six years to compete directly with Tim Hortons—an American-owned, but Canadian-operated chain that is considered to be somewhat of a national institution in Canada.[11] Canada is a profitable market because the country has more doughnut shops per capita than any other country. Tim Hortons was already the second-largest food service company in Canada, with 17 percent of quick-service restaurant sales. It had driven out much of the competition through efficient service and aggressive tactics, such as opening identical drive-through outlets on opposite sides of the same street to attract customers traveling in either direction. Krispy Kreme is another large company, with $448.1 million in sales in 2001 and 192 stores across 32 states.

As Krispy Kreme managers made the decision to move north to Canada, Tim Hortons' managers were expanding south, focusing on U.S. border cities such as Detroit and Buffalo. The company had also invaded Krispy Kreme's territory by opening two stores in West Virginia and one in Kentucky. Both companies engaged in product differentiation, with Tim Hortons emphasizing its product diversity—soups and sandwiches as well as doughnuts—while Krispy Kreme focused on its signature product—hot doughnuts. Tim Hortons also relied on its Canadian roots to ward off the competition from its U.S. competitor by using "We never forget where we came from" as its advertising theme in Canada. The doughnut battle in Canada appears to be between these two oligopolistic competitors, who are directly countering each other's strategies. Dunkin' Donuts Inc., the world's largest

---

[10] Joe Guy Collier, "Cola Wars Aren't Just About Cola Any More," *Atlanta Journal-Constitution*, March 28, 2008.

[11] Joel Baglole, "Krispy Kreme, Tim Hortons of Canada Square Off in Each Other's Territory," *Wall Street Journal*, August 23, 2001.

doughnut chain, with 5,146 stores in 39 countries, has been in Canada since 1961, but owns only 6 percent of the Canadian doughnut/coffee shops.

Tim Hortons has continued its expansion in the United States, confronting both Krispy Kreme and Dunkin' Donuts. In 2007 most of its 340 stores in the United States were near the Canadian border in Michigan, Ohio, and upstate New York. By the end of 2008, the company had a goal of 500 U.S. stores, assuming it could establish a presence in New England, the home of Dunkin' Donuts. Although Hortons' style was more similar to Dunkin' than Starbucks, the company has tried to differentiate itself from Dunkin' by offering more comfortable seats, china mugs, and cheaper coffee. Hortons has a strong association with coffee, although little name recognition in the United States. The company has been encouraging its franchisees to get involved with local communities by sponsoring sports teams and summer camps.[12]

Dunkin' Donuts had also been trying to expand in the South, the West, and overseas by designing stores similar to coffeehouses and adding more sandwiches. This change in strategy came at a time when McDonald's had moved toward selling lattes and cappuccinos to the same type of customer. The challenge for Dunkin' was to decide how much style to add to its brand. Some of the new stores were painted in coffee-colored hues until long-time customers indicated they wanted more of the old bright pink and orange. A new hot sandwich was renamed a "stuffed melt" after customers complained that calling it a "panini" was too fancy. Research showed that Dunkin's customers were unpretentious and disliked the more stylized chains such as Starbucks. This research concluded that the Dunkin "tribe" members wanted to be part of the crowd, while members of the Starbucks tribe had a desire to stand out as individuals. Dunkin managers also decided to keep the goal of moving its customers through the cash register line in two minutes compared with Starbuck's goal of three minutes.[13]

The Parcel and Express Delivery Industry

United Parcel Service (UPS) and Federal Express (FedEx) control approximately 80 percent of the U.S. parcel and express delivery services, with UPS having a 53 percent market share and FedEx a 27 percent share. Although these two firms are normally intense rivals, in early 2001 they formed an alliance to keep a third competitor, the German firm Deutsche Post AG, out of the U.S. market.[14] Both companies filed protests with the U.S. Department of Transportation, alleging that the German company was trying to get around U.S. laws to subsidize an expansion in the United States with profits from its mail monopoly in Germany. The U.S. companies contended that it was unfair for the German firm, which is partially owned by the German government, to compete in the United States because the U.S. Postal Service is not allowed to deliver packages in other countries. Deutsche Post AG owns a majority stake in Brussels-based DHL International Ltd., which has a stake in its U.S. affiliate, DHL Airways of Redwood City, California. UPS and FedEx contended that DHL International and Deutsche Post AG had essentially taken control of DHL Airways, placing that company in violation of federal laws prohibiting foreign ownership of more than 25 percent of a U.S. air carrier.

UPS and FedEx were trying to block expansion of the German firm in the United States at the same time the U.S. companies were trying to expand in Europe. That

---

[12] Douglas Belkin, "A Canadian Icon Turns Its Glaze Southward," *Wall Street Journal*, May 15, 2007.

[13] Janet Adamy, "Dunkin' Donuts Tries to Go Upscale, But Not Too Far," *Wall Street Journal*, April 8, 2006; Janet Adamy, "Dunkin Donuts Whips Up a Recipe for Expansion," *Wall Street Journal*, May 3, 2007.

[14] Rick Brooks, "FedEx, UPS Ask U.S. to Suspend DHL Flights, Freight Forwarding," *Wall Street Journal*, January 24, 2001; Rick Brooks, "FedEx, UPS Join Forces to Stave Off Foreign Push into U.S. Delivery Market," *Wall Street Journal*, February 1, 2001.

expansion had been countered by Deutsche Post AG, as the German firm lowered its parcel-delivery prices in light of increased U.S. competition. UPS and FedEx faced relatively weak competition in the U.S. delivery market and were attempting through coordinated behavior to block entry by the German competitor.

DHL did enter the U.S. package delivery industry in 2003, although the company was still unprofitable in 2007. DHL captured 7 percent of the U.S. market by 2005 when it announced that it was "not setting out to create another UPS or FedEx." The company's reputation suffered from a difficult hub consolidation in 2005 that cost it customers and revenue. In spring 2008, DHL announced that it was planning to transfer its North American air-parcel deliveries to UPS and cut its U.S. network capacity on the ground by one-third. In November 2008, the company announced that it was ending its domestic U.S. deliveries by January 2009, while continuing delivery and pickup of international shipments. Blaming its cutbacks on both competition from UPS and FedEx and the declining economy, DHL planned to shut its 18 U.S. ground hubs, reduce the number of delivery stations from 412 to 103, and eliminate 9,500 jobs.[15]

Oligopoly Models

Economists have developed a variety of models to capture different aspects of the interdependent behavior inherent in oligopoly, although none of the models incorporates all elements of oligopolistic behavior. The many models can be divided into two basic groups: noncooperative and cooperative models. In **noncooperative oligopoly models**, managers make business decisions based on the strategy they think their rivals will pursue. In many cases, managers assume that their rivals will pursue strategies that inflict maximum damage on competing firms. Managers must then develop strategies of their own that best respond to their competitors' strategies. The implication of many noncooperative models is that firms would be better off if they could cooperate or coordinate their actions with other firms.

This outcome leads to **cooperative oligopoly models**—models of interdependent oligopoly behavior that assume that firms explicitly or implicitly cooperate with each other to achieve outcomes that benefit all the firms. Although cooperation may benefit the firms involved, it can also set up incentives for cheating on the cooperative behavior, and it may be illegal. The above discussion of UPS and FedEx shows that oligopolists may engage in noncooperative behavior with each other and cooperative behavior to keep out further competition.

Noncooperative oligopoly models
Models of interdependent oligopoly behavior that assume that firms pursue profit-maximizing strategies based on assumptions about rivals' behavior and the impact of this behavior on the given firm's strategies.

Cooperative oligopoly models
Models of interdependent oligopoly behavior that assume that firms explicitly or implicitly cooperate with each other to achieve outcomes that benefit all the firms.

Noncooperative Oligopoly Models

Let's now look at several models of noncooperative oligopoly behavior in which managers of competing firms make judgments and assumptions about the strategies that will be adopted by their rivals.

The Kinked Demand Curve Model

One of the simplest models of oligopoly behavior that incorporates assumptions about the behavior of rival firms is the **kinked demand curve model**, shown in Figure 9.1. The kinked demand curve model assumes that a firm is faced with two

Kinked demand curve model
An oligopoly model based on two demand curves that assumes that other firms will not match a firm's price increases, but will match its price decreases.

---

[15] Andrew Ward, "DHL Reins In Its Ambitions in U.S. Market," *Financial Times*, May 18, 2005; William Hoffman, "Debating DHL's Gains," *Traffic World*, May 21, 2007; Corey Dade, "FedEx Cuts Outlook as Conditions Worsen," *Wall Street Journal*, March 21, 2008; Mike Esterl and Corey Dade, "DHL Sends an SOS to UPS in $1 Billion Parcel Deal," *Wall Street Journal*, May 29, 2008; Corey Dade, Alex Roth, and Mike Esterl, "DHL Beats a Retreat from the U.S.," *Wall Street Journal*, November 8, 2008.

FIGURE 9.1

Kinked Demand Curve Model of Oligopoly

The kinked demand curve model of oligopoly incorporates assumptions about interdependent behavior and illustrates why oligopoly prices may not change in reaction to either demand or cost changes.

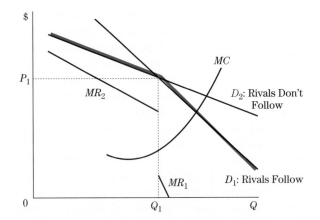

demand curves: one that reflects demand for its product if all rival firms follow the given firm's price changes (D_1) and one that reflects demand if all other firms do not follow the given firm's price changes (D_2). Demand curve D_1 is relatively more inelastic than demand curve D_2 because D_1 shows the effect on the firm's quantity demanded if all firms follow its price change.

For example, if the firm considers raising the price above P_1, its quantity demanded will depend on the behavior of its rival firms. If other firms match the price increase, the firm will move along demand curve D_1 and have only a slight decrease in quantity demanded. However, if the rival firms do not match the price increase, the firm will move along demand curve D_2 and incur a much larger decrease in quantity demanded.

The same principle holds for price decreases. If the firm lowers its price below P_1 and other firms follow, the increase in quantity demanded will move along demand curve D_1. If other firms do not match the price decrease, the firm will have a much larger increase in quantity demanded, as it will move along the relatively more elastic demand curve, D_2.

The behavioral assumption for managers of the firm in this model is that other firms will behave so as to inflict maximum damage on this firm. This means that other firms will not follow price increases, so that only the given firm has raised the price, but other firms will match price decreases so as to not give this firm a competitive advantage. This assumption means that the portions of the two demand curves relevant for this firm are D_2 for prices above P_1 and D_1 for prices below P_1. Thus, the firm faces a kinked demand curve, with the kink occurring at price P_1.

The implications of this kinked demand curve model for profit maximization can be seen by noting the shape of the marginal revenue curve. The portion of MR_2 that is shown in Figure 9.1 is relevant for prices above P_1, whereas the illustrated portion of MR_1 is relevant for prices below P_1. These are the marginal revenue curves that correspond to demand curves D_2 and D_1 in those price ranges. The marginal revenue curve is discontinuous at price P_1, where the kink occurs in the demand curve. Given the marginal cost curve shown in Figure 9.1, the profit-maximizing level of output is Q_1 and the optimal price is P_1.

As you can see in Figure 9.1, the marginal cost curve could shift up and down within the discontinuous portion of the marginal revenue curve and the profit-maximizing price and quantity would not change. This outcome is different from the standard model of a firm with market power, as shown in Figure 8.1 in Chapter 8, where changes in demand and in either marginal revenue or marginal cost result in a new profit-maximizing price and quantity.

Likewise, if the demand curves shift out, but the kink remains at the same price, the profit-maximizing price will not change. The kinked demand curve model of oligopoly implies that oligopoly prices tend to be "sticky" and do not change as much as they would in other market structures, given the assumptions that a firm is making about the behavior of its rival firms. Critics have charged that prices in oligopoly market structures are not more rigid than in other types of markets. The kinked demand curve model also does not explain why price P_1 exists initially. However, we saw examples of firms testing different price changes to determine the behavior of their rivals in the airlines examples. The kinked demand curve model is one illustration of that behavior.

Game Theory Models

Game theory incorporates a set of mathematical tools for analyzing situations in which players make various strategic moves and have different outcomes or payoffs associated with those moves. The tool has been applied to oligopoly behavior, given that the outcomes in this market, such as prices, quantities, and profits, are a function of the strategic behaviors adopted by the interdependent rival firms. Games can be represented by payoff tables, which show the strategies of the players and the outcomes associated with those strategies.

Game theory
A set of mathematical tools for analyzing situations in which players make various strategic moves and have different outcomes or payoffs associated with those moves.

Dominant Strategies and the Prisoner's Dilemma   The most well-known game theory example is the prisoner's dilemma, which is illustrated in Table 9.2. The example in Table 9.2 assumes that two outlaws, Bonnie and Clyde, have been captured after many years on a crime spree. They are both taken to jail and interrogated separately, with no communication allowed between them. Both Bonnie and Clyde are given the options outlined in Table 9.2, with Bonnie's options shown in bold. If neither one confesses to their crimes, there is only enough evidence to send each of them to prison for two years. However, if Bonnie confesses and Clyde does not, she will be given no prison term, while her evidence will be used to send Clyde to prison for 10 years. Clyde is made the same offer if he confesses and Bonnie does not. If both individuals confess, they will each receive a five-year prison term.

We assume that even though Bonnie and Clyde have been partners in crime, each one will make the decision that is in his or her own best interest. Bonnie's best strategy if Clyde does not confess is to confess, as she will not receive a prison term in that case. If Clyde does confess, Bonnie's best strategy is also to confess, as she will go to prison for only 5 years instead of the 10 years she would receive if she did not confess.

Clyde's reasoning will be exactly the same. If Bonnie does not confess, he should confess, as he will not go to prison. If Bonnie does confess, Clyde should also confess to minimize his prison sentence. Thus, both partners are led to confess, and they each end up with a prison term of five years. Both would have been better off if neither had confessed. However, in the given example, they were not able to communicate with each other, so neither one could be certain that the other partner would not confess, given the incentives of the example. Both Bonnie and Clyde would have been better off if they could have coordinated their actions or if they could have trusted each other enough not to confess.

In game theory terms, both Bonnie and Clyde had a **dominant strategy**, a strategy that results in the best outcome or highest payoff to a given player no matter what

Dominant strategy
A strategy that results in the best outcome or highest payoff to a given player no matter what action or choice the other player makes.

TABLE 9.2 The Prisoner's Dilemma

		CLYDE	
		DON'T CONFESS	**CONFESS**
Bonnie	**Don't Confess**	**2 years,** 2 years	**10 years,** 0 years
	Confess	**0 years,** 10 years	**5 years,** 5 years

action or choice the other player makes. If both players have dominant strategies, they will play them, and this will result in an equilibrium (both confessing, in the above example). The prisoner's dilemma occurs when all players choose their dominant strategies and end up worse off than if they had been able to coordinate their choice of strategy. All players are prisoners of their own strategies unless there is some way to change the rules of the game. Thus, one of the basic insights of game theory is that cooperation and coordination among the parties may result in better outcomes for all players. This leads to the cooperative models of oligopoly behavior that we'll discuss later in the chapter. The prisoner's dilemma results may also be less serious in repeated games as learning occurs, trust develops between the players of the game, or there are clear and certain punishments for cheating on any agreement.

A business example of the prisoner's dilemma focuses on the strategies of cigarette companies for advertising on television before the practice was banned in 1970.[16] The choice for competing firms was to advertise or not; the payoffs in profits in millions of dollars to each company are shown in Table 9.3.

The outcomes in Table 9.3 are similar to those in the Bonnie and Clyde example in Table 9.2. Each company has an incentive to advertise because it can increase its profits by 20 percent if it advertises and the other company does not. Advertising for both companies is a dominant strategy, so the equilibrium is that both companies will advertise. However, this outcome leaves each of them with profits of $27 million compared with profits of $50 million if neither company advertised. Simultaneous advertising tends to cancel out the effect on sales for each company while raising costs for both companies. Yet neither company would choose not to advertise, given the payoffs that the other company would obtain if only one company advertised. The companies were caught in a prisoner's dilemma.

In this case, the rules of the game were changed by the federal government. In 1970, the cigarette companies and the government reached an agreement that the companies would place a health warning label on cigarette packages and would stop advertising on television in exchange for immunity from lawsuits based on federal law. This outcome was beneficial for the cigarette industry because it removed the advertising strategy from Table 9.3 and let all companies engage in the more profitable strategy of not advertising on television.

Nash Equilibrium   Many games will not have dominant strategies, in which the players choose a strategy that is best for them regardless of what strategy their rival chooses. In these situations, managers should choose the strategy that is best for them, given the assumption that their rival is also choosing its best strategy. This is the concept of a **Nash equilibrium**, a set of strategies from which all players are choosing their best strategy, given the actions of the other players. This concept is useful when there is only one unique Nash equilibrium in the game. Unfortunately, in many games, there may be multiple Nash equilibria.

Nash equilibrium
A set of strategies from which all players are choosing their best strategy, given the actions of the other players.

TABLE 9.3 Cigarette Television Advertising

		COMPANY B	
		DO NOT ADVERTISE	**ADVERTISE**
Company A	**Do Not Advertise**	**50**, 50	**20**, 60
	Advertise	**60**, 20	**27**, 27

Source: Roy Gardner, *Games for Business and Economics* (New York: John Wiley, 1995), 51–53. Copyright © 1995. Reprinted by permission of John Wiley & Sons, Inc.

---

[16] This example is drawn from Roy Gardner, *Games for Business and Economics* (New York: John Wiley, 1995), 51–53.

TABLE 9.4 Illustration of Unique Nash Equilibrium

		FIRM 2		
		DO NOT EXPAND	SMALL EXPANSION	LARGE EXPANSION
Firm 1	Do Not Expand	**18,** 18	**15,** 20	**9,** 18
	Small Expansion	**20,** 15	**16,** 16	**8,** 12
	Large Expansion	**18,** 9	**12,** 8	**0,** 0

Source: David Besanko, David Dranove, and Mark Shanley, *Economics of Strategy,* 2nd ed.
(New York: John Wiley, 2000), 37–40. Copyright © 2000. Reprinted by permission of John Wiley & Sons, Inc.

We illustrate a game with a unique Nash equilibrium in Table 9.4, where two firms are considering the effect on their profits of expanding their capacity.[17] Their choices are no expansion, a small capacity expansion, and a large capacity expansion. Expansion of capacity would allow a firm to obtain a larger market share, but it would also put downward pressure on prices, possibly reducing or eliminating economic profits. We assume that the decisions are made simultaneously with no communication between the firms and that the profits under each strategy (in millions of dollars) are shown in the table.

We can see in Table 9.4 that there isn't a dominant strategy for either firm. If Firm 2 does not expand or plans a small expansion, Firm 1 should plan a small expansion. However, if Firm 2 plans a large expansion, Firm 1 should not expand. The same results hold for Firm 2, given the strategies of Firm 1. Thus, there is not a single strategy that each firm should pursue regardless of the actions of the other firm. There is, however, a unique Nash equilibrium in Table 9.4: Both firms plan a small expansion. Once this equilibrium is reached, each firm would be worse off by changing its strategy.

However, as in the prisoner's dilemma, both firms would be better off if they could coordinate their decisions and choose not to expand plant capacity. In that situation, each firm would have a payoff of $18 million compared with the $16 million to each firm in the Nash equilibrium. However, that outcome is not a stable equilibrium. Each firm could increase its profits through a small expansion if it thought the other firm would not expand capacity. This strategy would lead both firms to plan a small capacity expansion, the Nash equilibrium. This example also shows the benefits of coordinated behavior among the firms.

The above examples of the prisoner's dilemma and Nash equilibrium are cases of simultaneous decision making. Strategies and outcomes differ if the decision making is sequential, with one side making the first move. In this case, an unconditional move to a strategy that is not an equilibrium strategy in a simultaneous-move game can give the first mover an advantage as long as there is a credible commitment to that strategy.[18]

For example, consider the rivalry between the United States and Japan to develop high-definition TV (HDTV). Although the United States has a technological advantage, it has fewer resources to commit to the project. Each country must decide between a low or high level of research and development (R&D). A high

---

[17] This example is drawn from David Besanko, David Dranove, and Mark Shanley, *Economics of Strategy,* 2nd ed. (New York: John Wiley, 2000), 37–40.

[18] The following example and a complete discussion of these issues in nonmathematical terms are found in Avinash K. Dixit and Barry J. Nalebuff, *Thinking Strategically: The Competitive Edge in Business, Politics, and Everyday Life* (New York: Norton, 1991). For a discussion of cooperative and noncooperative strategies, see Adam M. Brandenburger and Barry J. Nalebuff, *Co-opetition* (New York: Currency Doubleday, 1996).

TABLE 9.5 Payoffs for U.S. and Japanese HDTV R&D

		JAPANESE EFFORT	
		LOW	HIGH
U.S. Effort	Low	**4,** 3	**2,** 4
	High	**3,** 2	**1,** 1

Source: Avinash K. Dixit and Barry J. Nalebuff, *Thinking Strategically: The Competitive Edge in Business, Politics, and Everyday Life* (New York: Norton, 1991), 120–24. Copyright © 1991 by Avinash K. Dixit and Barry J. Nalebuff. Used by permission of W. W. Norton & Company, Inc. The best strategies are ranked as 4, while the worst strategies are ranked as 1.

level decreases the development time, but involves greater costs. The payoff matrix is shown in Table 9.5.

The worst scenario for both countries is a high-level race. The Japanese believe the United States is more likely to win such a race, while the United States dislikes the greater cost involved. This payoff is labeled 1 for both countries (lower right box). The second-worst outcome for each side (payoff 2) is to have a small R&D effort while the other country pursues a high level. The best outcome for Japan (payoff 4) is a high effort while the United States has a low effort, as this increases Japan's chance of winning. The best outcome for the United States is a low effort on both sides because the United States can then win at a lower cost.

For the United States, the low-effort strategy is dominant. However, because Japan anticipates this outcome, it will choose the high-level strategy. This results in the United States getting its second-worst payoff (2 in the upper right box) if the game is played simultaneously. However, if the United States makes an unconditional commitment to the high-level strategy, it gains a first-mover advantage. This is not the strategy the United States would play in a simultaneous game. However, this unconditional move changes the Japanese response to a low-effort strategy and gives the United States a payoff of 3 instead of 2. To make this a successful strategy, the United States must make a credible commitment to the high-level R&D effort, such as offering grants or subsidies to the companies engaged in such work.

Strategic Entry Deterrence

Strategic entry deterrence
Strategic policies pursued by a firm that prevent other firms from entering the market.

Limit pricing
A policy of charging a price lower than the profit-maximizing price to keep other firms from entering the market.

Another way that managers in oligopoly firms can try to limit competition from rivals is to practice **strategic entry deterrence**, or to implement policies that prevent rivals from entering the market.[19] One such policy is **limit pricing**, or charging a price lower than the profit-maximizing price in order to keep other firms out of the market. Figure 9.2 shows a simple model of limit pricing.

Figure 9.2 shows the graphs for an established firm and for a potential entrant into the industry. The existing firm is assumed to have lower costs, given a factor such as economies of scale. The profit-maximizing level of output for the established firm is Q_M, where marginal revenue equals marginal cost. The price is P_M, and the profit earned is represented by the rectangle $(P_M)AB(ATC_M)$. Because the established firm earns positive economic profit by producing at the profit-maximizing price (P_M), this profit will attract other firms into the industry. Price P_M lies above the minimum point on the average total cost curve of the potential entrant (ATC_{EN}). Thus, the positive economic profit shown in Figure 9.2 is not sustainable for the established firm over time due to entry.

---

[19] This discussion is based on F. M. Scherer and David Ross, *Industrial Market Structure and Economic Performance*, 3rd ed. (Boston: Houghton Mifflin, 1990), 356–71.

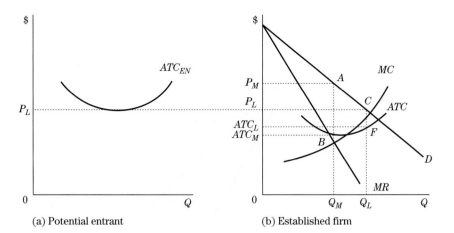

FIGURE 9.2
Limit Pricing Model
With limit pricing, an established firm may set a price lower than the profit-maximizing price to limit the profit incentives for potential entrants to the industry.

(a) Potential entrant   (b) Established firm

To thwart entry, the established firm can charge the limit price, P_L, or a lower price, rather than the profit-maximizing price P_M. The potential entrant would not find it profitable to enter at this price. The established firm could charge a price down to the point where its average total cost curve intersects its demand curve and still make positive or at least zero economic profit. The profit for the established firm at Q_L, which is represented by the rectangle $(P_L)CF(ATC_L)$, is lower than the profit at Q_M, but it is more sustainable over time.

However, these strategies must be credible, in that rivals must be convinced that the established firm will continue its policy of low prices. Even profits that exist at these prices may attract entry, particularly if potential entrants are able to adopt lower-cost technologies. Thus, many dominant oligopolists lose market share over time due to entry. The established firm loses the least amount of market share when it has a high market share, when economies of scale are important, and when the minimum efficient scale of production can satisfy a large fraction of industry demand.

When it introduced the Xerox 914 copier in 1959, the Xerox Corporation recognized that different degrees of competition and entry existed in the copier market based on volume of copies demanded. In the low-volume market, the company had no substantial cost advantage over competitors, so prices were set close to the profit-maximizing level with the expectation that market share would be lost to competitors. Twenty-nine firms entered this market between 1961 and 1967. In the medium- to high-volume market, Xerox had a modest to substantial cost advantage, so prices were set below the profit-maximizing level, but above the entry-deterring level. Entry by other firms was much less frequent in this market than in the low-volume market. By 1967, there were only 10 firms in the medium-volume market and 4 firms in the high-volume market. In the very high-volume market, Xerox enjoyed a substantial cost advantage protected by patents. In this market, the company was able to charge prices substantially exceeding costs for nearly a decade without attracting much entry.

Predatory Pricing

While limit pricing is used to try to prevent entry into the industry, **predatory pricing** is a strategy of lowering prices to drive firms out of the industry and scare off potential entrants. This strategy is not as widespread as often believed because the firm practicing predation must lower its price below cost and therefore incur losses itself with the expectation that these losses will be offset by future profits. The predatory firm must also convince other firms that it will leave the price below cost until the other firms leave the market. If the other firms

Predatory pricing
A strategy of lowering prices below cost to drive firms out of the industry and scare off potential entrants.

FIGURE 9.3

Predatory Pricing

Predation:

Japanese share of

market = Q_P − Q_US = NM = RG

Loss per unit to Japanese

firms = P_C − P_P = NR

Total loss to Japanese firms = NRGM

Postpredation:

U.S. price = P_US

Japanese price = P_J

Japanese share of

market = Q_PP − Q_US

Japanese profits = RTLS

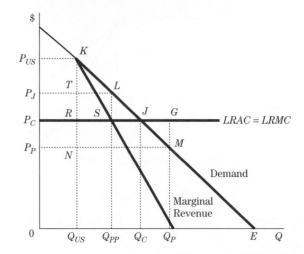

leave and the predatory firm raises prices again, it may attract new entry. If all firms have equal costs, the predatory firm may incur larger losses than rival firms. The legal standard for predatory pricing is often considered to be pricing below marginal cost, which is typically approximated as pricing below average variable cost, given the lack of data on marginal cost.

The basic issues of predatory pricing are illustrated in Figure 9.3.[20] This figure can be used to illustrate the issues in *Matsushita v. Zenith*, a court case in which the National Union Electric Corporation and Zenith Radio Corporation filed suit against Matsushita and six other Japanese electronic firms, accusing them of charging monopoly prices for televisions in Japan and then using those profits to subsidize below-cost television exports to the United States. In Figure 9.3, assume that P_C is the pre-predation competitive price for televisions in the United States and that it is equal to a constant long-run average and marginal cost. Quantity demanded at this price is Q_C. Suppose that the predatory price of the Japanese sellers is P_P and that in response to this price U.S. firms leave the market and cut back output, so that the total output produced by U.S. sellers is Q_{US}. Assume also that demand remains unchanged.

The total quantity demanded at the predatory price of P_P is Q_P, of which Q_{US} is supplied by U.S. firms. The Japanese firms must produce the remaining output, $Q_P - Q_{US}$. The loss to the Japanese firms is $P_C - P_P (= NR)$ per unit of output, which is the difference between the predatory price and long-run average cost. Thus, the total losses to the Japanese firms are represented by the area $NRGM$.

Assume that after predation is over, the U.S. firms are beaten back and continue to produce only output Q_{US}, which is sold at price P_{US}. The Japanese now face only the "residual" demand curve, which is KE on the demand curve. The marginal revenue curve associated with this residual demand curve intersects the long-run marginal cost curve at point S, so the Japanese will charge price P_J and produce output level $Q_{PP} - Q_{US}$. They will earn profits represented by the rectangle $RTLS$. These profits after recoupment ($RTLS$) must be greater than the losses suffered during predation ($NRGM$) for predatory pricing to be a successful policy. Although this outcome does not appear to be the case in Figure 9.3, this figure represents profits and losses for only one period. Actual benefits and costs must be measured over time, which may be a substantial number of years.[21]

---

[20] This diagram and the discussion of *Matsushita v. Zenith* are based on Kenneth G. Elzinga, "Collusive Predation: Matsushita v. Zenith (1986)," in *The Antitrust Revolution: Economics, Competition, and Policy*, ed. John E. Kwoka, Jr., and Lawrence J. White, 3rd ed. (New York: Oxford University Press, 1999), 220–38.

[21] This process involves calculating the time value of money or the present value of the benefits and costs occurring at different points in time. These concepts are typically covered in finance courses.

In the court case of *Matsushita v. Zenith*, the economic analysis indicated that the Japanese firms could never have earned profits sufficient to recoup their losses from the alleged predatory pricing, and, therefore, the court ruled for the Japanese firms. The success of a predatory pricing policy depends on

- How far the predatory price is below cost
- The period of time during which the predatory price is in effect
- The rate of return used for judging the investment in predatory pricing
- How many rivals enter the industry after predation ends
- The length of time over which recoupment of profits occurs

For both color and black-and-white televisions, an economic analysis showed that the Japanese firms would not be able to recoup their profits, given the size of the loss from the predatory pricing below cost and the relatively modest price increases possible during the recoupment period. However, even in the face of losses, predatory pricing in one market might still be rational if a firm achieves the reputation of being aggressive. This reputation can spill over and deter entry in other markets.

Cooperative Oligopoly Models

The second set of oligopoly models focuses on cooperative behavior among rivals. Our examples of both the prisoner's dilemma and the Nash equilibrium showed that the pursuit of individual strategies, while making assumptions about a rival's behavior, could leave both firms worse off than if they had been able to collaborate or coordinate their actions.

Cartels

The most explicit form of cooperative behavior is a **cartel**, an organization of firms that agree to coordinate their behavior regarding pricing and output decisions in order to maximize profits for the organization. Figure 9.4 illustrates this concept of cartel **joint profit maximization**. It also illustrates why cartel members have an incentive to cheat on cartel agreements. The potential to cheat exists because what is optimal for the cartel organization may not be optimal for the individual cartel members.

Model of Joint Profit Maximization   For simplicity, Figure 9.4 illustrates the joint profit maximization problem for a cartel composed of two members.

Cartel
An organization of firms that agree to coordinate their behavior regarding pricing and output decisions in order to maximize profits for the organization.

Joint profit maximization
A strategy that maximizes profits for a cartel, but that may create incentives for individual members to cheat.

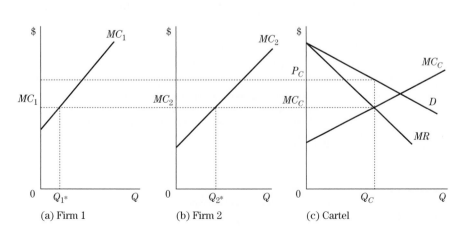

(a) Firm 1   (b) Firm 2   (c) Cartel

FIGURE 9.4
Cartel Joint Profit Maximization
A cartel maximizes the profits of its members by producing where marginal revenue equals marginal cost for the cartel and then allocating output among its members so that the marginal cost of production is equal for each member. This procedure can give cartel members the incentive to cheat on the cartel agreement.

Horizontal summation of marginal cost curves
For every level of marginal cost, add the amount of output produced by each firm to determine the overall level of output produced at each level of marginal cost.

We have assumed that both firms have linear upward sloping marginal cost curves, but that these curves are not identical. At every level of output, Firm 1's marginal cost is higher than Firm 2's marginal cost. The costs of production do typically vary among cartel members, which is a major cause of the cheating problem discussed below. The marginal cost curve for the cartel (MC_C) is derived from the summation of the individual firms' marginal cost curves, or the **horizontal summation of marginal cost curves**.[22] For every level of marginal cost measured on the vertical axis, we add the amount of output Firm 1 would produce at that marginal cost to the amount of output Firm 2 would produce at the same marginal cost to determine the cartel output at that cost. Repeating this process for various levels of marginal cost traces out the cartel marginal cost curve (MC_C).

For joint profit maximization, the cartel must determine what overall level of output to produce, what price to charge, and how to allocate the output among the cartel members. The demand and marginal revenue curves facing the cartel are shown in Figure 9.4c. The profit-maximizing level of output (Q_C) is determined by equating marginal revenue with the cartel's marginal cost. The profit-maximizing price is, therefore, P_C.

Allocating Output Among Cartel Members   The cartel must then decide how to allocate this total output, Q_C, among the two cartel members. The optimal allocation that minimizes the costs of production is achieved by having each firm produce output levels such that their marginal costs of production are equal. The intuition of this rule can be seen in Table 9.6. In this table, Firm 1's marginal cost is always double that of Firm 2. If the goal is to produce 20 units of output overall and each firm produces 10 units, $MC_1 = \$40$, $MC_2 = \$20$, and $TC_1 + TC_2 = \$300$. Firm 1 should produce less output, as it has the higher marginal cost, and Firm 2 should produce more output, as it has the lower marginal cost. As Firm 2 produces more output, its marginal cost increases, while Firm 1's marginal cost decreases as it produces less output. As shown in Table 9.6, the cost-minimizing allocation of output between the firms is $Q_1 = 6.67$ and $Q_2 = 13.33$, with $TC_1 + TC_2 = \$266.67$.

Applying this rule to Figure 9.4, we see that Firm 1 should produce output level Q_{1*} and Firm 2 should produce output level Q_{2*} so that their marginal costs of

TABLE 9.6 Equating Marginal Cost to Minimize Total Cost

	FIRM 1			FIRM 2	
Q	MC (\$)	TC (\$)	Q	MC (\$)	TC (\$)
5	20	50	5	10	25
10	40	200	10	20	100
15	60	450	15	30	225
20	80	800	20	40	400

This simple example is based on the following equations and the assumption of zero fixed costs:
$TC_1 = 2Q^2$, $MC_1 = 4Q$, $TC_2 = Q^2$, and $MC_2 = 2Q$.
To find the cost-minimizing method of producing a total of 20 units of output, solve the equations
$MC_1 = MC_2$ and $Q_1 + Q_2 = 20$.
The solution is $Q_1 = 6.67$, $MC_1 = \$26.68$, $TC_1 = \$88.98$, $Q_2 = 13.33$, $MC_2 = \$26.66$, and $TC_2 = \$177.69$.
$TC_1 + TC_2 = \$266.67$.

---

[22] This process is similar to the derivation of the market demand curve from individual firms' demand curves in Chapter 2.

production are equal to each other and to the cartel's marginal cost. The optimal outputs for Firms 1 and 2 are equal to the total cartel output ($Q_{1*} + Q_{2*} = Q_C$), as shown by the construction of the cartel marginal cost curve. This allocation rule for joint profit maximization is summarized in Equation 9.1:

9.1 $MC_1 = MC_2 = MC_C$

where

MC_1 = Firm 1's marginal cost

MC_2 = Firm 2's marginal cost

MC_C = cartel's marginal cost (derived from horizontal summation of the firms' marginal cost curves)

Cheating in Cartels   By solving the cartel joint profit-maximization problem, we can see the incentive for cheating in cartels. In Figure 9.4, the optimal level of output for Firm 1 is much less than the level of output for Firm 2. If Firm 1's marginal cost curve had intersected the axis above the value MC_C, its optimal allocation of output would have been zero. Joint profit maximization when firms have unequal costs of production implies that these firms' output shares will be unequal. If they are expected to sell this output at the cartel profit-maximizing price, the profits of the two firms will be quite different. Both firms have an incentive to expand output to the point where the cartel price (P_C) equals their marginal cost of production because this would be the best strategy for profit maximization by each individual firm.

Cartel Success   A cartel is likely to be the most successful when

1. It can raise the market price without inducing significant competition from noncartel members.
2. The expected punishment for forming the cartel is low relative to the expected gains.
3. The costs of establishing and enforcing the agreement are low relative to the gains.[23]

If a cartel controls only a small share of the market, it can expect significant competition from noncartel members. The existence of positive economic profits from the cartel pricing policy is also likely to attract more competition. In the United States, price- and output-fixing agreements were made illegal by the Sherman Antitrust Act of 1890. Germany, Japan, and the United Kingdom once permitted the formation of cartels that their governments thought would increase efficiency.

More recently, countries in the European Union have adopted antitrust laws similar to those in the United States. In these cases, with the expected punishment for explicit agreements very severe, firms must consider the expected costs and benefits of less formal behavior, to be discussed below. The costs of organizing a cartel will be lower if there are few firms involved, the market is highly concentrated, the firms are producing nearly identical products, and a trade association exists.

All of these factors lower the costs of negotiating and bargaining among the cartel members. Cartels try to prevent cheating by dividing the market into specific buyers and geographic areas or by agreeing to fix market shares. Contracts may include agreements to a buyer that the seller is not selling at a lower price to another buyer. Cartel agreements may also include a trigger price. If the market price drops below this trigger price, firms can expand output to their precartel levels or abandon the cartel agreement.

---

[23] This discussion is based on Dennis W. Carlton and Jeffrey M. Perloff, *Modern Industrial Organization*, 3rd ed. (Reading, Mass.: Addison-Wesley Longman, 2000), 121–50.

Well-Known Cartels: OPEC Perhaps the most well-known cartel is OPEC—the Organization of Petroleum Exporting Countries—founded by Saudi Arabia, Iran, Iraq, Kuwait, and Venezuela in 1960 to counter the market power of the major international oil companies.[24] During the early 1970s, world oil demand was at an all-time high, while the supply was increasingly concentrated in the low-production-cost countries of the Middle East. There was also a fringe of non-OPEC suppliers, but these countries faced substantially higher development and operating costs. In response to Western support for Israel during the Egyptian-Israeli War of 1973, OPEC instituted production cutbacks and an oil embargo against the West. The price of oil rose from less than $10 a barrel to over $30 per barrel as a result of this action. Another oil price increase occurred after the fall of the Shah of Iran in 1979. Oil demand in the United States declined sharply after the second price shock, and energy use in the European Union and Japan also began to decline. At the same time, oil output of OPEC member Venezuela and non-OPEC producers increased. The pricing behavior of the cartel resulted in the entry of new oil producers and changed consumer behavior, substantially weakening the cartel.

Saudi Arabia is the dominant player in the cartel, given its vast reserves of oil and its cost advantage in production. Thus, there are different incentives facing cartel members, as well as the competitive supply from non-OPEC members. OPEC members Saudi Arabia, Kuwait, and the United Arab Emirates have vast oil reserves, small populations, and large economies, so they are more conservative about selling oil for revenues than are poorer countries with large populations, such as Indonesia, Nigeria, and Algeria. OPEC's market share fell to 30 percent by 1985, largely due to production cutbacks by Saudi Arabia. Internal dissension about quotas occurred among OPEC members from the late 1980s to the 1990s. The major Arab oil producers expanded their output following the Gulf War in 1991, as bargaining power within OPEC seemed to be related to production capacity. Member quotas were raised in 1997 in anticipation of increased world demand. This did not materialize, so prices fell that year.

Since 2000, a similar pattern has continued, with OPEC members trying to enforce quotas, but with substantial competition from non-OPEC producers severely limiting the strength of the cartel.[25] In fall 2001, OPEC producers predicted that oil prices could fall to $10 per barrel. They argued that such a price drop might be the only way to make non-OPEC producers limit their output, which they had refused to do previously. OPEC members, excluding Iraq, had cut oil production by 290,000 barrels per day, but non-OPEC countries, such as Russia, Angola, and Kazakhstan, had increased output by 630,000 barrels per day. OPEC members reduced production in early 2002, but also pressured non-OPEC countries to do the same. Russia, Norway, Mexico, Oman, and Angola responded, but several months later Russia announced that it was planning to increase exports again. These actions on the part of both OPEC and non-OPEC members illustrate how difficult it is to maintain cartel behavior.

In fall 2006, there was again downward pressure on oil prices. OPEC had to decide what price to defend with a total limit on production and how to allocate quotas among members. OPEC officials publicly contradicted themselves over what type of system they were discussing. Many oil ministers suggested $55 per barrel of U.S. benchmark crude as the price the group would defend, although some wanted

---

[24] This discussion is based on Steven Martin, "Petroleum," in *The Structure of American Industry*, eds. Walter Adams and James Brock, 10th ed. (Upper Saddle River, N.J.: Prentice Hall, 2001), 28–56.
[25] "Non-OPEC Output Rose in November Weakening OPEC's Role in Oil Market," *Dow Jones Newswires*, December 13, 2001; "Russia Says It Will Phase Out Restrictions on Oil Exports," *Wall Street Journal*, May 19, 2002; Jim Efstathiou, "OPEC Members Wary of Looming Higher Non-OPEC Oil Supply," *Wall Street Journal*, May 20, 2002.

a price closer to $60. At this point OPEC had split into two camps. One group of countries, including Kuwait, Algeria, and Libya, were able to greatly exceed the individual production quotas OPEC had assigned each member. Other countries, such as Venezuela, Iran, and Indonesia, struggled to meet their quotas. Saudi Arabia had already been quietly trimming its output in the previous several months.[26]

By fall 2007, world demand drove oil prices to the $70 range in September and close to $100 per barrel by November. This created a different set of problems for the cartel. In September 2007, the cartel raised its output limits so that it would not appear to be benefiting while many of the world's economies slowed. Saudi Arabia, with its large reserves, again took the lead in increasing output. Many of the other countries were already pumping oil to the limit. At the OPEC meeting in November 2007, there was discussion about whether the current high prices were justified. The Saudi oil minister, the cartel's de facto leader, suggested he would prefer to see prices come down as did officials from the United Arab Emirates. However, Venezuela and Iran both defended the prices as fair. Venezuelan President Hugo Chavez also called for a return of the 1970s-style "revolutionary OPEC," although this view was not accepted by the Saudis.[27]

The Diamond Cartel   The international diamond cartel, which organizes the production side of the diamond market, may be the most successful and enduring cartel in the world.[28] DeBeers, the dominant company in the industry, was founded in 1880 and has been controlled by a single South African family, the Oppenheimers, since 1925. Eight countries—Botswana, Russia, Canada, South Africa, Angola, Democratic Republic of Congo, Namibia, and Australia—produce most of the world's gem diamonds under a system with an explicit set of rules. These countries adjust production to meet expected demand, stockpile excess diamonds, and sell most of their output to the Diamond Trading Company in London, which is owned by DeBeers.

Cecil Rhodes, the founder of DeBeers, realized from the start that the company needed to control the supply of diamonds to maintain their scarcity and perceived value and that the South African individual miners would be unable to control production. The solution was to organize a vertically integrated organization to manage the flow of diamonds from South Africa. Rhodes organized the Diamond Syndicate under which distributors would buy diamonds from him and sell them in agreed-upon numbers and at agreed-upon prices. This organization was taken over by the Oppenheimers, who, over the years, took new diamond producers into the fold. Demand was managed through the introduction of the slogan, "A diamond is forever," in 1948, which implicitly told customers that the product was too valuable ever to be resold and that diamonds equal love.

Even the controversy over "blood" or "conflict" diamonds benefited the cartel. Around the year 2000, activists began arguing that warlords in Sierra Leone, Liberia, the Congo, and elsewhere funded their brutal activities by the sale of diamonds and that these diamonds should be boycotted, a move that would have had a major impact on DeBeers. The end result of this controversy was the Kimberly Process, an international program begun in 2002 and supported by the producing countries, importing countries, nongovernmental organizations, the jewelry trade, and the United Nations. This program included a complex certification system for all diamonds regarding their origin and a commitment by all participants to adhere

---

[26] Bhushan Bahree, "A Slippery Debate Stirs in OPEC," *Wall Street Journal*, September 22, 2006; Chip Cummins, "Oil-Price Drop Challenges OPEC Unity," *Wall Street Journal*, October 19, 2006.

[27] Peter Fritsch and Oliver Klaus, "OPEC Seeks Soft Landing for Oil," *Wall Street Journal*, September 12, 2007; Neil King, Jr., "OPEC's Divisions Rise to Surface," *Wall Street Journal*, November 19, 2007.

[28] This discussion is based on Debora L. Spar, "Continuity and Change in the International Diamond Market," *Journal of Economic Perspectives* 20 (Spring 2006): 195–208.

to the rules of the system. DeBeers wholeheartedly supported this program because the end result was to keep excess supply off the market and prevent entry by new suppliers. Warlords and other small suppliers were kept out of the market, and the additional costs of tagging, monitoring, and auditing made entry more difficult for new and smaller players. Both DeBeers and the Canadian producers were the major beneficiaries of this program. Thus, even given all the changes that have impacted the diamond industry since the late 1800s, it "remains an industry dominated by a single firm and an industry in which, perhaps uniquely, all of the major players understand the extent to which their long-term livelihood depends on the fate and actions of the others."[29]

Tacit Collusion

Because cartels are illegal in the United States due to the antitrust laws, firms may engage in **tacit collusion**, coordinated behavior that is achieved without a formal agreement. Practices that facilitate tacit collusion include

Tacit collusion
Coordinated behavior among oligopoly firms that is achieved without a formal agreement.

1. Uniform prices
2. A penalty for price discounts
3. Advance notice of price changes
4. Information exchanges
5. Swaps and exchanges[30]

However, managers must be aware that many of these practices have been examined by the Justice Department and the Federal Trade Commission (FTC) to determine whether they have anticompetitive effects. Cases are often ambiguous because these practices can also increase efficiency within the industry.

Charging uniform prices to all customers of a firm makes it difficult to offer discounts to customers of a rival firm. This policy may be combined with policies that require that any decreases in prices be passed on to previous customers in a certain time period, as well as to current customers. This strategy decreases the incentives for a firm to lower prices. Price changes always cause problems for collusive behavior, as the firm that initiates the change never knows whether its rivals will follow.

Price leadership
An oligopoly strategy in which one firm in the industry institutes price increases and waits to see if they are followed by rival firms.

In some cases, there is formal **price leadership**, in which one firm, the acknowledged leader in the industry, will institute price increases and wait to see if they are followed. This practice was once very common in the steel industry. However, price leadership can impose substantial costs on the leader if other firms do not follow. A less costly method is to post advance notices of price changes, which allows other firms to make a decision about changing their prices before the announced price increase actually goes into effect. We will discuss this practice in more detail below.

Collusive behavior may also be strengthened by information exchanges, as when firms identify new customers and the prices and terms offered to them. This policy can help managers avoid price wars with rival firms. However, in the *Hardwood Case* (1921), lumber producers, who ran the American Hardwood Manufacturers Association, collected and disseminated pricing and production information. Although the industry was quite competitive, with 9,000 mills in 20 states and only 465 mills participating in the association, the Supreme Court ruled that the behavior violated the Sherman Antitrust Act, and the information exchange was ended.

Firms may also engage in swaps and exchanges in which a firm in one location sells output to local customers of a second firm in another location in return for the reciprocal service from the second firm. This practice occurs in the chemical, gasoline, and

---

[29] Ibid.
[30] This discussion is based on Carlton and Perloff, *Modern Industrial Organization*, 361–69.

paper industries, where the products are relatively homogeneous and transportation costs are significant. These swaps can allow firms to communicate, divide the market, and prevent competition from occurring.

The Ethyl Case   In the *Ethyl Case* (1984), the FTC focused on several facilitating practices that it claimed resulted in anticompetitive behavior among the four producers of lead-based antiknock compounds used in the refining of gasoline—the Ethyl Corporation, DuPont, PPG Industries, and Nalco Chemical Company.[31] The practices included advance notices of price changes, press notices, uniform delivered pricing, and most-favored-customer clauses. All four firms gave their customers notices of price increases at least 30 days in advance of the effective date. Thus, other firms could respond to the first increase before it was implemented.

Until 1977, the firms issued press notices about the price increases, which provided information to their rivals. All firms quoted prices on the basis of a delivered price that included transportation, and the same delivered price was quoted regardless of a customer's location. This delivered pricing strategy removed transportation costs from the pricing structure and simplified each producer's pricing format, making it easier to have a uniform pricing policy among the firms. The firms also used most-favored-customer clauses, in which any discount off the uniform delivered list price given to a single customer would have to be extended to all customers of that seller.

The effect of these clauses was to prevent firms from stealing rivals' customers by lowering prices to certain customers. This could easily happen in the antiknock compound industry because sales were made privately to each of the industrial customers and might not be easily detected by rivals. These clauses meant that the uncertainty about rivals' prices and pricing decisions was reduced. In this case, the FTC ruled against the industry, but the court of appeals overruled this decision. Much of the appellate court's decision was based on the fact that many of these practices were instituted by the Ethyl Corporation before it faced competition from the other rivals, and, therefore, the court concluded the purpose of these practices was not to reduce competition.

Airline Tariff Publishing Case   Similar issues regarding communication of advanced pricing information arose in the *Airline Tariff Publishing Case* (1994).[32] In December 1992, the Justice Department filed suit against the Airline Tariff Publishing Company (ATPCO) and eight major airlines, asserting that they had colluded to raise prices and restrict competition. The Justice Department charged that the airlines had used ATPCO, the system that disseminates fare information to the airlines and travel agency computers, to carry on negotiations over price increases in advance of the actual changes. The system allowed the airlines to announce a fare increase to take effect some number of weeks in the future.

Often the airlines iterated back and forth until they were all announcing the same fare increase to take effect on the same date. The Justice Department alleged that the airlines used fare basis codes and footnote designators to communicate with other airlines about future prices. The airlines argued that they were engaging in normal competitive behavior that would also benefit consumers, who were often outraged when the price of a ticket increased between the time they made the reservation and the time they purchased the ticket. The Justice Department believed that any benefits of these policies were small compared with the ability of the airlines to coordinate price increases.

[31] George A. Hay, "Facilitating Practices: The Ethyl Case (1984)," in *The Antitrust Revolution: Economics, Competition, and Policy*, ed. John E. Kwoka, Jr., and Lawrence J. White, 3rd ed. (New York: Oxford University Press, 1999), 182–201.
[32] Severin Borenstein, "Rapid Price Communication and Coordination: The Airline Tariff Publishing Case (1994)," in *The Antitrust Revolution: Economics, Competition, and Policy*, eds. John E. Kwoka, Jr., and Lawrence J. White, 3rd ed. (New York: Oxford University Press, 1999), 310–26.

Under the settlement of the case, the airlines cannot use fare basis codes or footnote designators to convey anything but very basic information, they cannot link different fares with special codes, and they cannot pre-announce price increases except in special circumstances. The settlement does not restrict what fares an airline can offer or when specific fares can be implemented or ended. Since this antitrust dispute, the airlines have engaged in pricing practices discussed in the previous news articles—that is, posting an increase on a Friday afternoon, waiting to see if the rivals respond, and then either leaving the increase in place or abandoning it by Monday morning.

Managerial Rule of Thumb

Coordinated Actions

Managers in oligopoly firms have an incentive to coordinate their actions, given the uncertainties inherent in noncooperative behavior. Their ability to coordinate, however, is constrained by a country's antitrust legislation, such as the prohibition on explicit cartels and the limits placed on many types of tacit collusion in the United States. There are also incentives for cheating in coordinated behavior. It is often the case that any type of behavior that moderates the competition among oligopoly firms is likely to be of benefit to them even if formal agreements are not reached. However, oligopolists, like all firms with market power, must remember that this power can be very fleeting, given the dynamic and competitive nature of the market environment. ■

Summary

In this chapter, we have focused on the interdependent behavior of oligopoly firms that arises from the small number of participants in these markets. Managers in these firms develop strategies based on their judgments about the strategies of their rivals and then adjust their own strategies in light of their rivals' actions. Because this type of noncooperative behavior can leave all firms worse off than if they coordinated their actions, there are incentives for either explicit or tacit collusion in oligopoly markets. Explicit collusive agreements may be illegal and are always difficult to enforce. Many oligopolists turn to forms of tacit collusion, but managers of these firms must be aware that their actions may come under scrutiny from governmental legal and regulatory agencies.

The discussion of market structure in Chapters 7, 8, and 9 has drawn on all the microeconomic concepts we developed in the first part of this text. We now use these concepts to analyze additional pricing policies managers can use to increase their firms' profits.

Key Terms

cartel, p. 239
cooperative oligopoly models, p. 231
dominant strategy, p. 233
game theory, p. 233
horizontal summation of marginal
    cost curves, p. 240

joint profit maximization, p. 239
kinked demand curve model, p. 231
limit pricing, p. 236
Nash equilibrium, p. 234
noncooperative oligopoly
    models, p. 231

oligopoly, p. 226
predatory pricing, p. 237
price leadership, p. 244
strategic entry deterrence, p. 236
tacit collusion, p. 244

Exercises

Technical Questions

1. The following graph shows a firm with a kinked demand curve.

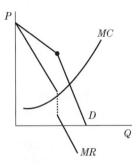

   a. What assumption lies behind the shape of this demand curve?
   b. Identify the firm's profit-maximizing output and price.
   c. Use the graph to explain why the firm's price is likely to remain the same, even if marginal costs change.

2. The following matrix shows strategies and payoffs for two firms that must decide how to price.

		Firm 2	
		Price High	Price Low
Firm 1	Price High	400, 400	−50, 700
	Price Low	700, −50	100, 100

   a. Does either firm have a dominant strategy, and if so, what is it?
   b. What is the Nash equilibrium of this game?
   c. Why would this be called a prisoner's dilemma game?

3. Some games of strategy are cooperative. One example is deciding which side of the road to drive on. It doesn't matter which side it is, as long as everyone chooses the same side. Otherwise, everyone may get hurt.

		Driver 2	
		Left	Right
Driver 1	Left	0, 0	−1000, −1000
	Right	−1000, −1000	0, 0

   a. Does either player have a dominant strategy?
   b. Is there a Nash equilibrium in this game? Explain.
   c. Why is this called a cooperative game?

4. A game that everyone knows is coin flipping. Suppose that Player 1 flips the coin (and is so skilled that he is able to flip it whichever way he wants) and Player 2 calls heads or tails. The winner gets $10 from the loser.

		Player 2 (call)	
		Heads	Tails
Player 1 (flip)	Heads	−10, 10	10, −10
	Tails	10, −10	−10, 10

   a. Does either player have a dominant strategy?
   b. Is there a Nash equilibrium in this game? Explain.
   c. Games like this are called *zero-sum games*. Can you explain why?

5. A monopolist has a constant marginal and average cost of $10 and faces a demand curve of $Q_D = 1000 − 10P$. Marginal revenue is given by $MR = 100 − 1/5Q$.

   a. Calculate the monopolist's profit-maximizing quantity, price, and profit.
   b. Now suppose that the monopolist fears entry, but thinks that other firms could produce the product at a cost of $15 per unit (constant marginal and average cost) and that many firms could potentially enter. How could the monopolist attempt to deter entry, and what would the monopolist's quantity and profit be now?
   c. Should the monopolist try to deter entry by setting a limit price?

6. Consider a market with a monopolist and a firm that is considering entry. The new firm knows that if the monopolist "fights" (that is, sets a low price after the entrant comes in), the new firm will lose money. If the monopolist accommodates (continues to charge a high price), the new firm will make a profit.

		Entrant	
		Enter	Don't Enter
Monopolist	Price High	20, 10	50, 0
	Price Low	5, −10	10, 0

   a. Is the monopolist's threat to charge a low price credible? That is, if the entrant has come, would it make sense for the monopolist to charge a low price? Explain.
   b. What is the Nash equilibrium of this game?
   c. How could the monopolist make the threat to fight credible?

7. The following graphs show a monopolist and a potential entrant.

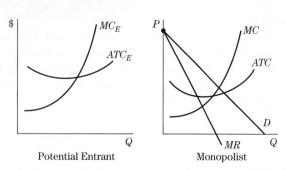

a. Label the monopolist's profit-maximizing price and quantity.
b. Identify a limit price that the monopolist could set to prevent entry.
c. How much does the monopolist lose by setting a limit price rather than the profit-maximizing price? Does that mean that this would be a bad strategy?

8. The following graphs show marginal cost curves for two firms that would like to form a cartel in the market in which they are selling.

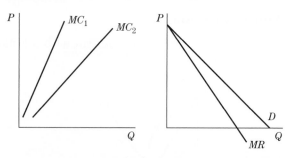

a. Use the two marginal cost curves to construct a combined marginal cost curve, and plot that on the market graph.
b. Label the cartel's profit-maximizing output and price, as well as the output of each firm.
c. Use your graphs to explain why each cartel member has an incentive to cheat on the agreement.

Application Questions

1. In current business publications, find examples of the continued oligopolistic behavior among the airlines similar to what we discussed in this chapter.

2. The following paragraphs provide a description of the competition between Xerox Corp. and Eastman Kodak Co.:[33]

> For most of their 40 years of coexistence as the two biggest companies in Rochester, NY, Xerox Corp. and Eastman Kodak Co. have been friendly neighbors who avoided poaching on each other's territory. Xerox copiers ruled the office; Kodak film owned the consumer. But digital convergence and financial problems have increasingly turned the two companies into rivals.
>
> In 2007 Xerox announced plans with Fujifilm Holdings Corp., Kodak's long-time rival, to put high-quality Xerox printers into retailers' photo minilabs. Xerox and Kodak already compete to sell color digital presses to commercial printers, a market that Xerox leads and Kodak entered about three years ago. Both companies regard the

commercial printing industry as a key strategic market. The new competition illustrates how rapidly changing technology can force companies to challenge corporations that once moved in parallel universes.

> The development of inkjet printers slashed demand for Xerox copiers, while digital cameras severely impacted Kodak's film business. Xerox barely avoided bankruptcy in 2001, while Kodak is still in the midst of a restructuring. Both companies hope that sales of ink and toner with digital color printing will provide the flow of revenue that black toner once did for Xerox and that film gave Kodak.

> Both companies face even greater competition from Hewlett-Packard Co. and Canon Inc., which are larger, more profitable, and have greater research and development budgets. Analysts say that Xerox's broad portfolio of digital printers gives it an advantage, but Kodak will soon start reselling some cheaper digital presses made by Canon. Xerox's deal with Fuji takes it into the heart of Kodak's traditional business—consumer photo printing. Kodak installed 80,000 photo kiosks where customers can make prints in retail stores around the world. Fuji focused on one-hour photo labs at Wal-Mart Stores Inc. and Walgreen Co.

---

[33] William M. Bulkeley, "When Neighbors Become Rivals," *Wall Street Journal*, February 22, 2007.

The competition between Kodak and Xerox is likely to increase. Kodak had not tried to enter Xerox's office market for a while, but it has introduced color inkjet multifunction devices that can print 22 color pages a minute, fast enough to attract some of the small-business offices that Xerox also targets.

Discuss how the oligopoly models presented in this chapter apply to the behavior of Xerox and Kodak.

3. The following describes the ice cream industry in summer 2003:[34]

Given the Federal Trade Commission's approval of Nestle's acquisition of Dreyer's Grand Ice Cream Inc., two multinationals, Nestle SA and Unilever, are preparing to engage in ice cream wars. Unilever, which controls the Good Humor, Ben & Jerry's, and Breyer's brands, holds 17 percent of the U.S. market, while Nestle, owner of the Haagen-Dazs and Drumstick brands, will control a similar share after buying Dreyer's.

Ice cream has long been produced by small local dairies, given the problems with distribution. Most Americans eat ice cream in restaurants and stores, although 80 percent of the consumption of the big national brands occurs at home. Both Unilever and Nestle want to move into the away-from-home market by focusing on convenience stores, gas stations, video shops, and vending machines, a strategy the rivals have already undertaken in Europe.

Five national brands—Haagen-Dazs, Nestle, Ben & Jerry's, Breyer's, and Dreyer's—are developing new products and flavors, focusing on single-serving products that carry profit margins 15 to 25 percent higher than the tubs of ice cream in supermarkets. The higher profit margins can open new distribution outlets. Although traditional freezer space is very costly, Unilever, Nestle, and Dreyer's have been pushing for logo-covered freezer cabinets in stores, given the higher profit margins.

Under the FTC settlement, Nestle will be allowed to keep Dreyer's distribution network, which delivers ice cream directly to more than 85 percent of U.S. grocers. Unilever must use middlemen to deliver most of its Good Humor and Breyer's products. Nestle can expand from Dreyer's supermarket base to cinemas and gas stations with little extra cost. The supermarket ties may also help Nestle enter grocers' competitive prepared-foods section, so that consumers can easily purchase ice cream along with their deli and hot foods. Nestle agreed to sell a number of Dreyer's secondary brands as part of the FTC approval. However, Nestle-Dreyer's will be able to sign more licensing agreements with the wider distribution network, and the combined company will be able to turn more of Nestle's candies into Dreyer's ice cream.

  a. Describe how the ice cream industry fits the oligopoly model.
  b. How does the government influence oligopolistic behavior?
  c. Do oligopolists always compete on the basis of price? Explain.

4. The following describes the toothpaste market in fall 2003:[35]

In fall 2003, Procter & Gamble Co. [P&G] launched an $80 million marketing campaign to promote a new Crest product, Whitening Expressions. P&G is trying to regain market share from Colgate-Palmolive Co. While Crest had success with its battery-operated toothbrushes and Whitestrips, the at-home tooth-whitening kits, it trailed Colgate in the toothpaste market with a 23 versus a 27 percent market share. Colgate achieved the highest market share in 1998 when it introduced its Total toothpaste, which promised to fight gum disease and whiten teeth. This battle has pushed other competitors out of the market. Unilever recently gave up its toothpaste business, selling its Close-Up and Mentadent brands.

Colgate is also introducing new products including different children's toothpastes and a new Total—Colgate Total Advanced Fresh Toothpaste. Both companies face the challenge of trying to get consumers to buy more of a product they use regularly already. They are focusing on characteristics such as beauty and taste. P&G is using celebrity chef Emeril Lagasse to promote Whitening Expressions. In focus groups, it also put microchips into toothbrushes and found that consumers brushed 20 percent longer with Whitening Expressions than with regular Crest. Research also showed that two new flavors, citrus and cinnamon, appealed to the Hispanic and African-American communities where Crest had lagged behind Colgate.

---

[34] Deborah Ball, "Ice Cream Rivals Prepare to Wage a New Cold War," *Wall Street Journal*, June 26, 2003.

[35] Sarah Ellison, "Crest Spices Up Toothpaste War with New Tastes," *Wall Street Journal*, September 15, 2003.

Describe the strategies used by these oligopolists to fight the toothpaste wars. How does this behavior draw on the discussion of consumer demand and behavior in Chapter 3?

5. The following describes the relationship between two major shipping companies hauling liquid chemicals:[36]

> Documents indicate that two shipping companies, Stolt-Nielsen SA and Odfjell ASA, colluded to divide up the market for transporting liquid chemicals across the sea. The companies discussed which shipping business each would bid for, route by route, even exchanging information on bid prices. Stolt officials also developed tables showing the increase in revenues from cooperation compared to all-out competition. The companies are unknown to most consumers, but they carry the chemicals that are used to make a variety of everyday products.

> Carriers are allowed to cooperate in certain ways. They may pool their capacity if they both carry chemicals for a given producer on the same route. They may form joint ventures to bid for a piece of business. However, cooperation to divide markets or set prices would fall outside these areas.

> The alleged collusion was in response to the Southeast Asian financial crisis of 1997, which depressed the volume of shipping, and a glut of new ships that decreased freight rates. Chemical company mergers also increased the producers' bargaining power, particularly the merger between Dow Chemical and Union Carbide in 2001. Each of the shipping companies had important pieces of business with each of the chemical companies that were merging. After the merger, either Stolt or Odfjell could be dislodged and price wars could break out. Documents indicate that officials of the two shipping companies held talks on dividing the pie, reviewing contracts around the world, trade lane by trade lane. Documents also indicate that the cooperation would keep freight rates 5 to 25 percent higher than otherwise. Stolt officials compared the economic costs of "going to war" with cooperation. On certain trade lanes, Stolt might benefit from

individual action, but lower rates overall would result if the cooperation was abandoned.

> Journals of company officials indicate that by April 2001, both companies were threatening price wars if the agreements could not be maintained. The journals are also filled with notations such as "no written agreements" or "no paper." Memos included the phrase, "Don't be seen as doing something together."

> In September 2006, Stolt was indicted by a federal grand jury in Philadelphia on charges of price fixing and other illegal cartel activities. Stolt-Nielsen was initially granted amnesty as part of a Justice Department's investigation into the chemical-shipping industry, but department officials revoked it in 2004 after determining the company wasn't meeting the terms of the deal. The indictment cites company activity between August 1998 and November 2002. If convicted, corporate officials could face up to three years of imprisonment, $350,000 individual fines, and $10 million in corporate fines.

Explain how the discussion of cartel behavior in this chapter relates to this shipping company case.

6. In February 2007, Russia and Iran, which hold nearly half the world's natural gas reserves, began talking about creating an OPEC-like organization for gas.[37] Although natural gas accounts for a growing share of global energy use, the nations that produce it have traditionally not worked together to influence markets. This natural gas cartel would be less threatening to the United States than to Europe because the U.S. obtains most of its gas within North America.

A previous effort to create an organization of gas exporters failed, and many are doubtful that this one would succeed. The Gas Exporting Countries Forum, which included Russia, Iran, and Qatar, was formed in 2001 but has not met since 2005. Discussion of a gas cartel appears to relate to dissatisfaction among gas suppliers with the emerging international gas market. After making billions of dollars of investment, gas suppliers are finding it "difficult to place all of this gas in the

---

[36] James Bandler, "Seagoing Chemical Haulers May Have Colluded on Rates," *Wall Street Journal*, February 20, 2003; Mark H. Anderson, "Shipper Stolt-Nielsen Is Indicted in U.S. Price-Fixing, Cartel Case," *Wall Street Journal*, September 6, 2006.

[37] Russell Gold and Gregory L. White, "Russia and Iran Discuss a Cartel for Natural Gas," *Wall Street Journal*, February 2, 2007.

market at a price they're comfortable with." India and China used their huge demand potential to negotiate lower long-term pricing. There is concern among gas suppliers that other Asian countries may resort to the same strategy. Russia's interest in a cartel is unusual because it never joined OPEC, possibly because it did not want to submit to quotas set by other countries. It also resisted calls to curtail oil output to support prices.

Discuss the reasons why this proposed cartel is likely to fail. Is the motivation for this cartel similar to that of the potato farmers' cooperative in Chapter 7? Explain.

On the Web

For updated information on the article at the beginning of the chapter, as well as other relevant links and information, visit the book's Web site at **www.pearsonhighered.com/farnham**

10 Pricing Strategies for the Firm

I n this chapter, we build on the concepts developed in Chapters 3, 8, and 9 to analyze how differences in demand and elasticity lead managers to develop various pricing strategies. We show how knowledge of price elasticity among different groups of customers or for various products enables managers to price discriminate, or charge different prices to these groups. Such a strategy can increase the firm's level of profit above that achieved by charging a single price for all units of a good.

We also discuss how a common managerial pricing strategy, markup pricing, can be consistent with our models of profit maximization based on the equality of marginal revenue and marginal cost, and we show how both of these pricing policies are related to the marketing literature.[1] We also examine why managers may not change prices immediately in response to changing demand and cost conditions, an issue that is significant for the macroeconomic analysis we present in the second half of the text.

We begin this chapter with the article "Seeking Perfect Prices, CEO Tears Up the Rules." This article discusses how one manufacturing company changed from simply setting prices on the basis of costs to using more complex schemes based on the willingness to pay by different groups of consumers for different products. We then discuss the theory of markup pricing and price discrimination and give numerous examples of how managers can use these techniques.

---

[1] Philip Kotler, *Marketing Management: The Millennium Edition* (Upper Saddle River, N.J.: Prentice Hall, 2000); Robert J. Dolan and Hermann Simon, *Power Pricing: How Managing Price Transforms the Bottom Line* (New York: Free Press, 1996).

Seeking Perfect Prices, CEO Tears Up the Rules

by Timothy Aeppel

Wall Street Journal, *March 27, 2007*

In early 2001, shortly after Donald Washkewicz took over as chief executive of Parker Hannifin Corp., he came to an unnerving conclusion. The big industrial-parts maker's pricing scheme was crazy.

For as long as anyone at the 89-year-old company could recall, Parker used the same simple formula to determine prices of its 800,000 parts—from heat-resistant seals for jet engines to steel valves that hoist buckets on cherry pickers. Company managers would calculate how much it cost to make and deliver each product and add a flat percentage on top, usually aiming for about 35%. Many managers liked the method because it was straightforward and gave them broad authority to negotiate deals.

But Mr. Washkewicz thought that Parker, which had revenues of $9.4 billion last year, had stuck itself in a profit-margin rut. No matter how much a product improved, the company often ended up charging the same premium it would for a more standard item. And if the company found a way to make a product less expensively, it ultimately cut the product's price as well. . . .

While touring the company's 225 facilities in 2001, Mr. Washkewicz had an epiphany: Parker had to stop thinking like a widget maker and start thinking like a retailer, determining prices by what a customer is willing to pay rather than what a product costs to make. Such "strategic" pricing schemes are used by many different industries. Airlines know they can get away charging more for a seat to Florida in January than in August. Sports teams raise ticket prices if they're playing a well-known opponent. Why shouldn't Parker do the same, Mr. Washkewicz reasoned.

Today, the company says its new pricing approach boosted operating income by $200 million since 2002. That helped Parker's net income soar to $673 million last year from $130 million in 2002. Now the company's return on invested capital has risen from 7% in 2002 to 21% in 2006, putting it on the verge of moving into the top 25% of Mr. Washkewicz's list comparing Parker with "peer" industrial companies. From the end of 2001 to present, Parker's shares have risen nearly 88% to about $86, compared to a 25% gain in the S&P 500.

For the past several years, many U.S. manufacturers have struggled to raise prices amid the growth of global competition and cost-cutting drives among customers. While this erosion of pricing power is often cited as a factor that helped tame inflation, it put a strain on U.S. manufacturing, which contributes 12% to the nation's gross domestic product.

Now, a growing number of manufacturers are trying to fight back by scrutinizing every assumption underlying their pricing strategies. Some companies like Intel Corp. have used strategic pricing schemes for well over a decade. But much of industrial America—60% of U.S. manufacturers, according to Thomas Nagle, a pricing consultant at the Monitor Group—still relies on oldfangled, "cost-plus" types of pricing methods such as the one Parker used.

Changing Parker's pricing was a complex undertaking. The company has tens of thousands of different types of products, often custom-engineered. The company estimates half of its offerings are specifically made for a single customer. And unlike retailers or airlines, a manufacturer generally can't see its rivals' prices. Discussing pricing with competitors is illegal, while published list prices from other manufacturers mean little in industrial markets, where most deals are negotiated. And pricing changes were certain to alienate some customers. . . .

It didn't help that Parker, like many manufacturers, has a conservative culture that treasures continuity. Founded in 1918 as a maker of hydraulic brakes for trucks, the company had a descendant of the founder as its chairman as recently as 1999. Today, Parker is a leading producer of industrial parts used in aerospace, transportation, and manufacturing. It makes components used in everything from the space shuttle to a mechanism that helped tilt a faux steamship for the movie *Titanic*. . . .

Mr. Washkewicz had just been made president and chief operating officer in early 2000 when he set out to visit all of Parker's facilities around the globe. He saw people boosting productivity, landing new accounts, and making shrewd acquisitions, even in the face of a deepening manufacturing recession. Yet the company never seemed to improve one key measure—the return on invested capital. On his list comparing Parker with "peer" industrial companies, the company failed to make the top 25% by that measure.

Mr. Washkewicz decided the company needed to revamp its whole approach. He mandated that every business adopt "lean" manufacturing to streamline production and overhaul the way Parker purchased materials from its suppliers. The last—and most crucial element—he targeted was pricing.

To his surprise, Mr. Washkewicz discovered that computer programs for calculating prices, adopted in the 1990s, were part of the problem. "It became the cookbook approach," he says. Managers typed in myriad costs, and the computer spit out a recommended base price which was used as the starting point in negotiations.

The cookbook approach might make sense for basic commodity products, where there is enough competition and little wiggle room. But what about the unique products that only Parker or a handful of others can offer?

Although he decided to adopt strategic pricing on his own, Mr. Washkewicz hired consultants to help each of Parker's businesses painstakingly study its full gamet of products and divide them into categories. "A" items were the high-volume commodities where there was at least one big competitor helping to shape prices. Other products were divided into "B," "C," and "D" items, which fell into increasingly narrow or specialized niches. The final and most narrow groups were "specials" and "classics" that only Parker produced.

What Mr. Washkewicz discovered was that about a third of Parker's products—a huge number—fell into niches where there was limited or no competition or where Parker offered some other unique value. Sometimes Parker could deliver the product faster. Sometimes Parker's product was just better.

By 2003, the business that makes industrial fittings, for example, had spent six months reviewing some 2,000 different items and gathered some 20,000 data points in total. The upshot: 28% of the parts, mostly metal fittings used in places like oil rigs and power plants, were priced too low. Overnight, Parker raised their prices anywhere from 3% to 60%, with the average increase about 5%. The fittings cost anywhere from $5 to $500 each.

Occasionally, the process led to price cuts. One type of hydraulic replacement filter, for instance, used on a wide range of industrial machines, saw a 15% price decrease when Parker realized that owners of the machines usually preferred to buy new filters from the makers of the machines, rather than an outside supplier like Parker.

The price increases were met with immediate protest. Many distributors complained, fearing they would be stuck footing the higher bill. Parker began running classes in 2005 to point out the unique attributes of various products to distributors, which in turn helps them justify passing on the higher prices to customers. . . .

Parker says most customers accepted the price increases, either because they had to or because they accepted the company's rationale. . . .

Each of Parker's 115 divisions now has a least one of its own pricing gurus—specialists who act as gatekeepers, and enforcers, of strategic pricing.

Sheila Konopka is the guru at the hydraulic valve division in Elyria, Ohio, which has four factories and sells $1.5 billion worth of valves in North America. "Before, everyone around here thought they were a pricing manager," she says. "If we could make 35% margin for a big order—that was great. Nobody asked: 'Why not 45%?'"

When it came to one line of Parker's high-pressure valves, the question was particularly appropriate. These valves handle extremely high pressure—up to 10,000 pounds of pressure per square inch—with almost no leakage. Most industrial valves operate at half or less that PSI and are prone to varying amounts of leaks. The high-pressure models are used for things like airplane doors and the mechanisms to raise and lower the flaps on the decks of aircraft carriers.

The company found it was able to increase prices for these items about 5% across the board because of their special attributes.

Parker's new approach has also helped it charge more for attributes that are difficult to quantify. It sometimes costs more, for instance, to produce a product in the U.S., which allows the supplier to deliver it more quickly and be more responsive. . . . Parker's pricing teams now examine these sort of extra services and attempt to attach values to them.

Parker continues finding ways to apply the new approach. The company, for instance, has integrated pricing into its innovation process—aiming to pinpoint and develop products that offer the most potential for price premiums.

"Once you start doing this, you never stop," says Mr. Washkewicz. "It's a different way of thinking that filters into everything."

 ## Case for Analysis

Manufacturing Pricing Strategies

This article discusses the shift by the CEO of Parker Hannifin Corp. from simple cost-based rules for markup pricing to a strategy of using information about customers' willingness to pay, especially for products produced uniquely by the company. In the past the company determined the cost of producing its tens of thousands of products and applied a standard markup above cost to determine the product prices. As noted in the article, "No matter how much a product improved, the company often ended up charging the same premium it would for a more standard item." In 2001 CEO Washkewicz realized that the company needed to "start thinking like a retailer" and use customer willingness to pay as a major factor in determining product prices. Prices would be marked up differentially from a simple cost approach for "basic commodity products, where there is enough competition and little wiggle room" to larger markups on "unique products that only Parker or a handful of others" could offer. The article shows the advantages to the company from the new approach with an increase in operating income by $200 million since 2002 and an increase in its return on invested capital from 7 to 21 percent.

The article also illustrates how a change in the company's mindset was needed to implement this new pricing strategy and how it was a major challenge, given the number of products Parker produced. Most customers accepted the price increases "either because they had to or because they accepted the company's rationale." Once managers became used to the new approach, they started applying it to product attributes that were more difficult to quantify and to the development of new products. The pricing strategy became "a different way of thinking that filters into everything." ▪

The Role of Markup Pricing

Markup pricing is a long-established business practice for determining product prices.[2] Under this procedure, firms estimate their costs of production and then apply a markup to the average cost to determine price. In some cases, the size of the markup is based on industry tradition, managers' experiences, or rules of thumb. For example, the rule of thumb in an electronics journal is that products sell for two and one-half times their production cost.[3] From a manager's perspective, markup pricing is considered a means of dealing with uncertainty in demand estimation, a method that is "fair" to both customers and firms, and a simplified approach to the pricing of large numbers of products, as the procedure involves only determining a product's average cost of production and then applying a percentage markup to that cost to determine the product price.

There has been much discussion about whether using a simplified rule of thumb, such as markup pricing, is consistent with the firm's goal of profit maximization, which we discussed in Chapter 7. Applying a *uniform* markup to all products would not be a profit-maximizing pricing strategy for a firm because this approach considers only the cost of production and does not incorporate information on demand and consumer preferences. However, many studies of managerial pricing decisions have shown that firms do not use a uniform markup for all products. According to Philip Kotler, common markups in supermarkets are 9 percent on baby foods, 14 percent on tobacco products, 20 percent on bakery products, 27 percent on dried foods and vegetables, 37 percent on spices and extracts, and 50 percent on greeting cards.[4] Markup dispersion can also exist within categories of goods. For example, Kotler found markups ranging from 19 to 57 percent within the spices and extracts category. In many of these cases, it appears that the size of the markup is related to what managers believe the market will bear, or, in economic terms, the price elasticity of demand.

In the following discussion, we show why a policy of applying larger markups to products that have less elastic demand helps firms maximize their profits. This discussion will proceed in three steps:

1. We establish a mathematical relationship between marginal revenue and the price elasticity of demand. (We showed this relationship graphically and numerically in Chapter 3, but we now derive it formally.)
2. We review the profit-maximizing rule of equating marginal revenue and marginal cost introduced in Chapter 7.

Markup pricing
Calculating the price of a product by determining the average cost of producing the product and then setting the price a given percentage above that cost.

---

[2] Markup pricing was first analyzed by Hall and Hitch in 1939 and then studied more extensively in the 1950s and 1960s. See R. L. Hall and Charles J. Hitch, "Price Theory and Business Behavior," *Oxford Economic Papers* 2 (May 1939): 12–45; A. D. H. Kaplan, Joel B. Dirlam, and Robert F. Lanzillotti, *Pricing in Big Business: A Case Approach* (Washington, D.C.: Brookings Institution, 1958); Robert F. Lanzillotti, "Pricing Objectives in Large Companies," *American Economic Review* 48 (December 1958): 921–40; Bjarke Fog, *Pricing in Theory and Practice* (Copenhagen: Handelshojskolens Forlag, 1994); and the literature cited in F. M. Scherer and David Ross, *Industrial Market Structure and Economic Performance*, 3rd ed. (Boston: Houghton Mifflin, 1990), chap. 7.

[3] Dolan and Simon, *Power Pricing*, 37.

[4] Philip Kotler, *Marketing Management: Analysis, Planning, Implementation, and Control*, 8th ed. (Englewood Cliffs, N.J.: Prentice Hall, 1994), 498–500; Kotler, *Marketing Management: The Millennium Edition*, 465–66.

3. We show how marking up a price above the average cost of production, where the markup is inversely related to the price elasticity of demand, is equivalent to pricing according to the profit-maximizing rule from economic theory (marginal revenue equals marginal cost). Thus, even though markup pricing is often considered a rule of thumb, applying it as described here is a profit-maximizing strategy for managers.

Marginal Revenue and the Price Elasticity of Demand

Equations 10.1 to 10.7 present a derivation of the relationship between marginal revenue—the change in total revenue from producing an additional unit of output (which we defined in Chapter 3)—and the price elasticity of demand.

10.1 $MR = \dfrac{(\Delta TR)}{\Delta Q}$

10.2 $\Delta TR = (P)(\Delta Q) + (Q)(\Delta P)$

10.3 $MR = P * \dfrac{\Delta Q}{\Delta Q} + Q * \dfrac{\Delta P}{\Delta Q}$

10.4 $MR = P + Q * \dfrac{\Delta P}{\Delta Q}$

10.5 $MR = \left[P + Q * \left(\dfrac{\Delta P}{\Delta Q}\right)\left(\dfrac{P}{P}\right) \right]$

10.6 $MR = P\left(1 + \dfrac{\Delta P}{\Delta Q} * \dfrac{Q}{P} \right)$

10.7 $MR = P\left(1 + \dfrac{1}{e_P} \right)$

Equation 10.1 is simply the definition of marginal revenue (*MR*)—the change in total revenue (*TR*) divided by the change in output or quantity (ΔQ), as we discussed in Chapter 3. Equation 10.2 describes the change in total revenue, which is the numerator of Equation 10.1. When lowering price and moving down a demand curve, total revenue changes because additional units of output are now sold at the lower price. This change in revenue is represented by the first right-hand term in Equation 10.2, $(P)(\Delta Q)$. Total revenue also changes because the previous quantity demanded is now sold at a lower price. This change is represented by the second right-hand term in Equation 10.2, $(Q)(\Delta P)$. Thus, Equation 10.2 is simply expressing the change in total revenue as price is lowered along a demand curve. In Chapter 3, we illustrated this concept in Figures 3.2 and 3.3 and with the second managerial rule of thumb for estimating price elasticity.

Equation 10.3 again presents the full definition of marginal revenue, using the definition of change in total revenue (ΔTR) from Equation 10.2. Equation 10.4 is a simplified version of Equation 10.3. In Equation 10.5, the last term of Equation 10.4 is multiplied by the term (*P/P*). Because this term equals 1, the value of the equation is not changed. Equation 10.6 simplifies Equation 10.5 by taking the price term outside the brackets and rearranging the other terms. The last term in Equation 10.6 is the inverse of the price elasticity of demand. This is expressed in Equation 10.7, which shows the formal relationship between marginal revenue and price elasticity: $MR = P[1 + (1/e_P)]$.

TABLE 10.1 Marginal Revenue and Price Elasticity of Demand

$$MR = P\left(1 + \frac{1}{e_P}\right)$$

VALUE OF ELASTICITY	VALUE OF MARGINAL REVENUE	NUMERICAL EXAMPLE
$|e_P| > 1$ Elastic	$MR > 0$	$e_P = -2;\ MR = P\left(1 + \frac{1}{-2}\right) = \frac{1}{2}P > 0$
$|e_P| < 1$ Inelastic	$MR < 0$	$e_P = -1/2;\ MR = P\left(1 + \frac{1}{-1/2}\right) = -P < 0$
$|e_P| = 1$ Unit elastic	$MR = 0$	$e_P = -1;\ MR = P\left(1 + \frac{1}{-1}\right) = 0$

The implications of this relationship are shown in Table 10.1. As we demonstrated graphically in Chapter 3, when demand is elastic, marginal revenue is positive; when demand is inelastic, marginal revenue is negative; and when demand is unit elastic, marginal revenue is zero. The numerical examples in Table 10.1 illustrate this relationship for different elasticity values.

The Profit-Maximizing Rule

The second step in our discussion of price elasticity and optimal pricing is to review the rule for profit maximization that we used in all of our market structure models in Chapters 7 through 9. To maximize profit, a firm needs to produce that level of output at which marginal revenue equals marginal cost. We now show how this rule, derived from economic theory and the mathematics of optimization, is consistent with the commonly used managerial technique of markup pricing *when the size of the markup is inversely related to the price elasticity of demand.*

Profit Maximization and Markup Pricing

We begin the discussion relating markup pricing to the profit-maximizing rule by reprinting Equation 10.7 and adding the profit-maximizing rule in Equation 10.8.

$$10.7 \quad MR = P\left(1 + \frac{1}{e_P}\right)$$

$$10.8 \quad MR = MC$$

We now substitute the definition of marginal revenue from Equation 10.7 into Equation 10.8 and rearrange terms, as shown in Equations 10.9 to 10.11.

$$10.9 \quad P\left(1 + \frac{1}{e_p}\right) = MC$$

$$10.10 \quad P = \frac{MC}{\left(1 + \frac{1}{e_P}\right)} = \frac{MC}{\frac{(e_P + 1)}{e_P}}$$

$$10.11 \quad P = \left(\frac{e_P}{1 + e_P}\right)MC$$

Equation 10.11 shows that the optimal price, which maximizes profits for the firm, depends on marginal cost and price elasticity of demand. Holding the marginal cost constant, the optimal price is *inversely* related to the price elasticity of demand. Firms usually base the price markups for their products on the average variable cost (variable cost per unit of output), not the marginal cost (the additional cost of producing an additional unit of output). In Chapter 5, we showed that marginal cost equals average variable cost if average variable cost is constant, which may be the case over a given range of output for many firms.[5] Given this assumption and drawing on Equation 10.11, we derive the formula for the optimal markup, m, in Equations 10.12 and 10.13 by substituting average variable cost for marginal cost in Equation 10.11, defining m, the markup procedure, in Equation 10.12, and solving for m in terms of the price elasticity of demand by relating Equations 10.11 and 10.12. The end result is presented in Equation 10.13. The implications of the formula in Equation 10.13 are shown in Table 10.2.

10.12   *P = average variable cost + (m)(average variable cost)*
     = (1 + m) average variable cost

10.13 $(1+m) = \dfrac{e_P}{(1+e_P)}$ or $m = \dfrac{-1}{(1+e_P)}$

Table 10.2 shows that as the price elasticity of demand increases in absolute value, the optimal markup, which maximizes profit for the firm, decreases in size. If the price elasticity of demand is –2.0, the optimal markup of price above cost is 100 percent, whereas it is only 10 percent if the price elasticity of demand is –11.0. A large price elasticity typically occurs when there are many substitutes for a given product, so the producer of that product is constrained in terms of how much price can be raised above cost without losing a substantial number of customers. The upper limit for the size of price elasticity, as described in Chapter 3, is infinitely or perfectly elastic demand, which, as shown in Table 10.2, results in no markup above the average cost of production. This is the case of the perfectly competitive firm that faces the horizontal or perfectly elastic demand curve. As we discussed in Chapter 7, perfectly competitive firms are price-takers, which cannot influence the price of the product. Therefore, perfectly competitive firms have no ability to mark up the price above cost.

You should also note that no values of elasticity less than 1 in absolute value are included in Table 10.2. Recall from Table 10.1 that these values of inelastic demand

---

TABLE 10.2 The Optimal Markup

$$m = \frac{-1}{(1+e_P)}$$

ELASTICITY (e_P)	CALCULATION	MARKUP
−2.0	$m = -[1/(1 - 2)] = +1.00$	1.00 or 100%
−5.0	$m = -[1/(1 - 5)] = +0.25$	0.25 or 25%
−11.0	$m = -[1/(1 - 11)] = +0.10$	0.10 or 10%
∞	$m = -[1/(1 - ∞)] = 0$	0.00 (no markup)

---

[5] If average variable cost is not constant, marginal cost may still not differ significantly from average cost in many cases. Firms may also mark up prices on the basis of long-run average cost, which, as we discussed in Chapter 6, is often constant and equal to long-run marginal cost.

occur where marginal revenue is negative. Because profit maximization is achieved where $MR = MC$, the profit-maximizing level of output never occurs where marginal revenue is negative. This theoretical result is consistent with the empirical price elasticity estimates in Chapter 3. Elasticity estimates for individual producers are greater than 1 in absolute value (elastic) even though estimates for the entire product category might be less than 1 (inelastic).

Business Pricing Strategies and Profit Maximization

In the 1950s and 1960s, the observed use of markup pricing by many companies generated an extensive debate about whether firms really pursued the goal of profit maximization. Doubts about this maximizing strategy were raised, particularly if firms simply used a given markup set by tradition or if they set prices to generate a given target rate of return that did not depend on market conditions.[6] The 1958 Lanzillotti study on the issue, which was based on interviews with officials in 20 large corporations, including Alcoa, A&P, General Electric, General Motors, Sears, and U.S. Steel, concluded that the goal of these companies was to earn a predetermined target rate of return on their investment. Prices were considered to be "administered" to achieve this goal. The implication was that major U.S. corporations selected a level of output to produce and priced it at a margin above cost that would earn a target rate of return on investment selected by the company.

In 1988, Kenneth Elzinga updated the Lanzillotti study to determine whether the firms included in the original research continued to target the same rates of return in subsequent years (1960 to 1984) as in the earlier period (1947 to 1955), and whether firms that specifically designated a target rate of return as the basis for their pricing policies had been able to achieve that return.[7] Elzinga found that most of the 20 original firms earned a lower rate of return in subsequent years compared with the original study period. He also found that companies that specifically stated a target rate of return typically did not meet that goal in the 1960 to 1984 period. In fact, several of the original companies either filed for bankruptcy or underwent reorganization in that latter period. Elzinga argued that firms responded to market forces in their price-setting behavior. He notes:[8]

> For a corporation to fail to meet an objective and then to settle for less also is consistent with the hypothesis that prices and profits are so powerfully influenced by market forces that firms cannot always systematically determine their own fate. . . . The differences in interfirm behavior Lanzillotti recorded in his sample reveal not so much differences in objectives or goals as variations in adaptive behavior to differing market circumstances.

Economist Bjarke Fog notes that prices can be determined along a continuum from complete reliance on costs only (a rigid markup or full cost approach) to the other extreme of reliance on demand only, with no reference to costs.[9] The inverse elasticity rule lies between these two extremes. Fog argues that there are examples of real-world pricing policies across this entire continuum. Thus,

---

[6] This debate is summarized in the following literature: Kaplan, Dirlam, and Lanzillotti, *Pricing in Big Business*; Lanzillotti, "Pricing Objectives in Large Companies"; M. A. Adelman, "Pricing Objectives in Large Companies: Comment," *American Economic Review* 49 (September 1959): 669–70; Alfred E. Kahn, "Pricing Objectives in Large Companies: Comment," *American Economic Review* 49 (September 1959): 670–78; Kenneth G. Elzinga, "Pricing Achievements in Large Companies," in *Public Policy Toward Corporations*, ed. Arnold A. Hegestad (Gainesville: University of Florida Press, 1988), 166–79; and Fog, *Pricing in Theory and Practice*.

[7] Elzinga, "Pricing Achievements in Large Companies."

[8] Ibid., 171, 176.

[9] Fog, *Pricing in Theory and Practice*, 73–81.

the profit-maximizing rule based on marginal analysis may be too complex to always apply in a world of imperfect information and uncertainty.

Markup Pricing Examples

Restaurant Industry   The divergence between the prices restaurants charge and the costs of producing the menu items goes far beyond the traditional view that the markup on liquor is much greater than the markup on food items. Markups on mussels can reach 650 percent, while those on salmon can exceed 900 percent.[10]

Restaurant owners typically aim for a price that is a 300 percent markup above the cost of the raw ingredients for their meals. However, various items on restaurant menus—such as gourmet seafood and certain cuts of beef—are so expensive that customers would not tolerate a 300 percent markup on those foods. Because restaurant owners cannot mark up these items by the desired amount, given the customers' price elasticity of demand, the owners must use even larger markups on less expensive items, including other meats, salmon, lettuce, and pasta. Restaurants have developed computer programs that allow owners to calculate the exact price of each ingredient in a dish and the overall cost of a single serving. Restaurant owners use these markup procedures based on price elasticity of demand because they see themselves operating in a very competitive industry with low profit margins.

Psychological factors also affect restaurant pricing. Pricing an item too low compared with other offerings might make customers think something is wrong with the item. Pricing an item too high simply means that people will not be willing to pay that price because it seems out of line compared with the rest of the items on the menu. Many people will not choose the least expensive item on the menu, so markups are often high on the next two or three higher-priced items.

Fixed-price meals also give restaurant owners greater pricing power. One Dallas, Texas, restaurant was able to mark up the price of its $90 prix fixe meal by 75 percent compared with a 66 percent markup on its a la carte menu.[11] This larger markup is based on customers' willingness to pay for the chef's key dishes and on cost advantages. Chefs can use fewer ingredients and purchase them in bulk for the more limited menus. The kitchens require a smaller staff and fewer stations, and the meals provide the opportunity to use food that might otherwise be thrown out.

Pricing in Professional Sports   We noted above that the markup pricing formula and the profit-maximizing rule imply that firms will never price where demand is inelastic. This rule may be modified when firms offer multiple products that are complementary. Although the ticket price for a Major League Baseball (MLB) game more than doubled between 1991 and 2002 and subjected team owners to criticism in the popular press, many studies have shown that tickets to sporting events are regularly priced in the inelastic range of demand. MLB ticket price elasticities range from –.06 to –0.93.[12]

Several explanations have been offered for this behavior. As with the 1950s business discussion above, some have questioned whether the goal of team owners is to maximize profits. Owners may receive satisfaction from controlling a professional sports team and may not be concerned with setting profit-maximizing prices. It is also possible that owners keep prices low in exchange for special political considerations from local governments, particularly regarding the public funding of stadiums. In the

---

[10] Eileen Daspin, "What Do Restaurants Really Pay for Meals?" *Wall Street Journal*, March 10, 2000.

[11] Mike Spector, "The Prix Fixe Is In," *Wall Street Journal*, October 7, 2006.

[12] This discussion is based on Anthony C. Krautmann and David J. Berri, "Can We Find It at the Concessions? Understanding Price Elasticity in Professional Sports," *Journal of Sports Economics* 8 (April 2007): 183–91.

National Football League, there is some evidence suggesting a trade-off between ticket prices and stadium subsidies. Lower prices in the short run may also be necessary to maximize profits over a longer time period by creating fan loyalty.

It has also been suggested that inelastic ticket pricing may be explained by recognizing that team owners do not derive revenue simply from ticket sales. If complementary sources of revenue can more than offset the lost revenue from selling tickets at lower prices, these pricing policies may be optimal. One important complementary source of revenue is that derived from concession stands. High prices of hot dogs and other baseball favorites may more than compensate for the lower revenue from ticket sales.

Managerial Rule of Thumb

Markup Pricing

Managers may use a simple cost-based pricing method to achieve an acceptable outcome, even if they do not earn the maximum amount of profits. However, most managers appear to explicitly or implicitly use some type of inverse price elasticity rule, which involves both demand and cost factors, in calculating their markups. This strategy will bring them closer to earning the maximum amount of profit possible. ■

Price Discrimination

We now discuss price discrimination, a pricing strategy closely related to markup pricing and one that is also dependent on the price elasticity of demand. We first illustrate the concept with several theoretical models, and we then discuss numerous managerial applications of this technique.

Definition of Price Discrimination

Price discrimination is the practice of charging different prices to various groups of customers that are not based on differences in the costs of production. This can entail charging different prices to different groups when the costs of production do not vary or charging the same price to different groups when there are differences in the costs of production.

There are three basic requirements for successful price discrimination.

1. Firms must possess some degree of monopoly or market power that enables them to charge a price in excess of the costs of production. Thus, price discrimination can be used by firms in all the market structures discussed in Chapter 1 *except* perfect competition, where the individual firm has no influence on price. Successful price discrimination results when competitors cannot undersell the price-discriminating firm in its high-priced market.
2. Firms must be able to separate customers into different groups that have varying price elasticities of demand. The costs of segmenting and policing the individual markets must not exceed the additional revenue earned from price discrimination.
3. Firms must be able to prevent resale among the different groups of customers. Otherwise, consumers who are charged a low price could resell their product to customers who are charged a much higher price. Price discrimination also should not generate substantial consumer resentment at the differential prices or be illegal.[13]

Price discrimination
The practice of charging different prices to various groups of customers that are not based on differences in the costs of production.

---

[13] Kotler, *Marketing Management. The Millennium Edition.*

These requirements are typically met in the airline industry. A small number of large airlines dominate the U.S. market, ensuring that these firms have market power. As noted previously, airline business and pleasure travelers have different elasticities of demand because pleasure travelers typically have much more flexibility in their schedules and are more price sensitive. Finally, resale can be prevented by requiring a specific name on the ticket, which will be monitored when the customer checks in for the flight, and by placing restrictions, such as a Saturday night stay, on the cheaper tickets. Price discrimination is always easier to implement for nondurable goods, such as an airline seat on a particular flight at a given time. Once the flight leaves, that good no longer exists and cannot be resold.

Figure 10.1 shows the variety of fares charged on a typical flight in the late 1990s. As you can see, the highest fare is often eight times greater than the lowest fare charged for the flight.

FIGURE 10.1

Airline Price Discrimination

Reprinted from Figure 8–2 in William G. Shepherd, "Airlines," in Walter Adams and James W. Brock (eds.), The Structure of American Industry, *10th ed. Upper Saddle River, NJ: Prentice Hall, Inc., 2001.*

Source: Adapted from the *New York Times,* 12 April 1998, Section 4, p. 2. Reproduced by permission of Pearson Education, Inc., Upper Saddle River, New Jersey.

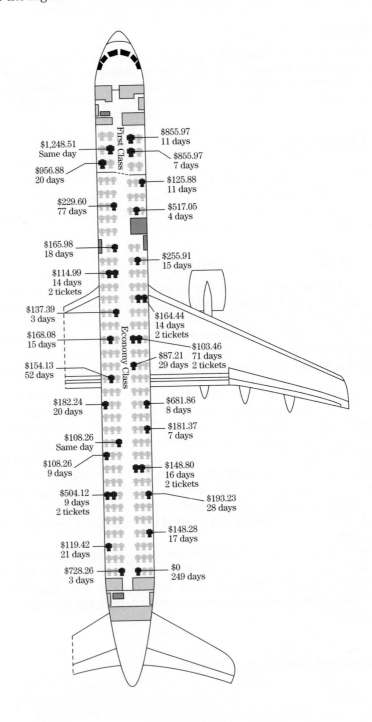

The airlines have made substantial investments in "yield management" computer software, which enables them to calculate how much different customers or groups of customers are willing to pay for their airline seats. Current yield management systems evaluate thousands of possible connections for each flight. Continental Airlines estimated that it increased its revenue by 0.5 to 0.7 percent, or around $50 million in 1999, using these systems.[14] The systems allowed Continental's pricing experts to open more seats to frequent flyer rewards or to post a special rate on the Internet to fill seats in a slow-selling market without having to offer an across-the-board fare reduction that would reduce profits in all markets. However, these systems can also make mistakes. In the spring of 1999, United Airlines' system overestimated demand for full-fare tickets and rejected reservations for less-expensive seats, resulting in a second-quarter revenue loss of at least $22 million.[15]

As noted in the third point for successful price discrimination, the power of the airlines to discriminate is not unlimited. Many businesses have started balking at the prices they have to pay for employee travel and are limiting travel, searching for discount fares that apply, or using substitutes for travel such as videoconferencing. In response, some airlines have begun offering discounts on full-fare coach seats aimed at business travelers. Test marketing has indicated that business travelers have become more price sensitive, so that future business fares may be only three times the amount of the discounted fares on average.[16]

By 2004 the difference between the average fare charged to business travelers and to leisure passengers had decreased dramatically. On the highly travelled New York to Los Angeles route, 15 percent of the passengers booked by the reservation company Sabre Holdings Corp. paid between $2,000 and $2,400 on average in June 2001, while only 3 percent paid that much in June 2004. Fifty-five percent paid between $200 and $400, up from 28 percent three years earlier. These changes resulted from both the increased use of discounted fares by business travelers and from greater competition among the airlines on these popular routes. The rise of low-cost carriers such as JetBlue Airways helped increase seat capacity 14 percent between 2001 and 2004 on the New York–Los Angeles route.[17]

Theoretical Models of Price Discrimination

Economists focus on three models of price discrimination—first-, second-, and third-degree—that illustrate the relationship of this strategy with demand and price elasticity. Before discussing each of these models and their implications, we describe how a demand curve illustrates consumer willingness to pay for a product and provides a rationale for price discrimination. Later in the chapter, we discuss other managerial applications of price discrimination, and we relate these approaches to strategies typically discussed in marketing courses.

Demand and Willingness to Pay   The standard assumption with a demand curve is that *all* units of a good are sold at whatever price exists in the market. We employed this assumption in our discussion of demand, price elasticity, and revenues in Chapter 3 and in the market models of Chapters 7, 8, and 9. In Figure 10.2, suppose that P_1 is the price of the good and Q_1 is the quantity demanded at that price. The amount of money spent on the good is price times quantity, or the area $0P_1BQ_1$. However, this area does *not* represent the total amount that consumers would be willing to pay for the good rather than go without it. That total willingness

[14] Scott McCartney, "Bag of High-Tech Tricks Helps to Keep Airlines Financially Afloat," *Wall Street Journal*, January 20, 2000.

[15] Ibid.

[16] Nicole Harris and Kortney Stringer, "Breaking a Taboo, Airlines Slash Traditionally Full Business Fares," *Wall Street Journal*, August 8, 2002; Scott McCartney, "Airlines Try Business-Fare Cuts, Find They Don't Lose Revenue," *Wall Street Journal*, November 22, 2002.

[17] Melanie Trottman, "Equalizing Air Fares," *Wall Street Journal*, August 17, 2004.

FIGURE 10.2

FIGURE 10.2
Demand, Willingness to Pay, and First-Degree Price Discrimination
The total amount consumers are willing to pay for Q_1 units of output is the area $0ABQ_1$, whereas the amount they actually pay at price P_1 is the area $0P_1BQ_1$. The difference is consumer surplus or area ABP_1. Under first-degree price discrimination firms are able to turn this consumer surplus into revenue.

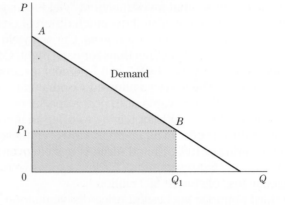

Marginal benefit
The valuation that a consumer places on each additional unit of a product, which is measured by the price of that product.

Total benefit
The total amount of money consumers are willing to pay for a product rather than go without the product.

to pay is represented by the area underneath the demand curve up to quantity Q_1, or area $0ABQ_1$. This difference between the amount actually paid when purchasing all units at price P_1 and the total amount consumers would be willing to pay results from the fact that the prices measured along a demand curve represent consumers' **marginal benefit** or valuation, the dollar value they attach to each additional unit of the product, as we show in the following example.

Table 10.3 shows a hypothetical demand schedule for oranges. If I observe you buying four oranges when the price of oranges is 25 cents, I can infer that you did not buy the fifth orange because it was worth less than 25 cents to you. (This argument assumes that you had more than a dollar in your pocket to spend on oranges.) If the price of oranges is 50 cents per orange and you buy only three oranges, I can infer that the third orange is worth at least 50 cents, but the fourth orange is worth less than 50 cents, but at least 25 cents because you bought the fourth orange when the price was 25 cents per orange. For simplicity, let's assume that the valuation of the fourth orange is exactly 25 cents and the third orange, 50 cents. With the same reasoning, the second orange is worth $0.75, and the first orange is worth $1.00. Thus, a market price reflects a consumer's marginal valuation or benefit, the amount of money he or she is willing to pay for the last or marginal unit consumed.[18]

If we add up all these valuations for each of the units, we obtain the total valuation, or the total amount consumers are willing to pay for all units. This dollar amount, represented by area $0ABQ_1$ in Figure 10.2, is the total willingness to pay, or the **total benefit** to consumers of that amount of output. If all units of output

TABLE 10.3 Individual Demand for Oranges (Hypothetical)

PRICE	QUANTITY DEMANDED
$0.25	4
$0.50	3
$0.75	2
$1.00	1

[18] Oranges were chosen in this example to illustrate the marginal benefit concept because income, for most people, is not a factor constraining their demand for oranges. It can be safely argued that the reason the consumer did not purchase the fifth orange, when oranges were priced at 25 cents per orange, is that the consumer did not value the fifth orange at 25 cents, *not* that the individual did not have the income to purchase the fifth orange. Oranges also illustrate the marginal concept because they are a small product about which the consumer would typically think in marginal terms and consider purchasing one more or one less orange.

are sold at price P_1, consumers actually pay the dollar amount represented by the area $0P_1BQ_1$. The difference between the two areas, area ABP_1, is called **consumer surplus**. It is derived from the fact that consumers typically do not have to spend the maximum amount they are willing to pay for a product. The existence of consumer surplus provides an opportunity for the price-discriminating manager to increase profits by turning some or all of the consumer surplus into revenue for the firm.

First-Degree Price Discrimination   Under **first-degree price discrimination**, a manager is able to charge the maximum amount that consumers are willing to pay for each unit of the product. Thus, the total revenue to the firm under first-degree price discrimination is the area $0ABQ_1$ in Figure 10.2 because the consumer surplus, area ABP_1, is turned into revenue for the firm. In the numerical example of Table 10.3, at a common price of $0.25 per orange, the consumer demands four oranges and the producer receives $1.00 in revenue. Under first-degree price discrimination (if it were possible), the firm charges $1.00 for the first orange, $0.75 for the second, $0.50 for the third, and $0.25 for the fourth, for a total revenue of $2.50. The consumer surplus, valued at $1.50, is turned into revenue for the firm.

We now illustrate the differences in a firm's revenue and profit that result when charging a single profit-maximizing price and engaging in first-degree price discrimination, using the numerical demand example from Chapter 3. We continue with this example to show different types of price discrimination throughout the remainder of the chapter.

Figure 10.3 shows the demand function $Q = 12 - P$ or $P = 12 - Q$, drawn from Chapter 3. It also shows the marginal revenue function $MR = 12 - 2Q$. We now assume that marginal cost (MC) is constant at $2 and, therefore, equal to average cost. Table 10.4 shows the calculation of the profit-maximizing quantity and price, total revenue, total cost, and profit, assuming both a single profit-maximizing price and first-degree price discrimination. We can see that first-degree price discrimination increases total revenue from $35 to $47.50 and profit from $25 to $37.50.

First-degree price discrimination is a largely hypothetical case because firms are not usually able to charge the maximum price consumers are willing to pay for each unit of a product. A close example of first-degree price discrimination might be an old country doctor who knew all his patients and their income levels and charged different prices for the same services provided to each patient or a psychologist who uses a sliding fee scale for different clients. Haggling over the price of a new or used car at an auto dealership is another example of a firm trying to get each customer to pay the maximum amount he or she is willing to spend on the automobile. This is accomplished by the salesperson taking a personal interest in the customer, "asking what the customer does for a living (ability to pay), how long he has lived in the area (knowledge of the market), what kinds of cars she has bought before (loyalty to a

Consumer surplus
The difference between the total amount of money consumers are willing to pay for a product rather than do without and the amount they actually have to pay when a single price is charged for all units of the product.

First-degree price discrimination
A pricing strategy under which firms with market power are able to charge individuals the maximum amount they are willing to pay for each unit of the product.

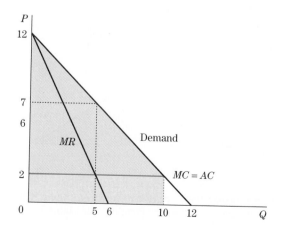

FIGURE 10.3
Profit Maximization and First-Degree Price Discrimination
Profit maximization where MR = MC *results in* P = $7, Q = 5, TR = $35, TC = $10, *and* π = $25. *Under first-degree price discrimination, the consumer surplus or the area of the triangle under the demand curve above a price of $7 is turned into revenue for the firm. This adds $12.50 to revenue and profit.*

TABLE 10.4 Numerical Example of Profit Maximization with a Single Price and First- and Second-Degree Price Discrimination

PROFIT MAXIMIZATION WITH A SINGLE PRICE	PROFIT MAXIMIZATION WITH FIRST-DEGREE PRICE DISCRIMINATION
$Q = 12 - P$ or $P = 12 - Q$	The firm turns the consumer surplus in the triangle at the top of Figure 10.3 into revenue:
$MR = 12 - 2Q$	Consumer surplus $= (1/2)(5)(12 - 7)$
$MC = AC = 2$	$= (1/2)(5)(5) = \$12.50$
$MR = MC$	New $TR = \$35.00 + \$12.50 = \$47.50$
$12 - 2Q = 2$	New $\pi = \$47.50 - \$10.00 = \$37.50$
$2Q = 10$	
$Q = 5$	**PROFIT MAXIMIZATION WITH SECOND-DEGREE PRICE DISCRIMINATION**
$P = \$7$	
	First 3 units: $P = \$9, Q = \$3, TR = \$27$
$TR = (P)(Q) = (\$7)(5) = \$35$	Second 2 units: $P = \$7, Q = \$2, TR = \$14$
$TC = (AC)(Q) = (\$2)(5) = \$10$	New $TR = \$27 + \$14 = \$41$
$\pi = TR - TC = \$35 - \$10 = \$25$	New $\pi = \$41 - \$10 = \$31$

particular brand), where she lives (value placed on the dealer's location), and whether she has looked at, or is planning to look at, other cars (awareness of alternatives)."[19] We discuss below how new technologies, including the Internet, are assisting firms in more closely approximating first-degree price discrimination.

Second-Degree Price Discrimination   **Second-degree price discrimination** involves firms charging the maximum price consumers are willing to pay for different blocks of output. It is often called *nonlinear pricing* because prices depend on the number of units bought instead of varying by customer. Each customer faces the same price schedule, but customers pay different prices depending on the quantity purchased. Quantity discounts are an example of second-degree price discrimination. This strategy is illustrated in Figure 10.4. If all Q_1 units in the figure are sold at price P_1, the revenue to the firm is the area $0P_1BQ_1$ (price times quantity). However, if the firm can sell the first block of units, $0Q_3$, at price P_3 and the second block of units, Q_3Q_2, at price P_2 and the third block of units, Q_2Q_1, at price P_1, the total

Second-degree price discrimination

A pricing strategy under which firms with market power charge different prices for different blocks of output.

FIGURE 10.4
Second-Degree Price Discrimination
Under second-degree price discrimination, firms charge the maximum price consumers are willing to pay for different blocks of output. Revenue to the firm equals area $0P_3CQ_3$ plus area Q_3EDQ_2 plus area Q_2FBQ_1.

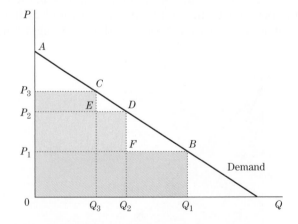

[19] Thomas T. Nagle and John E. Hogan, *The Strategy and Tactics of Pricing: A Guide to Growing More Profitably*, 4th ed. (Upper Saddle River, NJ: Pearson Prentice Hall, 2006), 65.

revenue to the firm is the area $0P_3CQ_3$ plus the area Q_3EDQ_2 plus the area Q_2FBQ_1, or the area of the three blocks underneath the demand curve. This area, which results from second-degree price discrimination, is larger than the area $0P_1BQ_1$, the revenue obtained by charging a single price for all units, but less than area $0ABQ_1$, the revenue from first-degree price discrimination. Electric utilities have used this form of price discrimination by charging different rates for various blocks of kilowatt hours of electricity.

Figure 10.5 and Table 10.4 show the numerical example of second-degree price discrimination. The profit-maximizing quantity with a single price is five units in Table 10.4. Assume now that the first three units can be sold at a price of $9 and the remaining two units at a price of $7. Total revenue is $27 for the first three units and $14 for the last two units, or a total of $41. Profit is now $31. Revenue and profit are greater than when a single price is charged, but less than under first-degree price discrimination.

For second-degree price discrimination to be successful, firms must prevent consumers from combining their demand in order to take advantage of lower prices that could be offered for quantity sales. In Europe, neighboring households often form a purchasing alliance to obtain quantity discounts for the purchase of home heating oil. They then convince the driver to unofficially deliver the oil to their individual homes, a strategy that has saved up to 9 percent on their heating bills. Even after including a tip for the driver's cooperation, this strategy can save consumers money and thwart the intended price discrimination.[20]

Third-Degree Price Discrimination **Third-degree price discrimination** is the most common form of price discrimination, in which firms separate markets according to the price elasticity of demand and charge a higher price (relative to cost) in the market with the most inelastic demand. There are different prices in different markets, but each consumer in a given market pays a constant amount for each unit purchased. This is the case of the airlines discussed above. We illustrate third-degree price discrimination with two markets in Figure 10.6, assuming that marginal cost is constant and equal in both markets and that demand is relatively more inelastic in Market 1 and more elastic in Market 2.

As we discussed with regard to Equation 10.8, profit maximization in each market is achieved where marginal revenue equals marginal cost in that market. Figure 10.6 shows a relatively inelastic demand curve, D_1, with its marginal revenue curve, MR_1, and a relatively more elastic demand curve, D_2, with its marginal revenue curve, MR_2. Quantity Q_1 maximizes profits for Market 1, while Q_2 maximizes profits for Market 2, as

Third-degree price discrimination
A pricing strategy under which firms with market power separate markets according to the price elasticity of demand and charge a higher price (relative to cost) in the market with the more inelastic demand.

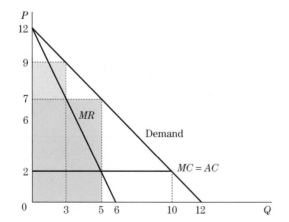

FIGURE 10.5
Profit Maximization and Second-Degree Price Discrimination
Under second-degree price discrimination, the first three units are sold at a price of $9, while the second two units are sold at a price of $7. Total revenue is $41. This strategy adds $6 to revenue and profit compared to charging a single price.

[20] Dolan and Simon, *Power Pricing*, 184–88.

FIGURE 10.6

Third-Degree Price Discrimination

Under third-degree price discrimination, firms separate markets according to the price elasticity of demand and charge a higher price (relative to cost) in the market with the more inelastic demand.

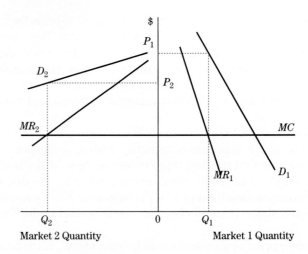

$MR = MC$ in each market at these output levels. The optimal price in each market is that price on the demand curve that corresponds to the profit-maximizing level of output, P_1 in Market 1 and P_2 in Market 2. As you see in Figure 10.6, the optimal price in Market 1, P_1, is higher than the optimal price in Market 2, P_2. Third-degree price discrimination results in a higher price being charged in the market with the relatively more inelastic demand. Charging the same price in both markets would result in lower profit because marginal revenue would not equal marginal cost in both markets at the levels of output corresponding to that common price.

Figure 10.7 and Table 10.5 illustrate the numerical example of third-degree price discrimination. In this case, the firm is able to separate its customers into two markets, the first with demand curve $Q_1 = 12 - P_1$ or $P_1 = 12 - Q_1$ and the second with demand curve $Q_2 = 20 - 2P_2$ or $P_2 = 10 - 0.5Q_2$. Marginal cost is again assumed to be constant, equal to 2, and equal to average cost. The calculation of maximum profit in each market is shown in Table 10.5.

Third-degree price discrimination results in a price of $7 being charged in Market 1 and a price of $6 being charged in Market 2. Market 1 has the relatively more inelastic demand curve, while the demand curve in Market 2 is relatively more elastic.[21] Thus, third-degree price discrimination results in a higher price being charged in the market

FIGURE 10.7

Profit Maximization and Third-Degree Price Discrimination

The firm will charge a higher price of $7 in Market 1, where demand is relatively more inelastic, and a lower price of $6 in Market 2, where demand is relatively more elastic.

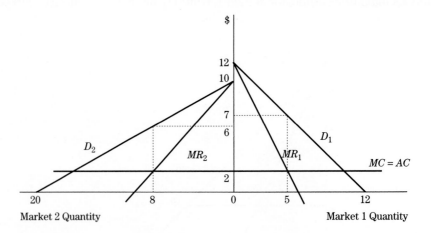

---

[21] Picking a common price of $6 for both markets and using the point price elasticity of demand formula from Chapter 3, the price elasticity in Market 1 is $[P/(P - a)] = [6/(6 - 12)] = -1.0$. In Market 2, the price elasticity is $[6/(6 - 10)] = -1.5$. Price elasticity is greater in Market 2 than in Market 1.

TABLE 10.5 Numerical Example of Profit Maximization and Third-Degree Price Discrimination

MARKET 1	MARKET 2
$Q_1 = 12 - P_1$ or $P_1 = 12 - Q_1$	$Q_2 = 20 - 2P_2$ or $P_2 = 10 - 0.5Q_2$
$MR_1 = 12 - 2Q_1$	$MR_2 = 10 - Q_2$
$MC = AC = 2$	$MC = AC = 2$
$MR_1 = MC$	$MR_2 = MC$
$12 - 2Q_1 = 2$	$10 - Q_2 = 2$
$Q_1 = 5$	$Q_2 = 8$
$P_1 = \$7$	$P_2 = \$6$
$TR_1 = (P_1)(Q_1 = (\$7)(5) = \$35$	$TR_2 = (P_2)(Q_2) = (\$6)(8) = \$48$
$TC_1 = (AC)(Q_1) = (\$2)(5) = \$10$	$TC_2 = (AC)(Q_2) = (\$2)(8) = \$16$
$\pi_1 = TR_1 - TC_1 = \$25$	$\pi_2 = TR_2 - TC_2 = \$32$
If $P_1 = \$6, Q_1 = 6$	If $P_2 = \$7, Q_2 = 6$
$TR_1 = (\$6)(6) = \$36$	$TR_2 = (\$7)(6) = \$42$
$TC_1 = (\$2)(6) = \$12$	$TC_2 = (\$2)(6) = \$12$
$\pi_1 = \$36 - \$12 = \$24$	$\pi_2 = \$42 - \$12 = \$30$

with relatively more inelastic demand. If the same price were charged in both markets, overall profit would decrease. Table 10.5 shows that charging a price of $6 in Market 1 would lower profit from $25 to $24, while charging a price of $7 in Market 2 would lower profit from $32 to $30.

Price Discrimination and Managerial Decision Making

There are numerous examples of real-world price-discrimination strategies that are based on the theoretical models presented in the previous section. The goal of these strategies is to earn more revenue for the firm than would be possible by charging the same price to all customers or for all units of the product. In many cases, this result is achieved by turning the consumer surplus the customer receives from a single-price policy into revenue for the firm through the price-discrimination strategy.

Personalized Pricing First-degree price discrimination has been called **personalized pricing** because the goal of the strategy is to determine how much each individual customer is willing to pay for the product and to charge him or her accordingly.[22] For example, Lexis-Nexis, the online database provider, is able to charge customers different prices based on the type and size of the subscribing organization, what databases are accessed and when, how much they are used, and whether information is printed or just viewed on the screen. Scanner technologies combined with the use of frequent-shopper cards allow grocery stores to monitor the buying habits and price sensitivity of individual customers for all the products they purchase. Automatic coupons, which lower the price for that customer, can be printed with the sales receipt for either the product purchased or relevant substitute or complementary goods. Grocery-industry veteran analyst Patrick Kiernan notes that "pricing is moving

Personalized pricing
Another name for first-degree price discrimination, in which the strategy is to determine how much each individual customer is willing to pay for the product and to charge him or her accordingly.

---

[22] Much of the following discussion is based on Carl Shapiro and Hal R. Varian, *Information Rules: A Strategic Guide to the Network Economy* (Boston: Harvard Business School Press, 1999). Personalized pricing, group pricing, and versioning are all terms developed by Shapiro and Varian. These issues have been updated in Hal R. Varian, Joseph Farrell, and Carl Shapiro, *The Economics of Information Technology, An Introduction* (Cambridge: Cambridge University Press, 2004).

from the product to the store to the individual consumer." He argues that soon the only people paying the posted or "insult price" at the grocery store will be newcomers to the store or individuals who value their privacy so highly that they will not use a frequent-shopper card to take advantage of the selective price reductions.[23]

The Internet offers many opportunities for personalized pricing. Amazon.com tracks the purchases of its customers, adjusts prices, and recommends additional related books in subsequent sessions. Computer companies use e-mail to announce special promotions for certain customers. Online pricing can reduce the costs of reprinting catalogs to adjust the prices of items in oversupply for given customers.

Analysts have estimated that up to 50 percent of online retailers are also using some type of sophisticated promotional targeting. Overstock.com has been displaying several thousand different promotions ranging from free shipping offers to discounted products to different visitors based on 40 attributes related to the shopper's session, including time of day as well as the shopper's presumed gender. eBay Inc. displays different homepages to shoppers based on their previous viewing habits while other customers are targeted by geography. Companies have examined keywords used on search engines such as Yahoo or Google to try to determine what offers are likely to be popular. Discounts that are targeted to first-time buyers mean that repeat customers may end up paying higher prices.[24]

Although many thought that the Internet might change the entire nature of retailing, there is some evidence that online retailing may be evolving into a competitive industry with low profit margins, similar to traditional offline retailing. In September 2000, Amazon.com faced a hostile consumer reaction when its customers learned through online chat boards that they were paying different prices for the same DVD movies. This policy was the result of a direct market test to gauge consumer price sensitivity. Amazon.com was forced to announce it would refund the difference between the highest and lowest prices offered in the market test. Even though this type of experimentation is undertaken on a regular basis in the real economy through differential catalog pricing, offline consumers are much less likely to be aware of these traditional retailing tactics.[25] Still, as we discussed in Chapter 8, the Internet does present online retailers with a number of opportunities to generate market power and gain some control over prices.

Group pricing
Another name for third-degree price discrimination, in which different prices are charged to different groups of customers based on their underlying price elasticity of demand.

Group Pricing   Third-degree price discrimination can be termed **group pricing** because it is based on the underlying differences in price elasticities among different groups of consumers. Dell Computer Corporation has made extensive use of this pricing strategy. In June 2001, its Latitude L400 ultralight laptop was listed at $2,307 on the company's Web page directed to small businesses, at $2,228 for sales to health care companies, and at $2,072 for sales to state and local governments.[26] Dell sales personnel continually canvassed their customers about their buying plans, their willingness to pay for new technology, and the options the customers were considering with Dell's rivals.

The company's price-discriminating strategy was aided by the company's close control over its costs of production at this time. Dell expected its suppliers to pass any cost reductions on to the company so that the reductions could be incorporated into Dell's pricing strategy. However, as we discussed in the opening article of Chapter 8, changes in consumer preferences and the nature of the competition in the personal computer market worked against Dell since this time period.

---

[23] David Wessel, "How Technology Tailors Price Tags," *Wall Street Journal*, June 21, 2001.
[24] Jessica E. Vascellaro, "Online Retailers Are Watching You," *Wall Street Journal*, November 28, 2006.
[25] David P. Hamilton, "The Price Isn't Right," *Wall Street Journal*, February 12, 2001.
[26] Gary McWilliams, "Dell Fine-Tunes Its PC Pricing to Gain Edge in Slow Market," *Wall Street Journal*, June 8, 2001.

Refinery officials have followed a similar strategy of using information on demand and elasticity to develop what the industry calls "zone pricing" for gasoline.[27] With this strategy, refineries charge dealers in different areas varying wholesale prices based on secret formulas that involve location, affluence of the customers in the area, and an estimate of what the local market will bear. The use of zone pricing can result in differential prices for gas stations that are located only a few miles apart. These stations may pay different prices even though they are supplied by the same refinery. It is estimated that Shell Oil has more than 120 zones in the state of Maryland alone. The price differences can change rapidly in response to changes in market conditions. Gasoline industry analysts have argued that there are three categories of gasoline consumers: "pricers, who will switch for a penny difference; switchers, who will do the same for two to three cents difference; and loyalists who follow the same patterns and may not even look at price."[28] Consumer behavior also varies by grade of gasoline. Price elasticity estimates of -6.0, -4.5, and -3.0 have been calculated for regular, mid-grade, and premium gasoline, respectively.[29]

Differential pricing on the basis of location is used in a variety of industries.[30] Health care professionals may have multiple offices in various parts of a city with varying fee schedules. Grocery chains often classify their stores by intensity of competition and use lower markups in those areas with more intense competition. Ski resorts near Denver typically use purchase location to segment the sales of lift tickets. Tickets purchased slope side are the most expensive because they are typically purchased by more affluent customers staying in the slope-side hotels and condos. Tickets cost approximately 10 percent less in the nearby town of Dillon, where there are cheaper accommodations. In Denver itself tickets can be purchased at grocery stores and self-serve gas stations for 20 percent discounts. These are attractive to area residents who know the market and are more price sensitive.

Pricing by location is also used by local governments to solve the problem of the lack of parking spaces in densely populated areas.[31] Seattle has abolished free street parking in a neighborhood just north of downtown, while London has meters that charge as much as $10 per hour. San Francisco has installed hundreds of street sensors to record the "parking events" across 200 parking spots. This technology would allow the city to charge the same rates as private lots for spaces near the stadium during a Giants game. The city has installed new kiosks that take credit cards as well as cash and increased the flat meter rate of $2 per hour to a four-hour rolling rate. This policy applies to areas with highly inelastic demand for parking spaces, while parking is likely to remain free and unrestricted in low-density areas and many residential neighborhoods.

Officials who manage the Eurotunnel, which allows customers to drive between Folkestone, England, and Calais, France, for a flat price, also use price discrimination. Prices that allow a customer to travel at any time of day are twice as high as those during the off-peak evening and night periods. Rates increase with the time elapsed between the outbound and return trips on the assumption that customers are willing to pay more to have their car with them on longer stays in the other country.[32]

Further Rationale for Group Pricing   Two other reasons for managers to use group pricing to attract additional customers are consumer **lock-in** and **network externalities**. Newspapers such as the *Wall Street Journal* offer reduced-rate student subscriptions to attract readers early in their careers, build

Lock-in
Achieving brand loyalty and a stable consumer base for a product by making it expensive for consumers to switch to a substitute product.

Network externalities
These result when the value an individual places on a good is a function of how many other people also use that good.

---

[27] Alexei Barrionuevo, "Secret Formulas Set Prices for Gasoline," *Wall Street Journal*, March 20, 2000.
[28] Keith Reid, "The Pricing Equation: Which Price Is Right?" *National Petroleum News* 92 (February 2000): 17.
[29] Ibid., 17.
[30] This discussion is based on Nagle and Hogan, *The Strategy and Tactics of Pricing.*
[31] Conor Dougherty, "The Parking Fix," *Wall Street Journal*, February 3, 2007.
[32] Nagle and Hogan, *The Strategy and Tactics of Pricing.*

loyalty, and make at least the psychological costs of switching to other news media relatively high. This is an example of consumer lock-in. Airline frequent flyer programs are another example of group price discrimination that may attract the customers, while the frequent flyer points raise the cost of switching to another airline. Network externalities arise when the value that an individual places on a good is a function of how many other people also use that good. Computer software is one of the best examples of this concept, given that businesses can function much more efficiently if everyone is using the same software. Selling the software at reduced prices to different groups or even giving it away may be a sound price-discrimination strategy if it enables that software to become the industry standard that all firms desire to use.

Versioning
Offering different versions of a product to different groups of customers at various prices, with the versions designed to meet the needs of the specific groups.

Versioning   **Versioning** is a price-discrimination strategy that has become much more widespread with the emergence of the information economy. Under this strategy, different versions of a product are offered to different groups of customers at various prices, with the versions designed to meet the needs of the specific groups. The advantage of this strategy is that consumers reveal their willingness to pay for the different versions of the product through the choices they make. Managers are able to learn about their customers without getting involved with the detailed consumer surveys or direct market tests discussed in Chapter 4.

Book publishers have long used versioning when they publish a hardcover edition of a book and then wait a number of months before the cheaper paperback edition is released. Those customers who must read the latest novel as soon as it is published will pay more to purchase the hardcover edition, while others with less intense preferences will wait and read the softcover edition. The same approach applies to first- and second-run movie theaters and the home video market.

Offering different versions of a product to casual versus more experienced users is a strategy used by Intuit for its Quicken financial software. Basic Quicken is available for approximately $20, whereas Quicken Deluxe sells for approximately $60. Product versions may also differ by their speed of operation, flexibility of use, and product capability and by the technical support offered for the product. Selling both online and offline versions of books and other publications is another variant of this strategy. In many cases, the online version is free, but is less convenient to use. Companies offer the online version to stimulate sales of the offline product.[33]

Bundling
Selling multiple products as a bundle where the price of the bundle is less than the sum of the prices of the individual products or where the bundle reduces the dispersion in willingness to pay.

Bundling   **Bundling** is a variant of product versioning in which the products are sold separately, but also as a bundle, where the price of the bundle is less than the sum of the prices of the individual products. Microsoft Office bundles its products together, but also sells them separately. If two products are bundled, such as a word processing package and a spreadsheet, the strategy is to get consumers to purchase both products because the incremental price for the second product is less than what it would be if they purchased the products separately. The firm attracts sales that it might not otherwise obtain with the individual pricing of the products because some customers will pay the small incremental price, but not the full price of the additional product.

Bundling is also a profitable strategy if it reduces the dispersion in the willingness to pay for the products, particularly if the dispersion is less for the bundle than for the individual components of the bundle. We illustrate this case in Table 10.6.

Table 10.6 shows the maximum price two customers are willing to pay for a computer and a printer. If the firm sells the components separately, it should charge a price of $800 for the computer and $250 for the printer. In this case, both consumers will buy both the computer and the printer, and the firm will earn revenue totaling $2,100 [($800 × 2) + ($250 × 2)]. Charging a higher price for either component means that

---

[33] For a detailed discussion of all these strategies, see Shapiro and Varian, *Information Rules*, 37–80.

TABLE 10.6 Bundling

CUSTOMER	COMPUTER	PRINTER
1	$1,000	$250
2	$800	$300

only one customer will purchase each component. However, if the firm bundled the components and sold the bundle for $1,100, each customer would purchase the bundle, and the firm would receive $2,200 in revenue. Bundling reduces the dispersion in willingness to pay. If the firm could price discriminate between the two customers and charge each a different price, total revenue would increase to $2,350. Bundling becomes an optimal strategy if the firm must charge all customers the same price.

Coupons and Sales: Promotional Pricing   The use of coupons and sales, or **promotional pricing**, is another example of price discrimination. These are effective pricing strategies because they focus on different price elasticities of demand, but also impose costs on consumers. Those individuals who clip coupons or watch newspaper advertisements for sales are more price sensitive than consumers who do not engage in these activities, and they are also willing to pay the additional costs of the time and inconvenience of clipping the coupons and monitoring the sale periods. This strategy is beneficial for the firm because it does not have to lower the price of its products for all customers and lose additional revenue.

Promotional pricing
Using coupons and sales to lower the price of the product for those customers willing to incur the costs of using these devices as opposed to lowering the price of the product for all customers.

Firms have become much more adept at using sales or markdowns to clear out excess inventory by using software designed to determine the size, number, and timing of the optimal markdowns of the price. This issue has always been a dilemma for retail firms, who do not want to sacrifice revenues by lowering the price too soon, but who do not want to be left with excess inventory that may never sell at the end of the season. Marked-down goods accounted for only 8 percent of department store sales in the 1970s, but increased to around 20 percent by 2001. The software programs used by retail firms are similar to the yield management programs that the airlines use for price discrimination on airline seats.

For example, ShopKo Stores, a discount chain system similar to Target Corporation, has used the Markdown Optimizer software to test the markdown strategy for 300 of its products. The company ended up using fewer markdowns than it had previously, but increased its sales of the test products by 14 percent compared with a year earlier. The gross profit margin for this merchandise increased by 24 percent, and the company sold 13 percent more of each product at the regular price than it had previously. Predicted markdowns ranged from 25.7 percent at high-volume superstores to 46.3 percent in the lowest-volume stores. Use of the program not only took advantage of differing price elasticities of demand, but also saved labor costs by having fewer markdowns. ShopKo estimated that it cost 18 cents to change the price on a single garment tag and 24 cents to change a shelf label.[34]

Two-Part Pricing   Another price-discrimination strategy that managers can use to increase their profits is **two-part pricing**. With this strategy, consumers are charged a fixed fee for the right to purchase the product and then a variable fee that is a function of the number of units purchased. This is a pricing strategy used by buyers clubs, athletic facilities, and travel resorts where customers pay a membership or admission fee and then a per-unit charge for the various products, services, or activities as members.

Two-part pricing
Charging consumers a fixed fee for the right to purchase a product and then a variable fee that is a function of the number of units purchased.

---

[34] Amy Merrick, "Retailers Try to Get Leg Up on Markdowns with New Software," *Wall Street Journal*, August 7, 2001.

FIGURE 10.8
Profit Maximization and Two-Part Pricing
With two-part pricing, firms charge consumers a fixed fee for the right to purchase a product and then a variable fee that is a function of the number of units purchased.

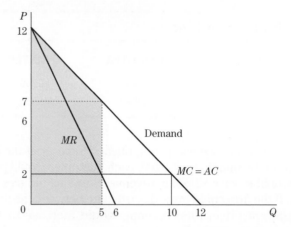

This strategy can be more profitable for a firm than simply charging the profit-maximizing price for all units of the product or service. To demonstrate this outcome, we draw again on the numerical example presented earlier in Table 10.4 and Figure 10.3. In that example, which we now show in Figure 10.8, we determined that $25 is the maximum profit that can be earned when all five units of output are sold at the profit-maximizing price of $7.

Suppose instead that the firm sets the price equal to the marginal and average cost of $2. The consumer now demands 10 units of the product. The total revenue of $20 just equals total cost, so the firm earns no profit on these units. However, the amount of consumer surplus at a price of $2 is the triangular area underneath the demand curve, but above the price line. The numerical value of the consumer surplus in this triangular area is $(0.5)(10)(12 - 2) = \$50$ (the area of the triangle). This represents the difference between the consumer's total willingness to pay for the 10 units and the amount actually paid. Thus, the firm can charge a fixed fee of up to $50 for the right to purchase the product at a price of $2 per unit. As long as this fee is greater than $25 (the maximum profit earned under the single-price strategy), the firm's profits are greater with the two-part pricing strategy than with the single-price strategy. As with first-degree price discrimination or personalized pricing, this strategy attempts to turn consumer surplus into revenue for the firm. However, with any price-discrimination strategy, managers must also evaluate the administrative costs of that strategy compared with the single-price approach.

Price Discrimination Summary   Table 10.7 summarizes the types of price discrimination we have just discussed.

Unsuccessful Price Discrimination   Price discrimination may not be successful if the strategy causes substantial consumer resentment or a negative reaction from competitors. Coca-Cola Company's testing in 1999 of a vending machine that would automatically raise prices for its drinks in periods of increased and more inelastic demand, such as extremely hot weather, is such an example.[35] This price discrimination would have been achieved through the use of a temperature sensor and a computer chip. The process could also work in the opposite direction, thus lowering the price of a can of soda during periods of slow demand. Coke officials proposed this strategy because vending machines had become an increasingly important source of profits for both Coke and its competitor, Pepsico.

As might be expected, the proposed strategy drew many negative comments about its fairness and appropriateness. One beverage analyst commented, "What next? A machine that X-rays people's pockets to find out how much change they have and

---

[35] Constance L. Hayes, "Variable-Price Coke Machine Being Tested," *New York Times*, October 28, 1999.

TABLE 10.7 Types of Price Discrimination

TYPE	DESCRIPTION
First-degree or personalized pricing	Charging each individual the maximum amount he or she is willing to pay for each unit of the product.
Second-degree	Charging the maximum price consumers are willing to pay for different blocks of output.
Third-degree or group pricing	Separating the markets into different groups of consumers and charging a higher price (relative to cost) in the market with the more inelastic demand. Sometimes called zone pricing.
Versioning	Offering different versions of a product to different groups of customers at various prices, with the versions designed to meet the needs of the specific groups.
Bundling	Selling products separately, but also as a bundle, where the price of the bundle is less than the sum of the prices of the individual products.
Promotional pricing	Using coupons and sales to lower the price to customers with more elastic demands, but also imposing costs on these customers.
Two-part pricing	Charging consumers a fixed fee for the right to purchase a product and then a variable fee that is a function of the number of units purchased.

raises the price accordingly?" Pepsi officials also took advantage of this move to develop a counter strategy: "We believe that machines that raise prices in hot weather exploit consumers who live in warm climates. . . . At Pepsi, we are focused on innovations that make it easier for consumers to buy a soft drink, not harder."[36]

Price discrimination based on observation may also be counterproductive. Hotel managers often believe they can segment the market by being responsive to those customers who complain about the price. This strategy would involve offering a regular room rate first, then going to a small discount such as one based on an AAA membership if the customer resists, and finally, if there is excess capacity, finding a special block of discounted rooms. However, customers who complain are rarely the most price-sensitive. Business travelers love to negotiate and brag to each other about the great deals they obtain. Customers who do not complain are more likely to be leisure travelers who are more price-sensitive, but who do not know the game of bargaining. They will simply hang up the phone and call an economy motel.[37]

Marketing and Price Discrimination

Numerous examples of price discrimination strategies also exist in the marketing literature, although they may be called by different names. For example, in *Marketing Management*, Philip Kotler discusses discriminatory pricing as presented above, but then devotes other sections of his pricing chapter to geographical pricing, price discounts, promotional pricing, two-part pricing, and product-bundling pricing, all of which are examples of price discrimination.[38] Other marketing texts and articles have similar coverage.[39] Market researchers Dolan and Simon cite the case of the differential price elasticities of large versus small customers purchasing industrial

---

[36] Ibid.

[37] Nagle and Hogan, *The Strategy and Tactics of Pricing.*

[38] Kotler, *Marketing Management: The Millennium Edition*, 471–78.

[39] See Kent B. Monroe, *Pricing: Making Profitable Decisions*, 2nd ed. (New York: McGraw-Hill, 1990); and Gerard J. Tellis, "Beyond the Many Faces of Price: An Integration of Pricing Strategies," *Journal of Marketing* 50 (October 1986): 146–60. More theoretical and conceptual discussions of these issues are found in Gary L. Lilien, Philip Kotler, and K. Sridhar Moorthy, *Marketing Models* (Englewood Cliffs, N.J.: Prentice Hall, 1992); and Timothy M. Devinney, *Issues in Pricing: Theory and Research* (Lexington, Mass.: Lexington Books, 1988).

air-pollution test equipment.[40] Large customers, those who purchased over 1,000 units, were estimated to have a price elasticity of –2.20, while small buyers, those who purchased less than 100 units, had an elasticity of –1.54. These differences in elasticities resulted in firms charging medium-sized customers 24 percent less and large customers 36 percent less than small customers. Dolan and Simon note that firms have to be careful when using price-discrimination strategies, as they may be pricing very close to the maximum price that consumers are willing to pay.

A marketing analysis can often build on the economics of markup pricing and price discrimination to develop more effective competitive strategies and avoid either forgone profits or noncompetitive prices.[41] For example, when Glaxo introduced Zantac ulcer medication in 1983 to compete with SmithKline Beecham's Tagamet, the number one ulcer medicine and the best-selling drug in the world, conventional markup pricing above cost suggested a lower price for Zantac than Tagamet. However, a marketing analysis of the perceived value to the consumer resulted in a price 50 percent higher than for Tagamet. Zantac had a superior product performance with an easier schedule of doses, fewer side effects, and fewer reactions with other drugs. This analysis proved correct, as Zantac became the market leader within four years.

In a second case, Northern Telecom believed its Norstar telephone system was superior to the competition, but could not be sold at the higher price that a conventional markup would dictate. The Norstar system was priced comparably to its competitors, and the company then examined its costs to determine how to make a profit. As Northern's competitors lowered their prices, Northern was able to decrease its costs so that both its profit margins and its share of the market increased.

Macroeconomics and Pricing Policies

The ability of different firms to mark up price above cost based on the price elasticity of demand is also influenced by overall macroeconomic conditions. The long-run economic expansion in the late 1990s made consumers less cost conscious and more value and status conscious. Thus, their demand for many products became more price inelastic. In May 2000, the Federal Reserve policy of higher interest rates to slow the economy was influenced by the perception that firms were beginning to be able to raise prices and maintain them. The economy appeared to be heating up enough to start another round of inflation.

In 1999, Johns Manville Corporation attempted to raise prices on its insulation and roofing products, but was unable to do so because customers threatened to switch suppliers. A year later, as economic growth was sustained, the company raised prices by as much as 5 percent on many products. UCB Chemical Corporation of Smyrna, Georgia, was also able to raise the prices of its inputs for inks, packaging, and fiber optics in spring 2000 for the first time since 1997. While some of these price increases resulted from passing higher costs of production along to consumers, the firms' increased ability to raise prices from greater and more inelastic demand also played a major role.[42]

This ability to raise prices, however, differed significantly among sectors of the economy. During this period of time, Eastman Kodak Company and Sears, Roebuck either tried to raise prices that could not be maintained or did not

---

[40] Dolan and Simon, *Power Pricing*, 174–75.

[41] The following examples are drawn from Robert J. Dolan, "How Do You Know When the Price Is Right?" *Harvard Business Review* (September–October 1995): 174–83.

[42] Jacob M. Schlesinger and Yochi J. Dreazen, "Producers Start to Raise Prices, Stirring Fear in Inflation Fighters," *Wall Street Journal*, May 16, 2000.

attempt to increase prices. Delta Airlines also found itself in this situation, given the availability of information on the Internet about prices of competitor airlines. Demand for other products became more inelastic because there had been decreases in the number of producers in several industries. Consolidation in the paper industry allowed P. H. Glatfelter Company of York, Pennsylvania, to raise prices 15 percent after five years of no increases.

With the slowing economy in 2007 and 2008, firms were again faced with a decreased ability to raise prices and with the possibility of having to offer discounts even if they cut into profit margins. The chief economist of the International Council of Shopping Centers noted that retailers "need to think about promoting more heavily to try to drive traffic." High-end shoppers were also focusing more on bargains. Although Saks Inc. reported a 4.1 percent increase in same-store sales in January 2008, the company noted that customers were shifting more of their spending to sales events. Discount chains and warehouse clubs performed relatively better during this period than did department stores and specialty-apparel chains.[43]

The ability of firms to raise prices in the face of demand and cost changes has been a key issue in our microeconomic models of market structure. The models of imperfect competition imply that firms would change their prices as either demand or cost conditions changed. Much empirical data question this result.

The survey of firms' pricing and cost behavior by Alan Blinder and his colleagues that we discussed in Chapter 5 indicated that the median number of price changes for a typical product in a given year is only 1.4 and that half of all price changes occur no more than once a year.[44] Price changes typically lag about three months behind changes in either demand or cost.

In the survey, the most important reason firms gave for price rigidity was the fear that other firms would not follow price increases by a given firm. We discussed this behavior in Chapter 9 on oligopoly. Firms also found other ways to clear the market in response to changing demand and cost conditions, such as varying delivery lags, sales effort, product quality, and quality of service. These forms of nonprice competition, which act as substitutes for price changes, were important in most sectors of the economy surveyed by Blinder and his colleagues. Firms may also have tacit or implicit contracts with their customers not to raise prices when markets are tight. These implicit contracts may be intended to reduce consumers' search and shopping costs, or they may result from a concern for "fairness" in the pricing process.

Recent studies of pricing changes in both the United States and Europe have found that prices of many goods and services do not respond immediately to changing demand and supply conditions.[45] Prices seem to change far less frequently in some European countries (Austria, Belgium, Finland, France, Germany, Italy, Luxembourg, the Netherlands, Portugal, and Spain) than in the United States, with the average duration of a price spell ranging from four to five quarters in Europe, twice as long as in the United States. The frequency of price changes

---

[43] Amy Merrick and Kevin Kingsbury, "Retail Squeeze Felt Far Beyond Malls," *Wall Street Journal*, February 8, 2008.

[44] Alan S. Blinder, Elie R. D. Canetti, David E. Lebow, and Jeremy B. Rudd, *Asking About Prices: A New Approach to Understanding Price Stickiness* (New York: Russell Sage Foundation, 1998), 84–105

[45] Emmanuel Dhyne, Luis J. Alvarez, Herve Le Bihan, Giovanni Veronese, Daniel Dias, Johannes Hoffmann, Nicole Jonker, Patrick Lunnemann, Fabio Rumler, and Jouko Vilmunen, "Price Changes in the Euro Area and the United States: Some Facts from Individual Consumer Price Data," *Journal of Economic Perspectives* 20 (Spring 2006): 171–92; Luis J. Alvarez, Emmanuel Dhyne, Marco Hoeberichts, Claudia Kwapil, Herve Le Bihan, Patrick Lunnemann, Fernando Martins, Roberto Sabbatini, Harald Stahl, Philip Vermeulen, and Jouko Vilmunen, "Sticky Prices in the Euro Area: A Summary of New Micro-Evidence," *Journal of the European Economic Association* 4 (April–May 2006): 575–84; Campbell Leith and Jim Malley, "A Sectoral Analysis of Price-Setting Behavior in U.S. Manufacturing Industries," *The Review of Economics and Statistics* 89 (May 2007): 335–42.

varies substantially across products. Energy products and unprocessed food have frequent price changes, while processed food, nonenergy industrial goods, and services have infrequent changes. Goods with relatively large inputs of labor are subject to less frequent price adjustments. There is no evidence of general downward price rigidity, although price decreases are less common in services. Price changes are generally not synchronized across products, even within the same country. These studies found that the use of implicit contracts was the most important reason preventing a rapid adjustment of prices. Firms tried not to jeopardize their customer relationships. Other explanations for the lack of price adjustments included explicit contracts that were costly to renegotiate, marginal costs that did not vary significantly, and the desire of firms not to change prices unless their competitors did so. These behaviors that result in price rigidity, or sticky prices, have implications for the macroeconomic analysis of the economy that we discuss in the second half of this text.[46]

Summary

In this chapter, we analyzed how knowledge of the price elasticity of demand for different products or among different groups of customers is fundamental to developing optimal pricing strategies. We illustrated the role of price elasticity in two common pricing strategies: markup pricing and price discrimination. We also highlighted the linkages between the economics of pricing and the role of marketing in developing competitive strategies.

We reviewed cost and profit maximization concepts in this chapter because average and marginal costs form the basis for markup pricing, price discrimination, and profit determination. Managers may have to look at the cost side of their operation to improve profits if they have little ability or are unable to change prices. We also noted that there are a number of reasons why managers may not immediately change their prices in response to changes in demand and cost conditions.

This chapter completes our discussion of the microeconomic topics of demand, pricing, cost, and market structure. We now turn to an analysis of the macroeconomic environment in which firms and managers operate that builds on many of the concepts and issues developed in the first part of the text.

Key Terms

bundling, p. 272

consumer surplus, p. 265

first-degree price
    discrimination, p. 265

group pricing, p. 270

lock-in, p. 271

marginal benefit, p. 264

markup pricing, p. 255

network externalities, p. 271

personalized pricing, p. 269

price discrimination, p. 261

promotional pricing, p. 273

second-degree price
    discrimination, p. 266

third-degree price
    discrimination, p. 267

total benefit, p. 264

two-part pricing, p. 273

versioning, p. 272

---

[46] The increase in online commerce may change these results. In a study comparing online pricing behavior with that of brick-and-mortar stores selling books and CDs that are easily identified by their ISBN codes, the authors found that online menu costs are considerably smaller and therefore price changes are more frequent and in smaller amounts. See Erik Brynjolfsson and Michael Smith, "Frictionless Commerce: A Comparison of Internet and Conventional Retailers," *Management Science* 46 (2000): 563–85.

Exercises

Technical Questions

1. Given each of the following price elasticities, determine whether marginal revenue is positive, negative, or zero.

   a. -5

   b. -1

   c. -0.5

2. Given each of the following price elasticities, calculate the optimal markup.

   a. -15

   b. -8

   c. -3

3. Suppose a firm has a constant marginal cost of $10. The current price of the product is $25, and at that price, it is estimated that the price elasticity of demand is -3.0.

   a. Is the firm charging the optimal price for the product? Demonstrate how you know.

   b. Should the price be changed? If so, how?

4. The individual demand for a slice of pizza at Sam's Pizza is given by $Q_D = 6 - P$. Assume the marginal cost of a slice is constant at $1.00 and the marginal revenue (MR) function is $6 - 2Q$.

   a. What is the profit-maximizing price and quantity if Sam's sells all slices at a single price? What profit per customer will be earned?

   b. Suppose that Sam's decides to sell pizza at cost and charge a fixed price for this option. What quantity will a customer demand at the market price? What is the maximum fixed price Sam's can charge for this option?

5. Suppose that individual demand for a product is given by $Q_D = 1000 - 5P$. Marginal revenue is $MR = 200 - 0.4Q$, and marginal cost is constant at $20. There are no fixed costs.

   a. The firm is considering a quantity discount. The first 400 units can be purchased at a price of $120, and further units can be purchased at a price of $80. How many units will the consumer buy in total?

b. Show that this second-degree price-discrimination scheme is more profitable than a single monopoly price.

6. An airline estimates that the price elasticity of demand for business travelers (who travel on weekdays) is -2, while the price elasticity of demand for vacation travelers (who travel on weekends) is -5. If the airline price discriminates (and costs are the same), what will be the ratio of weekday to weekend prices?

7. A monopolist sells in two geographically divided markets, the East and the West. Marginal cost is constant at $50 in both markets. Demand and marginal revenue in each market are as follows:

$$Q_E = 900 - 2P_E$$
$$MR_E = 450 - Q_E$$
$$Q_W = 700 - P_W$$
$$MR_W = 700 - 2Q_W$$

   a. Find the profit-maximizing price and quantity in each market.

   b. In which market is demand more elastic?

8. A cable company offers two basic packages: sports and kids, and a combined package. There are three different types of users: parents, sports fans, and generalists. The following table shows the maximum price that each type of consumer is willing to pay for each package.

	Sports Package	Kids Package
Parents	10	50
Sports Fans	50	10
Generalists	40	40

   a. If the cable company offers any one package for $50 or the combined bundled package for $70, who will buy each package?

   b. Explain why the company will make a higher profit with this method than if the bundled package option were not offered.

Application Questions

1. In the current business media, find examples of firms similar to Parker Hannifin Corp. in this chapter's opening news article that changed from pricing based on cost to strategies that also incorporated information on the price elasticity of demand.

2. The following discussion focuses on the change in production and selling strategies of Timken Co.,

the Canton, Ohio, firm that is a major producer of bearings:[47]

> To counter the low prices of imports, Timken Co. in 2003 began bundling its bearings with other parts to provide industrial business customers with products specifically designed for their needs. Timken had begun bundling prelubricated, preassembled bearing packages for automobile manufacturers in the early 1990s. Evidence indicated that companies that sold integrated systems rather than discrete parts to the automobile manufacturers increased their sales. Other industrial customers put the same pressure on Timken in the late 1990s to lower prices, customize, or lose their business to lower-priced foreign suppliers. Manufacturers are increasingly combining a standard part with casings, pins, lubrication, and electronic sensors. Installation, maintenance, and engineering services may also be included.
>
> Suppliers, such as Timken, saw this as a means of increasing profits and making themselves more indispensable to the manufacturers. The strategy also required suppliers to remain in proximity with their customers, another advantage over foreign imports. This type of bundling does require significant research and development and flexible factories to devise new methods of transforming core parts into smart assemblies. The repackaging is more difficult for industrial than automobile customers because the volumes of production are smaller for the former. Timken also had to educate its customers on the variety of new products available.
>
> Timken has an 11 percent share of the world market for bearings. However, imports into the U.S. doubled to $1.4 billion in 2002 compared with $660 million in 1997. Timken believes that the uniqueness of its product helps protect it from foreign competition. However, the company still lobbied the Bush administration to stop what it calls the dumping of bearings at low prices by foreign producers in Japan, Romania, and Hungary.

a. What factors in the economic environment in addition to foreign imports contributed to Timken's new strategy in 2002 and 2003?

b. How does this strategy relate to the discussion of bundling presented in the chapter? What additional factors are presented in this case?

3. The following discussion pertains to the pricing policies of Linear Technology Corp.:[48]

> The semiconductor industry's Linear Technology Corp. has maintained strong profitability by operating at the fringes where competition is low and margins are high. This midsize company makes 7,500 arcane, unglamorous products that solve real-world problems for a long list of customers, including analog chips that are too cheap for customers to haggle over, but perform chores too important to ignore. Many of Linear's chips cost less than 50 cents to build and sell for three to four times as much, but customers seldom complain about the markup.
>
> Linear made a 39% profit on its $1.1 billion sales in 2006, more than five times the average for U.S. industrial companies. However, other bigger chip makers, including Texas Instruments Inc., Richtek Technology Corp. of Taiwan, and Freescale Semiconductor Inc. of Austin, Texas, are now moving into the market and others may follow. Unlike in the digital chip world, in which a single winning design bought by a few big customers can yield huge profits, Linear would rather see its order book packed with small to midsize orders from companies too busy to haggle over prices. Intermec Inc., which makes mobile data scanners, uses Linear chips to obtain extra life from its devices' batteries. The chips' total cost is less than 5% of the materials budget. Performance is crucial for this company; price is not.
>
> Traditionally the dozen or so major analog chip companies have tiptoed around one another's product lines, helping keep profit margins high. Each company established its strength decades ago, making it easy to extend existing product families and deepen relations with longtime customers. "We chip away a little at each others' specialties," says Jerald Fishman, chief executive of Analog Devices. "But there isn't a lot of direct competition."

Discuss how price elasticity of demand influences the pricing strategies of Linear Technology Corp. What market model best describes this industry? Explain.

4. Discuss how the following strategies relate to the price-discrimination principles presented in this chapter.[49]

> Wildeck, Inc., began manufacturing storage-rack protectors used to keep forklifts from damaging

---

[47] Carlos Tejada, "The Allure of Bundling," *Wall Street Journal*, October 7, 2003.

[48] George Anders, "In a Tech Backwater, a Profit Fortress Rises," *Wall Street Journal*, July 10, 2007.

[49] Timothy Aeppel, "Amid Weak Inflation, Firms Turn Creative to Boost Prices," *Wall Street Journal*, September 18, 2002.

the corners of racks on factory floors about five years ago. However, a competitor began producing a similar product made from lighter steel that was priced 15 percent lower. Instead of lowering its price, Wildeck introduced a "lite" version of its protectors that sold for less than the competitor's product. Customers who inquired about the lite version were told the advantages of the heavier-duty product and often ended up buying the original. This strategy helped Wildeck hold its market share and institute a 5 percent price increase.

The Union Pacific railroad developed its "blue streak" service in September 2001 that promised to get shipments from Los Angeles to Atlanta in five days. This strategy allowed the railroad to compete more directly with truckers and charge up to a 40 percent premium over regular rail service. However, the service costs increased only slightly for Union Pacific.

5. Publishers have traditionally sold textbooks at different prices in different areas of the world. For example, a textbook that sells for $70 in the United States might sell for $5 in India.[50] Although the Indian version might be printed on cheaper paper and lack color illustrations, it provides essentially the same information. Indian customers typically cannot afford to pay the U.S. price.

   a. Use the theories of price discrimination presented in this chapter to explain this strategy.
   b. If the publisher decides to sell this textbook online, what problems will this present for the pricing strategy? How might the publisher respond?

6. Tolls on approximately one-third of the 5,000 miles of highway, bridges, and tunnels in the United States increased in 2005.[51] Tolls went from $2.00 to $3.00 on seven bridges in the San Francisco Bay Area. The Pennsylvania Turnpike increased the average fare by 43 percent, while the New York State Thruway increased its tolls by 25 percent for cars and 35 percent for trucks. Tolls on the Thruway were supposed to be removed a decade ago when the bonds that financed the construction of the highway were paid off. However, these plans were changed when state officials decided they wanted the Thruway to finance another highway that is toll-free. For people who want to avoid toll roads, the costs are not insignificant. Alternatives may be less-direct routes that go through densely packed downtowns or sprawling suburbs. The number of cars using the Pennsylvania Turnpike decreased by less than 1 percent after the toll increase. Road officials need to use toll revenue for repairs and maintenance. They are trying to soften the impact of higher tolls with smaller increases for drivers that pay electronically using a transponder mounted on the car windshield that deducts tolls from a customer's prepaid account.

   a. Why are tolls a popular source of revenue from the viewpoint of road officials?
   b. What is the impact of maintaining tolls on the New York State Thruway?
   c. What is the price elasticity of demand for use of the Pennsylvania Turnpike?

---

[50] This example is drawn from Shapiro and Varian, *Information Rules*, 44–45.

[51] Daniel Machalaba, "Steep Increases Set for Toll Roads," *Wall Street Journal*, April 12, 2005.

On the Web

For updated information on the *Wall Street Journal* article at the beginning of the chapter, as well as other relevant links and information, visit the book's Web site at **www.pearsonhighered.com/farnham**

11 Measuring Macroeconomic Activity

This chapter begins Part 2 of the text, where the focus changes from the microeconomic factors influencing managers—prices, costs, and market structure—to factors arising in the larger *macroeconomic* environment, such as the overall level of income and output produced in the economy, the price level, and the level of employment and unemployment. The latter factors are affected by the spending decisions of individuals and organizations throughout the entire economy. Thus, macroeconomic analysis focuses on the aggregate behavior of different sectors of the economy. However, as we noted in Chapter 1, changes in the macro environment affect individual firms and industries through the microeconomic factors of demand, production, cost, and profitability. Industries and firms react to macroeconomic changes by taking actions based on the microeconomic tools we discussed in the first part of the text.

We begin this chapter with the *Wall Street Journal* article "Factory Slowdown Sets Off Alarm; Contraction Shows Limits of Recent Export Strength, Heightens Recession Fears." This article describes the impact of the downturn in overall economic activity in the United States in late 2007 and early 2008 on different manufacturing firms and the strategies these firms developed to cope with changes in the macro environment.

We then describe the framework used to measure overall economic activity or *gross domestic product* (GDP). We use this framework to develop the aggregate macroeconomic model that includes the components in Chapters 11 through 15. We'll then describe commonly used measures of the price level and the level of output and employment in the economy and relate these concepts to the major issues facing policy makers. Although managers cannot influence the macroeconomic environment, they need to understand the policies that change that environment to determine whether they need to modify their competitive strategies.

Factory Slowdown Sets Off Alarm; Contraction Shows Limits of Recent Export Strength, Heightens Recession Fears

by Timothy Aeppel and Sudeep Reddy

Wall Street Journal, *January 3, 2008*

A key measure of U.S. manufacturing contracted sharply in December, in a sign that recent strength in export-related businesses is being swamped by problems in housing and other parts of the domestic economy.

Until now, factories have shown resilience in the face of housing turmoil and high oil prices, in large part because exports of products like airplanes and mining machines helped offset slumping sales of domestically oriented items such as lawn mowers and wallboard. But the latest figures from the factory floor are heightening recession worries and confirm the view that the slowdown is spilling over to a growing list of goods-producing industries.

The Institute for Supply Management reported that its index of factory activity fell to 47.7 in December from 50.8 in November—far lower than most economists were predicting and the lowest reading since April 2003. A reading below 50 indicates contraction. The index of new orders, a gauge for future business, fell even more sharply to 45.7. . . .

The report sent the stock market down sharply and raised new doubts about whether the economy's recent pattern of relying on more export-led growth would keep the broader economy out of recession. It also underscored the widening effect of the credit crunch. The slump in housing and credit problems have chilled consumer spending and appear to be prompting many businesses to curb or delay investments—bad news for factories that make machines and equipment. . . .

A key question looms: Will businesses and consumers pull back further, spurring a broader decline in economic activity? The slump in housing-related sectors, from construction to mortgage finance, is already depressing overall employment. And the latest ISM report showed that export-related activity tumbled last month. That could mean exports are nearing the limit of their ability to offset steep declines in other sectors.

"I think we're looking at a very tough year ahead in manufacturing, and possibly two years," said Dan Ariens, chief executive of Ariens Co., a Brillon, Wis.-based lawn-mower maker. The company's sales are linked partly to housing, since people buying new homes need new yard tools. . . .

Ariens gets about 30% of its sales from Canada and other countries where sales have enjoyed a nice boost from the declining dollar. "But the other 70% of our business is flat or down," he said.

Factories outside the U.S. face a slowdown that is less severe. J.P. Morgan, which publishes a monthly index for global manufacturing activity, announced yesterday that this measure fell 0.8 point to 51.4—the lowest reading in more than four years. "Manufacturing activity in Canada, the U.K., and the euro area also is being buffeted by tighter credit conditions, but the head winds are less intense" than in the U.S., said economist David Hensley.

In many ways, the picture for U.S. manufacturing is the inverse of the last big slowdown—when manufacturing suffered a deeper, longer decline than the rest of the economy. In 2000, factories faced a strong dollar that choked off exports and a huge overhang of inventories and capacity.

This time, factories had been a bright spot. David Rosenberg, North American economist at Merrill Lynch, said the decline in the dollar has "supercharged the competitiveness" of manufacturers, prompting them to shift toward exports. At the same time, more foreign producers are setting up shop or expanding in the U.S., boosting direct foreign investment in the U.S. by more than 11% in the past year.

The question for manufacturers is whether the strength in foreign markets will be eclipsed by growing problems at home. Most of what is made by U.S. factories is consumed domestically, so exports can only go so far in taking up slack.

Still, some manufacturers remain relatively upbeat. "Obviously there are some potholes, but I'm actually optimistic," said James Lekin, CEO of M.S. Willett Inc. in Cockeysville, Md., a closely held metal fabricator and tool-and-die producer.

M.S. Willett has seen a falloff in orders from Harley-Davidson Inc., one of its biggest customers. But that has been offset by growth in other business, mainly from big multinationals with growing export businesses. "We're also directly exporting more ourselves to our existing customer base," said Mr. Lekin, who recently sent machinery to Denmark, Canada, and Brazil.

But exports aren't lifting all boats. USG Corp., the Chicago-based maker of wallboard, recently warned that falling demand for housing as well as softening repair and remodeling markets is "significantly reducing" sales and profits. The company closed factories and cut 1,100 jobs and said it is "prepared to make further adjustments to our operations as necessary."

Similar problems are visible at furniture factories, appliance companies and metal fabricators closely linked to housing and the domestic auto industry.

Residential-construction spending fell 2.4% in November to an annualized $492 billion, the Commerce Department said yesterday. This is down 17.5% from a year ago. Nonresidential construction rose more than 2% in November. Public-sector construction also increased, but how long that will continue remains in doubt, since many state and local governments face budget cuts because of declines in real-estate taxes.

Case for Analysis

Impact of Macro Environment Changes on Manufacturing Firms

This article focuses on the impact of the slowing economy in 2007 and 2008 on the U.S. manufacturing sector. A key measure of factory activity from the Institute for Supply Management (ISM) fell lower than most economists expected and into a range indicating a contraction of the economy. The concern was that the demand for manufacturing output, which had been sustained by export-related businesses, was being overwhelmed by the problems in the U.S. housing sector and the credit markets. These factors had slowed consumer spending and were causing many businesses to halt or delay investments in plant and equipment.

Export-related businesses had been prospering due to strong growth in the rest of the world and the declining value of the dollar, which made imports more expensive and exports cheaper. Companies such as M.S. Willett Inc., a metal fabricator and tool-and-die producer, had experienced a decrease in orders from U.S. firms such as Harley-Davidson Inc., but increased business from big multi-nationals with growing export businesses. Other companies, such as USG Corp., a wallboard manufacturer, had experienced declining sales and profits, given the negative conditions in the U.S. housing market. The article notes, however, that conditions facing the manufacturing sector differed from those in 2000 when a higher value of the dollar decreased the demand for U.S. exports and firms had excess inventories and unused manufacturing capacity. The examples in the article also illustrate how firms are affected differently by changes in the overall macro environment, which have arisen from shifts in consumer spending, business investment, and the value of the dollar. ▪

Measuring Gross Domestic Product (GDP)

Gross domestic product
The comprehensive measure of the market value of all currently produced final goods and services within a country in a given period of time by domestic and foreign-supplied resources.

Circular flow
The framework for the aggregate macroeconomic model, which portrays the level of economic activity as a flow of expenditure from consumers to firms or producers as consumers purchase goods and services produced by these firms. This flow then returns to consumers as income received from the production process.

Mixed economy
An economy that has both a private (household and firm) sector and a public (government) sector.

Just as we needed the framework of demand, supply, and markets to understand the impact of microeconomic variables on managers' competitive strategies, we need a framework to understand the variables influencing the overall level of economic activity. The most closely watched measure of economic activity is **gross domestic product (GDP)**, the market value of all currently produced final goods and services within a country in a given period of time by domestic and foreign-supplied resources. The framework underlying GDP is the **circular flow**, which is derived from the market transactions we studied in Part 1 of the text. All of these transactions were exchanges of income for goods and services between demanders (consumers or households) and suppliers (producers or firms). In market transactions, consumers use a certain amount of their income to pay producers an amount equal to the market price of the goods and services times the quantity purchased, and the consumers receive the goods and services in return. Thus, there is a flow of expenditure from consumers to producers and a flow of goods and services in the opposite direction, from producers to consumers. Producers then use this revenue from the sale of the products to pay for the inputs used in producing the goods and services. Thus, there is a flow of income from firms to households who own these inputs and a flow of real resources from households to firms. Households use this income to again purchase other goods and services—hence, the name *circular flow*.[1]

The Circular Flow in a Mixed, Open Economy

Figure 11.1 illustrates the circular flow in a mixed, open economy.[2] A **mixed economy** has both a private (household and firm) sector and a public (government) sector,

---

[1] Income and expenditure are flows that occur over a period of time. This flow concept differs from the stock of wealth or debt that may result from this process. If consumers save some of their income, this action adds to their stock of wealth or the amount of financial assets they have at a point in time. If consumers' expenditure exceeds their income, they have to borrow the difference, and their stock of debt increases. Stocks (wealth, debt) are measured at a point in time, whereas flows (income, expenditure, saving) are measured over time.

[2] The model in Figure 11.1 is reproduced from Figure 1.2 in Chapter 1.

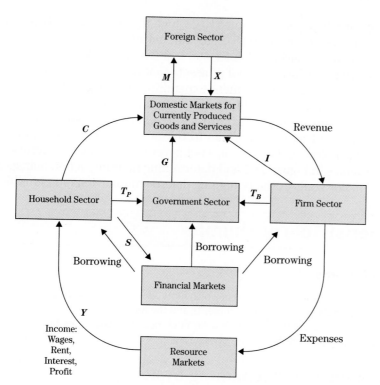

FIGURE 11.1
GDP and the Circular Flow
The circular flow is the framework that forms the basis for the aggregate macroeconomic model of the economy.
C = *consumption spending*
I = *investment spending*
G = *government spending*
X = *export spending*
M = *import spending*
Y = *household income*
S = *household saving*
T_P = *personal taxes*
T_B = *business taxes*

whereas a private economy has only the household and firm sector. An **open economy** has domestic and foreign sectors, while a closed economy has only a domestic sector.

Figure 11.1 shows the household and firm sector of the economy. Firms sell currently produced goods and services in the domestic markets in the top part of the figure, and households use part of their income on consumption expenditures (C) for these products. These expenditures become revenue for the firms, which is used to pay the firms' expenses of production. These transactions occur in the resource markets in the bottom part of Figure 11.1, where firms purchase all of the inputs (labor, machinery, land, and so on) used to produce their goods and services. These payments to the factors of production occur as wages, rent, interest, and profits, which then become income (Y) to the household sector. This income is used to finance further consumption in another round of the circular flow. We show only the flow of income and expenditure in Figure 11.1, not the flow of goods, services, and resources, which occurs in the opposite direction of the arrows in the figure.

Figure 11.1 also incorporates investment expenditure (I) by the firm sector, spending by all levels of government (G), and the foreign sector (export spending, X, by foreign residents on domestically produced goods and services and import spending, M, by domestic residents on foreign goods and services). We are measuring GDP using the **expenditure** or **output approach** when we add consumption (C), investment (I), government (G), and net export expenditure (F)—which is export spending (X) minus import spending (M)—as shown in the top half of Figure 11.1. These components equal the **aggregate expenditure** (E) on the output produced in the economy, or $E = C + I + G + X - M$.

The economic activity in Figure 11.1 can also be measured by the **earnings** or **income approach**, which focuses on the flow of income in the bottom half of Figure 11.1. Given the circular flow, aggregate expenditure (E) on the output in the economy must equal the income (Y) earned from producing this output, or $E = Y$. Thus, throughout the remainder of this text, we use the terms *aggregate expenditure, output,* and *income* interchangeably.

Figure 11.1 also shows the three major uses that households make of their income. They first pay personal taxes (T_P) to support government activities. This

Open economy
An economy that has both domestic and foreign sectors.

Expenditure or output approach
Measuring overall economic activity by adding the expenditure on the output produced in the economy.

Aggregate expenditure
The sum of consumption, investment, government, and net export spending on the total amount of real output produced in an economy in a given period of time, which equals the income generated from producing and selling that output.

Earnings or income approach
Measuring overall economic activity by adding the earnings or income generated by selling the output produced in the economy.

leaves them with disposable income (Y_d), which they either spend on consumption goods and services (C) or save (S). The amount of income that is saved typically flows to the financial markets (banks, stock and bond markets, and other financial institutions), where it forms a pool of assets that can be borrowed by either firms or governments to finance investment expenditure (I) or government expenditure (G). Thus, government expenditure (G) is financed through personal taxes on households (T_P), business taxes on firms (T_B), and borrowing. Households may also borrow in the financial markets to finance consumption expenditure (C). However, households, on balance, are net savers. Analyzing the factors that affect all of the variables in Figure 11.1 and determining their impact on managers' strategies are the major goals of the remaining macroeconomic chapters in this text.

Managerial Rule of Thumb

Spending Patterns

The overall macroeconomic environment in which firms operate is influenced by aggregate spending decisions of consumers, businesses, governments, and the foreign sector. Changes in these spending patterns can have a substantial effect on a firm's competitive strategies because they alter the economic environment in which that firm does business. ■

National Income Accounting Systems

National income accounting system

A system of accounts developed for each country, based on the circular flow, whose purpose is to measure the level of economic activity in that country.

National Income and Product Accounts

The U.S. national income accounting system, operated by the Bureau of Economic Analysis (BEA) in the U.S. Department of Commerce.

Economists and forecasters use a **national income accounting system** to measure economic activity in real-world economies that is based on the circular flow concept. In the United States, these accounts are called the **National Income and Product Accounts** and are produced by the Bureau of Economic Analysis (BEA) in the U.S. Department of Commerce.[3] This accounting system uses the market prices of goods and services to weigh the relative value of all output produced. Thus, if the price of a pound of coffee is twice that of a loaf of bread, production of the pound of coffee will receive twice the value in the national income accounts. On the income side, the national income accounts include payments to all factors of production, including wages, rents, interest, and profit.

As we noted previously, the overall measure of economic activity in the United States, the gross domestic product (*GDP*), is the market value of all currently produced final goods and services over a period of time within the borders of the United States, whether produced by American or foreign-supplied resources.[4] GDP estimates are prepared quarterly by the BEA and published on its Web site (www.bea.gov) and in its monthly journal, the *Survey of Current Business*. The

---

[3] For a comprehensive discussion of the National Income and Product Accounts, see J. Steven Landefeld, Eugene P. Seskin, and Barbara M. Fraumeni, "Taking the Pulse of the Economy: Measuring GDP," *Journal of Economic Perspectives* 22 (Spring 2008): 193–216.

[4] Gross domestic product differs slightly from the measure used previously in the National Income and Product Accounts, gross national product (GNP), which is the value of all currently produced final goods and services over a period of time using resources of U.S. residents, no matter where produced. GNP includes and GDP excludes the income of U.S. residents and corporations earned abroad (interest, dividends, and reinvested profits) minus the earnings of foreign residents on their investments in the United States. The National Income and Product Accounts assume that these net earnings measure the net contribution of U.S.-owned investments abroad to the production of goods and services in other countries. GDP, therefore, is the value of goods and services produced within the United States, while GNP is the value of goods and services produced by residents of the United States. The United States switched to the GDP accounting system in 1992 to make the National Income and Product Accounts consistent with the national income accounting systems of other industrialized countries. The difference between the two measures is extremely small, approximately one-half of 1 percent of GDP in 2001. Throughout this text, we will use the current GDP accounting system.

estimates are based on data gathered from surveys of households, businesses, and governments and from tax and regulatory reports submitted to various government agencies. These data may be collected weekly, monthly, quarterly, or annually.

Because there is a need to get the GDP estimates published as soon as possible, the initial or advanced estimate, which is published at the beginning of each quarter during the year for the quarter just completed, is followed by a series of revisions in the two subsequent months based on data not originally available. These preliminary and final estimates are followed by annual revisions in the three succeeding years and a benchmark revision on a periodic five-year schedule. The five-year benchmark revisions are made consistent with a data series carried back to 1929.[5]

Characteristics of GDP

GDP is the value of economic activity—a *monetary* measure of economic activity that includes only *final* goods and services and excludes market transactions that do not relate to the *current* production of goods and services. In the United States, GDP is calculated in dollar terms, whereas local currencies are used for other countries. As we noted above, market prices are used to weight the different goods and services included in GDP, so the value of GDP is a function of both the prices and the quantities of the goods produced in a given time period.

GDP includes the **final goods and services** (sold to end-users), but not any **intermediate goods and services** (used in the production of other goods and services). Although it might be possible to count all final goods and services produced in a given time period, it would be difficult to determine which goods and services are consumed by their end-users and which are used in the further production of other goods and services. Thus, to calculate GDP, government statisticians use the **value-added approach**. In this approach, only the value added in each stage of production (raw materials to semifinished goods to final products) is counted for inclusion in GDP. If the value of all intermediate and final goods were included in the GDP, there would be substantial double-counting of the nation's output.

For example, suppose that you buy a cup of coffee at Dunkin' Donuts for $1.00. Suppose also that Dunkin' Donuts pays $.60 for the coffee beans. The cost of the cup, the labor to serve the customer, and the profit to the company constitute the other $.40. Does GDP increase by $1.00 or $2.00 ($0.60 + $0.40 + $1.00) when this cup of coffee is produced and sold? The correct answer is $1.00 because that is the value of the final good purchased by the customer. This amount can be calculated by the value-added approach: $.60 is the value added by all other businesses to get the coffee beans to Dunkin' Donuts, and then an additional $.40 is added by Dunkin' Donuts when it turns the raw coffee beans into a cup of coffee. Counting both the intermediate good (raw coffee beans) and the final product (a cup of coffee) would overstate the contribution to GDP.

GDP for any time period includes only those goods and services currently produced in that period. Therefore, any secondhand sales are excluded. For example, even though there are many market transactions for used cars each year, these transactions are not included in the current year's GDP. To include them would result in double-counting because these automobiles were already counted in the year in which they were produced.[6] GDP also does not include any financial security

Final goods and services
Goods and services that are sold to their end-users.

Intermediate goods and services
Goods and services that are used in the production of other goods and services.

Value-added approach
A process of calculating the value of the final output in an economy by summing the value added in each stage of production (i.e., raw materials to semifinished goods to final products).

---

[5] This discussion of the National Income and Product Accounts is based primarily on Charles L. Schultze, *Memos to the President: A Guide Through Macroeconomics for the Busy Policymaker* (Washington, D.C.: Brookings Institution, 1992); and Norman Frumkin, *Tracking America's Economy*, 3rd ed. (Armonk, N.Y.: Sharpe, 1998).

[6] Although the production of the used automobile is not included in current GDP, any services performed by the salesperson or any repairs to the car represent value added by a used car dealer and are included in current GDP.

transactions, such as the buying and selling of stocks and bonds. These financial transactions represent changes in the claims of ownership of existing assets, not the production of new goods and services. These transactions also cancel each other out because when you purchase the asset, someone else sells it.

GDP does not include most nonmarket activities that are not recorded in output or input market transactions. These activities include legal activities, such as unpaid housework done by a spouse, and illegal activities, such as prostitution and the sale of drugs. The latter activities are considered part of the **underground economy**, or those economic transactions that cannot be easily measured because they are not reported on income tax returns and other government economic surveys. Researchers have made a variety of attempts to measure the size of the underground economy. They have employed both direct methods—including studies of the compliance with income tax laws in reporting business incomes—and indirect methods—using information suggesting attempts to hide income, such as using cash rather than checks for transactions, as there is no paper or electronic trail with cash transactions. Estimates of the effect of underreporting of the underground economy on the national income accounts have ranged from 1 to 33 percent of GDP. Measuring the underground economy is a continuing problem for government statisticians.

The Bureau of Economic Analysis does calculate an **imputed value** for certain expenditures for which there are no market transactions. For example, if an individual rents a house, there is an explicit market transaction in which rent is paid to the landlord in return for the housing services. Individuals who own their homes also receive these housing services, but pay no explicit rent. The BEA *imputes* a rental value for these housing services and includes that figure in personal consumption expenditures, which are part of the GDP.

Transfer payments are also not included in the calculation of GDP. Transfer payments represent the transfer of income among individuals in the economy, but do not reflect the production of new goods and services. Transfer payments can be both public (Social Security, welfare, and veterans' payments) and private (transfers among members of a family). Public transfer payments are recorded in government budgets, but they are excluded from GDP because they do not represent payment for newly produced goods and services.

Underground economy
Economic transactions that cannot be easily measured because they are not reported on income tax returns or other government economic surveys.

Imputed value
An estimated value for nonmarket transactions, such as the rental value of owner-occupied housing, included in GDP.

Transfer payments
Payments that represent the transfer of income among individuals in the economy, but do not reflect the production of new goods and services.

Real Versus Nominal GDP

Because GDP is a monetary measure that weights currently produced goods and services according to their market prices, GDP can increase from year to year because

1. The prices of goods and services produced increase, while quantities are held constant.
2. The quantities of goods and services increase, while the prices are held constant.
3. Both prices and quantities increase, the typical case.

These factors create a difference between nominal and real GDP. **Nominal GDP** is the value of goods and services measured in current year prices, whereas **real GDP** is the value of goods and services measured in constant prices. Real GDP is nominal GDP adjusted for price level changes.[7]

Table 11.1 illustrates the difference between nominal and real GDP with BEA data for 2000 and 2001. These years were chosen for this example because the BEA defined 2000 as the base year, making real and nominal GDP equal at $9,817.0 billion. In 2001, nominal GDP increased to $10,128.0 billion, or 3.17 percent, while real GDP

Nominal GDP
The value of currently produced final goods and services measured in current year prices.

Real GDP
The value of currently produced final goods and services measured in constant prices, or nominal GDP adjusted for price level changes.

---

[7] For example, a 6 percent increase in nominal GDP could consist of a 6 percent increase in real goods and services and a 0 percent increase in prices, a 0 percent increase in real goods and services and a 6 percent increase in prices, or a 3 percent increase in real goods and services and a 3 percent increase in prices.

TABLE 11.1 Nominal Versus Real GDP

VARIABLE	2000	2001
Nominal GDP	$9,817.0 billion	$10,128.0 billion
Percent change		3.17
Real GDP	$9,817.0 billion	$9,890.7 billion
Percent change		0.76
GDP deflator (price changes)	100	102.40
Percent change		2.40

increased only to $9,890.7 billion, or 0.76 percent. The **GDP deflator**, which is defined as (nominal GDP/real GDP) × 100, compares the price of each year's output of goods and services to the price of that same output in a base year (2000, in this case). From 2000 to 2001, the price level, or the GDP deflator, increased by 2.40 percent. We can see in Table 11.1 that the percentage increase in nominal GDP is approximately equal to the percentage increase in the price level plus the percentage increase in real GDP, or the amount of real goods and services.[8]

Real GDP is considered a better measure of economic well-being than nominal GDP because increases in real GDP represent larger amounts of goods and services available for the individuals in that economy. Nominal GDP could increase solely from an increase in the price level, without any increase in goods and services. Individuals are not better off if they have no more goods and services, but have to pay higher prices for them. Figure 11.2 shows U.S. nominal and real GDP for 1985 to 2007, with 2000 as the base year (as in Table 11.1). Nominal GDP is greater than real GDP after 2000, but it is less than real GDP before the base year.

GDP deflator

A measure of price changes in the economy that compares the price of each year's output of goods and services to the price of that same output in a base year.

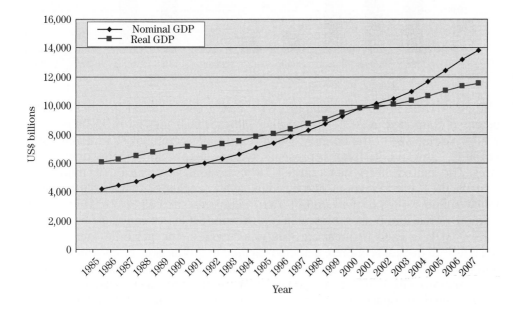

FIGURE 11.2
U.S. Nominal vs. Real GDP
(2000 = 100)
The difference between nominal GDP measured in current year prices and real GDP measured in constant prices.
Source: www.bea.gov, NIPA tables.

---

[8] Real GDP measures the increase in goods and services produced over time, while holding prices constant at the level of a base year. The BEA used to change the base year every three to four years. It now uses a chain-type price index in calculating the change in real GDP from year to year, which incorporates the average price of the goods in both years. The prices of both years are "chained" or multiplied together and averaged with a geometric mean. The continual updating of the base years with this approach reduces the problems regarding the distortion that changes in relative prices and quantities can cause in calculating real GDP.

FIGURE 11.3A
2005 Nominal Gross Domestic Product (GDP) for Selected Countries
The differences in nominal GDP for selected countries.
Source: www.worldbank.org. Reprinted by permission of World Bank via Copyright Clearance Center.

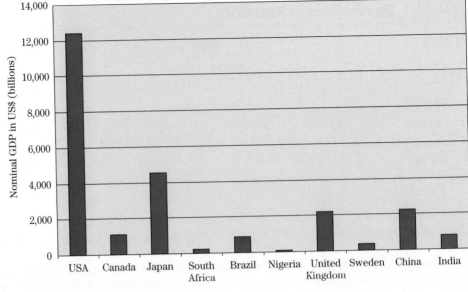

FIGURE 11.3B
2005 Nominal Gross National Income (GNI) per Capita for Selected Countries
The differences in GNI per capita for selected countries.
Source: www.worldbank.org. Reprinted by permission of World Bank via Copyright Clearance Center.

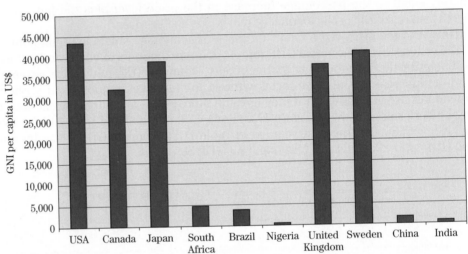

Business cycles
The periodic increases and decreases in overall economic activity reflected in production, employment, profits, and prices.

Expansion
The rising phase of a business cycle, in which the direction of a series of economic indicators turns upward.

Recession
The falling phase of a business cycle, in which the direction of a series of economic indicators turns downward.

Figures 11.3a and 11.3b compare GDP and gross national income (GNI) for selected countries in 2005.[9] The dollar value of GDP in Figure 11.3a is closely related to the size of the country. However, the per capita gross national income graph in Figure 11.3b better represents average output and income across countries. The United States has a large GDP in both absolute and per capita terms. Canada, the United Kingdom, and Sweden have a relatively small absolute GDP, but much higher values in per capita terms. Countries such as South Africa, Brazil, Nigeria, China, and India rank low in both absolute and per capita terms.

Real GDP is used to measure **business cycles**, the periodic increases and decreases in overall economic activity reflected in production, employment, profits, and prices. These business cycles are primarily associated with advanced industrialized nations with highly developed product and financial sectors. Analysts usually refer to the rising phase of a business cycle as an **expansion** and the falling phase as a **recession**. The Cambridge, Massachusetts–based National Bureau of Economic Research (NBER) is the private, nonprofit research organization that officially designates when a recession occurs.

---

[9] Remember that we can measure a country's level of economic activity from either the expenditure (GDP) or the income side (GNI).

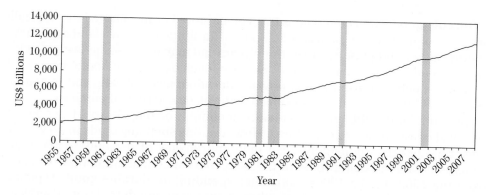

FIGURE 11.4
U.S. Real GDP and Recessions
The relationship between real GDP and recessions, the falling phase of a business cycle in which the direction of a series of economic indicators turn downward.
Source: www.bea.gov; www.nber.org

Figure 11.4 shows real GDP and the officially designated recessions from 1955 to 2003. Although the popular definition of a recession is a decline in real GDP for two quarters in a row, the NBER Business Cycle Dating Committee designates a recession as beginning the month when a broad spectrum of economic indicators turns downward. These indicators include business sales, industrial production, the unemployment rate, nonfarm employment and hours worked, and personal income, in addition to the trends in real GDP. An expansion is designated in the month in which the overall direction of these indicators turns upward. Although, as noted in the opening news article, the slowing U.S. economic activity was evident in late 2007 and throughout 2008, it was not until November 2008 that the NBER Business Cycle Dating Committee officially declared the date of the beginning of the recession as December 2007.[10]

Alternative Measures of GDP

As we discussed earlier and illustrated in Figure 11.1, the level of economic activity or GDP can be calculated by either the expenditure/output approach (the top half of Figure 11.1) or the earnings/income approach (the bottom half of Figure 11.1). Let's examine both measures in turn for the U.S. economy.

The Expenditure or Output Approach   The expenditure or output approach focuses on spending on currently produced goods and services by four major sectors of the economy:

1. Personal consumption expenditures, or consumption (C)
2. Gross private domestic investment, or investment (I)
3. Government consumption expenditures and gross investment, or government (G)
4. Net export spending (F), which equals export spending (X) minus import spending (M)

Personal Consumption Expenditures[11]   Personal consumption expenditures are the largest component of GDP, typically averaging around two-thirds of the total. These consumption expenditures are subdivided into three categories:

* Durable goods
* Nondurable goods
* Services

Personal consumption expenditures
The total amount of spending by consumers on durable goods, nondurable goods, and services in a given period of time.

---

[10] National Bureau of Economic Research Business Cycle Dating Committee. "Determination of the December 2007 Peak in Economic Activity," December 11, 2008. www.nber.org.
[11] The discussion of the components of GDP is based largely on Frumkin, *Tracking America's Economy*; and Albert T. Sommers, with Lucie R. Blau, *The U.S. Economy Demystified*, 3rd ed. (New York: Lexington Books, 1993).

Durable goods
Commodities that typically last three or more years, such as automobiles, furniture, and household appliances.

Nondurable goods
Commodities that last less than three years and may be consumed very quickly, such as food, clothing, and gasoline.

Services
Noncommodity items, such as utilities, public transportation, private education, medical care, and recreation.

Durable goods are commodities that can be stored or inventoried that typically last three or more years, such as automobiles, furniture, and household appliances. **Nondurable goods** last less than three years and may be consumed very quickly, such as food, clothing, and gasoline. **Services** include noncommodity items such as utilities, public transportation, private education, medical care, and recreation that cannot be stored and are consumed at the place and time of purchase.

Spending on durable goods typically accounts for only 12 to 14 percent of personal consumption expenditures. However, this spending tends to be volatile over time because consumers can delay purchases of durable goods under adverse economic conditions. In the six economic expansions that occurred from the 1960s to the 1990s, consumer spending on durable goods typically increased two to three times faster than spending on nondurables and services. Spending on durable goods declined in all six recessions during this period, while spending on nondurables declined in only three of the recessions. In those recessions when spending on both types of goods declined, the decline in spending on durable goods was much steeper.

The stability and the amount of spending on nondurables and services mean that overall personal consumption expenditures tend to be more stable across business cycles than other components of GDP, such as investment and net export spending. From 1959 to 2002, consumer spending on services increased from 40 percent to 59 percent of personal consumption expenditure, while spending on nondurables decreased from 47 percent to 29 percent.[12]

Gross Private Domestic Investment Spending   **Gross private domestic investment spending**, a second component of GDP expenditure, has a very specific meaning in the National Income and Product Accounts. It includes

1. Business or nonresidential fixed investment (i.e., the purchase of structures, equipment, and software by firms)
2. Residential fixed investment (i.e., the purchase of new housing by households and landlords)
3. Changes in business inventories, goods that are produced, but not sold in a given year

Gross private domestic investment spending
The total amount of spending on nonresidential structures, equipment, and software; residential structures; and business inventories in a given period of time.

Although individuals often say they are making an "investment" when they place some of their income in a savings account or mutual fund, these financial transactions are only portfolio allocations and are not considered to be investment in the national income accounts.

Business fixed investment
Spending on the structures, equipment, and software that provide the industrial capacity to produce goods and services for all sectors of the economy.

Business fixed investment encompasses the spending on structures, equipment, and software that provide the industrial capacity to produce goods and services for all sectors of the economy. This investment spending includes all privately owned buildings (factories, offices, stores); nonbuilding structures (roads, power plants, telephone lines, oil and gas wells); and machinery, computers, and other equipment lasting two or more years. These structures and equipment are used in new businesses and also replace and modernize existing capital facilities, as these facilities depreciate or wear out over time. Business fixed investment spending ranged from 9 to 11 percent of GDP from the 1950s to the 1990s, with structures accounting for 3 to 4 percent and equipment for 6 to 7 percent. Equipment has come to dominate this type of spending, given that equipment tends to deteriorate or become outmoded more quickly than structures. Firms can also rearrange the use of their structures to increase efficiency without investing in new buildings.

In 1999, the Bureau of Economic Analysis began counting software as part of nonresidential fixed investment, given that the average service life of software is three to five years. Previously, embedded or bundled software was included in

---

[12] Norman Frumkin, *Tracking America's Economy*, 4th ed. (Armonk, NY: M.E. Sharpe, 2004).

investment, but not software purchases by business and government. Three types of software are now treated as business investment: prepackaged software sold in standard form and intended for nonspecialized uses; custom software specifically designed for a business enterprise or government unit; and own-account software, consisting of in-house expenditures for new or enhanced software created by a business or government for its own use.[13]

Residential fixed investment includes the spending on new construction of privately owned single-family and multifamily permanent housing units, mobile homes, nonhousekeeping dormitories, and fraternity and sorority houses, as well as improvements such as additions to, alterations of, and major replacements to existing residential structures. This category of spending also includes brokers' commissions on the sale of new and existing housing. Residential investment spending is dominated by the construction of new housing units.

Changes in business inventories are typically the smallest component of gross private domestic investment, but one of its most volatile elements. Inventories represent goods that have been produced in a given period of time, but not sold. If an automobile is added to a firm's inventory during a given year, the BEA treats this transaction as though the firm has purchased the good. This "purchase" has a positive effect on GDP in that year, as it reflects current production. If the automobile is sold to a consumer the following year, there is negative business inventory investment. This sale is subtracted from GDP because it does not represent the production of current goods and services.[14]

Some business inventory changes are planned, as when a firm wants to maintain a relatively constant rate of output so as not to shut down a production line even though demand for the product may be seasonal. However, other inventory changes are unplanned. Firms may anticipate a certain rate of sales that fails to materialize because consumers decided to spend less than anticipated. We will see in subsequent chapters that unplanned inventory adjustment plays a major role in our model of the macro economy.

Government Consumption Expenditures and Gross Investment   **Government consumption expenditures and gross investment** include federal, state, and local government purchases of finished products plus all direct purchases of resources. Government expenditures are divided into two categories:

1. Consumption: Current outlays for goods and services and depreciation charges on existing structures and equipment
2. Investment: Capital outlays for newly acquired structures and equipment

Government spending includes purchases of goods and services from private industry, the wages paid to public-sector workers, and depreciation charges on structures and equipment. The wages of government workers, such as police officers and firefighters, are used as a proxy for the value of the output they produce because that output is not bought and sold in the marketplace.

Although this category of spending includes all three levels of government—federal, state, and local—the level of expenditure included in the National Income and Product Accounts is smaller than that included in the budgets of

Residential fixed investment
Spending on newly constructed housing units, major alterations of and replacements to existing structures, and brokers' commissions.

Changes in business inventories
Changes in the amount of goods produced, but not sold in a given year.

Government consumption expenditures and gross investment
The total amount of spending by federal, state, and local governments on consumption outlays for goods and services and for depreciation charges for existing structures and equipment and on investment capital outlays for newly acquired structures and equipment in a given period of time.

---

[13] Brent R. Moulton, Robert P. Parker, and Eugene P. Seskin, "A Preview of the 1999 Comprehensive Revision of the National Income and Product Accounts," *Survey of Current Business* (August 1999), 7–20; *Recognition of Business and Government Expenditures for Software as Investment: Methodology and Quantitative Impacts, 1959–98* (May 2000), available at www.bea.gov.

[14] Personal consumption expenditures do include the net purchase—purchase less sales—of used goods from the business and government sectors. Negative changes in business inventories cancel these transactions, so that GDP includes only currently produced goods and services. See U.S. Department of Commerce, Bureau of Economic Analysis, *Personal Consumption Expenditures*, Methodology Paper Series, no. MP-6 (Washington, DC.: U.S. Government Printing Office, June 1990).

these organizations. Given the definition of GDP, only expenditures related to the current production of goods and services are included in the national income accounts. Thus, as noted earlier, all transfer payments are excluded from government expenditure in the national income accounts. These transfers include payments to individuals for Social Security, unemployment compensation, and income maintenance; federal grants to state and local governments and state grants to local governments; interest on government debt; foreign aid; and government loans less repayments.

In 2001, federal government expenditures measured by the national income accounts encompassed approximately 25 percent of the expenditures included in the federal budget.[15] Thus, the GDP measure of government consumption and investment expenditures substantially understates the impact of government on the economy. Items excluded from government spending do typically reappear in subsequent years' GDP expenditure figures. The transfer income from Social Security and other income maintenance programs becomes part of personal consumption expenditure. Grants to state and local governments appear as part of their consumption and investment expenditures. Foreign aid may become part of net export spending, while interest payments will be translated into domestic and foreign spending on goods and services.

Net Export Spending   The final category of GDP measured from the expenditure or output approach is **net export spending**, which is the difference between spending by other countries on domestically produced goods and services (**export spending**) and spending by domestic residents on goods and services produced in the rest of the world (**import spending**). Export spending is added to U.S. GDP because it represents spending on goods and services currently produced in this country by individuals in the rest of the world. However, import spending is subtracted from GDP because it represents spending by U.S. citizens on goods and services produced in the rest of the world. Net export spending represents the net expenditure from abroad for domestically produced goods and services, which provides income for domestic producers.

Net export spending can be either positive or negative depending on the balance between exports and imports. Net export spending can be a relatively small figure, even if the export and import flows are relatively large, as long as the two spending categories are relatively the same size. Foreign trade in goods includes agricultural, mineral, and manufactured items, while services include travel, transportation, royalties and licensing fees, insurance, telecommunications, and business services. This spending category also includes U.S. military sales contracts, direct defense expenditures, and miscellaneous U.S. government services.

Table 11.2 shows U.S. GDP for the year 2007 measured by the expenditure or output approach.[16] In Table 11.2, we can see that consumption spending was 70.3 percent of GDP in 2007. Changes in business inventories were negative and accounted for approximately 0.2 percent of gross private domestic investment. Given the definition of federal government spending used in the National Income and Product Accounts, state and local government spending was 1.7 times the amount of federal spending. Imports exceeded exports by $708 billion in 2007, resulting in a negative balance of trade.

Although Table 11.2 provides a good description of the composition of GDP, analysts and managers are most interested in the rate of growth of real GDP and its components because these changes may alter a firm's competitive strategy in the

Net export spending
The total amount of spending on exports minus the total amount of spending on imports in a given period of time.

Export spending
The total amount of spending on goods and services currently produced in one country and sold abroad to residents of other countries in a given period of time.

Import spending
The total amount of spending on goods and services currently produced in other countries and sold to residents of a given country in a given period of time.

---

[15] U.S. Congressional Budget Office, *The Budget and Economic Outlook: Fiscal Years 2003–2012* (Washington, D.C.: U.S. Government Printing Office, January 2002).

[16] This table shows nominal GDP or GDP measured in 2007 dollars to get a consistent set of measures with GDP measured from the earnings or income approach in Table 11.3.

TABLE 11.2 Gross Domestic Product and Its Components, 2007 Expenditure or Output Measurement

COMPONENT	VALUE IN BILLIONS OF DOLLARS (% OF GDP)
GROSS DOMESTIC PRODUCT (GDP)	**13,807.5**
PERSONAL CONSUMPTION EXPENDITURES (C)	**9,710.2 (70.3)**
Durable goods	1,082.8
Nondurable goods	2,833.0
Services	5,794.4
GROSS PRIVATE DOMESTIC INVESTMENT (I)	**2,130.4 (15.5)**
Fixed investment	2,134.0
Nonresidential	1,503.8
Structures	480.3
Equipment and software	1,023.5
Residential	630.2
Change in inventories	−3.6
GOVERNMENT CONSUMPTION EXPENDITURES AND GROSS INVESTMENT (G)	**2,674.8 (19.4)**
Federal	979.3
National defense	662.2
Nondefense	317.1
State and local	1,695.5
NET EXPORTS OF GOODS AND SERVICES (F)	**−707.8 (−5.1)**
Exports (X)	1,662.4 (12.0)
Goods	1,149.2
Services	513.2
Imports (M)	2,370.2 (17.2)
Goods	1,985.2
Services	385.1

Source: U.S. Department of Commerce, Bureau of Economic Analysis, *National Income and Product Account Tables,* Table 1.1.5, Gross Domestic Product. Available at www.bea.gov/bea/national/nipaweb.

future. Figure 11.5 shows the annual growth rate percentages for real GDP from 2000 to 2008. This figure clearly shows the effects of the recession in 2001, the gradual recovery in 2002 and 2003, and the slowing of economic activity in 2007 and 2008.

Figure 11.6 presents average annual growth rates for the components of real GDP for this same time period. This figure shows that consumer spending on nondurable good and services remained relatively constant over the period, whereas investment spending was extremely volatile. The major cause of the 2001 recession was the drop in investment spending, particularly on structures and equipment and software. Residential construction spending held up in the first part of the decade. However, the negative growth rates for residential investment in 2007 and 2008 show the impact of the collapse of the housing market and the effect of the turmoil in credit markets during this period. Figure 11.6 also illustrates the major changes in export and import spending that can occur over relatively short periods of time. The positive impact of the lower value of the

FIGURE 11.5

Real GDP Growth (annual growth rates in %)

Value of newly produced final goods and services adjusted for changes in the price level (base year 2000). Real GDP data are important measures of the rate of change in percentage terms of the quantity of economic output over quarters and years.
Source: Federal Reserve Economic Data (FRED II), Economic Research, Federal Reserve Bank of St. Louis, http://research.stlouisfed.org/fred2/.

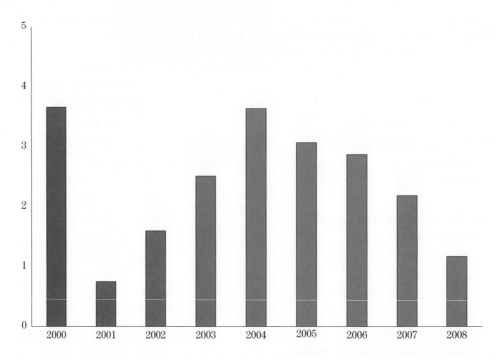

National income

Income that is generated from the sale of the goods and services that are produced in the economy and that is paid to the individuals and businesses who supply the inputs or factors of production.

Compensation of employees

The wages and salaries and the fringe benefits paid by employers to employees.

dollar and foreign economic growth on U.S. export spending, as noted in the opening article, can be seen in Figure 11.6.

The Income or Earnings Approach   We stated earlier that GDP measured using the expenditure or output approach must equal GDP measured using the income or earnings approach, or $E = Y$. **National income** is the income generated from the sale of the goods and services produced in the economy and paid to the individuals and businesses who supply the inputs or factors of production. This amount, shown in the bottom half of Figure 11.1 and in Table 11.3, is composed of the following categories:

1. **Compensation of employees:** The wages and salaries, the Social Security payments made by employers, and the employer contributions for fringe

FIGURE 11.6

Average Growth of Real GDP Components—2000 to 2008 (annual growth rates in %)

The large differences in the percentage annual growth rates of the components of real GDP.
Source: Federal Reserve Economic Data (FRED II), Economic Research, Federal Reserve Bank of St. Louis, http://research.stlouisfed.org/fred2/.

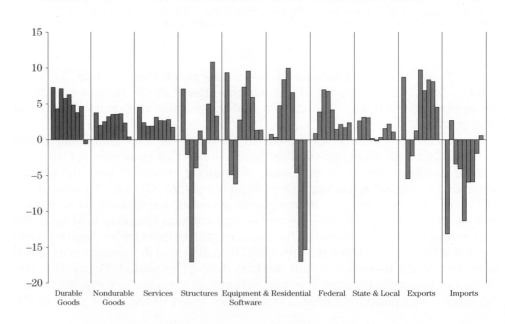

TABLE 11.3 Gross Domestic Product and Its Components, 2007 Earnings or Income Measurement

COMPONENT	VALUE IN BILLIONS OF DOLLARS (% OF NATIONAL INCOME)
GROSS DOMESTIC PRODUCT	**13,807.5**
Less: Depreciation expenditures	1,618.0
Less: Statistical discrepancy	−81.4
EQUALS: NATIONAL INCOME	**12,270.9**
Compensation of employees	7,812.3 (63.6)
Proprietor's income	1,056.2 (8.6)
Rental income	40.0 (0.3)
Corporate profits	1,642.4 (13.4)
Net interest	664.4 (5.4)
Less: Income earned, but not received	4,321.0
Plus: Income received, but not earned	3,713.3
EQUALS: PERSONAL INCOME	**11,663.2**
Less: Personal taxes	1,492.8
EQUALS: DISPOSABLE INCOME	**10,170.5**
Personal consumption expenditure ($9,710.2) plus other outlays ($402.9)	10,113.1
Personal saving	57.4

Source: U.S. Department of Commerce, Bureau of Economic Analysis, *National Income and Product Account Tables,* Table 1.7.5, Relation of Gross Domestic Product, Gross National Product, Net National Product, National Income, and Personal Income; Table 1.12, National Income by Type of Income; Table 2.1, Personal Income and Its Disposition. Available at www.bea.gov/national/nipaweb.

benefits such as health insurance and pensions. Employee compensation is the largest component of national income, typically around 60 to 70 percent of the total.

2. **Proprietors' income:** The income of unincorporated businesses, such as medical practices, law firms, small farms, and retail stores.
3. **Rental income:** The income households receive from the rental of their property.
4. **Corporate profits:** The excess of revenues over costs for the incorporated business sector of the economy.
5. **Net interest:** The interest private businesses pay to households for lending money to the firms minus the interest the businesses receive plus interest earned from foreigners.

We can see in Table 11.3 that GDP does not equal national income until depreciation expenditures to replace existing capital equipment are subtracted and a statistical adjustment is made for the discrepancy that arises from the use of different data sources to calculate GDP from the expenditure approach and from the income approach.[17]

Proprietors' income
The income of unincorporated businesses, such as medical practices, law firms, small farms, and retail stores.

Rental income
The income households receive from the rental of their property.

Corporate profits
The excess of revenues over costs for the incorporated business sector of the economy.

Net interest
The interest private businesses pay to households for lending money to the firms minus the interest businesses receive plus interest earned from foreigners.

---

[17] Depreciation expenditures are included in the expenditure side of GDP, but they are not paid out as income, so they must be subtracted to derive national income from GDP on the income side. There are also minor adjustments for business transfer payments, net subsidies for government enterprises, and net foreign factor income.

Personal income
Income received by households that forms the basis for personal consumption expenditures.

Disposable income
Personal household income after all taxes have been paid.

Saving
That portion of households' disposable income that is not spent on consumption goods and services.

Relative prices
The price of one good in relation to the price of another good.

Table 11.3 also shows **personal income**, an important component of macroeconomic analysis, because it forms the basis for the personal consumption expenditures of the household sector. To derive personal income from national income, we must subtract income that is earned, but not received by households and add income that is received, but not currently earned by the households.[18]

Personal income can be further reduced to **disposable income**, which is current household income after all personal taxes have been paid (see Figure 11.1). The most important personal taxes affecting disposable income are income taxes, particularly the federal income tax. We express this relationship in Equation 11.1.

11.1 $Y_d = Y - T_P$

where

Y_d = disposable income

Y = personal income

T_P = personal taxes, primarily the federal income tax

Households then divide their disposable income between personal consumption expenditures (C) and **saving** (S), which is that portion of their disposable income that is not currently spent.[19] This relationship is shown in Equation 11.2:

11.2 $Y_d = C + S$

where

Y_d = disposable income

C = personal consumption expenditures

S = saving

Personal income and taxes, disposable income, personal consumption expenditures, and saving for 2007 are all shown in Table 11.3. Changes in disposable income and consumption expenditures are particularly important for managers because spending on durable goods, nondurable goods, and services represents revenue to the business firms in the economy. Changes in these variables helped various industries recover from the 2001 recession and were crucial in determining how much the economy slowed down in 2007 and 2008.

Other Important Macroeconomic Variables

Two other variables are important in our discussion of the macroeconomic environment and its effects on managerial decisions: measures of the absolute price level and the labor force. From the labor force, we can derive the level of employment or unemployment in the economy.[20]

Price Level Measures

In Chapter 1, we noted that microeconomics focuses on relative prices, whereas macroeconomics focuses on the absolute price level. **Relative prices** show the price

[18] Income that is earned but not received includes taxes on production and imports, undistributed corporate profits (or retained earnings), business contributions to social insurance programs such as Social Security, and any wages that have been accrued but not yet paid. Income that is received but not currently earned includes government transfer payments that were excluded from the expenditure side of GDP, but that are part of personal income; business transfer payments; and interest paid to households from nonbusiness sources. Government transfer payments include Social Security payments, unemployment insurance, food stamps, Medicare, Medicaid, and other income maintenance programs.

[19] Remember that saving is a flow concept because it represents that portion of a flow of current income that is not spent on durables, nondurables, and services (consumption expenditure). This is contrasted with wealth or the stocks of assets that households have at a given period of time.

[20] This discussion is based largely on Frumkin, *Tracking America's Economy*.

of one good in relation to the price of another good. All of our discussion in Part 1 of the text centered on relative prices as we examined demand, supply, production, and cost in different market structures. The **absolute price level** is a measure of the overall price level in the economy. Various indices are used to measure the prices of all goods and services and how these prices change over time—that is, the rate of **inflation**, a sustained increase in the price level over time, or **deflation**, a sustained decrease in the price level over time. In this chapter, we focus on three major indices: the GDP deflator, the Consumer Price Index, and the Producer Price Index.

Absolute price level
A measure of the overall level of prices in the economy using various indices to measure the prices of all goods and services.

Inflation
A sustained increase in the price level over time.

Deflation
A sustained decrease in the price level over time.

The GDP Deflator   We defined the GDP deflator in our earlier discussion of real versus nominal GDP (see Table 11.1). The GDP deflator, illustrated in Figure 11.7, compares the price of each year's output of real goods and services to the price of that same output in a base year. It is a broad measure of price changes because it reflects the changes in consumption patterns over time included in GDP. The GDP deflator incorporates shifts in tastes and spending patterns as consumers substitute between new and older products and react to relative price changes of various products.

Table 11.4 shows the different rates of price increases among the components of GDP. Of particular importance is the personal consumption price deflator because this is the primary index that the Federal Reserve analyzes in deciding how to influence interest rates.[21] Note, however, the divergence in the rate of price increases among the components of personal consumption expenditures. The price index for durable goods fell over this period, while the index for services increased faster than GDP. The price index for nonresidental fixed investment increased, while that for residential fixed investment fell. The price level for state and local governments increased more rapidly than that for the federal government.

The Consumer Price Index (CPI)   The **Consumer Price Index (CPI)**, shown in Figure 11.8, is probably the most well-known measure of the absolute price level. Developed by the Bureau of Labor Statistics (BLS) and available at www.bls.gov/cpi/, the CPI measures the combined price consumers pay for a fixed market basket of goods and services in a given period relative to the combined price of an identical group of goods and services in a base period. The CPI

Consumer Price Index (CPI)
A measure of the combined price consumers pay for a fixed market basket of goods and services in a given period relative to the combined price of an identical basket of goods and services in a base period.

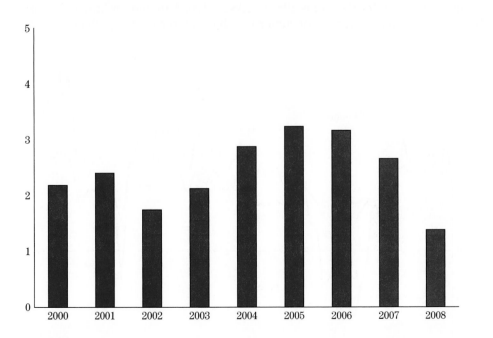

FIGURE 11.7
Annual Percentage Change in the GDP Deflator (ratio of current $ to chained $2000 = 100 − % change)
Nominal GDP/Real GDP—The deflator reflects continuing shifts in tastes and spending patterns because it accounts for actual spending as new or substitute products replace old ones and as consumers choose between higher- and lower-priced products or between items with slow or rapid price increases.
Source: Federal Reserve Economic Data (FRED II), Economic Research, Federal Reserve Bank of St. Louis, http://research.stlouisfed.org/fred2/.

---

[21] For example, see the section "Prices," in Board of Governors of the Federal Reserve System, *Monetary Policy Report to the Congress*, February 27, 2008.

TABLE 11.4 Price Deflators for GDP and Its Components, 2000–2006

VARIABLE	2000	2001	2002	2003	2004	2005	2006
GDP	100	102.40	104.19	106.40	109.46	113.00	116.57
Personal consumption expenditure	100	102.09	103.54	105.60	108.39	111.59	114.68
Durable goods	100	98.11	95.77	92.37	90.70	90.02	88.86
Nondurable goods	100	101.53	102.09	104.15	107.63	111.56	114.99
Services	100	103.26	106.02	109.38	112.93	116.73	120.73
Gross private domestic investment	100	101.00	101.61	103.16	106.69	111.12	115.09
Nonresidential	100	99.68	99.51	99.59	100.90	103.78	106.96
Residential	100	97.71	95.96	94.91	94.60	94.53	94.49
Government	100	102.54	105.51	109.85	114.75	121.44	127.34
Federal	100	101.91	105.63	110.10	115.32	120.91	125.62
State and local	100	102.87	105.43	109.71	114.43	121.76	128.37
Exports	100	99.63	99.27	101.43	105.00	108.80	112.54
Imports	100	97.50	96.34	99.69	104.53	111.12	115.61

Source: U.S. Department of Commerce, Bureau of Economic Analysis, *National Income and Product Accounts Tables*, Table 1.1.9, Implicit Price Deflators for Gross Domestic Product. Available at www.bea.gov/national/nipaweb.

uses a fixed market basket of goods that reflects the consumption patterns of a "typical" consumer in the base year. The base period is defined either as a single year or as a period of years, and the base period index is set equal to 100. All movements of the indicator indicate percentage changes from the base period. The formula for calculating the percentage change between two periods is

$$11.3 \quad \frac{\text{Period 2}}{\text{Period 1}} - 1.0 \times 100$$

The base period for the CPI is 1982 to 1984 = 100. A three-year base period is used by the BLS so that unusual consumer purchase patterns in any given year do not

FIGURE 11.8
Trends in Selected Inflation Rates (annual percentage changes of monthly data using the CPI and PPI)
Consumer Inflation—The Consumer Price Index (CPI) is a measure of the average change over time in the prices paid by urban consumers for a market basket of consumer goods and services.
Wholesale Inflation—The Producer Price Index (PPI) for finished goods measures the average change over time in the selling prices received by domestic producers of goods and services. PPIs measure price change from the perspective of the seller.
Source: Federal Reserve Economic Data (FRED II), Economic Research, Federal Reserve Bank of St. Louis, http://research.stlouisfed.org/fred2/.

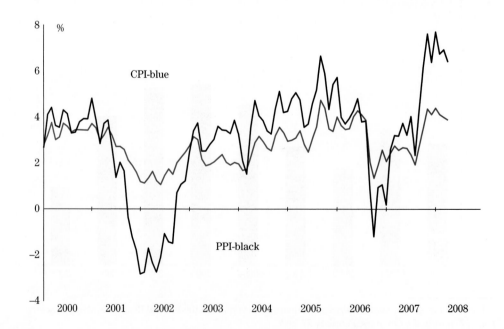

distort the index. The prices recorded are the actual transaction prices of the items in the fixed market basket of goods, including sales taxes, premiums on and discounts from listed prices, and import duties. The proportions for the various items in this fixed market basket, or the weights for each category of spending, are based on the dollar sales volume of each item in the base period and are derived from surveys of households in various geographic areas around the country. Prices for the goods and services included in the CPI are collected from 50,000 housing units and 23,000 retail and service establishments in 87 urban areas located throughout the country. Prices of fuels and some other items are obtained every month in all 87 locations. Prices of most commodities and services are collected every month in the three largest geographic areas and every other month in most areas. Data, which are obtained through personal visits and phone calls by BLS representatives, are presented both seasonally adjusted and unadjusted. Seasonally adjusted data are usually preferred because they eliminate the effect of changes, such as price movements from varying weather conditions, production cycles, model revisions, holidays, and sales, that normally occur at the same time and in about the same magnitude every year.[22]

Although the weights are updated periodically, the fixed market basket procedure creates a number of problems in the CPI over time. One problem is substitution bias. As we learned in our microeconomic analysis in Part 1, consumers will demand various quantities of goods and services in response to changes in their relative prices. Thus, consumers are likely to adjust their purchases more quickly than what is reflected in the relative weights of the expenditure categories in the CPI. This outcome means that the CPI may not reflect the actual price increases faced by consumers over time. The U.S. Bureau of Labor Statistics (BLS) has estimated that this lag in the index raises the annual CPI inflation rate 0.15 percentage point higher than would occur if the weights were updated every year.[23]

A second problem is that the CPI may not adjust adequately for changes in the quality of goods over time and for the introduction of new goods. If the quality of goods in the market basket improves over time and their prices increase, the index may not recognize that the price increase actually resulted from an increase in the quality of the product. A fixed market basket of goods also does not allow for the introduction of new goods until that market basket is revised at some point in the future.

Analysts and policy makers sometimes focus on the **core rate of inflation**, a measure of absolute price changes that excludes changes in energy and food prices. This core rate of inflation may more accurately reflect the underlying forces causing price increases rather than the special factors influencing food and energy prices. For example, food prices may fluctuate due to changes in the weather and other natural conditions, including floods and hurricanes, while energy prices are influenced by how well the Organization of Petroleum Exporting Countries maintains control over oil pricing behavior by its members and nonmembers, factors we discussed in Chapter 9.

There can be significant changes in the component categories of the CPI that can be masked by focusing only on the changes in the overall index. Table 11.5 presents the categories of the CPI that have experienced the largest price decreases and increases from 2001 to 2002 and from 1999 to 2002.

Although the overall CPI increased at approximately a 1 to 2 percent annual rate from 1999 to 2002, an estimated 30 percent of the hundreds of component categories experienced price decreases from 2001 to 2002.[24] Most of the categories with the largest increases in prices in Table 11.5 were services, while goods accounted for

Core rate of inflation
A measure of absolute price changes that excludes changes in energy and food prices.

---

[22] Bureau of Labor Statistics, "Consumer Price Index: May 2008," news release, June 13, 2008, www.bls.gov/cpi.
[23] The GDP deflator incorporates the changes in consumption patterns over time that are included in GDP and does not use the fixed weights of the CPI approach.
[24] Jon E. Hilsenrath and Lucinda Harper, "Deflation Makes a Comeback as Economy Keeps Sputtering," *Wall Street Journal*, August 13, 2002.

TABLE 11.5 Consumer Price Index Categories with the Largest Changes, 1999–2002

PRICE DECREASES (% CHANGE)	2001–2002	1999–2002	PRICE INCREASES (% CHANGE)	2001–2002	1999–2002
Personal computers	−28.9	−26.5	Cigarettes	8.8	12.1
Gasoline	−14.6	7.4	Wine away from home	7.8	4.9
Televisions	−10.3	−9.5	Hospital services	7.5	6.4
Ship fares	−6.8	−8.2	Ice cream	7.1	3.6
Computer software	−5.4	−5.2	Motor vehicle insurance	7.0	3.2
Audio equipment	−4.9	−3.4	Educational books	6.9	6.0
Cellular telephone services	−4.8	−9.4	Legal services	6.6	5.5
Dishes and flatware	−4.3	−3.6	Repair of household items	6.4	5.4
Window coverings	−4.2	−2.2	Motor oil and coolant	6.3	5.0
Toys	−4.1	−5.5	Veterinarian services	6.3	6.5
Coffee	−3.9	−2.8	College tuition	6.1	4.8
Clocks and lamps	−3.1	−3.8	Delivery services	5.9	5.8
Apparel	−2.7	−1.8	Prescription drugs	5.8	5.2
Furniture and bedding	−2.6	−1.2	Admission to sporting events	5.3	6.0
Sports equipment	−2.5	−3.2	Child care and nursery school	5.1	5.2
Photographic equipment	−2.4	−2.5	Cable television	4.7	4.5
Long-distance telephone	−2.3	−4.3	Funeral expenses	4.7	3.6
Airline fares	−2.0	4.0	Medical care	4.6	4.2
Video cassettes and discs	−1.8	−3.2	Nursing homes and adult daycare	4.6	4.6
Hotels and motels	−1.4	2.0	Rent of primary residence	4.5	3.9

Source: Jon E. Hilsenrath and Lucinda Harper, "Deflation Makes a Comeback as Economy Keeps Sputtering," *Wall Street Journal*, August 13, 2002. Copyright © 2002 Dow Jones & Co. Reprinted by permission of Dow Jones & Co. via Copyright Clearance Center.

most of the price decreases. However, there were exceptions to both trends. Air fares, hotel rates, car rental rates, and cellular telephone services experienced price decreases, while cigarettes and wine experienced price increases. Thus, a variety of changes in relative prices can occur at the industry and firm (micro) level, while the CPI is used to measure the overall trend in absolute prices at the macro level.

Producer Price Index (PPI)
A measure of the prices firms pay for crude materials; intermediate materials, supplies, and components; and finished goods.

The Producer Price Index (PPI) The **Producer Price Index (PPI)**, also illustrated in Figure 11.8, shows the rate of price increases at an earlier stage in the production process than the CPI and is a measure of the prices firms pay for intermediate goods and services. The PPI focuses on price changes of domestically produced goods and excludes services, construction, and imported goods. There are actually three indices reflecting different stages of production:

1. Crude materials for further processing (including corn, soybeans, cattle, crude petroleum, and timber)
2. Intermediate materials, supplies, and components (such as textiles, electric power, paper, glass, motor vehicle parts, and medical and surgical devices)
3. Finished goods (including fruits, meat, apparel, furniture, appliances, automobiles, and machinery)

From 1980 to 1996, the crude materials index was the most volatile, while the finished goods index varied the least. The prices of crude materials are likely to be subject to shocks from natural disasters such as floods and droughts and from social and political events such as strikes, revolutions, and wars. Crude materials are often traded in very competitive auction markets, where the forces of demand

and supply change rapidly and have an immediate effect on prices. Intermediate and final goods are further removed from these supply shocks, given their stage in the production process.[25]

Measures of Employment and Unemployment

Economists, policy makers, and managers are also concerned about the levels of employment and unemployment in an economy. The U.S. Bureau of Labor Statistics (BLS) has developed a specific set of statistics for categorizing the employment status of the population, which is shown in Figure 11.9 for 2006.[26]

The BLS obtains employment information from a monthly survey of a sample of approximately 60,000 households called the Current Population Survey (CPS). One-fourth of the households in the sample are changed each month. Persons are not asked directly whether they are employed or unemployed, but are asked a series of questions intended to determine their employment status.

The basic framework for calculating the number of employed and unemployed persons begins with the number of noninstitutionalized persons in the United States who are 16 years of age or older and who are not members of the U.S. armed forces. This definition excludes those persons who are confined to institutions, such as nursing homes or jails; those who are too young to work; and those who

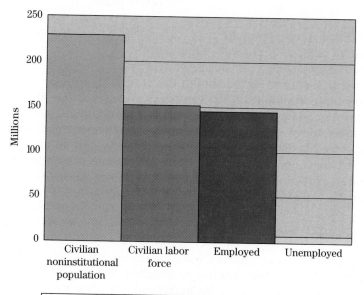

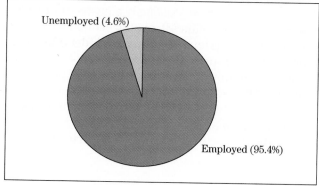

FIGURE 11.9

Labor Force Characteristics, 2006
The civilian labor force is composed of those individuals 16 years of age and over who are working in a job (employed) or who are actively seeking employment (unemployed).
Source: Bureau of Labor Statistics, http://stats.bls.gov.

---

[25] Although the PPI is used as a macro measure of the absolute price level, changes in intermediate input prices affect firms' costs and methods of production, as described in Part 1 of the text.
[26] U.S. Department of Labor, Bureau of Labor Statistics, www.stats.bls.gov.

Labor force

Those individuals 16 years of age and over who are working in a job or actively seeking employment.

Employed

Persons 16 years of age and over who, in the survey week, did any work as an employee; worked in their own business, profession, or farm; or worked without pay at least 15 hours in a family business or farm.

Unemployed

Persons 16 years of age and over who do not currently have a job, but who are actively seeking employment.

are in the armed forces. The BLS then subtracts those who are not actively seeking work, such as students, homemakers, and retirees, from this noninstitutionalized population. These individuals are not counted in the labor force.

The remaining group is defined as the **labor force**, which is divided into the employed and the unemployed. **Employed** persons are those who did any work at all as paid employees; persons working in their own business, profession, or farm; persons working at nonpaid jobs in a family business or farm for at least 15 hours a week; and persons temporarily absent from their jobs due to illness, vacation, or other reasons. Persons with more than one job are counted only once, in their primary job. **Unemployed** persons are defined as those who were not working during the survey week, were available to work except for temporary illness, and had actively looked for work during the four-week period preceding the survey week. Actively seeking work means having a job interview, contacting an employer about an interview, sending out resumes, placing or answering job advertisements, or consulting job registers.

In 2006, there were 229 million persons in the civilian noninstitutional population, of which 151.7 million or 66.2% were in the labor force. Of these, 144.7 million were employed and 7 million were unemployed.

The unemployment rate is calculated as follows:

$$11.4 \quad \textbf{Unemployment rate} = \frac{\textbf{number of unemployed}}{\textbf{labor force}} \times 100$$

Thus, for 2006 the unemployment rate was 7 million / 151.7 million, or 4.6 percent. By November 2008, the number of unemployed persons had increased to 10.3 million, and the unemployment rate had risen to 6.7 percent.[27]

Because the labor force includes both the employed and the unemployed, the unemployment rate is influenced by the number of individuals who are seeking, but cannot find work and by the size of the labor force. Persons 16 years of age or over who have looked for work in the past 12 months, but who are not currently seeking work because they believe that jobs are unavailable in their area or line of work or because they believe they would not qualify for existing job openings are considered to be **discouraged workers** who are not in the labor force. Discouraged workers are not considered unemployed because they are not actively seeking employment, but they are of concern to macroeconomic policy makers. The number of discouraged workers increased from 259,000 in November 2007 to 608,000 in November 2008.[28]

Over the course of a year, seasonal events, such as changes in weather, increased or decreased production, harvests, major holidays, and the opening and closing of schools, can cause significant changes in the nation's labor force, employment, and unemployment. These data can be seasonally adjusted for these events so that other nonseasonal factors, such as declines in overall economic activity and changes in the labor force participation of various groups, can be identified more easily. Seasonally adjusted data are more appropriate for the analysis of overall economic activity.[29]

One goal of macroeconomic policy is to promote full employment of the country's labor force. However, this policy does not seek to obtain a zero unemployment rate. Some unemployment will always exist as workers change jobs and move in and out of the labor force. Policy makers are also concerned with expanding output and employment but without exerting pressure on the price level. They often target the

Discouraged workers

Persons 16 years of age and over who are not currently seeking work because they believe that jobs in their area or line of work are unavailable or that they would not qualify for existing job openings.

---

[27] U.S. Department of Labor, Bureau of Labor Statistics, *News: The Employment Situation: November 2008.* Available at www.bls.gov.
[28] Ibid.
[29] Ibid.

natural rate of unemployment, or the minimum level of unemployment that can be achieved without causing inflation to accelerate.[30] Estimates of the natural rate of unemployment have changed over time, given differences in economic conditions and labor market institutions. Estimates rose from 3 to 4 percent in the 1960s to 6 to 7 percent in the 1970s. By the mid-1990s, estimates had declined to between 5.2 and 6.3 percent. In the late 1990s and in 2000 and 2001, there was extensive debate about whether this rate was even lower. Changes in the natural rate of unemployment are related to changes in the composition of the labor force and to increases in the productivity of the economy over time.[31]

Natural rate of unemployment
The minimum level of unemployment that can be achieved with current institutions without causing inflation to accelerate.

Managerial Rule of Thumb

Price Level and Unemployment

Managers need to be aware of how both the price level and the level of unemployment are changing. Changes in these variables can affect the demand and customer base for their products and production costs. Large changes in these variables are also likely to result in policy changes that influence the overall macroeconomic environment. ■

Major Macroeconomic Policy Issues

We end this chapter by discussing the major macroeconomic policy issues that are of concern to economists and policy makers. We then discuss the implications of these issues for managers and their firms.

What Factors Influence the Spending Behavior of the Different Sectors of the Economy?

Spending decisions by the four major sectors of the economy are the primary determinants of the overall level of GDP:

1. Household personal consumption expenditure or, for simplification, consumption (C)
2. Business gross private domestic investment expenditure, or investment (I)
3. Government consumption expenditure and gross investment, or government (G)
4. Net exports of goods and services (F), or export expenditure (X) minus import expenditure (M)

Economists and policy makers are concerned about the factors that influence the spending behavior of the individuals or organizations in these different sectors. The opening *Wall Street Journal* article presented some of these factors, such as the effect of the turmoil in the housing and credit markets on consumption spending and the impact of domestic versus foreign activity on investment spending. There are various indicators of economic activity in each of these sectors, such as the Institute for Supply Management index of factory activity, not all of which move in the same direction. This divergence makes it difficult for both policy makers and managers to determine exactly where the economy is headed and can lead to differences in forecasts of future economic activity.

---

[30] The natural rate of unemployment is also called the non-accelerating inflation rate of unemployment (NAIRU).
[31] Thomas B. King and James Morley, "In Search of the Natural Rate of Unemployment," *Journal of Monetary Economics*, 54 (March 2007): 550–564.

How Do Behavior Changes in These Sectors Influence the Level of Output and Income in the Economy?

Equilibrium level of output and income
The level of aggregate output and income where there is a balance between spending and production decisions and where the economy will stay unless acted on by other forces.

Once we understand the factors influencing the spending patterns of the different sectors of the economy and the data used to measure these factors, we can determine the resulting level of output and income. We call this outcome the **equilibrium level of output and income**, the level toward which the economy is moving and at which it will stay unless a shock causes the economy to deviate from equilibrium.

Equilibrium implies a balance between the spending and production decisions in the economy. For example, in December 2008, Chrysler LLC confirmed that it would suspend all manufacturing operations for at least a month "in an effort to align production and inventory with U.S. market demand."[32] This behavior itself can change the equilibrium level of output and income in the economy. Thus, we need to know what factors determine equilibrium and how the economy moves from a disequilibrium situation to one of equilibrium.[33]

Can Policy Makers Maintain Stable Prices, Full Employment, and Adequate Economic Growth over Time?

Policy makers are concerned with keeping the country's resources fully employed while maintaining an environment with relatively stable prices and avoiding either inflation or deflation. The economy tends to experience increases and decreases in activity, given the interactions among the spending decisions of individuals in the various sectors. One of the specific goals of policy makers is to keep the economy as close to full employment as possible without setting off a period of inflation as output and employment move close to the capacity of the economy. In the short run, there is often a trade-off between the level of unemployment and a stable price level. As the economy moves closer to full employment, there will be upward pressure on both wages and prices, which can cause the price level to increase.

The policy goals of full employment and stable prices have been established for both Congress and the Federal Reserve System by the Employment Act of 1946 and the Full Employment and Balanced Growth Act of 1978 (the Humphrey-Hawkins Act). The 1946 legislation requires government institutions to promote "maximum employment, production, and purchasing power." The 1978 act requires the chairman of the Federal Reserve System to appear before Congress twice a year to present the central bank's forecast for the economy and to discuss its future policies.

Both high unemployment and high inflation impose costs on the economy. High unemployment results in lost output. For individuals, unemployment means lost income, a deterioration in skills if the unemployment is prolonged, and a loss of self-worth. These factors can cause social unrest if the unemployment rate is substantial, as in the Great Depression of the 1930s, and they can result in increased crime and other antisocial behaviors during recessions.

Inflation and deflation also impose costs on the economy in terms of planning for the future and the establishment of contracts. Inflation can redistribute income

---

[32] Lauren Pollock and Neal E. Boudette, "Chrysler to Close Manufacturing Plants for a Month Starting Friday," *Wall Street Journal*, December 17, 2008.

[33] Although the variables and level of analysis are quite different, the process we follow to understand these factors is similar to that which we followed to understand the forces of demand, supply, and equilibrium in individual markets, which we discussed in Part 1 of the text. We also examined forces causing changes in market equilibrium in those chapters.

between those who can raise their prices and wages and those who are unable to do so. Individuals living on fixed incomes from pensions or investments will be worse off if these sources of income do not increase with the inflation rate. Borrowers gain and lenders lose with inflation because the payments on loans, such as home mortgages, may not increase with inflation. Inflation results in uncertainty about what the real purchasing power of money will be in the future. It creates difficulties in writing contracts for future payments, and high inflation may even undermine individuals' faith in their government and economic system. Inflation reduces managerial efficiency, as managers are forced to spend time and resources to protect their firms against inflation.

Although the U.S. economy has not experienced a period of prolonged deflation since the Great Depression of the 1930s, falling prices can cause business profits to decrease and employees to be laid off if the price decreases result from a lack of spending in the economy. Borrowers lose and lenders gain in a deflationary environment. Firms may not be able to pay off their debts and may go into bankruptcy, further cutting wages and employment.[34]

Over longer periods of time, policy makers are concerned with the amount of economic growth or increase in real GDP, as this growth has a substantial impact on the well-being of individuals in the economy. In the short run, over several years in the future, the main focus of economic policy makers is on influencing expenditures (the demand side of the economy) to promote full employment with low inflation. Over longer periods of time, policy interest focuses more on the capacity of the economy to produce more goods and services (the supply side of the economy). These issues relate to increasing the quality, quantity, and productivity of the inputs of production.

How Do Fiscal, Monetary, and Balance of Payments Policies Influence the Economy?

Given these policy goals, managers need to understand how spending in each of the sectors of the economy and the overall level of economic activity are affected by **fiscal policy**, or changes in taxes and government spending by the executive and legislative branches of government; **monetary policy**, or changes in the money supply and interest rates by the Federal Reserve, the country's central bank; and **balance of payments issues**, or changes in the rate at which different countries' currencies can be exchanged for each other and in the flow of goods and services and financial assets among countries.

Policy makers in a country's legislative and executive institutions use taxes and government expenditures as tools to influence the growth of GDP, among other goals. These tools include policies that influence aggregate expenditure (the demand side of the economy) and policies that affect incentives to work, save, and invest (the supply side of the economy). The central bank, which is independent from the government in the United States, uses its control over the money supply to change interest rates and credit conditions in order to influence consumer and business spending. All of these institutions must respond to changes in a country's **currency exchange rate**, the rate at which one country's currency can be exchanged for that of another; the **trade balance**, the relationship between a country's exports and imports; and **capital flows**, the buying and selling of existing real and financial assets among countries.

Fiscal policy

Changes in taxes and spending by the executive and legislative branches of a country's national government that can be used to either stimulate or restrain the economy.

Monetary policy

Policies adopted by a country's central bank that influence interest rates and credit conditions, which, in turn, influence consumer and business spending.

Balance of payments issues

Issues related to the relative value of different countries' currencies and the flow of goods, services, and financial assets among countries.

Currency exchange rate

The rate at which one country's currency can be exchanged for that of another.

Trade balance

The relationship between a country's exports and imports, which may be either positive (exports exceed imports) or negative (imports exceed exports).

Capital flows

The buying and selling of existing real and financial assets among countries.

---

[34] Greg Ip, "Inside the Fed, Deflation Is Drawing a Closer Look," *Wall Street Journal*, November 6, 2002.

What Impact Do These Macro Changes Have on Different Firms and Industries?

As we have noted throughout this chapter, managers have little influence over the macro environment, but their competitive strategies and the profitability of their firms are influenced by macroeconomic events. Some of these events are the outcomes of specific monetary and fiscal policies, while others result from changes in the behavior of individuals, both domestically and around the world.

Managers need to understand and anticipate changes in the macro environment. They may do so by purchasing the services of various economic forecasting firms or by developing their own in-house forecasting capacity. In either case, they will focus on the variables described in this chapter and the remainder of the text. Managers also need to realize that their firms will be affected differentially by macroeconomic changes. The opening news article noted that firms with export business were less affected by the economic slowdown in 2007 and 2008 than those that depended primarily on demand in the United States. Firms that sell in international markets will be more influenced by factors such as fluctuating currency exchange rates than are those firms operating only in domestic markets. Some firms and industries are more sensitive to changes in interest rates than others. However, all firms will be affected by changes in the overall level of economic activity or GDP. As discussed in the opening news article, managers must be prepared to revise their competitive strategies in light of changing conditions in the macroeconomic environment.

Managerial Rule of Thumb

Competitive Strategies and the Macro Environment

The impact of the macro environment on competitive strategies may vary substantially among firms and industries. Managers need to develop the ability to forecast and anticipate changes in the macro environment by either purchasing services from forecasting firms or developing their own in-house forecasting capacity. ■

Summary

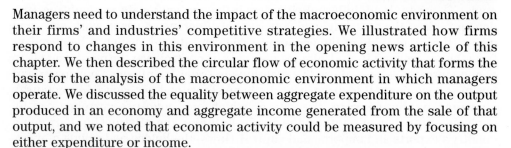

Managers need to understand the impact of the macroeconomic environment on their firms' and industries' competitive strategies. We illustrated how firms respond to changes in this environment in the opening news article of this chapter. We then described the circular flow of economic activity that forms the basis for the analysis of the macroeconomic environment in which managers operate. We discussed the equality between aggregate expenditure on the output produced in an economy and aggregate income generated from the sale of that output, and we noted that economic activity could be measured by focusing on either expenditure or income.

We then analyzed the national income accounting system used in the United States to measure gross domestic product and its components. We also discussed measures of the price level and the level of employment and unemployment. We then related these variables to the major macroeconomic goals of policy makers, and we discussed how changes in macro events influence managerial strategies.

In the next chapter, we begin our analysis of the aggregate macroeconomic model that will help managers understand the spending decisions of individuals in different sectors of the economy, how these decisions lead to an equilibrium level of aggregate output and income, and why that equilibrium changes over time.

Key Terms

absolute price level, p. 299

aggregate expenditure, p. 285

balance of payments
    issues, p. 307

business cycles, p. 290

business fixed
    investment, p. 292

capital flows, p. 307

changes in business
    inventories, p. 293

circular flow, p. 284

compensation of
    employees, p. 296

Consumer Price Index
    (CPI), p. 299

core rate of inflation, p. 301

corporate profits, p. 297

currency exchange rate, p. 307

deflation, p. 299

discouraged workers, p. 304

disposable income, p. 298

durable goods, p. 292

earnings or income
    approach, p. 285

employed, p. 304

equilibrium level of output and
    income, p. 306

expansion, p. 290

expenditure or output
    approach, p. 285

export spending, p. 294

final goods and services, p. 287

fiscal policy, p. 307

GDP deflator, p. 289

government consumption
    expenditures and gross
    investment, p. 293

gross domestic product
    (GDP), p. 284

gross private domestic
    investment spending, p. 292

import spending, p. 294

imputed value, p. 288

inflation, p. 299

intermediate goods and
    services, p. 287

labor force, p. 304

mixed economy, p. 284

monetary policy, p. 307

national income, p. 296

national income accounting
    system, p. 286

National Income and Product
    Accounts, p. 286

natural rate of
    unemployment, p. 305

net export spending, p. 294

net interest, p. 297

nominal GDP, p. 288

nondurable goods, p. 292

open economy, p. 285

personal consumption
    expenditures, p. 291

personal income, p. 298

Producer Price Index
    (PPI), p. 302

proprietors' income, p. 297

real GDP, p. 288

recession, p. 290

relative prices, p. 298

rental income, p. 297

residential fixed
    investment, p. 293

saving, p. 298

services, p. 292

trade balance, p. 307

transfer payments, p. 288

underground
    economy, p. 288

unemployed, p. 304

value-added approach, p. 287

Exercises

Technical Questions

1. Do government statisticians calculate GDP by simply adding up the total sales of all business firms in one year? Explain.

2. Evaluate whether *all* of the following are considered to be investment (*I*) in calculating GDP.

    a. The purchase of a new automobile for private, nonbusiness use

    b. The purchase of a new house

    c. The purchase of corporate bonds

3. Explain whether transfer payments, such as Social Security and unemployment compensation, are counted as government spending in calculating GDP.

4. Is it true that the value of U.S. imports is added to exports when calculating U.S. GDP because imports reflect spending by Americans? Explain.

TABLE 11.E1 Nominal Versus Real GDP

YEAR	COFFEE (CUPS)		MILK (GALLONS)		GDP (NOMINAL,REAL)
2007	Price	Quantity	Price	Quantity	
(The base year)	$1.00	10	$2.00	20	
Expenditure					
2008 (Case 1)	Price	Quantity	Price	Quantity	
	$1.50	10	$4.00	20	
Expenditure					
2008 (Case 2)	Price	Quantity	Price	Quantity	
	$1.00	15	$2.00	40	
Expenditure					
2008 (Case 3)	Price	Quantity	Price	Quantity	
	$1.50	15	$4.00	40	
Expenditure					

5. Is real GDP defined as "the value of aggregate output produced when the economy is operating at full employment"? Explain.

6. Suppose an economy produces only two goods, cups of coffee and gallons of milk, as shown in Table 11.E1:

   a. Calculate the expenditure on each good and the nominal and real GDP for 2007, the base year.

   b. Repeat this exercise for each of the three alternative cases (1, 2, and 3).

   c. Explain the differences between nominal and real GDP in each of these cases.

7. Adding to Table 11.1, if real GDP in 2002 were $10,048.8 billion and nominal GDP in 2002 were $10,469.6 billion, calculate the percentage change from 2001 to 2002 in nominal GDP, real GDP, and the price level. What is the value of the GDP deflator in 2002?

Application Questions

1. Drawing on current business publications, discuss whether current strategies in the manufacturing sector are similar to or different from those described in the opening article of this chapter that pertained to late 2007. How do changes in the macro environment influence these strategies?

2. From the Bureau of Economic Analysis Web page (www.bea.gov), compare real GDP for 1960, 1970, 1980, 1990, and 2000. Show the percentage change in real GDP over each of those decades. Do the percentages of GDP spent on consumption (C), investment (I), government (G), exports (X), and imports (M) differ significantly among those years? Are there changes in the balance of trade over the period? Explain.

3. From the Bureau of Economic Analysis Web page (www.bea.gov), construct a table showing the annual percentage change in real GDP, gross private domestic investment (I), nonresidential fixed investment, and residential fixed investment from 2000 to 2008. Discuss how the changes

in these variables show the differences between the recession of 2001 and the recession in 2007 and 2008 that is discussed in the news article that opened this chapter.

4. Find an article in a current business publication that discusses revisions in the GDP data. How significant were these revisions for your example?

5. From the Bureau of Labor Statistics Web page (www.bls.gov/cpi), find the answers to the following questions:

   a. How is the CPI used?

   b. How is the CPI market basket determined?

   c. What goods and services does the CPI cover?

   d. How are CPI prices collected and reviewed?

6. From the Bureau of Labor Statistics Web page (www.bls.gov/cps), find the annual averages of the employment status of the civilian noninstitutional population from 1940 to date. Construct a table and chart showing the size of the civilian noninstitutional population, the civilian labor

force, the number of employed, the number of unemployed, and the unemployment rates for 1969, 1982, 1992, 2000, 2003, and 2007. Discuss how these variables differed in those time periods.

7. From the National Bureau of Economic Research Web site (www.nber.org), find the official beginning and ending dates of the recessions that have occurred since 1965. Which recession was the longest and which was the shortest?

8. Drawing on current business publications, find an article in which either fiscal or monetary policy makers were describing their goals of maintaining stable prices, full employment, and adequate economic growth over time. Which goal was the most important at the time your article was written?

On the Web

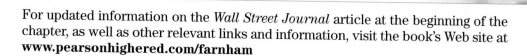

For updated information on the *Wall Street Journal* article at the beginning of the chapter, as well as other relevant links and information, visit the book's Web site at **www.pearsonhighered.com/farnham**

12

Spending by Individuals, Firms, and Governments on Real Goods and Services

I

n this chapter, we begin to develop the aggregate macroeconomic model that will help managers understand the macroeconomy and answer the questions posed at the end of the previous chapter:

- What factors influence the spending behavior of the different sectors of the economy?
- How do the behavior changes in these sectors influence the level of output and income in the economy?
- Can policy makers maintain stable prices, full employment, and adequate economic growth over time?
- How do fiscal, monetary, and balance of payments policies influence the economy?
- What impact do these macro changes have on different firms and industries?

In Chapter 11, we focused on the national income accounting problems of defining gross domestic product and its components based on the underlying circular flow concept. We now turn our attention to building the aggregate macroeconomic model that *explains* the spending decisions of the different sectors of the economy: We begin this chapter by discussing the *Wall Street Journal* article, "Jobs Data Suggest U.S. Is in Recession; Largest Payroll Fall in Five Years Spurs New Stimulus Talk."

Jobs Data Suggest U.S. Is in Recession; Largest Payroll Fall in Five Years Spurs New Stimulus Talk

by Sudeep Reddy

Wall Street Journal, *March 8, 2008*

U.S. employers shed 63,000 jobs last month, the most in five years, reinforcing a widening view that the U.S. is falling into recession. Among economists and politicians, the debate is shifting to how deep the downturn will be and how to ease it.

The jobs dropoff came after the nation lost 22,000 jobs in January, the Labor Department said. In the past, such back-to-back monthly employment declines have occurred only around recessions.

Coming amid continued turmoil in the financial and credit markets, the report sent stocks lower, with the Dow Jones Industrial Average falling 146.70 points Friday to close at 11,893.69. The index lost 3% for the full week. . . .

Easing the worries slightly, the Federal Reserve said it is stepping up efforts to restore credit markets to health by injecting cash into money markets and making larger direct loans to banks.

The Fed's actions were an effort to bring down interest rates banks charge to one another and stabilize the market for mortgage-backed securities, whose falling prices have lowered the value of the collateral posted by firms that hold large quantities of them. . . . As banks demand more collateral and the firms are forced to sell assets, prices fall further. . . .

Before the employment report, many economists had said the labor market, while weakening, wasn't signaling that the economy was in a recession. Many changed their tune Friday, saying it's probable the U.S. economy, punished by falling home prices and troubles at financial institutions, is already in a recession.

Private-sector jobs fell by 101,000, the third straight month of declines. The February unemployment rate edged down to 4.8% from 4.9%, but only because some job-seekers quit looking for work. . . .

Administration officials said they were confident conditions would improve as tax rebates that are part of the recent $152 billion economic-stimulus law begin to reach consumers. . . .

Democratic presidential candidates seized on the jobs report to contend that the Bush administration has botched its handling of the economy and that additional measures are needed.

Mr. [Lawrence] Summers, a Democrat, said federal officials should begin planning now for more stimulus measures. He said state and local governments should consider buying foreclosed homes to rent them and look at ways to reduce the principal owned by mortgage borrowers to avoid foreclosures. He said the government may need to guarantee, for a fee, municipal bonds and student loans because distressed markets are making it tough for borrowers to find credit.

Fed Chairman Ben Bernanke has made a similar proposal on mortgages, urging some lenders to reduce the principal, or outstanding balance, on home loans.

The Fed is expected to cut interest rates again to prop up the economy. Futures markets anticipate the Fed will cut its target for the federal-funds rate, charged on overnight loans between banks, by 0.75 percentage point from its current 3% when it meets March 18.

Fed officials, while agreeing on the need for easing, believe they have done a lot already and that cutting as deeply as markets expect could aggravate inflation concerns, perhaps through a weaker dollar. That suggests they would prefer a half-point cut. But weakening markets and economic data could force them to deliver the larger cut, as has happened in the past. . . .

How much the economy continues to deteriorate remains uncertain. Corporate balance sheets are still relatively strong, and business inventories are already lean enough that they aren't expected to show the sharp declines that accompanied the 2001 recession.

At the same time, housing-price declines and rising energy costs are adding to the troubles in the job market and putting at risk consumer spending, which accounts for more than 70% of economic activity. . . .

A declaration of a 2008 recession, if one occurs, probably would not come before the summer. The National Bureau of Economic Research, the academic group that dates recessions, tends to wait until it can definitely mark the starting point of a contraction. The bureau announced the beginning of the last recession in March 2001 eight months after the fact—by which point, it determined later, the recession was already over. . . .

Case for Analysis

Expenditure on Real Goods and Services and Employment Effects

This article describes the changes in the U.S. economy that occurred in 2007 and 2008 as the economy slowed and headed into a recession. The article discusses changes in all sectors of the economy, *consumption, investment, government*, and *net export spending*, and the impact of these changes on the level of U.S. employment. The article highlights the *fiscal policy* response of the Congress and the Bush administration to the declining economic conditions, the $152 billion economic-stimulus package passed in February 2008. The impact of the Federal Reserve's *monetary policy* on interest rates is described as well as the Fed's dual concerns about both slowing economic growth and possible rising inflation. The *exchange rate* impact of monetary policy on the value of the dollar and its effect on real spending is also mentioned. Throughout the article there is a sense of uncertainty about whether the data actually show that the United States is headed into or is already in a recession. The article notes that the National Bureau of Economic Research (NBER) Business Cycle Dating Committee did not officially mark the beginning of the recession in March 2001 until eight months later—after, as it was eventually determined, the recession was over. As discussed in Chapter 11, it was not until November 2008 that the NBER committee declared that the next recession began in December 2007.[1] ∎

Framework for Macroeconomic Analysis

As with the microeconomic models in Part 1 of the text, the aggregate model we use in macroeconomic analysis provides a framework for managers to examine changes in the macro environment. This model helps managers interpret the vast amount of macroeconomic data released by the government and other sources, as illustrated in the opening news article.

Focus on the Short Run

Potential GDP
The maximum amount of GDP that can be produced at any point in time, which depends on the size of the labor force, the number of structures and the amount of equipment in the economy, and the state of technology.

In the last chapter, we briefly discussed the differences between short-run and long-run macroeconomic models. In the short run, a period of up to several years into the future, macroeconomic policy focuses primarily on the demand or expenditure side of the economy. **Potential GDP**, or the maximum amount of output that can be produced, varies little, if at all, over this period of time. Potential GDP depends on the size of the labor force, the number of structures and the amount of equipment in the economy, and the state of technology, factors that do not change rapidly over the short run. Thus, the short-run macroeconomic policy goal is managing aggregate expenditure to keep the economy close to its potential output and the labor force fully employed without setting off an increase in the price level or an inflationary spiral. As the economy approaches full employment and potential GDP, there is a tendency for prices and wages to rise. Because the goal of policy makers is to maintain both stable prices and high employment and output, short-run macroeconomic policy focuses on minimizing fluctuations around potential GDP. To achieve this goal, policy makers emphasize the demand side of the economy, using monetary and fiscal policies to either stimulate or reduce aggregate expenditures around a relatively fixed target, as noted in the opening article.

Over a longer-run period, macroeconomic policy focuses more on potential GDP, or the supply side of the economy. Potential GDP can change over time because the size of the labor force, the number of structures and the amount of equipment, and

---

[1] National Bureau of Economic Research Business Cycle Dating Committee. "Determination of the December 2007 Peak in Economic Activity," December 11, 2008, www.nber.org.

the state of technology change. The standard of living of a society over long periods of time depends on increases in potential real GDP.[2] Therefore, long-run macroeconomic policies concentrate on incentives for increasing productivity and the potential output of the economy. These policies include education and training programs to increase the quality of the labor force and tax incentives for businesses to increase investment and for workers to increase their participation in the labor force and their hours worked.

Some of these policies may have both demand- and supply-side effects. For example, tax incentives to stimulate business investment spending influence aggregate expenditure in the short run. The incentives should also increase the capacity of the economy to produce over the long run, as investment spending focuses on structures and equipment that can be used to produce goods and services in the future. Thus, investment spending plays a dual role, influencing both the demand and the supply sides of the economy. Much debate over macroeconomic investment expenditure policies centers on the size of the short-run (demand) versus long-run (supply) effects of these policies.

This text focuses on *short-run macroeconomic models* because managers and their firms are most affected by short-run factors. Managers' competitive strategies are influenced by changes in the macroeconomic environment over the next few months, quarters, and years, and not in the more distant future, because most business planning horizons are in the three- to five-year range. Managers need to be able to understand how changes in monetary and fiscal policies or international events affect the environment in which they operate and may create opportunities or impediments for their current competitive strategies.[3]

Analysis in Real Versus Nominal Terms

As we discussed in the previous chapter, changes in aggregate expenditure and gross domestic product can be measured in either **real terms** or **nominal terms**, depending on whether the price level is assumed to be constant or allowed to vary. As we build the aggregate model, we assume in this and the next chapter that the price level is constant. Thus, any changes in aggregate expenditure represent changes in real income and output (more or fewer real goods, services, and income). Although inflation (a general increase in the price level) represents a major policy problem for most industrialized countries, we will not discuss this problem until we fully develop aggregate demand and aggregate supply in Chapter 14. This simplification of assuming that prices are constant in Chapters 12 and 13 allows us to focus on the behavioral factors influencing real spending in the various sectors of the economy before introducing price-level changes.

Real terms
Measuring expenditures and income with the price level held constant, so that any changes in these values represent changes in the actual amount of goods, services, and income.

Nominal terms
Measuring expenditures and income with the price level allowed to vary, so that changes in these values represent changes in the actual amount of goods, services, and income; changes in the price level; or a combination of both factors.

Treatment of the Foreign Sector

Because export and import spending on currently produced goods and services is included in gross domestic product or aggregate expenditure, we incorporate this aspect of the foreign sector in this and the next two chapters. However, we wait to discuss other international issues, such as the flows of financial assets among countries and currency exchange rate determination, until Chapter 15.

---

[2] Remember the differences in GDP and national income per capita among the various countries in Figures 11.3a and 11.3b in the previous chapter.

[3] For a complete discussion of both short- and long-run macroeconomic models, see Robert J. Gordon, *Macroeconomics*, 10th ed. (New York: Addison-Wesley, 2006); Olivier Blanchard, *Macroeconomics*, 5th ed. (Upper Saddle River, N.J.: Prentice Hall, 2009); Richard T. Froyen, *Macroeconomics: Theories and Policies*, 8th ed. (Upper Saddle River, N.J.: Prentice Hall, 2005); and N. Gregory Mankiw, *Macroeconomics*, 6th ed. (New York: Worth Publishers, 2007).

FIGURE 12.1
The Aggregate Macroeconomic Model
The components of the aggregate macroeconomic model.

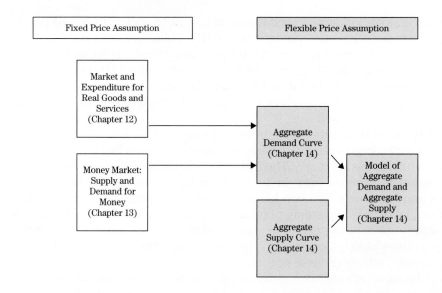

Outline for Macroeconomic Analysis

Figure 12.1 presents a framework for developing the short-run aggregate macroeconomic model. (We will refer back to this framework in the following chapters.) We begin this chapter by analyzing the factors influencing real aggregate expenditure and defining the equilibrium level of expenditure and income. In Chapter 13, we analyze the money market and the factors influencing the demand for and supply of money. The crucial link between the real and monetary sides of the economy is the interest rate, which we discuss in Chapter 14. We then relax the fixed price assumption to derive the aggregate demand curve, and we develop the concept of aggregate supply, which incorporates variables determining the size of potential GDP. Combining aggregate demand with aggregate supply allows us to fully develop the short-run aggregate macroeconomic model that incorporates all the factors influencing both the level of real income and output (real GDP) and the price level.

The Components of Aggregate Expenditure

Aggregate expenditure
The sum of personal consumption expenditure, investment expenditure, government expenditure, and net export expenditure in a given period of time.

Let's look at the components of **aggregate expenditure** as established by the U.S. Bureau of Economic Analysis (BEA): personal consumption expenditure (C), investment expenditure (I), government expenditure (G), and net export expenditure (F), or export spending (X) minus import spending (M).

Personal Consumption Expenditure

Personal consumption expenditure
The amount of spending by households on durable goods, nondurable goods, and services in a given period of time.

Personal consumption expenditure is the amount of spending by households on durable goods, nondurable goods, and services in a given period of time. It is influenced by the level of real income in the economy and by a number of other factors, such as the turmoil in the housing market, as noted in the opening article of this chapter.

The Relationship Between Personal Consumption Expenditure and Income   Personal consumption expenditure (C) on currently produced goods and services is determined primarily by the level of disposable income, or income net of personal taxes ($Y_d = Y - T_P$, where Y_d is disposable income, Y is personal income, and T_P represents personal taxes).[4] This concept, called the **consumption function**, was introduced by John Maynard Keynes, the father of modern macroeconomics, in his 1936 book *The General Theory of Employment, Interest, and Money*. The theory of the consumption function also assumes that as disposable income increases, consumption spending increases by a smaller amount. This assumption means that the **marginal propensity to consume (*MPC*)**, which is defined as $\Delta C/\Delta Y_d$ or $\Delta C/\Delta(Y - T_P)$, is less than 1. All other variables that affect consumption expenditure are assumed to be constant when defining the consumption function. In 2002, economists at Wells Fargo & Company attributed 75 percent of consumer spending to income, while those at the Conference Board used a 90 percent figure.[5]

The impact of changes in overall real income on individual firms' and managers' strategies depends on the factors affecting the demand for that firm's product that we discussed in Part 1. For example, in November 2008, retailers reported that same-store sales fell 2.7 percent compared with the previous year, the largest decrease since 1969. However, Wal-Mart's same-store sales increased 3.4 percent, given its low prices and strong food sales. Costco Wholesale Corp. lagged behind Wal-Mart because it derived more of its sales from higher-priced jewelry and electronics. Year-end reports indicated that holiday sales of luxury goods fell 21.2 percent in 2008 compared with an increase of 7.5 percent in 2007. Electronics and appliance sales decreased 26.7 percent compared with a 2.7 percent gain in 2007, while sales of women's apparel declined 22.7 percent compared with a 2.4 percent drop in 2007.[6]

Household **saving (*S*)**, as defined in Chapter 11, is the amount of disposable income that households do *not* spend on the consumption of goods and services. Therefore, $S = Y_d - C$ or $C + S = Y_d$. The **marginal propensity to save (*MPS*)**, which is defined as $\Delta S/\Delta Y_d$ or $\Delta S/\Delta(Y - T_P)$, equals $1 - MPC$.

The Level of Personal Taxes   As just noted, consumption depends on disposable income, or personal income less personal taxes. Therefore, any increases or decreases in taxes will influence consumption spending. For example, Congress passed the Economic Growth and Tax Relief Reconciliation Act of 2001 in June 2001 to help offset the effects of the economic downturn that occurred early that year. To speed up the effects of this tax cut on personal consumption expenditure, $300 and $600 rebate checks were mailed to households in the summer of 2001.[7]

In May 2003, Congress passed another tax cut designed to further stimulate the economy. This legislation affected personal taxes by cutting tax rates across the board, increasing the child care credit, and reducing the tax penalty on married couples. A number of provisions in the bill were scheduled to expire after several years.[8]

In February 2008, Congress passed and President Bush signed a $168 billion economic-stimulus bill designed to slow the decline in economic activity. Taxpayers received up to $600 for individuals or $1,200 for married couples,

Consumption function
The fundamental relationship in macroeconomics that assumes that household consumption spending depends primarily on the level of disposable income (net of taxes) in the economy, all other variables held constant.

Marginal propensity to consume (*MPC*)
The additional consumption spending generated by an additional amount of real income, assumed to take a value less than 1.

Saving (*S*)
The amount of disposable income that households do *not* spend on the consumption of goods and services.

Marginal propensity to save (*MPS*)
The additional household saving generated by an additional amount of real income, which equals $1 - MPC$.

---

[4] We noted in Chapter 11 that households receive some income in the form of transfer payments, income that results from transfers among individuals or governments and not from the production of goods and services. The variable T_P is actually personal taxes net of any transfer income. For simplicity, we assume that transfers are zero in the model and refer to T_P as taxes. We also assume that taxes are lump sum and do not depend on the level of income.

[5] Bernard Wysocki, Jr., "Forget the Wealth Effect: Income Drives Spending," *Wall Street Journal*, August 12, 2002.

[6] Jennifer Saranow, Ann Zimmerman, and Kevin Kingsbury, "Retail Sales Notch Biggest Drop in 39 Years," *Wall Street Journal*, December 5, 2008; Ann Zimmerman, Jennifer Saranow, and Miguel Bustillo, "Retail Sales Plummet," *Wall Street Journal*, December 26, 2008.

[7] U.S. Congressional Budget Office, *The Budget and Economic Outlook: Fiscal Years 2003–2012* (Washington, D.C.: U.S. Government Printing Office, January 2002).

[8] Shailagh Murray, "House, Senate Hammer Out $350 Billion Tax-Relief Deal," *Wall Street Journal*, May 23, 2003; Greg Ip and John D. McKinnon, "Tax Plan Would Boost Growth, But Would Also Widen Deficits," *Wall Street Journal*, May 23, 2003.

amounts that phased out at higher income levels. Millions of individuals who did not pay income taxes but who had incomes of at least $3,000 received smaller rebates.[9]

The effect of a tax cut on consumption expenditures depends on whether the cut is temporary or permanent and on who receives the cut. Temporary tax changes are likely to be much less effective than permanent changes in influencing consumption spending because individuals may not change their spending behavior in response to a temporary change in taxes. Economists have estimated that over a one-year time frame, a temporary tax change will have only a little more than half the impact of a permanent change of equal size and a tax rebate will have only 38 percent as much impact.[10]

By fall 2008, economists estimated that the February 2008 tax cut had only a small impact on the economy because consumers saved the rebates rather than spending them, given the temporary nature of the program. The economic stimulus bill offset the declining economy only slightly in the second and third quarters of 2008.[11]

The Real Interest Rate   We argue later in the chapter that the real interest rate is a primary determinant of business investment spending. However, changes in interest rates can also influence consumer spending, particularly for durable goods such as automobiles and large appliances, for which consumers may have to borrow. For example, automobile dealers' zero percent financing and other incentives largely drove the 6.1 percent increase in consumer spending in the fourth quarter of 2001 that helped the economy come out of recession.[12]

When the Fed began its extensive interest rate cutting in September 2007 to try to offset problems in the housing market, rates on home-equity lines of credit, automobile loans, and credit cards all decreased. Home equity loan rates dropped from 8.25 to 6.27 percent between September 2007 and March 2008, although some companies, such as Countrywide Financial Corp. and Washington Mutual Inc., reduced or froze the amount of credit available to certain borrowers to protect themselves against falling home values and rising delinquencies. Credit card rates fell from 13.97 to 12.36 percent in this period, although some consumers began encountering their floor rates, predetermined points below which the rates charged would not decrease regardless of what happened to other interest rates in the economy. Automobile loan rates decreased from 7.72 to only 7.22 percent, a reflection of the heavy manufacturer incentives already being offered.[13]

It is the **real interest rate**, or the **nominal interest rate** adjusted for expected inflation, that influences both consumers' and firms' spending decisions. This is another application of real versus nominal variables and the influence of a constant versus a changing price level, which we discussed in Chapter 11. Lenders will charge borrowers a nominal interest rate (i), which is based on the real interest rate (r) and the expected rate of inflation. The real interest rate, which is necessary

Real interest rate
The nominal interest rate adjusted for expected inflation, which is the rate that influences firms' investment decisions.

Nominal interest rate
The real interest rate plus the expected rate of inflation, which may differ substantially from the real interest rate during periods of inflation.

---

[9] Sarah Lueck, "Congress Approves Economic-Stimulus Bill," *Wall Street Journal*, February 8, 2008.

[10] Shailagh Murray and John D. McKinnon, "Instant Tax Cuts to Stimulate Economy Have Fizzled, Even Backfired in Past," *Wall Street Journal*, April 4, 2001. Consumer behavior can be different than anticipated. When President George Bush announced in January 1992 that he was reducing the amount of tax withheld from paychecks, few economists expected that this change would stimulate consumption spending. A research study later showed that 43 percent of those who responded to a telephone survey said they would spend most of the increase in take-home pay and that this program would have a moderate effect in stimulating the economy. See Matthew D. Shapiro and Joel Slemrod, "Consumer Response to the Timing of Income: Evidence from a Change in Withholding," *American Economic Review* 85 (March 1995): 274–83.

[11] Sudeep Reddy, "Congress Postpones Stimulus Plan to '09," *Wall Street Journal*, November 21, 2008; John B. Taylor, "Why Permanent Tax Cuts Are the Best Stimulus," *Wall Street Journal*, November 25, 2008.

[12] "Economy Surged 5.8% in 1st Quarter as Businesses Slowed Inventory Cuts," *Wall Street Journal*, April 26, 2002.

[13] Jeff D. Opdyke and Jane J. Kim, "Why Only Some See Benefit from Fed's Cuts," *Wall Street Journal*, March 19, 2008.

to induce them to make the loan and give up the use of their funds, would exist even if prices were stable. However, in times of inflation, lenders will add a premium to the real interest rate to compensate them for the fact that they will be paid back in dollars that have less purchasing power.

For example, in 1978, nominal interest rates averaged 8 percent, but the rate of inflation was 9 percent. Although nominal interest rates were high, the real interest rate was actually negative 1 percent. In early 1999, nominal rates were approximately 4.75 percent, while the inflation rate was 2 percent. Thus, the real interest rate in 1999 was 2.75 percent. The real rate was actually higher in the period of low inflation than in the period of high inflation.[14]

Consumer Confidence   Consumer confidence also affects consumer spending decisions such that decreases in confidence might make consumers restrain their spending, endangering the recovery from a recession or helping one to occur. There are two measures of consumer confidence: the **Consumer Sentiment Index (CSI)**, prepared by the University of Michigan, and the **Consumer Confidence Index (CCI)**, prepared by the Conference Board, a nonprofit, nonpartisan research organization that monitors consumer confidence and business expectations about the future.[15] The CSI is published monthly and combines households' attitudes in three areas into one index:

1. Expected business conditions in the national economy for one and five years ahead
2. Personal financial conditions compared with the previous year and the next year
3. Consumer confidence regarding the purchase of furniture and major household appliances

The CCI, on the other hand, includes households' perceptions of general business conditions, available jobs in the households' local area, and expected personal family income in the coming six months. The CCI samples 5,000 households with a mail survey, whereas the CSI uses a telephone survey of 500 households. The CSI includes the purchase of big-ticket items, while the CCI asks about employment conditions. Figure 12.2 shows the CSI and the unemployment rate for the period 2000–2008.

In February 2008, the Conference Board announced that the CCI fell from a value of 87.3 in January to 75.0 (1985 = 100) a month later. With the exception of the war in Iraq in 2003, this was the lowest level of the index in nearly 15 years. By October 2008, the CCI had fallen to an all-time low of 38.8. The index rose slightly in November 2008 to 44.9, although consumers remained extremely pessimistic.[16]

There is continuing debate about how well these confidence indices actually predict changes in consumer spending. Most economists argue that broad changes in the indices over time are related to changes in consumption spending, but that the indices will not provide an exact prediction of consumer spending changes, particularly on a month-to-month basis. One study, which compared simple statistical models with and without the consumer confidence and sentiment indexes, found that including these indexes provided only a slight improvement in the forecasts.[17]

Consumer Sentiment Index (*CSI*)
An index, based on a telephone survey of 500 households conducted by the University of Michigan, that measures households' attitudes regarding expected business conditions, personal financial conditions, and consumer confidence about purchasing furniture and major household appliances.

Consumer Confidence Index (*CCI*)
An index, based on a mail survey of 5,000 households conducted by the Conference Board, that measures households' perceptions of general business conditions, available jobs in the households' local area, and expected personal family income in the coming six months.

---

[14] Federal Reserve Bank of San Francisco, *U.S. Monetary Policy: An Introduction.* Available at www.frbsf.org/publications/federalreserve/monetary/index.htm.

[15] Frumkin, *Tracking America's Economy*, 4th ed.; http://www.conference-board.org/economics/ConsumerConfidence.cfm.

[16] "The Conference Board Consumer Confidence Index Declines 12 Points; Expectations Fall to 17-Year Low," *PR Newswire*, February 26, 2008; "The Conference Board Consumer Confidence Index Improves Moderately, But Present Situation Worsens," November 25, 2008, www.conference-board.org.

[17] Norman Frumkin, *Guide to Economic Indicators*, 2nd ed. (Armonk, N.Y.: Sharpe, 1994), 76–82; Frumkin, *Tracking America's Economy*, 4th ed.; "Consumer Spending: A Sentimental Journey?" *Wall Street Journal*, April 8, 2002.

FIGURE 12.2
Consumer Sentiment and the Unemployment Rate
The University of Michigan's Consumer Sentiment Index is an indicator of major turning points in the business cycle.
The unemployment rate is the percent of the labor force not employed and actively seeking work; the labor force includes adult (16 years of age and older), noninstitutional, civilian workers.
Source: Federal Reserve Economic Data (FRED II), Economic Research, Federal Reserve Bank of St. Louis, http://research.stlouisfed.org/fred2/.

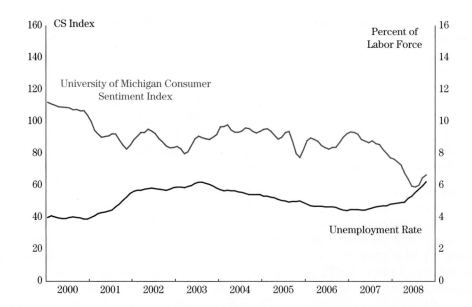

Consumer confidence was of particular concern to managers and analysts in the period following the terrorist attacks of September 2001 and at the time of the Iraq war in March 2003.[18] As discussed in Part 1 of the text, consumer demand in the hotel, travel, and tourism industries decreased substantially in the days following the terrorist attacks. This was the period when the automobile industry responded by offering zero percent financing initiatives to offset the lack of demand resulting from the ongoing recession and the attacks. The opening days of the Iraq war in March 2003 did not appear to have a major impact on consumer confidence and spending behavior. Research on the confidence and sentiment indexes has suggested that consumers did not view the 1993 World Trade Center bombing and the 1995 Oklahoma City bombing as significantly affecting the overall economy, but the Persian Gulf War lowered the indexes by 14 and 8 points, respectively. The September 11th terrorist attacks did not appear to have an effect separate from that of the ongoing recession at that time.[19]

Wealth   Households can also finance consumption expenditures out of their existing stock of wealth.[20] The wealth effect of the stock market during the economic expansion of the late 1990s had a significant impact on household spending.[21] From 1989 to 1999, the real value of tangible assets increased 14 percent, the real value of financial assets other than stocks increased 38 percent, but the real value of stocks increased 262 percent. This wealth effect often means that consumers spend more in the current period due to the increase in the value of their retirement accounts, not because they are actually drawing down on these retirement accounts.

The decline in stock market wealth was a restraining influence on consumption spending in 2001.[22] The turmoil in the financial and credit markets also affected

---

[18] "Terrorist Attacks Briefly Stalled Economy, Federal Reserve Says," *Wall Street Journal,* October 24, 2001; "Despite the War in Iraq, Consumers Keep Buying," *Wall Street Journal,* March 24, 2003.

[19] C. Alan Garner, "Consumer Confidence after September 11," as reported in Frumkin, *Tracking America's Economy,* 4th ed., 140–141.

[20] As we discussed in Chapter 11, saving is the amount of a flow of income that is not spent by consumers in a given period of time. This process of saving results in changes in the amount of consumer wealth, which may take the form of savings accounts, money market funds, and/or financial investments in stocks, bonds, other securities, and real estate.

[21] Yochi J. Dreazen, "Stocks Make Up Almost a Third of Household Wealth in the U.S.," *Wall Street Journal,* March 14, 2000; James M. Poterba, "Stock Market Wealth and Consumption," *Journal of Economic Perspectives* 14 (Spring 2000): 99–118.

[22] Board of Governors of the Federal Reserve System, *Monetary Policy Report to Congress* (Washington, D.C.: Federal Reserve System, February 27, 2002).

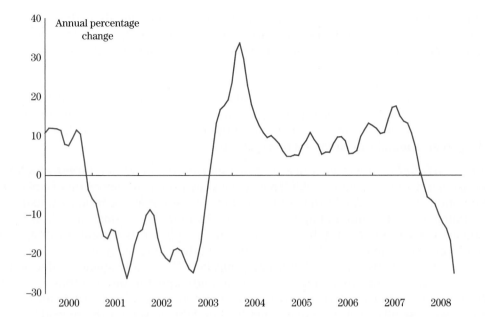

FIGURE 12.3
Stock Market Returns
The decline in stock market wealth was a restraining influence on consumption spending in the recession of 2001 and the economic slowdown of 2007–2008.
Source: Federal Reserve Economic Data (FRED II), Economic Research, Federal Reserve Bank of St. Louis. http://research.stlouisfed.org/fred2/

stock prices in 2007 and 2008. Figure 12.3 shows the annual percentage change in the Standard & Poors stock index from 2000 to 2008.

Several studies have reported that there is a greater wealth effect on consumer expenditure from the capital gains in housing than from the stock market. On average a dollar increase in housing wealth increases consumption spending by seven cents while the effect for financial wealth is approximately three cents.[23] This wealth effect became a particular issue in 2007 and 2008 with the upheaval in the housing and mortgage markets and the decline in the stock market in the fall of 2008. In December 2008, the Federal Reserve reported that U.S. household net worth fell 4.7 percent to $56.5 trillion in the third quarter of 2008, the fourth straight quarterly decline. Household net worth was 11 percent lower than a year earlier.[24]

Consumer Credit   The availability of consumer credit also influences personal consumption spending. If an item is purchased on credit, the entire cost of the item is counted as a personal consumption expenditure at the time the purchase is made. The Federal Reserve Board monitors the use of consumer credit (a flow variable), or loans to households by banks, credit companies, and retail stores that cover items such as automobiles, credit cards, home improvements, education, vacations, and recreational vehicles.[25] From 1960 to 1996, there was a positive relationship between the percentage change in consumer credit outstanding and consumer expenditures. However, there was also substantial year-to-year variation in this relationship between the use of consumer credit and consumption spending, suggesting that other factors, such as household income and consumer confidence, play a larger role in influencing personal consumption expenditures.[26]

The availability of consumer credit was a major factor in the slowing of the U.S. economy in 2007 and 2008. The credit crisis began when the housing market collapsed and homeowners began to default on mortgages in record numbers.

---

[23] Frumkin, *Tracking America's Economy*, 4th ed.; N. Kundan Kishor, "Does Consumption Respond More to Housing Wealth Than to Financial Market Wealth? If So, Why?" *Journal of Real Estate Finance and Economics*, 35 (2007): 427–48.

[24] Phil Izzo, Brenda Cronin, and Sudeep Reddy, "Debt Shows First Drop as Slump Squeezes Consumers," *Wall Street Journal*, December 12, 2008.

[25] Jon Hilsenrath, "Consumer Credit Rose by $7.3 Billion in May," *Wall Street Journal*, July 9, 2003.

[26] Norman Frumkin, *Tracking America's Economy*, 3rd ed. (Armonk, N.Y.: Sharpe, 1998), 122–23.

Many of these were subprime mortgages issued to individuals with bad credit records and requiring little money down. Because these mortgages were packaged into complex securities, the losses were spread throughout the financial system. In response, banks and other institutions tightened their lending standards on both prime mortgages and home-equity lines of credit. Concerns about defaults also affected interest rates and the availability of credit cards and student loans. In December 2008, the Federal Reserve reported that growth in consumer credit slowed to an annual rate of 1.2 percent in the third quarter of 2008, down from a 3.9 percent annual rate in the second quarter.[27]

Level of Debt   Increased use of consumer credit creates a larger stock of consumer debt outstanding, which may have a restraining influence on future consumption spending. The burden of this debt is measured as the ratio of consumer installment credit outstanding to disposable income. When this ratio increases, consumers will eventually become reluctant to add to their debt burden, and banks and other lenders will become stricter in their lending practices. However, it is unclear exactly where this turning point lies. Household spending decisions are influenced more by changes in income and expected income than by debt burden. Consumer credit debt burden rose slowly from 1959 to 1996, although there were strong cyclical movements in this debt ratio over the period.[28] The wealth effect, particularly from the stock market, can at least partially offset this debt burden effect on consumer spending.

As noted above, distrust in the ability of consumers to pay back credit card and other forms of debt affected lenders' decisions to offer credit in late 2007 and early 2008. Given that 7.6 percent of credit card balances were reported either 60 days late or in default in December 2007, the number of approved credit card applications dropped from 40 to 33 percent. Borrowers were typically charged higher late fees and interest rates and faced more caps on borrowing limits.[29]

In December 2008, the Federal Reserve reported that U.S. households decreased the amount of their debt at a 0.8 percent annual rate, the first drop in debt since the central bank started collecting this information in 1952. Although this change might be a positive long-run trend, it had a negative impact on consumer spending at that time.[30]

The Consumption Function   This discussion of all the factors influencing personal consumption expenditure can be summarized in the generalized consumption function shown in Equation 12.1:

12.1 $C = f(Y, \ T_P, \ r, \ CC, W, \ CR, \ D)$
$$(+)(-)(-)\ \ (+)(+)(+)\ (-)$$

where

C = personal consumption expenditure

Y = personal income

T_P = personal taxes

r = real interest rate

CC = consumer confidence

W = consumer wealth

---

[27] Scott Patterson, "How the Credit Mess Squeezes You," *Wall Street Journal,* March 2, 2008; Daniel Gross, "Borrowers Are Out in the Cold; It's No Longer Just People with Bad Credit Who Are Feeling the Squeeze. Americans with Good Credit at All Income Levels Are Now Caught in a Full-Blown Credit Crunch," *Newsweek,* March 3, 2008; *Monetary Report to Congress,* February 27, 2008; Izzo et al. December 12, 2008.

[28] Frumkin, *Tracking America's Economy,* 3rd ed., 123–25.

[29] Gross, *Newsweek,* March 3, 2008.

[30] Izzo et al., December 12, 2008.

CR = available consumer credit

D = consumer debt

In this notation, consumption expenditure is expressed as a function of income, holding constant the other variables in the consumption function. The relationship between C and Y will determine the slope of the consumption function, while changes in the other variables will cause a shift in the consumption function.[31] The plus sign under the income variable shows that the consumption function will have a positive slope. The signs under the other variables show how the consumption function will shift when those variables change. A plus sign indicates a positive or upward shift of the function, whereas a negative sign indicates a negative or downward shift. This notation will be used throughout the macroeconomic portion of this text.

Equation 12.2 shows a linear consumption function:

12.2 $C = C_0 + c_1Y$

where

C_0 = autonomous consumption expenditures

c_1 = marginal propensity to consume

Y = personal income

Equation 12.2 is the form of the consumption function we will use throughout our macroeconomic analysis. The constant term, C_0, represents **autonomous consumption expenditures**, or those consumption expenditures that are determined by the factors in Equation 12.1 other than income. The effects of all of these factors in Equation 12.1, which we discussed above, are combined to form the constant term in Equation 12.2. The variable c_1 in Equation 12.2 is the slope term that represents the marginal propensity to consume, or the proportion of the increase in real income households will spend on durables, nondurables, and services. These expenditures are **induced consumption expenditures**, as they result from changes in real income in the economy. This distinction between autonomous and induced expenditures also applies to the other components of aggregate expenditure we discuss later in the chapter.[32]

The linear consumption function is illustrated in Figure 12.4a. Autonomous consumption expenditures are represented by the vertical distance, C_0. The slope, c_1, is $\Delta C/\Delta Y$, or the marginal propensity to consume. Changes in any of the other variables in Equation 12.1 will cause the consumption function to shift in the direction indicated in that equation. The marginal propensity to consume for this type of consumption function has been estimated to be approximately 0.75.[33]

Gross Private Domestic Investment Expenditure

As we discussed in the previous chapter, **gross private domestic investment** includes spending on business structures, equipment, and software; residential

Autonomous consumption expenditures
Consumption expenditures that are determined by factors other than the level of real income in the economy.

Induced consumption expenditures
Consumption expenditures that result from changes in the level of real income in the economy.

Gross private domestic investment
The total amount of spending on nonresidential structures, equipment, and software; residential structures; and business inventories in a given period of time.

---

[31] This is the same notation we used for the demand and supply analysis in Chapter 2. As in that chapter, the *f* symbol means the variable on the left side of the equation "is a function of" or depends on the variables on the right side of the equation.

[32] In Equation 12.2, personal taxes (T_P) are combined in the C_0 term because we are assuming that taxes do not depend on the level of income.

[33] Consumption functions estimated over longer periods of time have marginal propensities to consume closer to 0.90 and a zero vertical intercept. Economists have argued that these long-run consumption functions result from the upward shift of short-run consumption functions over time. See David C. Colander and Edward M. Gamber, *Macroeconomics* (Upper Saddle River, NJ: Prentice Hall, 2002), 341–54.

FIGURE 12.4

The Components of Aggregate Expenditure

Consumption, investment, and import spending are all assumed to be a function of the level of real income. Government spending and export spending are assumed to be determined by factors other than the level of real income.

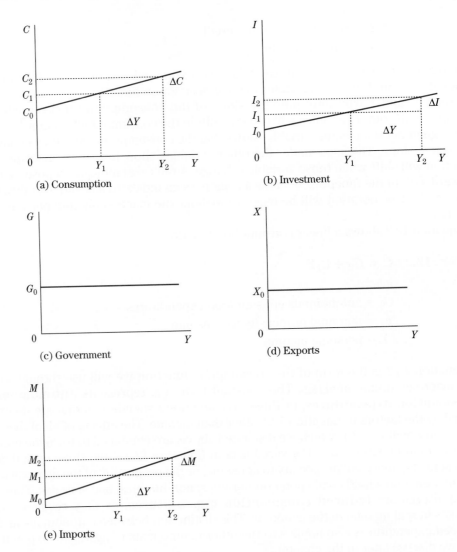

(a) Consumption

(b) Investment

(c) Government

(d) Exports

(e) Imports

housing; and changes in business inventories. Firms invest in structures, equipment, and software to provide the capacity to produce increased amounts of goods and services as the economy grows, to replace capital goods that have worn out or become obsolete, to adopt new cost-saving production methods, or to produce new, higher-quality products. Residential housing spending is related to the level of income and interest rates in the economy, while inventory spending is largely a function of the overall level of economic activity. Thus, a variety of factors influence gross private domestic investment spending.

Business Investment Spending and Real Income   Investment spending on structures and equipment is related to the level of real income and output in the economy.[34] The portion of investment spending related to the replacement of existing capital facilities tends to be relatively stable over time. However, additions to the capital stock can be much more volatile because firms want new facilities to meet expected sales, but they do not want excess capacity. If businesses are expecting a certain constant rate of growth of real income or GDP,

[34] The discussion of investment spending is based on Charles L. Schultze, *Memos to the President: A Guide Through Macroeconomics for the Busy Policymaker* (Washington, D.C.: Brookings Institution, 1992); Frumkin, *Tracking America's Economy*; Barry P. Bosworth, *Tax Incentives and Economic Growth* (Washington, D.C.: Brookings Institution, 1984); and Robert J. Gordon, *Macroeconomics*, 7th ed. (Reading, Mass.: Addison Wesley Longman, 1998).

they plan a rate of investment expenditure corresponding to this growth rate. However, if the economy's growth rate slows, business investment expenditures may actually decline, even though the economy's growth rate has only slowed and not actually declined.

Likewise, business investment can accelerate very rapidly if the growth rate of the economy increases, making business investment more volatile than overall economic growth. Business spending on structures and equipment expanded more rapidly than GDP in five of the six economic expansions between the 1960s and the 1990s, and it declined more rapidly than GDP in five of the six recessions during that time period. Investment spending on new plant and equipment can be deferred because firms can continue operating with existing structures and equipment even if the production process is not the most efficient and is unable to meet sudden surges in demand for the firm's products.

Stimulated by tax cuts and low interest rates, consumer spending first propelled the economy out of the 2001 recession. However, by early 2005, it appeared that business investment spending was also stimulating the economy even though a temporary tax break for business investment had expired in December 2004. After falling sharply during the 2001 recession and stagnating for several years, business-related construction rose in 2004 and 2005 because the excess capacity that previously existed had been absorbed.[35]

In the second half of 2007, business fixed investment rose at an annual rate of 8.5 percent, driven by a double-digit increase in expenditures on nonresidential construction. Some of this spending reflected a catch-up from the weakness in this sector during the first half of the decade. This growth differed from the 2003–2005 period when spending on equipment and software drove most of the business fixed investment. By the end of 2007, funds for business investment were being affected by the credit crisis that had begun in the housing sector and was spilling over to other areas.[36] The effects of the 2008 recession on investment were evident later that year. In the third quarter of 2008, real nonresidential fixed investment spending decreased 1.5 percent in contrast to an increase of 2.5 percent in the second quarter. Spending on nonresidential structures increased 6.6 percent compared with the previous quarterly increase of 18.5 percent, while equipment and software spending decreased 5.7 percent compared with a 5.0 percent decrease in the second quarter.[37]

The Real Interest Rate   The real interest rate affects the cost of new capital goods and spending on new residential homes. The rate of return on an investment must be greater than the cost of financing that investment. For a firm, this principle holds whether it is actually borrowing money and paying an explicit interest rate for the use of the funds or whether it is using its own internal funds or retained earnings. In the latter case, the market interest rate represents the opportunity cost of the firm using its own funds, as those funds could have been invested elsewhere at the market interest rate. A firm's investment expenditures are inversely related to market interest rates. A firm will undertake an investment with a 5 percent expected rate of return if the market interest rate is 4 percent, but not if it is 8 percent.[38]

---

[35] Timothy Aeppel and Kemba Dunham, "Business Shows Stronger Role in Driving Growth," *Wall Street Journal*, March 7, 2005.

[36] *Monetary Report to Congress*, February 27, 2008; Conor Dougherty, "Business Spending Eases Worries," *Wall Street Journal*, April 26, 2007.

[37] U.S. Bureau of Economic Analysis, "Gross Domestic Product: Third Quarter 2008 (Preliminary) News Release," November 25, 2008.

[38] As we discussed with consumption spending, the real interest rate will differ from the nominal interest rate in periods of inflation.

The response to interest rate changes differs between consumption and the various components of investment. Simulations have shown that an unanticipated tightening in monetary policy that raises interest rates first impacts final demand, which falls relatively quickly after a change in policy. Production then starts to decrease, implying that inventories first rise and then fall, contributing to a decrease in overall GDP. Residential investment experiences the earliest and sharpest declines, with spending on both durable and nondurable consumer goods following closely behind. A monetary tightening eventually causes fixed business investment to decline, but this decrease lags behind the changes in housing and consumer durable spending.[39]

Businesses whose products require customer borrowing are very sensitive to interest rate changes. For example, the Wisconsin-based Manitowoc Company produces construction cranes whose prices range from $500,000 to $6 million, so most purchases require financing. During the recession of 2001, the company was forced to build cranes in 50 to 60 days instead of the 120 days that had been typical in the past because their customers were placing orders only after a contract was signed for a construction job instead of six months in advance in anticipation of the signing.[40]

Business Taxes   Business taxes also affect the cost of capital investment for firms. Taxes levied on a firm's earnings, such as the corporate income tax, raise the effective cost of funds. If a firm has to pay some of its return on investment to the government, this return must be higher to justify making the investment.

The government also uses policies such as investment tax credits to stimulate business investment. The effects of these policies on business investment are typically modest and occur over a long period of time. One study estimated that a 10 percent decrease in the cost of capital from an investment tax credit would increase gross investment in GDP by 0.5 percentage point during the five-year period subsequent to the change.[41] This result implies that the increase in annual investment is approximately equal to the loss in tax revenues from the tax credit. The effect of taxes on investment decisions depends on whether these decisions are influenced more by expected sales and income or by the cost of capital and the interest rate. The role of the cost of capital is influenced by the degree to which firms can substitute capital for other inputs of production. **Relative prices**—here, the cost of capital versus the cost of other inputs—play a greater role the more firms are technologically able to substitute capital for other inputs.

The 2003 tax cut we discussed previously affected businesses as well as households. The tax bill included a reduction in the top tax rate on stock dividends from 38.6 percent to 15 percent, as well as a reduction in the tax rate on capital gains, the increased value of assets that are sold, from 20 percent to 15 percent. Businesses were also allowed to write off investment expenses more quickly, giving them greater incentives for investment spending.[42]

Although most of the economic-stimulus package passed by Congress in February 2008 was designed to stimulate consumer spending, tax incentives to allow businesses to write off equipment purchases made in 2008 more quickly and to give small firms greater ability to write off their expenses were included in the bill. These incentives were only temporary, which would limit their impact, and

Relative prices
The price of one good in relation to the price of another good.

---

[39] Ben S. Bernanke and Mark Gertler, "Inside the Black Box: The Credit Channel of Monetary Policy Transmission," *Journal of Economic Perspectives* 9 (Fall 1995): 27–48.

[40] Louis Uchitelle, "Thriving or Hurting, U.S. Manufacturers Brace for the Worst," *New York Times*, March 2, 2001.

[41] Bosworth, *Tax Incentives and Economic Growth*, 109–10.

[42] Greg Ip and John D. McKinnon, "Tax Plan Would Boost Growth, But Would Also Widen Deficits," *Wall Street Journal*, May 23, 2003.

[43] Sarah Lueck, "Congress Approves Economic-Stimulus Bill," *Wall Street Journal*, February 8, 2008; Patrice Hill, "Stimulus Package Seen as Cushion," *McClatchy-Tribune Business News*, February 14, 2008.

might also simply cause a shift in investment spending plans from 2009 to 2008. Other business tax breaks, such as renewable-energy incentives and a provision allowing companies including home builders to obtain tax refunds from previous years when they were profitable, were debated but not included in the final bill.[43]

Expected Profits and Business Confidence   Firms make capital investments with the expectation that these investments will contribute to future profits. Thus, decisions about adding to capacity are influenced by expectations about the profits that can be obtained from these investments. Expectations about future profits are affected by judgments about whether past rates of profits can be sustained in the future. Rising profits and expanding markets stimulate business confidence and expectations that capital investments will pay off in the future. Increased profits also provide more internal funds to finance capital investments and are a major factor in lenders' and investors' decisions to provide external funds to the firm.

Expectations of large profits helped fuel economic growth during the late 1990s, but resulted in overcapacity in many industries, including computers, chemicals, autos, aircraft, and plastics. Although the recession of 2001 was relatively mild in terms of its effect on GDP, corporate profits declined by 15.9 percent during the year, one of the largest declines since World War II. These changes influenced many business investment decisions.[44]

The terrorist attacks in September 2001 further impacted business confidence and profit expectations. Responding to a survey in October 2001, more than a quarter of the 669 finance officers polled indicated they were postponing capital expenditures as a result of the attacks.[45] Even by April 2002, executives were still wary about future profits and were focusing more on cost-cutting measures than on plant expansion.[46]

Forecasters monitor executives' statements about their expected future profits as an indicator of where the economy is headed.[47] For example, the Conference Board measures business as well as consumer confidence through quarterly surveys of more than 100 chief executives in a wide variety of U.S. industries. This survey asks executives to assess both current economic conditions and conditions in their own industry versus those six months ago and to give their expectations for both the economy and their industry for the following six months.[48]

In January 2008, when the slowdown in the U.S. economy was becoming widely apparent, the Conference Board reported that its Measure of CEO Confidence fell to 39 in the final quarter of 2007 after declining to 44 in the third quarter. The last time the measure fell below 40 was in the final quarter of 2000. This decrease in business confidence was attributed to the trouble in the housing and credit markets, the volatility in the financial markets, and increases in energy prices. In 2008, the measure remained at 39 in the second quarter and 40 in the third quarter, levels associated with recession.[49]

Capacity Utilization   Business investment in new structures and equipment also depends on the stock of capital goods on hand and how much they are utilized. **Capacity utilization rates (*CURs*)** are prepared monthly by the Federal Reserve

Capacity utilization rates (*CURs*)

The ratio of production to capacity calculated monthly for the manufacturing, mining, and electric and gas utilities industries and used as an indicator of business investment spending on structures and equipment.

---

[44] Louis Uchitelle, "Wary Spending by Executives Cools Economy," *New York Times*, May 14, 2001.

[45] Joann S. Lubin, "Businesses Delay Projects in Wake of Terror Attacks," *Wall Street Journal*, November 13, 2001.

[46] Jon E. Hilsenrath, "Businesses Sing Bottom-Line Blues As Profit Crunch Haunts Recovery," *Wall Street Journal*, April 1, 2002.

[47] Greg Ip, "A Few Economic Cues Should Show When Current Recession Will End," *Wall Street Journal*, January 4, 2002.

[48] Conference Board, "Chief Executives' Confidence Retreats," October 3, 2002. Available at www.conference-board.org/cgi-bin.

[49] Conference Board, "CEO Confidence Declines Again, The Conference Board Reports," January 15, 2008; "CEOs Still Lacking Confidence, The Conference Board Reports," October 16, 2008. Available at www.conference-board.org/cgi-bin.

Board for the manufacturing, mining, and electric and gas utilities industries. The CUR is the ratio of production (the numerator) to capacity (the denominator). For example, if a factory can produce 1,000 automobiles per month and is currently producing 750, its utilization rate is 75 percent. Higher CURs give firms the incentive to expand capacity through investment in new structures and equipment. Forecasters often estimate that there is a CUR threshold level at about 83 to 85 percent. Above this threshold, businesses increase investment in structures and equipment in order to expand capacity to meet anticipated demand for their products. Below this threshold, businesses are assumed to cut back on capital spending and concentrate on replacing inefficient and outmoded facilities. The Federal Reserve also looks at this threshold as an indicator of inflationary pressure in the economy, as firms are utilizing most of their existing capacity. The newer just-in-time inventory management methods used by many firms may change the role of capacity utilization in influencing business investment because fewer structures are needed to hold inventories. Figure 12.5 shows CURs for 2000 to 2008.

Residential Investment Spending   As we discussed in Chapter 11, spending on new residential construction is included as investment even though most of this spending is done by households and is part of household wealth. Similar to business fixed investment, residential investment is in long-lived structures that depreciate over time. BEA statisticians also consider that households are in the business of owning a home.

Both long- and short-term factors affect residential investment spending.[50] Demographic variables, such as trends in population, migration, and household formulation, are the major factors influencing new housing construction over the long run. Household formation is affected by marriage and divorce rates, adult children moving in or out of their parents' homes, and the sharing of structures by unrelated individuals. Other factors influencing long-run housing construction include the replacement of houses lost from the existing inventory and the demand for second homes. Short-term factors include the effects of business cycle expansions and recessions on employment, interest rates, and inflation. The housing market is particularly sensitive to changes in mortgage interest rates. Thus, income and the real interest rate are important influences on the residential construction component of gross private domestic investment.

FIGURE 12.5

Resource Utilization and Constraints

The Federal Reserve's monthly index of industrial production and the related capacity indexes and capacity utilization rates cover manufacturing, mining, and electric and gas utilities. The industrial sector, together with construction, accounts for the bulk of the variation in national output over the course of the business cycle.

A capacity utilization rate approaching 85% is generally regarded as a trigger for accelerating inflation.

Source: Federal Reserve Economic Data (FRED II), Economic Research, Federal Reserve Bank of St. Louis, http://research.stlouisfed.org/fred2/.

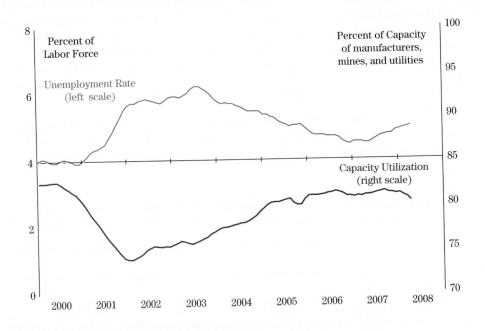

[50] Frumkin, *Tracking America's Economy*, 4th ed.

The residential housing market was the crucial sector in the slowdown of economic activity that began in the summer of 2007 and continued into 2008. Beginning in the early years of the decade, both private lenders and government agencies, such as Freddie Mac and Fannie Mae, began promoting mortgages to subprime borrowers with poor credit records to buy homes with little or no money down. It is estimated that the percentage of subprime borrowers who did not fully document their income and assets increased from about 17 percent in early 2000 to 44 percent in 2006. Repayment of these loans was based on the premise that housing prices would continue to increase. These loans were also packaged into complex securities that were bought and sold throughout the financial system. When housing prices deflated in 2007, borrowers defaulted on their loans and financial institutions were left holding securities of uncertain value. Major investment banks took huge losses as they wrote down the value of these securities and their stock prices sank. These actions set off a crisis of confidence in which lenders either refused to make loans or did so only under much tighter conditions. Although the Federal Reserve lowered its targeted short-term interest rates a full three percentage points between September 2007 and March 2008, mortgage interest rates were only about a quarter of a percentage point lower, given the reluctance of lenders to make loans. The end result was that housing starts and the sale of new homes in early 2008 were less than half of their respective peaks in 2006 and housing prices were flat or declined in most areas. Real residential fixed investment spending declined throughout 2008: 25.1 percent in the first quarter, 13.3 percent in the second quarter, and 17.6 percent in the third quarter.[51] Figure 12.6 shows housing starts and mortgage rates for the period 2000 to 2008.

Inventory Investment   Inventory investment is more volatile than other forms of investment spending because inventories can be increased and decreased

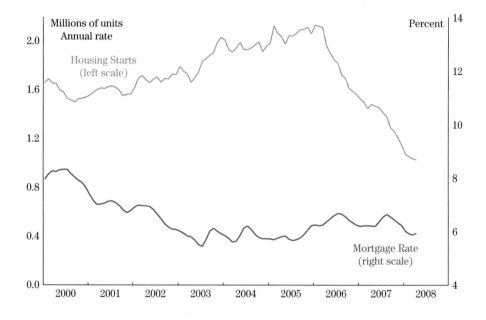

FIGURE 12.6
Housing Starts and Mortgage Rates
Residential investment spending is strongly influenced by mortgage interest rates.
Source: Federal Reserve Economic Data (FRED II), Economic Research, Federal Reserve Bank of St. Louis, http://research.stlouisfed.org/fred2/.

---

[51] Greg Ip, James R. Hagerty, and Jonathan Karp, "Housing Bust Fuels Blame Game," *Wall Street Journal*, February 27, 2008; Scott Patterson, "How the Credit Mess Squeezes You," *Wall Street Journal*, March 2, 2008; Jeff D. Opdyke and Jane J. Kim, "Why Only Some See Benefit from Fed's Cuts," *Wall Street Journal*, March 19, 2008; Testimony, Chairman Ben S. Bernanke, *Semiannual Monetary Report to the Congress* Before the Committee on Financial Services, U.S. House of Representatives, February 27, 2008; U.S. Bureau of Economic Analysis News Release, November 25, 2008.

[52] Schultze, *Memos to the President*, 78–79.

[53] Alan S. Blinder and Louis J. Maccini, "Taking Stock: A Critical Assessment of Recent Research on Inventories," *Journal of Economic Perspectives* 5 (Winter 1991): 73–96.

relatively quickly. Mistakes in inventory holdings can be reversed with less cost than incorrect decisions regarding the construction of new structures. Similar to nonresidential business investment, inventories are closely related to sales and the level of income in the economy. Although inventory spending is typically only approximately 1 percent of GDP, since World War II, changes in inventory investment have contributed more than twice as much to fluctuations in GDP than any other single component.[52] A decrease in inventory investment has accounted for 87 percent of the drop in GDP during the average postwar recession in the United States.[53]

The concern at the end of 2007 was housing inventories. The Federal Reserve chairman testified in February 2008 that homebuilders, "still faced with abnormally high inventories of unsold homes, are likely to cut the pace of their building activity further, which will subtract from overall growth and reduce employment in residential construction and closely related industries."[54] In December 2008, he noted that inventories of unsold new homes were still close to their record high, suggesting that residential construction was likely to "remain soft in the near term."[55]

At the end of 2008, inventories of unsold automobiles were also a major problem. Chrysler LLC announced that it would stop all manufacturing operations for at least a month, while General Motors Corp., Toyota Motor Corp., and Honda Motor Co. all announced steep production cuts. Toyota had already shut one of the two manufacturing lines at its San Antonio plant that we discussed in Chapter 6.[56]

Investment spending function

The functional relationship between investment spending and income, holding all other variables that influence investment spending constant.

Investment Spending Function   The **investment spending function**—the functional relationship between investment spending and income, holding all other variables that influence investment spending constant—is shown in Equation 12.3:

12.3 $I = f(Y, r, T_B, PR, CU)$
$$(+)(-)\ (-)(+)\ (+)$$

where

I = investment spending

Y = real income

r = real interest rate

T_B = business taxes

PR = expected profits and business confidence

CU = capacity utilization

A linear relationship between investment spending and income is shown in Figure 12.4b and Equation 12.4.

12.4 $I = I_0 + i_1 Y$

where

I_0 = autonomous investment expenditure

i_1 = marginal propensity to invest

Y = real income

The slope of the investment function, i_1 in Equation 12.4, shows how investment spending changes with changes in income, or the marginal propensity to invest.

---

[54] Testimony, Chairman Ben S. Bernanke, February 27, 2008.

[55] Board of Governors of the Federal Reserve System, Speech, Chairman Ben S. Bernanke at the Federal Reserve System Conference on Housing and Mortgage Markets, Washington, D.C., December 4, 2008.

[56] Lauren Pollock and Neal E. Boudette, "Chrysler to Close Manufacturing Plants for a Month Starting Friday," *Wall Street Journal*, December 17, 2008; Yoshio Takahashi and Kate Linebaugh, "Toyota Sees First Loss in 70 Years," *Wall Street Journal*, December 23, 2008.

These are induced investment expenditures. The vertical intercept, I_0, shows autonomous investment expenditures determined by the other factors in Equation 12.3 that are unrelated to income. The effects of all of these factors from Equation 12.3, discussed above, are combined to form the constant term, I_0, in Equation 12.4.[57]

Government Expenditure

As noted in Chapter 11, **government expenditure** in the national income accounts includes both consumption and investment expenditures by all levels of government—federal, state, and local—but does not include transfer payments from government to government or from government to individuals. For modeling purposes, we assume that all government expenditure is autonomous or determined by factors other than the level of real income in the economy. Government expenditure policy is determined by the legislative and executive institutions at all levels of government. The interplay of these institutions, political agendas, and unexpected events, such as the terrorist attacks in September 2001, influences the level of government spending as recorded in the national income accounts.

Federal government spending on homeland security and the Iraq war in spring 2003 had an expansionary effect on the economy although, given the existing excess capacity, much of the spending kept firms profitable and prevented layoffs instead of causing them to increase output. War spending benefited particular areas of the country, such as metropolitan Washington, D.C., the Gulf Coast, and Southern California, and certain industries including aerospace and high-technology companies.[58]

The federal budget proposed by President George W. Bush in 2008 focused on increases in security-related spending versus spending on other programs. The president proposed an increase in security-related funding—for national defense, homeland security, and international affairs—of 8.2 percent, while nonsecurity spending, primarily on social services and other domestic programs, would increase by 0.3 percent. The budget proposed major reductions or elimination of 151 programs that included education, health, and job-training programs for the states.[59]

Federal government spending is also used as an instrument of **fiscal policy**—changes in taxes and government expenditure designed to pursue the macroeconomic goals of full employment and low inflation. These spending changes can still be considered as autonomous—the result of policy decisions and not the level of real income.[60] The impact of fiscal policy and many political debates regarding the amount and types of government spending depend on the relationship between government revenue and expenditure or whether there is a **budget surplus** (revenue greater than expenditure) or **deficit** (revenue less than expenditure). Figure 12.7 shows the relationship between federal government revenue and expenditure for the period 2000 to 2008.

Government expenditure
The total amount of spending by federal, state, and local governments on consumption outlays for goods and services, depreciation charges for existing structures and equipment, and investment capital outlays for newly acquired structures and equipment in a given period of time.

Fiscal policy
The use of expenditure and taxation policies by the federal government to pursue the macroeconomic goals of full employment and low inflation.

Budget surplus/deficit
The relationship between federal government revenue and expenditure with a surplus indicating revenue greater than expenditure and a deficit indicating revenue less than expenditure.

---

[57] Different combinations of these factors affect the three components of investment spending as noted in the discussion above.
[58] John D. McKinnon and Anne Marie Squeo, "Shaky Economic Times Limit Bang of New Defense Spending," *Wall Street Journal*, April 15, 2003.
[59] John D. McKinnon and Michael M. Phillips, "Bush Budget Sets Stage for Battle on Tax Cuts," *Wall Street Journal*, February 5, 2008.
[60] This is a simplifying assumption used in the model. Some government expenditures, such as unemployment compensation, act as automatic stabilizers because they rise when real income falls and vice versa. Income taxes also act as automatic stabilizers. See Alan J. Auerbach and Daniel Feenberg, "The Significance of Federal Taxes as Automatic Stabilizers," *Journal of Economic Perspectives* 14 (Summer 2000): 37–56; and Darrel Cohen and Glenn Follette, "The Automatic Fiscal Stabilizers: Quietly Doing Their Thing," *FRBNY Economic Policy Review*, April 2000, 35–68.

FIGURE 12.7
Federal Government Budget
The relationship between federal government revenue and expenditure determines whether there is a budget surplus or deficit.
Source: Federal Reserve Economic Data (FRED II), Economic Research, Federal Reserve Bank of St. Louis, http://research.stlouisfed.org/fred2/.

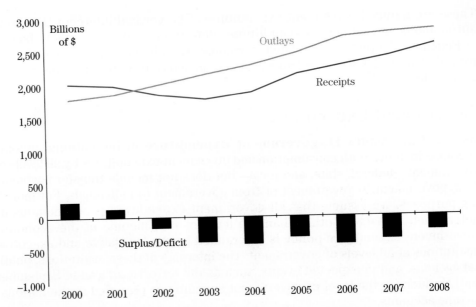

The assumptions about government spending are incorporated in the government spending function in Equations 12.5 and 12.6 and in Figure 12.4c:

12.5 $G = f(Y, \text{Policy})$
            (0)   (+)

where
> G = government spending
> Y = real income
> Policy = institutional policy decisions at all levels of government

12.6 $G = G_0$

where
> G = government expenditure
> G_0 = autonomous government expenditure

Both the equations and the figure show that government spending is assumed to be determined only by policy decisions and not by the level of real income in the economy. Autonomous government spending, G_0, is represented by the horizontal line in Figure 12.4c.

Net Export Expenditure

Net export expenditure
The difference between export spending on domestically produced goods and services by individuals in other countries and import spending on foreign-produced goods and services by domestic residents in a given period of time.

Net export expenditure is the difference between export spending on domestically produced goods and services by individuals in other countries and import spending on foreign-produced goods and services by domestic residents. Import spending is subtracted from domestic GDP because it is spending by domestic residents on goods and services produced in other countries.

Export Expenditure   The determinants of export expenditures are shown in Equations 12.7 and 12.8 and in Figure 12.4d.

12.7 $X = f(Y, Y^*, R)$
            (0) (+) (−)

where
> X = export expenditure
> Y = domestic real income

$Y^* =$ foreign GDP or real income

$R =$ currency exchange rate

12.8 $X = X_0$

where

$X =$ export spending

$X_0 =$ autonomous export spending

We assume that export expenditures are unaffected by the level of domestic GDP or real income, but are positively influenced by the level of real income or GDP in the rest of the world. As economic activity in foreign economies increases, those individuals will spend some of that income on U.S. domestically produced goods and services. Thus, U.S. export spending is not affected by U.S. real income, but is influenced by the economic activity of its major trading partners, such as Japan and the European Union.

Export spending is also influenced by the **currency exchange rate**, or the rate at which one nation's currency can be exchanged for that of another, which is determined in foreign exchange markets. In this text, we define the exchange rate, R, as the number of units of foreign currency per U.S. dollar. As R increases, the dollar appreciates, and more units of foreign currency can be purchased for a dollar. If R decreases, the dollar depreciates, and fewer units of foreign currency can be purchased for a dollar. If the dollar appreciates against a foreign currency such as the Japanese yen, the yen depreciates against the dollar. Fewer dollars can be purchased for a given number of yen.

Tables 12.1 and 12.2 show the effects of both the depreciation and the appreciation of the dollar on U.S. exports and imports. Table 12.1 shows the depreciation of the U.S. dollar against the Japanese yen that occurred between January 2007 and January 2008. This change made U.S. exports less expensive and imports more expensive, so that exports increased and imports decreased. The opposite case held for the U.S. dollar and the yen between January 2005 and January 2006 in Table 12.2. The dollar appreciated against the yen, so that U.S. exports became more expensive and imports less expensive, which caused exports to decrease and imports to increase. Thus, export spending is inversely related to the currency exchange rate in Equation 12.7.

Currency exchange rate
The rate at which one nation's currency can be exchanged for that of another, which is determined in foreign exchange markets.

TABLE 12.1 Effect of Dollar Depreciation on Exports and Imports

$R = ¥/\$$	DOMESTIC PRICE	JAN 07: $R = 120$	JAN 08: $R = 108$	EFFECT
U.S. exports—computers	$10,000	¥1,200,000	¥1,080,000	X increases
U.S. imports—Japanese cars	¥2,000,0000	≈ $16,700	≈ $18,500	M decreases

TABLE 12.2 Effect of Dollar Appreciation on Exports and Imports

$R = ¥/\$$	DOMESTIC PRICE	JAN 05: $R = 103$	JAN 06: $R = 115$	EFFECT
U.S. exports—computers	$10,000	¥1,030,000	¥1,150,000	X decreases
U.S. imports—Japanese cars	¥2,000,000	$19,400	$17,400	M increases

Equation 12.8 and Figure 12.4d show the level of export spending as autonomous or represented by a horizontal line. The level of this spending is determined by the level of foreign income and the exchange rate, not by the level of domestic real income.

Import Expenditure   The determinants of import expenditures are shown in Equations 12.9 and 12.10 and in Figure 12.4e.

12.9 $M = f(Y, R)$
$$(+)(+)$$

where

M = import spending

Y = domestic real income

R = currency exchange rate

12.10 $M = M_0 + m_1 Y$

where

M = import spending

M_0 = autonomous import spending

m_1 = marginal propensity to import

Y = domestic real income

The level of U.S. import spending is affected by the level of domestic real income, as U.S. residents will spend part of any increase in their income on goods and services produced by countries in the rest of the world.[61] Thus, the import spending line in Figure 12.4e has a positive slope, which is the marginal propensity to import (m_1) in Equation 12.10. Autonomous import spending, M_0, is influenced by the currency exchange rate, R. For example, as R increases or the U.S. currency appreciates against the yen, the level of spending on imports from Japan will increase because U.S. residents can purchase more yen for every dollar. This change causes M_0 to increase in both Equation 12.10 and Figure 12.4e.

Net Exports   In 2001, real U.S. exports decreased 11 percent due to slower economic growth abroad, the continued appreciation of the dollar, and the significant decrease in global demand for high-tech products. Exports declined in most major categories of goods, with the largest decreases in high-tech capital goods and other machinery. Import spending declined 8 percent in 2001, largely due to the slowing of the U.S. economy.[62]

Many companies felt the effects of the strong or appreciated dollar in 2001. For example, Gaylord Container Corporation, a Deerfield, Illinois, producer of liner board, which is used to make cardboard boxes, lost customers in Europe because it could not compete with Scandinavian and Canadian producers on price. The company then focused more on the U.S. market, where the increased competition from producers in similar situations pushed prices down, forcing the company to cut its workforce.[63]

Opposite effects occurred at the end of 2007. During the second half of 2007, net exports added almost one percentage point to U.S. GDP growth. Exports of goods and services increased at an 11 percent annual rate, given the effects of solid growth in foreign economies and the depreciation of the dollar. There were sizeable increases in the exports of automobiles, agricultural goods, and capital goods, especially aircraft. The growth of imports decreased to about 1.5 percent in 2007, down from a 3.75 percent increase in 2006, given the slowing U.S. economy and the

---

[61] All sectors of the economy import goods and services. BEA statisticians aggregate these import expenditures into one number, which is then subtracted from total export spending.

[62] Board of Governors of the Federal Reserve System, *Monetary Report to the Congress*, February 27, 2002.

[63] Jon E. Hilsenrath, "Die-Hard Dollar Causes Damage for U.S. Exporters," *Wall Street Journal*, March 20, 2001.

depreciation of the dollar. Imports of capital goods were strong, but the growth of most other major categories declined.[64]

This depreciation of the dollar benefited U.S. firms selling abroad but hurt companies in other countries. Even with the slower rate of consumer spending in the United States in early 2008, the manufacturing sector had not weakened in the manner typical of a recession, given that manufacturers export nearly half of their output. U.S. exports of financial, accounting, legal, and other services also increased significantly during this period. Japanese firms, however, were negatively impacted by the depreciated dollar. Toyota Motor Corp. estimated that its operating profit declined by 35 billion yen, or about $350 million, every time the dollar's value decreased by one yen. A February 2008 survey of purchasing managers in countries using the euro also found that the growth in their new export orders increased at the weakest rate in 33 months. When the euro was introduced, one euro bought less than a dollar, but in March 2008, a euro bought more than $1.56.[65]

Aggregate Expenditure and Equilibrium Income and Output

We now combine the components discussed above to define aggregate expenditure and the equilibrium level of income and output.

Aggregate Expenditure

Aggregate expenditure (E) represents the planned spending on currently produced goods and services by all sectors of the economy, as shown in Equation 12.11:

12.11 $E = C + I + G + X - M$

> *where*
> E = aggregate expenditure
> C = consumption expenditure
> I = investment expenditure
> G = government expenditure
> X = export spending
> M = import spending

The general form of the **aggregate expenditure function**, which is the relationship between aggregate expenditure and income, holding all other variables constant, is shown in Equation 12.12:

Aggregate expenditure function
The relationship between aggregate expenditure and income, holding all other variables constant.

12.12 $E = f(Y, T_P, r, CC, W, CR, D, T_B, PR, CU, G, Y^*, R)$
$$(+)(-)(-)(+)(+)(+)(-)(-)\ (+)(+)(+)(+)\ (-)$$

> *where*
> E = aggregate expenditure
> Y = real income
> T_P = personal taxes
> r = real interest rate
> CC = consumer confidence
> W = consumer wealth

---

[64] *Monetary Policy Report to the Congress*, February 27, 2008.
[65] James C. Cooper, "A Plug for a Leaky Economy," *Business Week*, March 3, 2008; Yuka Hayashi and Joanna Slater, "Japan Economy Quakes Anew As Yen Soars Against Dollar," *Wall Street Journal*, March 14, 2008.

$$CR = \text{consumer credit}$$
$$D = \text{consumer debt}$$
$$T_B = \text{business taxes}$$
$$PR = \text{expected profits}$$
$$CU = \text{capacity utilization}$$
$$G = \text{government spending}$$
$$Y^* = \text{foreign GDP or real income}$$
$$R = \text{currency exchange rate}$$

Equation 12.12 includes all the variables affecting each component of aggregate expenditure drawn from Equations 12.1, 12.3, 12.5, 12.7, and 12.9. Aggregate expenditure is a function of real income, holding constant all the other variables in Equation 12.12. A change in any of these variables would cause a shift in the expenditure function.

Equation 12.13 is the linear version of the aggregate expenditure function in Equation 12.12.[66]

12.13 $\quad E = E_0 + (c_1 + i_1 - m_1)Y$

> *where*
> $E = $ aggregate expenditure
> $E_0 = $ sum of all autonomous expenditure components
> $c_1 = $ marginal propensity to consume
> $i_1 = $ marginal propensity to invest
> $m_1 = $ marginal propensity to import
> $Y = $ real income

Figure 12.8 shows a graph of Equation 12.13. The vertical intercept in Figure 12.8 is autonomous aggregate expenditure, E_0, from Equation 12.13. A change in any of the variables other than real income (Y) in Equation 12.12 will cause E_0 in Equation 12.13 to change and the aggregate expenditure function in Figure 12.8 to shift. For example, an increase in consumer confidence, all else assumed constant, will shift the aggregate expenditure function up (higher aggregate expenditure at every level of income), while an increase in personal taxes will shift the aggregate expenditure line down (lower aggregate expenditure at every level of income).[67]

FIGURE 12.8

Aggregate Expenditure Function
The vertical intercept, E_0, represents autonomous aggregate expenditure that is determined by factors other than real income. The slope of the function shows how various expenditures are induced by increases in real income.

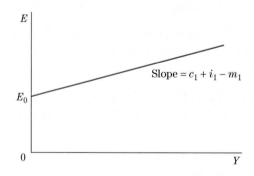

$$E$$
$$\text{Slope} = c_1 + i_1 - m_1$$
$$E_0$$
$$0 \qquad\qquad Y$$

---

[66] $E = C + I + G + X - M$

$E = C_0 + c_1Y + I_0 + i_1Y + G_0 + X_0 - M_0 - m_1Y$

$E = C_0 + I_0 + G_0 + X_0 - M_0 + c_1Y + i_1Y - m_1Y$

$E = E_0 + (c_1 + i_1 - m_1)Y$, where $E_0 = C_0 + I_0 + G_0 + X_0 - M_0$

[67] In this example, we have assumed that personal taxes, T_P, are not a function of the level of real income. Given the importance of the federal income tax in the U.S. economy, this assumption is unrealistic. If taxes are both autonomous and a function of income ($T_P = T_0 + tY$, where T_0 represents autonomous personal taxes and t is the tax rate applied to income), both the slope and the vertical intercept of the aggregate expenditure function are affected by taxes. This change does not affect the underlying analysis developed here.

The slope of the aggregate expenditure function in Equation 12.13 and Figure 12.8 is the sum of the marginal propensities to consume, invest, and import. The slope shows how various expenditures are induced by increases in real income. Higher marginal propensities to consume and invest out of income make the slope of the line steeper. A larger marginal propensity to import makes the aggregate expenditure function flatter because imports are subtracted from domestic GDP.

Equilibrium Level of Income and Output

We now use the aggregate expenditure function to define the equilibrium level of income and output. We first show why this equilibrium level exists and how income and output levels will change if the economy is in a disequilibrium state. We then discuss and illustrate changes in equilibrium levels of income and output.[68]

Definition of Equilibrium   The **equilibrium level of income and output** is that level of income at which the desired spending by all sectors of the economy just equals the value of the aggregate output produced and the income received from that production. At any other level of income, desired spending either exceeds the value of the output produced or is insufficient to purchase all of that output. In symbolic terms, equilibrium is shown in Equation 12.14:

12.14 $E = Y$

We can also use the definition in Equation 12.14 to define equilibrium in terms of injections into and leakages from the circular flow of economic activity. An **injection** is any supplement to consumer spending, the main component of the circular flow, that increases domestic aggregate output and income. Injections include business investment spending, government spending, and spending by foreigners on domestic exports, which represent additions to the circular flow of economic activity. **Leakages** are any uses of current income for purposes other than purchasing current domestically produced goods and services. Leakages, which include saving, tax payments (both personal and business), and spending on imports, represent withdrawals from the circular flow of economic activity.

In equilibrium, injections must equal leakages in the economy. There will be no tendency for income to either increase or decrease if this condition holds. The alternative definitions of equilibrium are shown in Table 12.3 for our model of an open, mixed economy.

Simplified Illustration of Equilibrium Income and Output   We first illustrate equilibrium income with the following simplified aggregate expenditure function, Equation 12.15, which is based on Equation 12.13:

12.15 $E = E_0 + c_1 Y$

> *where*
> E = aggregate expenditure
> E_0 = sum of all autonomous expenditure components
> c_1 = marginal propensity to consume
> Y = real income

Equilibrium level of income and output
The level of income or, equivalently, the aggregate output where the desired spending by all sectors of the economy just equals the value of the aggregate output produced and the income received from that production.

Injections
Any supplement to consumer spending that increases domestic aggregate output and income.

Leakages
Any uses of current income for purposes other than purchasing currently produced domestic goods and services.

TABLE 12.3 Equilibrium in the Open, Mixed Economy Model

$E = Y$	INJECTIONS = LEAKAGES
$C + I + G + X - M = C + S + T$	$I + G + X = S + T + M$

Note: Total taxes equal personal plus business taxes or $T = T_P + T_B$.

---

[68] This analysis was developed by John Maynard Keynes and is usually called the Keynesian model.

In Equation 12.15, we assume that all investment and import expenditures are autonomous and, therefore, not dependent on income, so that the i_1 and m_1 terms in Equation 12.13 equal zero. We also assume that taxes are lump sum or not a function of the level of income. All autonomous expenditures in Equation 12.15 are included in E_0, while c_1 equals the marginal propensity to consume.

We illustrate equilibrium in Figure 12.9, where E_I is an aggregate expenditure function with autonomous expenditure E_0 and a slope equal to the marginal propensity to consume (c_1). The aggregate expenditure function is a behavioral relationship that shows planned or desired expenditure by all sectors of the economy as a function of real income. The other line in the graph is a 45-degree line drawn from the origin, a theoretical construct that enables us to define equilibrium. At all points on the 45-degree line, aggregate expenditure (E) equals real income (Y) by definition. Equilibrium is defined as that level of income (Y_E) where the aggregate expenditure line crosses the 45-degree line (point A in Figure 12.9). Only at this level of income and output is the desired expenditure equal to the value of output produced and income generated.[69]

Adjustment Toward Equilibrium   It may be easiest to understand the concept of equilibrium if we examine what happens when the economy moves from one equilibrium to another. In Figure 12.10, suppose the starting equilibrium is at point A. This equilibrium level of income will change when any of the factors affecting autonomous expenditures in Equation 12.12 change. Changes in these factors will cause a shift in the aggregate expenditure function, as illustrated in Figure 12.10. In this figure, an increase in autonomous aggregate expenditures

FIGURE 12.9

Equilibrium Level of Income

Equilibrium is that level of real income, Y_E, where the aggregate expenditure line, E_I, crosses the 45° line. Only at this level of income and output is desired expenditure just equal to the value of the output produced and income generated.

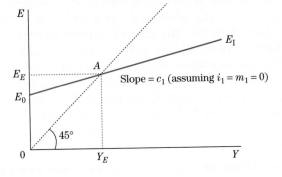

FIGURE 12.10

Changes in Equilibrium

An increase in autonomous aggregate expenditure from E_0 to E_1 shifts the aggregate expenditure line from E_I to E_{II}, resulting in an increase in the equilibrium level of income from Y_{E1} to Y_{E2}. The change in income is greater than the change in expenditure due to the multiplier effect.

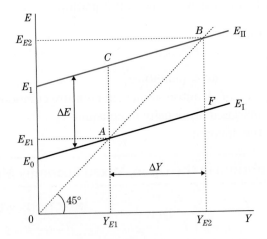

---

[69] Figure 12.9 is often called the Keynesian cross.

from E_0 to E_1 shifts the aggregate expenditure function from E_I to E_{II}. The original equilibrium, point A on E_I, is no longer an equilibrium because the desired spending (point C) is now greater than income and output at income level Y_{E1}. At this level of real income, individuals and governments now want to purchase more real goods and services than are currently produced. To meet this desired spending, firms have to draw down on their existing inventories of goods. This spending on inventories, or **unplanned inventory decrease**, represented by the distance CA in Figure 12.10, gives firms the incentive to increase production, which generates more real income and results in more aggregate expenditure or a movement along E_{II}. This incentive to increase production exists until reaching point B on aggregate expenditure function E_{II}, where the desired spending equals the amount of real output produced and income generated.

Unplanned inventory decrease
An unexpected decrease in inventories that occurs when desired aggregate expenditure exceeds the level of output currently produced.

The opposite situation exists if we begin our analysis at point B on aggregate expenditure function E_{II} with equilibrium income Y_{E2}. Suppose that autonomous expenditures decrease from E_1 to E_0, so that the aggregate expenditure function shifts down from E_{II} to E_I. Desired or planned expenditure at income level Y_{E2} is now represented by point F, a point below the 45-degree line. At point F, desired aggregate expenditure is less than the amount of currently produced goods and services. Firms cannot sell all of their goods, so there is an **unplanned inventory increase**, represented by the distance BF. This value of goods is put into firms' inventory. This situation then gives firms the incentive to decrease production, which generates lower real output and income and less aggregate expenditure (a movement along E_I). Firms have the incentive to continue decreasing production until desired expenditure just equals output and real income (point A). Thus, point A represents the new equilibrium level of income and output.

Unplanned inventory increase
An unexpected increase in inventories that occurs when desired aggregate expenditure is insufficient to purchase the level of output currently produced.

Numerous examples of inventory adjustment to a new equilibrium are reported in the *Wall Street Journal* and other business publications.[70] In describing the conditions leading to the recession in 2001, the *Wall Street Journal* reported:

> Manufacturers were largely blindsided by the dramatic drop in demand for their products and left holding too much inventory. To compensate, they slashed production faster than demand was falling. It happened with far greater speed and determination than in past slowdowns, especially among industrial manufacturers in the Midwest.[71]

Inventories are then drawn down before production is increased again. In the fourth quarter of 2001, James Glassman of J.P. Morgan Chase estimated that inventories were falling at a rate of 7 to 8 percent. CNW Marketing Research estimated that at least 70,000 automobile sales did not occur in December 2001 because dealers did not have the cars in inventory. In January 2001 18 of Ford Motor Company's 22 North American plants were idle, but by January 2002, all were in operation again to begin production for current sales and to replenish inventories.[72]

In early 2008 industry analysts estimated that light vehicle sales for the coming year would be 15.4 million or 2.5 percent less than anticipated. To minimize unintended inventory accumulation, Chrysler announced that it would broaden its traditional two-week shutdown in summer 2008 to include the entire company. Toyota Motor Corp. stated that it would cut production of big pickup trucks and sport-utility vehicles at two of its U.S. plants.[73]

---

[70] Remember from Chapter 11 and our earlier discussion in this chapter that changes in inventories are counted as investment spending (I) in the national income accounts.

[71] Clare Ansberry, "Manufacturers Are Showing Some Faint Signs of Recovery," *Wall Street Journal*, December 6, 2001.

[72] Greg Ip, "A Few Economic Cues."

[73] John D. Stoll and Josee Valcourt, "Woes Continue to Thwart Auto Makers," *Wall Street Journal*, March 14, 2008.

TABLE 12.4   Factors Causing Changes in Aggregate Expenditure (E) and Equilibrium Income (Y) (derived from Equation 12.12)

	INCREASE IN E, Y		DECREASE IN E, Y	
FACTOR	IMPACT ON EXPENDITURE COMPONENT		FACTOR	IMPACT ON EXPENDITURE COMPONENT
Decrease T_P	Increase C		Increase T_P	Decrease C
Decrease r	Increase C, I		Increase r	Decrease C, I
Increase CC	Increase C		Decrease CC	Decrease C
Increase W	Increase C		Decrease W	Decrease C
Increase CR	Increase C		Decrease CR	Decrease C
Decrease D	Increase C		Increase D	Decrease C
Decrease T_B	Increase I		Increase T_B	Decrease I
Increase PR	Increase I		Decrease PR	Decrease I
Increase CU	Increase I		Decrease CU	Decrease I
Increase G	Increase G		Decrease G	Decrease G
Increase Y^*	Increase X		Decrease Y^*	Decrease X
Decrease R	Increase X, Decrease M		Increase R	Decrease X, Increase M

The factors that can cause changes in aggregate expenditure and equilibrium income are summarized in Table 12.4. A change in any of these variables will cause the aggregate expenditure line, E_I, in Figure 12.10 to shift.

The Multiplier   You can see in Figure 12.10 that the increase in equilibrium income from Y_{E1} to Y_{E2} (ΔY) is greater than the increase in autonomous expenditure (ΔE) when aggregate expenditure increases from E_0 to E_1. This is the multiplier effect of a change in autonomous expenditure.

We illustrate the multiplier by substituting the aggregate expenditure function, Equation 12.15, into the equilibrium Equation 12.14, and solving for Y in Equations 12.16 through 12.19:

$$12.16 \quad Y = E_0 + c_1 Y$$

$$12.17 \quad Y - c_1 Y = E_0$$

$$12.18 \quad Y(1 - c_1) = E_0$$

$$12.19 \quad Y = \frac{E_0}{(1 - c_1)}$$

Multiplier
The multiple change in income and output that results from a change in autonomous expenditure.

Equation 12.19 shows that the equilibrium level of income is the level of autonomous expenditures multiplied by the term $1/(1 - c_1)$, where c_1 is the marginal propensity to consume. This term is called the **multiplier** because it shows the multiplied change in real income and output resulting from a change in autonomous expenditure. With $i_1 = m_1 = 0$, the size of the multiplier depends on the size of the marginal propensity to consume. Thus, if the marginal propensity to consume is 0.75, the multiplier is 4. Any increase in autonomous expenditure will generate an increase in equilibrium income four times as large.

The multiplier effect results from the fact that an increase in autonomous expenditure represents an injection of new spending into the circular flow of economic activity. For example, if the injection is an increase in government spending, an equal increase in income will be generated. If the marginal propensity to consume is 0.75, consumers will spend 75 percent of that increase in income. This will generate a further increase in income, of which consumers will spend 75 percent. This process will continue, with the increase in consumer spending becoming smaller in each round. The end result is a multiple increase in income determined by the size of the marginal propensity to consume and the term $1/(1 - MPC)$.[74]

In the complete model of Equation 12.13, where investment and import spending are also a function of income, the size of the multiplier is shown by Equation 12.20.

12.20 $$m = \frac{1}{1 - (c_1 + i_1 - m_1)} = \frac{1}{1 - c_1 - i_1 + m_1}$$

> *where*
>
> m = multiplier
> c_1 = marginal propensity to consume
> i_1 = marginal propensity to invest
> m_1 = marginal propensity to import

The size of the multiplier increases if the marginal propensity to invest, i_1, is greater than zero, as there is an additional injection into the circular flow from induced investment spending. If the marginal propensity to import, m_1, is greater than zero, the multiplier is decreased because induced import spending represents a leakage from the circular flow.

To compare this result with the simple multiplier ($c_1 = 0.75$, $m = 4$), assume that $c_1 = 0.75$, $i_1 = 0.1$, and $m_1 = 0.25$. In this case, the multiplier, $m = 1/[1 - (0.75 + 0.1 - 0.25)] = 1/0.4 = 2.5$. The simple multiplier is increased with the injection of induced investment spending, but reduced with the leakage of import spending.[75]

Appendix 12A presents a simple numerical example illustrating the equilibrium level of income, changes in that equilibrium, and the multiplier in a mixed, open economy.

Effect of the Interest Rate on Aggregate Expenditures

Although all the variables influencing aggregate expenditure in Equation 12.12 and Table 12.4 are important, we want to extend our discussion of the role of the real interest rate, given that this variable is influenced by the monetary policy of a country's central bank. Changes in monetary policy have an impact on real variables in the economy in the short-run framework we are examining in this text through interest rate changes. This is why managers must pay attention to Federal Reserve policy and the statements that are made by the Federal Reserve chair and the presidents of the Federal Reserve banks.

Recall from our discussion of aggregate expenditure that some components of both consumption and investment spending are influenced by the real interest rate. Figure 12.11a introduces the **interest-related expenditure (IRE) function**, which shows planned consumption and investment spending as a function of the real interest rate, all else held constant. We have drawn this function as linear, although it could also be curved. The important point is that it is a downward

Interest-related expenditure (*IRE*) function
The function that shows the inverse relationship between planned consumption and investment spending and the real interest rate, all else held constant.

---

[74] The increase in income, $\Delta Y = [\Delta G + (MPC)\Delta G + (MPC)^2 \Delta G + (MPC)^3 \Delta G + \ldots] = [1 + (MPC) + (MPC)^2 + (MPC)^3 + \ldots]\Delta G$. The multiplier, $\Delta Y/\Delta G = [1 + (MPC) + (MPC)^2 + (MPC)^3 + \ldots]$. The latter is an infinite geometric series that reduces to $1/(1 - MPC)$. If $\Delta G = 20$ and $MPC = 0.75$, $\Delta Y = [20 + (.75)(20) + (.75)^2(20) + (.75)^3(20) + \ldots] = [20 + 15 + 11.25 + 8.4375 + \ldots] = 80$.
[75] If taxes (T) also depend on the level of income, the multiplier is reduced by this further leakage from the circular flow.

FIGURE 12.11

Interest-Related Expenditure and Equilibrium in the Real Goods Market

Interest-related consumption and investment spending are determined in Figure 12.11a by changes in the real interest rate. This spending then influences the equilibrium level of real income in Figure 12.11b.

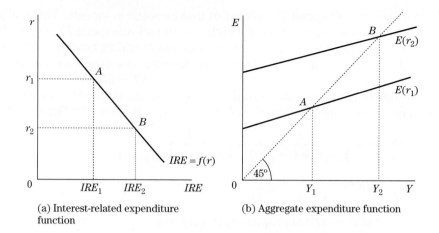

(a) Interest-related expenditure function

(b) Aggregate expenditure function

sloping function showing an inverse relationship between the interest rate and planned consumption and investment expenditure, as both households and businesses will undertake less interest-related spending at a higher interest rate.[76]

We use the interest-related expenditure function in Figure 12.11a to show the impact of changes in the interest rate on the aggregate expenditure equilibrium in Figure 12.11b. Start with interest rate r_1, which generates planned interest-related spending IRE_1 in Figure 12.11a. This planned consumption and investment spending is included in the aggregate expenditure function $E(r_1)$ in Figure 12.11b. Equilibrium with this aggregate expenditure function occurs at point A and income level Y_1, as this is the point where the expenditure function crosses the 45-degree line in Figure 12.11b.

We can repeat this process for a lower interest rate, r_2, in Figure 12.11a. This lower interest rate results in larger planned interest-related spending, IRE_2 (point B). In Figure 12.11b, this autonomous change in investment spending shifts the aggregate expenditure line up from $E(r_1)$ to $E(r_2)$, resulting in a new equilibrium level of income, Y_2, at point B. This derivation shows that lower interest rates are consistent with higher equilibrium levels of income due to the increased consumption and investment spending that is generated by the lower rate.

All of the variables in Equation 12.12 and Table 12.4 cause the aggregate expenditure function to shift as shown in Figure 12.10. However, the real interest rate is the one variable that is the continuing focus of the monetary policy of a country's central bank.

Summary

In this chapter, we examined the factors influencing real aggregate expenditure in the economy, many of which were discussed in the opening news article of the chapter. We described the components of aggregate expenditure—that is, consumption, investment, government, export, and import spending—and analyzed the factors influencing those components using examples from news articles and descriptions of managers' decisions and changes in strategies. We then defined the

---

[76] Although household consumption expenditure and the components of business investment spending may be affected differentially by changes in the real interest rate, the *IRE* function shows the total amount of this interest-related spending at any given interest rate.

equilibrium level of income and discussed how this level of income would change. We described the multiplier effect of a change in autonomous expenditure on equilibrium income. Finally, we used the interest-related expenditure function and the aggregate expenditure function to show how changes in interest rates from the monetary policy of a country's central bank can influence the equilibrium level of aggregate expenditure.

In the next chapter, we examine the monetary side of the economy to determine how changes in money supply and demand affect the interest rate. We then integrate the real and monetary sides of the economy in Chapter 14 to develop the full aggregate model that managers can use to determine how macro changes influence their firms and industries.

Appendix 12A Numerical Example of Equilibrium and the Multiplier

Table 12.A1 shows the autonomous spending components in the model (C_0, I_0, G_0, X_0, M_0) and the marginal propensities (c_1, i_1, m_1) that determine induced consumption, investment, and import spending. The equilibrium level of income ($350 billion) is calculated in the equations and illustrated in the middle part of the table. Only at this level of income is desired or planned spending by all sectors of the economy ($C + I + G + X - M$) equal to the level of income and output produced. At income levels less than $350 billion, desired spending is greater than the level of income and output produced, so there are unplanned inventory decreases and a tendency for income and output to increase. At income levels above $350 billion, desired spending is less than the level of income and output. There are unplanned inventory increases, and the tendency is for income and output to decrease.

We also illustrate the injection-leakage approach to equilibrium in the bottom part of Table 12.A1. In a mixed, open economy, the injections of investment, government, and export spending ($I + G + X$) must equal the leakages of saving, taxes, and import spending ($S + T + M$) in equilibrium. This condition holds only at the equilibrium level of income of $350 billion in Table 12.A1, where investment plus government plus export spending ($60 + $25 + $40 = $125 billion) equals saving plus taxes plus import spending ($-12.5 + 0 + $137.5 = $125 billion). At any other level of income, there will be a tendency for output and income to either increase or decrease, given the imbalance between injections and leakages.

Note that the concept of equilibrium refers to planned or desired investment spending. As we discussed in Chapter 11, from the viewpoint of national income accounting, aggregate expenditure must equal income, given the definition of the circular flow. This accounting identity holds even when the economy is not in equilibrium, as inventory changes are counted as part of investment spending. For example, when income is $250 billion in Table 12.A1, aggregate planned expenditure ($C + I + G + X - M$) is $290 billion, so the economy is not in equilibrium. Planned or desired spending is greater than the value of currently produced goods and services. However, actual expenditure equals actual income generated because the $40 billion decrease in inventories is counted as part of investment spending. This $40 billion represents investment spending on goods that were produced in previous years, so it must be subtracted from current GDP. Measured aggregate expenditure ($290 billion minus $40 billion) equals income of $250 billion. This example illustrates the difference between the accounting

TABLE 12.A1 Equilibrium in a Mixed, Open Economy (billions $)

SPENDING COMPONENTS

$$C_0 = 100, I_0 = 25, G_0 = 25, X_0 = 40, M_0 = 50, T = 0$$

MARGINAL PROPENSITIES

$$c_1 = 0.75, i_1 = 0.10, m_1 = 0.25$$

AGGREGATE EXPENDITURE

$$E = C_0 + c_1Y + I_0 + i_1Y + G_0 + X_0 - M_0 - m_1Y$$

$$E = C_0 + I_0 + G_0 + X_0 - M_0 + (c_1 + i_1 - m_1)Y$$

$$E = 100 + 25 + 25 + 40 - 50 + (0.75 + 0.10 - 0.25)Y$$

$$E = 140 + 0.6Y$$

EQUILIBRIUM

$$Y = E$$

$$Y = 140 + 0.6Y$$

$$Y - 0.6Y = 140$$

$$0.4Y = 140$$

$$Y_E = 350$$

Y	C = 100 + 0.75Y	S = Y − C = −100 + 0.25Y	I = 25 + 0.1Y	G_0 = 25	X_0 = 40	M = 50 + 0.25Y	C + I + G + X − M	UNPLANNED INVENTORY ADJUSTMENT	CHANGE IN INCOME AND OUTPUT
250	287.5	−37.5	50	25	40	112.5	290	−40	Increase
300	325	−25	55	25	40	125	320	−20	Increase
350	**362.5**	**−12.5**	**60**	**25**	**40**	**137.5**	**350**	**0**	**None**
400	400	0	65	25	40	150	380	+20	Decrease
450	437.5	12.5	70	25	40	162.5	410	+40	Decrease

Y	I	G	X	TOTAL INJECTIONS	S	T	M	TOTAL LEAKAGES	INJECTION LEAKAGE BALANCE
250	50	25	40	115	−37.5	0	112.5	75	INJ > LK
300	55	25	40	120	−25	0	125	100	INJ > LK
350	**60**	**25**	**40**	**125**	**−12.5**	**0**	**137.5**	**125**	**INJ = LK**
400	65	25	40	130	0	0	150	150	INJ < LK
450	70	25	40	135	12.5	0	162.5	175	INJ < LK

identity of $E = Y$ and the behavioral relationship inherent in the equilibrium concept of $E = Y$.

Changes in aggregate expenditure and equilibrium income are illustrated in Table 12.A2, in which we assume that government expenditure has increased by $60 - billion. This change has caused aggregate expenditure to increase, so that the new equilibrium level of income is $500 billion. The $60 billion increase in government expenditure resulted in a $150 billion increase in equilibrium income or a multiplier of 2.5. Calculating the multiplier with Equation 12.20 also results in a value of 2.5.

TABLE 12.A2 Changes in Aggregate Expenditure and Equilibrium Income and Output in a Mixed, Open Economy (based on model in Table 12.A1—billions $)

INCREASE GOVERNMENT EXPENDITURE BY $60 BILLION

SPENDING COMPONENTS

$C_0 = 100, I_0 = 25, G_0 = 85, X_0 = 40, M_0 = 50, T = 0$

MARGINAL PROPENSITIES

$c_1 = 0.75, i_1 = 0.10, m_1 = 0.25$

AGGREGATE EXPENDITURE

$E = C_0 + c_1Y + I_0 + i_1Y + G_0 + X_0 - M_0 - m_1Y$

$E = C_0 + I_0 + G_0 + X_0 - M_0 + (c_1 + i_1 - m_1)Y$

$E = 100 + 25 + 85 + 40 - 50 + (0.75 + 0.10 - 0.25)Y$

$E = 200 + 0.6Y$

EQUILIBRIUM

$Y = E$

$Y = 200 + 0.6Y$

$Y - 0.6Y = 200$

$0.4Y = 200$

$Y_E = 500$

MULTIPLIER

$\Delta Y = 500 - 350 = 150$

$\Delta G = 85 - 25 = 60$

$\Delta Y/\Delta G = 150/60 = 2.5$

$m = 1/[1 - (0.75 + 0.10 - 0.25)] = 1/[1 - 0.6] = 1/0.4 = 2.5$

Appendix 12B Algebraic Derivation of the Aggregate Expenditure Function

We use the linear spending equation from each sector of the economy to develop an algebraic aggregate expenditure function.

Consumption Spending (C)

12.B1 $C = c_0 + c_1(Y - T_P) - c_2r + c_3CC + c_4W + c_5CR - c_6D$

where

C = personal consumption expenditure

c_0 = other factors influencing consumption

Y = personal income

T_P = personal taxes

$$r = \text{real interest rate}$$
$$CC = \text{consumer confidence}$$
$$W = \text{consumer wealth}$$
$$CR = \text{available consumer credit}$$
$$D = \text{consumer debt}$$
$$c_1 \text{ to } c_6 = \text{coefficients for the relevant variables}$$

12.B2 $C = C_0 + c_1 Y$

where

$$C_0 = [c_0 - c_1 T_P - c_2 r + c_3 CC + c_4 W + c_5 CR - c_6 D]$$
$$c_1 = \text{marginal propensity to consume}$$

Investment Spending (I)

12.B3 $I = i_0 + i_1 Y - i_2 r - i_3 T_B + i_4 PR + i_5 CU$

where

$$I = \text{investment spending}$$
$$i_0 = \text{other factors influencing investment spending}$$
$$Y = \text{real income}$$
$$r = \text{real interest rate}$$
$$T_B = \text{business taxes}$$
$$PR = \text{expected profits and business confidence}$$
$$CU = \text{capacity utilization}$$
$$i_1 \text{ to } i_5 = \text{coefficients for the relevant variables}$$

12.B4 $I = I_0 + i_1 Y$

where

$$I_0 = [i_0 - i_2 r - i_3 T_B + i_4 PR + i_5 CU]$$
$$i_1 = \text{marginal propensity to invest}$$

Government Spending (G)

12.B5 $G = G_0$

where

$$G = \text{government expenditure}$$
$$G_0 = \text{autonomous government expenditure}$$

Export Spending (X)

12.B6 $X = x_0 + x_1 Y^* - x_2 R$

where

$$X = \text{export expenditure}$$
$$x_0 = \text{other factors influencing export expenditure}$$
$$Y^* = \text{foreign GDP or real income}$$

R = currency exchange rate

x_1, x_2 = coefficients of the relevant variables

12.B7 $X = X_0$

where

$X_0 = [x_0 + x_1 Y^* - x_2 R]$

Import Spending (M)

12.B8 $M = m_0 + m_1 Y + m_2 R$

where

M = import spending

m_0 = other factors influencing import spending

Y = domestic real income

R = currency exchange rate

m_1, m_2 = coefficients of the relevant variables

12.B9 $M = M_0 + m_1 Y$

where

$M_0 = [m_0 + m_2 R]$

m_1 = marginal propensity to import

Aggregate Expenditure (E)

12.B10 $E = C + I + G + X - M$

12.B11 $E = C_0 + c_1 Y + I_0 + i_1 Y + G_0 + X_0 - M_0 - m_1 Y$

where

E = aggregate expenditure

Y = real income

C_0 = autonomous consumption expenditure

I_0 = autonomous investment expenditure

G_0 = autonomous government expenditure

X_0 = autonomous export expenditure

M_0 = autonomous import expenditure

c_1 = marginal propensity to consume

i_1 = marginal propensity to invest

m_1 = marginal propensity to import

12.B12 $E = C_0 + I_0 + G_0 + X_0 - M_0 + c_1 Y + i_1 Y - m_1 Y$

12.B13 $E = E_0 + (c_1 + i_1 - m_1)Y$

where

$E_0 = [C_0 + I_0 + G_0 + X_0 - M_0]$

c_1 = marginal propensity to consume

i_1 = marginal propensity to invest

m_1 = marginal propensity to import

Key Terms

Exercises

Technical Questions

1. Describe the difference between autonomous expenditure and induced expenditure. Which sectors of the economy are assumed to have both types of spending and which are not? Explain your answer.

2. Describe the effect of the currency exchange rate on export and import spending.

3. Explain how the aggregate expenditure function shifts in response to changes in each of the following variables:

   a. The real interest rate increases.
   b. Consumer confidence decreases.
   c. Higher taxes are imposed on business profits.
   d. The economies of many countries in the rest of the world go into recessions.

4. Evaluate the following statements as to whether they are true or false:

   a. The multiplier means that changes in wealth have a larger effect on consumption spending than changes in consumer confidence.
   b. Both an increase in government spending (G) and an increase in personal taxes (T_P) will shift the aggregate expenditure function in the same direction.
   c. The national income accounts show that real income (Y) *always* equals real expenditure (E), given the definition of the circular flow of economic activity. Thus, the economy must *always* be in equilibrium because that is *also* where $Y = E$.

5. Given the following variables in the open economy aggregate expenditure model, autonomous consumption (C_0) = 200, autonomous investment (I_0) = 200, government spending (G_0) = 100, export spending (X_0) = 100, autonomous import spending (M_0) = 100, taxes (T_P) = 0, marginal propensity to consume (c_1) = 0.8, marginal propensity to invest (i_1) = 0.1, and marginal propensity to import (m_1) = 0.15,

   a. Calculate the equilibrium level of income for the open economy aggregate expenditure model.
   b. If there is an increase in autonomous import expenditure from 100 to 200 resulting from an increase in the currency exchange rate, calculate the new equilibrium level of income and the value of the multiplier.
   c. Compared with the original equilibrium in part a, if the government decides to impose taxes (T_P) of 100, calculate the new equilibrium level of income.
   d. *Hint:* Remember that consumption has an autonomous component and is a function of disposable income, Y_d, where $Y_d = Y - T_P$.

6. In the aggregate expenditure model, assume that the consumption function is given by $C = 800 + 0.8(Y - T_P)$, that planned investment (I) equals 200, and that government purchases (G) and taxes (T_P) each equal 200. Assume that there is no import or export spending.

 a. Calculate the equilibrium level of income.
 b. If government purchases (G) increase by 100 (all else held constant), calculate the new equilibrium level of income and the value of the multiplier.
 c. Compared with the original equilibrium, if both government expenditure (G) and taxes (T_P) increase by 100, so that the government budget remains balanced, does the equilibrium level of income remain unchanged? Explain your answer.

Application Questions

1. Use the aggregate expenditure model developed in this chapter to explain the following statements from the opening news article of the chapter:

 a. "Coming amid continued turmoil in the financial and credit markets, the report sent stocks lower, with the Dow Jones Industrial Average falling 146.70 points Friday to close at 11,893.69."
 b. "Administration officials said they were confident conditions would improve as tax rebates that are part of the recent $152 billion economic-stimulus law begin to reach consumers."
 c. "The Fed is expected to cut interest rates again to prop up the economy."

2. Redraw Figures 12.11a and 12.11b to illustrate the effects on the resulting equilibrium level of income from *each* of the following changes:

 a. A greater sensitivity of interest-related consumption and investment expenditure to changes in the interest rate.
 b. A larger multiplier in the aggregate expenditure model.

3. Go to the Web site of the Conference Board (www.conference-board.org) and find the latest release of the Consumer Confidence Index. How has the index changed since its last release? What is the expected impact of this change on the economy?

4. A number of articles in the *Wall Street Journal* reported that the strong dollar, combined with the recession of 2001, forced many U.S. manufacturers to develop better methods to produce and sell their products. Use the discussion of the macro model in this chapter to explain why businesses would have implemented such changes in strategies.

5. What were the key provisions of the economic stimulus bill passed by Congress in February 2008? What further changes in fiscal policy have occurred since this time?

6. The opening article of this chapter described changes in the number of jobs and employment early in 2008. How does this description compare with the current status of the labor market and employment?

On the Web

For updated information on the *Wall Street Journal* article at the beginning of the chapter as well as other relevant links and information, visit the book's Web site at **www.pearsonhighered.com/farnham**

13

The Role of Money in the Macro Economy

I n the last chapter, we discussed the factors influencing aggregate spending on real goods and services in the different sectors of the economy $(C + I + G + X - M)$. This expenditure is based on the circular flow concept illustrated in Figure 11.1. In this chapter, we discuss how money and the monetary policy of a country's central bank influence interest rates. This discussion focuses on the financial markets in the bottom part of Figure 11.1, where various financial assets (i.e., stocks, bonds, Treasury securities) are bought and sold. We then integrate the real and monetary sides of the economy in the next chapter to show how monetary policy influences interest rates, which affects spending on real goods and services and the competitive strategies of firms producing those products.

We begin this chapter with the *Wall Street Journal* article "Credit Worries Ease as Fed Cuts, Hints at More Relief." This article discusses the role of the Federal Reserve System, the U.S. central bank, in influencing interest rates and the impact of interest rate changes on the economy in March 2008. After summarizing the article, we define the term *money* and show how the supply of money in the economy is influenced by both depository institutions and the Federal Reserve. We describe the various tools the Federal Reserve uses to change the money supply and interest rates. Treating money as a commodity, similar to the goods and services we discussed in Chapter 2, we develop a model of the money market that includes the supply and demand for money, and we examine the resulting equilibrium price or interest rate in this market. We then show how changes in money demand and/or supply cause changes in this interest rate.

Credit Worries Ease as Fed Cuts, Hints at More Relief

by Greg Ip

Wall Street Journal, *March 19, 2008*

Copyright © 2008 Dow Jones & Co. Reprinted by permission of Dow Jones & Co. via Copyright Clearance Center.

WASHINGTON—The Federal Reserve continued its two-front attack on the credit crunch with a steep rate cut, and hinted at more to come.

The cut was less than financial markets wanted. But in a sign the Fed's prior efforts to boost lending through unconventional means may be getting some traction, stocks soared, buoyed by earnings reports from two big investment banks.

The Fed cut its short-term interest-rate target 0.75 percentage point to 2.25%, not the full point that markets had been expecting. It was the largest disappointment the Fed has delivered to markets since the central bank began cutting rates in September. The move was also a signal that because of the Fed's concerns about inflation, it expects its other initiatives to bear more of the burden of stimulating growth. . . .

The dollar improved against both the euro and the Japanese yen after the Fed announcement. The U.S. currency has fallen sharply in recent weeks as global investors questioned the Fed's commitment to resisting inflation, a worry that has sent money pouring into gold, oil, and other inflation hedges. . . .

Though less than expected, the interest-rate cut was substantial. Yesterday was only the second time the Fed has cut so much since it began announcing its rate moves in 1994. The central bank now has cut short-term interest rates a full three points since September, the fastest pace of easing in decades.

This reflects the speed with which a slump in housing and subprime mortgages has spiraled into a broad credit crunch, weakening financial institutions and making it harder for a broad swath of businesses and households to borrow. . . .

Recognizing that, the Fed signaled in its end-of-meeting statement that the prospect of more rate cuts remains on the table. "The outlook . . . has weakened further," it said. "Consumer spending has slowed and labor markets have softened. Financial markets remain under considerable stress, and the tightening of credit conditions and the deepening of the housing contraction are likely to weigh on economic growth." It said "downside risks to growth remain," and the Fed will "act in a timely manner as needed."

Nonetheless, the Fed has increasingly come to view that lower rates alone won't restore order to the financial markets and prevent a severe recession. It has rolled out even more creative and aggressive attempts to infuse cash into market corners where it normally doesn't operate, culminating in Sunday's decision to lend to investment banks from its "discount window," a privilege previously reserved for commercial banks. Chairman Ben Bernanke also has publicly backed action to use public money to stem a tide of mortgage defaults and foreclosures. . . .

Meanwhile, the Bush administration, which has so far resisted using large amounts of public money to save borrowers and lenders from bad loans, may be ready to compromise with Democrats on a more activist approach to the housing crisis. . . .

With the economy continuing to weaken, the Fed remains concerned about what some officials describe as an "adverse feedback loop" of economic weakness, tighter lending and further weakness. It is thus likely to cut interest rates again.

But the elevated concern about inflation in the statement suggests the Fed does think it's getting close to the bottom in interest rates. Some analysts speculate the Fed could trim rates before its next scheduled meeting on April 29–30, but many think that's unlikely unless the outlook or markets get markedly worse. . . .

The Fed also lowered the rate charged on direct "discount window" loans it makes available to banks and—since Sunday—to investment banks. It slashed the rate to 2.5% from 3.25%, keeping it a quarter-point above the federal funds rate. Commercial banks began lowering their prime interest rates, to which some variable-rate loans are tied, to 5.25% from 6%.

Highlighting the depth of the Fed's inflation concerns, two of the 10 voting members of the policy-setting Federal Open Market Committee voted against the 3/4 point cut. Charles Plosser and Richard Fisher, presidents of the Federal Reserve Banks of Philadelphia and Dallas, "preferred less aggressive action at this meeting," the Fed said.

A worsening of both inflation and economic growth in the past month has made FOMC decisions more fractious. Each of the past five rate-cut decisions has triggered at least one dissent—one favoring a bigger cut and the others favoring less. Yesterday's was the first meeting with two dissents since 2002. . . .

The economy is hardly out of the woods. Investor confidence remains fragile just days after the Fed made an unprecedented loan to prevent the collapse of Bear Stearns Cos., exposing how deeply the credit squeeze had penetrated the U.S. financial system. Sunday's statement that the Fed would lend to investment banks, and on the same terms as to commercial banks, was the boldest step the central bank has taken so far to employ its own balance sheet to take some of the riskier debt off the hands of financial institutions. . . .

Case for Analysis

Federal Reserve Monetary Policy

This is one of many articles that appeared in the *Wall Street Journal* in 2008 that described the actions of the Federal Reserve and the Federal Open Market Committee (FOMC) to stem the economic downturn that had resulted from the collapse of the housing market in 2006 and the ensuing credit crisis in the financial markets in 2007 and 2008. The article notes that although the FOMC decreased its short-term interest target by 0.75 percentage point to 2.25 percent at its March meeting, less than investors had expected, the interest rate target had decreased a full three points since September 2007, the fastest rate of decline in decades. The article also mentions that the Fed used another tool of monetary policy, the discount rate, to influence the economy. It lowered the discount rate it charged on loans to banks from 3.25 to 2.5 percent. The Fed signaled that more interest rate cuts were possible because "downside risks to growth remain" and the Fed will "act in a timely manner as needed."

Given the severity of the credit crisis and the reluctance of many financial institutions to make loans even with the lower rates, the Fed also took other steps to increase liquidity in the financial system which included a decision to open its discount window loans to investment banks, a policy that previously applied only to commercial banks. Federal Reserve Chairman Ben Bernanke had also stated his support for the use of public funds to halt the wave of mortgage defaults and foreclosures that had been occurring.

Even with all this concern about whether the economy was in or headed into a recession, members of the FOMC were also concerned about the Fed's other goal of preventing inflation from increasing. Two of the ten voting members of the FOMC voted against the three-quarter point rate cut at the March meeting. Given the dual policy concerns of maintaining both economic growth and price stability, the range of opinions among FOMC members had widened with at least one dissent in each of the previous five rate-cut decisions.

All Federal Reserve policies changed drastically in the summer and fall of 2008 in response to the increased tightening of credit markets and the bankruptcy or near-collapse of major investment banks and other financial institutions. These changes, which will be described in this chapter and Chapter 14, resulted in the more aggressive use of traditional monetary tools and the development of a variety of new nontraditional programs.[1] ■

Money and the U.S. Financial System

Before discussing monetary policy and the U.S. financial system, let's define the commodity that we call money.

Definition of Money

Money

The stock of financial assets that can easily be used to make market transactions and that serves as a medium of exchange, a unit of account, and a store of value.

Money is the stock of financial assets that can be easily used as the medium of exchange for market transactions. It helps facilitate the buying and selling of goods and services, actions that are the essence of a market economy. Money can be defined most clearly in terms of the functions it performs because it serves as a medium of exchange, a unit of account, and a store of value.

Money as a Medium of Exchange　As just noted, money functions as a medium of exchange because it simplifies market transactions. In a **barter system**, goods and services are exchanged directly without a common unit of account. The problem with this system is that each individual has to find another person who wants to exchange the needed commodities, a task that would be very difficult in a

Barter system

A system in which goods and services are exchanged directly without a common unit of account.

---

[1] For summaries of these issues, see "The Financial Crisis: A Timeline of Events and Policy Actions," St. Louis Federal Reserve Bank, www.stls.frb.org/timeline/pdf/CrisisTimeline.pdf; Board of Governors of the Federal Reserve System, Speech, Chairman Ben S. Bernanke at the Greater Austin Chamber of Commerce, Austin, Texas, December 1, 2008, www.federalreserve.gov; and Neil Willardson, "Actions to Restore Financial Stability," Federal Reserve Bank of Minneapolis, www.minneapolisfed.org/banking/about/willardson.pdf.

modern industrialized economy with large numbers of individuals and commodities. An individual might directly exchange yard work for automobile repair with his or her neighbor without the use of money, but lawn maintenance services and automobile repair shops would not be able to serve all their customers if they did not use money as a medium of exchange.

Money as a Unit of Account As a unit of account, money provides the terms in which the prices of goods and services are quoted and debts are recorded. In the United States, the current price of a gallon of milk is approximately $3.00, while the price of a pound of margarine is around $1.00. Dollars are the unit of account in which we measure the relative prices of different goods and services. If we used something else as the unit of account, such as loaves of bread, all prices would be quoted in terms of loaves.

Money as a Store of Value Money also functions as a store of value that can be used for future market purchases. Bread would not serve this purpose well over long periods of time because it would become stale and moldy and would be bulky to maintain. Even with paper currency, countries must make certain that their money actually does hold its value over time in terms of its purchasing power. In times of rapid inflation, individuals can lose faith in the value of their money.

Measures of the Money Supply

Given that money is defined in terms of its functions and its ability to facilitate market transactions, there are various measures of the money supply. Table 13.1 illustrates these measures, which are often called *monetary aggregates*, for the United States.

TABLE 13.1 Measures of the U.S. Money Supply

MEASURE	DESCRIPTION	VALUE (JAN 2008) SEASONALLY ADJUSTED (BILLIONS $)
C: CURRENCY	Coins held outside the Treasury, the Federal Reserve banks, and depository institutions, as well as paper money—Federal Reserve notes	758.0
M1: C PLUS:		
Checkable deposits	Deposits in checking accounts (demand deposits)	292.5
Travelers' checks	Checks that can be used as cash issued by nondepository institutions such as American Express	6.2
Other checkable deposits	Negotiable orders of withdrawal (NOWs) and automatic transfer service (ATS) account balances	307.9
Total M1		*1,364.6*
M2: M1 PLUS:		
Money market mutual fund shares	Shares of funds that invest in short-term financial assets and have check-writing privileges	1,006.1
Savings accounts	Interest-bearing accounts with no checking privileges	3,903.2
Small time deposits	Accounts of less than $100,000, such as certificates of deposit, that have fixed maturities and penalties for early withdrawal	1,224.5
Total M2		*7,498.3*

Sources: Board of Governors of the Federal Reserve System. *The Federal Reserve System: Purposes and Functions* (Washington, D.C.: Board of Governors, 2005) (available at www.federalreserve.gov); Roger LeRoy Miller and David VanHoose, *Money, Banking, and Financial Markets* (Cincinnati, Ohio: South-Western, 2001, 23–30); Federal Reserve Statistical Release, Table 1, Money Stock Measures, H.6 (508), available at www.federalreserve.gov.

Liquidity
The ability of a financial asset to be used to immediately make market transactions.

Demand deposits
Another name for checking accounts or checkable deposits, one of the major components of the M1 measure of the money supply.

These measures of the money supply differ in terms of their **liquidity**, or their ability to be used immediately to make market transactions. M1 is the most commonly used definition of the money supply because it includes the most liquid components. Coins and paper money are almost always accepted for market transactions, while checks and travelers' checks are accepted in many situations.[2] Checking accounts are called **demand deposits** because they can be withdrawn on demand. Money market mutual fund shares and savings accounts are less liquid because these assets must typically be converted to cash or checking account deposits to be used for market transactions. Check-writing privileges from these additional M2 components are generally either restricted or limited to larger transactions. Time deposits in M2 are typically not immediately available for transactions without withdrawal penalties being imposed. Table 13.1 shows the substantial differences in the sizes of the different monetary aggregates.[3]

The most liquid components of the money supply best satisfy the medium of exchange function of money. The less liquid components and other financial instruments may act better as a store of value because they pay interest or higher rates of interest on the principal amount of the asset. We'll discuss later in the chapter how individuals make decisions on the amount of their assets to hold in the form of money versus other financial instruments.

Depository Institutions and the Fractional Reserve Banking System

Depository institutions
Institutions that accept deposits from individuals and organizations, against which depositors can write checks on demand for their market transactions and that use these deposits to make loans.

Federal Deposit Insurance Corporation (FDIC)
The government regulatory institution that supervises the activities of depository institutions in the United States and provides depositors with accounts up to a certain amount (currently $250,000) with a guarantee that they will receive their funds even in the event of a bank failure.

Depository and other financial institutions act as intermediaries to channel income that is saved in the circular flow process to funds that are available for business investment spending and to finance government expenditure and household borrowing (see Figure 11.1 in Chapter 11). Although a wide variety of institutions serve this role, the approximately 8,000 depository institutions in the United States play a special role regarding the money supply. Depository institutions accept deposits, backed by the **Federal Deposit Insurance Corporation (FDIC)**, from individuals and organizations against which the depositors can write checks on demand for their market transactions. The FDIC is the government regulatory institution that supervises the activities of depository institutions in the United States and provides depositors with accounts up to a certain amount (increased from $100,000 to $250,000 in October 2008) with a guarantee that they will receive their funds even in the event of a bank failure.[4]

---

[2] As stated in the Coinage Act of 1965, "All coins and currencies of the United States (including Federal Reserve notes and circulating notes of Federal Reserve banks and national banking associations) . . . shall be legal-tender for all debts, public and private, public charges, taxes, duties and dues." However, there is no federal law mandating that individuals or organizations must accept currency or coins as payment for goods and services. A bus system may refuse to accept payment for fares in pennies or dollars. Gas stations and convenience stores may not accept bills larger than $20. These restrictions are legal as long as a notice is posted and a transaction has not already begun. See Federal Reserve Board, *Frequently Asked Questions (FAQs)* (available at www.federalreserve.gov/faq.htm).

[3] Until March 2006, there was an M3 component of the money supply which consisted of M2 plus time deposits exceeding $100,000, institutional money funds, repurchase agreements, and eurodollars (one-day dollar-denominated deposits in foreign depository institutions and in foreign branches of American depository institutions). The Board of Governors stopped reporting this monetary aggregate in March 2006 due to data collection costs and to the fact that M3 did not prove essential for policy making and monetary analysis. See Edward Nelson, "Goodbye to M3," *Monetary Trends*, Federal Reserve Bank of St. Louis, April 2006.

[4] Depository institutions include commercial banks, savings banks, savings and loan associations, and credit unions as well as U.S. branches and agencies of foreign banks and other domestic banking entities that engage in international transactions. For ease of explanation, we will call these institutions banks. See Board of Governors of the Federal Reserve System. *The Federal Reserve System: Purposes and Functions* (Washington, D.C.: Board of Governors, 2005).

Banks earn income by loaning out these deposits and charging interest for the loans. However, banks need to keep some of their deposits in reserve as depositors write checks and make withdrawals from their accounts. Banks in the United States operate in a **fractional reserve system**, in which the central bank or the Federal Reserve requires them to keep only a fraction of their deposits as reserves, either as cash in their vaults or as non-interest-bearing deposits at the Federal Reserve. This fraction is the **reserve requirement**, rr, or required reserves divided by demand deposits. Banks have the incentive to loan out excess reserves because they earn revenue by charging interest on these loans. Moreover, by using their excess reserves to make loans, banks actually create more money in the financial system.

If banks operated under a 100 percent reserve system, they would not be able to create any further money. For example, in Case 1 in Table 13.2, Bank One would have to hold a $100 deposit in its entirety as reserves against withdrawals of that $100. Suppose under a fractional reserve system, banks are required to hold only 10 percent of their deposits as reserves. This means that in Case 2 in Table 13.2, Bank One can loan out $90 of the original $100 and keep only $10 in reserve. If that $90 is deposited by the borrower in another bank in the system (Bank Two), only 10 percent or $9 needs to be held as reserves. Bank Two can loan out an additional $81. Thus, subsequent loans can be made with the declining amount of excess reserves left after each round of required reserves. The end result of this process is to increase the money supply by a **simple deposit multiplier** that is based on the size of the reserve requirement (rr), as shown in Equation 13.1.

13.1 $d = [(1 - rr) + (1 - rr)^2 + (1 - rr)^3 + \ldots] = [(1/rr)]$

where

d = simple deposit multiplier

rr = reserve requirement

In the example above, $rr = .10$, so the simple deposit multiplier is 10. The original $100 deposit is converted to $1,000 of new money.

The actual money multiplier (mm) differs from the simple deposit multiplier (d), given the possible decisions by banks to hold reserves in excess of those required and by individuals to hold assets in cash rather than bank deposits, as shown in Table 13.3. In this table, the **money supply** is defined as currency plus demand deposits, or M1 from Table 13.1. The **monetary base** is defined as currency plus reserves. Some of these reserves are required by the central bank (which we discuss in more detail below), so the monetary base is a policy variable of the central bank. Banks may also choose to hold reserves in excess of what is required if they see a greater level of withdrawals or if they are reluctant to make loans, given unease over future economic conditions or the creditworthiness of current borrowers.

Fractional reserve system
A banking system in which banks are required to keep only a fraction of their deposits as reserves.

Reserve requirement
Required reserves kept in banks' vaults or as deposits at the Federal Reserve divided by demand deposits or the fraction of deposits banks are required to keep as reserves.

Simple deposit multiplier
The amount by which the money supply can be increased in a fractional reserve banking system, which equals (1/rr), where rr is the reserve requirement.

Money supply
Currency plus checkable accounts or demand deposits (M1).

Monetary base
Currency plus reserves (both required and excess), a variable controlled by central bank policy.

TABLE 13.2 The Fractional Reserve Banking System

CASE 1: 100 PERCENT RESERVE REQUIREMENT		CASE 2: 10 PERCENT RESERVE REQUIREMENT	
BANK ONE BALANCE SHEET		**BANK ONE BALANCE SHEET**	
ASSETS	LIABILITIES	ASSETS	LIABILITIES
Reserves: $100	Deposits: $100	Reserves: $10	Deposits: $100
		Loans: $90	
		BANK TWO BALANCE SHEET	
		ASSETS	LIABILITIES
		Reserves: $9	Deposits: $90
		Loans: $81	

TABLE 13.3 **The Money Multiplier**

Money supply (M) = currency (CU) + demand deposits (DD)

Monetary base (B) = currency (CU) + required reserves (RR) + excess reserves (ER)

Money multiplier (mm) = $\dfrac{\text{Money supply }(M)}{\text{Monetary base }(B)} = \dfrac{CU+DD}{CU+RR+ER}$

Divide the numerator and denominator by DD:

Money multiplier (mm) = $\dfrac{(CU/DD)+(DD/DD)}{(CU/DD)+(RR/DD)+(ER/DD)} = \dfrac{c+1}{c+rr+e}$

> *where*
> c = currency/deposit ratio
> rr = reserve requirement
> e = excess reserve ratio

Money multiplier

The money multiplier, mm—which is usually smaller than the simple deposit multiplier, d—reflects individuals' decisions to hold some of their assets in cash rather than deposit them in a checking account and banks' decisions to hold excess reserves.

The **money multiplier** (mm) reflects the fact that money creation will be less if banks choose to hold reserves in excess of what is required or if individuals choose to hold some of their assets in cash rather than deposit them in a bank where they can be expanded through the money creation process.[5]

Table 13.4 shows the differences between the simple deposit multiplier and the money multiplier. With $rr = 0.1$, the simple money multiplier is 10. However, if individuals hold 10 percent of their assets as cash, the money multiplier is reduced to 5.5. In addition, if banks hold an additional 10 percent in excess reserves, the money multiplier is reduced to 3.667.

Figure 13.1 shows the relationship between the monetary base (currency plus required reserves plus excess reserves), the policy tool of the central bank, and the money supply (currency plus demand deposits). As shown in the figure, currency is transmitted dollar for dollar from the monetary base to the money supply. However, excess reserves in the monetary base can be used to expand demand

---

TABLE 13.4 **Differences Between the Simple Deposit Multiplier and the Money Multiplier**

SIMPLE DEPOSIT MULTIPLIER, $d = 1/rr$	**MONEY MULTIPLIER, $mm = (1 + c)/(c + rr + e)$**
where	*where*
rr = reserve requirement	c = currency deposit ratio
$rr = 0.1$	rr = reserve requirement
$d = 1/0.1 = 10$	e = excess reserve ratio
	EXAMPLE 1
	$c = 0.1; rr = 0.1; e = 0$
	$mm = (1 + 0.1)/(0.1 + 0.1 + 0) = (1.1)/(0.2) = 5.5$
	EXAMPLE 2
	$c = 0.1; rr = 0.1; e = 0.1$
	$mm = (1 + 0.1)/(0.1 + 0.1 + 0.1) = (1.1)/(0.3) = 3.667$

---

[5] In Table 13.2, if Bank One holds an extra 10 percent of its deposits as additional reserves, then it has only $80 to make loans that will create further money. Alternatively, if the customers receiving the original $90 in loans keep 10 percent or $9 in currency and deposit only $81 in Bank Two, that bank keeps $8.10 in reserves and has only $72.90 to loan out to other customers.

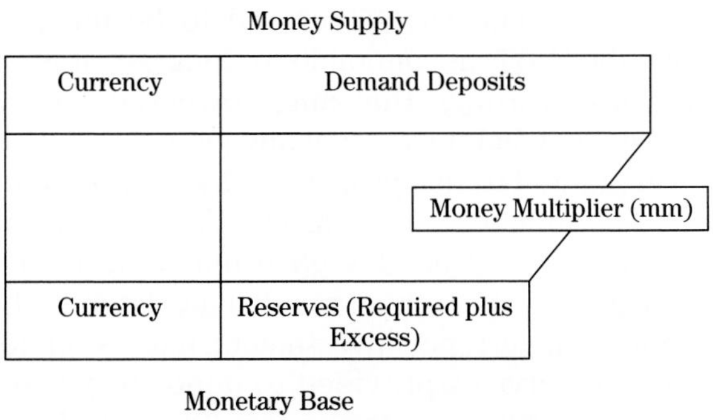

Money Supply

Currency	Demand Deposits
Currency	Reserves (Required plus Excess)

Money Multiplier (mm)

Monetary Base

FIGURE 13.1
The Monetary Base and the Money Supply
The monetary base (currency, required and excess reserves), a policy tool of the central bank, influences the money supply through the money multiplier.

deposits and the money supply through the money multiplier. Any central bank policy that changes reserves will change the money supply.

The Central Bank (Federal Reserve)

The **Federal Reserve System**, or just the **Fed**, is the central bank in the United States.[6] It was created in 1913 to help provide stability to the country's financial system. The Fed both implements monetary policy and helps regulate and operate the country's financial system. The system consists of the 7 members of the Board of Governors located in Washington, D.C., 12 Federal Reserve District Banks in major cities across the country, and approximately 4,000 member banks.[7] The members of the Board of Governors are appointed by the president and confirmed by the Senate. They are appointed for nonrenewable 14-year terms, with their appointments staggered so that one term expires on January 31 of each even-numbered year. The chairman and vice chairman of the Board are also appointed by the president and confirmed by the Senate for four-year terms.

The 12 Federal Reserve District Banks and their 25 branches undertake a variety of functions, including operating a nationwide payments system, regulating and supervising member banks, distributing currency and coins for the country, and serving as bankers for the U.S. Treasury. Each district bank has a board of directors chosen from both the public and the commercial banks that are part of the Federal Reserve System. The district banks provide economic information from across the country to the Federal Reserve System. This information is summarized in the **Beige Book**, which is published eight times a year and includes information on current economic conditions gathered from the banks' staff and interviews with business contacts, economists, market experts, and other sources. Topics in the Beige Book include consumer spending, services and tourism, construction and real estate, manufacturing, banking and finance, labor markets and prices, and agriculture and natural resources.

Banks that are members of the Federal Reserve System include all national banks chartered by the federal government through the Office of the Comptroller of the Currency in the Department of the Treasury and state banks that elect to become members of the system if they meet the standards set by the Board of Governors. Member banks must subscribe to stock in their regional Federal Reserve Bank, and they vote for some of the directors of their Federal Reserve Bank.

Federal Reserve System (Fed)
The central bank in the United States that implements monetary policy and helps regulate and operate the country's financial system.

Beige Book
A publication of the Federal Reserve System that includes information on current economic conditions gathered from the Federal Reserve banks' staff and interviews with business contacts, economists, market experts, and other sources.

---

[6] This discussion is based on *The Federal Reserve System: Purposes and Functions* (Washington, D.C.: Board of Governors of the Federal Reserve System, 2005) (available at www.federalreserve.gov); Federal Reserve Bank of San Francisco; *U.S. Monetary Policy: An Introduction* (available at www.frbst.org/publications/federalreserve/monetary/index.htm); and Roger LeRoy Miller and David VanHoose, *Money, Banking, and Financial Markets* (Cincinnati, Ohio: South-Western, 2001), 592–623.

[7] The Federal Reserve District Banks are located in the following cities: 1st District—Boston; 2nd District—New York; 3rd District—Philadelphia; 4th District—Cleveland; 5th District—Richmond; 6th District—Atlanta; 7th District—Chicago; 8th District—St. Louis; 9th District—Minneapolis; 10th District—Kansas City; 11th District—Dallas, and 12th District—San Francisco.

The Federal Reserve System was structured to be independent within the government. Although the Fed is accountable to Congress, it is insulated from day-to-day political pressures through the long, staggered terms of the Board of Governors, which extend beyond the term of any individual U.S. president. District bank presidents are appointed to five-year terms by the board of directors of each bank and not through the political process. The Federal Reserve System derives most of its income from interest on U.S. government securities that it acquires through open market operations, which we discuss later in the chapter. It also derives income from foreign currency investments, interest on loans to depository institutions, and fees for services provided to depository institutions. The Fed returns any earnings net of expenses to the U.S. Treasury. In 2003, this payment totaled $22 billion. This financing arrangement makes the Fed independent of the political process by which Congress funds federal government agencies.

The Fed is, however, ultimately accountable to Congress and comes under government audit and review. The Fed chairman and other members of the system meet regularly with administration officials and report to Congress on monetary and regulatory issues.

Federal Open Market Committee (FOMC)
The Federal Reserve body that has the primary responsibility for conducting monetary policy.

The **Federal Open Market Committee (FOMC)** has the primary responsibility for conducting monetary policy. The FOMC has 12 members: the seven members of the Board of Governors, the president of the Federal Reserve Bank of New York, and four other Federal Reserve Bank presidents who serve one-year terms on a rotating basis. The remaining district bank presidents participate in the FOMC meetings, which are held eight times a year in Washington, D.C., but do not vote on policy decisions.

Tools of Monetary Policy

The Federal Reserve cannot influence income, output, and inflation directly. Instead, it engages in policy actions that influence the level of interest rates in the economy. Changes in interest rates influence real spending and output through the mechanisms we discussed in Chapter 12. Fed policy focuses either on changing interest rates directly or on changing bank reserves, which then affects interest rates. The Federal Reserve uses three main tools for monetary policy changes: open market operations, the discount rate, and reserve requirements. We will discuss these tools first and then describe the nontraditional approaches the Fed developed to deal with the credit and financial crisis of 2008.

Open market operations
The major tool of Fed monetary policy that involves the buying and selling of government securities on the open market in order to change the money supply and influence interest rates.

Open Market Operations **Open market operations**, the major tool of Fed policy, involve the buying and selling of government securities on the open market (not on an organized stock exchange) by the Federal Reserve Bank of New York under the direction of the FOMC. The Fed engages in open market operations to influence the amount of reserves held by commercial banks, which, in turn, influences the **federal funds rate**, the rate banks charge each other for loans of reserves to meet their minimum reserve requirements. Banks are required to hold between 3 and 10 percent of their demand deposits as reserves, whether as cash in their vaults or as non-interest-bearing deposits with the Fed. They may also hold additional or excess reserves for clearing overnight checks or other purposes.

Federal funds rate
The interest rate that commercial banks charge each other for loans of reserves to meet their minimum reserve requirements.

Federal funds market
The private financial market where banks borrow and loan reserves to meet the minimum reserve requirements.

If a bank needs additional reserves, it can borrow them at the federal funds rate from other banks in a private financial market called the **federal funds market**. Most loans in this market mature within one or two days, some within only a few hours. If increased reserves are supplied to this market, the federal funds rate will fall, making it easier for banks to borrow additional reserves and continue making loans. Changes in the federal funds rate are also reflected in other interest rates that influence real spending.

If the Fed engages in **expansionary monetary policy**, its goal is to stimulate the economy and increase the rate of growth of real GDP. This goal is achieved by increasing the amount of bank reserves in the system and lowering the federal funds rate, which also tends to lower other interest rates in the economy. If the Fed wants the federal funds rate to fall, it will buy government securities from a bank. It pays for these securities with a check drawn on itself. When the selling bank presents the check for payment, the Fed increases the reserves in the account of the bank, and, thus, the total reserves in the banking system increase. This action differs from banks' purchases and sales of securities to each other because the Fed action represents a net addition of reserves to the banking system rather than a redistribution of existing reserves among the banks.

Interest rates in the rest of the economy will tend to fall along with the federal funds rate. The Fed's purchase of government securities or bonds tends to drive up the price of bonds, which lowers their rate of interest (r) or current yield. Bonds are debt securities sold by governments, municipalities, corporations, and federal agencies to finance their activities. Households and institutions purchase them as a financial asset that pays interest income. The interest payment or coupon rate of the bond is typically fixed as a percent of the price or face value of the bond.

However, bonds are resold in competitive secondary markets, where their prices fluctuate according to the forces of demand and supply. If you purchase a new bond for $1,000 that pays $50 per year, the rate of return, or interest rate, is $50/$1,000, or 5 percent. If the price of that $1,000 bond increases in the secondary markets to $1,250 due to an increase in the demand for bonds, the current yield is lowered to 4 percent ($50/$1,250). Likewise, if the price of the bond should fall to $800, the interest rate yield is 6.25 percent ($50/$800). Thus, even though the Fed's actions have the greatest direct impact in the federal funds market, the impact on interest rates spills over into other financial markets.

Contractionary monetary policy has the opposite effect, slowing the rate of growth of real GDP by decreasing the amount of reserves in the banking system and raising the federal funds and other interest rates. When the Fed wants the federal funds rate to increase, it sells government securities. Banks pay the Fed for these securities with their reserves, which leaves fewer reserves in the banking system and causes the federal funds rate to rise. It is this dollar-for-dollar exchange of reserves for government securities that makes open market operations the most powerful and flexible tool of Fed monetary policy.

Table 13.5 shows the *intended* federal funds rate and changes in these rates from 2003 to 2008. These are the targeted federal funds rates set on the various meeting dates of the FOMC indicated in the table. The table shows that these targeted rates are typically changed gradually in response to varying economic conditions that reflect business and managerial decisions across the country.

In January 2001, in response to the slowing economy, the Fed began a series of rate cuts from the 6.50 percent targeted rate that had been in place since May 2000. The targeted rate was gradually lowered throughout 2001 and 2002 to a 1.0 percent rate in June 2003, given the continued uncertainty about the economic recovery.

One year later in June 2004, the Fed began a series of steady quarter-point increases in the federal funds rate that lasted until a target rate of 5.25 percent was reached in June 2006. This policy recognized that the 1.0 percent rate was too stimulating once the economy began to grow on its own and was far below that needed for long-term price stability. The Fed maintained the 5.25 percent rate throughout the first half of 2007, even in the face of the developing problems in the housing and subprime mortgage markets. As noted in the opening article of this chapter, the impact of these factors on economic growth became apparent by summer 2007, and the Fed began a series of rapid cuts in the federal funds rate in September 2007 that lasted into 2008, including some that occurred before the regularly scheduled meetings of the FOMC.

Expansionary monetary policy
Federal Reserve policy to increase the rate of growth of real GDP by increasing the amount of bank reserves in the system and lowering the federal funds and other interest rates.

Contractionary monetary policy
Federal Reserve policy to decrease the rate of growth of real GDP by decreasing the amount of bank reserves in the system and raising the federal funds and other interest rates.

TABLE 13.5 Intended or Targeted Federal Funds Rates

DATE	INCREASE (BASIS POINTS)	DECREASE (BASIS POINTS)	LEVEL (PERCENT)
2008			
December 16		75–100	0.00–0.25
October 29		50	1.00
October 8		50	1.50
April 30		25	2.00
March 18		75	2.25
January 30		50	3.00
January 22		75	3.50
2007			
December 11		25	4.25
October 31		25	4.50
September 18		50	4.75
2006			
June 29	25		5.25
May 10	25		5.00
March 28	25		4.75
January 31	25		4.50
2005			
December 13	25		4.25
November 1	25		4.00
September 20	25		3.75
August 9	25		3.50
June 30	25		3.25
May 3	25		3.00
March 22	25		2.75
February 2	25		2.50
2004			
December 14	25		2.25
November 10	25		2.00
September 21	25		1.75
August 10	25		1.50
June 30	25		1.25
2003			
June 25		25	1.00

Source: Federal Reserve Board, Federal Open Market Committee, *The Intended Federal Funds Rate* (available at www.federalreserve.gov/fomc/fundsratre.htm).

As noted in the opening article, by March 2008 the targeted rate was a full 3 points below the rate in September 2007. At this time there was still concern that lower rates might cause inflationary pressures. By fall 2008, inflationary expectations had receded as the consumer price index fell 1 percent from September to October, while credit markets were still frozen and economic activity continued to slow. The FOMC lowered the targeted rate to 1 percent in October 2008, a step that included an unprecedented coordinated rate cut by six major central banks. In December 2008, the FOMC cut the targeted rate to historic lows between zero and one-quarter percentage point.[8]

The December 2008 Beige Book reflected these weak economic conditions. All Federal Reserve districts reported decreases in retail and vehicle sales, subdued tourism spending, declining manufacturing activity, weak housing and labor markets, and contracted lending.[9]

The FOMC also undertakes the buying and selling of government securities to counteract other influences on the banking system's reserves that are unrelated to monetary policy. These **technical factors** include changes in the amount of currency in circulation and in the size of U.S. Treasury balances at the Federal Reserve Banks. For example, individuals hold more currency during the holiday shopping season, so commercial banks must replenish their vault cash during these periods to maintain their reserves. The amount of U.S. Treasury reserves at the Fed can also change in response to individual and corporate income tax receipt dates and scheduled Social Security payments. Changes in reserves in response to these technical factors may either support or offset overall Fed monetary policy.

Technical factors
Other influences on the commercial banking system's reserves that are unrelated to Fed monetary policy.

The Fed buys and sells securities outright through auctions in which securities dealers submit bids to buy or sell securities of the type and maturity that the Fed has stipulated. Orders are arranged by price, and the Fed purchases or sells as many securities as are needed for the particular policy action. The Fed may also engage in actions that only temporarily affect the supply of reserves in the banking system.[10]

The FOMC engages in securities transactions almost daily after analysis of economic conditions by the staff of the Board of Governors and the Federal Reserve Bank of New York. Once a policy is established, staff members at the Open Market Trading Desk of the New York Federal Reserve Bank contact some of the approximately three dozen securities dealers (called primary dealers) that work with the bank to execute the transactions that either credit or debit the dealers' banks and change the amount of reserves in the banking system. Short-term temporary operations are much more common than outright transactions due to daily fluctuations in the factors influencing the demand for reserve balances.

The FOMC reports its actions in the minutes of its meetings, which are published on the Federal Reserve Web page, and in press releases. For example, the press release for the December 16, 2008, meeting notes that[11]

> The Federal Open Market Committee decided today to establish a target range for the federal funds rate of 0 to 1/4 percent.
>
> Since the Committee's last meeting, labor market conditions have deteriorated, and the available data indicate that consumer spending, business investment, and

[8] Jon Hilsenrath and Kelly Evans, "Prices Post Rare Fall; A New Test for the Fed," *Wall Street Journal*, November 19, 2008; Jon Hilsenrath and Sudeep Reddy, "Fed Signals More Action as Slump Drags On," *Wall Street Journal*, December 2, 2008; Jon Hilsenrath, "Fed Cuts Rates Near Zero to Battle Slump," *Wall Street Journal*, December 17, 2008.

[9] "Summary of Commentary on Current Economic Conditions by Federal Reserve District," December 2008, www.federalreserve.gov/fomc/beigebook/2008/20081203/fullreport20081203.pdf.

[10] If a temporary addition is needed, the Fed engages in short-term repurchase agreements, in which it buys securities from dealers who agree to repurchase them at a specified date and price. Most repurchase agreements mature within seven days, while some are completed overnight. To absorb reserves temporarily, the Fed engages in matched-sale purchase transactions, in which there is a contract for an immediate sale to, and a matching contract for future repurchase from, all securities dealers. These agreements also usually do not exceed seven days in length.

[11] Board of Governors of the Federal Reserve System, Press Release, December 16, 2008. When it publishes each FOMC press release, the online *Wall Street Journal* also includes a feature, "Parsing the Fed," in which analysts make a detailed comparison of the language in the current press release with the previous one. Many financial market participants perform the same type of analysis as they try to determine the future course of Fed policy.

industrial production have declined. Financial markets remain quite constrained and credit conditions tight. Overall, the outlook for economic activity has weakened further.

Meanwhile, inflationary pressures have diminished appreciably. In light of the declines in the prices of energy and other commodities and the weaker prospects for economic activity, the Committee expects inflation to moderate further in coming quarters.

The Federal Reserve will employ all available tools to promote the resumption of sustainable economic growth and to preserve price stability. In particular, the Committee anticipates that weak economic conditions are likely to warrant exceptionally low levels of the federal funds rate for some time.

The focus of the Committee's policy going forward will be to support the functioning of financial markets and stimulate the economy through open market operations and other measures that sustain the size of the Federal Reserve's balance sheet at a high level. As previously announced, over the next few quarters the Federal Reserve will purchase large quantities of agency debt and mortgage-backed securities to provide support to the mortgage and housing markets, and it stands ready to expand its purchases of agency debt and mortgage-backed securities as conditions warrant. The Committee is also evaluating the potential benefits of purchasing longer-term Treasury securities. Early next year, the Federal Reserve will also implement the Term Asset-Backed Securities Loan Facility to facilitate the extension of credit to households and small businesses. The Federal Reserve will continue to consider ways of using its balance sheet to further support credit markets and economic activity,

The FOMC has made its decision process more transparent over time, almost turning the monetary stance announced in these briefings into another policy tool. In 1994, the FOMC began releasing a statement when it changed its targeted interest rate and, in 1998, it began announcing major shifts in its policy "bias" to raise or lower interest rates. In January 2000, these statements about policy bias were replaced by an assessment of the "balance of risks" affecting the economic policy goals of price stability and stable economic growth, which we discussed in Chapter 11.

Discount rate

The interest rate the Federal Reserve charges banks that borrow reserves at the Fed's discount window.

The Discount Rate   The **discount rate** is the interest rate the Fed charges banks that borrow reserves at the Fed's discount window. An increase in this rate indicates contractionary monetary policy, making it more expensive for banks to borrow reserves, whereas lowering the discount rate signals expansionary policy. In the 1920s, the discount rate was the primary tool for Fed monetary policy. However, as financial markets became more developed and sophisticated, open market operations became the main policy tool. Currently, changes in the discount rate have a largely symbolic or announcement effect, indicating the direction of change in Fed policy. Because there is only a relatively small amount of borrowing at the discount window, any changes in this rate have only modest effects on the funding costs of depository institutions. Banks have been reluctant to borrow at the discount window, given that Fed discount officers routinely monitor their requests and the securities market also pays close attention to the volume of discount window borrowing.

On January 9, 2003, the Fed instituted a new dual discount rate policy, under which a lower rate is charged on primary credit for banks in sound fiscal condition, while a higher rate is charged on secondary credit for banks that do not qualify for primary credit. The primary rate is typically set 1 percentage point above the federal funds rate targeted by the FOMC, while the secondary rate is set 50 basis points above the primary rate. Under this new system, called a Lombard facility, financially sound banks do not have to exhaust other sources of funds in order to obtain a discount window loan. In most cases Federal Reserve Banks do not require depository institutions to justify their requests for very short-term primary credit, while loans under the secondary credit program entail a higher level of Reserve Bank administration and oversight. This change has had little impact on monetary policy, which continues to be determined primarily by Fed open market operations.[12] However, as noted in the opening article of this chapter, in March 2008, the Fed also opened its discount window to investment banks to help ease the credit crisis that was occurring in the financial markets.

Table 13.6 lists the discount rates for several time periods. The discount rate is set by the Federal Reserve, as opposed to the federal funds rate, which is influenced by Fed actions. The concurrent changes in the discount rate and the targeted federal funds rate from 2004 to the present can be seen in Table 13.6. By fall 2008, the primary credit program was temporarily changed to allow primary credit loans for periods up to 90 days instead of just overnight or for very short periods. The spread of the discount rate over the federal funds rate was reduced to 25 basis points, and the Fed developed a program, the Term Auction Facility, under which predetermined amounts of credit were auctioned to depository institutions for

TABLE 13.6 Discount Rates in Selected Periods

PERIOD IN EFFECT	PERCENT PER ANNUM
12/16/08–	0.50^a
10/29/08 to 12/15/08	1.25^a
10/08/08 to 10/28/08	1.75^a
4/30/08 to 10/07/08	2.25^a
03/18/08 to 4/30/08	2.50^a
01/22/08 to 01/30/08	4.00^a
11/01/07 to 12/12/07	5.00^a
08/17/07 to 09/18/07	5.75^a
06/29/06 to 08/17/07	6.25^a
06/26/03 to 6/30/04	2.00^a
01/09/03 to 06/25/03	2.25^a
11/07/02 to 01/08/03	0.75
12/13/01 to 11/06/02	1.25
09/17/01 to 10/02/01	2.50
08/22/01 to 09/16/01	3.00
12/19/90 to 01/31/91	6.50
02/24/89 to 12/18/90	7.00
10/13/81 to 11/01/81	14.0
12/05/80 to 05/04/81	13.0

[a]These are the primary rates under the new dual discount rate policy established January 9, 2003; they have been repositioned to be above the federal funds target rate. The policy was designed to improve the operation of the discount window for implementing monetary policy and providing a backup source of funds for depository institutions.

Source: Federal Reserve Bank of Minneapolis. *Discount Rates—Historic Through Present* (available at www.minneapolisfed.org/research/data/us/disc.cf and at http://www.frbdiscountwindow.org/discountwindowbook.cfm.

---

[12] See Deborah LaGomarsino, "Fed Approves Major Shift in How It Lends to Banks," *Wall Street Journal,* November 1, 2002; "The Fed Is Set to Roll Out a Revamped Lending Plan," *Wall Street Journal,* January 7, 2003; Federal Reserve Board, "Discount Window Frequently Asked Questions" (available at http://www.frbdiscountwindow.org/faqs); Federal Reserve Bank of New York, "The Discount Window" (available at http://www.newyorkfed.org/abouthefed); *The Federal Reserve System Purposes & Functions,* 2005.

FIGURE 13.2

Selected Interest Rates

The prime rate, which banks charge their best customers, is set by commercial banks, whereas the federal funds rate is determined by market forces but influenced by the FOMC. Source: Federal Reserve Economic Data (FRED II), Economic Research, Federal Reserve Bank of St. Louis, http://research.stlouisfed.org.fred2/.

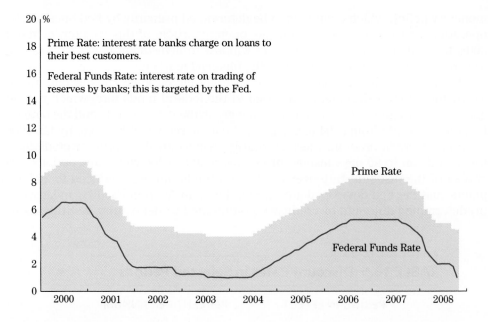

Prime rate

The interest rate that banks charge on loans to their best customers.

terms of up to 84 days. These Federal Reserve actions were designed to help increase liquidity in the financial markets and ease the ongoing credit crisis.[13]

Figure 13.2 shows the federal funds rate and the **prime rate**, which is the rate banks charge on loans to their best customers, from 2000 to 2008. The prime rate is shown as a step function, as banks set their prime rate on the basis of the discount rate established by the Fed. These are announced rates that remain in effect until they are changed by the Fed and the commercial banks. The federal funds rate, shown by the solid line in the table, is the *actual* federal funds rate, as opposed to the *intended or targeted* rate in Table 13.5. The Federal Reserve does not set the federal funds rate, which is determined by market forces in the federal funds market, but it does use its monetary tools to influence that rate in the direction set by the FOMC.

A decrease in the targeted federal funds rate (expansionary monetary policy) typically results in the lowering of other short-term interest rates, particularly those for automobile loans, home-equity lines of credit, adjustable-rate mortgages, and some credit cards. For example, the Federal Reserve's targeted federal funds rate cut in November 2002 made it easier for automobile companies to extend the zero percent financing that had been prevalent since the terrorist attacks in September 2001. The rate on most home-equity lines of credit follows the prime rate. Some credit card rates decrease with expansionary monetary policy, although many cards have fixed interest rates or floors under their adjustable rates. Long-term fixed mortgage rates typically do not respond directly to changes in the targeted federal funds rate, as new mortgage rates tend to follow movements in the rates on long-term securities such as 10-year Treasury notes.[14]

Reserve Requirements   The Depository Institutions Deregulation and Monetary Control Act of 1980 made all depository institutions—commercial banks, savings banks, savings and loan associations, credit unions, and U.S. agencies and branches of foreign banks—subject to the Fed's reserve requirements, whether or not they were Federal Reserve member banks. As we discussed above, these requirements

[13] Bernanke speech, December 1, 2008.

[14] Ruth Simon, "Will the Fed's Rate Cut Pay Off for Consumers?" *Wall Street Journal*, November 7, 2002; Ruth Simon and Zachery Kouwe, "Why a Rate Cut Might Hurt You," *Wall Street Journal*, June 25, 2003.

regulate the fraction of deposits that these banks and other institutions must hold either as cash in their vaults or as deposits at the Federal Reserve. Raising the reserve requirements has a contractionary effect on the economy, because banks will be able to make fewer loans and the money supply will either contract or expand less rapidly. As of January 2009, the first $10.3 million of deposits are not subject to reserve requirements, deposits up to $44.4 million have a 3 percent requirement, and deposits above that amount have a 10 percent requirement.[15] Thus, the requirements are structured to have less impact on small financial institutions. The use of reserve requirements as an active tool of monetary policy was more prevalent in the 1960s and 1970s than at present. Because even small changes in reserve requirements can have a major effect on the amount of reserves required, this tool is not appropriate for day-to-day changes in monetary policy.

Banks typically have an incentive to minimize their reserve levels because reserves held as either cash or deposits in an account with the Fed have traditionally not earned interest. The reserve requirements are typically higher than the level banks would impose on themselves for liquidity reasons, although there is some recent evidence that the reserve requirements may have become less binding as computer technology has allowed banks to temporarily "sweep" deposits from one type of account to another, which reduces the required reserve levels.[16] In October 2008, the Fed announced a new policy of paying interest on required reserve balances and excess balances. This policy was designed to help the FOMC target the federal funds rate by decreasing the incentives for institutions to trade balances in the market at rates much below that paid on the excess balances.[17]

Appendix 13A presents a graphical discussion of the effect of the Fed's monetary instruments on the federal funds rate and the market for bank reserves.

Nontraditional Approaches   In response to the recession and credit crisis of 2008, the Federal Reserve also developed an unprecedented set of lending programs and initiatives. The Fed worked with the Treasury to facilitate the acquisition of the investment bank Bear Stearns by J.P. Morgan Chase and to stabilize an insurer, American Intercontinental Group (AIG), and Citigroup. The Fed also supported actions by the Federal Housing Finance Agency and the Treasury to place the government-sponsored enterprises, Fannie Mae and Freddie Mac, into conservatorship and to assist troubled depository institutions. The Fed supported creation of the Emergency Economic Stabilization Act of 2008 to provide resources to strengthen the financial system. All of these actions doubled the assets in the Federal Reserve's balance sheet between August 2007 and December 2008.[18]

Managerial Rule of Thumb

Federal Reserve Policy

Managers must watch Federal Reserve policy statements and actions to judge where the economy is headed and how monetary policy will influence economic activity. The actions of the FOMC regarding the federal funds rate are the best guides to the direction of overall monetary policy. ∎

---

[15] Federal Reserve Board, "Reserve Requirements" (available at www.federalreserve.gov/ monetarypolicy/ reservereq.htm).

[16] Paul Bennett and Stavros Peristian, "Are U.S. Reserve Requirements Still Binding?" *FRBNY Economic Policy Review*, May 2002, 53–68; *The Federal Reserve System Purposes & Functions*, 2005.

[17] The Federal Reserve Board, "Reserve Requirements," www.federalreserve.gov/monetarypolicy/reservereq. htm; Federal Reserve Bank of New York, "FAQs about Interest on Reserves and the Implementation of Monetary Policy," www.newyorkfed.org/markets/ior_faq.html.

[18] Bernanke speech, December 1, 2008; Willardson, Federal Reserve Bank of Minneapolis, December 2008.

Equilibrium in the Money Market

Now that we have presented the fundamentals of the banking system and the operation of the Federal Reserve, we will use this background to develop a model of the money market, which we use to analyze the supply of money, the demand for money, and equilibrium in the money market.

The Supply of Money

Our discussion in the previous section focused on the Federal Reserve System's control over the money supply. An increase in the money supply, primarily through the open market buying of government securities, has the effect of lowering the federal funds rate, given the increased reserves in the banking system. This effect also causes other interest rates, such as the prime rate and rates on automobile and home-equity loans, to fall. For now, we assume that the Fed has perfect control over the money supply and can cause it to change a given amount with certainty. This assumption is a simplification we use for our model building. We discuss the problems involved with the real-world implementation of monetary policy in the next chapter.

Nominal money supply (M_S)
The money supply (M1), controlled by the Federal Reserve, which is defined in dollar terms.

Real money supply (M_S/P)
The nominal money supply divided by the price level, which expresses the money supply in terms of real goods and services and which influences behavior.

Real Versus Nominal Money Supply   We also note that the Fed controls the **nominal money supply (M_S)**, which is the dollar value of the M1 measure of the money supply shown in Table 13.1. The Fed influences the money supply primarily through the open market operations that we discussed above. However, it is the **real money supply**, which is the nominal money supply divided by the price level (P), or ***M_S/P***, that influences the economic behavior of individuals in an economy, as we show in the following simplified example.

We can illustrate the difference between the nominal and real money supplies in terms of a simple example involving one good, a can of soda, and the money carried in your pocket, your nominal money supply. Suppose that you normally drink 2 cans of soda per day and the price per can is $1.00. If you carry $2.00 in your pocket (the nominal money supply or M_S), your real money supply is (M_S/P_S) = ($2.00/$1.00) = 2 cans of soda. This real money supply, defined in terms of goods rather than dollars, is what influences behavior. If a friend gives you an extra $2.00 tomorrow, your nominal money supply increases to $4.00, and your real money supply increases to 4 cans of soda, assuming the price of soda is constant. You may consider this to be an excess supply of money if you consume only 2 cans of soda per day, and you may put that extra $2.00 into another form of financial asset. Thus, an increase in the nominal money supply results in an increase in the real money supply if the price level is constant.

In a second example, suppose that tomorrow you have only $2.00 in your pocket, but that the price of a can of soda falls to $0.50. In this case, your real money supply is also 4 cans of soda. Your real money supply has increased to 4 cans of soda even though your nominal money supply has remained constant at $2.00. Thus, an increase in the real money supply also occurs if the nominal money supply is constant, but the price level decreases. You again have an excess supply of money because you now need to carry only $1.00 in your pocket to buy 2 cans of soda.

Our analysis of money supply and demand will be undertaken in real terms or in terms of the goods and services that can be purchased with a given nominal money supply and price level. Our models focus on the nominal money supply (M1) controlled by the Federal Reserve and a measure of the absolute price level (P) for the entire economy, which we discussed in Chapter 11. However, the principles in these models are the same as those in the above one-good, one-price, and personal money supply examples.

Real Money Supply Function   The real money supply function is shown in Equations 13.2 and 13.3.

13.2 $RLMS = M_S/P$

> *where*
> $RLMS$ = real money supply
> M_S = nominal money supply
> P = price level

13.3 $RLMS = M_S/P = f(r,\ M_S,\ P)$
$$\qquad\qquad\qquad\qquad (0)\,(+)\,(-)$$

> *where*
> $RLMS$ = real money supply
> r = real interest rate
> M_S = nominal money supply (controlled by Federal Reserve policy)
> P = price level

Equation 13.2 is the definition of the real money supply, whereas Equation 13.3 shows the general relationship among the real money supply, the real interest rate, the nominal money supply, and the price level. As with our notation throughout this text, the f symbol means that the variable on the left side of the equation is a function of or depends on the variables on the right side of the equation. The first variable on the right-hand side of Equation 13.3 determines the slope or shape of the curve, while the other variables cause the curve to shift. Equation 13.3 states that the real money supply does not depend on the interest rate. It is determined only by the price level and Federal Reserve policy regarding the nominal money supply. If the Federal Reserve engages in expansionary open market operations (or decreases the discount rate or the reserve requirement) and the price level is constant, the increase in the nominal money supply causes the real money supply to increase. If the price level decreases, all else held constant, the real money supply also increases, as in the soda example presented above.

Figure 13.3 illustrates two real money supply functions on a graph showing the real interest rate (r) and real money balances (M/P). Both money supply curves are vertical, indicating that the money supply is not a function of the interest rate. The initial money supply curve, $RLMS_1$, is determined by Federal Reserve policy. An increase in the real money supply is shown by a shift of the curve from $RLMS_1$ to $RLMS_2$, as real money balances increase from $(M_S/P)_1$ to $(M_S/P)_2$. This increase in real money balances could result from either an increase in the nominal money supply (M_S) by the Federal Reserve or a decrease in the price level (P).

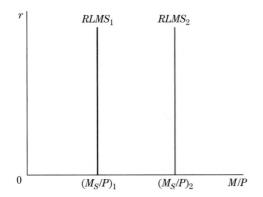

FIGURE 13.3
Real Money Supply Functions
Either an increase in the nominal money supply (M_S) by the Federal Reserve or a decrease in the price level (P) will cause the real money supply function to shift from $RLMS_1$ to $RLMS_2$.

The Demand for Money

Real money demand
The demand for money in real terms, which is a function of the real interest rate and the level of real income.

Equation 13.4 shows a generalized **real money demand** function.[19]

$$\textbf{13.4} \quad RLMD = M_D/P = f(r, \ Y)$$
$$(-)(+)$$

where

$RLMD$ = real money demand

M_D = nominal money demand

P = price level

r = real interest rate

Y = real income

The demand for money in real terms focuses on the portfolio decision that individuals make in terms of holding assets in the form of money versus other types of securities. To illustrate this portfolio allocation decision, we assume, for simplicity, that there are two assets that individuals can hold. One is a liquid asset, money (currency and checkable or demand deposits), which pays them no interest. The second asset is illiquid and represents all other financial assets. For simplicity, we term this asset a government bond, which pays a positive interest rate, r.[20] Individuals hold money because it is liquid and enables them to engage in market transactions. Bonds are less liquid because they cannot immediately be used for market transactions, but they pay a positive rate of return. Thus, the interest rate represents the opportunity cost of holding assets in the form of money.[21] At higher interest rates, individuals will hold fewer assets in the form of money or will demand a smaller quantity of money because they do not want to sacrifice the interest they could earn on the bonds. At lower interest rates, the opportunity cost of holding money is less, so a larger quantity of money will be demanded. Thus, as shown in Equation 13.4, the quantity of money demanded and the interest rate are inversely related.

Real money demand also depends on the level of real income (Y) in the economy. As income increases, there is a larger level of output produced and more expenditure on that output. Individuals demand more money to finance the increased number of market transactions associated with the higher levels of income, output, and expenditure. Thus, the real demand for money is positively related to the level of real income in the economy.

Figure 13.4 shows two money demand functions, $RLMD_1$ and $RLMD_2$. Each money demand function in Figure 13.4 is downward sloping, showing the inverse relationship between the quantity of money demanded and the interest rate. Thus, for demand function $RLMD_1$, real money balances demanded at interest rate r_1 are $(M/P)_1$, while a larger quantity of real balances, $(M/P)_2$, is demanded at the lower

---

[19] The demand for money balances is expressed in real terms, as with the previous discussion of the money supply and the soda example. We assume people are aware of price level changes and demand nominal money balances (M_D) in order to maintain their real purchasing power (M_D/P). If you drink 2 cans of soda per day and the price of a can increases from $1.00 to $2.00, your nominal money demand increases from $2.00 to $4.00. However, your real money demand is the same in both cases ($2.00/$1.00 equals 2 cans of soda, or $4.00/$2.00 equals 2 cans of soda). Real money demand depends on the real interest rate and real income, but not the price level.

[20] Although checking accounts may pay some interest on the amount deposited, this interest rate is typically lower than what can be earned on other financial investments, such as money market funds and mutual funds. Thus, it is reasonable to characterize the asset allocation choice as between an asset with zero interest (money) and one with a positive rate of interest (bond).

[21] Technically, it is the nominal interest rate, i, that influences the demand for money and the real interest rate, r, that influences investment and consumption spending. If the rate of inflation is very low, these two rates are approximately equal.

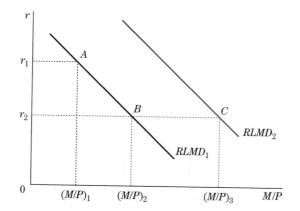

FIGURE 13.4
Real Money Demand Functions
A change in the interest rate, all else held constant, causes a movement along a given money demand curve (RLMD$_1$). A change in income or other autonomous factors influencing money demand shifts the curve from RLMD$_1$ to RLMD$_2$.

interest rate, r_2. The demand functions are drawn as straight lines, although they could be curved. Demand function $RLMD_1$ corresponds to real income level Y_1. If real income increases from Y_1 to Y_2, the money demand function shifts out to $RLMD_2$. There is a larger demand for money, $(M/P)_3$, at any given interest rate (r_2) with money demand function $RLMD_2$, given the larger number of transactions associated with the higher level of income.

Although income and the interest rate are the two major determinants of the demand for money, other autonomous factors can also shift the money demand curve.[22] For example, financial innovations, such as the use of ATMs and electronic banking, have caused a decrease in the demand for money and a leftward shift of the money demand curve at any given interest rate and level of income. In the past, individuals had to travel to a bank or other financial institution to transfer money from a mutual fund or savings account into their checking account or make a withdrawal from an account. Now this can be done electronically or with an ATM. This means that individuals demand less money at any given interest rate and level of income because they can easily transfer funds into their checking accounts from other securities that pay interest.

Equilibrium in the Money Market

As with the markets we studied in Chapter 2, equilibrium in the money market occurs at that interest rate where the quantity of money demanded equals the quantity of money supplied. At any other rate, there will be market disequilibrium, where the imbalance between demand and supply will set forces into motion that bring the market back to equilibrium.[23]

Change in the Supply of Money

We illustrate the process of restoring equilibrium in the money market by showing an increase in the real money supply in Figure 13.5. This change could result from either an increase in the nominal money supply by the Federal Reserve or a decrease in the price level. The original equilibrium in the money market in Figure 13.5 is at point A and interest rate r_1. Suppose there is an increase in the nominal money supply by the Fed, assuming a constant price level. This policy change shifts the money supply curve from $RLMS_1$ to $RLMS_2$. Point A' represents the disequilibrium point where there is an excess supply of money at interest rate r_1.

To understand individual behavior in reaction to this excess supply of money, we assume that an individual is faced with the choice of holding bonds that pay a positive

---

[22] For simplicity, we do not show these factors in Equation 13.4.
[23] The equilibrium price in the money market is the interest rate. Also, the Federal Reserve is the monopoly supplier of money in this market.

FIGURE 13.5

Increase in the Real Money Supply

Beginning at the original equilibrium (point A), an increase in the real money supply from RLMS₁ to RLMS₂ causes the interest rate to fall from r₁ to r₂ to restore equilibrium in the money market (point B).

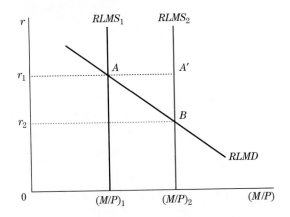

rate of interest or holding money that pays no interest.[24] Also remember, as we discussed previously, that the price of a bond is inversely related to its interest rate or current yield. At point A' and interest rate r_1 in Figure 13.5, individuals demand less money than the amount supplied. They want to hold more bonds and less money, so they will buy bonds with their excess supply of money, which drives up the price of bonds. This, in turn, drives down the current yield or interest rate. However, at a lower interest rate, individuals desire to hold more of their assets in the form of money, given the lower opportunity cost, so that their quantity demanded of money increases. The market is pushed toward a new equilibrium at point B and interest rate r_2 as individuals move down the money demand curve.[25]

The effect of the increase in the money supply is to lower the interest rate from r_1 to r_2. Likewise, a decrease in the money supply from $RLMS_2$ to $RLMS_1$ shifts the curve in the opposite direction, from point B and interest rate r_2 to point A and a higher equilibrium interest rate, r_1. Figure 13.5, therefore, can be used to illustrate the effect of a monetary policy change by the Federal Reserve.

The increase in the real money supply in Figure 13.5 could also result from a decrease in the price level, with the nominal money supply held constant. As illustrated in the soda examples, a decrease in the price level increases the purchasing power of the money supply. We portray this change with the shift of the real money supply curve from $RLMS_1$ to $RLMS_2$ in Figure 13.5. The end result is also a decrease in the interest rate from r_1 to r_2.

Change in the Demand for Money

Equilibrium in the money market can change if the demand for money shifts. Figure 13.6 illustrates an increase in the demand for money resulting from a change in income. The initial equilibrium in Figure 13.6 is with money demand curve $RLMD_1$ at point A and interest rate r_1. This money demand curve corresponds to income level Y_1. If income increases from Y_1 to Y_2, there is an increased demand for money, or a shift in the money demand curve to $RLMD_2$ in order to finance the additional transactions associated with the higher level of income. After the increase in demand, point A is no longer an equilibrium point, as there is now excess demand for money at interest rate r_1 (point A'). At point A', individuals want to hold more of their assets as money than they currently do at this interest rate. To satisfy this excess demand for money, individuals sell bonds to obtain money. This increased supply of bonds drives down the price of bonds in the bond

---

[24] As noted above, we are using bonds to represent all types of financial instruments that individuals and organizations may purchase.

[25] Review the soda and personal money supply examples again if you need help in understanding this process.

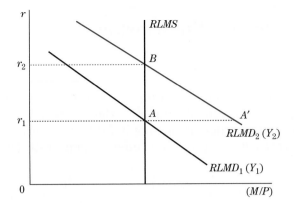

FIGURE 13.6
Change in the Demand for Money
Beginning at the original equilibrium at point A, an increase in the demand for money due to an increase in real income from Y_1 to Y_2 results in an increase in the interest rate from r_1 to r_2 to restore equilibrium at point B.

market. The decrease in the price of bonds means that the current yield or the effective interest rate on the bonds increases. However, with higher interest rates, individuals will desire to hold less of their assets as cash, given the increased opportunity cost. The quantity demanded of money will decrease as individuals move up money demand curve $RLMD_2$ in Figure 13.6 toward a new equilibrium at point B and interest rate r_2.

Although a change in income is the primary factor causing the money demand curve to shift, any other autonomous changes in money demand will also shift the curve, with the same result in terms of interest rate changes. An increase in money demand results in a higher interest rate in order to restore equilibrium in the money market, whereas a decrease in money demand results in a lower interest rate in order to restore equilibrium.

Overall Money Market Changes

Shifts in the demand for and/or supply of money change equilibrium interest rates in the money market. These interest rate changes then affect managerial and consumer spending decisions and the equilibrium level of income through the interest-related expenditure and aggregate expenditure functions, as we discussed in Chapter 12. The opening article of this chapter focused on the Fed's actions to cut interest rates in 2007 and 2008 that were aimed at stimulating the economy to prevent or lessen the impact of a recession resulting from the collapse of the housing market and the credit crisis in the financial markets. We will examine all of these issues in more detail in the next chapter.

Summary

In this chapter, we have examined the effects of money and monetary policy on the economy. We first analyzed the role of money in the banking system. We then discussed the role of the Federal Reserve and its tools for implementing monetary policy. Next we developed a model of the money market, analyzing both the demand and the supply of money. We showed how an equilibrium interest rate resulted in the money market and how that rate could change. Changes in interest rates affect managerial decisions because they influence the cost of borrowing for the firm and they change consumer spending patterns.

We are now ready to develop the overall aggregate macroeconomic model that integrates the real and monetary sides of the economy and helps managers understand how changes in the macro environment affect their competitive strategies.

Appendix 13A Monetary Tools and the Market for Bank Reserves

Figure 13.A1 summarizes the effect of the monetary instruments of the Federal Reserve on the federal funds rate and the market for bank reserves. Figure 13.A1a shows the demand and supply for bank reserves and equilibrium in the market, which determines the federal funds rate (*FFR*). Banks are

FIGURE 13.A1

Effect of Monetary Tools in the Market for Bank Reserves

FFR = *federal funds rate*

Q_{OMO} = *quantity of reserves established by open market operations*

D_{RES} = *demand for bank reserves*

S_{RES} = *supply of bank reserves*

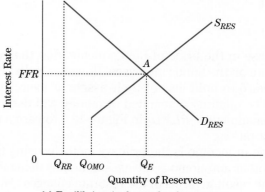

(a) Equilibrium in the market for reserves

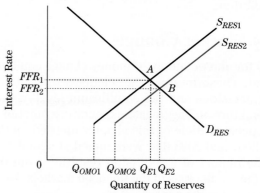

(b) Change in open market operations

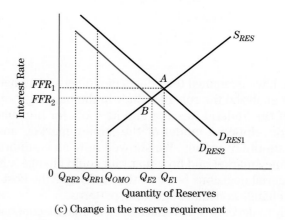

(c) Change in the reserve requirement

required to hold the quantity of reserves indicated by Q_{RR}. If the cost of borrowing or the interest rate decreases, they will have an incentive to borrow more reserves to guard against unforeseen contingencies. Thus, the demand curve for bank reserves slopes downward. The supply of reserves is established by Fed open market operations (Q_{OMO}). Banks with excess reserves will supply more reserves to the federal funds market as the interest rate increases. Thus, the supply curve for reserves is upward sloping.

Equilibrium in the reserves market is determined by the forces of demand and supply, which are influenced by the Fed's monetary instruments. Figure 13.A1b shows an increase in the supply of reserves, represented by the shift of the supply curve from S_{RES1} to S_{RES2}, which lowers the federal funds rate from FFR_1 (point A) to FFR_2 (point B). This shift in the supply curve results from open market operations that increase reserves from Q_{OMO1} to Q_{OMO2}. Figure 13.A1c illustrates a decrease in the reserve requirement, which lowers the amount of reserves that banks must maintain from Q_{RR1} to Q_{RR2}. This change shifts the demand curve for reserves to the left, as fewer reserves are required at any interest rate. The changes illustrated in Figures 13.A1b and 13.A1c result in a lower federal funds rate, which has an expansionary effect on the economy.

Key Terms

barter system, p. 352

Beige Book, p. 357

contractionary monetary
    policy, p. 359

demand deposits, p. 354

depository institutions, p. 354

discount rate, p. 362

expansionary monetary
    policy, p. 359

Federal Deposit Insurance
    Corporation (FDIC), p. 354

federal funds market, p. 358

federal funds rate, p. 358

Federal Open Market
    Committee (FOMC), p. 358

Federal Reserve System (Fed),
    p. 357

fractional reserve system, p. 355

liquidity, p. 354

monetary base, p. 355

money, p. 352

money multiplier, p. 356

money supply, p. 355

nominal money supply (M_S),
    p. 366

open market operations, p. 358

prime rate, p. 364

real money demand, p. 368

real money supply (M_S/P), p. 366

reserve requirement, p. 355

simple deposit multiplier, p. 355

technical factors, p. 361

Exercises

Technical Questions

1. Explain which of the following are counted as part of the money supply (M1):

   a. Checking account deposits
   b. Stocks
   c. Savings account deposits
   d. Government bonds

2. What is a fractional reserve banking system? What is its role in the monetary side of the economy?

3. If the reserve requirement (rr) is 0.2, what is the simple deposit multiplier? If, in addition, the currency deposit ratio (c) is 0.05 and the excess reserve ratio (e) is 0.15, what is the money multiplier? Explain why the money multiplier differs from the simple deposit multiplier.

4. What are the three tools the Federal Reserve uses to change the money supply and interest rates in the economy? Which of these tools is most important and why?

5. Explain which of these interest rates the Federal Reserve sets:
   a. The discount rate
   b. The federal funds rate
   c. The prime rate

6. In each of the following cases, explain whether the statements are true or false:
   a. If the real money demand is greater than the real money supply, interest rates must rise to reach equilibrium in the money market as people sell bonds to obtain more money.
   b. The federal government's control of the money supply, which influences interest rates, is the primary tool that policy makers use to impact the macro economy.
   c. A decrease in the reserve requirement decreases the money supply because banks have fewer reserves.
   d. The real money demand curve shows how households and businesses change their spending in response to changes in the interest rate.
   e. Both an increase in the nominal money supply by the Federal Reserve and an increase in the price level will cause the real money supply curve to shift to the right.

Application Questions

1. In current business publications or on the Federal Reserve Web site (www.federalreserve.gov/ FOMC), find the press release from the most recent meeting of the FOMC. What is the targeted federal funds rate? How does the FOMC evaluate the balance of risks between its goals of price stability and sustainable economic growth? How do the conditions in your article compare with those in March 2008 in the article that opened this chapter?

2. Drawing on articles in the *Wall Street Journal* and other business publications, evaluate the following statement: "What the FOMC says is becoming as important as what it does regarding monetary policy implementation." Find the "Parsing the Fed" feature in the online *Wall Street Journal* for the most recent FOMC press release. Does this feature support the statement in quotes?

3. On the Federal Reserve Web site (www. federalreserve.gov/FOMC/beigebook), find the latest version of the Beige Book that summarizes economic conditions in your Federal Reserve district. Summarize those conditions and relate them to current FOMC policy.

4. On the Federal Reserve Web site (www. federalreserve.gov/FOMC), find the minutes of the most recent FOMC meeting. (Minutes of a given meeting are published after the next scheduled meeting, so they lag behind the press releases of the most recent meeting.) Summarize the factors that led to the decision regarding the targeted federal funds rate at that meeting.

5. Building on Figures 13.5 and 13.6, show how equilibrium in the money market would change:
   a. If money demand is less sensitive to the interest rate or
   b. If there is a greater responsiveness of money demand to changes in income

On the Web

For updated information on the *Wall Street Journal* article at the beginning of the chapter, as well as other relevant links and information, visit the book's Web site at **www.pearsonhighered.com/farnham**

14

The Aggregate Model of the Macro Economy

I n the previous two chapters, we discussed spending on real goods and services by individuals, firms, and governments and the influence of money and Federal Reserve monetary policy on the economy. All of this discussion was in real terms because we assumed that prices were constant in this framework. In real-world economies, the price level changes, and inflation can be a serious policy problem. In addition, the framework in Chapters 12 and 13 focused solely on the expenditure or demand side of the economy. The price level and potential output in the economy are also influenced by supply-side factors. We need to develop the full model of aggregate demand and supply to address these problems, so that managers have a framework for analyzing the entire range of macroeconomic factors that influence their firms and industries.

We begin this chapter with the *Wall Street Journal* article "Fears of Stagflation Return as Price Increases Gain Pace." We'll use the aggregate model we develop in the chapter to analyze the issues raised in this article by developing an aggregate demand curve based on our earlier framework and introducing the concept of aggregate supply to examine the constraints on expenditure imposed by the supply side of the economy.

Fears of Stagflation Return as Price Increases Gain Pace

by Greg Ip

Wall Street Journal, *February 21, 2008*

The U.S. faces an unwelcome combination of looming recession and persistent inflation that is reviving angst about stagflation, a condition not seen since the 1970s.

Inflation is rising. Yesterday the Labor Department said consumer prices in the U.S. jumped 0.4% in January and are up 4.3% over the past 12 months, near a 16-year high. Even stripping out sharply rising food and energy costs, prices rose 0.3% in January, driven by education, medical care, clothing, and hotels. They are up by 2.5% from the previous year, a 10-month high.

The same day brought a reminder of possible recession. The Federal Reserve disclosed that its policy makers lowered their forecast for economic growth this year to between 1.3% and 2%, half a percentage point below the level of their previous forecast, in October. They blamed a further slowdown on the slump in housing prices, tighter lending standards and higher oil prices. They warned the economy's performance could fall short of even that lowered outlook. . . .

A simultaneous rise in unemployment and inflation poses a dilemma for Fed Chairman Ben Bernanke. When the Fed wants to fight unemployment, it lowers interest rates. When it wants to damp inflation, it raises them. It's impossible to do both at the same time.

Stagflation, a term coined in the United Kingdom in 1965, defined the years from 1970 to 1981 in the U.S. Inflation rose to almost 15%. The economy went through three recessions. Unemployment reached 9%. Fed Chairman Paul Volcker finally conquered inflation, but only by dramatically boosting interest rates, causing a severe recession in 1981–82.

Today's circumstances are far from that. Inflation is lower. Unemployment has risen, but only to 4.9%.

Yet there are similarities. As in the 1970s, surging commodity prices are leading the way. Crude oil rose to $100.74 a barrel yesterday, a new nominal high and close to its 1980 inflation-adjusted high. Wheat prices have hit a record. And, as in the 1970s, the rate at which the U.S. economy can grow without generating inflation has fallen, because of slower growth in both the labor force and in productivity, or output per hour of work.

The biggest difference is that in the 1970s, the Fed was unwilling, or thought itself unable, to bring inflation down. The Fed today sees achieving low inflation as its primary mission. . . .

Members of the Federal Open Market Committee, the Fed's policy committee, raised their forecasts for both the overall inflation rate and the "core" rate, which excluded food and energy, by 0.3 percentage points from October, their latest forecast revealed. Yet they dialed back their rhetorical concern. The officials pronounced risks on inflation to be "balanced"—in other words, they felt inflation, should it differ from their forecast, was as likely to be lower as it was higher. . . .

Higher inflation is still a possibility. Food and energy costs could keep rising, instead of flattening out as futures markets currently anticipate. Companies could succeed in passing those costs onto consumers. . . .

The declining dollar, while boosting U.S. exports, is adding to inflation pressure, as goods priced in foreign currencies become relatively more expensive. Prices for imports from China jumped 0.8% in January, the largest monthly increase since the Labor Department began reporting the data in 2003. . . .

In the U.S., stagflation scares are more common than actual stagflation. Core inflation rose after the start of recessions in both 1990–91 and 2001, but then trended down as unemployment kept rising.

The only generally agreed period of stagflation in the U.S. came in the 1970s. Its seeds were planted in the late 1960s, when President Johnson revved up growth with spending on the Vietnam War and his Great Society programs. Fed Chairman William McChesney Martin, meanwhile, failed to tighten monetary policy sufficiently to rein in that growth.

In the early 1970s, President Nixon, with the acquiescence of Fed Chairman Arthur Burns, tried to get inflation down by imposing controls on wage and price increases. The job became harder after the Arab oil embargo dramatically drove up energy prices, and overall inflation, in 1973. Mr. Burns persistently underestimated inflation pressure: In part, he did not realize the economy's potential growth rate had fallen, and that an influx of young, inexperienced baby boomers into the work force had made it harder to get unemployment down to early-1960s levels.

As a result, even when he raised rates, pushing the economy into a severe recession in 1974–75, inflation and unemployment didn't fall back to the levels of the previous decade. . . .

In a speech in 1979, a year after he stepped down, Mr. Burns blamed his failure on a political environment that wouldn't tolerate the high interest rates necessary to rein in inflation. As the Federal Reserve tested how far it could raise rates, he said, "it repeatedly evoked violent criticism" from the White House and Congress.

Such political risks are smaller but not entirely absent for Mr. Bernanke in this election year. . . .

Still, Mr. Bernanke has reiterated the importance of not repeating the 1970s. He and his colleagues believe a persistent escalation of inflation is likely only if workers and firms come to expect the elevated inflation rate to persist, and set their wages and prices accordingly. . . .

Thus far, Fed officials have taken comfort that surveys and bond-market behavior suggest the public expects the inflation rate to fall. But expected inflation, as measured by trading of inflation-protected Treasury bonds, has jumped since the Fed

declared in early January that supporting growth would be a more important focus than holding down inflation. . . .

On the other hand, surveys of consumer predictions about inflation show no corresponding jump. And most important, wage gains had not accelerated. Since labor is the largest component of business costs, a wage-price spiral would likely be a prerequisite for stagflation. . . .

 Case for Analysis

Multiple Factors Influence Economic Activity

This article focuses on the dual goals of the Federal Reserve of maintaining both adequate economic growth and a low level of inflation. The article notes that there are typically trade-offs between these conditions so that lowering interest rates typically stimulates the economy. If this policy is maintained too long, however, rapid economic growth generates inflation, which must then be reduced with higher interest rates.

During the 1970s, both of these conditions existed simultaneously due to price increases generated by the Vietnam War spending in the 1960s and the oil embargo imposed by the Organization of Petroleum Exporting Countries (OPEC) in the 1970s. The economy's potential growth rate, which is influenced by factors on the supply side of the economy, had also fallen, making it more difficult to achieve both price stability and high employment. Inflation was finally reduced when the Fed substantially raised interest rates, causing the severe recession of 1981–82.

The challenge for Fed policy makers in early 2008 was to accurately judge how much to stimulate the economy to offset the negative influences of the decrease in household wealth from declining home prices, the lack of consumer confidence, and the tight conditions in the credit and financial markets. High oil and commodity prices combined with slowing productivity made this a more difficult task than in other periods. However, by late 2008, commodity prices had stabilized, consumer prices were falling, and the economic downturn had become more severe. The model we develop in this chapter will show how all of these factors interact to create the challenges for Fed policy, and why this policy may change significantly in response to volatile economic conditions. ■

The Model of Aggregate Demand and Supply

As noted above, policy makers are concerned with the macro goals we first described in Chapter 11: maintaining stable prices, full employment, and a sustainable rate of economic growth over time. In summer 2002, the Fed's focus was on stimulating the economy as it emerged from the 2001 recession, even though Fed policy makers knew that the targeted federal funds rate at that time was not consistent with maintaining low inflation in the long run. In late 2007 and early 2008 the concern was how to stimulate the economy to prevent or minimize a recession while not increasing inflationary pressures. There was also discussion at this time that the Fed's traditional policy of using open market operations to lower interest rates would not be sufficient to boost spending and income, given that much of the slowdown in economic activity was due to a lack of confidence in financial institutions and in the mortgage and housing markets. These factors increased in importance in late 2008, requiring new nontraditional responses from the Fed.

To fully analyze these and other policy issues, we need the complete macroeconomic model of aggregate demand (*AD*) and aggregate supply (*AS*), which allows us to consider the impact of changes in real spending and monetary policy on both the level of real output and the price level. We first derive the aggregate demand curve and show how it shifts. After discussing the concept of aggregate supply and potential output, we then integrate both concepts into the complete macroeconomic model of the economy.

The Aggregate Demand Curve

The **aggregate demand curve** shows alternative combinations of the absolute price level (P) and real income (Y) or GDP that result in simultaneous equilibrium in both the real goods and the money markets. We established the concept of equilibrium in the real goods market in Chapter 12 and in the money market in Chapter 13. By itself, the aggregate demand curve does not show where the economy will actually operate. The aggregate demand curve gives the total amount of real goods and services (real GDP) that will be demanded by all sectors of the economy (household, business, government, and foreign) at different price levels.

Aggregate demand curve
The curve that shows alternative combinations of the price level (P) and real income (Y) that result in simultaneous equilibrium in both the real goods and the money markets.

Deriving the Aggregate Demand Curve   As background for deriving the aggregate demand curve, let's review the impact on the money market of a change in the price level. In Chapter 13, we noted that a change in the real money supply results from either a change in the nominal money supply by the Federal Reserve or a change in the price level. In Figure 14.1, we illustrate the effect of a decrease in the price level from P_1 to P_2, holding the nominal money supply constant. The initial equilibrium in the money market is at interest rate r_1, or point A. The decrease in the price level causes the real money supply to increase from $RLMS_1$ to $RLMS_2$. The interest rate must fall to r_2, or point B, to restore equilibrium in the money market. Thus, a decrease in the price level, holding the nominal money supply constant, causes the real money supply to increase and the interest rate to fall, whereas an increase in the price level, all else held constant, causes the real money supply to decrease and the interest rate to rise.

Figure 14.2 reproduces the interest-related expenditure function and the aggregate expenditure function from Figure 12.11 in Chapter 12. These functions show that at interest rate r_1, there is interest-related consumption and investment expenditure IRE_1, which results in an equilibrium level of income Y_1 (point A in these figures). If the interest rate decreases to r_2, interest-related consumption and investment expenditure increases to IRE_2, which results in a higher equilibrium level of income Y_2 (point B in these figures).

Figure 14.3 uses these concepts to derive the aggregate demand curve. The axes of this graph are the price level (P) and the level of real income (Y). Point A in Figure 14.3 corresponds to equilibrium point A in the money market in Figure 14.1 with interest rate r_1 and price level P_1 and to equilibrium point A in the real goods market in Figure 14.2 with interest-related expenditure IRE_1 and level of real income Y_1. Thus, point A in Figure 14.3 shows a price level P_1 and a level of real income Y_1 such that there is simultaneous equilibrium in both the real goods market and the money market.

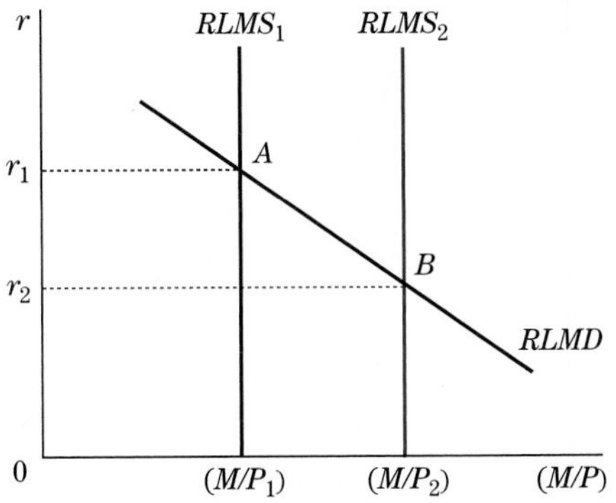

FIGURE 14.1
Change in the Price Level and the Effect on the Money Market
A decrease in the price level from P_1 to P_2 causes the real money supply to increase from $RLMS_1$ to $RLMS_2$. Equilibrium moves from point A to point B, and the interest rate falls from r_1 to r_2.

FIGURE 14.2

Interest-Related Expenditure and Equilibrium Income

A decrease in the interest rate from r_1 to r_2 increases interest-related consumption and investment expenditure from IRE_1 to IRE_2 and equilibrium income from Y_1 to Y_2.

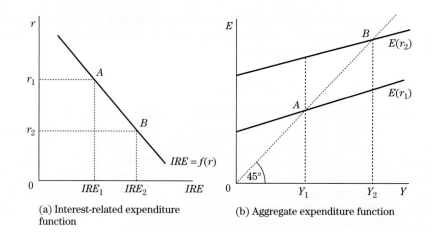

(a) Interest-related expenditure function

(b) Aggregate expenditure function

Point B in Figure 14.3 shows a lower price level P_2 and a larger level of real income Y_1. The decrease in the price level has caused the real money supply curve in Figure 14.1 to shift to the right, which has resulted in a lower interest rate r_2 to restore equilibrium in the money market (point B). This lower interest rate r_2 has stimulated more interest-related consumption and investment expenditure IRE_2 in Figure 14.2, which has increased the equilibrium level of real income to Y_2 (point B). Thus, point B in Figure 14.3 shows another combination of the price level and real income level such that there is simultaneous equilibrium in the real goods and money markets. Points A and B therefore represent points on an aggregate demand curve, AD. This curve slopes downward, indicating that a larger level of real income is consistent with a lower price level and a smaller level of real income is consistent with a higher price level.

Shifting the Aggregate Demand Curve   The aggregate demand curve can shift as a result of deliberate policy actions by the Federal Reserve (monetary policy) or the national government (fiscal policy) or as a result of other autonomous spending changes in the economy.

Monetary Policy   Figure 14.4 shows the effects of expansionary monetary policy on the aggregate demand curve. In this figure, the original equilibrium at point A on aggregate demand curve AD_1 corresponds to point A in Figure 14.3.

Suppose that the Federal Reserve engages in expansionary monetary policy by increasing the nominal money supply. This is represented by a rightward shift of the real money supply curve, as in Figure 13.5 in Chapter 13. As described in that chapter, this increased supply of money results in a lower interest rate for equilibrium in the money market. The lower interest rate from the expansionary monetary policy generates interest-sensitive investment and consumption spending and a higher equilibrium level of real income Y_2.

FIGURE 14.3

Deriving the Aggregate Demand Curve

If the price level decreases from P_1 to P_2 with the nominal money supply, M_{S1}, constant, the real money supply increases, which lowers the interest rate and increases equilibrium income. Equilibrium moves from point A (price level P_1 and real income level Y_1) to point B (price level P_2 and real income level Y_2). The AD curve traces out these alternative points of equilibrium.

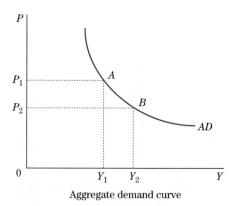

Aggregate demand curve

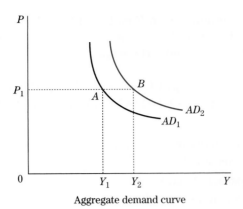

Aggregate demand curve

FIGURE 14.4
Expansionary Monetary and Fiscal Policy and the Aggregate Demand Curve
An increase in the nominal money supply by the Federal Reserve from M_{S1} to M_{S2} (assuming a constant price level, P_1) lowers the interest rate and increases the equilibrium level of income. Since the new equilibrium point B is at the same price level (P_1) as point A, but represents a larger level of income, point B must lie on a separate aggregate demand curve. Thus, an increase in the money supply causes the AD curve to shift to the right. Expansionary fiscal policy also results in a higher equilibrium level of income at the same price level and is represented by a rightward shift in the AD curve.

Note that this example assumes that only the nominal money supply changed from Federal Reserve action and that the price level (P_1) has not changed. Thus, point B in Figure 14.4 corresponds to income level Y_2 and price level P_1. It is clear that point B cannot lie on the original aggregate demand curve AD_1 because the point represents the same price level, but a larger level of real income. If this analysis is repeated for another initial equilibrium, we trace out a second aggregate demand curve, AD_2, in Figure 14.4. Thus, expansionary monetary policy by the Federal Reserve causes the aggregate demand curve to shift to the right, resulting in increased aggregate demand at any given price level. Similarly, contractionary monetary policy causes the aggregate demand curve to shift to the left with less aggregate demand at any price level.

Comparing Figure 14.3 with Figure 14.4, we can see that in both cases, there is a change in the real money supply. In Figure 14.3, there is a change in the price level, but we assume the nominal money supply is held constant. Because the interest rate changes and there is a change in interest-related expenditure and equilibrium income, there is a movement along the aggregate demand curve, AD. In Figure 14.4, the Federal Reserve increases the nominal money supply at the same price level. This change lowers the interest rate and increases equilibrium income, but results in a shift of the aggregate demand curve from AD_1 to AD_2 because the price level has not changed.

Fiscal Policy   Figure 14.4 also shows the effect of expansionary fiscal policy (increasing government spending or lowering taxes) on the aggregate demand curve. Starting at point A, expansionary fiscal policy results in a higher equilibrium level of income Y_2 at the same price level P_1 (point B).[1] We see that this point cannot lie on the same aggregate demand curve as point A because it represents a higher level of income at the same price level. Point B lies on a new aggregate demand curve, AD_2. Thus, expansionary fiscal policy results in a rightward shift of the aggregate demand curve. Likewise, contractionary fiscal policy (decreasing government spending or increasing taxes) causes a leftward shift of the aggregate demand curve.

Other Autonomous Spending Increases   Other autonomous spending increases in any sector of the economy will have the same effect on aggregate demand, as illustrated in Figure 14.4. These spending increases cause a rightward shift of the AD curve. Likewise, decreases in autonomous spending cause a leftward shift of the AD curve.

---

[1] This result is based on the aggregate expenditure function and the multiplier effect that we discussed in Chapter 12.

These factors are summarized in Equation 14.1, which gives the general *AD* relationship in terms of the variables influencing autonomous consumption, investment, government, export, and import spending.

14.1 $AD: Y = f(P, T_P, CC, W, CR, D, T_B, PR, CU, G, Y^*, R, M_S)$
$$(-)\ (-)\ (+)\ (+)\ (+)\ (-)\ (-)\ (+)\ (+)\ (+)(+)\ (-)(+)$$

where

Y = real income

P = price level

T_P = personal taxes

CC = consumer confidence

W = consumer wealth

CR = consumer credit

D = consumer debt

T_B = business taxes

PR = expected profits and business confidence

CU = capacity utilization

G = government spending

Y^* = foreign GDP or real income

R = currency exchange rate (foreign currency per dollar)

M_S = nominal money supply (influenced by Federal Reserve policy)

The relationship between the left-hand variable, Y, and the first right-hand variable, P, in Equation 14.1 shows the shape of the aggregate demand curve (downward sloping). Other right-hand variables cause the aggregate demand curve to shift either rightward $(+)$ or leftward $(-)$. Both fiscal policy tools (government spending, G, and taxes, T) and monetary policy tools (Federal Reserve control of the nominal money supply) are included as variables in Equation 14.1. Note, however, the large number of other variables in the equation that also influence aggregate demand, *but are not under the control of any policy maker.* Forecasting the effects of changes in these other variables in order to develop sound fiscal and monetary policies is the major challenge facing policy makers, as discussed in the opening article of this chapter. Determining the impact of changes in all of these variables on a firm's competitive strategy is one of the major tasks of a manager.

Table 14.1 summarizes the effects of all the variables in the model on the *AD* curve, while Table 14.2 presents policy descriptions from the *Wall Street Journal* and other publications of how each variable influences aggregate demand.

Fiscal and Monetary Policy Implementation

The shift of the aggregate demand curve in Figure 14.4 from fiscal and monetary policy makes it appear as though using fiscal and monetary policy tools to influence the level of economic activity is a very mechanical and precise process. Although this is the case in the models, nothing could be further from the truth in the real world.

Fiscal Policy Changes   Fiscal policy changes result from a complex political process involving the president, his administration, and the Congress. Because there are so many people involved in this process, any changes in government expenditure or taxes meant to stimulate or contract the economy may take weeks or months to be approved by both the Senate and the House of Representatives and then sent to the president for his signature. Discussion of

TABLE 14.1 Factors Causing Shifts in the *AD* Curve

AD CURVE SHIFTS OUT TO THE RIGHT	*AD* CURVE SHIFTS BACK TO THE LEFT
HOUSEHOLD CONSUMPTION SPENDING (*C*)	**HOUSEHOLD CONSUMPTION SPENDING (*C*)**
Decrease in personal taxes (T_P)	Increase in personal taxes (T_P)
Increase in consumer confidence (*CC*)	Decrease in consumer confidence (*CC*)
Increase in consumer wealth (*W*)	Decrease in consumer wealth (*W*)
Increase in consumer credit (*CR*)	Decrease in consumer credit (*CR*)
Decrease in consumer debt (*D*)	Increase in consumer debt (*D*)
BUSINESS INVESTMENT SPENDING (*I*)	**BUSINESS INVESTMENT SPENDING (*I*)**
Decrease in business taxes (T_B)	Increase in business taxes (T_B)
Increase in expected profits and business confidence (*PR*)	Decrease in expected profits and business confidence (*PR*)
Increase in capacity utilization (*CU*)	Decrease in capacity utilization (*CU*)
GOVERNMENT SPENDING (*G*)	**GOVERNMENT SPENDING (*G*)**
Increase in government spending (*G*)	Decrease in government spending (*G*)
FOREIGN SECTOR SPENDING (*X, M*)	**FOREIGN SECTOR SPENDING (*X, M*)**
Increase in the level of foreign GDP or real income (Y^*)	Decrease in the level of foreign GDP or real income (Y^*)
Decrease in the currency exchange rate (*R*)	Increase in the currency exchange rate (*R*)
FEDERAL RESERVE POLICY	**FEDERAL RESERVE POLICY**
Increase in the nominal money supply	Decrease in the nominal money supply

tax and spending changes is often more related to the political philosophy of the Democratic and Republican parties than to specific macroeconomic goals. Debate also focuses on the issue of whose spending and taxes will be changed.[2] In some cases, at the beginning of a new fiscal year, federal agencies are authorized to undertake spending only on a temporary basis because the president and Congress have not agreed on the desired level of spending.

Fiscal policy takes even longer to have an impact on the economy after the changes are passed by Congress and signed by the president. Newly appropriated expenditures have to become part of a federal agency's budget, contracts must be established, programs must be funded, and employees must be hired. The impact of federal income tax changes depends on whether withholding rates from paychecks are changed and rebates are mailed out to consumers during the year or whether individuals must wait until April of each year, when federal income taxes are due, to determine the impact of any tax law changes.

When Congress passed the economic-stimulus bill in February 2008, it was considered a rare bipartisan effort to use fiscal policy to quickly stimulate the economy. Even so, there was partisan debate over the provisions of the bill. Democrats tried unsuccessfully to create a more expansive package that would have extended unemployment benefits, increased funding for home-heating subsidies for the poor, and given $500 checks to millions of Social Security recipients. Analysts noted that the bill would probably not hold off a recession because the rebate checks would

---

[2] When President George W. Bush introduced his tax proposal in January 2003, which focused on reducing taxes on business profits and dividends, the plan was attacked by Democrats who argued that it gave too many benefits to the wealthy. The actual tax bill, greatly modified from the original proposal, was not approved by Congress until May 2003. See John D. McKinnon and Shailagh Murray, "Bush Tax Plan Draws Fire from Democrats, Industries," *Wall Street Journal*, January 7, 2003; Shailagh Murray, "House, Senate Hammer Out $350 Billion Tax-Relief Deal," *Wall Street Journal*, May 23, 2003.

TABLE 14.2 Policy Descriptions of the Variables Influencing Aggregate Demand

HOUSEHOLD CONSUMPTION SPENDING (C)

PERSONAL TAXES (T_P)	"Recession will be difficult to avoid, even with . . . the $152 billion stimulus package President Bush signed into law yesterday, but economists say the extraordinary measures will help to cushion any downturn and promote a speedy recovery. Experience with tax rebates in 2001 shows that consumers will quickly spend 60 percent or more of rebate checks the Treasury sends out between May and July. . . . Because consumers account for about 70 percent of economic activity, that will give an important boost to growth." (*McClatchy-Tribune Business News*, February 14, 2008)
CONSUMER CONFIDENCE (CC)	"The Conference Board Consumer Confidence Index, which had declined in January, fell sharply in February. The Index now stands at 75.0 (1985 = 100), down from 87.3 in January. . . . The weakening in consumers' assessment of current conditions, fueled by a combination of less favorable business conditions and a sharp rise in the number of consumers saying jobs are hard to get, suggests that the pace of growth in early 2008 has slowed even further." (*PR Newswire*, February 26, 2008)
CONSUMER WEALTH (W)	"Until this month, the Fed had expected the troubles in the housing and mortgage markets wouldn't spill over to the broader economy. . . . That changed in January with news that consumer spending, employment and manufacturing activity had all downshifted. . . . The possibility that falling house prices will lead to more defaults and foreclosures, loss of bank capital, tighter lending and yet further declines in prices is now Mr. Bernanke's dominant concern." (*WSJ*, January 31, 2008)
CONSUMER CREDIT (CR)	"As in past credit dry spells, high-risk corporations and homeowners with poor credit face the prospect of paying more for debt. But in this, the first debt drought of the 21st century, the impact is evident in unexpected places. Due to the well-documented subprime losses and to the generally weak housing market, caution has spread to the entire home-lending industry. In the Federal Reserve's January survey, 55 percent of U.S. banks said they had tightened lending standards on prime mortgages in the past three months, while 60 percent had done so for home-equity lines of credit." (*Newsweek*, March 3, 2008)
CONSUMER DEBT (D)	"[The economic downturn] couldn't come at a worse time for U.S. homeowners. American household debt has more than doubled in a decade to $13.8 trillion at the end of 2007 from $6.4 trillion in 1999, the vast majority of it in mortgages and home equity lines, according to Fed data." (*WSJ*, March 15, 2008)

BUSINESS INVESTMENT SPENDING (I)

BUSINESS TAXES (T_B)	"Two tax breaks retained in the final [economic stimulus] legislation would allow businesses to write off equipment purchases made this year more quickly and give small firms greater ability to write off their expenses." (*WSJ*, February 8, 2008)
EXPECTED PROFITS AND BUSINESS CONFIDENCE (PR)	"The Conference Board Measure of CEO Confidence, which had declined to 44 in the third quarter 2007, fell to 39 in the final quarter of 2007. . . . The last time the Measure fell below 40 was in the final quarter of 2000. . . . CEOs' confidence in the state of the U.S. economy continues to wither and is now at a seven-year low," says Lynn Franco, director of The Conference Board Consumer Research Center." (*The Conference Board*, January 15, 2008)
CAPACITY UTILIZATION (CU)	"Data on industrial production in January are expected to show a modest 0.1% rise on the heels of December's flat reading. Economists expect the capacity-utilization rate to be unchanged from November at 81.4%, which is below the inflation danger zone." (*WSJ*, February 15, 2008)

GOVERNMENT SPENDING (G)

GOVERNMENT SPENDING (G)	"Overall, Mr. Bush used the budget to burnish his legacy as both a fiscal conservative and a security hawk. For the year that starts Oct. 1, it boosts overall security-related funding—for defense, homeland security, and international affairs—by a combined 8.2% from the current fiscal year to about $595 billion. By contrast, nonsecurity spending, mostly social services and other domestic programs, would rise by just 0.3% to $393 billion." (*WSJ*, February 5, 2008)

FOREIGN SECTOR SPENDING (X, M)

LEVEL OF FOREIGN GDP OR REAL INCOME (Y^*)	"Can foreign trade keep the U.S. economy afloat? So far it's doing a yeoman's job, especially in support of manufacturing and corporate profits. Through the end of last year export growth showed few signs of cooling, despite some emerging softness in a few overseas markets. . . . The big question is exports: How much will the U.S. slowdown depress overseas economies and the demand for U.S.-made products?" (*Business Week*, March 3, 2008)

TABLE 14.2 Continued

CURRENCY EXCHANGE RATE (R)	"The dollar's dive deepened, touching record lows against the euro and the Swiss franc, and barreling to a level not seen in more than 12 years against the yen. In recent weeks, the faltering U.S. economy and intensifying turmoil in credit markets have caused the dollar to weaken with renewed speed, much as it did last fall. The acceleration creates a host of problems world-wide, starting in Japan, where a stronger yen threatens the country's exporters and increases the likelihood that the world's No. 2 economy will slow significantly. . . . European exporters, too, will feel the pinch." (*WSJ*, March 14, 2008)
FEDERAL RESERVE POLICY	
NOMINAL MONEY SUPPLY (M_S)	"The Fed, Mr. Bernanke said, has cut interest rates 'substantially further' in response to the slowdown. The fed-funds rate now sits at just 2.25%, down three full percentage points since September. Those rate cuts, as well as efforts to boost liquidity in credit markets, 'will help to promote growth over time and to mitigate the risks to economic activity,' he said, adding that 'much necessary economic and financial adjustment has already taken place.'" (*WSJ*, April 2, 2008)

Sources: Patrice Hill, "Stimulus Package Seen as Cushion," *McClatchy-Tribune Business News*, February 14, 2008; "The Conference Board Consumer Confidence Index Declines 12 Points; Expectations Fall to 17-Year Low," *PR Newswire*, February 26, 2008; Greg Ip, "Fed Moves to Curb Risk of Recession," *Wall Street Journal*, January 31, 2008; Daniel Gross, "Borrowers Are Out in the Cold; It's No Longer Just People with Bad Credit Who Are Feeling the Squeeze. Americans with Good Credit at All Income Levels Are Now Caught in a Full-Blown Credit Crunch," *Newsweek*, March 3, 2008; Liz Rappaport and Justin LaHart, "Debt Reckoning: U.S. Receives a Margin Call," *Wall Street Journal*, March 15, 2008; Sarah Lueck, "Congress Approves Economic-Stimulus Bill," *Wall Street Journal*, February 8, 2008; "CEO Confidence Declines Again, the Conference Board Reports," *The Conference Board*, January 15, 2008; "Modest Rise Forecast for Industrial Output," *Wall Street Journal*, February 15, 2008; John D. McKinnon and Michael M. Phillips, "Bush Budget Sets Stage for Battle on Tax Cuts," *Wall Street Journal*, February 5, 2008; James C. Cooper, "A Plug for a Leaky Economy; Rising Exports and Declining Imports Have Sharply Narrowed the Trade Gap, So Far Helping to Keep the U.S. from Sinking into Recession," *Business Week*, March 3, 2008; Yuka Hayashi and JoAnna Slater, "Dollar's Swift Decline Threatens Europe, Japan," *Wall Street Journal Europe*, March 14, 2008; Brian Blackstone, "Bernanke Says Contraction Possible, But Most Adjustment Is Complete," *Wall Street Journal*, April 2, 2008.

not be mailed until May or June 2008. Many economists argued that the economy was already in a recession in March 2008.[3]

Most of the discussion over President Bush's $3.1 trillion budget proposal, also in February 2008, centered on whether the Bush tax cuts of 2001 and 2003 would be made permanent or allowed to expire as scheduled in 2010. The tax cuts of 2001 and 2003 included broad reductions in the income tax rate, tax breaks on dividends and capital gains, and a gradual elimination of the estate tax. The partisan nature of the debate over federal expenditure and taxation was apparent upon release of the budget proposal. President Bush reiterated his position that his fiscal policies would balance the budget by 2012, ending the series of deficits during his administration. The Senate Democratic leader called the proposal "fiscally irresponsible and highly deceptive, hiding the cost of the war in Iraq while increasing the skyrocketing debt."[4]

In December 2008, President-elect Barack Obama's economic policy team worked on an economic stimulus package to send to Congress that totaled between $675 and $775 billion over 2 years. The package included a tax cut, aid to state governments, and funding for traditional infrastructure, school construction, energy efficiency, broadband access, and health-information technology.[5]

Some aspects of federal expenditures and taxes act as **automatic stabilizers** for the economy. These features tend to automatically slow the economy during times of high economic activity and boost the economy during periods of recession. For example, certain expenditures, such as unemployment compensation and

Automatic stabilizers
Features of the U.S. federal government expenditure and taxation programs that tend to automatically slow the economy during times of high economic activity and boost the economy during periods of recession.

---

[3] Sarah Lueck, "Congress Approves Economic-Stimulus Bill," *Wall Street Journal*, February 8, 2008; Patrice Hill, "Stimulus Package Seen as Cushion," *McClatchy-Tribune Business News*, February 14, 2008. As we noted in Chapter 11, the National Bureau of Economic Research (NBER) Business Cycle Dating Committee officially declared in November 2008, that the recession began in December 2007.

[4] John D. McKinnon and Michael M. Phillips, "Bush Budget Sets Stage for Battle on Tax Cuts," *Wall Street Journal*, February 5, 2008.

[5] Jonathan Weisman, "Stimulus Package Heads Toward $850 billion," *Wall Street Journal*, December 18, 2008.

Nondiscretionary expenditures
Federal government expenditures, for programs such as unemployment compensation, that increase or decrease simply as a result of the number of individuals eligible for the spending programs.

Discretionary expenditures
Federal government expenditures for programs whose funds are authorized and appropriated by Congress and signed by the president, where explicit decisions are made on the size of the programs.

Progressive tax system
An income tax system where higher tax rates are applied to increased amounts of income.

welfare payments, are **nondiscretionary expenditures**. These expenditures increase automatically during periods of economic downturn. For example, during a recession, as more individuals lose their jobs, unemployment compensation expenditures increase simply because more individuals qualify for the program.

Spending on these programs differs from **discretionary expenditures**, such as spending on defense or education programs, where the government spending must be authorized by Congress and funds appropriated for the programs. The tax system can also act as an automatic stabilizer. The U.S. federal income tax system is a **progressive tax system**, where higher tax rates are applied to higher income. This means that in times of greater economic activity, more taxes will be collected, which has a restraining effect on the economy. The Congressional Budget Office has estimated that every $1.00 decline in GDP produces a $0.25 decrease in federal revenues and an $0.08 increase in federal spending for interest payments, unemployment compensation, and similar programs.[6] Thus, federal spending and taxation both affect and are influenced by the overall level of economic activity.

Monetary Policy Changes　Monetary policy is considered to be a more precise tool than fiscal policy for influencing economic activity, given that most monetary policy changes result from Federal Open Market Committee (FOMC) operations, as described in Chapter 13. Even though these open market operations can take place on a daily basis, this does not mean that there is a definitive impact on the economy from these changes.

The Fed always has to react to other changes that are occurring in the economy. Therefore, any targeted federal funds rate may become outdated by other changes in the economy and around the world. Although monetary policy focuses on the federal funds rate, an entire structure of interest rates exists in the economy. Most consumers are much more affected by changes in mortgage and personal loan rates than by the federal funds rate. Managers are influenced by the prime rate and other rates on business loans. Although interest rates tend to move together, there is not a strict correlation between them. Interest rates on different securities depend on the risk of default (or risk structure) and the length of time to maturity (or term structure) of the security. Higher interest rates are generally charged on more risky investments and on securities that have longer maturities. Thus, interest rates on long-term bonds (20 or 30 years) are generally higher than those on short-term bonds (a few months to a few years). Monetary policy focuses on the federal funds and other short-term interest rates, with the understanding that there will be similar effects on long-term rates. This outcome might not always occur. For example, if contractionary monetary policy causes short-term interest rates to rise to slow the economy, long-term interest rates might actually fall if investors think future inflation might be less than expected.[7]

Spending changes on real goods and services that result from changes in monetary policy may vary by sector and take time to move through the economy. In a study[8] estimating the effect of a 1 percent decline in the federal funds rate, which assumed the decline remained in place indefinitely, Federal Reserve staff concluded that most of the effect on inventory investment would be felt rather quickly. According to the study, about two-fifths of the effect on residential construction would occur in the first year after the interest rate decrease and three-quarters of the effect would be felt by

---

[6] Charles L. Schultze, *Memos to the President: A Guide Through Macroeconomics for the Busy Policymaker* (Washington, D.C.: Brookings Institution, 1992), 203–205.

[7] President Clinton's deficit-reducing budget of January 1993 reduced investors' fears of future budget deficits enough that lower long-term interest rates resulted in the bond market. This change helped stimulate the economy and offset the need for as much monetary expansion by the Fed to lower the federal funds rate. See Alan S. Blinder and Janet L. Yellen, *The Fabulous Decade: Macroeconomic Lessons from the 1990s* (New York: Century Foundation Press, 2001), 15–24.

[8] Schultze, *Memos to the President*, 186.

the end of the third year. However, only one-quarter of the effect on net exports and only one-twentieth of the effect on business plant and equipment spending would occur in the first year of the rate decrease. Overall, less than one-third of the effect would be felt in the first year and less than half by the end of the second year.

The implementation of monetary policy has also changed over time. In the past, the Fed targeted the size of the money supply (M1). However, the demand for money became less stable over time as financial markets were deregulated and more types of near money (M2) came into use. These changes made M1 a less useful target. Thus, Fed policy shifted to focus on the federal funds rate rather than the monetary aggregates.

Fed policy is often characterized as "leaning against the wind." To avoid serious policy mistakes, the Fed usually adopts a gradualist approach. In a recessionary situation, the Fed will typically not try to close the entire gap between current GDP and potential output. That way, policy will not overstimulate the economy. Monetary policy is typically more sensitive to possible inflation and may react more quickly to inflationary expectations and pressures than to signs that the economy is slowing.[9]

The Fed can act quickly in special situations, as in the days following the terrorist attacks of September 11, 2001. Immediately after the attacks, the Fed announced that the Federal Reserve System was functioning normally and that the discount window was available to meet liquidity needs. Borrowing increased to a record $45.5 billion by the next day. To maintain liquidity in the system, the FOMC cut the targeted federal funds rate the following week and at each subsequent meeting through the end of 2001.[10]

The Fed also acted quickly in early 2008 to moderate the effects of the slowing economic activity. As noted in Chapter 13, the Federal Open Market Committee lowered its targeted federal funds rate seven times between September 2007 and April 2008. In March 2008 the Fed allowed investment banks as well as depository institutions to borrow from its discount window; it agreed to take $29 billion of securities from the books of Bear Stearns Company to help J.P. Morgan Chase & Co. acquire the firm; and it offered hundreds of billions of its Treasury securities in exchange for hard-to-value mortgage-backed securities, which had been the source of much of the crisis in the financial markets.[11] We also discussed in Chapter 13 how the Fed continued its aggressive policy throughout 2008 to provide liquidity to the financial system and to fight the effects of the recession through the use of both traditional and newly developed policy tools.

Interaction of Monetary and Fiscal Policy   The final level of interest rates and real income in the economy typically depends on the Federal Reserve's reaction to fiscal policy or other autonomous changes in spending, which, in turn, relates to the Fed's policy goals of maintaining full employment, stable prices, and smooth economic growth. For example, an increase in spending either from expansionary fiscal policy or from some other autonomous spending change in the consumer, business, or foreign sectors would result in a higher equilibrium level of real income and a higher interest rate. The latter occurs because the higher level of real income increases the demand for money, as discussed in Chapter 13, which increases the interest rate.

If the Fed believes that the increase in real income is appropriate, given its policy goals, it holds the money supply constant. The end result is a higher interest rate and an increased level of real income. However, the Fed's goal might be to hold the

---

[9] Ibid., 187–188.

[10] Board of Governors of the Federal Reserve System, *Monetary Policy Report to the Congress* (February 27, 2002), available at www.federalreserve.gov.

[11] Greg Ip, "Central Bank Offers Loans to Brokers, Cuts Key Rate," *Wall Street Journal*, March 17, 2008; Justin LaHart, "Busy Fed Might Need to Reload," *Wall Street Journal*, March 27, 2008.

interest rate constant, such as in a recessionary situation where the Fed is trying to stimulate the economy by maintaining a low targeted federal funds rate. In this case, the Fed needs to increase the money supply to lower the interest rate and further increase income by shifting the *AD* curve.

Crowding out

The decrease in consumption and investment interest-related spending that occurs when the interest rate rises as government spending increases.

There might also be a concern about **crowding out**, the decrease in interest-related spending of consumers and businesses that occurs when the interest rate rises from increased government spending. If government spending increases without an increase in taxes, the government must borrow funds in the financial markets, driving up interest rates that then impact consumer and managerial spending decisions. Much of the political debate in spring 2003 over the increased federal government expenditure for the war in Iraq and the tax cut implemented by President Bush centered on the effects of these fiscal policy changes on long-term interest rates. Although these rates were at a 45-year low at that time, some policy makers expressed concern that increased government borrowing would compete with the private sector, driving up interest rates and reducing private investment.[12]

The Fed's goal can also be to hold the level of income constant in response to a change in fiscal policy or a change in autonomous spending because it is concerned about inflationary pressures arising from the increased spending. In this case, the Fed engages in contractionary monetary policy, reducing the money supply and raising interest rates.

After the presidential election in 1992, President Bill Clinton became convinced that reducing the federal budget deficit through a combination of spending cuts and tax increases was a high priority due to the crowding-out effects of deficit spending and possible financial calamities that might result from continued high deficits. This contractionary policy, reflected in the budget Clinton proposed in February 1993, could have slowed the economy (a leftward shift of the *AD* curve). However, the bond market reacted favorably with lower long-term rates, and the Fed continued its policy of targeting a federal funds rate of 3 percent until February 1994. Because the inflation rate was around 3 percent during this period, the real federal funds rate was approximately zero, representing expansionary monetary policy. By February 1994, the Fed was convinced that the economy was growing above trend on its own and that an increase in the federal funds rate was needed to gradually slow the growth rate and prevent possible future inflation. Although President Clinton was upset that the Fed began raising targeted interest rates barely six months after his politically sensitive deficit reduction package passed Congress, he maintained a hands-off policy toward the Fed.[13]

The Aggregate Supply Curve

Aggregate supply curve

The curve that shows the price level at which firms in the economy are willing to produce different levels of real goods and services and the resulting level of real income.

Up to this point, our analysis has focused solely on aggregate expenditure or the demand side of the economy. The simple multiplier, the equilibrium level of income, and the aggregate demand (*AD*) curve all illustrate spending decisions by the various sectors of the economy—the consumer, business, government, and foreign sectors. To complete the aggregate macroeconomic model, we now need to examine the supply side of the economy.

Aggregate production function

The function that shows the quantity and quality of resources used in production, the efficiency with which resources are used, and the existing production technology for the entire economy.

The **aggregate supply curve** shows the price level at which firms in the economy are willing to produce different amounts of real goods and services or real income. An aggregate supply curve can have different shapes depending on the time frame of the analysis and the underlying assumptions of various models. Aggregate supply curves are based on an underlying **aggregate production function** for the economy as a

---

[12] Greg Ip and John D. McKinnon, "Tax Plan Would Boost Growth, But Would Also Widen Deficits," *Wall Street Journal*, May 23, 2003.
[13] Blinder and Yellen, *The Fabulous Decade*, 15–26.

whole. Similar to the individual firm production functions that we examined in Chapter 5, the aggregate production function incorporates information on

1. The quantity and quality of resources used in production (labor, capital, raw materials, and so on)
2. The efficiency with which resources are used
3. The production technology that exists at any point in time

However, the aggregate production function reflects production or supply possibilities for the economy as a whole. At any point in time, there is a maximum amount of real goods and services that can be produced, given the above factors. This is called the level of **potential output (GDP)**, or the full-employment level of output (GDP). Given the circular flow model, there is a maximum level of real income corresponding to the level of potential output.[14]

The equilibrium level of real income and output and the price level that exist in the economy at any point in time are determined by the interaction of aggregate demand and aggregate supply, which we model as the intersection point of the aggregate demand and supply curves. This **aggregate demand–aggregate supply equilibrium** is stable unless forces cause either curve to shift. In real-world economies, the aggregate demand curve, in particular, shifts often, so this equilibrium can change fairly quickly.

The shape of the aggregate supply curve and the level of potential output will determine whether this aggregate demand–aggregate supply equilibrium is considered desirable by policy makers in terms of the macroeconomic policy goals we discussed in Chapter 11: maintaining stable prices, a high level of employment, and smooth economic growth over time. The equilibrium level of output may lie far enough below the level of potential output that policy makers will use expansionary fiscal and monetary policies to stimulate the economy to generate more output and employment. On the other hand, the equilibrium output may lie above the potential level of output, causing inflationary pressures. In this case, policy makers will use contractionary policies to slow the economy. Most macroeconomic policy making, therefore, is concerned with influencing the equilibrium level of real output and the rate of change in the price level (inflation).

The equilibrium level of output changes as both the economy's aggregate demand curve and its aggregate supply curve shift. Because aggregate supply changes much more slowly than aggregate demand, we first examine changing aggregate demand with differently shaped aggregate supply curves. This process is the short-run policy problem faced by Federal Reserve officials and by the president and his administration, as was discussed in the article opening this chapter. The shape of the aggregate supply curve depends on the time frame of the model and the assumptions about how firms respond to price changes. Macroeconomists continue to debate these issues.[15]

Short-Run Aggregate Supply Curve (Horizontal and Upward Sloping) Figure 14.5 presents the aggregate demand–aggregate supply (*AD–AS*) model using a **short-run aggregate supply curve** with a horizontal portion and an upward sloping portion. The horizontal portion of the short-run aggregate supply curve reflects production in a range substantially below potential or full-employment output (Y_f), where firms can change the level of output produced without a change in the absolute price level. The economy's resources are not fully

Potential output (GDP)
The maximum amounts of real goods and services or real income (GDP) that can be produced in the economy at any point in time based on the economy's aggregate production function.

Aggregate demand–aggregate supply equilibrium
The equilibrium level of real income and output and the price level in the economy that occur at the intersection of the aggregate demand and supply curves.

Short-run aggregate supply curve
An aggregate supply curve that is either horizontal or upward sloping, depending on whether the absolute price level increases as firms produce more output.

---

[14] Potential or full-employment output is the output level produced when unemployment is at the natural rate or the nonaccelerating inflation rate of unemployment (NAIRU). Review Chapter 11 for further discussion. Remember that we use the terms *real GDP, output,* and *income* interchangeably because real GPD can be measured from either the expenditure/output or earnings/income approach.

[15] For a discussion of these debates and the models of aggregate supply that go beyond the scope of this book, see David C. Colander and Edward N. Gamber, *Macroeconomics* (Upper Saddle River, N.J.: Prentice-Hall, 2002); and N. Gregory Mankiw, *Macroeconomics*, 6th ed. (New York: Worth, 2007).

FIGURE 14.5

Aggregate Demand–Aggregate Supply Equilibrium with Short- and Long-Run Aggregate Supply Curves

An increase in aggregate demand with a horizontal aggregate supply curve results only in an increase in real output, while an aggregate demand increase with an upward sloping aggregate supply curve results in an increase in both real output and the price level.

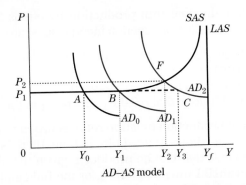

AD–AS model

Keynesian model

A model of the aggregate economy, based on ideas developed by John Maynard Keynes, with a horizontal short-run aggregate supply curve in which all changes in aggregate demand result in changes in real output and income.

employed, so that firms can increase the amount of real output produced and real income generated without having to bid resources away from other uses. This means that firms can produce more real output without an increase in their unit costs; thus, they do not need to charge higher prices for their products. Firms supply all the output that is demanded by the different sectors of the economy at a constant price level. This horizontal portion of the short-run aggregate supply curve is often called the **Keynesian model** because it reflects the economic conditions of worldwide depression that existed when John Maynard Keynes developed his macroeconomic analysis in the 1930s.

The initial equilibrium occurs at point A in Figure 14.5 where aggregate demand curve AD_0 intersects the horizontal short-run aggregate supply curve with price level P_1 and real income level Y_0. We then illustrate an increase in aggregate demand from AD_0 to AD_1, which results from either a policy change or an autonomous spending increase. The new equilibrium, point B, occurs at the same price level, but a larger level of real income, Y_1. Thus, with a horizontal short-run aggregate supply curve, all changes in aggregate demand result in changes in real income and output with no change in the price level.

The concept of equilibrium in Figure 14.5 implies that if aggregate demand does not increase from AD_0 to AD_1, the level of income in the economy will remain at Y_0. For example, in the Great Depression of the 1930s, the equilibrium level of income was substantially below the level of potential income and output. Researchers have attributed the Great Depression in the United States to a series of shocks that shifted aggregate demand to the left. The depression began in mid-1929 as a result of the tight Federal Reserve monetary policy, which raised interest rates in order to dampen the speculation on the U.S. stock market (causing a shift to the left of the AD curve). Interest-sensitive industries such as residential construction began to decline first. The stock market crash in October 1929 then led to a collapse in domestic consumption and investment spending as consumers and businesses became uncertain about the future and stopped purchasing durable goods (causing a further shift to the left of the AD curve). The decline in output in the first 18 months of the Great Depression was almost as large as in most previous and subsequent recessions combined.[16]

The short-run aggregate supply curve slopes upward as real income and output approach the economy's potential output. This upward sloping short-run aggregate supply curve occurs because firms' input costs rise when they have to bid resources away from competing uses, as most inputs are becoming fully employed. As input costs rise, firms charge higher prices for their products, and the absolute price level begins to increase. Firms will produce more real output only as the price level increases.

Figure 14.5 also illustrates the upward sloping aggregate supply curve. Starting at point B, we again show that expansionary fiscal policy or an autonomous

---

[16] Christina D. Romer, "The Nation in Depression," *Journal of Economic Perspectives* 7 (Spring 1993): 19–39.

spending increase causes a shift of the aggregate demand curve from AD_1 to AD_2. If the price level did not rise, equilibrium would be at point C at price level P_1 and income level Y_3.

However, in this case, the aggregate supply curve is upward sloping. The price level rises as output increases, given that the economy is approaching the full-employment level of output. The final equilibrium in Figure 14.5 is at point F, with price level P_2 and income level Y_2. Part of the increase in aggregate demand results in an increase in the price level rather than an increase in real output. This outcome occurs because the increase in the price level creates a smaller real money supply which causes the interest rate to rise. This increase in the interest rate chokes off some interest-related spending, thereby increasing real income only to Y_2 and not to Y_3.

The short-run aggregate supply curve can be expressed as Equation 14.2:

14.2   Short-run AS: $P = f(Y_f,$ Resource costs$)$
$$\qquad\qquad\quad (0) \qquad\quad (+)$$

where

$$P = \text{price level}$$
$$Y_f = \text{full-employment or potential output}$$
$$\text{Resource costs} = \text{costs of the resources or inputs of production}$$

Equation 14.2 shows that the price level is a function of the costs of the resources or inputs of production. Changes in these costs unrelated to overall demand will cause the short-run AS curve to shift up or down. If the cost of a major resource such as oil increases, a higher price level will be needed at every level of income to induce firms to supply that output. The level of potential or full-employment GDP (Y_f) does not change because the factors determining potential output (resources, efficiency, and technology) are fixed in the short run.

Long-Run Aggregate Supply Curve (Vertical)   Figure 14.5 also shows a **long-run aggregate supply curve**, which is vertical at the level of potential or full-employment output. This level of output is determined by the amount of resources, the efficiency with which they are used, and the level of technology in the economy. Because these factors are constant in the short run, the full-employment level of output represents a constraint on increases in aggregate demand. As aggregate demand increases beyond AD_2 in Figure 14.5 (and the short-run AS curve slopes upward and approaches the long-run AS curve), any increases in spending will result in smaller increases in real output and larger increases in the price level. With a vertical aggregate supply curve, any further increases in aggregate demand result only in a higher price level and no increase in real output.[17]

This figure, therefore, illustrates the ongoing policy dilemma of the Federal Reserve. If the Fed uses monetary policy to shift aggregate demand and increase

Long-run aggregate supply curve
A vertical aggregate supply curve that defines the level of full employment or potential output based on a given amount of resources, efficiency, and technology in the economy.

---

[17] Remember that the focus of this text is explaining short-run fluctuations in income, output, and price level. In the long-run analysis of the economy, it is assumed that firms produce at their maximum sustainable output, so that the economy operates at its potential level of output. It is also assumed that prices are completely flexible in the long run. Therefore, any changes in aggregate demand in the long run can result only in changes in the price level, not in the level of real output and income. This model is called the Classical model because it reflects the beliefs about the economy held by the classical economists before John Maynard Keynes. These economists believed that any deviations of real output from potential output were only temporary because prices would adjust to bring the economy back to potential output. For example, if aggregate demand decreased and was insufficient to generate the full potential level of output at the current price level, classical economists believed the price level would fall sufficiently that the economy would return to that level of output. Likewise, if aggregate demand increased and exceeded potential output, the price level would rise sufficiently to bring the economy back to the level of potential output and income.

output and employment, it may stimulate the economy too much, setting off an inflationary spiral. The Fed also needs to judge what changes in private-sector behavior would cause aggregate demand to increase on its own, reducing the need for further monetary intervention.

The long-run aggregate supply curve is defined in Equation 14.3:

$$\textbf{14.3} \quad \textbf{Long-run } AS\text{: } Y_f = f\,(P, \textbf{Resources}, \textbf{Efficiency}, \textbf{Technology})$$
$$\qquad\qquad\qquad\quad \textbf{(0)} \qquad \textbf{(+)} \qquad\quad \textbf{(+)} \qquad\qquad \textbf{(+)}$$

where

Y_f = full-employment or potential output

P = price level

Resources = amount of inputs in the economy used to produce final goods and services

Efficiency = means by which resources are combined to minimize the cost of production

Technology = state of knowledge in the economy on how to produce goods and services

Equation 14.3 implies that the long-run aggregate supply curve is vertical and not influenced by the price level. It can be shifted right or left over time by changes in the amount of resources available to produce final goods and services, by increased efficiency in minimizing the costs of production, or by the development of new technologies for producing goods and services.

Shifting Aggregate Supply The policy dilemma of the Federal Reserve discussed above is made more complicated because both the short- and the long-run aggregate supply curves can shift.

Shifts in Short-Run Aggregate Supply The short-run aggregate supply curve will shift as a result of productivity changes and changes in the costs of the inputs of production that are independent of overall demand changes. These changes have to be widespread throughout the economy, such as the oil price increases caused by the OPEC oil embargo during the 1970s, to have an influence on the absolute price level. We illustrate such a supply-side shock to the economy in Figure 14.6. In this figure, assume that the original equilibrium is at point A, the intersection of the AD_1 and SAS_1 curves, with income level Y_1 and price level P_1. We represent the oil price increase by the shift of the aggregate supply curve from SAS_1 to SAS_2. Firms' unit costs have increased, and they charge higher prices to cover those costs. Because these increases are widespread throughout the economy, the absolute price level rises to P_2. Given aggregate demand curve AD_1, the level of real income is reduced to Y_2 at point B. The higher price level

FIGURE 14.6

Change in Short-Run Aggregate Supply
The short-run aggregate supply curve shifts up due to major increases in the costs of production unrelated to demand, such as increases in the price of oil, resulting in a higher price level and a lower level of real output.

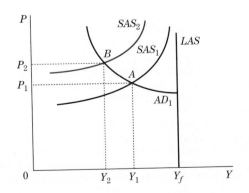

and increased prices (inflation), when combined with lower real output and income (stagnation), are called **stagflation**.

As was discussed in the opening article of this chapter, stagflation represents a major dilemma for policy makers. To deal with the problem of inflation, policy makers would need to use contractionary monetary or fiscal policy to shift the aggregate demand curve to the left. However, this policy would result in a still lower level of real income and output even further from potential output. If the policy goal is to focus on the stagnation problem, expansionary monetary or fiscal policy would be needed. However, expansionary policy would shift the aggregate demand curve to the right and would result in a higher price level and possible inflation. Thus, in the case of stagflation, policy makers are forced to choose between alternative policy goals. In the late 1970s, the Federal Reserve implemented a deliberate contractionary monetary policy to decrease the inflation generated by the oil price shocks earlier in the decade. This action resulted in recessions in 1980 and 1981, but a lower inflation rate was also achieved.[18]

Shifts in Long-Run Aggregate Supply   The long-run aggregate supply curve can also shift over time if there are increases in the amount of inputs (labor, land, capital, and raw materials) in the economy and increases in technology and efficiency. These increases in long-run aggregate supply are favorable to the economy, as shown in Figure 14.7.

The original equilibrium in Figure 14.7 is at the intersection of aggregate demand curve AD_1 and short-run aggregate supply curve SAS_1 (point A, with price level P_1 and income level Y_1). Given that the SAS_1 curve begins to slope upward because the economy is nearing the full-employment output, Y_{f1}, an increase in aggregate demand to AD_2 results in an increase in the price level to P_2 and an increase in real output and income to only Y_2.

However, if the long-run aggregate supply curve shifts and the full-employment level of output increases from Y_{f1} to Y_{f2}, given increases in the quantity and quality of the economy's productive resources and new technology, output can expand farther along short-run aggregate supply curve SAS_2 at a constant price level P_1 before the price level again begins to rise as Y_{f2} is approached. With this increase in long-run aggregate supply, the increase in aggregate demand from AD_1 to AD_2 results in an

Stagflation
Higher prices and price increases (inflation) combined with lower real output and income (stagnation), resulting from a major increase in input prices in the economy.

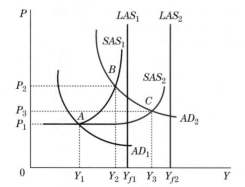

FIGURE 14.7
Change in Long-Run Aggregate Supply
Shifts in the long-run aggregate supply curve result from changes in the quantity and quality of resources and the introduction of new technology. Any increase in aggregate demand will result in a larger increase in real output and a smaller increase in the price level if the long-run aggregate supply curve also shifts out.

[18] There were seven occasions in the post–World War II era when the Fed deliberately engaged in restrictive monetary policy to reduce the level of inflation. Industrial production declined 9.6 percent between 1979 and 1982 due to the monetary shocks of August 1978 and October 1979. However, production would have risen 9.3 percent in the absence of those shocks. The Fed had little mandate to fight the peacetime inflation of the 1970s by inducing a recession until the end of the decade, when there were increased fears about the costs of inflation. See Christina D. Romer, "Changes in Business Cycles: Evidence and Explanations," *Journal of Economic Perspectives* 13 (Spring 1999): 23–44; and J. Bradford De Long, "America's Peacetime Inflation: The 1970s," in *Reducing Inflation: Motivation and Strategy*, ed. Christina D. Romer and David H. Romer (Chicago: University of Chicago Press, 1997), 247–280.

equilibrium at point C, at a lower price level, P_3, and a larger real output and income level, Y_3. Thus, increases in long-run aggregate supply can assist the Fed in reaching its policy goals. Much of the macroeconomic policy debate in the late 1990s centered on understanding the reasons why aggregate demand kept increasing, pushing unemployment lower without generating sustained inflation. Many analysts attributed these desirable outcomes to the increased productivity in the economy from computers and other electronic technology, or the new economy effect.

Some research on this new economy effect has focused on measuring the changes in the natural rate of unemployment, or the nonaccelerating inflation rate of unemployment (NAIRU), which we defined in Chapter 11. Decreases in the NAIRU represent a rightward shift of the long-run aggregate supply curve because the economy can produce more output and reach a lower level of unemployment without incurring an increase in the rate of inflation. These studies have shown that the NAIRU started at approximately 5.4 percent in 1960, increased up to a peak of 6.8 percent in 1979, and then declined to approximately 4.9 percent in 2000.[19] Various factors contributed to this trend. The proportion of the labor force aged 16 to 24 increased from 17 percent in 1960 to 24 percent in 1978 and then fell back to 16 percent in 2000. These changes in the composition of the labor force could have impacted the NAIRU because younger workers have higher unemployment rates than older workers. Increasing incarceration rates and more generous disability insurance payments may have also caused individuals with higher unemployment rates to leave the labor force, making the trade-off with inflation more favorable.

While these trends explained much of the decline in the NAIRU up to 1995, subsequent decreases were probably related to increases in productivity in the economy resulting from the increased use of computers and the Internet. Given these productivity gains, firms were able to respond to workers' wage increases without raising prices. Average annual growth in output per hour of work was 1.5 percent over the period 1974–95, but increased to 2.6 percent between 1996 and 2000.[20]

Stephen Oliner and Daniel Sichel have estimated that of the 1 percentage point acceleration in labor productivity that occurred between the periods 1991–95 and 1996–99, 0.45 percentage point was attributed to the growing use of information technology capital throughout the nonfarm business sector of the economy. Rapidly improving technology for producing computers contributed another 0.26 percentage point to the acceleration. However, the growth in other capital services per hour explained almost none of the acceleration. These researchers concluded that information technology had been the primary factor behind the sharp increase in productivity growth in the late 1990s.[21]

More recent productivity estimates show that information technology played a less important role in productivity growth after 2000 than it did in the 1990s. Researchers estimated that productivity growth from 2007 to 2017 might average 2.4 percent per year, a rate that was relatively rapid for the United States from a historical perspective but below average for the decade after 1995. These analysts

---

[19] Laurence Ball and N. Gregory Mankiw, "The NAIRU in Theory and Practice," *Journal of Economic Perspectives* 16 (Fall 2002): 115–136; Robert J. Gordon, "Foundations of the Goldilocks Economy: Supply Shocks and the Time-Varying NAIRU," *Brookings Papers on Economic Activity* 2 (1998): 297–333; Douglas Staiger, James H. Stock, and Mark W. Watson, "Prices, Wages, and the U.S. NAIRU in the 1990s," in *The Roaring Nineties: Can Full Employment Be Sustained?* eds. Alan B. Krueger and Robert Solow (New York: Sage Foundation and Century Foundation Press, 2001), 3–60.

[20] Ball and Mankiw, "The NAIRU in Theory and Practice."

[21] Stephen D. Oliner and Daniel E. Sichel, "The Resurgence of Growth in the Late 1990s: Is Information Technology the Story?" *Journal of Economic Perspectives* 14 (Fall 2000): 3–22. See also Erik Brynjolfsson and Lorin M. Hitt, "Beyond Computation: Information Technology, Organizational Transformation and Business Performance," *Journal of Economic Perspectives* 14 (Fall 2000): 23–48; Robert J. Gordon, "Does the 'New Economy' Measure Up to the Great Inventions of the Past?" *Journal of Economic Perspectives* 14 (Fall 2000): 49–74; and Blinder and Yellen, *The Fabulous Decade.*

noted that there was little likelihood that the U.S. economy would revert to the lower rates of productivity growth that existed in the 1970s and 1980s.[22]

Using the Aggregate Model to Explain Changes in the Economy from 2001 to 2002 and from 2007 to 2008

Managers can use the aggregate macroeconomic model we have developed in Chapters 11 to 14 to analyze changes in the macro environment in any time period.[23] We now illustrate the use of the model to examine changes in the U.S. economy from 2001 to 2002 and again from 2007 to 2008.

Changes from 2001 to 2002   The U.S. economy entered a recession in March 2001. Although the recession was officially declared to have ended in November 2001, the economy experienced slow real GDP growth, low inflation, and rising unemployment through the end of 2002.[24] This performance resulted from changes in several factors throughout the period:

- Increased productivity
- Increased employment costs
- A continuous increase in the money supply
- A strong dollar
- A decrease in stock market wealth
- Declining levels of consumer and business confidence
- Increased home-equity and mortgage refinancings
- Declining interest rates
- Increased government spending for defense and homeland security
- Slow growth in foreign economies

Figure 14.8a illustrates the impact of these factors for 2001–2002 using the AD–AS model. Point A is the initial equilibrium determined by the intersection of the AD_{01} and SAS_{01} curves in Figure 14.8a with price level P_{01} and real income level Y_{01}. The full-employment level of output is given by Y_{f01}. The impact of changes in the above variables is shown by the curves labeled "02" in Figure 14.8a and in Table 14.3. All of these changes are derived from our aggregate macro model.

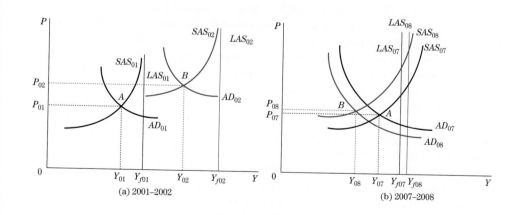

(a) 2001–2002

(b) 2007–2008

FIGURE 14.8

Using the Aggregate Model

The changes in the economy from 2001 to 2002 and from 2007 to 2008 are illustrated in the AD–AS model.

---

[22] Dale W. Jorgenson, Mun S. Ho, and Kevin J. Stiroh, "A Retrospective Look at the U.S. Productivity Growth Resurgence," *Journal of Economic Perspectives* 22 (Winter 2008): 3–24.

[23] Both the general and specific equations of the aggregate macro model are summarized in Appendix 14A.

[24] Jon E. Hilsenrath, "Despite Job Losses, Recession Is Officially Declared Over," *Wall Street Journal*, July 18, 2003.

TABLE 14.3 Impact of Changes in the Aggregate Model

CURVE	VARIABLE	SPENDING COMPONENT(S)	SHIFT OF CURVE
AD_{02}	1. Dollar increases in value	1. Exports decrease; imports increase	1. Left
	2. Stock market wealth decreases	2. Consumption decreases	2. Left
	3. Confidence decreases	3. Consumption and investment decrease	3. Left
	4. Home equity increases	4. Consumption increases	4. Right
	5. Government spending increases	5. Government spending increases	5. Right
	6. Foreign GDP increases	6. Exports increase	6. Right
	7. M_S increases	7. Lower interest rates increase consumption/investment	7. Right
AS_{02}	8. Productivity increases	8. —	8. Long-run right
	9. Employment costs increase	9. —	9. Short-run up
AD_{08}	10. Housing wealth decreases	10. Consumption decreases	10. Left
	11. Confidence decreases	11. Consumption and investment decrease	11. Left
	12. Credit crisis in financial markets	12. Residential investment decreases	12. Left
	13. Government spending slows	13. Government spending slows	13. Left
	14. M_S increases	14. Lower interest rates increase consumption/investment	14. Right
	15. Dollar decreases in value	15. Exports increase; imports decrease	15. Right
	16. Foreign GDP increases	16. Exports increase	16. Right
AS_{08}	17. Employment costs increase	17. —	17. Short-run up
	18. Energy/commodity prices increase	18. —	18. Short-run up
	19. Productivity increases	19. —	19. Long-run right

We can see in Table 14.3 that the variables influencing the *AD* curve have conflicting impacts. Some cause the *AD* curve to shift to the right, while others cause it to shift to the left. Thus, the final location of the curve and the final impact on the price level and the level of real output and income depend on the magnitude of the changes in the variables, which is what managers need to forecast.

We can see in Figure 14.8a that aggregate demand increased from 2001 to 2002 as a result of changes in both the real goods and monetary sides of the economy. Real GDP increased 2.75 percent in 2002.[25] Real household personal consumption expenditures increased 2.5 percent, approximately the same as in 2001, but down substantially from the more than 4 percent average growth in previous years. Although decreases in stock market wealth and consumer confidence had negative effects on consumer spending, these effects on aggregate demand were offset by the increases in home-equity wealth, increased government spending, and the lower interest rates resulting from the Fed's increase in the money supply.

Real residential investment spending increased 6 percent in 2002, the largest gain in several years. Business investment in equipment and software increased 3 percent in 2002, supported by the low interest rates, but spending on structures declined sharply, particularly for office and industrial building due to a lack of business confidence and uncertainty about world events. Federal government spending increased 7 percent in 2002, and the federal budget turned from surplus to deficit, thus increasing government borrowing. These effects translate into a rightward shift of the *AD* curve in Figure 14.8a.

---

[25] This discussion is based on Board of Governors of the Federal Reserve System, *Monetary Report to the Congress* (February 11, 2003), available at www.federalreserve.gov.

In 2001, stagnant real GDP in the United States and abroad resulted in declines of 11.5 percent in U.S. exports and 8 percent in U.S. imports. Moderate growth in these economies resulted in export and import spending increases of 5 and 9 percent, respectively, in 2002. The exchange rate of the dollar appreciated approximately 13 percent from January 2000 to February 2002. This trend, which had a positive effect on imports and a negative effect on exports, had restrained GDP growth during the boom period before the 2001 recession. Although the dollar began to decline in 2002, the continued effects of its previous appreciation over the prior two years contributed to the faster growth of imports than exports in 2002.

Both the short- and long-run aggregate supply curves also shifted over this period. Increased employment costs resulted in an upward shift of the short-run aggregate supply curve in Figure 14.8a. At the same time, increased productivity caused the long-run aggregate supply curve to shift to the right from Y_{f01} to Y_{f02}. These effects combined to keep inflation low, as shown by the increase in the price level from P_{01} to P_{02} in Figure 14.8a. Unemployment increased, as the shifts in aggregate demand did not keep pace with the shifts in aggregate supply so that the difference between actual and potential output in 2002 was larger than in 2001.

The increased labor productivity of 3.75 percent in 2002 may have resulted from better use of previous capital investments and organizational innovations stimulated by the weak profit situation. Although the employment cost index for private nonfarm businesses rose 3.25 percent in 2002, health insurance costs, which were 6 percent of overall compensation, rose 10 percent in 2002 compared with a 9 percent increase in each of the previous two years.

Changes from 2007 to 2008   Macroeconomic conditions were quite different in the 2007–2008 period, given the concern about whether the economy was headed into a recession and how that could be prevented. As noted in the chapter's opening article, there was also speculation about stagflation.

The major changes occurring in the economy over this period, illustrated in Table 14.3, were:

- A decrease in home prices and consumer wealth
- Decreased consumer and business confidence
- A credit crisis in the financial markets
- Slower rate of growth in federal government spending
- A continuous increase in the money supply to lower interest rates
- A decrease in the value of the dollar
- Growth in foreign economies

The effect of these changes on aggregate demand and supply are shown in Figure 14.8b.

The negative effects of the decrease in housing prices that impacted consumer wealth, the loss of consumer and business confidence, and the decrease in residential investment due to the collapse of the subprime mortgage market and tightening credit standards that we discussed in Chapters 12 through 14 are all summarized in the leftward shift of the aggregate demand curve. We have shown these changes as a decrease in real income from 2007 to 2008. Real GDP growth was negative in the fourth quarter of 2007 and the third quarter of 2008 and slightly positive in the first and second quarters of 2008.[26] Countering these trends were the decline in the value of the dollar, which increased U.S. exports and decreased imports, and the continued growth in foreign economies that strengthened exports. U.S. imports decreased due to the slowing United States economy. From August 2007 to December 2008,

---

[26] U.S. Bureau of Economic Analysis, News Release, November 25, 2008.

the Federal Reserve was actively engaged in open market operations and other nontraditional steps to lower interest rates to stimulate consumption and investment spending and to strengthen the financial institutions operating in the housing and mortgage markets to restore confidence and increase lending.

Although the economy held up well in the first half of 2007, the strains in the housing and financial markets began to have their effect in the fourth quarter.[27] The decline in residential investment reduced the annual growth rate of real GDP in the second half of 2007 by more than 1 percentage point. Overall consumption spending in 2007 was sustained first by the lagged effects of the increases in household wealth in 2005 and 2006. However, the effects of the decreases in housing prices, declines in stock prices, and the sharply higher energy prices on consumption became apparent by the end of the year.

The external sector provided significant support to the U.S. economy in the second half of 2007. Net exports added approximately 1 percentage point to U.S. GDP growth during that period. Exports expanded at about an 11 percent annual rate, while imports growth decreased to about 1.5 percent in 2007 from a 3.75 percent increase in 2006.

Productivity in the nonfarm business sector rose 2.5 percent in 2007, up from a 1.5 percent annual rate in the preceding three years. This is the reason that we show a small rightward shift in the *LAS* curve in Figure 14.8b. The employment cost index for private industry workers increased 3 percent in 2007. This increase combined with the increases in energy and commodity prices is represented by the upward shift of the *SAS* curve in Figure 14.8b. The final equilibrium for 2008 at point *B* shows the potential for stagflation discussed in the opening article.

The downturn in economic activity continued throughout 2008. Real GDP decreased in the third quarter of 2008 due to decreases in personal consumption expenditure, residential fixed investment, and equipment and software. These changes were partially offset by positive contributions from federal government spending, private inventory investment, exports, nonresidential structures, and state and local government spending. Decreased import spending also had a slight positive effect on growth. Although the Fed had lowered its targeted interest rate to almost zero, it was also attempting to loosen credit by lending to damaged financial market institutions and by purchasing mortgage-backed securities. Concerns over stagflation had dissipated by this time as consumer prices posted their second straight monthly drop in November 2008.[28]

Impact of Macro Changes on Managerial Decisions

The macro changes from 2001 to 2002 and from 2007 to 2008 discussed in the previous section had different impacts on various firms and industries, which we now illustrate. In all cases, as we noted in Chapter 11, changes in the macroeconomic environment affect individual firms and industries through the microeconomic factors of demand, production, cost, and profitability. Firms develop new strategies to respond to these macro changes by using the microeconomic tools we discussed in Part 1 of this text. Their responses also depend on the market environment in which they operate.

As we discussed in Chapters 2 and 7, firms in a highly competitive environment have little or no influence on the price of their product, so they must concentrate on the cost side to stay competitive in the face of both market and macro environment changes. This was exactly the case for the firms in the copper industry in the opening discussion of Chapter 2. One of the biggest impacts on the copper industry was the

---

[27] This discussion is based on *Monetary Report to the Congress*, February 27, 2008.

[28] U.S. Bureau of Economic Analysis, News Release, November 25, 2008; Jon Hilsenrath, "Fed Cuts Rates Near Zero to Battle Slump," *Wall Street Journal*, December 17, 2008.

decrease in copper demand in 1997 and 1998, resulting from the 1997 collapse of the Southeast Asian economies.[29] The recessions and currency devaluations in these countries had a significant impact on the global copper industry. Firms survived either by keeping their costs of production below the declining price of copper or by consolidating with other firms.

The downturn in economic activity and low inflation in the United States and the tremendous global competition faced by many U.S. firms in 2002 forced managers in firms with market power to develop innovative methods of increasing profits, many involving the price discrimination strategies we discussed in Chapter 10 or the greater attention to costs we discussed in Chapter 5.[30] For example, in responding to an order for 500 2-inch locating fasteners and 10 1.75-inch versions, Jergens, a Cleveland-based industrial equipment company, actually calculated the additional cost of producing the 10 odd-sized fasteners from scratch and charged for them accordingly. Under more favorable economic conditions, the company would have simply covered the additional cost itself and charged the same price for the entire batch of fasteners. Companies also developed methods to make better use of their existing capital stock or found ways to make less expensive future investments.[31] For example, Boeing Company began making parts without using a foundry to build tools and dies by layering one level of powdered metal on top of another with a laser's heat.

Oligopolistic industries often engage in more intense competition to increase market share during economic downturns. For example, Kimberly Clark Corporation, the leading diaper manufacturer in the United States, tried to increase its profits in summer 2002 by instituting a 5 percent price increase by decreasing the number of diapers in each package of its Huggies while cutting the price less.[32] Kimberly Clark executives expected that its arch-rival, Procter & Gamble Company, would follow with a similar increase in the price of its Pampers, as it had done in the past. Procter & Gamble was faced with a prisoner's dilemma situation similar to the ones we discussed in Chapter 9. If the company did not lower its price to match that of Kimberly Clark, it might lose significant market share. If it did so, both companies might decrease their profits, while maintaining relatively the same market shares.

Procter & Gamble's response to the Kimberly Clark move was to maintain the price of its Pampers, but also to keep the same number of diapers in each package for several more months and to strongly market this strategy. The company engaged in heavy promotion and increased the value of its discount coupons. The strategy worked for Procter & Gamble, as Kimberly Clark was forced to cancel its price increase before it really went into effect and to match some of Procter & Gamble's promotions.

The above examples show how managers have adapted to changes in the macroeconomic environment. Yet, as we have noted throughout this text, another managerial strategy is to try to change that environment. When the value of the dollar was high compared to the yen and the euro, American companies lobbied the U.S. government for policies that would cause the dollar to depreciate and, therefore, help increase exports. With the dollar depreciating in the foreign exchange markets in 2002, many of these manufacturers turned their attention to Asian governments

[29] We discuss this situation in Southeast Asia in more detail in Chapter 15.

[30] Timothy Aeppel, "Amid Weak Inflation, Firms Turn Creative to Boost Prices," *Wall Street Journal*, September 18, 2002.

[31] Clare Ansberry, "A Cloud over the Recovery: Businesses' New Frugal Ways," *Wall Street Journal*, October 16, 2002.

[32] This discussion is based on Sarah Ellison, "In Lean Times, Big Companies Make a Grab for Market Share," *Wall Street Journal*, September 5, 2003.

that tried to keep their own currencies low against the dollar in order to promote their exports to the United States.[33]

The decline in economic activity in 2007 and 2008 also caused many firms to reevaluate their competitive strategies to determine how best to deal with the slowing economy.[34] J.C. Penney Co. announced that it expected declining sales in both March 2008 and for the entire first quarter. The company was assessing its new American Living line of apparel and home goods created by Polo Ralph Lauren Corp. because these products cost more than other similar items at Penney's and comparable products at Kohl's.

Many retailers also felt the impact of the slowing economy in late 2007 and early 2008. Stores reported poor retail sales in January 2008, and many chains announced plans to close hundreds of units and cut thousands of jobs.[35] These trends continued throughout 2008 with retail sales falling 5.5 percent in November and 8.0 percent in December compared with a year earlier. Even large price discounting could not offset the decline in overall consumer spending. During the holiday season, many retailers changed their advertising strategies to focus on loyal customers rather than attempting to attract new ones to their stores.[36]

For some companies that were already struggling, the economic slowdown only made managerial decisions more complex. Sears and Kmart had faced declining sales and profits as they struggled to distinguish themselves from Kohl's, J.C. Penney, Target, and Wal-Mart Stores. These rivals had been chipping away at Sears' clothing, appliance, and home-products businesses with better selection, shopping experiences, and prices. Sears' share of major U.S. appliance sales declined both from the increased competition and from the collapse of the housing market.[37]

By December 2008, the Big Three United States automobile makers, General Motors, Ford, and Chrysler, had all appealed to Congress for $34 billion in loans or lines of credit to help them survive the recession and the car-industry downturn. The political debate centered over whether government assistance would help the companies avoid collapse or whether structured bankruptcies would be the better course of action. In November 2008, United States new-vehicle sales fell 37 percent from the previous month.[38]

Measuring Changes in Aggregate Demand and Supply

Both policy makers and managers use a variety of economic data to assess the future direction of the economy. As noted in the opening article and illustrated in the previous examples, many of these variables give conflicting views on where the economy is headed. Forecasting is made more difficult by the differences in collection and benchmarking among the various data series.[39] For example, payroll statistics are derived from business and government reports that are checked once

---

[33] Michael M. Phillips, "U.S. Manufacturers Lobby Against Asian Rate Strategies," *Wall Street Journal*, January 24, 2003.

[34] Sudeep Reddy, Cheryl Lu-Lien Tan, and Neal Boudette, "Personal Spending Up Mere 0.1%, But Inflation Pressures Are Muted," *Wall Street Journal*, March 29, 2008.

[35] Amy Merrick and Kevin Kingsbury, "Retail Squeeze Felt Far Beyond Malls," *Wall Street Journal*, February 8, 2008.

[36] Emily Steel, "Marketers Reach Out to Loyal Customers," *Wall Street Journal*, November 26, 2008; Ann Zimmerman, Jennifer Saranow, and Miguel Bustillo, "Retail Sales Plummet," *Wall Street Journal*, December 26, 2008.

[37] Gary McWilliams, "Why Sears Must Engineer Its Own Makeover," *Wall Street Journal*, January 15, 2008.

[38] John D. Stoll, Matthew Dolan, Jeffrey McCracken, and Josh Mitchell, "Big Three Seek $34 Billion Aid," *Wall Street Journal*, December 3, 2008; Gregg Hitt and Matthew Dolan, "Detroit Bailout Hits a Bumpy Road," *Wall Street Journal*, December 5, 2008.

[39] Daniel Altman, "Data in Conflict: Why Economists Tend to Weep," *New York Times*, July 11, 2003.

a year against unemployment insurance records. The statistics for the number of employed people are derived from a sampling of households that is benchmarked with the Census only once a decade. Data reporting for some series is voluntary, and it may be difficult to persuade new companies to participate in the process. Reported income data are much more reliable for wages and profits than for other forms of income.[40]

Over the years, The Conference Board, a leading economic research group, has developed a series of economic indicators that it uses to monitor the tendency of the economy to move from upward expansion to downward recession and then back again.[41] **Leading indicators**, such as manufacturing, employment, monetary, and consumer expectation statistics, are economic variables that generally turn down before a recession begins and turn back up before a recovery starts. **Coincident indicators**, including employment, income, and business production statistics, tend to move in tandem with the overall phases of the business cycle. **Lagging indicators**, such as measures of inflation and unemployment, labor costs, and consumer and business debt and credit levels, turn down after the beginning of a recession and turn up after a recovery has begun.

These leading, coincident, and lagging indicators are based on the concept that expectations of future profits are the driving force of the economy. If business executives are confident that sales and profits will rise, they will expand production of goods and services and investment in structures and equipment. These actions generate increased economic activity overall. Negative expectations about profits will cause the reverse effects and are likely to cause the economy to experience a downturn. The components of the different indicators are shown in Table 14.4.

Most of these indicators correspond to variables we have already discussed in our analysis of either the market for real goods and services or the money market. The role of these indicators in predicting recessions or expansions is not precise. For the leading indicators, the lead time in signaling the beginning of a recession varied from 8 to 15 months for the recessions from 1960 to 1980. Statistical analysis suggests that a tendency for a decline of 1 to 2 percent in the leading composite index, together with a decline of at least half of the component indicators for a six-month period, is a general indicator of a forthcoming recession.[42]

In December 2008, the Conference Board announced that the U.S. leading index decreased 0.4 percent, the coincident index decreased 0.3 percent, and the lagging index increased 0.1 percent in November 2008. The decrease in the leading index was due mainly to large declines in building permits and stock prices and increases in initial unemployment claims. The decline in the coincident index resulted from a large contraction in employment and a smaller drop in industrial production.[43]

We noted in Chapter 13 that the Federal Reserve Open Market Committee bases its monetary policy decisions on the economic data in its Beige Book, which the district banks collect from businesses and other contacts. Managers may also develop their own company-specific indicators. For example, the Kohler Company was surprised when the economic downturn hit in fall 2000 because the company's

Leading indicators
Economic variables, such as manufacturing, employment, monetary, and consumer expectation statistics, that generally turn down before a recession begins and turn back up before a recovery starts.

Coincident indicators
Economic variables, including employment, income, and business production statistics, that tend to move in tandem with the overall phases of the business cycle.

Lagging indicators
Economic variables, including measures of inflation and unemployment, labor costs, and consumer and business debt and credit levels, that turn down after the beginning of a recession and turn up after a recovery has begun.

---

[40] These data and forecasting problems were even more severe before the development of the National Income and Product Accounts in the 1930s. Even in the late 1920s, most of the country's leading economists were unable to forecast the Great Depression of the 1930s, largely due to the lack of current, standardized data on the U.S. economy. See Cynthia Crossen, "Pre-Depression Indicators Forecasted Rosy Economy," *Wall Street Journal*, August 6, 2003.

[41] This discussion is based on Norman Frumkin, *Tracking America's Economy*, 3rd ed. (Armonk, N.Y.: Sharpe, 1998), 300–317; and U.S. Business Cycle Indicators, www.conference-board.org.

[42] Frumkin, *Tracking America's Economy*, 3rd ed.

[43] The Conference Board, U.S. Leading Economic Indicators and Related Composite Indexes for November 2008, December 18, 2008, www.conference-board.org/economics/bci.

TABLE 14.4 Leading, Coincident, and Lagging Economic Indicators

Leading indicators	1. Average weekly hours, manufacturing
	2. Average weekly initial claims for unemployment
	3. Manufacturers' new orders, consumer goods, and materials
	4. Index of supplier deliveries—vendor performance
	5. Manufacturers' new orders, nondefense capital goods
	6. Building permits, new private housing units
	7. Stock prices, 500 common stocks
	8. Money supply, M2 (constant dollars)
	9. Interest rate spread, 10-year Treasury bonds less federal funds
	10. Index of consumer expectations
Coincident indicators	1. Employees on nonagricultural payrolls
	2. Personal income less transfer payments (constant dollars)
	3. Industrial production
	4. Manufacturing and trade sales (constant dollars)
Lagging indicators	1. Average duration of unemployment
	2. Inventories to sales ratio, manufacturing and trade (constant dollars)
	3. Labor cost per unit of output, manufacturing (monthly change)
	4. Average prime rate charged by banks
	5. Commercial and industrial loans outstanding (constant dollars)
	6. Consumer installment credit outstanding to personal income ratio
	7. Consumer price index for services (monthly change)

Source: U.S. Business Cycle Indicators, www.conference-board.org.

leading indicator had been its sales of bathroom and kitchen fixtures, which traditionally began to fall six months before the economy slowed.[44] This decrease in sales did not occur before this downturn. Rather, the first impact of the slowdown in economic activity appeared not in any of the company's 43 factories, but in the two luxury hotels the company operated in Kohler, Wisconsin, where business meeting reservations were cancelled.

Managerial Rule of Thumb

Judging Trends in Economic Indicators

Managers need to be able to react to both policy changes and other aggregate spending changes in order to determine the optimal strategies for their firms and industries. They need to examine and make judgments about the trends in a variety of economic indicators. This process is made more complex because, at any point in time, different indicators may give conflicting signals as to the future direction of the economy. Many business and financial publications and Web sites provide data and analyses that can help managers develop their own forecasts of future economic activity. ■

---

[44] Louis Uchitelle, "Thriving or Hurting, U.S. Manufacturers Brace for the Worst," *New York Times*, March 2, 2001.

Summary

This chapter has brought together and integrated the variables and relationships managers need to understand the determination of income, output, interest rates, and price level in the aggregate demand/aggregate supply (*AD/AS*) model of the economy. This model integrates spending decisions on real goods and services with the monetary side of the economy and then incorporates price-level and supply-side changes. We examined the effects of both fiscal and monetary policy changes and shifts in autonomous expenditures on the level of interest rates, prices, and real income in the economy. We also discussed the major issues involved in implementing fiscal and monetary policy, the impact of macro environment changes on different firms and industries, and the problems both managers and forecasters face in using various economic indicators to predict future economic changes.

Although we have integrated export and import spending and currency exchange rates into our aggregate demand–aggregate supply model, in Chapter 15 we examine the determination of currency exchange rates and the factors affecting other international financial flows. After we have discussed these international economic issues, we will again use the aggregate macro model in Chapter 16 to develop two case studies to further illustrate how changes in the macro environment influence managerial strategies.

Appendix 14A Specific and General Equations for the Aggregate Macro Model

Specific Equation	General Equation
Personal Consumption Expenditure	**Personal Consumption Expenditure**
$C = c_0 + c_1(Y - T_P) - c_2 r + c_3 CC + c_4 W + c_5 CR - c_6 D$	$C = f(Y, \ T_P, \ r, \ CC, \ W, \ CR, \ D)$
	$\quad\quad (+)(-)(-)(+)(+)(+)(-)$
where	*where*
$\quad C$ = personal consumption expenditure	$\quad C$ = personal consumption expenditure
$\quad c_0$ = other factors influencing consumption	$\quad Y$ = real income
$\quad Y$ = real income	$\quad T_P$ = personal taxes
$\quad T_P$ = personal taxes	$\quad r$ = real interest rate
$\quad r$ = real interest rate	$\quad CC$ = consumer confidence
$\quad CC$ = consumer confidence	$\quad W$ = consumer wealth
$\quad W$ = consumer wealth	$\quad CR$ = consumer credit
$\quad CR$ = consumer credit	$\quad D$ = consumer debt
$\quad D$ = consumer debt	
$\quad c_1$ to c_6 = coefficients for the relevant variables	
Gross Private Domestic Investment	**Gross Private Domestic Investment**
$I = i_0 + i_1 Y - i_2 r - i_3 T_B + i_4 PR + i_5 CU$	$I = f(Y, \ r, \ T_B, \ PR, CU)$
	$\quad\quad (+)(-)(-) \ (+) \ (+)$
where	*where*
$\quad I$ = investment spending	$\quad I$ = investment spending
$\quad i_0$ = other factors influencing investment spending	$\quad Y$ = real income
$\quad Y$ = real income	$\quad r$ = real interest rate
$\quad r$ = real interest rate	$\quad T_B$ = business taxes
$\quad T_B$ = business taxes	$\quad PR$ = expected profits and business confidence
$\quad PR$ = expected profits and business confidence	$\quad CU$ = capacity utilization
$\quad CU$ = capacity utilization	
$\quad i_1$ to i_5 = coefficients for the relevant variables	

(continued)

Specific Equation	**General Equation**

GOVERNMENT EXPENDITURE

$G = G_0$

where

G = government expenditure
G_0 = autonomous government expenditure determined
    by public policy

GOVERNMENT EXPENDITURE

$G = f(Y, \text{Policy})$
   (0) (+)

where

  G = government expenditure
  Y = real income
Policy = public policy determining autonomous expenditure

EXPORT EXPENDITURE

$X = x_0 + x_1 Y^* - x_2 R$

where

  X = export expenditure
  x_0 = other factors influencing export expenditure
  Y^* = foreign GDP or income
  R = currency exchange rate (units of foreign currency per unit
    of domestic currency)
  x_1, x_2 = coefficients of the relevant variables

EXPORT EXPENDITURE

$X = f(Y, Y^*, R)$
  (0)(+)(−)

where

  X = export expenditure
  Y = real income
  Y^* = foreign GDP or income
  R = currency exchange rate (units of foreign currency per unit
    of domestic currency)

IMPORT EXPENDITURE

$M = m_0 + m_1 Y + m_2 R$

where

  M = import spending
  m_0 = other factors influencing import spending
  Y = real domestic income
  R = currency exchange rate (units of foreign currency per unit
    of domestic currency)
  m_1, m_2 = coefficients of the relevant variables

IMPORT EXPENDITURE

$M = f(Y, R)$
  (+)(+)

where

  M = import spending
  Y = real domestic income
  R = currency exchange rate (units of foreign currency per unit
    of domestic currency)

AGGREGATE EXPENDITURE

$E = C_0 + c_1 Y + I_0 + i_1 Y + G_0 + X_0 - M_0 - m_1 Y$
$E = C_0 + I_0 + G_0 + X_0 - M_0 + c_1 Y + i_1 Y - m_1 Y$
$E = E_0 + (c_1 + i_1 - m_1)Y$

where

  E = aggregate expenditure
  C_0 = autonomous consumption expenditure
  Y = real income
  I_0 = autonomous investment expenditure
  G_0 = autonomous government expenditure
  X_0 = autonomous export expenditure
  M_0 = autonomous import expenditure
  E_0 = sum of all autonomous expenditure components
  c_1 = marginal propensity to consume
  i_1 = marginal propensity to invest
  m_1 = marginal propensity to import

AGGREGATE EXPENDITURE

$E = f(Y, T_P, r, CC, W, CR, D, T_B, PR, CU, G, Y^*, R)$
  (+)(−)(−)(+)(+)(+)(−)(−)(+)(+)(+)(+)(−)

where

  E = aggregate expenditure
  Y = real income
  T_P = personal taxes
  r = real interest rate
  CC = consumer confidence
  W = consumer wealth
  CR = consumer credit
  D = consumer debt
  T_B = business taxes
  PR = expected profits
  CU = capacity utilization
  G = government spending
  Y^* = foreign GDP or real income
  R = currency exchange rate

REAL MONEY SUPPLY

$RLMS = M_S/P$

where

$RLMS$ = real money supply
  M_S = nominal money supply
    P = price level

REAL MONEY SUPPLY

$RLMS = f(r, \text{FR Policy or } M_S, P)$
   (0)   (+)   (−)

where

    $RLMS$ = real money supply
      r = real interest rate
FR Policy or M_S = nominal money supply controlled by the Federal Reserve
     P = price level

REAL MONEY DEMAND

$RLMD = M_D/P = d_0 - d_1 r + d_2 Y$

where

$RLMD$ = real money demand
  M_D = nominal money demand
    P = price level
    d_0 = other factors influencing money demand
    r = real interest rate
    Y = real income
  d_1, d_2 = sensitivity of money demand to the real interest rate and real income

REAL MONEY DEMAND

$RLMD = M_D/P = f(r, Y)$
       (−)(+)

where

  $RLMD$ = real money demand
    M_D = nominal money demand
     P = price level
     r = real interest rate
     Y = real income

Specific Equation	General Equation
	AGGREGATE DEMAND CURVE

$$AD: Y = f(P,\ T_P, CC,\ W,\ CR,\ D,\ T_B,\ PR, CU, G,\ Y^*,\ R, \text{FR Policy})$$
$$(-)(-)(+)(+)(+)(-)(-)(+)(+)(+)(-)\quad(+)$$

where

- Y = real income
- P = price level
- T_P = personal taxes
- CC = consumer confidence
- W = consumer wealth
- CR = consumer credit
- D = consumer debt
- T_B = business taxes
- PR = expected profits and business confidence
- CU = capacity utilization
- G = government spending
- Y^* = foreign GDP or real income
- R = currency exchange rate (units of foreign currency per dollar)
- FR Policy = Federal Reserve policy (the nominal money supply)

Key Terms

aggregate demand–aggregate
supply equilibrium, p. 389
aggregate demand curve, p. 379
aggregate production
function, p. 388
aggregate supply curve, p. 388
automatic stabilizers, p. 385
coincident indicators, p. 401

crowding out, p. 388
discretionary expenditures,
p. 386
Keynesian model, p. 390
lagging indicators, p. 401
leading indicators, p. 401
long-run aggregate supply
curve, p. 391

nondiscretionary
expenditures, p. 386
potential output, p. 389
progressive tax system, p. 386
short-run aggregate supply
curve, p. 389
stagflation, p. 393

Exercises

Technical Questions

1. Explain why the aggregate demand curve represents a series of equilibria.

2. Explain how each of the following changes would shift the aggregate expenditure function (Chapter 12) and the aggregate demand curve (Chapter 14):

   a. An increase in personal taxes

   b. An increase in expected profits and business confidence

   c. A decrease in the level of foreign GDP or real income

   d. A decrease in the nominal money supply by the Federal Reserve

3. A change in the real money supply can result either from a change in the nominal money supply through Federal Reserve policy (holding the price level constant) or from a change in the price level (holding the nominal money supply constant). The change in the nominal money supply causes a shift of the aggregate demand curve, whereas a change in the price level causes a movement along the aggregate demand curve. Explain.

4. Evaluate whether each of the following statements is true or false, and explain your answer:

   a. The short-run aggregate supply (SAS) curve slopes upward because households spend more as their incomes increase.

b. The long-run aggregate supply curve can never shift.

c. Either a decrease in the nominal money supply by the Federal Reserve, all else held constant, or an increase in the price level, all else held constant, will shift the aggregate demand (*AD*) curve to the left.

d. The Keynesian portion of the short-run aggregate supply (*SAS*) curve would be relevant during a recessionary situation.

e. Stagflation occurs when the aggregate demand (*AD*) curve shifts out on the upward sloping portion of the short-run aggregate supply (*SAS*) curve.

5. In a closed (no foreign sector), mixed economy with stable prices, if we assume that consumption (*C*) and investment (*I*) spending do *not* depend on the interest rate (*r*), can we conclude that

a. The interest-related expenditure (*IRE*) function is vertical?

b. Monetary policy has *no* effect on real income and output?

Explain your answers.

6. If the economy is operating on the upward sloping portion of the short-run aggregate supply (*SAS*) curve, show that an increase in aggregate demand (*AD*) from expansionary fiscal policy will result in an increase in both real income (*Y*) and the price level (*P*).

Application Questions

1. Describe how the following quotes from the article that opened this chapter relate to the *AD–AS* model:

a. "The U.S. faces an unwelcome combination of looming recession and persistent inflation that is reviving angst about stagflation, a condition not seen since the 1970s."

b. "[The Federal Reserve] blamed a further slowdown on the slump in housing prices, tighter lending standards and higher oil prices."

c. "And, as in the 1970s, the rate at which the U.S. economy can grow without generating inflation has fallen, because of slower growth in both the labor force and in productivity, or output per hour of work."

d. "Higher inflation is still a possibility. Food and energy costs could keep rising. Companies could succeed in passing these costs onto consumers . . ."

e. "The declining dollar, while boosting U.S. exports, is adding to inflation pressure, as goods priced in foreign currencies become relatively more expensive."

2. Find one or more articles in the *Wall Street Journal* or other business publications that describe changes in fiscal and monetary policies in the United States. Discuss how these policies relate to the model of aggregate demand and aggregate supply and the issues involved in implementing the policies.

3. Update Table 14.2 with more recent policy descriptions of the variables influencing aggregate demand drawn from the *Wall Street Journal* and other current business publications.

4. Using both the sources in the footnotes in this chapter and updated articles from the literature, discuss the debate over the rate of increase in productivity in the economy and the impact that productivity changes have on real GDP and the price level.

5. Find the most recent summary of the survey of economic forecasters in the *Wall Street Journal*. What are the predictions for changes in real GDP and its major components, inflation, and unemployment? Describe the degree of consensus among the various forecasters.

On the Web

For updated information on the *Wall Street Journal* article at the beginning of the chapter, as well as other relevant links and information, visit the book's Web site at **www.pearsonhighered.com/farnham**

15

International and Balance of Payments Issues in the Macro Economy

We have been discussing international issues throughout the macroeconomic section of this text. For example, we introduced imports and exports as components of the circular flow in Chapter 11. We also discussed the determinants of import and export spending in the analysis of spending on real goods and services in Chapter 12. We showed in Chapters 12 and 14 how changes in these variables cause the *AD* curve to shift, influencing the equilibrium level of income in the economy.

We begin this chapter with the *Wall Street Journal* article "Rescuing Dollar Raises Potential Policy Tug of War," which discusses issues regarding the decline in the value of the dollar relative to other currencies, the impact of this change on the economy, and possible policy action to influence the value of the dollar. We then review the definition of exchange rates from Chapter 12 and examine their impact on imports and exports in more detail. Next we focus on the balance of payments accounts, the accounting system used to measure all international transactions. We present a simple model of foreign exchange markets that we then use to show the impact of both flexible and fixed exchange rate systems. Finally, we present more complex, real-world examples of how these balance of payments issues influence the decisions of foreign and domestic policy makers and the competitive strategy of managers and firms responding to changes in the international economic environment.

Rescuing Dollar Raises Potential Policy Tug of War

by Craig Karmin

Wall Street Journal, *March 18, 2008*

With the U.S. dollar tumbling to its lowest level against the yen since 1995 and hitting another record low against the euro, some traders and analysts wonder whether the Treasury Department may soon have to intervene to brake the currency's fall, something it was last forced to do in the mid-1990s.

But currency interventions have a mixed record of success around the world. In this case, if the Treasury decided to act, it might find itself moving in the opposite direction of an even more powerful market force: the Federal Reserve.

When a government intervenes in currency markets, it buys or sells a currency depending on the direction in which it wants it to move. In this case, the Treasury would be forced to buy dollars, constraining their supply, to slow or halt the pace of its decline.

When the Fed lowers interest rates, as it has been doing aggressively in recent months, it is effectively pumping dollars into the financial system.

When the Fed meets today, it is expected to reduce its target on the federal funds rate by at least three-quarters of a percentage point, and perhaps by as much as a full point. That move could further pressure the dollar.

In addition to pumping extra dollars into the global financial system, it would increase the gap between U.S. and European interest rates, which makes holding foreign currencies more attractive to investors. The actions could also fuel investor fears that the crisis is deepening, further weighing on the dollar. . . .

The euro has increased 8% this year against the dollar, while the U.S. currency has declined by 12% against the yen. . . .

Analysts say any government intervention in the currency market that failed to achieve its goal of slowing the decline would be far worse than none at all. It would embolden speculators to increase their bets on the buck's fall, believing that governments couldn't stop them.

Stephen Jen, a currency analyst with Morgan Stanley, said for government intervention to work, European monetary officials not only would have to coordinate with Washington and Tokyo in buying dollars on the open market, the European Central Bank also would have to change its stance on interest rates. At minimum, he said, the ECB would have to shift its outlook on interest-rate increases to neutral from leaning toward further increases.

This may not happen until the ECB is convinced that inflation in the 17-nation zone is slowing from the 3.3% annual rate recorded in February. However, it is possible that the ECB could shift gears in anticipation of a slowdown, as it did in the middle of 2001, Mr. Jen added.

For investors who think the slowing U.S. economy and bubbling credit crisis indicate further dollar weakness, even intervention might not be enough to scare them off. "We would use it as a way to sell more dollars," said Jonathan Clark, vice chairman of FX Concepts, a hedge fund based in New York that specializes in currency trading.

Certainly not everyone in the U.S. government would favor currency intervention, in part for philosophical reasons that oppose intervening in the market. The weak dollar has also helped increase U.S. exports and has played a role in starting to reduce the massive current-account deficit.

But after six years in which the dollar's decline has been relatively orderly, in recent days the selloff has picked up speed alongside the collapse of Bear Stearns and heightened fears that the credit crisis is intensifying.

Even if the worst case doesn't materialize, the dollar's continued depreciation can increase U.S. inflation, push commodity prices higher world-wide and undercut U.S. stocks and bonds by making them less attractive to foreign investors. . . .

Interventions don't always work. In 1992, George Soros became known as the "Man Who Broke the Bank of England" after his bets against the pound undercut government efforts to defend the currency and forced a devaluation.

But they have also marked important turning points in currency markets in the past. The Plaza Accord in 1985 successfully stemmed a powerful dollar rally against the yen and the German mark, while the Louvre Accord two years later helped stop the dollar's decline.

Case for Analysis

Value of the U.S. Dollar

This article discusses the concern that a country's government has in the value of its currency relative to other major currencies. In this case, the issue was the declining value of the U.S. dollar relative to the yen and the euro. Since 2007, the dollar had declined 8 percent against the euro and 12 percent against the yen. There was discussion in the financial markets that the U.S. Treasury might intervene and buy dollars in the currency markets to halt the decline in its value. Analysts noted that U.S. action would need to be coordinated with European and Japanese monetary officials, and that this policy could be counter to domestic monetary policies of the European Central Bank and the U.S. Federal Reserve. As discussed in the previous two chapters, the goal of U.S. monetary policy during 2007 and 2008 was to stimulate the economy through lower interest rates, a policy that tended to decrease the value of the dollar. The article also mentioned that the lower value of the dollar helped stimulate U.S. economic growth by increasing U.S. exports and began reducing the large U.S. current-account deficit. Finally, the article indicated that moves by any central bank in the currency markets could be offset by speculation and the actions of the thousands of other currency traders in these markets. ■

Exchange Rates

Because companies and individuals in the United States trade with countries having different currencies, we need some way to compare these currencies. Japanese producers want to receive yen when selling their products abroad, while U.S. firms want to be paid in dollars. Thus, how much one currency is worth in terms of another is an additional factor affecting a firm's competitive strategy.

Currency exchange rate
How much of one currency can be exchanged for another or the price of one currency in terms of another.

As we discussed in Chapter 12, the simplest definition of the **currency exchange rate** is how much of one currency can be exchanged for another (for example, how many Japanese yen you can exchange for one U.S. dollar). This definition can also be stated as the price of one currency in terms of another—that is, how much one currency costs in terms of another.

How exchange rates are described is often a source of confusion. In some sources, the exchange rate is defined as units of foreign currency per dollar, whereas other sources define it as dollars per unit of foreign currency. Sometimes units on the vertical axis of a graph showing exchange rates are inverted, depending on the definition used. In this text, we define the exchange rate, R, as the number of units of foreign currency per unit of domestic currency or, from the U.S. perspective, per U.S. dollar. Therefore, $1/R$ is the number of dollars per unit of foreign currency. This definition has the most intuitive appeal because we define an appreciation in the domestic currency as an increase in R and a depreciation as a decrease in R.

Trade-weighted dollar
An index of the weighted exchange value of the U.S. dollar versus the currencies of a broad group of major U.S. trading partners.

The first two rows of Table 15.1 show exchange rates for the U.S. dollar compared to the euro and the Japanese yen in January 2005 and January 2006. The third row presents the **trade-weighted dollar**, an index of the weighted exchange value of the U.S. dollar versus the currencies of a broad group of major U.S. trading partners. The currencies included in the trade-weighted or broad index are those of economies whose bilateral shares of U.S. imports or exports exceed 0.5 percent. Trade with these economies accounts for over 90 percent of total U.S. imports and exports.[1]

The bold numbers in Table 15.1 use our definition of the exchange rate, R (the foreign currency price of domestic currency or foreign currency units per dollar).

---

[1] Mico Loretan, "Indexes of the Foreign Exchange Value of the Dollar," *Federal Reserve Bulletin*, Winter 2005, 1–8.

TABLE 15.1 Exchange Rates

CURRENCY	R (UNITS OF FOREIGN CURRENCY PER $)		1/R ($ PER UNIT OF FOREIGN CURRENCY)	
	January 2005	January 2006	January 2005	January 2006
Euro (E)	0.76	0.82	1.31	1.21
Japanese yen (¥) ($/100¥)	103	115	0.97	0.87
Trade-weighted $ ($/100 units)	109	110	0.92	0.91
	January 2007	January 2008	January 2007	January 2008
Euro (E)	0.77	0.68	1.30	1.47
Japanese yen (¥) ($/100¥)	120	108	0.83	0.93
Trade-weighted $ ($/100 units)	108	98	0.93	1.02

Source: Federal Reserve Statistical Release, *Foreign Exchange Rates (Monthly)*, www.federalreserve.gov/releases/g5.

In January 2005, $1 could be exchanged for 0.76 euros; in January 2006, $1 could be exchanged for 0.82 euros. Thus, between these two dates, the dollar appreciated against the euro (a dollar *will buy more* euros; a dollar *can be exchanged for more* euros; the dollar *is more expensive in terms of* the euro; the dollar *has strengthened against* the euro). Using our definition of the exchange rate, as R increases, the domestic currency *appreciates* (referred to as **currency appreciation**). The table also shows that the dollar appreciated against the Japanese yen and the currencies of the United States' major trading partners over this period.

The bottom half of Table 15.1 shows that the dollar depreciated against the euro, the yen, and the trade-weighted currencies between January 2007 and January 2008 (a dollar *will buy less* yen; a dollar *can be exchanged for fewer* yen; the dollar *is cheaper in terms of* the yen; the dollar *has weakened against* the yen). Thus, using our definition of the exchange rate, as R decreases, the domestic currency depreciates (referred to as **currency depreciation**).

The nonbold numbers in Table 15.1 show the exchange rate values using the inverse of R ($1/R$, the domestic price of foreign currency or dollars per foreign unit). The numbers show that from January 2005 to January 2006, the euro and the yen *depreciated* against the dollar (these currencies now cost *less* in terms of the dollar), while these currencies *appreciated* against the dollar (they now cost *more* in terms of the dollar) between January 2007 and January 2008. Thus, when the dollar appreciates against the yen or the euro, by definition, the yen and the euro depreciate against the dollar, and vice versa.[2]

Table 15.2 shows the effect of dollar appreciation and depreciation on a hypothetical example of U.S. exports and imports. Technically, this relationship involves the **real exchange rate**, e^*, which is the **nominal exchange rate**, R (or the value at which one currency can be exchanged for another), times the ratio of the domestic price level to the foreign price level or $e^* = R(P_d/P_f)$. If we assume that the foreign price level is constant, as we did with the domestic price level in our analysis of real spending in Chapter 12, and we set the price level indices so $P_d = P_f = 1$, then $e^* = R$.

Currency appreciation
One currency can be exchanged for more units of another currency or the value of R increases.

Currency depreciation
One currency can be exchanged for fewer units of another currency or the value of R decreases.

Real exchange rate
The nominal exchange rate times the ratio of the domestic price level to the foreign price level.

Nominal exchange rate
The value at which one currency can be exchanged for another, or R.

---

[2] In the Federal Reserve Statistical Release of monthly foreign exchange rates, most data are in the form of currency units per U.S. dollar. However, data for the euro, the Australian and New Zealand dollars, and the United Kingdom pound are reported as U.S. dollars per currency unit. See www.federalreserve.gov/releases/g5.

TABLE 15.2 Effect of Dollar Appreciation and Depreciation on U.S. Exports and Imports

$R = ¥/\$$	DOMESTIC PRICE	JAN 05: $R = 103$	JAN 06: $R = 115$	EFFECT ON EXPORTS (X) AND IMPORTS (M)
U.S. exports: Computers	$10,000	¥1,030,000	¥1,150,000	X decreases
U.S. imports: Japanese cars	¥2,000,000	≈ $19,400	≈ $17,400	M increases
		JAN 07: $R = 120$	JAN 08: $R = 108$	
U.S. exports: Computers	$10,000	¥1,200,000	¥1,080,000	X increases
U.S. imports: Japanese cars	¥2,000,000	≈ $16,700	≈ $18,500	M decreases

Movements in the nominal exchange rate, R, are reflected in the real exchange rate, e^*. We use this simplifying assumption throughout the analysis.[3]

As you can see in Table 15.2, as the dollar appreciates against the yen, U.S. exports such as computers become more expensive in terms of the number of yen required to pay the domestic price in dollars, while U.S. imports such as cars become cheaper in terms of the number of dollars required to pay the Japanese price in yen. This result implies that as R increases, the volume of exports (X) decreases, while the volume of imports (M) increases, all else held constant. The opposite case holds for a dollar depreciation. As the dollar depreciates against the yen, each dollar trades for fewer yen, so it takes more dollars to pay for Japanese cars that are priced in yen. However, fewer yen are needed for U.S. exports priced in dollars. This means that as R decreases, the volume of exports (X) increases, while the volume of imports (M) decreases, all else held constant.

Figure 15.1 shows the effect of the exchange rate on net exports (exports minus imports), or the **balance of trade**, from 2000 to 2008. The exchange rate is measured

Balance of trade
The relationship between a country's export and import spending, which can be positive if there is a trade surplus (exports exceed imports) or negative if there is a trade deficit (imports exceed exports).

FIGURE 15.1
Balance of Trade and the Exchange Rate
An appreciating dollar typically causes the balance of trade or net exports to become more negative, while a depreciating dollar has the opposite effect.
Source: Federal Reserve Economic Data (FRED II), Economic Research, Federal Reserve Bank of St. Louis, http://research.stlouisfed.org/fred2/.

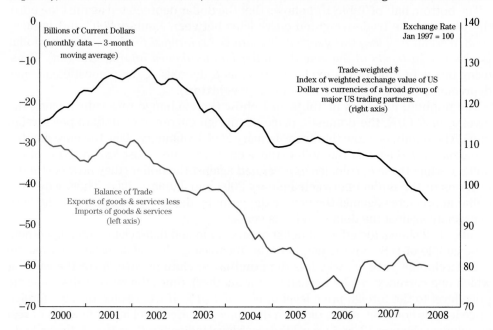

---

[3] For most of the last 30 years, the U.S. inflation rate did not vary substantially from the average inflation rate of its major trading partners. Thus, the real and nominal exchange rates moved together. See Charles Schultze, *Memos to the President: A Guide Through Macroeconomics for the Busy Policymaker* (Washington, D.C.: Brookings Institution, 1992), 101–103; and Imad A. Moosa, *Exchange Rate Regimes: Fixed, Flexible or Something in Between?* (New York: Palgrave Macmillan, 2005). Moosa reports correlations of 0.96, 0.88, and 0.65 between the nominal and real exchange rates for the U.S. dollar and the Canadian dollar, the Japanese yen, and the British pound for the period 1974–2004.

TABLE 15.3 Determinants of Exports and Imports

EXPORTS	IMPORTS	NET EXPORTS
$X = f(Y, Y^*, R)$	$M = f(Y, R)$	$F = f(Y, Y^*, R)$
$(0)(+)(-)$	$(+)(+)$	$(-)(+)(-)$

on the right axis as the weighted exchange value of the U.S. dollar versus the currencies of a broad group of major U.S. trading partners (R or units per dollar). The left axis shows the balance of trade, or exports minus imports. Figure 15.1 depicts the relationship between changes in the value of the dollar and net exports. An appreciating or strong dollar has a positive effect on U.S. imports and a negative effect on U.S. exports. This causes the balance of trade, or net exports, to become more negative (2000–2002). Net exports become less negative when the value of the dollar declines for an extended period (2006–2008) because exports increase while imports decrease.

These relationships are summarized in Table 15.3

> *where*
> X = export spending
> M = import spending
> F = net export spending (export minus import spending = $X - M$)
> Y^* = income in the rest of the world
> Y = income in the United States
> R = exchange rate as defined above (units of foreign currency per dollar)

As in earlier chapters, the notation is read as follows: Exports (imports, net exports) "are a function of" the variables inside the parentheses. The positive and negative signs show whether the variables in the parentheses are directly ($+$) or inversely ($-$) related to the variable on the left. U.S. exports are not related to the level of U.S. income, but are directly or positively related to the level of income in the rest of the world and inversely or negatively related to the exchange rate. U.S. imports are directly or positively related to both the level of U.S. income and the exchange rate. Therefore, net exports (exports minus imports) are

1. Negatively related to income in the United States (an increase in U.S. income causes imports to increase, but has no effect on exports and, therefore, causes net exports to decrease)
2. Positively related to income in the rest of the world (an increase in foreign income has no impact on U.S. imports, but causes U.S. exports and, therefore, net exports to increase)
3. Negatively related to R (an increase in R will cause exports to decrease, imports to increase, and, therefore, net exports to decrease)

Each of these relationships is defined assuming all else is held constant, as we have done throughout this text.

Managerial Rule of Thumb

Currency Exchange Rates

Managers are influenced by currency exchange rates because these exchange rates influence the prices of both the firm's inputs and its outputs if the firm sells its products or purchases its inputs abroad. An increase in a country's exchange rate hurts domestic firms that export to other countries, but helps firms that import their inputs from abroad. ∎

Equilibrium in the Open Economy

Before discussing how international transactions are measured, we'll review the concept of the equilibrium level of income and output as applied to a mixed, open economy. These relationships, first developed in Chapter 12, are expressed in Equations 15.1 through 15.4:

15.1 $E = Y$

15.2 $C + I + G + X - M = C + S + T$

15.3 $I + G + X = S + T + M$

15.4 $X - M = (S - I) + (T - G)$

where

E = aggregate expenditure
Y = real income
C = consumption expenditure
I = investment expenditure
G = government expenditure
X = export spending
M = import spending
S = saving
T = total taxes

Drawing on the circular flow relationships developed in Chapters 11 and 12, planned aggregate expenditure in the economy must equal aggregate income in equilibrium (Equation 15.1). Aggregate expenditure (E) represents the sum of consumption (C), investment (I), government (G), and export (X) minus import (M) spending. Households use aggregate income (Y) for consumption spending (C), saving (S), or taxes (T) (Equation 15.2). Simplifying and rearranging terms in Equation 15.2 leads to Equation 15.3, which shows injections to and leakages from the circular flow of U.S. economic activity. In a mixed, open economy, injections are investment, government, and export spending, while leakages are saving, taxation, and import spending.

In Equation 15.4, we have rearranged the terms in Equation 15.3 to show net exports, or the trade balance, on the left side of the equation. The right side shows the relationship between saving and investment in the private sector (the level of private saving) and the relationship between government spending and taxation in the public sector (the level of public saving). Because Equation 15.4 is based on the previous equations and represents an equilibrium condition for the economy, the trade balance must equal the level of private and public saving in the country.

If there is a **trade surplus** ($X - M > 0$) in the United States, the net saving on the right side of Equation 15.4 must be positive. Individuals and institutions in the United States are *lending* these savings abroad. They do so by purchasing foreign real and financial assets. This process represents a **capital outflow (k_o)** from the United States to the rest of the world. Likewise, if there is a **trade deficit** ($X - M < 0$), the net saving on the right side of Equation 15.4 must be negative. Individuals and institutions in the United States are *borrowing* from abroad. They do so by selling real and financial assets to foreigners. This process represents a **capital inflow (k_i)** to the United States. The **net capital flow ($K_N = k_i - k_o$)** must, therefore, match the

Trade surplus
Occurs when a country's export spending exceeds the spending on its imports.

Capital outflow (k_o)
A lending of a country's savings that occurs when the country has a trade surplus and its citizens purchase real and financial assets from abroad.

Trade deficit
Occurs when a country's import spending exceeds the spending on its exports.

Capital inflow (k_i)
Borrowing from another country that occurs when the country has a trade deficit and its citizens sell real and financial assets to foreigners.

Net capital flow ($K_N = k_i - k_o$)
The difference between capital inflows and outflows, which must match the trade balance, or export spending minus import spending.

trade balance $(X - M)$.[4] If exports just equal imports, there are no net capital flows between the United States and the rest of the world.[5]

U.S. International Transactions in 2007 (Balance of Payments)

U.S. international transactions are reported in the **balance of payments (BP) accounting system**, a record of *all* transactions between residents of the reporting country and residents of the rest of the world over a period of time, usually one year. This is an accounting system similar to the GDP accounts for a given country. We noted in Chapter 11 that GDP measures the market value of all *currently produced* final goods and services in a country for a given year. Because export and import spending flows are for currently produced goods and services in the United States and other countries, these expenditures are included in the GDP accounts. They are also included in the *BP* accounts because they are international transactions. However, there are capital flows between countries that reflect the buying and selling of *existing* real and financial assets. These transactions do not represent current production and are not included in the GDP accounts, but they are included in the *BP* accounts.

Table 15.4 shows the U.S. *BP* accounts for 2007 (all figures are measured in billions of dollars). A receipts item, which represents a flow of income to the United States, is listed as a positive number, whereas a payment item, which represents a flow from the United States to the rest of the world, is listed as a negative number. The *BP* accounts are divided into two sections: the current account and the financial account.

The Current Account

The **current account** measures the current flows of goods, services, investment income, and unilateral transfers between the United States and the rest of the world. U.S. exports of goods and services are listed as a positive amount because they generate income flowing to the United States, while imports are listed as a negative amount because income flows from the United States to the rest of the world to pay for imported goods and services. The trade balance (net exports or exports minus imports) was −$709 billion in 2007.

The second major category in the current account is **net investment income**, which is the difference between the interest income or receipts earned on investments in the rest of the world by U.S. residents and the payments to foreigners on the investments they have made in the United States.[6] As you can see in Table 15.4, net investment income was $74 billion in 2007. **Unilateral transfers** represent

Balance of payments (BP) accounting system
A comprehensive measure of all economic activity between a country and the rest of the world.

Current account
A measure of the current flows of goods, services, investment income, and unilateral transfers between a country and the rest of the world.

Net investment income
The difference between the interest income or receipts earned on investments in the rest of the world by the residents of a given country and the payments to foreigners on investments they have made in the given country.

Unilateral transfers
Flows of goods, services, and financial assets, such as foreign aid, from one country to another in which nothing of significant economic value is received in return.

---

[4] This relationship can also be seen with the alternative definition of equilibrium: $Y = E$. It follows that $Y = (C + I + G) + (X - M)$ or $Y - (C + I + G) = (X - M)$. If $(X - M) > 0$, then $Y > (C + I + G)$. Additional expenditures are needed for equilibrium. These are obtained by U.S. households and institutions purchasing real and financial assets from abroad (capital outflow). If $(X - M) < 0$, then $Y < (C + I + G)$. In this case, additional income is needed for equilibrium. This income is achieved by the sale of U.S. real and financial assets to foreigners (capital inflow).

[5] We use K_N to represent net financial capital flows in the macro model of Part 2 of this text. This is distinct from the use of K to represent the capital input in the production function of Part 1. K in the production function refers to real physical capital inputs in a production process that change as a result of investment spending by firms. K_N refers to the buying and selling of existing real and financial assets in response to differential rates of return and other factors.

[6] The current account includes the income on these financial investments. The dollar amounts of the actual investments in the United States and the rest of the world are included in the financial account below.

TABLE 15.4 U.S. Balance of Payments, 2007 (billion $)

CURRENT ACCOUNT TRANSACTIONS

Exports of goods and services	$ 1,628	
Imports of goods and services	−2,337	
Trade balance		$−709
Receipts on U.S. assets abroad	782	
Payments on foreign assets in United States	−708	
Net investment income		74
Unilateral transfers		−104
Current account balance		−739

FINANCIAL ACCOUNT TRANSACTIONS

Change in U.S. holdings of foreign assets (k_o)	−1,206	
Change in foreign holdings of U.S. assets (k_i)	1,864	
Statistical discrepancy	81	
Net capital flows to United States		$ 739

Source: Christopher L. Bach, "U.S. International Transactions in 2007," *Survey of Current Business* (April 2008): 22–47. Available at www.bea.gov/international.

flows of goods, services, and financial assets in which nothing of significant economic value is received in return. These include government military and nonmilitary transfers, such as foreign aid, private and government pensions to U.S. citizens living abroad, and gifts sent abroad by individuals and nonprofit organizations. These amounts totaled $104 billion in 2007 and were recorded as a negative item because they represented payments abroad. The net balance on the current account in 2007 was –$739 billion.

The Financial Account

Financial account

A measure of the change in the stock of real assets (buildings, property, etc.) and financial assets (bank deposits, securities, etc.) held by a country's residents in foreign countries and by foreigners in the given country.

The **financial account** measures changes in the stock of assets held by U.S. residents in foreign countries and by foreigners in the United States. The financial account includes both financial assets (bank deposits, securities, etc.) and real assets (buildings, property, etc.). In the international economy, financial account transactions or capital *flows* result from changes or differences in interest rates among countries or in rates of return among various types of financial and/or real assets as residents adjust their *stocks* of assets in search of the highest returns. If interest rates are higher in the United States than in the rest of the world, financial capital flows to the United States. There will be capital outflows from the United States if U.S. interest rates are lower than those in the rest of the world.[7]

As noted above, capital inflows (k_i) arise when U.S. residents sell real and financial assets to residents of the rest of the world; capital outflows (k_o) occur when U.S. residents buy real and financial assets from residents of the rest of the world. As you can see in Table 15.4, the change in foreign holdings of U.S. assets

---

[7] Capital flows are also affected by other factors, such as the political stability in different countries, profit potential, and credit conditions. For example, capital flows to and from the United States were much greater in the first half of 2007 than in the second half of the year, given the disruptions in the U.S. financial markets we have discussed throughout the macro chapters in this text. See Christopher L. Bach, "U.S. International Transactions in 2007," *Survey of Current Business* (April 2008): 22–47. Available at www.bea.gov/international.

(a capital inflow or positive number) was greater than the change in U.S. holdings of foreign assets (a capital outflow or negative number) by $658 billion. This positive balance on the financial account is equal to the negative balance on the current account with the exception of the statistical discrepancy noted in the table and discussed later in the chapter. This equality did not happen by chance. It *must* hold for equilibrium in the balance of payments. If the current flows of goods and services, investment income, and unilateral transfers are greater from the United States to the rest of the world than vice versa (a negative balance on the current account), there must be an offsetting positive balance on the financial account, representing a net capital inflow into the United States. Thus, a negative balance of trade, which represents the largest component of the current account, must be financed by U.S. borrowing from the rest of the world (an increase in foreign holdings of U.S. assets).

Revenue or T-Account

It may be easier to understand these balance of payments relationships by reorganizing the data in Table 15.4 into a **revenue or T-account.** All international transactions can be classified in one of two ways. Either they generate receipts (income) to U.S. residents, or they generate payments (expenses) by U.S. residents. These transactions can be listed in a revenue or T-account (shown in Table 15.5), which, following the accounting concept of the income statement, records international transactions as either expense-generating items (listed on the left-hand or debit side) or income-generating items (listed on the right-hand or credit side).

Revenue or T-account
An accounting statement that shows expense-generating items on the left-hand or debit side and income-generating items on the right-hand or credit side.

Because the *BP* account records *all* transactions between U.S. residents and residents of the rest of the world, the left-hand side of the *BP* T-account must equal the right-hand side (total expenditures must equal total income). Table 15.6 puts the 2007 balance of payments information from Table 15.4 into the revenue or T-account form. This T-account approach combines elements from the *BP* current

TABLE 15.5 Revenue or T-Account for Balance of Payments

DEBIT (−)	CREDIT (+)
U.S. residents' payments (expenses) to residents of the rest of the world	U.S. residents' receipts (income) from residents of the rest of the world

TABLE 15.6 Revenue or T-Account for 2007 Balance of Payments (billion $)

PAYMENTS		RECEIPTS	
(IMPORT-TYPE TRANSACTIONS: DEBIT [−])		(EXPORT-TYPE TRANSACTIONS: CREDIT [+])	
Imports of goods & services	$2,337	Exports of goods & services	$1,628
Payments on foreign assets in United States	708	Receipts on U.S. assets abroad	782
Unilateral transfers	104		
Change in U.S. holdings of foreign assets	1,206	Change in foreign holdings of U.S. assets	1,864
		Statistical discrepancy	81
Total	$4,355	Total	$4,355

TABLE 15.7 T-Account Summary of 2007 Balance of Payments (billion $)

PAYMENTS (EXPENDITURE)		RECEIPTS (INCOME)	
Imports (M)	$3,149	Exports (X)	$2,410
Capital outflows (k_o)	1,206	Capital inflows (k_i)	1,945
Total expenditure	$4,355	Total income	$4,355

and financial accounts into import-type transactions or payments to the rest of the world (debits) and export-type transactions or receipts from the rest of the world (credits). Items that had a negative value in the 2007 balance of payments accounts (Table 15.4) are recorded in Table 15.6 on the payments or debit side of the T-account, whereas items that had a positive value in the *BP* accounts are recorded here on the receipts or credit side of the T-account.

As we noted earlier, the totals on both sides of Table 15.6 must be equal. The **statistical discrepancy (SD)** arises from the fact that data collection is not perfectly efficient. We cannot account for every single transaction between U.S. residents and residents of the rest of the world. Because the discrepancy is usually attributed to short-term capital flows, we can include an SD value of 81 under the heading of "Change in foreign holdings of U.S. assets."

Generalizing the transactions in Table 15.6 results in Table 15.7. In this table and the examples that follow, we assume that there is perfectly efficient data collection or that the statistical discrepancy equals zero. In Table 15.7, total expenditure is the sum of imports and capital outflows ($M + k_o$), while total income is the sum of exports and capital inflows ($X + k_i$). Because income equals expenditure, income minus expenditure equals zero. Substituting the components gives us Equation 15.5, while rearranging the terms gives Equation 15.6. Equation 15.6 is simply the equation for net exports ($F = X - M$) plus the equation for net capital flows ($K_N = k_i - k_o$). Thus, the balance of payments is the sum of the balance on the current account plus the balance on the financial account, or $BP = F + K_N = 0$. These balances must be equal and offsetting so that their sum equals zero. The balance of payments equation (15.6) and the balance of payments account in Table 15.4 separate the above transactions into flows affecting current income or current GDP (trade flows) and flows involving existing assets (capital flows).[8]

> **15.5** $(X + k_i) - (M + k_o) = 0$
>
> **15.6** $BP: (X - M) + (k_i - k_o) = 0$

Deriving the Foreign Exchange Market

Given the importance of exchange rates in influencing exports, imports, and GDP, we'll now show how exchange rates are determined using concepts from the *BP* accounts. We'll use a simple two-country model of the United States and Japan to derive the foreign exchange market, and we'll use the revenue or T-account approach to show the quantity supplied and quantity demanded of both dollars ($)

Statistical discrepancy (SD) The imbalance between the capital and current accounts in the balance of payments statement or between payments and receipts in the revenue or T-account that arises from inefficient data collection.

---

[8] For a discussion of the issues surrounding the size of the U.S. trade deficit, see Catherine L. Mann, *Is the U.S. Trade Deficit Sustainable?* (Washington, D.C.: Institute for International Economics, 1999); Catherine L. Mann, "Perspective on the U.S. Current Account Deficit and Sustainability," *Journal of Economic Perspectives* 16 (Summer 2002): 131–52; and Masaru Yoshitomi, "Global Imbalances and East Asian Monetary Cooperation," in *Toward an East Asian Exchange Rate Regime*, eds. Duck-Koo Chung and Barry Eichengreen (Washington, DC: The Brookings Institution, 2007), 22–48.

and yen (¥). This is similar to the microeconomic demand and supply analysis for specific products that we developed in Chapter 2. However, in the foreign exchange market, the commodity is a currency, and the price is the exchange rate between two currencies.

The Demand for and Supply of Dollars in the Foreign Exchange Market

We start first with the income side of the international transactions revenue account (see Table 15.7). To pay for U.S. goods and services—both newly produced goods and services (U.S. exports, X) and existing real and financial assets (U.S. capital inflows, k_i)—Japanese residents *demand* $ by supplying their own currency, ¥, to the foreign exchange market. They sell ¥ and buy $. Alternatively, U.S. residents receive ¥ when they sell their goods to Japanese residents. Because yen are not U.S. currency, U.S. residents take their ¥ to the foreign exchange market and exchange them for $ (i.e., they buy $ with ¥). The income side of the revenue account shows the quantity demanded of dollars (see Table 15.8).

A similar analysis holds for the expense or payments side of the revenue account in Table 15.7. To pay for Japanese goods and services—both newly produced goods and services (U.S. imports, M) and existing real and financial assets (U.S. capital outflows, k_o)—U.S. residents need ¥. They *supply* $ to the foreign exchange market in exchange for ¥. Alternatively, Japanese residents receive $ when they sell their goods to U.S. residents and take these $ to the foreign exchange market to acquire their own currency, ¥. Either way, these transactions give rise to a quantity supplied of dollars (see Table 15.9).[9]

These results can be summarized in the following demand and supply functions (Equations 15.7 and 15.8) for dollars in the foreign exchange market:

15.7 $Q^d{}_\$ = f(X, k_i)$

15.8 $Q^s{}_\$ = f(M, k_o)$

Equation 15.7 states that the quantity of dollars demanded in the foreign exchange market is a function of the level of the receipts- or income-side factors in

TABLE 15.8 Demand for Dollars in Foreign Exchange Market

UNITED STATES SELLS TO JAPAN	IF JAPAN PAYS IN $	IF JAPAN PAYS IN ¥	RESULT
In foreign exchange market	Japan sells ¥ to buy $	United States sells ¥ to buy $	$Q^d{}_\$$

TABLE 15.9 Supply of Dollars in Foreign Exchange Market

UNITED STATES BUYS FROM JAPAN	IF UNITED STATES PAYS IN $	IF UNITED STATES PAYS IN ¥	RESULT
In foreign exchange market	Japan sells $ to buy ¥	United States sells $ to buy ¥	$Q^s{}_\$$

[9] Note that this discussion includes the supply of and demand for $ and ¥ only in the foreign exchange market, not the domestic money market.

TABLE 15.10 T-Account, Supply of and Demand for Dollars

$Q^s{}_\$$	$Q^d{}_\$$
M	X
k_o	k_i

Table 15.7 (that is, the amount of exports and the level of capital inflows). The quantity of dollars supplied in the foreign exchange market (Equation 15.8) is a function of the payments- or expenditure-side factors in Table 15.7 (that is, the amount of imports and the level of capital outflows). These relationships are also shown in T-account form in Table 15.10. The determinants of exports, imports, and capital flows were developed above and are expressed in Table 15.11.

U.S. exports are positively related to the level of income in Japan and negatively related to the exchange rate. U.S. imports are positively related to both the level of U.S. income and the exchange rate. The last two relationships in Table 15.11 show the influence of differences in interest rates on U.S. capital inflows and outflows. Capital inflows occur if U.S. interest rates are higher than those in Japan; outflows occur when Japanese interest rates exceed those in the United States.[10]

Substituting these relationships into the dollar demand and supply equations (15.7 and 15.8) gives us Equations 15.9 and 15.10:

15.9 $Q^d{}_\$ = f(R, Y_{\text{Japan}}, r_{\text{US}} > r_{\text{Japan}})$
$$\phantom{Q^d{}_\$ = f(}(-) \quad (+) \qquad (+)$$

15.10 $Q^s{}_\$ = f(R, Y_{\text{US}}, r_{\text{US}} < r_{\text{Japan}})$
$$\phantom{Q^s{}_\$ = f(}(+) \ (+) \qquad (+)$$

If we make the simplifying assumptions that interest rates in both countries are equal ($r_{\text{US}} = r_{\text{Japan}}$) and that incomes are constant in the United States and Japan, we can use all of these relationships to derive a *hypothetical* foreign exchange (or dollar) market (see Figure 15.2), where R is the price of $ in terms of ¥ (measured on the vertical axis) and $Q_\$$ is the quantity of dollars (measured on the horizontal axis).[11] As we discussed when first introducing demand functions, the demand for dollars is a function of the price, *holding all else constant*. The demand curve for dollars in the foreign exchange market is downward sloping. In Figure 15.2, a movement *down along* the D_0 curve shows the quantity of dollars demanded increasing as the exchange rate, R, decreases. As the exchange rate decreases and the dollar depreciates, U.S. exports become cheaper for Japanese residents. A greater demand for exports creates an increase in the quantity of dollars demanded

TABLE 15.11 Determinants of Exports, Imports, and Capital Flows

$X = f(Y_{\text{Japan}}, R)$	$M = f(Y_{\text{US}}, R)$	$k_i = f(r_{\text{US}} > r_{\text{Japan}})$	$k_o = f(r_{\text{US}} < r_{\text{Japan}})$
(+) (−)	(+)(+)	(+)	(+)

---

[10] This notation shows capital inflows and outflows as positive numbers and focuses on interest rate differentials between countries.

[11] Other factors, including the political environment in different countries and speculation by currency traders, can also influence the supply of and demand for various currencies. We ignore these factors in these simple models, but will discuss them in policy examples later in the chapter.

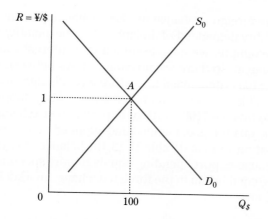

FIGURE 15.2

Foreign Exchange Market-Initial Equilibrium

Equilibrium in the foreign exchange (dollar) market is achieved at that exchange rate where the quantity demanded of dollars equals the quantity supplied of dollars.

to purchase those exports. Likewise, an increase in the exchange rate, R, all else held constant, makes U.S. exports more expensive for Japanese residents and results in a smaller quantity of dollars demanded to pay for those exports.

Changes in the other variables in Equation 15.9 cause a *shift* in the demand curve for dollars. With a higher level of Japanese income, there is a greater demand for U.S. exports and, thus, a greater demand for U.S. dollars at every exchange rate, R. This causes the demand curve, D_0 in Figure 15.2, to shift to the right. If interest rates in the United States are greater than those in Japan, there are higher capital inflows to the United States. This also creates a higher demand for U.S. dollars at every exchange rate, causing the demand curve, D_0, to shift to the right.

In the same way, the supply curve for dollars in the foreign exchange market is upward sloping. As the exchange rate increases and the dollar appreciates, all else held constant, imports become less expensive because more yen are obtained for each dollar. Thus, a movement *upward along* the S_0 curve shows the quantity of dollars supplied increasing because imports are becoming less expensive and more dollars are being supplied to the market to purchase those imports.

Changes in the other variables in Equation 15.10 result in a *shift* of the supply curve. If U.S. income increases, there is a greater demand for imports at every exchange rate. This results in an increased supply of dollars at every R to purchase those imports and, thus, a rightward shift of the supply curve in Figure 15.2. Similarly, if Japanese interest rates are higher than those in the United States, there are increased capital outflows to purchase Japanese financial instruments. This also causes an increased supply of dollars at every exchange rate and results in a rightward shift of the supply curve for dollars in Figure 15.2.

Equilibrium in the Foreign Exchange Market

Equilibrium in the foreign exchange market occurs at point A in Figure 15.2, at the price or exchange rate $R = 1$, where $Q^d{}_\$ = Q^s{}_\$ = 100$. The balance of payments effects of this equilibrium in the dollar foreign exchange market in Figure 15.2 can be summarized in Equation 15.11 and Table 15.12.

15.11 $BP = (X - M) + K = (100 - 100) + 0 = 0$

TABLE 15.12 U.S. International Transactions

$Q^s{}_\$$	$Q^d{}_\$$
M 100	X 100
k_o 0	k_i 0
100	100

Equilibrium in the foreign exchange market means that at the price or exchange rate $R = 1$, the quantity demanded of dollars equals the quantity supplied of dollars. In this simplified example, we have assumed that interest rates are equal in the United States and Japan, so there are no capital flows between the countries ($k_i = k_o = 0$). Therefore, $100 is demanded in the foreign exchange market to finance $100 worth of exports. This is exactly matched by the $100 supplied to the foreign exchange market to finance $100 worth of imports. The exchange rate or price necessary to equate the quantities demanded and supplied in this example is $R = 1$. As shown in both Equation 15.11 and Table 15.12, the balance of payments accounts are in equilibrium because export spending equals import spending and there are no capital flows. Thus, equilibrium in the foreign exchange market implies a balance of payments equilibrium.

Managerial Rule of Thumb

The Foreign Exchange Market

The foreign exchange market operates in the same manner as a competitive market for other goods and services. There are demand and supply factors for each currency, and the resulting price in the market is the currency exchange rate. Because the foreign exchange market is very competitive, exchange rates are constantly changing. These changes influence the costs of production and the prices of products for firms that buy and sell in international markets. ■

Exchange Rate Systems

Figure 15.2, Equation 15.11, and Table 15.12 all show equilibrium in the foreign exchange market and the balance of payments accounts. Yet this equilibrium is easily disturbed when there are changes in the factors influencing the demand for and supply of currencies in the foreign exchange market. If we continue our simple two-country example with the United States and Japan and we assume that interest rates are equal in both countries, changes in the demand for dollars will result primarily from changes in Japanese income (which influence the amount of U.S. exports), and changes in the supply of dollars will result primarily from changes in U.S. income (which influence the amount of U.S. imports). As in the microeconomic section of this text, these changes in demand and supply result in *shifts* of the curves, not movements along the curves. In any market, with a shift of a demand or supply curve, there will be a new equilibrium price if the market is allowed to operate freely.

Flexible exchange rate system

A system in which currency exchange rates are determined strictly by the forces of demand for and supply of the currencies and there is no intervention by any country's central bank in order to influence the level of exchange rates.

There are two major types of exchange rate systems that countries can use: flexible and fixed. In a **flexible exchange rate system**, the exchange rate is determined strictly by the interaction of the supply of and the demand for currencies. This means that a payments imbalance (a net surplus or a net deficit) cannot arise in the overall balance of payments accounts. The equilibrium price will always be established in the foreign exchange markets, which results in equilibrium in the balance of payments accounts.[12] Under a flexible exchange rate system, there is no intervention by the central bank of any country in order to influence the level of the exchange rate.

Countries may not always want their exchange rates to be subject to the forces of demand and supply for various political and economic reasons. Because an exchange rate influences the levels of a country's imports and exports, which are

---

[12] Any deficit in the current account must be matched by a corresponding surplus in the financial account, and vice versa.

components of aggregate demand, domestic policy makers may want to hold that rate at a particular level or within a certain range to achieve given domestic policy goals related to the level or growth of GDP. The unpredictable volatility of a floating exchange rate may reduce international trade and investment, given the difficulty of writing contracts, and may cause firms and workers hurt by exchange rate swings to demand tariffs, quotas, and other forms of import protection from their governments. It is often believed that an announcement of a fixed exchange rate may also help governments resist political pressures for overly expansionary macroeconomic policies.[13]

Thus, countries may operate under a **fixed exchange rate system**, which applies either to a **gold standard**, where central banks agree to buy or sell gold to keep the exchange rates at a certain level, or to a **managed float**, where central banks buy and sell foreign currencies in the foreign exchange market to maintain or stabilize the exchange rate. In either of these cases, payments imbalances can arise in the balance of payments accounts because there is disequilibrium in the foreign exchange markets. External forces are attempting to alter exchange rates through shifts in the demand for and supply of currencies, while policy makers are attempting to hold the exchange rates constant.

The **International Monetary Fund (IMF)** and the **World Bank**, the two major international organizations focusing on international financial and development issues, were created at the Bretton Woods conference in 1944. The countries participating in the conference also established a system of fixed exchange rates under which their currencies were tied to the U.S. dollar, which was directly convertible to gold at a price of $35 per ounce. This system, which lasted until 1971, when the United States abandoned the gold standard, then led to a system of more flexible exchange rates, in which countries let the value of their currencies float in given ranges.

As of 1995, only a small number of countries had maintained or pegged a tightly fixed exchange rate against any currency for five years or more. The fixed rate countries were primarily small tourism economies, oil sheikdoms, and politically dependent principalities. These countries typically subordinated their monetary policies to, rather than coordinating them with, the monetary policies of their partner countries. Data from 1991 to 1999 for the IMF's member countries indicate that the percentage of countries with "hard pegs" increased from 16 to 24 percent and those with floating currencies increased from 23 to 42 percent, while those with intermediate or "soft pegs" decreased from 62 to 34 percent. Hard pegs include currency boards, which are formal mechanisms for fixing exchange rates, and situations where countries are part of a currency union or have formally adopted the currency of another country. Soft pegs include situations where the exchange rate is allowed to shift gradually over time or within a rate band, which may also shift over time.[14]

Fixed exchange rate system

A system in which the central banks of various countries intervene in the foreign exchange market to maintain or stabilize currency exchange rates.

Gold standard

A fixed rate system in which central banks agree to buy and sell gold to keep exchange rates at a given level.

Managed float

A fixed rate system in which central banks buy and sell foreign currency to maintain exchange rates at a given level.

International Monetary Fund (IMF)

An international financial organization created at the Bretton Woods conference in 1944 that helps coordinate international financial flows and can arrange short-term loans between countries.

World Bank

An international financial organization created at the Bretton Woods conference in 1944 that helps developing countries obtain low-interest loans.

---

[13] Maurice Obstfeld and Kenneth Rogoff, "The Mirage of Fixed Exchange Rates," *Journal of Economic Perspectives* 9 (Fall 1995): 73–96; Guillermo A. Calvo and Frederic S. Mishkin, *The Mirage of Exchange Rate Regimes for Emerging Market Countries*, NBER Working Paper Series, no. 9808 (Cambridge, Mass.: National Bureau of Economic Research, June 2003); Moosa, *Exchange Rate Regimes*, 63–89.

[14] Obstfeld and Rogoff, "The Mirage of Fixed Exchange Rates"; Stanley Fischer, "Distinguished Lecture on Economics in Government—Exchange Rate Regimes: Is the Bipolar View Correct?" *Journal of Economic Perspectives* 15 (Spring 2001): 3–24. There are numerous definitional problems involved with these classifications. Based on data from the 2003 IMF *Annual Report on Exchange Arrangements and Exchange Restrictions*, Moosa reports that 48 percent of countries have fixed exchange rates, 44 percent have flexible exchange rates, and 8 percent have intermediate regimes. However, these classifications are based on what countries report to the IMF, which may not be what they actually do. Many developing countries that report floating rates may actually have rather rigid rates. See Moosa, *Exchange Rate Regimes*, 21–23. For an analysis of countries that have moved to more flexible systems, see Inci Otker-Robe and David Vavra, and a team of economists, *Moving to Greater Exchange Rate Flexibility: Operational Aspects Based on Lessons from Detailed Country Experiences* (Washington, DC: International Monetary Fund, 2007).

Flexible Exchange Rate System

We illustrate the differences between flexible and fixed exchange rate systems by building on the simplified two-country example of the United States and Japan developed in Figure 15.2, Equation 15.11, and Table 15.12. Assume for simplicity that U.S. decision makers use expansionary fiscal and monetary policies to raise domestic income *while maintaining prices and interest rates at their current levels.*[15] Also assume that no policy action is taken in Japan in response to this U.S. action (everything else is held constant). Thus, we are assuming that interest rates continue to be equal between the two countries, so that there are no capital flows between them. However, with increased income, U.S. residents will increase their demand not only for domestically produced goods and services (consumption expenditures), but also for foreign goods and services (import spending). This larger U.S. income increases the demand for U.S. imports *at every exchange rate.* At each exchange rate (R), U.S. residents want to supply a larger amount of dollars to exchange for yen to purchase these imports.

In Figure 15.3, this change in behavior is shown as a rightward shift of supply curve S_0 to supply curve S_1. As noted above, the supply curve for dollars in the foreign exchange market is drawn assuming a given level of U.S. income. We are illustrating an increase in U.S. income from a domestic economic policy change, which causes the demand for imports to increase and results in a rightward shift in the supply curve for dollars, given the above assumption of a constant interest rate and prices. The same result would occur with changes in any of the other variables affecting real spending (as discussed in Chapter 14).

In Figure 15.2, at the original exchange rate, $R = 1$, the demand for dollars equals the supply of dollars because desired exports equal desired imports. In Figure 15.3, assume the demand for imports increases to $150 due to increased U.S. income. This causes a balance of payments deficit in the United States because imports equal $150, while exports equal $100, or $BP = (X - M) = (\$100 - \$150) = -\$50$. In the dollar or foreign exchange market, the U.S. balance of payments deficit is represented by the distance AB, an excess supply of dollars ($Q^s{}_\$ = 150 > 100 = Q^d{}_\$$). More dollars are supplied to the market at every exchange rate to purchase these imports, resulting in a shift of the supply curve for dollars. The demand curve for dollars does not shift because we assume that Japanese income has not changed.

FIGURE 15.3

Foreign Exchange Market, Increase in U.S. Income

An increase in U.S. income, all else held constant, results in an increased supply of dollars in the foreign exchange market. Under a flexible exchange rate system, this increased supply of dollars results in a lower exchange rate or a depreciation of the dollar.

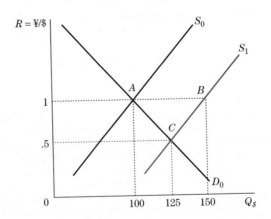

---

[15] Using the aggregate macro model, these changes are represented by an increase in aggregate demand from the fiscal policy change, which results in a higher level of equilibrium income and interest rate combined with an increase in the money supply by the Federal Reserve so that the final interest rate remains unchanged. The scenario also assumes that the *SAS* curve is horizontal so that the price level does not change.

Under a flexible exchange rate system, this disequilibrium situation means that market pressures will force the exchange rate down (the dollar will depreciate or be worth less). At $R = 1$, the quantity supplied of dollars is greater than the quantity demanded of dollars. As R falls, the effect on U.S. exports is shown as a movement along the D_0 curve from point A to C. As the translated price of U.S. goods decreases, Japanese residents increase the quantity of dollars demanded to purchase the now-cheaper exports. Also, as R falls, the effect on U.S. imports is shown as a movement along the new supply curve, S_1, from point B to C. As R falls, the translated price of Japanese goods increases, thereby cutting off some of the increase in quantity of dollars supplied resulting from the increase in U.S. income. The final equilibrium is at point C in the foreign exchange market at a lower exchange rate, $R = 0.5$. Because this is an equilibrium exchange rate, the quantity of dollars demanded again equals the quantity supplied. This result also means that the balance of payments accounts are in equilibrium, with imports and exports equal at $125. Thus, flexible exchange rates automatically eliminate a balance of payments disequilibrium. These results are summarized in Equation 15.12 and Table 15.13.

15.12 $BP = (X - M) + K = (125 - 125) + 0 = 0$

Fixed Exchange Rate System

Under a fixed exchange rate system, the central banks of different countries intervene in foreign exchange markets to maintain exchange rates between the countries at a given level or within a predetermined range. To do so, they must use their **reserve assets**, which include gold certificates, special drawing rights, the reserve position in the IMF, and holdings of foreign currencies. Changes in this account are labeled as "Changes in Official Reserve Assets" in the international transactions and balance of payments accounts. The function of this account is to accommodate any payments imbalances that arise from autonomous transactions of the household, business, and government sectors of the economy, excluding the actions of central banks. Changes in reserve assets are a policy tool used to equate the quantity supplied and quantity demanded of dollars and other currencies, so as to maintain or influence the exchange rate between these currencies.[16]

Reserve assets
Assets, including foreign currencies and gold certificates, that central banks use to maintain exchange rates between countries at a given level or in a predetermined range.

To illustrate a fixed exchange rate system, we use the example from the previous section on flexible exchange rates. Assume that U.S. policy makers use domestic expansionary policies under the same conditions as in the previous example (U.S. income increases with no change in prices or interest rates and no Japanese policy response). This leads, as before, to a U.S. balance of payments deficit of $50 (i.e., an excess supply of dollars because imports exceed exports by $50, as illustrated by the distance AB in Figure 15.3). Now assume that the central banks of these countries, the Federal Reserve and the Bank of Japan, want to maintain the

TABLE 15.13 U.S. International Transactions, Increase in U.S. Income

POINT A		POINTS A–B		POINT C	
M 100	X 100	M 150	X 100	M 125	X 125
k_o 0	k_i 0	k_o 0	k_i 0	k_o 0	k_i 0
100	100	150	100	125	125

---

[16] Reserve assets are included in the financial account numbers in Table 15.4. Because they are so small compared to the other flows, they essentially round to zero.

FIGURE 15.4

Federal Reserve Intervention

To maintain a fixed exchange rate in response to an increased supply of dollars, the Federal Reserve must increase the demand for dollars by selling its reserve assets for dollars.

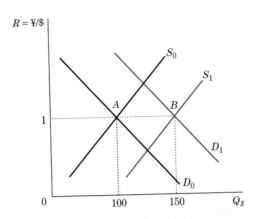

exchange rate at $R = 1$ for domestic policy reasons. They must intervene in the foreign exchange market to counter the market forces that are exerting downward pressure on the exchange rate, as shown in Figure 15.3. Distance AB in Figure 15.3 represents a disequilibrium situation. To maintain the exchange rate at $R = 1$, the Federal Reserve must change this to an equilibrium situation.

Because the distance AB in Figure 15.3 represents an excess supply of dollars or a balance of payments deficit, with expense transactions (imports) exceeding receipts transactions (exports), the Federal Reserve needs to generate receipts (income) of $50 in order to restore equilibrium. To do so, it *sells* reserve assets (RA), gold or yen (foreign currency), for dollars. At every exchange rate, the Federal Reserve increases the demand for dollars by supplying yen from its reserve assets to the foreign exchange market. This action is shown in Figure 15.4, as the original D_0 curve shifts to the right to intersect point B at $R = 1$ and $Q_\$ = 150$. Note that the shift from S_0 to S_1 resulted from the increase in U.S. income, an autonomous increase from the perspective of the Federal Reserve (even though it resulted from domestic U.S. economic policy). The shift from D_0 to D_1 results from the sale of reserve assets by the Federal Reserve, an accommodating increase resulting from a direct policy action by the Federal Reserve.[17]

Balance of payments equilibrium is restored through this policy action, as illustrated in Equation 15.13 and Table 15.14.

$$15.13 \quad BP = (X - M) + K + RA = (100 - 150) + 0 + 50 = 0$$

In the case of a fixed exchange rate system, the balance of payments equilibrium is restored not from a change in the exchange rate, but from a policy

TABLE 15.14 U.S. International Transactions, Federal Reserve Intervention

POINT A		POINTS A–B		POINT B	
M 100	X 100	M 150	X 100	M 150	X 100
k_o 0	k_i 0	k_o 0	k_i 0	k_o 0	k_i 0
					RA 50
100	100	150	100	150	150

---

[17] This change might also result because the Bank of Japan does not want the yen to appreciate (as the dollar depreciates), so it buys dollars on the foreign exchange market.

action by the central bank. The selling of reserve assets by the Federal Reserve creates an increased demand for dollars, which maintains the exchange rate at $R = 1$ in Figure 15.4, instead of allowing it to fall to $R = 0.5$, as shown in Figure 15.3. Both Equation 15.13 and Table 15.14 show the effect of the change in reserve assets in restoring balance of payments equilibrium. The selling of reserve assets by the central bank to buy dollars is an income- or receipts-generating transaction and is, therefore, included on the right-hand side of the revenue account in Table 15.14.

The Effect on the Money Supply

With a fixed exchange rate system, such as a gold standard, a central bank's intervention in the foreign exchange market will have certain effects on the country's domestic money supply. If the United States and Japan are on a gold standard (assume, for simplicity, $1 = ¥1 = 1$ oz. gold), gold is the central banks' reserve asset that backs bank reserves, which, in turn, back the money stock. With the U.S. balance of payments deficit, the Federal Reserve will buy back the excess supply of dollars from the Bank of Japan with gold. Therefore, gold flows out of the United States to Japan. As the United States is losing gold, the domestic money supply will decrease based on the money multiplier. The reverse process occurs in Japan (that is, the money stock increases with the inflow of gold). The important point is that a continual balance of payments deficit in any country can be sustained only as long as the country's gold reserves hold out. This is one of the reasons that countries around the world eventually abandoned the gold standard.

In terms of a managed float, where the Federal Reserve uses holdings of foreign currencies to influence the exchange rate, the same effect on the money stock *may* occur. The previous conclusion will also hold: With a fixed exchange rate, continual balance of payments deficits can be sustained only as long as a country's foreign currency reserves hold out. Although a central bank's reserve assets include both gold and foreign currencies, in the modern banking system the money stock is no longer backed by gold. Government securities are the main source of bank reserve funds.

Sterilization

In the previous section, we noted that a country's money stock *may* decrease as a result of a balance of payments deficit. This will not be the case if the Federal Reserve sterilizes the effects of the balance of payments deficit. The previous example discussed a nonsterilized intervention, where the Federal Reserve allowed the country's balance of payments position to affect the domestic money stock. This may not be desirable, given domestic economic goals. Under a **sterilized intervention**, the Federal Reserve takes action to offset the balance of payments deficit's (or surplus's) effect on the domestic money stock through open market operations. In the case of a loss of reserves due to foreign exchange market operations, which would decrease the domestic money supply, the Federal Reserve can buy securities in the open market to increase the domestic money supply. This is the same type of operation it would follow if it wanted to increase the money supply for purely domestic reasons. Sterilized interventions typically result in only modest, if any, effects on exchange rates, given that relative money supplies are not changed with these procedures.[18]

Sterilized intervention
Actions taken by a country's central bank to prevent balance of payments policies from influencing the country's domestic money supply.

---

[18] Obstfeld and Rogoff, "The Mirage of Fixed Exchange Rates." For details of sterilization procedures, see Board of Governors of the Federal Reserve System, *The Federal Reserve System Purposes & Functions* (Washington, DC: Board of Governors, 2005).

Policy Examples of International Economic Issues

We now discuss several policy examples that illustrate the use of fiscal, monetary, and balance of payments policies with flexible and fixed exchange rate systems. We focus on

1. The U.S. economy from 1995 to 2000 and from 2007 to 2008
2. Policies regarding the euro from 1999 to 2003 and from 2007 to 2008
3. The impact of currency devaluations and the collapse of the economies of Southeast Asian countries in 1997
4. The debate over the weak Chinese yuan from 2003 to the present

Unlike in our previous discussion of fixed and flexible exchange rates in the simplified U.S.–Japan model, we will focus on all the variables influencing the demand for and supply of various currencies including political factors and speculation. We also discuss the impact of these international macro changes on managerial strategies.

The U.S. Economy, 1995–2000

From 1995 to 2000, the U.S. economy experienced relatively high GDP growth with low inflation and decreasing unemployment. This period has been called the "Goldilocks economy" and the "fabulous decade" because real GDP growth rates averaged 4.0 percent over the period, productivity increases were twice as high as in the 1973–90 period, unemployment declined to 4.1 percent in 2000, and inflation averaged 2.9 percent over the period.[19] Much of this growth was driven by the wealth effect of the stock market on consumption spending and by productivity increases, which stimulated business investment spending. During the 1995–97 period, the Fed kept the targeted federal funds rate at approximately 5.5 percent, given that the productivity increases were allowing the economy to grow without increasing inflationary pressures. The Fed actually lowered the targeted rate in 1998 to deal with the fallout from the Southeast Asian financial crisis (discussed below) and did not begin raising rates to restrain the economy until 1999.

The United States essentially followed a flexible exchange rate policy during this period. We model this situation in the foreign exchange market in Figure 15.5. We illustrate the foreign exchange market with the dollar versus the euro so that we can discuss the euro in more detail in the next section.

FIGURE 15.5
Exchange Rates and Aggregate Expenditure: The U.S. Economy, 1995–2000
Downward pressure on the value of the dollar from increased imports is represented by the shift of the supply curve from S_0 to S_1. This trend was more than offset by the increased capital inflows shifting the demand curve from D_0 to D_1.

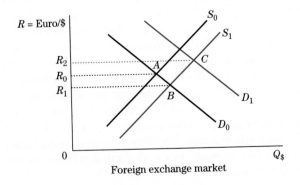

Foreign exchange market

---

[19] Alan S. Blinder and Janet L. Yellen, *The Fabulous Decade: Macroeconomic Lessons from the 1990s* (New York: Century Foundation Press, 2001), v–vi.

In Figure 15.5, the initial equilibrium in the foreign exchange market is at point A with exchange rate R_0. The increase in consumption and investment spending from 1995 to 2000 results in a higher equilibrium level of real income and a higher interest rate.[20] If we assume that the U.S. interest rate was originally equal to that in the rest of the world, the U.S. interest rate is now higher than that of other countries. The increase in real income has two effects in the foreign exchange market.[21] As we discussed in our earlier example (Figure 15.3), an increase in U.S. income results in an increase in import spending. This means that U.S. residents are supplying more dollars to the foreign exchange market, placing downward pressure on the exchange rate. This change is modeled as a shift of the supply curve from S_0 to S_1 in Figure 15.5 with a decrease in the exchange rate to R_1 (point B). However, the new higher interest rate in the U.S. now causes capital inflows as investors search for the highest returns, resulting in an increase in the demand for U.S. dollars, which drives up the exchange rate.

In the 1995–2000 period, the net effect of these two forces in the U.S. economy was an increase in the exchange rate or a "strong dollar," represented by R_2 in Figure 15.5 (point C). This increase in R in turn causes imports to increase and exports to decrease, restraining the growth in income. Thus, the effect of the strong dollar at this time was to help hold back the economy in the face of the strong private-sector spending increases. This exchange rate effect actually made the job of the Fed easier because it was unnecessary for the Fed to increase the targeted federal funds rate as quickly to restrain the economy. Many U.S. policy makers, including Secretary of the Treasury Lawrence Summers, announced their support for a strong dollar policy during this period.[22] This example shows the feedback effects of the exchange rate on real spending in the economy.

Although the example presented here focused on increased spending from the private sector, the same outcome would occur if the spending increase resulted from expansionary fiscal policy. Expansionary fiscal policy also causes an increase in real income and the interest rate. Suppose that the domestic interest rate is greater than that in the rest of the world and that capital is mobile, so there are large flows. This interest rate change increases capital inflows, which pushes up the exchange rate. A higher exchange rate (increased imports, decreased exports) then partially offsets the expansionary fiscal policy. If capital is less sensitive to interest rate changes and, therefore, less mobile, the effect of expansionary fiscal policy is felt through the increased income, which increases import spending. This change puts downward pressure on the exchange rate, which causes a further increase in income.

The U.S. Economy, 2007–2008

The macroeconomic events in the U.S. economy in 2007 and 2008 and their impact in the international sector were almost the exact opposite of what we just described for the period 1995 to 2000. As we have noted in all of the macro chapters in the text, the collapse of the housing market and the credit crisis in the financial markets that began in 2007 caused consumers and businesses to pull back on their

---

[20] Remember from our discussion in Chapters 13 and 14 that, in the absence of a change in monetary policy, an increase in spending generates a higher level of income, which results in a higher interest rate due to the increased demand for money to finance the transactions at the higher level of income.

[21] Using r_{Europe} and Y_{Europe} to represent the interest rate and income level in Europe, we can restate Equations 15.9 and 15.10 for the demand for and supply of dollars:

$$Q^d{}_\$ = f(R, Y_{\text{Europe}}, r_{\text{US}} > r_{\text{Europe}}) \text{ and } Q^s{}_\$ = f(R, Y_{\text{US}}, r_{\text{US}} < r_{\text{Europe}})$$
$$\quad\;\; (-)\;\; (+) \qquad (+) \qquad\qquad\quad (+)\;\; (+) \qquad (+)$$

[22] Joseph Kahn and Edmund L. Andrews, "Major Central Banks Step In to Shore Up the Ailing Euro," *New York Times*, September 22, 2000.

spending. This decrease in autonomous expenditure resulted in a lower level of real income and a lower interest rate, given the decreased demand for money at the lower level of income.[23]

The lower level of real income had two effects on the currency exchange rate. With lower income, there were fewer imports, which decreased the quantity of dollars supplied to the foreign exchange market, shifting the supply curve to the left and causing the exchange rate, R, to rise. If the original U.S. interest rate were equal to that in the rest of the world, the new lower interest rate resulted in increased capital outflows to the rest of the world in search of higher returns. This caused an increase in the supply of dollars to the foreign exchange market to finance these outflows, which would lower the exchange rate. In addition, as we have noted, the Federal Reserve began increasing the money supply in September 2007 to lower interest rates and achieve a targeted federal funds rate of 2.00 percent in April 2008. The domestic goal was to stimulate the economy, but the international effect of the lower interest rates was to generate further capital outflows, which also put downward pressure on the currency exchange rate. Throughout much of 2007, foreign economies had remained strong, which generated more U.S. exports, increased the demand for dollars in the foreign exchange market, and put upward pressure on the exchange rate. Although these were countervailing impacts on the exchange rate, the overall effect was that the exchange rate decreased and the dollar depreciated. The dollar had been declining gradually since 2003, but the decline became more pronounced in 2007 and 2008.

It was this decline that led to the discussion in the opening article of this chapter of the possibility that the Federal Reserve might intervene in the foreign exchange market to support the value of the dollar. As the article noted, this change would put foreign exchange policy at odds with domestic monetary policy and would require coordination with other central banks. It could also be offset by speculators, such as the manager of a New York hedge fund in the article who stated that "we would use it [the currency intervention] as a way to sell more dollars." Thus, investors who had lost confidence in the strength of the U.S. economy and the value of the dollar were placing further downward pressure on the value of the currency.

The overall effect of the lower value of the dollar was to decrease U.S. imports and increase U.S. exports. This development had a positive effect on the U.S. trade deficit and the balance of payments. U.S. exports increased at about an 11 percent annual rate in 2007, while the growth in imports decreased to about 1.5 percent. These changes in exports and imports combined with somewhat higher net investment income made the current account deficit decline on an annual basis in 2007 for the first time since 2001.[24] Although there is always concern that a lower value of the dollar may increase inflation due to higher import prices, this effect had become less pronounced due to the fact that foreign exporters often lower their prices to keep them constant after the currency effect to maintain U.S. market share. Although a 10 percent decline in the value of the dollar might be expected to increase import prices by 10 percent, the actual pass-through is 25 percent or less. This lower pass-through rate, which declined from a high of 50 percent in the mid-1970s to the 1990s, means that the Federal Reserve can stimulate the U.S. economy through lower interest rates with less concern about inflation from higher import prices. How a depreciated dollar affects imports always depends on the specific product. Prices of luxury products often stay relatively constant as manufacturers accept lower profits, while airlines, which operate on smaller margins, are more

---

[23] This is the exact opposite of the process we described in footnote 20.

[24] Board of Governors of the Federal Reserve System, *Monetary Policy Report to the Congress*, February 27, 2008.

likely to raise prices. Price increases of raw materials, such as steel and other commodities, tend to be passed through at a 90 percent rate or more because they are priced in global markets.[25]

Japan was particularly affected by the "weak" dollar and the resulting "strong" yen during this period, given that more than half of its 2.1 percent growth in 2007 was derived from exports. Expectations for a strong recovery from its long economic decline decreased, and investors' lack of confidence in the Japanese economy caused its stock market to decline 19 percent from January to March 2008.[26]

Numerous firms were affected by the continuing decline of the dollar. Toyota Motor Corp. announced that the lower value of the dollar had caused its group operating profit to decline by 20 billion yen ($194 million) in the fourth quarter of 2007. Larger losses were expected for the first quarter of 2008. Sony admitted in early 2008 that it would not reach its target of a 5 percent operating profit margin due to the "weak" dollar and the slowing U.S. economy. Exporters in other parts of Asia were also vulnerable to these changes.[27]

By fall 2008, most European countries had fallen into recession. The combined economies of the fifteen countries using the euro shrank 0.2 percent in the third quarter for a second straight quarterly decline. The International Monetary Fund (IMF) estimated that global economic growth would increase just 2.2 percent in 2009, a rate the IMF traditionally considered to be a recession. Much of the decline resulted from the credit crisis that began in the United States. The Fed's lowering of its target interest rate to almost zero in December 2008 put more downward pressure on the value of the dollar as investors received little return for investments denominated in dollars. This change benefited the United States economy by making exports cheaper, but caused concern in both Japan and Germany regarding their recessions.[28]

Effects of the Euro in the Macroeconomic Environment

There has been major policy discussion regarding the value of the euro, the common European currency, since its introduction by the European Union on January 1, 1999. Debates about the euro during this initial period focused on its value relative to other currencies, particularly the U.S. dollar; trade imbalances and capital flows between the United States and Europe; the interaction between the value of the euro and other economic events, such as increasing oil prices; and political and psychological factors related to the value of the euro. We first discuss the implications of these issues for different national economies using the balance of payments and foreign exchange models developed in this chapter. We then examine how managers and firms respond to these international macroeconomic issues in terms of their competitive strategies and profitability.

Most discussions of the euro take the perspective of Europe as the domestic economy and define the exchange rate, R, as dollars per euro. In this chapter, we have used the United States as the domestic economy and defined the exchange

[25] Sudeep Reddy, "The Weak Dollar Isn't the Inflation Driver It Once Was," *Wall Street Journal*, November 19, 2007.

[26] Yuka Hayashi and JoAnna Slater, "Dollar's Swift Decline Threatens Europe, Japan," *Wall Street Journal*, March 14, 2008.

[27] Yuka Hayashi and Laura Santini, "Japan Inc. Pays Price for Weak Dollar; Reliance on Exports Crimps Profit Growth and the Nikkei Index," *Wall Street Journal*, March 5, 2008; Mariko Sanchanta, "Weak Dollar Forces Sony into Climbdown on Profit Margin," *Financial Times*, February 1, 2008.

[28] Joellen Perry, Alistair MacDonald, and Sudeep Reddy, "Global Push to Beat Economic Downturn," *Wall Street Journal*, November 7, 2008; David Gauthier-Villars and Michael M. Phillips, "Europe Tips into Recession," *Wall Street Journal*, November 15, 2008; Joanna Slater, "With Rates Near 0%, Dollar Is Dumped," *Wall Street Journal*, December 17, 2008; Joanna Slater, "Weaker Dollar Worries Japan, Germany," *Wall Street Journal*, December 29, 2008.

FIGURE 15.6

Euro Market

The euro market is usually analyzed from the European perspective. The exchange rate, defined as dollars per euro, is determined by the demand for and supply of euros. Downward pressure on the value of the euro is shown by the shift of the supply curve from S_0 to S_1. The intervention to hold up the value of the euro is shown by the shift of the demand curve from D_0 to D_1.

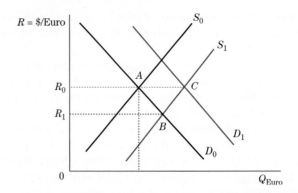

rate as units of foreign currency per dollar. We can easily modify Equations 15.9 and 15.10 and Figure 15.2 to the European perspective, as shown in Equations 15.14 and 15.15 and Figure 15.6. The exchange rate, R, in this discussion is now units of foreign currency per unit of domestic currency, or dollars per euro. Thus, the foreign exchange model in this chapter can be applied to any economy, provided the perspective taken in the demand and supply equations and graphs is that of the domestic economy and currency.

$$15.14 \quad Q^d_{Euro} = f(R, Y_{US}, r_{Europe} > r_{US})$$
$$\qquad\qquad\quad (-)\ (+)\qquad\quad (+)$$

$$15.15 \quad Q^s_{Euro} = f(R, Y_{Europe}, r_{Europe} < r_{US})$$
$$\qquad\qquad\quad (+)\ \ (+)\qquad\quad (+)$$

Equations 15.14 and 15.15 show the factors affecting the demand for and supply of euros: the exchange rate, income in the United States and Europe, and interest rate differentials. Figure 15.6 shows an initial equilibrium in the euro foreign exchange market at point A. The policy concern in Europe had been the long decline in the value of the euro after it was introduced on January 1, 1999.

The major factor causing this decline was the interest rate differential between the United States and Europe.[29] The higher U.S. interest rates and the attractive investment opportunities from the booming stock market in the late 1990s resulted in huge capital outflows from Europe to the United States. As shown in Equation 15.15 and Figure 15.6, higher interest rates and better investment opportunities in the United States caused the supply curve for euros to shift to the right from S_0 to S_1 as investors supplied euros to the foreign exchange market in exchange for dollars for U.S. financial capital transactions. This resulted in downward pressure on the value of the euro in dollar terms (exchange rate R_1 at point B). The fact that the U.S. economy was growing faster than the European economies created more U.S. investment opportunities for European investors and contributed to the capital flows from Europe to the United States. This inflow of foreign financial investment to the United States is consistent with the discussion of the balance of trade deficit and equilibrium in the open economy, as noted in Equation 15.6 in this chapter. The continuing U.S. balance of trade deficit must be financed by capital inflows from abroad.[30]

---

[29] This discussion is based on the following sources: Michael R. Sesit and G. Thomas Sims, "Sagging Euro Puts Upward Pressure on Inflation by Fueling Price Raises," *Wall Street Journal*, October 26, 2000; David Wessel, "Foreign Purchasing of U.S. Securities Fell in Quarter, but Remains Healthy," *Wall Street Journal*, September 19, 2000; Michael M. Phillips and G. Thomas Sims, "U.S. Joins Europe in Intervention to Help Support Faltering Euro," *Wall Street Journal*, September 25, 2000; and Jacob M. Schlesinger and Craig Karmin, "No Safe Haven: Dollar's Slide Reflects Wariness About U.S.," *Wall Street Journal*, June 3, 2002.

[30] Remember that the United States had a current account deficit and a financial account surplus, while the European countries had a current account surplus and a financial account deficit.

The European Central Bank (ECB) attempted to intervene in the foreign exchange markets in order to bolster the value of the euro. The lower value of the euro put upward pressure on inflation in Europe by increasing the price of imported goods, particularly oil. Thus, there was an attempt to maintain a fixed or at least a higher exchange rate with the U.S. dollar, with all of the associated problems that we discussed earlier. In mid-September 2000, the ECB began selling foreign currencies and buying euros. The United States joined Europe in an intervention to increase the value of the euro in late September 2000. This intervention occurred at the initiative of the ECB, even though the United States had been pursuing a "strong-dollar" policy, which had benefited that country by keeping imports cheap and attracting financial inflows to offset the trade deficit, as discussed previously. The intervention was undertaken quickly and secretly in order to have maximum effectiveness in the foreign exchange markets. We represent this intervention in Figure 15.6 by the shift of the demand curve from D_0 to D_1, with a new equilibrium at point C.

By 2002, changes in the U.S. economy had caused the dollar to decrease in value against the euro and other currencies. Given the recession and the corporate scandals in the United States, foreign investors began searching for investment opportunities elsewhere. With a decreased demand for investment in the United States, foreign investors demanded fewer dollars, causing the value of the dollar to decrease against the euro and the yen. As noted previously, given the problems in U.S. housing and financial markets, the dollar declined sharply against the euro, the yen, and the trade-weighted currency index in 2007 and 2008.

Euro Macro Environment Effects on Managerial Decisions

The Europeans claimed that the Fed in the United States participated in the September 2000 currency intervention because it was concerned about the impact of the lower value of the euro on U.S. business profits and the U.S. stock market. Various U.S. companies had been making public statements about the impact of the euro on their performance.[31]

Multinational companies can use currency gains in one part of the world to offset losses elsewhere. They have hedging options in the financial markets and can also develop other competitive strategies. For example, one of Gillette's razor blade factories in China began searching for raw materials in Europe, where the weak euro made their prices look cheaper.[32] If a U.S. corporation believes that the dollar will continue to appreciate when it changes foreign earnings back into dollars, it will typically purchase a futures contract or hedge, which allows it to lock into an exchange rate beforehand so that the company will not lose profits from a devalued currency.[33]

Small firms typically have more difficulty handling currency value changes than large firms. A 10 percent increase in price in euro terms as the currency depreciated resulted in the loss of a $2 million boat order in June 2000 by Hatteras Yachts, Inc., in North Carolina. For this company, European sales made up 8 percent of its $150 million total and thus had a major impact on the company.[34]

In the United States, the higher value of the dollar forced many companies to find new production methods and other means to cut costs as they encountered both an appreciating currency, which limited exports, and the recession of 2001 and 2002,

---

[31] Christopher Cooper, "Euro's Continued Slide Plagues Many Multinational Companies," *Wall Street Journal*, May 30, 2000.

[32] Ibid.

[33] Tyler Lifton and John Parry, "U.S. Firms Can Reap Rewards of Weak Dollar with Hedging," *Wall Street Journal*, November 20, 2002.

[34] Christopher Cooper, "Euro's Drop Is Hardest for the Smallest," *Wall Street Journal*, October 2, 2000.

which reduced aggregate demand in the United States.[35] Automatic Feed Company of Napoleon, Ohio, a company producing machinery used in automobile plants, undertook the most extensive product redesign in the company's 52-year history. Other companies developed much more extensive marketing efforts to find new customers and give them better service.

The appreciation of the euro and the depreciation of the dollar that occurred in 2002 created an opposite set of results. U.S. manufacturers who sold in Europe benefited from the dollar's decline. European firms with the largest sales in North America, such as those selling automobiles and pharmaceuticals, worried about their ability to compete.[36]

The steep decline of the dollar against the euro in late 2007 and early 2008 also caused concern among European policy makers, politicians, and businesses. A survey of purchasing managers in countries using the euro in February 2008 found that the growth in new export orders rose at the smallest rate in 33 months. Although Volkswagen had been attempting to challenge Toyota as the world's dominant mass-market automobile producer, the depreciation of the dollar was likely to result in losses in the U.S. market.[37]

Southeast Asia: An Attempt to Maintain Fixed Exchange Rates

Although the Southeast Asian financial crisis of 1997 resulted from a number of factors, it presents a vivid illustration of the difficulty, or impossibility, of maintaining fixed exchange rates in the face of speculation and other downward pressures on the value of a country's currency in the foreign exchange market. We discuss these issues with reference to Thailand, where the 1997 crisis began when the baht, the Thai currency, came under speculative attack and the markets lost confidence in the economy.[38] Similar developments then occurred in Korea, Indonesia, and Malaysia. The resulting recession in these crisis countries spread to Hong Kong, Singapore, the Philippines, and Taiwan. By 1998, there was evidence of a worldwide growth slowdown, with the IMF estimating world growth at only 2 percent compared with 4.3 percent anticipated one year earlier. As noted above, the Federal Reserve in the United States responded by lowering the federal funds rate target to help prevent both a global and a domestic crisis. We also discussed the effect of these macroeconomic changes in Southeast Asia on the copper industry in Chapters 2 and 14.

Thailand had experienced high growth rates throughout much of the 1990s, driven by strong increases in consumption and investment spending. However, there were a number of warning signals that developed before 1997. To maintain the high growth rates, there were public guarantees to many private investment

[35] Timothy Aeppel, "U.S. Dollar, Strong Despite the Recession, Tests the Ingenuity of U.S. Manufacturers," *Wall Street Journal*, January 22, 2002.
[36] Jon Hilsenrath, "Dollar's Drop Could Be Good, Bad, or Both for the U.S. Economy," *Wall Street Journal*, May 23, 2002; Michael R. Sesit, "Weak Greenback Pressures Earnings of European Firms," *Wall Street Journal*, January 23, 2003.
[37] Richard Milne and John Reed, "Weak Dollar Puts Brake on Volkswagen in US," *FT.com*, March 5, 2008; Yuka Hayashi and JoAnna Slater, "Dollar's Swift Decline Threatens Europe, Japan," *Wall Street Journal Europe*, March 14, 2008.
[38] This section is based on Morris Goldstein, *The Asian Financial Crisis: Causes, Cures, and Systemic Implications* (Washington, D.C.: Institute for International Economics, June 1998); Giancarlo Corsetti, Paolo Pesenti, and Nouriel Roubini, "What Caused the Asian Currency and Financial Crisis?" *Japan and the World Economy* 11 (1999): 305–373; IMF, *Recovery from the Asian Crisis and the Role of the IMF—An IMF Issues Brief* (Washington, D.C.: IMF, June 2000); and Nouriel Roubini and Brad Setser, *Bailouts or Bail-Ins? Responding to Financial Crises in Emerging Economies* (Washington, DC: Institute for International Economics, 2004).

projects through government control and subsidies. Given the climate of political favoritism, the markets came to believe that high returns on investment were "insured" against adverse changes in the economy. Investment expectations came to be based on unreal expectations about the growth of long-run output. A weak banking sector with lax supervision and weak regulation compounded this situation. There was much international lending to unsound financial institutions, such as finance and securities companies, particularly in real estate markets. Domestic banks borrowed from foreign banks in order to lend to domestic investors who were not necessarily creditworthy.

The Thai government also ran a large current account deficit, averaging 6 percent of GDP in each year over the 1990s. As discussed throughout this chapter, a current account deficit needs capital inflows to be sustained. The size of a current account deficit that can be sustained depends on both a country's willingness to pay and its creditors' willingness to loan. Although there were signs that the profitability of many of these investments was low, lending continued over much of the period.

The nominal exchange rate of the Thai baht was fixed at 25.2 to 25.6 to the U.S. dollar during the period 1990–97, largely to provide the stability necessary to encourage the external financing of domestic projects. However, the U.S. dollar appreciated, particularly after spring 1995, so that the real exchange rate of the baht also appreciated. This appreciation, which had a negative effect on exports and a positive influence on imports, resulted in slower growth in the Thai economy in 1995–96 and an increase in the current account deficit to 8.5 percent of GDP. Much of the foreign investment in Thailand was in volatile short-term debt rather than more stable long-term foreign direct investment.

In June 1997, Thai officials discovered that the stock of international reserves effectively available to support the currency was a tiny fraction of that officially stated. These reserves were insufficient to maintain the value of the baht and prop up the fragile banking and finance system. Speculators lost confidence and began to sell off the baht, resulting in a decrease in its value of 25 percent by the end of July, compared with the beginning of the year, and 34 percent by the end of August. The Thai government was forced to announce a managed float of the baht. The real estate bubble collapsed, bankrupting many finance companies who were further hurt by the depreciation of the baht because they had borrowed in foreign currency. Although the initial reaction of Thai authorities was not to contract the money supply and raise interest rates because they were concerned about the impact of high interest rates on the fragile banking and financial system, this policy was not sustainable. High interest rates to attract foreign investment and prevent further currency attacks and reform of the banking system were two key conditions for IMF assistance, which began in August 1997. These higher interest rates, combined with limited exports to a weak Japanese economy, forced Thailand into a recession. The competitive devaluations and recessions in the other Asian crisis countries then started to spread farther around the world, as noted above.

The changes in the Thai economy are modeled in Figure 15.7 where the targeted exchange rate for the baht is represented by R_0 at the initial equilibrium point A with baht demand and supply curves D_0 and S_0. The downward pressure on the value of the baht, first from the role of imports and the large current account deficit and then from the massive selling of baht by speculators in 1997, is represented by the shift of the supply curve from S_0 to S_1 and the decrease in the exchange rate to R_1 (point B). To maintain the fixed exchange rate, R_0, Thai officials first used their foreign exchange reserves to increase the demand for the baht from D_0 to D_1 (point C). This policy proved insufficient in the face of the speculation, and as a condition for IMF assistance, the central bank was forced to use contractionary monetary policy and raise interest rates in order to attract foreign investment. As noted above, this policy forced the country into recession.

FIGURE 15.7
Illustration of Thailand Financial Crisis
Downward pressure on the Thai baht is represented by the shift of the supply curve from S_0 to S_1. The effect of the intervention and the contractionary monetary policy is shown by the shift of the demand curve from D_0 to D_1.

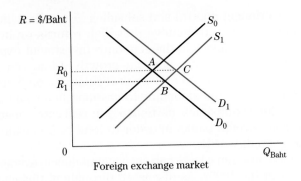

Foreign exchange market

Macro and Managerial Impact of the Chinese Yuan Since 2003

In 2003, the value of the Chinese yuan relative to the dollar became both an economic and a political issue in the United States.[39] The policy of the Chinese central bank was to keep the yuan at 8.28 to the dollar through the tightly controlled Shanghai foreign exchange market. Although there was a high level of foreign investment in China, which tended to push up the value of the yuan, the central bank sold enough yuan to keep it stable against the dollar. The value of the yuan stimulated Chinese exports and hurt imports into the country, thus impacting U.S. manufacturers. For example, the Iowa-based family-owned Shine Brothers Corporation blamed the low value of the yuan and Chinese subsidies for a deterioration in its scrap-metal recycling business. Although many U.S. manufacturers lobbied the Bush administration to pressure China to let its currency rise, these attempts were initially rebuffed by Chinese officials.

However, not all U.S. businesses were expected to gain from a stronger yuan. For example, the New Balance Athletic Shoe Company made 60 percent of the 40 million pairs of shoes it sold each year in China. An increase in the value of the yuan would increase the cost of labor and raw materials used in producing the shoes. Large companies, such as Wal-Mart Stores, Inc., and Johnson & Johnson, that invested, manufactured, and financed businesses in China and other foreign countries also expected to be adversely affected by a rise in the value of the yuan. Thus, the strategies of large multinational companies do not always coincide with the interests of workers in their home countries or with those of smaller companies that market only domestically.

Since this period, China's economy has continued to be stimulated by domestic and foreign investment and by exports and a trade surplus. China's trade surplus in 2007 was equivalent to about 8 percent of its GDP compared with 2 percent at the beginning of the decade. Although the Chinese government traditionally promoted exports, it announced in late 2007 that it would start encouraging imports as well by imposing taxes on exports of several types of products, such as refined metals, and speeding up the appreciation of the yuan. The currency rose 6.9 percent against the U.S. dollar in 2007 compared with a 3.5 percent gain in 2006. Still, the country was concerned with the slowdown in U.S. economic growth in 2007 and 2008. Manufacturers in Shengzhou, a city south of Shanghai that claims to make 40 percent of the world's neckties, noted

---

[39] Peter Wonacott and Leslie Chang, "As Fight Heats Up over China Trade, Business Is Split," *Wall Street Journal*, September 4, 2003; Peter Wonacott and Michael M. Phillips, "China Won't Let Currency Rise, Quickly Rebuffing U.S. Request," *Wall Street Journal*, September 3, 2003.

the declining U.S. orders and worried that the rising yuan would price them out of the market.[40]

Policy Effectiveness with Different Exchange Rate Regimes

The previous examples point out several important issues regarding the role of monetary and fiscal policies in the open economy. In an open economy with global capital markets and mobile capital, which flows to countries with the highest interest rates, a country has control over either its domestic money supply or the exchange rate, *but not both variables*.[41] To maintain a fixed exchange rate, a country loses control over its domestic money supply. For example, most central banks can find the foreign exchange reserves to fight a devaluation of their currency brought about by currency speculators if these banks are willing to make this task the primary goal of their monetary policy. Using foreign exchange reserves to bolster the value of a currency ("defending the dollar" is the term often used in the United States) results in decreases in the domestic money supply and higher interest rates, which then can have a negative impact on consumption, investment, and aggregate demand. To offset a speculative attack against a fixed exchange rate, a country has to make a credible commitment to this policy, regardless of the consequences to the economy. Speculators know that most governments are not willing to do this and that the central banks will typically abandon a fixed exchange rate, as was the case in Thailand.[42]

If the exchange rate is allowed to vary, monetary policy is effective in stimulating the economy. Expansionary monetary policy results in an increase in income that increases imports and lowers the exchange rate. This change has a further expansionary effect on real spending (a shift of the *AD* curve). Expansionary monetary policy also lowers domestic interest rates, which results in less capital inflow and a decreased demand for domestic currency. This change also lowers the exchange rate. Indeed, in comparing the fiscal and monetary policy examples, we can see that monetary policy is more effective than fiscal policy in stimulating the economy under a flexible exchange rate system, whereas monetary policy is not effective under a fixed exchange rate system. The effects of the different exchange rate regimes on achieving equilibrium in the open economy are summarized in Table 15.15.[43]

TABLE 15.15 Effects of Exchange Rate Systems

FLEXIBLE	FIXED	
The exchange rate automatically adjusts to eliminate *BP* disequilibrium ($Q_s = Q_d$).	The domestic money supply automatically adjusts to eliminate *BP* disequilibrium (through flows of gold or currency).	
	The Fed does nothing, allowing M_S to adjust.	The Fed sterilizes (through open market operations) and maintains *BP* disequilibrium.

---

[40] Andrew Batson, "World Economy Threatens China Growth," *Wall Street Journal*, January 12, 2008; JoAnna Slater, "Weak Dollar Feels New Stress," *Wall Street Journal*, March 11, 2008; Marcus Walker, James Hookway, John Lyons, and James T. Areddy, "U.S. Slump Takes Toll Across Globe," *Wall Street Journal*, April 3, 2008.

[41] This problem is often characterized as the "inconsistent trinity" or the "open-economy trilemma." A country cannot simultaneously maintain fixed exchange rates, have an open capital market, and use monetary policy to pursue domestic policy goals. See Maurice Obstfeld, "The Global Capital Market: Benefactor or Menace," *Journal of Economic Perspectives* 12 (Fall 1998): 9–30.

[42] Obstfeld and Rogoff, "The Mirage of Fixed Exchange Rates."

[43] For a detailed presentation of the arguments for and against both fixed and flexible exchange rates, see Moosa, *Exchange Rate Regimes*, 63–89.

Summary

In this chapter, we discussed international and open economy issues in more detail than in earlier chapters. We first developed a model of the open economy and defined balance of payments concepts. We then presented a model of the foreign exchange market to show the factors influencing currency exchange rates and the impact of fixed and flexible exchange rate policies.

At the end of the chapter, we discussed the impact of currency value changes on both national economies (in the United States, Europe, and Southeast Asia) and the competitive strategies of different types of firms. Managers need to understand the impact of international economic events on the level of economic activity in the domestic economy and in those countries where they have substantial markets. Managers must also be able to analyze the implications of these changes for the competitive strategies of their own firms and those of their major competitors. We discuss these issues further in the cases presented in Chapter 16.

Appendix 15A Specific and General Equations for the Balance of Payments

Specific Equation	**General Equation**
EXPORT EXPENDITURE	**EXPORT EXPENDITURE**
$X = x_0 + x_1 Y^* - x_2 R$	$X = f(Y, Y^*, R)$
	$\quad\;\;(0)(+)(-)$
where	*where*
$\quad X$ = export expenditure	$\quad X$ = export expenditure
$\quad x_0$ = other factors influencing export expenditure	$\quad Y$ = real domestic income
$\quad Y^*$ = real foreign GDP or income	$\quad Y^*$ = real foreign GDP or income
$\quad R$ = currency exchange rate (units of foreign currency per unit of domestic currency)	$\quad R$ = currency exchange rate (units of foreign currency per unit of domestic currency)
$\quad x_1, x_2$ = coefficients of the relevant variables	
IMPORT EXPENDITURE	**IMPORT EXPENDITURE**
$M = m_0 + m_1 Y + m_2 R$	$M = f(Y, R)$
	$\quad\;\;(+)(+)$
where	*where*
$\quad M$ = import expenditure	$\quad M$ = import expenditure
$\quad m_0$ = other factors affecting import expenditure	$\quad Y$ = real domestic income
$\quad Y$ = real domestic income	$\quad R$ = currency exchange rate (units of foreign currency per unit of domestic currency)
$\quad R$ = currency exchange rate (units of foreign currency per unit of domestic currency)	
$\quad m_1, m_2$ = coefficients of the relevant variables	
NET EXPORT EXPENDITURE	**NET EXPORT EXPENDITURE**
$F = X - M$	$F = f(Y, Y^*, R)$
$F = x_0 + x_1 Y^* - x_2 R - m_0 - m_1 Y - m_2 R$	$\quad\;\;(-)(+)(-)$
$F = F_0 + x_1 Y^* - m_1 Y - (x_2 + m_2)R$	*where*
where	$\quad F$ = net export expenditure
$\quad F$ = net export expenditure	$\quad Y$ = real domestic income
$\quad X$ = export expenditure	$\quad Y^*$ = real foreign GDP or income
$\quad M$ = import expenditure	$\quad R$ = currency exchange rate (units of foreign currency per unit of domestic currency)

Specific Equation	General Equation

x_0 = other factors influencing export expenditure
Y^* = real foreign GDP or income
R = currency exchange rate (units of foreign currency per unit of domestic currency)
x_1, x_2 = coefficients of the relevant variables
m_0 = other factors affecting import expenditure
Y = real domestic income
m_1, m_2 = coefficients of the relevant variables
$F_0 = x_0 - m_0$ = other factors influencing net export expenditure

NET CAPITAL FLOW

$K = k(r - r^*)$

where

K = net capital flow
k = interest sensitivity of capital flows
r = domestic interest rate
r^* = interest rate in the rest of the world

NET CAPITAL FLOW

$K = k_i - k_o$

$k_i = f(r > r^*)$
$(+)$

$k_o = f(r < r^*)$
$(+)$

where

K = net capital flow
k_i = capital inflows
k_o = capital outflows
r = domestic interest rate
r^* = interest rate in the rest of the world

Key Terms

balance of payments (BP) accounting system, p. 415

balance of trade, p. 412

capital inflow (k_i), p. 414

capital outflow (k_o), p. 414

currency appreciation, p. 411

currency depreciation, p. 411

currency exchange rate, p. 410

current account, p. 415

financial account, p. 416

fixed exchange rate system, p. 423

flexible exchange rate system, p. 422

gold standard, p. 423

International Monetary Fund (IMF), p. 423

managed float, p. 423

net capital flow ($K_N = k_i - k_o$), p. 414

net investment income, p. 415

nominal exchange rate, p. 411

real exchange rate, p. 411

reserve assets, p. 425

revenue or T-account, p. 417

statistical discrepancy (SD), p. 418

sterilized intervention, p. 427

trade deficit, p. 414

trade surplus, p. 414

trade-weighted dollar, p. 410

unilateral transfers, p. 415

World Bank, p. 423

Exercises

Technical Questions

1. Show the effect of dollar appreciation and depreciation with the euro on the price of U.S. exports and imports by updating Table 15.2 on the next page.

2. Evaluate whether the following statements are true or false, and explain your answer:

   a. A trade deficit occurs when the government spends more than it receives in tax revenue.

   b. In an open, mixed economy, the equilibrium level of GDP occurs when planned saving equals planned investment.

   c. An increase in interest rates in the rest of the world will lead to a stronger dollar.

   d. Under a fixed exchange rate system with global capital flows, monetary policy is ineffective. However, under a flexible exchange rate system, monetary policy is typically more effective than fiscal policy in increasing real GDP.

TABLE 15.2   Effect of Dollar Appreciation and Depreciation on U.S. Exports and Imports

R = EURO/$	DOMESTIC PRICE	JAN 05: R = 0.76	JAN 06: R = 0.82	EFFECT ON EXPORTS (X) AND IMPORTS (M)
U.S. exports: Televisions	$1,000			
U.S. imports: European cars	Euro 25,000			
		JAN 07: R = 0.77	JAN 08: R = 0.68	
U.S. exports: Televisions	$1,000			
U.S. imports: European cars	Euro 25,000			

3. If the U.S. economy is operating near full employment and the exchange rate increases (the dollar appreciates), explain why the Federal Reserve will be *less inclined* to raise interest rates.

4. In a flexible exchange rate system, explain why a country whose income grows faster than that of its trading partners can expect its exchange rate to fall or the value of its currency to depreciate.

5. Using the simple model of Table 15.12, explain why there is a balance of payments equilibrium when export spending equals import spending. What is the more general condition for equilibrium in the balance of payments?

6. In the foreign exchange market, explain which variables cause a movement along the demand for dollars curve and which variables cause the curve to shift. Repeat the exercise for the supply of dollars curve.

Application Questions

1. In current business publications or on the Bureau of Economic Analysis international accounts Web page (www.bea.doc.gov/bea/international), find the latest statistics on the balance of payments (both the current and the financial accounts). How do the balance of payments figures compare with those for 2007 in Table 15.4?

2. On the Bureau of Economic Analysis international accounts Web page, find statistics on the current direct foreign investment in the United States. What are the categories of this investment, and how have they changed in recent years?

3. Based on the discussion in this chapter, update the controversy over the value of the Chinese yuan in foreign currency markets. Is China still using central bank foreign exchange policy to maintain the value of the yuan? What is the current policy of the United States on this issue?

4. What is the current value of the euro relative to the U.S. dollar? What macro policies are the countries in the European Union following regarding their economies, and how do these policies affect the value of the euro?

5. Find examples in current news publications similar to those in this chapter of the strategic responses of individual businesses to changes in currency exchange rates. Are these firms adapting to the changing international environment, or are they engaged in political action to try to modify that environment?

On the Web

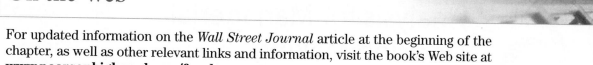

For updated information on the *Wall Street Journal* article at the beginning of the chapter, as well as other relevant links and information, visit the book's Web site at **www.pearsonhighered.com/farnham**

16 Combining Micro and Macro Analysis for Managerial Decision Making

I n this chapter, we draw on both the microeconomic analysis we developed in Part 1 and the macroeconomic analysis in Part 2 to analyze the challenges to managerial decision making arising from changes in the business environment.

We begin this chapter with the article "Drive-Through Tips for China," which discusses the current strategy of McDonald's Corp. to expand its operations in China by promoting drive-through restaurants. This strategy relates back to the production and cost issues of fast-food restaurants in the United States that we discussed in Chapter 5. We show how this strategy is based on changing tastes and lifestyles of Chinese consumers and how future growth in China by McDonald's and other U.S. companies will be influenced by current macroeconomic conditions in that country and in the United States.

We then reintroduce the case of Wal-Mart's expansion in Mexico that we discussed in Chapter 1. We now have the full set of microeconomic and macroeconomic tools needed to analyze this case. We will review the microeconomic factors we discussed in Chapter 1, and we will discuss the impact of Mexico's currency crisis and peso devaluation in 1994 on Wal-Mart's entry into the country. We will also analyze the impact of the macroeconomic developments we have discussed in Chapters 11 through 15 on Wal-Mart's current strategy in Mexico.

We end the chapter by emphasizing the major theme of this text: *Changes in the macro environment affect individual firms and industries through the microeconomic factors of demand, production, cost, and profitability.* Firms can either try to adapt to these changes or undertake policies to try to modify the environment itself.

Drive-Through Tips for China

by Gordon Fairclough and Geoffrey A. Fowler

Wall Street Journal, *June 30, 2006*

The restaurant placemats tout "a brand new way of dining. It's fashionable and time-saving"—and it is one way McDonald's Corp. is trying to explain drive-through eating to Chinese consumers.

Executives of the restaurant chain plan to announce today a deal with China's largest gas retailer, state-owned Sinopec Group, to build drive-throughs at filling stations across this increasingly car-obsessed country. With the agreement, McDonald's can expand rapidly along highways and in fast-growing suburbs outside China's sprawling cities, where cars are becoming ever more popular.

"We see the future of China with cars, communities and houses spreading out," says Jeffrey Schwartz, chief executive of McDonald's China business. "We think the potential for drive-throughs is huge."

McDonald's has coined a new, Chinese name for drive-through, *De Lai Su*, which translates roughly as Come and Get It Fast. When the company opened its first three drive-throughs in China last year, it aired a TV commercial—with a young couple in a green convertible ordering food from their car—and printed up fliers with instructions for using the drive-through.

At the time, employees were deployed in the parking lots to direct drivers to the drive-through lane. McDonald's also has tried to demystify the process by having customers place their orders with a person, rather than through a speaker as is common in the U.S. and other countries.

The company is also looking into new ways to make foods—especially traditional Chinese dishes—more portable, so they can more easily be consumed in the car. A Shanghai drive-through restaurant is testing a "rice burger," patties of beef or chicken sandwiched between two cakes of compressed rice.

A greater proportion of McDonald's China sales comes from chicken than in the U.S. In China, about 50% is chicken, 40% is beef and 10% is fish. The company sells a range of foods made specifically for the China market, including corn, spicy chicken wings and triangle wraps: beef or chicken and vegetables and rice wrapped in a tortilla-type wrapper.

It isn't clear that China's eating culture will mix well with American grab-and-go lifestyle. Traditionally, Chinese customers haven't favored takeout food, preferring to sit down for leisurely meals. Today, just 10% of the business at fast-food restaurants in China is take-away. . . .

McDonald's is betting that will change as personal incomes rise, lifestyles become busier and more and more people own cars. Last year, more than three million new cars hit Chinese streets, and auto sales were up 54% in the first quarter of this year. . . .

Yum Brands Inc.'s KFC fried-chicken chain—McDonald's main competitor in China—opened the country's first drive-through in 2002 and added a second in Shanghai last year, but business has been lackluster and the company hasn't announced specific plans to open more. The company will likely add more drive-throughs in the future. . . .

McDonald's first foray into drive-throughs has been limited as well. Now, with the Sinopec deal, McDonald's will hold an advantage in one of KFC's struggles: finding real estate where you can drive in and out. . . .

Drive-throughs are key to McDonald's strategy of boosting its market share in China, which slid to 8.7% in 2004, the most recent year for which figures are available, from 10% in 2002. . . . KFC's market share climbed to 15.8% from 13.8% over the same period.

"China is extremely important to McDonald's globally," says Michael Roberts, McDonald's Corp.'s president and chief operating officer. McDonald's in coming years plans to open more restaurants here than in any other country, capitalizing on China's embrace of car culture. . . .

McDonald's has spent much of its time in China learning to slow down from its fast-paced U.S. roots. The company's new restaurants have Internet connections, play areas for children and special seating for their mothers, all of which are designed to reinforce their role as gathering places. . . .

McDonald's, which opened its first restaurant in China in 1990, expects to have more than 1,000 outlets by the time of the Beijing summer Olympics in 2008. By comparison, KFC has more than 1,600 stores. McDonald's says it expects more than half of its future restaurants in China will be equipped with drive-throughs—in addition to regular dining rooms and free parking to attract suburban car owners.

Mr. Schwartz says drive-through customers account for about 30% of sales at the three outlets that have them. That compares with about 60% drive-through sales at U.S. McDonald's. . . .

Drive-throughs seem to be gaining snob appeal, because target customers are members of the car-owning middle class. . . .

Case for Analysis

McDonald's Use of Drive-Throughs in China

This article focuses on how McDonald's Corp. has developed its competitive strategy in China by focusing on the changing lifestyles and the new automobile-driven culture of Chinese consumers. Although the company opened its first restaurant in China in 1990, it developed the drive-through concept there only in recent years, opening its first drive-through in 2005 as a major part of its strategy to compete with Yum Brands Inc.'s KFC fried-chicken chain. The number of KFC restaurants in China far outnumbers the McDonald's outlets. However, McDonald's 2006 agreement with Sinopec, China's largest gas retailer, to build drive-throughs at gas stations across the country may give McDonald's a competitive edge.

The article focuses primarily on the microeconomic issues of consumer demand, production and cost, and market strategy. However, the current macroeconomic environment in China and the United States is likely to influence the success of McDonald's strategy and that of other multinational corporations in China. Let's use the microeconomic framework of Part 1 of this text and the macroeconomic models of Part 2 to analyze the points raised in the article. ■

Microeconomic Influences on McDonald's in China

As we discussed in Part 1 of this text, managers in firms with market power can develop competitive strategies that focus either on consumer demand and the revenue derived from the sale of its products or on production technology and the costs of production. Increases in revenue and decreases in costs both help managers increase a firm's profits (the difference between total revenue and total cost). Unlike those who manage perfectly competitive firms, which cannot influence the price of the product, such as the farmers we discussed in the opening article of Chapter 7, managers in firms with market power typically develop strategies that involve both the demand and the supply sides of the market.

McDonald's Corp. announced in March 2008 that it had posted a 12 percent increase in February same-store global sales. Same-store sales in the United States rose 8.3 percent, driven by a strong performance from the breakfast, coffee, and "everyday value" offerings. European sales increased 15 percent based on results from the United Kingdom, France, Germany, and Russia, where increased revenue was derived from the premium beef and chicken selections and the products' affordability. Sales in the Asia/Pacific, Middle East, and African regions increased 11 percent with particularly strong results in Australia, China, and Japan. McDonald's managers claimed that the availability of "locally relevant and affordable" menu items was the source of the increased sales in these regions.[1]

Consumers and Markets

The fact that sales increased more rapidly in other countries than in the United States shows the importance of entering and understanding foreign markets to U.S. multinational corporations.[2] In the opening article of the chapter, Michael Roberts, McDonald's Corp.'s president and chief operating officer, notes that "China is extremely important to McDonald's globally." In January 2008, McDonald's executives announced plans to open 125 outlets in China during 2008, an increase of

---

[1] Donna Kardos, "McDonald's Posts 12% Rise in February Same-Store Sales," *Wall Street Journal*, March 10, 2008.

[2] A case study of the microeconomic and macroeconomic factors influencing McDonald's strategies in the United States is included in Appendix A of this chapter for comparison with these international issues.

18 percent from 2007. Half of the new outlets would have drive-through windows, which would double the number of McDonald's drive-through windows in China. Approximately 28 percent of sales were derived from drive-through customers at the 60 Chinese outlets offering this service compared with 63 percent of such sales in U.S. outlets. The president of McDonald's for Asia, the Middle East, and Africa noted that the Chinese were quick to embrace the drive-through concept, and he stated, "I'm wishing we had drive-throughs 10 years ago."[3]

Still, as the opening article pointed out, there was a period of adjustment for the drive-through innovation in China. Customers had to be taught how to use the drive-through window. Many outlets had customers place their orders through a person rather than a speaker to demystify the procedure. In the United States, as discussed in Chapter 5, McDonald's pioneered the use of call centers to further increase efficiency in the drive-through process. Thus, the amount of cost-cutting technical innovation that can be introduced into a production process is a function not only of the technology itself but also of consumer acceptance.

McDonald's has confronted a number of other major issues regarding consumer tastes and acceptance in this market. One of the most important issues has been whether to adapt its products to the Chinese market or to keep a U.S.-based menu. The article that opened this chapter, written in June 2006, noted that the company was testing a "rice burger" and that it sold a range of foods made specifically for the Chinese, including triangle wraps of beef or chicken and vegetables and rice wrapped in a tortilla. However, by September 2006 when the company introduced the Quarter Pounder in China, it shifted strategy to emphasize traditional American hamburgers as opposed to specialties for the Chinese market.[4] The company discontinued the rice burgers and triangle wraps as it began pushing the Quarter Pounder. However, the Chinese Quarter Pounder is not identical to the U.S. version because it uses cucumbers rather than pickles and tomatoes and a spicy sauce more appealing to the Chinese. These changes resulted from tests of more than 16 variations on consumers, emphasizing the importance of the techniques to determine consumer preferences that we discussed in Chapter 4.

The Quarter Pounder introduction was supported by an advertising campaign that focused on beef as luxurious, healthy, and even sexy. Billboard ads featured a close-up of a woman's lips, while door ads showed a woman running her hands over a man's flexed biceps. TV commercials were even racier. "In one spot, a man and a woman eat Quarter Pounders, and close-up shots of the woman's neck and mouth are interspersed with images of fireworks and spraying water. The actors suck their fingers. The voice-over says: 'You can feel it. Thicker. You can taste it. Juicier.'"[5]

This campaign was important in a country with China's population, particularly given the fact that half of McDonald's sales in China had been of chicken products with beef making up only 35 percent. Beef typically costs more in China, and customers view it as a luxury good. However, market research and successful promotions for the Big Mac convinced McDonald's executives of the need for a change in strategy. The chief executive of McDonald's China operations stated, "We need to own beef. It's who we are. It's how we started."[6]

This changing strategy was part of a move to reverse a sliding market share for McDonald's in China and to compete more vigorously with Yum Brands' KFC, which focused more on foods specifically designed for the Chinese market. Average sales per McDonald's restaurant in China had been about half of what they were in the United States. Although McDonald's managers still made some concessions to local

---

[3] Mei Fong, "McDonald's Steps Up China Plan," *Wall Street Journal*, January 30, 2008.
[4] Gordon Fairclough and Janet Adamy, "Sex, Skin, Fireworks, Licked Fingers—It's a Quarter Pounder Ad in China," *Wall Street Journal*, September 21, 2006.
[5] Ibid.
[6] Ibid.

tastes, such as adding a corn cup and eliminating Diet Coke, which was not selling, these changes involved tweaking and adding side dishes rather than reshaping McDonalds's core menu. As incomes increased in China, beef consumption increased more rapidly than that of pork or chicken. These trends, combined with consumer research, convinced McDonald's executives that the company should emphasize its American roots. According to one executive, "People want McDonald's to be a Western brand. . . . When people come to us, they want an alternative to what they can get everywhere else."[7]

The article opening this chapter noted that Chinese customers traditionally did not favor take-out food and preferred to sit down for leisurely meals. Restaurants were often places for family gatherings and appointments with friends. McDonald's and KFC have both capitalized on this social aspect of the Chinese restaurant experience. Due to the Cultural Revolution, most restaurants in the 1970s looked similar inside and out, had a canteen mentality in management, and offered poor service and unpleasant dining experiences. When KFC and McDonald's opened their outlets in Beijing, customers were impressed by their beautiful appearances and brightly lit, climate-controlled interiors. Years of economic reform and improved living standards meant that many Chinese now had discretionary income. Dining out became a popular form of entertainment, and the cleanliness of the McDonald's and KFC outlets became an important issue.[8]

Other social issues were also important. There is pressure within Chinese culture for people holding banquets at restaurants to compete with neighboring tables on the basis of offering the guests the most expensive dishes and alcoholic beverages. To avoid competition and potential embarrassment, people would pay extra fees to reserve a private room. McDonald's became a good alternative for consumers with lower incomes because the menu was limited and all items were of similar value. McDonald's also evolved into a setting where people could define themselves as part of the middle class. Surveys and interviews showed that young professionals came to McDonald's in small groups or with their significant others and would spend an hour or more in the restaurant. Studies also indicated that women were more likely than men to eat at fast-food restaurants because they enjoyed ordering their own food and participating in conversation while dining. In formal Chinese restaurants, men order food for their female companions and control the conversation.[9]

McDonald's has traditionally been popular among Chinese children. The Chinese policy of one child per family has had the effect of turning single children into "fussy little emperors" who are the center of attention of their parents and relatives, so McDonald's actively marketed to children. Restaurants typically had a public relations staff available to answer questions. There were often several female receptionists who were called "Aunt McDonald" by children who knew Ronald McDonald as Uncle McDonald. The Aunt McDonalds learned the names of regular customers, chatted with families at the restaurants, and established relationships with the children. They would record information about the children in their "Book of Little Honorary Guests," send them birthday wishes, and visit their schools. Research interviews indicated that parents would often bring their children to McDonald's even if they themselves did not like the food or could barely afford it. One mother explained that she wanted her daughter to learn English and brought her to McDonald's to experience American culture as an investment for the future.[10]

---

[7] Ibid.

[8] Yunxiang Yan, "McDonald's in Beijing: The Localization of Americana," in *Golden Arches East: McDonald's in East Asia* (2nd ed.), James L Watson (ed.) (Stanford: Stanford University Press, 2006); Yunxiang Yan, "Of Hamburger and Social Space: Consuming McDonald's in Beijing," in *The Consumer Revolution in China*, Deborah S. Davis (ed.) (Berkeley: University of California Press, 2000).

[9] Yan, "McDonald's in Beijing;" Yan, "Of Hamburger and Social Space."

[10] Yan, "McDonald's in Beijing;" Yadong Luo, *How to Enter China: Choices and Lessons* (Ann Arbor, MI: The University of Michigan Press, 2001).

Economic and Political Issues

McDonald's had to confront both technical and political issues with its production decisions in its entry into China. Entry into Beijing was accomplished through an equity joint venture with the Beijing General Corp. of the Agriculture Industry and Commerce United Co. (Beijing's Department of Agriculture). This investment, begun in 1991, was to last 20 years. McDonald's chose this partner because it was controlled by the Chinese government, which enabled the company to receive agricultural subsidies. McDonald's used the Department of Agriculture's connections to cope with barriers concerning agricultural products, but also for other supplier relationships and distributional channels. These relationships helped McDonald's overcome entry barriers that the Chinese government placed on foreign companies acquiring natural resources within the country. McDonald's typically relied on independent suppliers who were required to meet and maintain the company's standards and specifications. As early as 1983, it began using apples from China to supply its restaurants in Japan. Thereafter, it began building up distribution and processing facilities in northern China. McDonald's also worked with Chinese farmers to teach them how to grow potatoes that could be used to make their french fries.[11]

There are many other examples of the political risk that McDonald's encountered with its entry into China. In 2004, Meng Sun became the first McDonald's franchisee in China. As noted above, most McDonald's and KFC restaurants are company-owned or operated in joint ventures with local companies. As part of the conditions for entry into the World Trade Organization, China was required to set a framework for everything from the recruitment and vetting of prospective entrepreneurs to the protection of brand and property rights. Western companies traditionally thought they could lose control of their trade secrets and brands by offering franchises in China, which offered few legal protections. New government rules made franchises more enticing to Chinese business people. Approximately 60 percent of McDonald's outlets outside the United States are franchised. Potential owners have to spend at least a year working at virtually every post in a restaurant. In 2001 McDonald's opened a Hong Kong branch of its Hamburger University to teach management practices.[12]

McDonald's has, of course, been a primary target among several multinational corporations of anticorporation, anticapitalist, and antiobesity campaigns. In August 2002, two New York teenagers sued McDonald's for making them fat. Although the judge dismissed the suit, many trial lawyers, nutritionists, and anticorporate activists have since argued that purveyors of food should be held responsible for the long-term health consequences of their products, just as tobacco firms were called to account for cigarette damage. The Center for Science in the Public Interest has asked the FDA to put tobacco-style warning labels on sugary beverages. Similar antiobesity campaigns have spread to Korea and Hong Kong.[13] To respond to this backlash around the world, McDonald's entered a partnership with Chinese educational authorities to give nutrition classes in elementary schools. The company created a Ronald McDonald clown show for schools that combined encouragement of physical activity with educational materials about nutrition. These shows were presented in thousands of Chinese schools.[14]

---

[11] Luo, *How to Enter China*; Yan, "Of Hamburger and Social Space."

[12] Steven Gray and Geoffrey A. Fowler, "China's New Entrepreneurs: McDonald's and KFC Race to Recruit More Franchisees as Rules Are Standardized," *Wall Street Journal*, January 25, 2005.

[13] James L. Watson, "McDonald's as a Political Target: Globalization and Anti-globalization in the Twenty-First Century," in *Golden Arches East: McDonald's in East Asia*, (2nd ed.), James L. Watson (ed.) (Stanford: Stanford University Press, 2006).

[14] Geoff Dyer, "Ronald Helps McDonald's Head Off China Backlash," *Financial Times*, London, November 25, 2006.

Food safety and other health issues are always problems for firms in this sector of the economy. In 2003 McDonald's raised the price of its Big Mac in China as much as 4 percent, but denied a report that suggested the price increase was to cover expenses related to severe acute respiratory syndrome (SARS). Restaurants had suffered from the SARS outbreak as people avoided public places, especially in Beijing.[15] One of the reasons that food prices surged in China in late 2007 and early 2008 was the increased price of pork after pig herds were hit by porcine "blue ear" disease in 2007.[16]

Multinational corporations always confront local legislation and institutions in terms of hiring and employment practices. McDonald's announced it was raising wages for restaurant crews 12 to 56 percent above China's minimum wage guidelines as of September 1, 2007. The All-China Federation of Trade Unions had accused the company of violating labor laws by underpaying part-time workers in Guangzhou. The company was absolved of wrongdoing, but it received negative publicity over the incident. McDonald's was able to offset these costs by lowering other costs, such as for paper, through increased economies of scale resulting from its expansion over time.[17]

In reaction to the implementation of the new labor law legislation in January 2008, many small- and medium-sized companies asked lawmakers to reconsider clauses regarding casual labor, which would allow them more flexibility in hiring temporary workers. The Labour Resources Intermediary Association argued that these companies helped keep unemployment rates under control by acting as intermediaries in providing employment for migrants. The association's chairman noted that if the law were strictly enforced, "there is a risk that some 30 percent of this labour force, or 15 million workers, would be left without jobs."[18]

McDonald's planned a major promotional effort regarding the Summer Olympics in China in 2008. The plan involved global advertising to showcase the company's history of feeding athletes and competitions in 30 countries to select 200 children for trips to the games.[19] At that time, this strategy was seen as a balancing act between the increased exposure from the games versus any negative fallout from the protests against the Chinese government that began when the Olympic flame traveled around the world in March 2008.[20] The lack of major protests at the games greatly benefited the company. McDonald's reported an 8.5 percent increase in August 2008 global same-store sales with its gain in the United States boosted by the Olympic-themed Southern Style Chicken Sandwich. The company's 10 percent growth in the Asia-Pacific, Middle East, and African regions was driven by extended hours and Olympic-related marketing.[21]

China's environment also raises problems for multinational corporations. In many Chinese cities, a thick shroud of pollution literally blocks out the sun much of the time. Acid rain reduces agricultural yields and eats away at buildings and infrastructure. Air pollution has been estimated to reduce the country's output by 3 to 7 percent per year, largely due to respiratory ailments that keep workers at home. China's water supply is also in a perilous state, given ever-increasing industrial and agricultural use. The amount of water available per capita is only a quarter

---

[15] "Food Brief: McDonald's Corp." *Wall Street Journal*, June 10, 2003.

[16] "China Economy: Price Surge," *The Economist*, The Economist Intelligence Unit, March 11, 2008.

[17] Mei Fong, "McDonald's Aims to Boost China Image with Wage Rise," *Wall Street Journal*, August 7, 2007.

[18] "China Regulations: Labour-Law Worries," *The Economist Intelligence Unit*, February 13, 2008.

[19] Emily Bryson York, "What's on McDonald's Olympic-Marketing Menu," *Advertising Age*, March 3, 2008.

[20] "China Politics: Political Risk Takes Centre Stage," *The Economist*, The Economist Intelligence Unit, March 14, 2008; "China Politics: Tibet Dilemma," *The Economist*, The Economist Intelligence Unit, March 17, 2008.

[21] Shara Tibken, "McDonald's Olympic Offerings Help Boost Same-Store Sales," *Wall Street Journal*, September 9, 2008.

of the global average. Ground water is pumped out much faster than it is being replenished. Not even Beijing treats all of its sewage, while other cities treat none at all. The World Bank has estimated that China's air and water pollution costs $100 billion per year or about 5.8 percent of its GDP.[22]

Macroeconomic Influences on Managers in China

As we discussed in Chapter 11, the major macroeconomic questions facing any economy are the following:

- What factors influence the spending behavior of the different sectors of the economy?
- How do the behavior changes in these sectors influence the level of output and income in the economy?
- Can policy makers maintain stable prices, full employment, and adequate economic growth over time?
- How do fiscal, monetary, and foreign exchange policies influence the economy?
- What impact do these macro changes have on different firms and industries?

China has transformed itself from a minor economy with little trade with the outside world in the 1970s and 1980s to the world's third largest trading nation after the United States and Germany.[23] China's GDP passed the $2 trillion mark in 2005 with GDP annual growth averaging 10 percent since 2003. Agricultural reform and the growth of village enterprises stimulated GDP during the 1980s, and this was followed by improvements in manufacturing and services. The economy opened up further in the 1990s with GDP growth at double-digit rates. Authorities, concerned about increasing inflation, clamped down on wages and prices to dampen economic growth, which still remained in the 6–8 percent range. Entry into the World Trade Organization created a substantial surge in trade and investment, especially in the exporting of toys, textiles, and other light manufactures. Imports rose but with a strong emphasis on raw materials, oil, and investment equipment. This pattern of trade led to a massive rise in China's trade surplus versus its key export partners. Investment is largely domestically financed out of profits reflecting a high domestic savings rate. Foreign direct investment played a significant role in the 1990s and remains about 5–6 percent of total investment funds, particularly in the manufacturing for export markets.

In the fourth quarter of 2007, China's GDP still rose strongly, up 11.2 percent in that quarter, but at a slightly reduced rate from summer 2007. Inflation dropped back to 6.5 percent. Strong job and income growth as well as new wealth resulted in a retail sales growth rate of 20 percent in the fourth quarter of 2007.

In early 2008 the National People's Congress, China's top legislature, debated how to deal with the problem of increasing inflation. The People's Bank of China had increased interest rates six times in 2007, given concerns that bouts of inflation had triggered social unrest in the past. Much of the surge in inflation in 2007 was due to food prices that increased by 23 percent. Policy makers also worried that if China raised interest rates at the same time the United States cut them, there would be larger capital inflows into China and the extra liquidity could worsen inflationary pressures.[24]

---

[22] "China Economy: A Large Black Cloud," *The Economist*, March 14, 2008.

[23] The following discussion is based on "China," *Oxford Economic Country Briefings*, January 25, 2008.

[24] "Revaluation by Stealth: China Is Allowing Its Currency to Rise More Rapidly. Why?" *The Economist*, January 10, 2008; "China Economy: A Slightly More Useful Talking Shop," *The Economist*, The Economist Intelligence Unit, March 13, 2008; "China Economy: Sweet and Sour Pork," *The Economist*, The Economist Intelligence Unit, March 14, 2008.

China's total trade in 2007 rose 23.5 percent from the previous year to U.S. $2.2 trillion. Despite the bad publicity China received over the quality and safety of various products, its overall export performance was not appreciably affected. China's trade surplus of U.S. $262 billion increased 48 percent in 2007. As China's range of exports increased, it faced more conflict with other countries. In July 2007, the South American trading bloc, Mercosur, raised import tariffs on Chinese footwear from 20 to 35 percent at the request of Brazilian shoemakers. The same month, Taiwan's finance ministry said it was imposing an antidumping tax of 43.5 percent on Chinese footwear imports for five years.[25]

As discussed in Chapters 11–15, the global economic climate deteriorated significantly by fall 2008. In November 2008, China announced an economic stimulus package of $586 billion aimed at increasing domestic demand and averting a global recession. The plan included spending on housing, infrastructure, agriculture, health care, and social welfare, as well as a tax deduction for business capital spending. China's GDP expanded 9 percent in the third quarter of 2008, the slowest rate in five years. Growth in exports continued to moderate from declining United States demand, while import growth slowed from the decline in Chinese economic activity.[26]

In December 2008, China's central bank announced its fifth interest rate cut in just over three months. The bank pledged to use all available means to stimulate the economy impacted by its most significant shock in a decade. Although inflation from surging food prices had been the important policy issue at the beginning of 2008, the collapse in global and local commodity prices decreased China's consumer price inflation in November 2008 to its lowest rate in nearly 2 years. The November rate marked the fourth consecutive month-on-month fall in China's consumer price index.[27]

Much of China's $586 billion stimulus package was to be directed toward building highways, railroads, and airports. Infrastructure spending had been increasing at an annual rate of 20 percent for the previous 30 years, a major factor behind China's explosive economic growth. Domestic investment spending had contributed 4–6 percentage points of China's 10 percent average annual growth rate. Thirty thousand miles of expressways were built since the late 1990s, while plans called for China's highway system to reach 53,000 miles by 2020, exceeding the 47,000 miles of the U.S. interstate system.[28]

It was this change, of course, that led to McDonald's making the drive-through window a major part of its competitive strategy in China, particularly in terms of surpassing KFC in the number of stores operated in the country. McDonald's had also been facing more competition from local fast-food chains. After improving their décor, hygiene, and service, many local fast-food restaurants had become as crowded as McDonald's sites.[29] Thus, McDonald's continued to face competitive challenges from multinational and local sources and from the changing macroeconomic environment.

[25] "China Economy: The Trouble with Another Banner Year," *The Economist*, The Economist Intelligence Unit, March 4, 2008.

[26] Andrew Batson, "China Sets Big Stimulus Plan in Bid to Jump-Start Growth," *Wall Street Journal*, November 10, 2008; Andrew Batson and Norihiko Shirouzu, "Weak China Data Show Why Beijing Acted Fast," *Wall Street Journal*, November 12, 2008.

[27] Andrew Batson, "China Data Spark Deflation Worries," *Wall Street Journal*, December 12, 2008; James T. Areddy, "China Cuts Interest Rates for Fifth Time Since September," *Wall Street Journal*, December 23, 2008.

[28] Andrew Batson, "China Bets Highways Will Drive Its Growth," *Wall Street Journal*, November 11, 2008.

[29] "McDonald's Wants to Surpass KFC in Store Number," *SinoCast China Business Daily News*, London, February 21, 2008; Luo, *How to Enter China: Choices and Lessons*.

Wal-Mart in Mexico Revisited

In the opening case in Chapter 1, we discussed the microeconomic and macroeconomic factors that influenced Wal-Mart's entry into Mexico in 1991 and the success of the company in that country in subsequent years. Having now covered all of these economic principles in more detail in Chapters 2–15, we will review the issues that have influenced Wal-Mart's competitive strategies and use this textbook's macro model to discuss the impact of changes in the macro environment on Wal-Mart's behavior.

Microeconomic Influences on Wal-Mart in Mexico

Analysts have noted that the impact of Wal-Mart in Mexico should be viewed within the context of the political and economic changes that occurred in the country over the past 30 years. Mexico went through a period of urban growth that resulted in an 80 percent urbanization rate. The liberalization of Mexican political and economic life resulted in the decentralization of the Mexican government and encouraged consumption patterns resembling those in developed countries.

Nature of the Market

The first U.S.-style supermarket, Aurrera, opened in Mexico in 1958 during a period of changing consumption patterns among the middle class, resulting from Mexican laborers bringing back new ideals of consumption from the United States from the bracero program in which these workers were contracted to work. The success of Aurrera led to the creation of another supermarket called Superama. During the 1960s Aurrera shifted its operations to warehouse-based retail, while in 1972 CIRFA, the retail-based conglomerate, gained control of both Aurrera and Superama. The first Wal-Mart store in Mexico was a Sam's Club in Mexico City that was a joint venture with CIFRA.[30]

Mexico's system of regional supermarket monopolies remained intact until the 1980s when the country's entrance into the General Agreement on Tariffs and Trade (GATT) led to consolidation, the development of national supermarket chains, and partnerships with international retailers. When Wal-Mart arrived in Mexico, the food retailing sector was composed of a handful of national supermarket chains and several large regional food retailers that primarily served upper- and middle-class households in Mexico City and along the northern border. In anticipation of the North American Free Trade Agreement (NAFTA), several international retailers, including Carrefour, Ahold, and Wal-Mart, formed joint ventures and strategic alliances with Mexican firms. This caused foreign direct investment (FDI) in the retail sector to increase from 6 percent of total FDI to 11 percent in 1991. Many U.S. companies with access to information on NAFTA negotiations began looking to form partnerships with Mexican companies at this time. The Mexican market was attractive because of its proximity, size, and recent urbanization, which had led to supermarket growth in other countries.[31]

---

[30] Margath A. Walker, David Walker, and Yanga Villagomez Velazquez, "The Wal-Martification of Teotihuacan: Issues of Resistance and Cultural Heritage," in *Wal-Mart World: The World's Biggest Corporation in the Global Economy.* Stanley D. Brunn (ed.) (New York: Taylor & Francis Group, 2006), 213–224.

[31] James J. Biles, "Globalization of Food Retailing and the Consequences of Wal-Martization in Mexico," in *Wal-Mart World: The World's Biggest Corporation in the Global Economy,* Stanley D. Brunn (ed.) (New York: Taylor & Francis Group, 2006), 343–355; Manual Chavez, "The Transformation of Mexican Retailing with NAFTA," *Development Policy Review,* 2002, 20(4): 503–513.

NAFTA, which took effect in 1994, created a hospitable environment for companies seeking to expand globally. It banned restrictions on foreign business ownership and lowered trade barriers, which benefited global retailers who were building competitive advantage with large-scale integrated systems of purchasing and distribution of products. Wal-Mart's joint venture with CIFRA flourished, and the companies expanded their collaboration. Mexico experienced an economic crisis in 1994, which led to the devaluation of the peso. When the economy began to recover in 1997, Wal-Mart purchased the majority share of CIFRA at an exchange rate–depressed price and formed Wal-Mart de Mexico (Walmex). The company then embarked on an aggressive expansion that doubled its sales between 1997 and 2003.[32]

Wal-Mart entered Mexico with expectations of an experience similar to that in the United States. One analyst noted at the time that Wal-Mart "will ride Mexico the way they rode the U.S." with company plans being "no different from what they're doing here" but with greater opportunities for growth in discount retailing.[33] Wal-Mart had success with its stores along the Texas-Mexico border, so it was anticipated that the company understood the Mexican consumer. However, it appeared in the early years that retail outlets were growing faster in Mexico than the buying power of their potential customers. When Wal-Mart opened a supercenter in Monterrey in 1993, it was criticized for charging 15–20 percent more than the Wal-Mart in Laredo, Texas, two hours by car to the north. At this time, transportation costs from the United States were high and many duties had not yet been phased out. The company also lacked leverage with Mexican vendors that gave it an advantage in the United States. Distribution systems were different in Mexico, where thousands of suppliers shipped directly to stores rather than to retailer warehouses. Wal-Mart was also faced with ambivalent preferences for U.S. goods. The Mexican news media warned about shoddy foreign goods, and some consumers were moved by the spirit of Mexican nationalism to purchase domestically produced goods. Wal-Mart also contended with differences in lifestyles. Mexicans often shop at neighborhood butcher shops, bakeries, tortillerias, fruit stands, and egg shops because these products are considered to be fresher. At this time most Mexican consumers did not own automobiles and had very small refrigerators that could not store a week's worth of groceries. Thus, Wal-Mart's features that worked to its advantage in the United States (large size, thousands of products, ample parking) did not transfer to Mexico.[34]

Kmart, which followed Wal-Mart into Mexico, avoided some of these problems first by hiring a Mexican native to run its stores. Unlike Wal-Mart, Kmart had a branch bank inside its stores to help consumers get access to cash in a country with interest rates over 30 percent and few credit card sales. Kmart imported only 20 percent of its goods compared with Wal-Mart's 40 percent imports. Wal-Mart sold mostly prepackaged cuts of meat and ground beef, American style, while Kmart's meat department had a huge walk-in refrigerator with a dozen sides of beef from which consumers could request specific cuts on the spot. Even hot dogs were wrapped in front of consumers to convey a sense of freshness. Kmart did not have a gardening department because most Mexicans had either tiny gardens or none at all, and they frequented enormous outdoor plant markets anyway.[35]

---

[32] Chris Tilly, "Wal-Mart Goes South: Sizing Up the Chain's Mexican Success Story," in *Wal-Mart World: The World's Biggest Corporation in the Global Economy*, Stanley D. Brunn (ed.) (New York: Taylor & Francis Group, 2006), 357–368.

[33] Bob Ortega, "Wal-Mart to Expand Mexican Business by Greatly Enlarging Cifra Venture," *Wall Street Journal*, June 1, 1992.

[34] Bob Ortega, "Tough Sale: Wal-Mart Is Slowed by Problems of Price and Culture in Mexico—Its New Stores Don't Have Slick U.S. Distribution; The Middle Class Is Small—Big Retail Battle Is Looming," *Wall Street Journal*, July 29, 1994.

[35] Ibid.

NAFTA also created an incentive for European and Asian manufacturers to build new plants in the NAFTA zone, giving Wal-Mart cheaper access to more foreign brands. For example, in 1998, Wal-Mart managers in Mexico City imported a few Sony 29-inch Wega flat-screen television sets for sale at $1,600, a price reflecting a 23 percent import duty and the cost of shipping the sets across the Pacific. The following year Sony build a giant Wega factory in the border town of Mexicali, allowing the company to ship televisions anywhere in the NAFTA zone duty free. By 2001 Wal-Mart was able to sell these television sets for $600, and the Wega line accounted for one-third of Sam's Club's electronics sales.[36]

Production and Cost Issues

Wal-Mart's efficiency in production in the United States has always resulted from its centralized distribution and information systems and databases that allow for tight control over costs. Wal-Mart managers have insisted that suppliers use Retail Link, a technology-based supply chain toolbox to enhance the efficiency of the distribution and supply system. In a typical supercenter, the company keeps 90,000 items in stock and evaluates the performance of these items through their stock-keeping unit (SKU) numbers. Wal-Mart also uses radio-frequency identification in the supply chain to enhance productivity. In the United States, Wal-Mart reduces costs through the intensive use of space, pressure on local governments and other entities to get the best deal, negotiations with suppliers to offer the lowest possible price and to continue to reduce prices, paying employees low wages with limited benefits, and discouraging unions.[37]

Wal-Mart operates ten distribution centers that channel goods to its supermarkets in Mexico. The company has established a procurement office in Mexico and organized a group of 200 domestic suppliers. These distribution centers allow the company to achieve economies of scale, reduce intermediation costs, and facilitate more efficient inventory management and application of just-in-time practices.[38] Because NAFTA has reduced the time and cost of shipping merchandise across the border, Wal-Mart has linked its Mexican distribution system to the one in the United States. Wal-Mart introduced a system of channeling deliveries from suppliers through centralized warehouses, requiring trucks to have appointment times and drivers to carry standard identification. Shipments were required to be on standardized pallets, shrink-wrapped with corner protectors, and subject to audits. These standards have diffused into other major chains.[39]

Wal-Mart also commands the lowest prices from its Mexican suppliers and has caused some of them to go into bankruptcy. An executive of a Mexican clothing manufacturer explained, "Wal-Mart maintains its profit margin. . . . They never reduce *their* margin. They *do* pass on savings in price, but at the expense of the manufacturer. . . . For example, they may tell you, 'We're going to sell shirts at a discount of 40 percent—you, the manufacturer, have to cut your price by 40 percent.' So the consumer benefits, but they're driving out of business the manufacturers that provide jobs."[40]

---

[36] David Luhnow, "Crossover Success: How NAFTA Helped Wal-Mart Reshape the Mexican Market—Lower Tariffs, Retail Muscle Translate into Big Sales; Middlemen Are Squeezed—'Like Shopping in the U.S.,'" *Wall Street Journal*, August 30, 2001.

[37] Steve Burt and Leigh Sparks, "Wal-Mart's World," in *Wal-Mart World: The World's Biggest Corporation in the Global Economy*, Stanley D. Brunn (ed.) (New York: Taylor & Francis Group, 2006), 27–43; Emek Basker, "The Causes and Consequences of Wal-Mart's Growth," *Journal of Economic Perspectives*, 2007, 21 (3): 177–189.

[38] Biles, "Globalization of Food Retailing and the Consequences of Wal-Martization in Mexico."

[39] Beata Smarzynska Javorcik, Wolfgang Keller, and James Tybout, "Openness and Industrial Responses in a Wal-Mart World: A Case Study of Mexican Soaps, Detergents, and Surfactant Producers," *NBER Working Paper #12457*, 2006.

[40] Tilly, "Wal-Mart Goes South: Sizing Up the Chain's Mexican Success Story."

Wal-Mart pays standard or above-standard wages for food retailing in Mexico, although the retail industry average wage of approximately $6.00 is below the economy-wide average of $14.55. Wal-Mart offers a year-end bonus double that is required by law, but otherwise offers only benefits required by Mexico's national labor law. Wal-Mart's compensation is not far out of line with other chains. However, Wal-Mart workers in Mexico report that they get paid only for full hours of work and that they may have to work added hours without pay.[41]

Competitive Strategies

Wal-Mart changed its retail model in Mexico by retaining CIRFA's multiple formats and local names, a segmented market strategy using different formats to target different consumers. Most of this segmentation was by income. The Bodega Aurrera stores were designed to appeal to low-income consumers with basic breads, while the Superama stores catered to the affluent with rich desserts and fancier display cases. Sales per square foot in the Mexican stores increased by 10 percent after these and other changes were made. In 2006 these same types of changes were introduced in Wal-Mart's U.S. stores. The U.S. market was considered to be more complex, so that segmentation involved ethnicity and lifestyle as well as income. Using the techniques described in Chapter 4 including census data and customer feedback, Wal-Mart managers researched its customers to break them into demographic groups. Most of the changes were in the company's suburban and urban areas.[42]

As discussed in the article in Chapter 1, one of Wal-Mart's most recent strategic innovations in Mexico was to open banks in its stores. In November 2007, Wal-Mart opened the first four branches of Banco Wal-Mart. The company had 22 bank locations in early 2008 and expected to have at least 80 by the end of that year. This development occurred at the same time that the U.S. Senate Banking Committee approved a bill that would prevent retailers from owning the type of bank charters that Wal-Mart had previously sought. Although Wal-Mart has been criticized for its interest rates in Banco Wal-Mart, 1 percent on savings accounts and 75 percent annually on consumer loans that can be used only to buy Wal-Mart items, *Business Week* reported that Mexican for-profit banks charge customers with poor credit between 50 and 120 percent annual interest rates. Wal-Mart executives argued that the Mexican bank was a way to provide banking services to customers who did not have access to affordable credit plans. It was expected that the Mexican government would regulate these banks similarly to the way banks were regulated in the United States.[43]

Wal-Mart's success in Mexico might be limited by three factors: (1) It took advantage of situations that might be difficult to replicate elsewhere; (2) competitors are successfully imitating its strategies; and (3) the polarization of Mexican society curtails retail strategies aimed primarily at a middle market.[44] As discussed previously, Wal-Mart began as a joint venture with CIFRA, a store that was already a leader. The peso devaluation allowed Wal-Mart to purchase a controlling share of CIFRA at an extremely low price. Wal-Mart also gained first-mover advantages by arriving in an area where the competition had not yet adopted its strategies.

Wal-Mart's three major competitors, Gigante, Comercial Mexicana, and Soriana, now offer a version of everyday low prices, have begun to implement automated distribution systems, are demanding discounts from their suppliers, and are carefully

---

[41] Ibid.

[42] Ann Zimmerman, "To Boost Sales, Wal-Mart Drops One-Size-Fits-All Approach," *Wall Street Journal*, September 7, 2006.

[43] Mark Friedman, "Wal-Mart Rolls Out Bank in Mexico," *Arkansas Business*, February 25, 2008.

[44] Chris Tilly, "Wal-Mart in Mexico: The Limits of Growth," in *Wal-Mart: The Face of Twenty-First Century Capitalism*, Nelson Lichtenstein (ed.) (New York: The New Press, 2006), 189–209.

specifying operating procedures. Soriana and Comercial Mexicana have recently begun to actively market to high-end clientele with their food choices. Soriana has built a strong regional base in the north and has a reputation for catering to Mexican tastes. Gigante and Comercial Mexicana are similar to Wal-Mart in that they are centrally located in Mexico City and have adapted Wal-Mart's strategies.[45]

Wal-Mart's approach of selling to a broad middle class may also face structural limits. One analyst noted that "Mexico is a land of haves and have-nots. It's a poor bet for an American broad-lines retailer that is mostly aimed at the middle class."[46] A Mexican minimum-wage earner must expend from three to twenty-five times as many hours as his or her U.S. counterpart to buy the same items. Thus, Wal-Mart is far less affordable in Mexico than in the United States. This polarization has meant that the percentage of Mexicans who state an overall preference for shopping in a supermarket dropped from 75 percent in 1993 to 56 percent in 2000 and 34 percent in 2003. Another source of competition for the large retailers continues to be the small-scale sellers in the informal sector of the Mexican economy. Mexicans have these other lower-cost options to the established retail chains, particularly for food, regular clothing, and general merchandise.[47]

Macroeconomic Influences on Wal-Mart in Mexico

As discussed previously, substantial political and economic liberalization took place in the Mexican economy over the past 40 years. These changes, combined with the currency crisis and peso devaluation in 1994, had substantial impacts on Wal-Mart's entry and success in Mexico.

The 1994 Currency Crisis

In 1988, the Mexican government passed an agreement called the "Pacto," which included commitments to reductions of the fiscal deficit, tightening of monetary policy, liberalization of trade, and an incomes policy that covered wages, prices, and exchange rates. The "Pacto" was successful in reducing inflation, but the use of nominal exchange rate-based stabilization resulted in recurring real appreciation of the peso because inflation was systematically higher than the target.[48]

The appreciation of the exchange rate exacerbated the amounts of capital inflows experienced by Mexico in the early 1990s. The capital inflows were a result of falling interest rates in the United States and Mexican government policies aimed at attracting private capital through the privatization of banks and negotiation for free trade with the United States. Portfolio capital became an important source of foreign savings, but the downside was that it responded more quickly to changes in the environment than direct investment. The capital inflows further increased the appreciation of the exchange rate which led to a decrease in savings

---

[45] Biles, "Globalization of Food Retailing and the Consequences of Wal-Martization in Mexico"; Tilly, "Wal-Mart Goes South: Sizing Up the Chain's Mexican Success Story."

[46] Ibid.

[47] Tilly, "Wal-Mart in Mexico: The Limits of Growth."

[48] This discussion is based on Nora Lustig, "The Mexican Peso Crisis: The Foreseeable and the Surprise," *Brookings Institution*, 1995. For other discussions of the Mexican peso crisis, see Riordan Roett (ed.), *The Mexican Peso Crisis: International Perspectives* (Boulder, CO: Lynne Rienner Publishers, 1996); Sebastian Edwards and Moises Naim (eds.), *Mexico 1994: Anatomy of an Emerging-Market Crash* (Washington, DC: Carnegie Endowment for International Peace, 1997); Paul Krugman (ed.), *Currency Crises* (Chicago: The University of Chicago Press, 2000); and Nouriel Roubini and Brad Setser, *Bailouts or Bail-Ins? Responding to Financial Crises in Emerging Economies* (Washington , DC: Institute for International Economics, 2004).

and an increase in investment. This was in part due to an expansion of credit by the banking sector that was not regulated. The gap in savings and investment resulted in a large current account deficit.

These factors contributed to an unhealthy cycle. The real exchange rate appreciated, causing the current account deficit to increase, which was financed by capital flows from abroad. Over time the capital flows put pressure on the real exchange rate and the cycle would begin again. If foreign financing slowed, Mexico would be in trouble, and some economists recommended the government change its exchange rate policy by widening the exchange rate band or increasing the daily depreciation of the exchange rate ceiling. The government did increase the daily depreciation of the exchange rate in October 1992, but not enough because the current account deficit continued to widen. The government expected that the current account deficit would be temporary, investment would continue, and productivity would grow.

In 1994, when the Federal Reserve increased interest rates in the United States, the net capital flows to Mexico were adversely affected. Capital reserves fell slowly during the uprising in the Chiapas and then quickly after the assassination of ruling party candidate, Luis Donaldo Colosio, in March 1994. The government made use of its international reserves as capital flowed out of the country and also issued more dollar-denominated short-term government debt called Tesobonos. Between December 1993 and December 1994, the composition of government debt changed from 70 percent peso-denominated debt and 7 percent Tesobonos to 10 percent peso-denominated debt and 87 percent Tesobonos. This shift shows that investors feared the exchange rate was not sustainable and preferred to hold Mexican debt in dollars.

Mexican monetary authorities tried to slow the decrease in international reserves by increasing domestic credit, which led to a decrease in domestic interest rates. As reserves were falling, the government decided on December 20, 1994, to devalue the peso by raising the ceiling of the band. Immediately after the announcement, the dollar reached the 4 peso ceiling and resulted in a huge flight of capital. Two days later, the peso was allowed to float and the bank would no longer reduce its reserves in order to maintain the value of the peso.

The currency crisis then led to a financial crisis because investors that had their funds in the stock market or other instruments denominated in pesos withdrew their capital as fast as possible. The government did not have a macroeconomic plan at the time of the devaluation. By the second week of January 1995, Mexico was on the verge of default and the financial markets of Latin America and other regions began to be affected. The devaluation and how it was handled resulted in an estimated loss of $30 billion for those that had invested in the stock market and government bonds.

It became evident that a rescue package was needed in order to halt the financial crisis, and at the end of January, the U.S. government announced that there would be loans extended from the United States ($20 billion), the IMF ($17.8 billion), and the Bank of International Settlements ($10 billion). Although the package stopped the selling of financial assets, it did not reinstate confidence. In order to restore credibility, the Mexican government had to put in place programs with realistic goals, keep interest rates positive, and conduct transparent monetary policy.

This scenario is quite similar to that of the financial crisis in Southeast Asia discussed in Chapter 15. Large current account deficits have to be financed by capital inflows from abroad. If these flows decrease due to higher interest rates in other countries and large amounts of import spending, there is downward pressure on a country's exchange rate.[49] This downward pressure can be

---

[49] Review the discussion of the demand and supply of currency in the foreign exchange market in Chapter 15.

intensified if investors lose confidence in a country's currency due to political and economic events. The original exchange rate can be maintained only as long as the reserves of the country's central bank are sufficient to support the currency through intervention in the foreign exchange market. Tighter fiscal and monetary policies are usually needed to maintain a higher exchange rate over longer periods of time.

As noted in Chapter 1, the peso devaluation caused Wal-Mart to suspend its ambitious expansion plans in Mexico until the country's economy showed signs of improvement. Wal-Mart had planned to open 13 Sam's Club warehouse stores and 12 supercenters in 1995. Wal-Mart also temporarily halted shipments from the United States to its 63 Mexican stores until the Mexican government gave permission for retailers to raise prices for imported goods to reflect their higher costs in pesos.[50] As noted above, the devaluation did enable Wal-Mart to purchase a controlling interest in CIFRA later in the decade.

Recent Macroeconomic Events

Mexico's economy is more stable in the first decade of the twenty-first century than it was previously. The ratio of capital inflows to GDP is below what it was in the early 1990s, and Mexico does not rely as much on short-term borrowing. Mexico's reserves are sufficient to meet its short-term obligations, and its debt has an average maturity of three years now, instead of nine months. In 1994, 85 percent of public debt was foreign owned, but that has decreased to 40 percent. Supervision of the banking sector has increased, and credit growth remains within reasonable limits. The twenty-first century has been a time of stable prices in comparison to the past. This is due to a constitutional amendment that was passed in 1994 that created a fully independent central bank whose primary goal is price stability. In addition, authorities no longer try to defend the peso, so it has essentially been floating for the past decade.[51]

The importance of U.S. business cycles in influencing output fluctuations in Mexico has increased with the expansion of trade between the two countries. Total trade grew from $90 billion in 1993 to approximately $350 billion in 2006. The United States is Mexico's largest trading partner. Approximately 85 percent of Mexico's exports go to the United States, while roughly 50 percent of its imports are from the United States. Mexico's exports to the United States are approximately one-quarter of its GDP.[52]

The Mexican economy suffered two years of stagnation when the American economy slowed in 2001. As expectations of a recession in the United States loomed in 2007, there were hopes that the Mexican economy could ride out a shallow recession. Mexican consumers were spending more than they did in the past. Mexico's credit market was growing modestly, and government-backed housing construction remained strong. The government gained approval for tax reform to pay for public investment in roads and other infrastructure.[53]

By fall 2008, the weak United States economy had lowered Mexico's growth rate. The Mexican government cut its 2008 estimates for GDP growth from

[50] Bob Ortega, "Wal-Mart Suspends Mexican Expansion; Other Firms Stick to More Modest Plans," *Wall Street Journal*, January 25, 1995.

[51] Erwan Quintin and Jose Jauquin Lopez, "Mexico's Financial Vulnerability: Then and Now," *Economic Letter: Insights from the Federal Reserve Bank of Dallas*, 2006, 1 (6): 1–7.

[52] Steve Phillips, Rodolphe Blavy, Lucia Juvenal, Luisa Zanforlin, Marco Espinosa, and Sebastian Sosa, "Mexico: Selected Issues," *IMF Country Report 07/387*, 2007.

[53] "Braced for Contagion," *The Economist*, September 27, 2007; "Time to Wake Up," *The Economist*, November 16, 2007.

2.8 percent to 2.4 percent and revised its 2009 estimates from 3 percent to 1.8 percent. Reduced exports to the United States were a key factor in these revisions as Mexico sold 80 percent of its exports to the United States. The Mexican central bank also cooperated with the U.S. Federal Reserve to increase liquidity in the financial system.[54]

Wal-Mart experienced the effects of the slowing U.S. economy in 2007 and 2008 on both sides of the Mexican border. In the United States, Wal-Mart attempted to attract Mexican and Mexican-American customers who send money to relatives in Mexico using the company's wire-transfer business. The Mexican central bank estimated that these transfers into the country increased only 0.6 percent in 2007 compared with 15 percent in 2006 and 21 percent in 2005. In May 2008, the central bank reported that remittances from the United States dropped 2.9 percent for the first quarter of 2008 compared with the same period in 2007. These money transfers from the United States were estimated to account for 5 percent of Mexico's consumer spending. Wal-Mart cited these reduced transfers as a source of slowing growth in its revenues in Mexico.[55]

In December 2008, Wal-Mart announced that its earnings for the third quarter increased 9.8 percent while sales rose 7.5 percent, results far better than most other United States retailers. Wal-Mart continued to use its economies of scale to drive down prices, undercut competitors, and squeeze costs out of its suppliers. The company also planned to continue its international expansion with five-year plans focusing on high-growth markets in Brazil and China.[56]

Summary

Both the cases of McDonald's in China and Wal-Mart in Mexico show how the interplay of microeconomic and macroeconomic factors influences managers' competitive strategies. For both of these companies, expansion abroad was a strategic move that helped offset slowing growth in the United States. However, both cases show how the companies had to understand consumer behavior in these countries and the nature of the competition from both local and international sources. Production and cost-cutting strategies that worked in the United States often had to be modified in the foreign setting. Both companies also faced risk from political and macroeconomic events in their developing markets.

Managers can use the tools and models presented in both Parts 1 and 2 of this text to understand the microeconomic concepts of demand, production, cost, and market structure and how these factors are influenced by the overall macroeconomic environment. Managers can develop industry and macroeconomic analyses similar to those in this chapter by combining the conceptual analysis in the text with data on firms, industries, and the macro economy. This process should enable managers to make better decisions and develop more successful competitive strategies as they attempt to cope with the complex and ever-changing economic environment.

---

[54] "A Slowing Mexican Economy," Economist.com, September 23, 2008; "Crisis Management in Mexico," Economist.com, November 12, 2008.

[55] Kris Hudson and Ana Campoy, "Hispanics' Hard Times Hit Wal-Mart; Results of U.S. Housing Slump Are Felt on Both Sides of Border with Mexico," *Wall Street Journal*, August 29, 2007; Miriam Jordan, "Fewer Latino Migrants Send Money Home, Poll Says," *Wall Street Journal*, May 1, 2008.

[56] Miguel Bustillo and Ann Zimmerman, "Wal-Mart Flourishes as Economy Turns Sour," *Wall Street Journal*, November 14, 2008.

Appendix 16A Competitive Strategy in the Fast-Food Industry

This case analyzes the fast-food industry, with a particular emphasis on McDonald's Corp. Although this industry was impacted by the recessions of 2001 and 2008, these factors interacted with the microeconomic forces of demand, production and cost, and market competition. Managers at McDonald's and its competitors had to focus on responding to the changing nature of demand for their products and on meeting new forms of competition.

Impact of the Changing Macro Environment

As we discussed in Chapters 11–15, the U.S. economy entered into a recession in March 2001 and again in December 2007. These downturns in economic activity forced all the fast-food companies to develop new strategies as discussed below. In December 2008, it appeared that McDonald's had weathered the recession better than many other companies, posting a 7.7 percent increase in sales at outlets open at least a year in November 2008. McDonald's attributed its success to its "Plan to Win" strategy that focused on improving results at existing locations. The global scope of its operations also helped offset weakness in particular countries.[57]

Shifting Product Demand

For much of 2001 and 2002, McDonald's faced a demand curve that shifted against its business for a number of reasons. Consumer tastes and preferences had been changing as more individuals became concerned about the high fat content of most fast foods. Lawsuits were launched claiming that the industry contributed to obesity and other health conditions in the population such as heart disease and high blood pressure. The industry was also under competitive threat from the emergence of "quick-casual" restaurants, such as Cosi and Panera Bread, which had no table service, but served higher-quality foods, such as sandwiches and salads, and charged higher prices. Although industry analysts expected that most quick-casual customers would be middle-aged baby boomers who could afford the higher prices, 37 percent of the quick-casual customers were 18 to 34 years old, the population segment that typically consumed the most fast food.[58]

This change in fast-food demand is shown in the demand curve shift in Figure 16A.1, which is based on the analysis we developed in Chapters 2 and 3. With the original

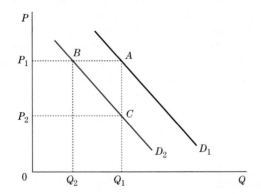

FIGURE 16A.1
Change in Demand in the Fast-Food Industry
To counter the decrease in demand from D₁ to D₂, fast-food managers must either try to shift the demand curve back out or lower price to increase quantity demanded. McDonald's and other fast-food companies have used both strategies.

---

[57] Janet Adamy, "McDonald's Sales Keep Growing," *Wall Street Journal*, December 9, 2008.
[58] Shirley Leung, "Fast-Food Chains' Price Cuts Only Get a Yawn from Diners," *Wall Street Journal*, November 11, 2002.

demand curve, D_1, in Figure 16.1, quantity Q_1 is demanded at price P_1. If the demand curve shifts to D_2 as a result of changing tastes and preferences, only quantity Q_2 will be demanded at price P_1, the situation described above. To restore the quantity demanded to Q_1, McDonald's can try to shift the demand curve to the right by influencing different variables in the demand function, by lowering the product price to increase the quantity demanded along demand curve D_2, or by using a combination of these strategies. The effectiveness of any strategy will depend on the consumer responsiveness or elasticity of the different variables in the demand function.

The Dollar Menu strategy of offering eight items for $1 each, which McDonald's undertook in fall 2002, was based on the assumption or hope that the price elasticity of demand is elastic or that the percentage change in quantity demanded is greater than the percentage change in price. In this situation, as we discussed in Chapter 3, a price decrease actually results in an increase in total revenue. The initial reaction to this strategy in early 2003 was that it was not working as expected. Some franchise owners reported that profits were declining from selling the discount items. Thus, demand for those items may actually have been inelastic, so that a decrease in price resulted in a decrease in total revenue. When McDonald's officials reported a fourth-quarter loss in 2002, the first quarterly loss in 38 years as a publicly traded company, they indicated they were reviewing the policy of keeping some of the big sandwiches, such as the Big 'N Tasty, on the Dollar Menu, given that these discounted items were decreasing sales of full-priced burgers, such as the Big Mac. Various industry and financial analysts argued that the Dollar Menu should be dropped or revised substantially because the discounting hurt not only McDonald's financial condition, but also that of the entire fast-food sector. However, an unconfirmed memo to franchisees indicated that McDonald's intended to allocate approximately 20 percent of its 2003 domestic advertising budget to the Dollar Menu in spite of the decrease in sales during the previous year, and especially during the fourth quarter when the Dollar Menu was advertised extensively.[59]

Given rising costs, McDonald's announced in November 2008 that it was pulling its double cheeseburger off its Dollar Menu and replacing it with a McDouble burger, which had one slice of cheese instead of two. This change was estimated to save six cents per burger. McDonald's kept the double cheeseburger on its regular menu and raised the suggested price to $1.19.[60]

Oligopolistic Behavior

McDonald's Corp. operates in a market structure with many competitors and substitute foods. However, it engages in oligopolistic behavior with its major fast-food competitors, especially Burger King and Wendy's.[61] McDonald's held 43.1 percent of the U.S. burger market in 2002, followed by Burger King (18.5 percent) and Wendy's (13.2 percent). Although the chains say they do not focus on each other as the main competition, their actions are definitely those of oligopolists. McDonald's introduction of its 8-item Dollar Menu with a $20 million advertising campaign in 2002 was followed by Burger King's offering of a menu of 11 items at 99 cents each. Burger King claimed it lost customers to McDonald's because the Big 'N Tasty and McChicken sandwiches on the Dollar Menu were twice as large as any sandwich on Burger King's 99-cent menu. Meanwhile, both chains were fighting the obesity issue. In September 2002, McDonald's announced it would use a different oil to

[59] Amy Zuber, "McD Plots Turnaround," *Nation's Restaurant News*, January 6, 2003, 1, 75.

[60] Janet Adamy, "McDonald's to Raise Burger's Price," *Wall Street Journal*, November 26, 2008; Adamy, *Wall Street Journal*, December 9, 2008.

[61] This discussion is based on Leung, "Fast-Food Chains' Price Cuts Only Get a Yawn"; and Shirley Leung, "Burger Wars Are Yielding Ground to Bigger Shakeups," *Wall Street Journal*, December 16, 2002.

reduce the trans-fatty acid in its fried foods, while Burger King introduced a veggie burger in the same year.

The companies matched each other on price cuts, cooking styles, and menu variety for many years. In 1998, McDonald's introduced its "Made for You" campaign, which involved a costly redesign of its kitchens to emulate Burger King's "Have It Your Way" style of assembling sandwiches to order. Previously, McDonald's had made batches of burgers and microwaved them at the time of a customer order. The company spent $181 million on this change, while franchisees spent an average of $30,000 on each restaurant. Although this kitchen change was designed to produce hotter and fresher food and more customized service, many franchisees found the kitchens too complicated, often requiring an increase in staff, which added to costs. In early 2003, it was still unclear whether there had been any increased sales growth from the "Made for You" innovation.

Thus, the strategic question for McDonald's managers is whether consumers care more about convenience, taste, or price. This is a question of the sensitivity of different variables in the consumer demand function.

In 2008, the fast-food rivals competed with new coffee strategies. Wendy's introduced a line of iced coffees and a new drink called Frosty-cino in August 2008. McDonald's rolled out its McCafe coffee drinks in more than 3,000 of its 14,000 United States locations. Based on focus group results, the company also began experimenting with new types of hot and cold drinks that would not be made with coffee, designed for people that like the idea of coffee drinks but not the actual taste. At McDonald's all drinks tended to have higher profit margins than food items.[62]

All the rivals also experimented with their menus and pricing. Wendy's, which was acquired by Triarc Cos., which also owned Arby's, planned to focus on customers aged 24 to 49, change its value menu in light of higher ingredient and labor costs, and improve its french fries, sandwich buns, and bacon. Wendy's also attempted to break into the breakfast business, which McDonald's had long dominated. Burger King tested a smaller $1.00 Whopper Jr. in response to higher ingredient costs.[63]

Strategies to Offset Shifting Demand

McDonald's has engaged in a variety of strategies to counter shifting demand. Sales of Happy Meals to children declined 6 to 7 percent over 2001 and 2002. This decline was critical to the company because Happy Meals accounted for 20 percent of the U.S. transactions, or approximately $3.5 billion in annual revenue.[64] Happy Meals also generated increased sales to adults. In some restaurants, the average adult order with a Happy Meal was 50 percent larger than those orders without a Happy Meal. McDonald's has dominated the market for children with its introduction of the Happy Meal in 1976 and in-store playgrounds in subsequent years. Burger King launched its Kids Meals only in 1990, and children's meals remain an insignificant business for Wendy's, Pizza Hut, KFC, and Taco Bell.

To counter this declining Happy Meal trend, McDonald's has considered offering a "Mom's Meal," with a gift for the mother who buys the Happy Meal for the child. Competitive strategy also focused on the toy that comes with the meal. In 2002, McDonald's began increasing the quality of its toys and adding toys with a greater

---

[62] Janet Adamy, "Wendy's Raises Its Coffee Profile," *Wall Street Journal*, September 8, 2008; Janet Adamy, "McDonald's Coffee Strategy Is Tough Sell," *Wall Street Journal*, October 27, 2008.
[63] Janet Adamy and Julie Jargon, "Burger King Battles Costs with Smaller Whopper Jr." *Wall Street Journal*, August 22, 2008; Janet Adamy, "Wendy's Comes Up with a New Strategic Recipe," *Wall Street Journal*, September 30, 2008.
[64] Shirley Leung and Suzanne Vranica, "Happy Meals Are No Longer Bringing Smiles to McDonald's," *Wall Street Journal*, January 31, 2003.

appeal to children. Part of the problem was that the chain had signed a 10-year agreement with Walt Disney Company that prohibited McDonald's from featuring promotions involving any Disney competitors. Thus, the lack of success of some Disney movies had a negative impact on Happy Meal sales. McDonald's officials were also concerned that children were becoming bored with traditional toys at an earlier age. The chain considered offering more interactive toys with the meals and installing Nintendo videogame stations in some markets. To counter parents' concerns about fast foods and childhood obesity, McDonald's considered offering a variety of menu additions, such as apple slices, fruit juices, peanut butter and jelly sandwiches, and carrot sticks.

In 2001 and 2002, McDonald's also tried to improve the quality of its service by hiring mystery shoppers to evaluate service, cleanliness, and food quality in more than 13,000 U.S. restaurants, using a single set of standards and measurements. Burger King used a similar type of grading system.[65] The question regarding this strategy was, again, the relative importance to the customer of service and cleanliness compared with price and the variety of menu items. A mystery shopper survey by the *Wall Street Journal* in 2001 found that the overall score for McDonald's was 81.9 percent compared with 80.1 percent at Burger King, 80.7 percent at Wendy's, and 77.1 percent at Taco Bell. Thus, customers may not be able to distinguish among the rival chains on the basis of this characteristic. It was also unclear what the impact on sales would be if the rating increased from 80 to 90 percent.

Expansion to Other Business Activities

Part of the McDonald's response to changing consumer tastes was to purchase or acquire ownership in more formal restaurant chains such as Boston Market, Chipotle Mexican Grill, and Donatos Pizza.[66] These purchases could help McDonald's counter revenue declines from its traditional restaurants. In 2002, McDonald's also began considering how to use its vast real estate network to sell items beyond food. The company is unique in the fast-food industry in that it owns much of its real estate or has it tied up in long-term leases, so it has to consider the opportunity cost of using the land to produce its traditional foods, as we discussed in Chapter 5. In 2002, McDonald's began an experiment with Freddie Mac, the mortgage finance agency, in which information about home ownership was provided to McDonald's customers by linking computers in the restaurants to Freddie Mac's own Web site. Analysts have suggested that the partnership with Walt Disney Company could result in McDonald's selling toys or offering travel planning to Disney parks.

Cost-Cutting Strategies

To cut costs in the face of declining demand and increased competition, many fast-food restaurants have focused on reducing paper napkin costs.[67] Some restaurants overstuffed the dispensers, making it difficult for customers to grab more than one

---

[65] Shirley Leung, "McDonald's Hires Mystery Eaters to Find Out What Ails Food Sales," *Wall Street Journal*, December 17, 2001; Amy Zuber, "Slow Economy Feeds Fast-Food Fight," *Nation's Restaurant News*, January 21, 2002, 28–29; Shirley Leung, "Kindler, Gentler Fast Food? Testing New Service Pushes," *Wall Street Journal*, January 7, 2003.

[66] Shirley Leung, "McDonald's Studies Using Outlets to Sell Items Other Than Food," *Wall Street Journal*, May 29, 2002.

[67] Shirley Leung, "Napkins Get Smaller and Scarcer as Fast-Food Places Trim Costs," *Wall Street Journal*, May 2, 2002.

napkin. Others placed the dispensers near cashiers so they could be monitored. Most fast-food chains have cut the size of their napkins from a standard 13 by 17 inches to 13 by 12 inches, reducing costs by 10 to 12 percent. Fast-food napkins have also gotten approximately 10 percent thinner in the past decade. McDonald's reduced the size of its napkins three times from 1997 to 2002 and began testing a 6.5-by-8.4-inch napkin. As with other input changes, there is always a balance between cutting costs and influencing demand. Napkins typically account for approximately 1 percent of a fast-food restaurant's total expenses, but they may impact 10 to 20 percent of customer-satisfaction scores. Making napkins more difficult to grab out of a dispenser may actually result in more consumption as consumers end up grabbing wads of napkins instead of one or two. One study found that customers typically ended up grabbing 9.25 napkins from the hard-to-pull dispensers.

Innovations for Different Tastes

Given varying tastes around the world, McDonald's has implemented a different strategy with its restaurants in France than in the United States.[68] French managers were convincing consumers to linger over their meals by installing chic interiors and music videos and by adding menu items such as a hot ham and cheese sandwich. While the chain was closing down restaurants worldwide, it opened a new outlet in France every six days in 2002. French customers typically spent $9 per visit compared with $4 in the United States, even though the price of a Big Mac was approximately the same in Paris as in New York City. McDonald's also designed its restaurants in France to blend in with the local architecture. Thus, the French strategy has been contrary to McDonald's history of consistency in the design of its restaurants and food offerings.

More recent managerial debates have focused on whether this French concept can be transferred to the United States. The question is whether McDonald's customers are primarily interested in quick service and cheap food, perhaps obtained mostly through a drive-in window, or whether more customers would respond to a comfortable setting and higher-quality food. In France and elsewhere in Europe, McDonald's has pushed its "Premier" line of sandwiches, priced 30 percent higher than the standard burger. The strategic issue is whether new customers can be attracted without alienating the old ones. Although Burger King pulled out of France in 1998, McDonald's restaurants have faced increased competition from chains serving fresh baguettes with ham and brie in a bistro setting.

Drawing on Previous Experience

McDonald's has in the past faced challenges similar to the ones described above.[69] The environmental impact of the company's use of polystyrene foam packages for its products became a major issue in the late 1980s. Even though McDonald's sponsored waste reduction campaigns and polystyrene foam recycling programs, the company continued to be on the defensive regarding environmental issues. In 1990, the company announced it was phasing out foam packaging in the United States, a move that would eventually save each restaurant approximately $2,000 per year. That year

---

[68] Shirley Leung, "McHaute Cuisine: Makeover Boosts McDonald's in France," *Wall Street Journal*, August 30, 2002; Carol Matlack and Pallavi Gogoi, "What's This? The French Love McDonald's? Gallic Twists Are Luring Crowds—and Giving the Parent a Boost," *Business Week*, January 13, 2003, 50.
[69] This discussion is based on John F. Love, *McDonald's: Behind the Arches*, rev. ed. (New York: Bantam, 1995).

McDonald's also developed a partnership and a comprehensive solid-waste-reduction action plan with the Environmental Defense Fund. These changes helped McDonald's turn a strategic problem into a competitive advantage.

The company also realized in the early 1990s that price and value were key strategic variables that needed greater attention. This change in strategy was brought about by both the recession of 1990–91 and price discounting by competitors such as Taco Bell, again showing the interaction of macro and micro influences on a firm's competitive strategy. McDonald's had traditionally viewed price discounting as a local market tactic and not part of a national marketing strategy. In 1991, McDonald's introduced several low-price menu leaders and its combination Extra Value Meals, supported by a $47 million advertising campaign. The company found that it could still be profitable with the lower prices by also focusing on cost reduction. The company began using a new filter powder to extend the life of the shortening used to cook french fries, which saved each restaurant $2,800 annually. Changing from a company-sponsored insurance program to eight approved insurance companies gave restaurant operators the flexibility to control costs through competitive bidding and resulted in an annual decrease in property and casualty insurance costs of $4,000 per restaurant. These two programs, combined with the savings from shifting to paper packaging, saved more than $80 million per year when applied to the more than 9,300 U.S. restaurants.

McDonald's was also able to lower the total average development cost of a U.S. restaurant by more than 27 percent from 1990 to 1993 by using better methods to determine the optimum size of the buildings and more cost-effective construction methods. The company developed the Series 2000 building, which is half the size of a traditional restaurant, but has a kitchen engineered to produce almost as much volume as a standard kitchen. These "mini" restaurants cost 30 percent less to build in 1991, but could handle 96 percent of the volume of a full-sized restaurant. The lower costs of these smaller units also opened up market niches in small towns and other areas that could not support traditional restaurants. As McDonald's expanded globally, it was able to achieve even greater economies of scale by purchasing supplies from around the world at the least cost. New Zealand cheese was flown to South America, while beef from Uruguay was distributed in Malaysia. The United States supplied potatoes for Hong Kong and Japan, while the sesame seeds for the buns were produced in Mexico. The company was often able to avoid currency problems through barter arrangements, as when it shipped Russian pies to Germany in return for packaging, lobby trays, and cleaning materials.

Statistical Estimation of Demand Curves

In Chapter 4, we contrasted the marketing approach of understanding consumer behavior and demand—by, for example, using expert opinion, consumer surveys, and test markets and pricing experiments—with the economic approach of statistically estimating a demand function. We have just described McDonald's attempts to learn about consumer behavior using these marketing methods. The company has used knowledge gained from observing consumers and experimenting with different demand variables to develop new competitive strategies, not all of which were successful. The statistical estimation of demand functions can give managers added insights on the role of the different variables influencing consumer demand.

The fast-food industry has long recognized that the convenience of its restaurants is a major factor influencing sales and consumer demand. Consumers want a consistent and standardized product, but it must be accessible in easily reached locations. Mark Jekanowski, James Binkley, and James Eales analyzed the role of accessibility versus other variables in an econometric study of fast-food demand in

1992.[70] These researchers based the study on the concept that consumers react to the "full price" of purchasing fast food, which consists of both the money price and the value of time spent in acquiring the food.

Using data on a cross-section of 85 metropolitan areas from the Census of Retail Trade and the decennial population census, these researchers used multiple regression analysis to estimate a fast-food demand function in which per capita fast-food consumption was assumed to be a function of market characteristics, prices and income, demographic characteristics, and regional indicators.

The market characteristic variables measure access to both fast-food outlets and competitor restaurants, which were subdivided into inexpensive (under $7 per check) and expensive restaurants. Food (grocery) store density was also included, as these stores compete with fast-food restaurants through their deli counters and prepared take-out meals. Gasoline consumption per capita and population density were included as proxies for travel distance and cost. The average fast-food price was based on the hamburger, pizza, and chicken outlets in the study areas. Prices of the substitute products, grocery store food and inexpensive and expensive restaurant meals, were also incorporated in the analysis. The female labor force participation rate was included as a measure of the opportunity cost of time, as consumption of food away from home is generally greater in households where the female family member works outside the home. Age variables were added to measure the targeting of fast food to children and differential consumption by other age groups. The effect of household size, educational background, and cultural differences among two minority groups were also tested in the analysis.

The statistical results showed that the coefficient of the fast-food outlet density variable was positive and significant, indicating that in 1992, restaurant accessibility was an important factor influencing the demand for fast food, independent of price and the other variables in the equation. The lack of statistical significance of the other density variables indicated that neither other types of restaurants nor food stores competed directly with fast-food restaurants on the basis of travel costs. For food purchased in grocery stores, the time involved in preparing that food for meals, which was not measured in the study, was probably a more important factor affecting fast-food demand than the time spent purchasing the food. The results also suggested that inexpensive restaurants were a poor substitute for fast-food outlets in terms of convenience. Gasoline consumption did not affect fast-food demand, perhaps because this variable focused on a single type of transportation. The sign and significance of the population density variable suggest that fast-food consumption might be negatively affected by the inconvenience associated with mobility in densely populated areas.

The fast-food price variable was significant and had its expected negative sign. However, none of the other price or income variables in this analysis was statistically significant. These results suggest that convenience, more than price, drives the demand for fast food. Other types of restaurants may provide the same or higher-quality food, even at similar prices. However, if consumers place a high value on their time and restaurant convenience, the full price of fast-food outlets is always lower.

The price elasticity of demand was estimated to be elastic, and the size of this elasticity estimate increased from 1982. This increased sensitivity to price could have resulted from the fact that product price became a larger proportion of the full price of consuming fast food, as travel costs decreased due to increased customer accessibility to fast-food outlets. The larger price elasticity could also have resulted from an increase in the number of substitute products from 1982 to 1992, especially microwaveable foods and prepared meals in grocery stores.

---

[70] This discussion is based on Mark D. Jekanowski, James K. Binkley, and James Eales, "Convenience, Accessibility, and the Demand for Fast Food," *Journal of Agricultural and Resource Economics* 26 (July 2001): 58–74.

The income elasticity of demand was estimated to be inelastic, although the variable was not statistically significant in the analysis. Other studies of the consumption of food away from home have also shown an inelastic income variable, indicating that consumption of these foods is not greatly affected by changes in income. These results support the above discussion, indicating that the problems of the fast-food industry are associated more with microeconomic demand and market changes than with changes in income arising from the overall macroeconomic environment.

How can these statistical results help McDonald's managers make better decisions? This study confirms fast-food managers' strategies of focusing on convenience as a major variable influencing consumer demand for their product. This result relates to the article in Chapter 5 of this text, which focused on improving the technology of fast-food windows in order to increase the flow of customers. The results also suggest that fast-food restaurants are not in direct competition with table service restaurants in the same price range, but may face more competition from prepared meals in grocery stores. Fast-food managers should consider increasing the number of restaurants in minority-populated areas. The results also indicate differences in fast-food consumption by geographical area, which means that managers should attempt to discover the reasons for these differences through marketing approaches designed to increase understanding of consumer behavior. Given the data available, this study was not able to evaluate many of the specific McDonald's strategies and problems discussed above, such as the introduction of Mom's Meals, the changing of the toys in the Happy Meals, and the increasing consumer concerns about the quality of fast food. However, more recent and more detailed data would allow marketers and economists to incorporate these factors into the types of models discussed here. As we noted in Chapter 4, combining both approaches to understanding consumer behavior can help managers develop better competitive strategies.

Summary: Macro and Micro Influences on the Fast-Food Industry

McDonald's Corp. and its competitors in the fast-food industry were influenced by the global downturn in economic activity in 2001 and 2002. However, more of their problems and strategies were influenced by microeconomic changes affecting this particular industry. Traditional fast food was under attack by competing "casual-quality" substitutes and by consumer concerns over the health impacts of the products. These factors would affect McDonald's competitive strategies even in the absence of an economic downturn. McDonald's and its competitors, who operate in an oligopolistic environment, must try to determine which variables—for example, price, quality, health concerns, convenience, speed of delivery, and ambiance of the restaurants—have the greatest influence on consumer demand.

The economic slowdown of 2007 and 2008 had similar impacts on McDonald's and the fast-food industry. In March 2008, the company reported the first decline in U.S. same-store sales in five years, although there was a rebound in April driven by menu variety, enhanced convenience, and value pricing.[71] The profit margins of many McDonald's franchisees were being squeezed by higher food and paper costs. As always, the impact on consumer behavior was a major factor influencing decisions about menus and pricing in response to these cost factors. Many restaurants were also considering international expansion following the lead of McDonald's and KFC as discussed in this chapter.[72]

---

[71] "McDonald's Reports Rise in Same-Store Sales," *Wall Street Journal*, May 9, 2008.
[72] Richard Gibson, "U.S. Restaurants Push Abroad," *Wall Street Journal*, June 18, 2008.

Exercises

Technical Questions

1. Describe the changing economic variables in China that influenced McDonald's expansion strategies.
2. What market model best describes the relationship between McDonald's and KFC in China? Explain.
3. What factors led to the Mexican currency crisis and peso devaluation in 1994?
4. Was Wal-Mart able to use the same strategies in Mexico as it did in the United States? Why or why not?

5. Regarding the discussion in Appendix A, when McDonald's introduced its Dollar Menu strategy in fall 2002, why was the company assuming or hoping that the demand for its products was elastic? Did this appear to be the case?
6. Based on the discussion in Appendix A, how did McDonald's development of its mini-restaurants improve its overall profitability?

Application Questions

1. Discuss how the two cases in this chapter illustrate the major theme of this text: *Changes in the macro environment affect individual firms and industries through the microeconomic factors of demand, production, cost, and profitability.* Drawing on current business publications, find some updated facts for each case that support this theme.
2. Compare and contrast McDonald's strategies in China with those of Wal-Mart in Mexico.
3. What role did the policies of various governments play in influencing the international expansion strategies of both McDonald's and Wal-Mart?

4. What variables other than price appear to have the biggest impact on the demand for McDonald's products? How much influence does the company have over these variables?
5. In recent business publications, find a case study in which changes in the macro environment play a major role in influencing a firm's competitive strategy. Contrast this with a second case in which micro factors play a more important role.

On the Web

For updated information on the *Wall Street Journal* article at the beginning of the chapter, as well as other relevant links and information, visit the book's Web site at **www.pearsonhighered.com/farnham**

Solutions to Even-Numbered Problems

Chapter 1

Technical Questions

2. Outputs are the final goods and services that firms and industries sell to consumers. Consumers create a demand for all of these goods and services. Inputs are the resources or factors of production that are used to produce the final outputs. Inputs include land, labor, capital, raw materials, and entrepreneurship. Firms' use of these inputs is related to the demand for their products.

4. In the model of perfect competition, firms are price-takers because it is assumed there are so many firms in each industry that no single firm has any influence on the price of the product. Each firm's output is small relative to the entire market, so that the market price is determined by the actions of all suppliers and demanders. In the other market models, firms have an influence over the price. If they raise the price of the product, consumers will demand a smaller quantity; if they lower the price, consumers will increase the quantity demanded.

6. Fiscal policies are implemented by the national government and involve changing taxes (T) and government expenditure (G) to stimulate or slow the economy. These decisions are made by the political institutions in the country. Monetary policies are implemented by a country's central bank—the Federal Reserve in the United States. These policies focus on changing the money supply in order to influence interest rates, which then affect real consumption, investment spending, and the resulting level of income and output.

Application Questions

2. In April 2008, the Economist Intelligence Unit predicted that Mexico's annual GDP growth would gradually accelerate toward a rate of 3.5 percent. However, Mexico's growth path will continue to be dependent on the U.S. economic cycle. U.S. growth affects not only Mexican gross fixed investment and exports, but also its employment, wages, and private consumption. Mexican economists state that Mexico is the most exposed country in the world to a U.S. slowdown. One of the major impacts on the Mexican economy is the remittance of money from Mexican immigrants working in the United States back to Mexico. The Central Bank of Mexico reported in May 2008 that remittances from the United States dropped 2.9 percent for the first quarter of 2008 compared with the same period in 2007. By fall 2008, the weaker United States economy was lowering Mexico's growth rate. The Mexican government cut its estimate for GDP growth from 2.8 percent to 2.4 percent. The Mexican central bank also cooperated with the United States Federal Reserve to increase liquidity in the financial system. See "Mexico: Country Forecast Summary," *EIU ViewsWire*, April 17, 2008; Jane Bussey, "Mexico Feels Our Economic Pain," *McClatchy-Tribune Business News*, April 7, 2008; Miriam Jordan, "Fewer Latino Migrants Send Money Home, Poll Says," *Wall Street Journal*, May 1, 2008; "A Slowing Mexican Economy," *EIA ViewsWire*, September 23, 2008; and "Crisis Management in Mexico," *EIA ViewsWire*, November 12, 2008.

4. Numerous examples can be found. In general, the more competitive the market is, the more firms will have to rely on reducing the costs of production, as they have less control over price. Firms with market power often use all types of strategies. For example, many restaurants responded to the economic slowdown in 2007 and 2008 by scaling back expansion plans, skimping on items like extra sauce and free sour cream, closing sites, and laying off workers. After examining rivals' portions of hash browns and french fries and analyzing leftovers, Vicorp, which owns 400-plus Village Inn and Bakers Square restaurants, cut back as much as an ounce from each serving of these foods with a projected annual savings of more than $500,000. See Jeffrey McCracken and Janet Adamy, "Restaurants Feel Sting of Surging Costs, Debt," *Wall Street Journal*, April 24, 2008.

Chapter 2

Technical Questions

2. a. Supply increases.
   b. Supply decreases.
   c. There is a decrease in the quantity supplied of computers (and no change in the supply curve).
   d. Supply decreases (because costs of production have increased).
   e. There is no change in supply, as consumer incomes are a determinant of demand.

4. a. X and Z are complements in production. We know this because there is a positive relationship between the price of good Z and the supply of good X (thus, as the price of Z rises, producers produce more X).
   b. $Q_S = -200 + 20P_X - 5P_I + 0.5P_Z$
      $= -200 + 20P_X - 5(10) + 0.5(20)$
      $= -240 + 20P_X$

   c.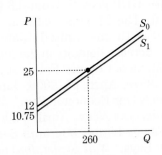

   d. Set $Q_S = 0$. The minimum price is $12.00.
   e. $Q_S = -240 + 20(25) = 260$.
   f. $Q_S = -200 + 20P_X - 5(5) + 0.5(20) = -215 + 20P_X$.

6. a. Demand increases (the price of a substitute has risen); equilibrium price and quantity rise.

   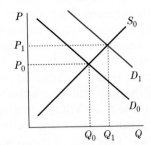

   b. Supply decreases (the price of an input has risen); equilibrium price rises and quantity falls.

   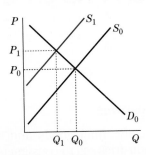

   c. Demand increases; equilibrium price and quantity rise.

   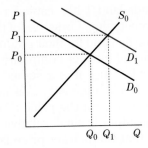

   d. Supply increases; equilibrium price falls and quantity rises.

   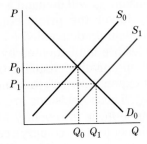

   e. Demand decreases; equilibrium price and quantity fall.

   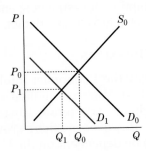

8. a. Because hamburger is an inferior good, demand will increase as incomes decrease, causing the price to rise (rightward shift of demand curve). The improvement in technology that lowers production costs causes supply to increase and tends to lower price (rightward shift of supply curve). With no further information, we know that the equilibrium quantity will rise, but the effect on price cannot be determined.

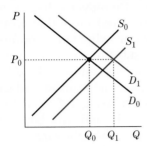

  b. The decrease in consumer incomes will cause demand to increase (for an inferior good), which will cause the price to rise, all other things held constant. If this effect is smaller than the effect of the improvement in technology (which will increase supply and cause the price to fall), then we may now be able to conclude that the equilibrium price of hamburger is likely to fall.

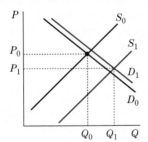

Application Questions

2. The boom in copper and other commodity prices continued through the first half of 2008. These high prices put immense pressure on geologists

and engineers in major mining companies to find new sources of copper, often in remote areas such as the Peruvian Andes. By April 2008, Rio Tinto employed 950 explorers worldwide and spent 15 percent more on exploration than it did five years earlier. Many global mining companies were playing catch-up after a long period of underinvesting in exploration for new mines. However, it can take years to get a new mine up and running. The high copper prices also continued to make manhole covers, pipes, wiring, and even public art projects made of bronze (whose main ingredient is copper) the targets of theft in many U.S. cities. However, in the summer and fall of 2008, the prices of copper and other commodities fell in response to the slump in global demand. See Robert Guy Matthews, "Hunters Comb Globe for a Hot Metal," *Wall Street Journal*, April 4, 2008; Sarah McBride, "Copper Caper: Thieves Nab Art to Sell for Scrap," *Wall Street Journal*, May 1, 2008; Allen Sykora, "Copper Is Vulnerable to Falling Further," *Wall Street Journal*, November 24, 2008.

4. a. The new demand for ethanol and biodiesel has raised the prices of corn, palm oil, sugar, and other crops from which these products are made. However, corn, palm oil, and sugar are also inputs to a variety of other foods such as beef, eggs, and soft drinks. These increased costs have caused a leftward shift of the supply curve for these foods, increasing their prices also.

  b. Increasing the amount of land under cultivation for food is represented by a rightward shift of the supply curve, which would lower food prices.

  c. Technological advances, such as better seed varieties, would lower the costs of food production, shift the supply curve to the right, and result in lower food prices.

  d. Rising incomes, particularly in China, increase the demand for food, resulting in higher food prices.

  e. A bumper crop, or a large increase in the supply of various commodities, may be necessary to keep food prices lower in India and China.

Chapter 3

Technical Questions

2. a. Price elasticity $= -1$ (unitary elasticity)
  b. Price elasticity $= -3.0$ (elastic)
  c. Price elasticity $= -0.33$ (inelastic)

4. a. $P_X = 250 - 1/2Q$
    $TR = PQ = (250 - 1/2Q)Q = 250Q - 1/2Q^2$

b.

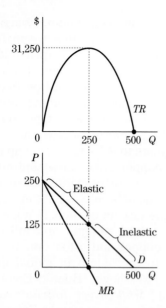

c. At $Q = 250$, $MR = 0$, and, thus, revenue is maximized. At that point, $P = \$125$, and, thus, $TR = \$31,250$.

d. The midpoint of the demand curve is at $Q = 250$, $P = \$125$. Above that point, demand is elastic, and below that point, demand is inelastic.

6. Demand is inelastic (and, thus, revenues will rise if you increase the price and fall if you lower it). Your good is a normal good and is income inelastic (or a necessity good). The related good is a substitute because a rise in the price of the other good causes an increase in demand for your product; the goods are fairly good substitutes as the demand for your product is elastic with respect to the price of the other good.

Application Questions

2. We can use the facts in the question to make inferences about the price elasticity of demand for walk-up, unrestricted business airfares.

   a. On the Cleveland–Los Angeles route, the decrease in fare resulted in about the same revenue as the higher fare. This implies a consumer price elasticity of demand around -1.00. At unit elasticity, any change in price results in no change in total revenue. On the Cleveland–Houston route, the decrease in price resulted in less revenue, but greater market share. Demand was inelastic on this route because quantity demanded increased as the price was lowered, but total revenue decreased. Demand was price elastic on the Houston–Oakland route because the lower airfares resulted in increased total revenue for Continental on this route.

   b. Consumer behavior differs on the three routes, but is also different from prior expectations. As discussed in the chapter, the airlines typically assumed that demand for business travel was inelastic, while demand for leisure travel was elastic. Under this assumption, airline companies did not decrease business fares because they believed they would have lost revenue in doing so.

   c. Many businesses have gotten tired of paying the high, unrestricted fares for their business travelers. Employees began searching for lower restricted fares that would meet their schedules or using videoconferencing or driving as a substitute for air travel. The terrorist attacks on September 11, 2001, also had a major impact on the airline industry, with many employees refusing to fly in the months following the attacks and with business only slowly recovering in the following years. All of these factors resulted in major changes in business traveler behavior and a probable increase in their price elasticity of demand. The above market tests show that business demand is actually price elastic in certain markets.

4. A price elasticity of demand for urban transit between -0.1 and -0.6 means that demand is inelastic for transit users. Thus, increased fares will result in higher revenue for local governments and transit authorities. This is the economic argument for raising transit fares. However, there may be political constraints on raising fares. The inelastic demand may result from the low income levels and lack of automobiles and other substitute forms of travel of transit riders. Voters may perceive increased fares as placing an unfair burden on these low-income riders. Transit authorities often obtain voter approval for new transit systems by promising not to raise fares for a certain number of years. Governmental decisions are typically based on many factors other than economic arguments.

6. The price elasticity of demand for the product of an individual firm is typically greater than the price elasticity for the product overall because the individual firm competes with all the other producers of the same product. There are more substitutes for the product of an individual firm than for the product overall. This outcome is most clearly shown in Table 3.7 for agricultural products. The demand for many of the products in the table is inelastic for the product overall, while the table shows a price elasticity of demand for individual producers ranging from -800 to $-31,000$ (extremely elastic). The price elasticity of demand for individual physicians is also much larger than that for medical or dental care as a

commodity. The demand for dental care may be inelastic, while the demand for care from any given dentist is price elastic, given the number of other dentists providing similar care.

8. The U.S. Postal Service raised Priority Mail rates by 16 percent, and Bear Creek Corporation reduced its package shipping by 15 to 20 percent. The implied price elasticity of demand (%ΔQ/%ΔP) ranges from $-15/16 = -0.94$ to $-20/16 = -1.25$. If this response

is typical for all Postal Service customers, revenues will either remain approximately the same or decrease, given that the price elasticity of demand is approximately unitary or price elastic. Particularly if the demand is elastic, the Postal Service will not be able to reduce its deficit by this strategy because revenues will decrease. Consumers will use Federal Express or UPS instead of the Postal Service to ship their packages.

Chapter 4

Technical Questions

2. The plotted data are simply price and quantity combinations for each of the 10 years. Although the data appear to indicate a downward sloping demand curve for potatoes, many factors other than the price of potatoes changed over this period. These factors included consumer incomes, the prices of other vegetables that could be substituted for potatoes, the introduction of packaged dried potatoes in grocery stores, and the changing tastes for french fries at fast-food outlets. Thus, each data point is probably on a separate demand curve for that year, and the data points in the figure result from shifts in those demand curves. To derive a demand curve from this time-series data, a multiple regression analysis should be run that includes other variables, such as income and the prices of substitute goods. Once these other variables are held constant statistically, the regression results can be used to plot the relevant demand curve showing the relationship between price and quantity demanded, all else held constant.

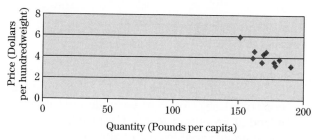

Quantity (Pounds per capita)

4. In multiple regression analysis, researchers try to include all the relevant variables that influence the demand for a product based on economic theory, market analysis, and common sense. The regression coefficients then show the effect of each variable, while statistically holding constant the effects of all other variables. Because each study is based on a limited set of data, researchers want to be able to generalize the results. Therefore, they

test hypotheses about whether each coefficient is significantly different from zero (i.e., whether the variable actually has a positive or negative effect on demand) in a statistical sense. If the variable is not significantly different from zero, its positive or negative coefficient is likely to result only from the given sample of data. The variable does not have an effect on demand in the larger population. Economic theory may give the researcher some knowledge of the expected sign of the variable (i.e., a price variable should have a negative coefficient in a demand equation). In many cases, however, the researcher does not know the expected sign of the variable, so the test is simply to determine whether the variable is significantly different from zero.

Application Questions

2. Test marketing and price experiments can be established so that consumer characteristics in addition to price, such as income and other demographics, can be varied in the different settings. Thus, consumer reaction to price can be measured while holding income constant in one setting and changing it to another level in a different setting. Individuals of various backgrounds can be specifically selected for different focus groups and laboratory experiments. Thus, test marketing, price experiments, focus groups, and laboratory experiments can be constructed to vary one characteristic (usually price), while holding other factors constant. Multiple regression analysis accomplishes this same task statistically. When variables are entered into a multiple regression analysis equation, their effects are statistically held constant. Each estimated coefficient shows the effect on the dependent variable of a one-unit change in an independent variable, holding the values of all other variables in the equation constant.

4. The estimating equation included variables measuring the monetary price of the cars as well as

variables measuring the search costs of subsequent visits to a dealer and whether a consumer repurchases the same brand of vehicle (which lowers search costs). Because these variables, as well as the monetary price variable, were statistically significant in the analysis, they indicate that consumers do consider the full price of purchasing an automobile and not just the monetary price.

Chapter 5

Technical Questions

2. a.

Capital (K)	Labor (L)	Total Product (TP)	Average Product (AP)	Marginal Product (MP)
10	0	0	—	—
10	1	25	25	25
10	2	100	50	75
10	3	220	73	120
10	4	303	76	83
10	5	357	71	54
10	6	392	65	35
10	7	414	59	22
10	8	424	53	10
10	9	428	48	4
10	10	429	43	1

b.

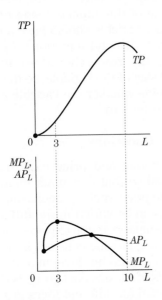

c. After the third worker (or output of 220), there are diminishing marginal returns.

d. Average product is maximized at an output level of 303.

4. a. Accounting profit is total revenue less explicit costs = $150,000 − [25,000 + 12,000 + 30,000 + 20,000] = $150,000 − 87,000 = $63,000.

b. Economic profit = total revenue − explicit costs − implicit costs
  = $150,000 − 87,000 − 50,000 − 5,000 = $8,000

6. a.

K	L	MP/TP	TFC	TVC	TC	AFC	AVC	ATC	MC
10	0	—/0	500	0	500	—	—	—	—
10	1	25/25	500	20	520	20	0.80	20.80	0.80
10	2	75/100	500	40	540	5	0.40	5.40	0.27
10	3	120/220	500	60	560	2.27	0.27	2.54	0.17
10	4	83/303	500	80	580	1.65	0.26	1.91	0.24
10	5	54/357	500	100	600	1.40	0.28	1.68	0.37
10	6	35/392	500	120	620	1.28	0.31	1.59	0.57
10	7	22/414	500	140	640	1.21	0.34	1.55	0.91
10	8	10/424	500	160	660	1.18	0.38	1.56	2.00
10	9	4/428	500	180	680	1.17	0.42	1.59	5.00
10	10	1/429	500	200	700	1.16	0.47	1.63	20.00

b.

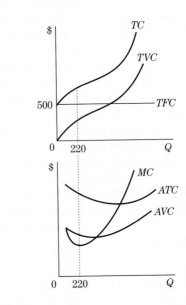

c. Average total cost is minimized at an output level of approximately 414 (or average total cost of $1.55). Average variable cost is minimized at an output level of approximately 303 (or average variable cost of $0.26).

8. An improvement in technology lowers (shifts rightward) marginal cost and all other cost curves (except fixed cost, which is not affected by marginal product). The minimum points on the average total and average variable cost curves will be at higher outputs and lower costs.

Application Questions

2. a. There will be diminishing returns in the drug manufacturing process because much of the testing for quality, gauging of dryness, and testing for bacterial contamination is done by hand. There are bottlenecks in terms of the fixed inputs—batches of chemicals that must be dried, the use of microscopes to count organisms. Adding more workers to the production process without increasing the fixed inputs will result in diminishing returns.

   b. The FDA allowed firms to maintain these types of production processes to maintain the quality and safety of the drugs. Pursuing this goal made the pharmaceutical companies very hesitant to change the production process and adopt new technologies because any change would require new FDA approval. The time and paperwork involved would probably put the company at a competitive disadvantage.

4. A change in a firm's total fixed costs of production will shift its average total cost (ATC) curve because $ATC = AFC + AVC$ and $AFC = TFC/Q$. Thus, an increase in total fixed cost will shift up the average total cost curve. Fixed costs do not influence the marginal costs of production. $MC = \Delta TC/\Delta Q = \Delta TVC/\Delta Q$. Marginal cost is influenced only by the variable costs, as fixed costs, by definition, do not change.

Chapter 6

Technical Questions

2.

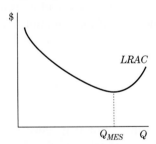

4. a. The minimum efficient scale should be at a high level of output.

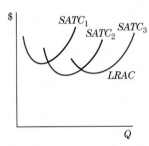

   b. The minimum efficient scale should be at a low level of output.

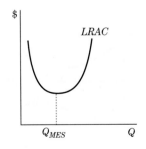

6. a.

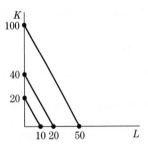

   b.

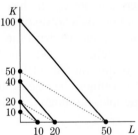

8. a. In the short run, with fixed capital, the firm cannot change its input mix because capital is fixed. Thus, the firm must employ exactly the same inputs if it wishes to produce the same quantity of output. However, the total cost of production will increase (new isocost line).

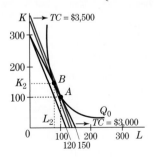

b. The firm's short-run cost curves will increase (shift leftward).

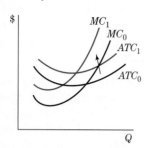

c. In the long run, with all factors variable, the firm will switch to an input mix with less labor and more capital. (Note also that the rise in costs may reduce the quantity that the firm wishes to produce.) The total cost of production will increase in order to produce the original level of output, but not by as much as when the input mix was held constant (part a). See graph for part a.

Application Questions

2. H.J. Heinz is developing sweeter tomatoes for its ketchup in response to the soaring price of high-fructose corn syrup, which accounts for about 10% of the cost of producing a bottle of ketchup. Heinz is paying 25% more for its corn syrup than it did two years ago. Tomatoes, which account for a third of the cost of making a bottle of ketchup, have also become more expensive, with the cost of growing an acre of tomatoes increasing from $1,800 to $2,300. Heinz has increased its budget for seed research and doubled the size of its seed research team to 30 people. Although the company has long focused on increasing tomato yields, it began putting an emphasis on developing sweeter tomatoes in the past two years as corn prices began rising. (*Source*: Julie Jargon, "Seeking Sweet Savings," *Wall Street Journal*, October 2, 2007.)

When the Ted Stevens Anchorage International Airport was planning a new concourse, Alaska Airlines insisted that the "one thing we don't want is a ticket counter." When Concourse C opened in 2004, it had only one, small traditional ticket counter for the 1.2 million passengers that checked in in that area in that year. The new design with self-service check-in machines and manned "bag drop" stations doubled Alaska's capacity, halved its staffing needs, and cut costs while speeding travelers through the building in far less time. Other airlines and other airports have copied these design changes to try to increase productivity and reduce costs. (*Source:* Susan Carey, "Case of the Vanishing Airport Lines," *Wall Street Journal*, August 9, 2007.)

4. Economies of scale suggest that large-scale production is cheaper than small-scale production or that the long-run average cost curve slopes downward. However, this large-scale production is cheaper only if a large amount of output is produced and sold. The huge fixed costs of large-scale production lower the average cost of automobiles only if they are spread out over a large number of autos. The plant that lies at the minimum point of a U-shaped long-run average cost curve does not have the lowest costs if only a small number of autos are produced. Automakers would be running plants at unprofitable rates if they did not have a large market share. This explains the behavior in the quote.

Chapter 7

Technical Questions

2. a.

Number of Worker Hours	Output (Q)	Fixed Cost (TFC)	Variable Cost (TVC)	Total Cost (TC)	Marginal Cost (MC)	Average Variable Cost (AVC)	Average Total Cost (ATC)
0	0	15,000	0	15,000	—	—	—
25	100	15,000	575	15,575	5.75	5.75	155.75
50	150	15,000	900	15,900	6.50	6.00	106.00
75	175	15,000	1,100	16,100	8.00	6.28	92.00
100	195	15,000	1,275	16,275	8.75	6.53	83.46
125	205	15,000	1,400	16,400	12.50	6.82	80.00
150	210	15,000	1,500	16,500	20.00	7.14	78.57
175	212	15,000	1,585	16,585	42.50	7.47	78.23

b. The firm will produce 205 units.

c. The firm's profit is $[(12.50)(205)] - 16,400 = 2,562.50 - 16,400 = -\$13,837.50$. The firm is losing money, but if it were to shut down, it would lose $15,000 (its fixed costs); thus, the loss-minimizing choice is to stay in business in the short run (as $P > AVC$).

d.

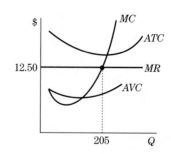

4. Supply curve S_2 is more elastic than supply curve S_1. We can infer this because, for a given change in price, the change in quantity supplied is far greater on supply curve S_2 (in other words, a given percentage change in price leads to a larger percentage change in quantity supplied).

6. a. The decrease in demand causes the price to fall to P_2. Thus, marginal revenue falls for the firms, and they will produce less and make a loss (as $P < ATC$).

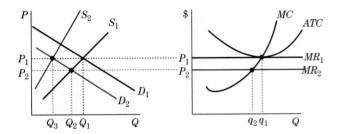

   b. Losses will induce firms to exit the industry, given enough time. Thus, industry supply will decrease, causing equilibrium price to rise and quantity to fall. This continues until the price rises to the original price, at which firms just break even, and there is no further incentive for exit. There will be fewer firms in the new long-run equilibrium, but each firm will produce the original quantity (q_1) and make zero economic profits.

Application Questions

2. a. The greater number of uses for cranberries increases the demand for the product, resulting in higher prices and greater profitability for cranberry producers.

   b. The factors creating a smaller crop of cranberries cause the supply curve to shift to the left, resulting in higher prices. We can infer from the statement that the demand for cranberries is probably inelastic, resulting in higher total revenue with the higher prices. Thus, profits decline by a smaller percent than the decrease in cranberry production.

   c. All of these health-related factors associated with consuming cranberries will increase the demand for the product, resulting in higher prices and profitability.

   d. Ocean Spray has been using the health benefits of cranberries to develop and promote a wider variety of cranberry drinks.

4. Overall, the statement is false. Information about a perfectly competitive firm's fixed costs is not needed to determine the profit-maximizing level of output. Profit maximization occurs at that level of output where marginal revenue equals marginal cost. In perfect competition, this is also the point where price equals marginal cost. Because marginal cost shows the change in total cost as output changes, it does not incorporate fixed costs. Fixed costs are relevant to determining the level of profit earned at that level of output. The relationship between price and average total cost determines whether profits are positive, zero, or negative. Because $ATC = AFC + AVC$, fixed costs are relevant for determining the level of profit.

Chapter 8

Technical Questions

2.

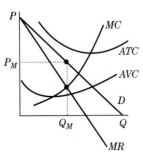

The ATC curve must be above the demand curve at all points.

4.

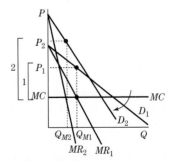

For simplicity, assume that marginal cost is constant. Persuasive advertising makes demand more inelastic (shifts from demand curve D_1 to D_2), and as elasticity decreases, the markup over marginal cost (and, thus, market power) is greater. However, advertising also increases fixed costs, and, thus, whether profit rises depends on the effectiveness of advertising relative to its cost.

6. a. The three-firm concentration ratio for Industry C is 75, whereas it is 95 for Industry D. In both industries, the four-firm concentration ratio is 100 because these firms account for the entire market.

   b. The HHI in Industry C is 2,500. The HHI for Industry D is 6,550.

   c. Although the four-firm concentration ratios are the same, the three-firm ratios and the HHI show that Industry D would be of more concern to antitrust authorities. The HHI is far higher due to the presence of one very large firm, which undoubtedly has more market power than any of the four equally sized firms in the other industry. Three firms control 95 percent of the market for Industry D and only 75 percent for Industry C.

8. Effective advertising may increase demand and make it more inelastic. But it also increases costs. Thus, advertising may lengthen the period during which the firm is able to make a positive profit, but with demand decreasing due to the entry of other firms and costs rising, in the long run, profits must be zero.

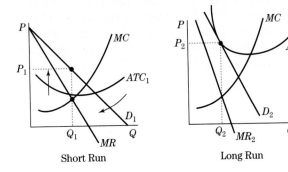

Short Run   Long Run

Chapter 9

Technical Questions

2. a. The dominant strategy for each firm is to price low (because no matter what the other firm does, you are better off pricing low).

   b. The Nash equilibrium is at (100, 100). At this point, neither firm has an incentive to change strategy, given what the other firm is doing.

   c. The firms would be collectively better off pricing high, but that is not an equilibrium. They are collectively worse off pricing low, and that is the only equilibrium of the game.

Application Questions

2. a. As the article notes, InBev hopes to gain from the economies of scale associated with the takeover. These are both giant companies that would gain more market power from the merger. They would be able to balance slow growth in mature markets with rapid growth in emerging markets. Both companies are interested in China, the world's largest beer market. The role of financial markets as a barrier to entry is also discussed. InBev has been able to raise financial capital due to its size and credit rating, even in financial markets that are still very unsettled.

   b. There may be different cultures between the two companies that would cause problems for a merger. InBev may not be able to wring as much savings out of Anheuser as it expects. There is already public resistance in the United States to the takeover of Anheuser by a foreign company. Members of the Busch family, who still run and hold stock in the company, appear to be opposed to the takeover.

4. Walgreen is pursuing new strategies, given the slowing growth in the traditional prescription market. It is expanding into the provision of health care with the Take Care clinics in its stores and plans to expand in worksites. It has also expanded into the specialty pharmacy sector that focuses on infusion drugs and drugs for infertility, cancer, and AIDS. Walgreen's rivals, Wal-Mart and CVS Caremark, have taken a different approach that emphasizes pharmacy benefit managers (PBMs). It is unclear at this time which approach will be more profitable in the ever-changing health care environment. Note the similarities and differences of these strategies with those of the independent pharmacies described under the model of monopolistic competition in the chapter.

4. a. There is no dominant strategy in this game because no single strategy is better in all cases.

   b. There is no Nash equilibrium in this game. In every case, one player would want to change strategy, knowing what the other player had chosen.

   c. All of the payoffs add up to zero (or to a constant sum). Whatever one player gains, the other loses, and, thus, there is no way for everyone to win.

6. a. If the entrant has already come in, the monopolist gets 20 if he prices high and 5 if he prices

low. It is not rational to price low once the entrant is in, and, thus, it is not a credible threat.

b. The Nash equilibrium is (20, 10), where the entrant comes in and the monopolist prices high.

c. The monopolist would have to make it more desirable to price low, even if the entrant comes in, perhaps by building a large plant or contracting to supply large amounts of output.

8. a. The total marginal cost curve is the horizontal sum of the two marginal costs.

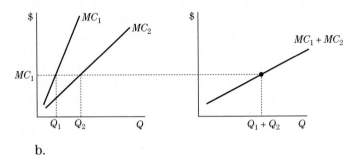

b.

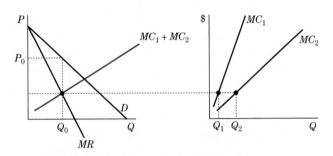

c. If each firm views the cartel price as fixed, then MR (for the firm) $> MC$, and each firm wishes to expand output. (Of course, if they do, the price must fall.)

Application Questions

2. Xerox and Kodak traditionally did not directly compete with each other, with Xerox focusing on office copying and Kodak on film for consumers. Both companies faced competitive threats, Xerox

from inkjet printers and Kodak from the development of digital cameras, which forced them into the same market, digital color printing. Both companies are located in Rochester, NY, which makes keeping secrets from each other difficult. Both companies also face competition from even bigger rivals, Hewlett-Packard and Canon. Xerox and Kodak are reacting to each other's strategies by developing a wide range of digital printers, but both companies face an uncertain future.

4. Procter & Gamble and Colgate are focusing on developing new products with different characteristics to sell more toothpaste to existing consumers and to appeal to new groups. Colgate gained the market advantage with its Total toothpaste, which promised to fight gum disease and whiten teeth. P&G's Crest responded with marketing that emphasized beauty and taste. The company used focus groups in a novel way to compare Whitening Expressions with regular Crest. P&G also researched the Hispanic and African American communities to determine what toothpaste characteristics would most appeal to these groups. Both companies focused on the variety of characteristics that influence consumer demand that we discussed in Chapter 3.

6. The proposed cartel is likely to fail because the natural gas producers have not been able to coordinate their behavior in the past. There are many sources of natural gas around the world, so alternative supplies would be available even if Russia and Iran formed a cartel. Because the United States obtains most of its gas from North America, it would be less vulnerable to this cartel's actions. The motivation for this cartel is similar to that of the potato farmers' cooperative in Chapter 7. Producers in both areas operate in an extremely competitive market with little control over price. Cooperative behavior is one way to try to overcome the volatility and uncertainty of a competitive market.

Chapter 10

Technical Questions

2. a. $m = -1/[1 + (-15)] = 1/14$ or 7%
   b. $m = -1/[1 + (-8)] = 1/7$ or 14%
   c. $m = -1/[1 + (-3)] = 1/2$ or 50%

4. a. $Q = 6 - P$ or $P = 6 - Q$, $MR = 6 - 2Q$,
   $MC = AC = 1$
   $MR = MC$
   $6 - 2Q = 1$
   $Q = 2.50$

$P = \$3.50$
$\pi = TR - TC = (\$3.50)(2.50) - (1)(2.50) = \$8.75 - 2.50 = \$6.25$

b. If $P = MC = AC = 1$, $Q = 5$ slices of pizza. The firm earns nothing on these slices because price equals AC. However, the firm can charge a fixed price for this option up to the maximum amount of the consumer surplus at $P = 1$. This is the area of the triangle under the demand curve and above $P = 1$. Consumer surplus is

$(0.5)(5)(6-1) = (0.5)(5)(5) = \$12.50$. If the firm charges a fixed price greater than \$6.25, but less than \$12.50, it will increase its profit with this two-part pricing strategy.

6. In the business market, the markup (over marginal cost) will be $-1/[1 + (-2)] = 100\%$. In the vacation market, the markup will be $-1/[1 + (-5)] = 25\%$. Thus, the ratio of weekday to weekend prices will be 100/25, or 4. Weekday prices will be four times higher than weekend prices.

8.

	Sports Package	Kids Package
Parents	10	50
Sports fans	50	10
Generalists	40	40

With the package option of any one package for \$50 or the combined bundled package for \$70, parents will buy the Kids package, sports fans will buy the Sports package, and generalists will buy both. (Note that generalists will not be willing to buy either package separately.) The level of profits depends, in general, on the number in each group and the value that each group places on each package, but this type of pricing exploits the value that certain consumers place on particular items and, at the same time, attracts more revenue by inducing others (the generalists) to buy the products, too.

Application Questions

2. Timken's strategy changed as a result of the recession in 2001 and the slow recovery thereafter, as well as of the increase in imports. More customers also began to demand the bundled products, so Timken responded in order to maintain their market position. The chapter discussion showed how bundling can increase a firm's revenues if it attracts customers who would not have purchased the individual components. Bundling is also successful if it reduces the dispersion in willingness to pay. The case presented additional factors, such as the change in production methods and the education of customers, necessary to make bundling a successful strategy. The case also showed that Timken engaged in political action as part of its competitive strategy.

4. Both of these cases are examples of versioning, developing specific products to meet the needs of different customers. In the Wildeck case, the "lite" version of the product attracted price-conscious customers who might have purchased from its competitor. However, many of these customers ended up purchasing the original product, helping Wildeck maintain its market share. The Union Pacific "blue streak" service focused on those customers who wanted faster service and were willing to pay for it. Union Pacific gained because the new service did not cost it much more than the regular service.

6. a. Tolls are popular from the viewpoint of road officials because demand appears to be price inelastic. There are typically few good substitutes for travel on interstate toll roads. As the toll increases, total revenue to the operating agency increases also.

   b. The impact of maintaining tolls on the New York State Thruway is that road-maintenance costs are borne by Thruway users rather than all taxpayers. This cross-subsidization policy can be controversial because users of the toll-free highway benefit, while Thruway users pay the cost.

   c. From the data given, the price elasticity of demand for use of the Pennsylvania Turnpike is $\%\Delta Q / \%\Delta P = -1\% / 43\% = -0.023$. This is very inelastic demand.

Chapter 11

Technical Questions

2. Of the three choices given, only the purchase of a new house is considered to be investment when calculating GDP. Investment refers to business purchases of tangible capital goods and software; all construction purchases, both residential and nonresidential; and changes in inventories in the national income accounts. The purchase of an automobile for private, nonbusiness use is treated as consumption spending. The purchase of corporate bonds represents the transfer of ownership of existing assets.

4. U.S. GDP measures the total market value of all final goods and services produced in the economy in one year. Imports are subtracted from exports when calculating GDP because they do not entail production in the United States.

6. Calculations are shown in the table on page 481. Nominal GDP and real GDP are the same (\$50) in the 2007 base year. Case 1 shows an increase in prices with no increase in quantities. Nominal GDP increase to \$95, while real GDP is constant at \$50. Case 2 shows an increase in quantities with no change in prices. Both real GDP and nominal GDP

TABLE 11.E1   Nominal Versus Real GDP

YEAR	COFFEE (CUPS)		MILK (GALLONS)		GDP
2007	Price	Quantity	Price	Quantity	
	$1.00	10	$2.00	20	
Expenditure	$10		$40		$50 (nominal)
					$50 (real)
2008 (Case 1)	Price	Quantity	Price	Quantity	
	$1.50	10	$4.00	20	
Expenditure	$15		$80		$95 (nominal)
					$50 (real)
2008 (Case 2)	Price	Quantity	Price	Quantity	
	$1.00	15	$2.00	40	
Expenditure	$15		$80		$95 (nominal)
					$95 (real)
2008 (Case 3)	Price	Quantity	Price	Quantity	
	$1.50	15	$4.00	40	
Expenditure	$22.50		$160		$182.50 (nominal)
					$95 (real)

increase to $95. Case 3 shows an increase in both prices and quantities. Both real GDP and nominal GDP increase, although the increase in nominal GDP is much greater.

Application Questions

2. The changes are shown in the following table:

Variable (billions $)	1960	1970	1980	1990	2000
Real GDP	$2,501.8	$3,771.9	$5,161.7	$7,112.5	$9,817.0
Consumption	$1,597.4	$2,451.9	$3,374.1	$4770.3	$6,739.4
	(63.9%)	(65.0%)	(65.5%)	(67.1%)	(68.7%)
Investment	$266.6	$427.1	$645.3	$895.1	$1,735.5
	(10.7%)	(11.3%)	(12.5%)	(12.6%)	(17.7%)
Government	$715.4	$1,012.9	$1,115.4	$1,530.0	$1,721.6
	(28.6%)	(26.9%)	(21.7%)	(21.5%)	(17.5%)
Exports	$90.6	$161.4	$323.5	$552.5	$1,096.3
	(3.6)	(4.3%)	(6.3%)	(7.8%)	(11.2%)
Imports	$103.3	$213.4	$310.9	$607.1	$1,475.8
	(4.1%)	(5.7%)	(6.0%)	(8.5%)	'(15.0%)

The percentage change in real GDP over each decade is

1960–1970	50.8%
1970–1980	36.8%
1980–1990	37.8%
1990–2000	38.0%

Consumption spending remained roughly constant at approximately two-thirds of GDP. Investment spending was more volatile. Although government spending decreased as a percent of GDP over the decade, remember that this spending does not include transfer payments. Export spending and import spending have become larger percentages of GDP over the period, signifying the increasing importance of the international economy to the United States. There was a trade surplus (export spending greater than import spending) only in 1980.

4. Advance estimates of GDP are fairly reliable. Studies have shown that initial estimates of real GDP successfully indicated the direction of change in GDP approximately 98 percent of the time; the direction of change in major GDP components about 88 percent of the time; whether GDP was accelerating or decelerating 75 percent of the time; and whether GDP growth was above, near, or below trend 80 percent of the time. The mean revision between the advance estimate and the latest estimate was only 0.4 percentage point over the 1983–2006 period. See J. Steven Landefeld, Eugene P. Seskin, and Barbara M. Fraumeni, "Taking the Pulse of the Economy: Measuring GDP," *Journal of Economic Perspectives* 22 (Spring 2008): 193–216; Dennis J. Fixler and Bruce T. Grimm, "The Reliability of the GDP and GDI Estimates," *Survey of Current Business* 88 (2008): 16–32.

6. The following table shows the labor force data: The percent of the population in the labor force has increased from 60 percent in 1969 to more

	Civilian Noninstitutional Population (thousands)	Civilian Labor Force (thousands) (% of population)	Number Employed (thousands)	Number Unemployed (thousands)	Unemployment Rate (%)
1969	134,355	80,734 (60.1)	77,902	2,832	3.5
1982	172,271	110,204 (64.0)	99,526	10,678	9.7
1992	192,805	128,105 (66.4)	118,492	9,613	7.5
2000	212,577	142,583 (67.1)	136,891	5,692	4.0
2003	221,168	146,510 (66.2)	137,736	8,774	6.0
2007	231,867	153,124 (66.0)	146,047	7,078	4.6

than 66 percent in 1992 and later years. The unemployment rate was very low during the booming periods of the late 1960s and the late 1990s. It increased substantially during the recessions of 1982 and 1991. The "jobless recovery" from the 2001 recession is evidenced by the relatively high unemployment rate in 2003. The 2007 figures had not yet shown the impact of the slowing economic activity in 2007 and 2008.

Chapter 12

Technical Questions

2. The currency exchange rate (R) is defined as the number of units of foreign currency per dollar. As R increases, U.S. imports become cheaper and exports become more expensive, so that import spending increases and export spending decreases. The opposite happens when R decreases. U.S. imports become more expensive and exports become cheaper, so that import spending decreases and export spending increases.

4. a. False. The multiplier measures the change in real income that results from a change in autonomous expenditure. The effect of an initial change in autonomous expenditure is multiplied because the expenditure becomes an additional round of income, of which households spend a certain amount, depending on the marginal propensity to consume. This expenditure generates subsequent declining rounds of income, of which households spend a fraction. The size of the multiplier depends on the marginal propensities to consume, invest, and import.

   b. False. An increase in government expenditure (G) represents an injection into the circular flow, or expansionary fiscal policy. This is an increase in autonomous expenditure that causes the aggregate expenditure function to shift up. An increase in taxes (T) represents a leakage out of the circular flow and causes a downward shift of the aggregate expenditure function.

   c. From the perspective of the national income accounts, real income always equals real expenditure, given the definition of the circular flow. We can measure economic activity either by the expenditure/output approach or by the income/earnings approach. This measurement identity does not mean that the economy is always in equilibrium. Equilibrium is achieved when the desired aggregate expenditure just equals the level of income and output produced and there are no unplanned inventory changes. If the economy is in disequilibrium and there are unplanned inventory changes, the accounting identity between income and expenditure still holds because inventory changes are counted as investment.

6. $C = 800 + 0.8(Y - T_P)$, $I = 200$, $G = T_P = 200$, $X = M = 0$
   a. $Y = C + I + G$
      $Y = 800 + 0.8(Y - 200) + 200 + 200$

8. The article should focus either on changes in taxes and government spending (fiscal policy) or on changes in the money supply in order to influence interest rates (monetary policy). The minutes and press releases issued following meetings of the Federal Open Market Committee contain a clear statement of the goals of price stability, full employment, and adequate economic growth and the Fed's assessment of future economic conditions.

$Y = 800 + 0.8Y - 160 + 400$

$Y = 1040 + 0.8Y$

$0.2Y = 1040$

$Y = 5{,}200$

b. $G = 300$

$Y = 1{,}140 + 0.8Y$

$0.2Y = 1{,}140$

$Y = 5{,}700$

Y increased by 500, while G increased by 100, so $m = 5$.

$m = 1/(1 - MPC) = 1/(1 - 0.8) = 1/(0.2) = 5$

c. $Y = 800 + 0.8(Y - 300) + 200 + 300$

$Y = 800 + 0.8Y - 240 + 500$

$Y = 1{,}060 + 0.8Y$

$0.2Y = 1{,}060$

$Y = 5{,}300$

Y increases by 100, so the equilibrium level of income increases even though $\Delta G = \Delta T_P$.

Application Questions

2. a. A greater sensitivity of interest-related consumption and investment expenditure to changes in the interest rate would make the IRE function flatter and result in a larger amount of interest-related expenditure for a given change in the interest rate. This would result in a larger change in equilibrium income.

b. A larger multiplier in the aggregate expenditure model would result in a higher level of equilibrium income for any given increase in interest-related expenditure.

4. As discussed in Chapter 11, a recession is the falling phase of a business cycle, in which the direction of a series of economic indicators turns downward. Real GDP typically falls for at least two quarters. The recession of 2001 caused a lack of consumer demand for many businesses, resulting in declining profits and employee layoffs. The fact that the dollar remained strong did not provide any relief for businesses producing in the United States and competing with foreign companies. The strong dollar decreased the price of U.S. imports and increased the price of exports. U.S. manufacturers had to look to other solutions, such as developing new methods to produce and sell their products, in order to counter the negative macroeconomic trends.

6. The news article describes the loss of jobs associated with the slowing economy early in 2008. Check the Web page of the Bureau of Labor Statistics (www.bls.gov) to find data and analysis of the current employment and unemployment situation.

Chapter 13

Technical Questions

2. A fractional reserve banking system is one in which banks are required to keep only a fraction of their deposits as reserves in the bank or on deposit with the Federal Reserve. This system allows them to use the excess reserves to make loans, which provide income to the bank. If these loans are redeposited in the banking system, the overall money supply is expanded. The size of the expansion relates to the size of the reserve requirement. The central bank, or Federal Reserve, influences the amount of reserves in the system, which changes the size of the money supply and prevailing interest rates.

4. The three tools are open market operations, the reserve requirement, and the discount rate. Open market operations, the most important tool, are the buying and selling of government securities, which influences the amount of reserves in the banking system and the federal funds rate that banks charge each other to borrow reserves. With expansionary monetary policy, the Federal Reserve buys securities, which increases the amount of reserves in the system and drives down the federal funds rates. Other short-term interest rates follow the federal funds rate. This stimulates interest-related consumption and investment expenditure and increases real income. Open market operations are the most flexible tool of monetary policy because they can be used on a daily basis. The Fed can also change the reserve requirement, regulating how much of their deposits banks must hold as reserves, and the discount rate, the rate the Fed charges banks to borrow reserves from the Fed. These are less-flexible tools that are not changed as frequently; they are used more for their announcement effects than as major tools of monetary policy.

6. a. True. If the real quantity of money demanded is greater than the real quantity of money supplied, individuals want to hold more of their assets in the form of money instead of bonds. They sell bonds to obtain money, which drives the price of bonds down and the interest rate up. As the interest rate rises, households want

to hold less money, and equilibrium in the money market is obtained at a higher interest rate. When the quantity of money demanded exceeds the quantity of money supplied, equilibrium is reached only at a higher interest rate.

b. False. The central bank, or the Federal Reserve, is the institution that controls the money supply and influences interest rates in the United States. The Federal Reserve is not part of the federal government (Congress and the administration). It was designed to be insulated from the political system in this country. The monetary policy of the Federal Reserve is used more than the fiscal policy of the federal government (taxes and expenditure) because it is a more flexible tool that can better deal with changing economic conditions.

c. False. A decrease in the reserve requirement increases the money supply because banks have more excess reserves to loan out. These excess reserves create further deposits, a fraction of which can also be loaned out. If the reserve requirement is 0.2, the simple deposit multiplier is $1/0.2 = 5$. If the reserve requirement decreases to 0.1, the simple deposit multiplier becomes $1/0.1 = 10$. This change results in a greater expansion of the money supply.

d. False. This statement is closer to a description of the interest-related expenditure and the aggregate expenditure functions in Chapter 12 that show the relationship between the interest rate and spending on real goods and services. The real money demand curve shows the quantity of money balances individuals wish to hold at different interest rates.

e. True/false. An increase in the nominal money supply by the Federal Reserve shifts the real money supply curve to the right. This change results in an increase in the real money supply. An increase in the price level causes a decrease in the real money supply, which shifts the real money supply curve to the left.

Application Questions

2. The statements that the FOMC makes after its meetings are becoming increasingly important indicators of future changes in monetary policy. Investors and forecasters analyze the wording of the statements to detect even subtle changes in policy. The "Parsing the Fed" feature for the April 30, 2008, FOMC press release noted that the change in the targeted federal funds rate from 2.25 to 2.00 percent was the seventh cut since September 2007, but it was "modest by recent standards." The statement said that the economy "remains weak" versus "has weakened further" in the March 2008 statement. The Fed now identified a business-spending slowdown in addition to weakening consumer spending and employment noted previously. The "substantial easing of monetary policy to date" language was new. Gone was the language regarding "downside risks to growth remain." This language signaled that the Fed might be ready to suspend its rate-cutting strategy. See "Spring Pause? Parsing the Fed," *Wall Street Journal*, April 30, 2008.

4. The minutes provide a detailed account of the factors influencing FOMC decisions.

Chapter 14

Technical Questions

2. a. An increase in personal taxes shifts the aggregate expenditure function down and the aggregate demand curve to the left.

b. An increase in expected profits and business confidence shifts the aggregate expenditure function up and the aggregate demand curve to the right.

c. A decrease in the level of foreign GDP or real income shifts the aggregate expenditure function down and the aggregate demand curve to the left.

d. A decrease in the nominal money supply by the Federal Reserve causes a decrease in the real money supply, which increases interest rates and lowers interest-related consumption and investment expenditure. This causes a downward shift in the aggregate expenditure function and a leftward shift of the aggregate demand curve.

4. a. False. The short-run aggregate supply curve slopes upward as real income and output approach the economy's potential output. This upward sloping short-run aggregate supply curve occurs because firms' input costs rise when they have to bid resources away from competing uses, as most inputs are becoming fully employed. As input costs rise, firms

charge higher prices for their products, and the absolute price level begins to increase. Firms will produce more real output only as the price level increases.

b. False. The long-run aggregate supply curve can also shift over time if there are increases in the amount of inputs (labor, land, capital, and raw materials) in the economy and increases in technology and efficiency.

c. True and false. A decrease in the nominal money supply by the Federal Reserve, all else held constant, does shift the aggregate demand (*AD*) curve to the left. This policy change causes the real money supply to decrease, resulting in a higher interest rate, which decreases interest-related expenditure and results in a lower equilibrium level of income at the same price level. An increase in the price level, all else held constant, results in an upward movement along a given *AD* curve. The increase in the price level decreases the real money supply, which results in a higher interest rate and a lower level of real income. This results in a movement along a given *AD* curve, as the nominal money supply is held constant and there is no change in Federal Reserve policy.

d. True. The Keynesian portion of the short-run aggregate supply (*SAS*) curve is the horizontal portion. The assumption is that real output can change from increases or decreases in spending (aggregate demand) without the price level changing. This would be most relevant in a recessionary situation, where there is significant unemployment and excess capacity. Increases in aggregate demand could result in increases in real output because there would be little tendency for wages and prices to rise in this case.

e. False. Stagflation occurs when there is an upward shift in the short-run aggregate supply (*SAS*) curve resulting from a supply shock, such as an increase in the price of oil. With a given aggregate demand (*AD*) curve, the resulting equilibrium is at a higher price level and a lower level of real output. The economy can both have inflation and be stagnating at a lower level of real output and employment.

6. With an upward sloping *SAS* curve, an increase in *AD* from expansionary fiscal policy results in both an increase in real income (*Y*) and an increase in the price level (*P*). There will be a smaller increase in real income than if the price level did not rise. This outcome occurs because the increase in the price level creates a smaller real money supply, which causes the interest rate to rise. This increase in the interest rate chokes off some interest-related spending, thereby increasing real income by a smaller amount.

Application Questions

2. Fiscal policy changes relate to decisions by the president and Congress on federal government spending and taxation. The president releases the proposed federal budget every January. Other fiscal policy changes may be proposed, such as the economic stimulus bill in February 2008. Monetary policy changes typically relate to ongoing decisions by the Federal Open Market Committee and are discussed regularly in all business publications.

4. Economists continue to debate the size and duration of the productivity increases from the investment in information technology (IT) that occurred in the late 1990s. The consensus appears to be that investments in information technology played a lesser role in productivity increases after 2000 than they did in the 1990s. It is always difficult to measure productivity changes due to problems in measuring changes in the quality of many goods and services. It can also be difficult to determine whether productivity changes are transitory or more permanent. See the research of Robert J. Gordon, Stephen Oliner and Daniel Sichel, Erik Brynjolfsson, Dale Jorgenson, and Kevin Stiroh.

Chapter 15

Technical Questions

2. a. False. A trade deficit occurs when import spending exceeds export spending. There is a government budget deficit when the government spends more than it receives in tax revenue. The two deficits often move together because government deficit spending stimulates the economy, which increases import spending.

b. False. The equality of planned saving and investment determines equilibrium in a closed (no foreign sector), private (no government sector) economy. This is a balance of leakages and injections in the economy. In an open, mixed economy, equilibrium occurs when $I + G + X = S + T + M$. In this chapter, we rewrote this condition as follows: $(X - M) = (S - I)$

$+ (T - G)$. This condition implies that the trade balance must equal the level of private and public saving in the country.

c. False. An increase in interest rates in the rest of the world leads to a weaker dollar. U.S. investors supply dollars to the foreign exchange market to purchase euros and yen in order to make financial investments in those countries with the higher interest rates. The increased supply of dollars drives down the value of the dollar in foreign exchange markets.

d. True. Under a fixed exchange rate policy with global capital flows, a country loses control of its money supply to maintain that exchange rate. To fight a devaluation of its currency, a country's central bank has to use its foreign exchange reserves to bolster the value of its currency. This typically results in a decreased domestic money supply and higher interest rates. Countries cannot usually make a credible commitment to this policy regardless of the consequences to the economy. Under a flexible exchange rate system, monetary policy is typically more effective than fiscal policy in increasing real GDP. Expansionary monetary policy increases real income, which increases import spending and lowers the exchange rate. This change has a further expansionary effect on real spending. Expansionary monetary policy also lowers domestic interest rates, which decreases the demand for domestic currency and lowers the exchange rate. While expansionary fiscal policy stimulates the economy and increases imports, which may lower the exchange rate, it also increases domestic interest rates, attracts financial capital, and increases the value of the currency. If this effect dominates (as it did in the late 1990s), the higher exchange rate will slow the growth in the economy.

4. If income in the United States grows faster than income in its major trading partners, U.S. imports will increase faster than exports. U.S. households and institutions will supply more dollars to the foreign exchange market to purchase those imports. The increase in the supply of dollars will drive the exchange rate down. If the economies of the trading partners begin to grow faster, that will increase the demand for U.S. exports, which will tend to drive up the demand for dollars and the currency exchange rate.

6. A change in the currency exchange rate (R) causes a movement along the demand curve for dollars. If R increases, imports become cheaper and exports more expensive. There is a smaller quantity of dollars demanded to purchase those exports, so the dollar demand curve slopes downward. The level of foreign income and the interest rate differential between the United States and the rest of the world cause the demand curve for dollars to shift. An increase in foreign income creates a greater demand for dollars at every exchange rate and shifts the demand curve to the right. If interest rates in the United States are higher than those in the rest of the world, there are higher capital inflows to the United States, creating an increased demand for dollars. The supply of dollars curve slopes upward. As the exchange rate increases, imports become cheaper. As import spending increases, the quantity of dollars supplied to the market increases, so there is a larger quantity supplied at a higher exchange rate. The supply of dollars curve shifts to the right if U.S. income increases. This increases import spending, so more dollars are supplied to the foreign exchange market at every exchange rate. If interest rates are higher in the rest of the world than in the United States, the supply of dollars in the foreign exchange market also increases as U.S. households and institutions purchase those foreign financial investments. This also shifts the supply of dollars curve to the right.

Application Questions

2. The direct foreign investment statistics on the Bureau of Economic Analysis Web page can be broken down by country and area of the world and by industry sector in the United States. Students should find data on how this investment differs by these categories.

4. The value of the euro and the macro policies of the European Union countries are discussed in the *Wall Street Journal* and other current business publications.

Chapter 16

Technical Questions

2. The oligopoly model best describes the relationship between McDonald's and KFC in China. The two companies have interdependent strategies in terms of restaurant openings, items included on the menu, and development of drive-throughs. McDonald's is trying to develop innovative strategies, given that KFC has the larger presence in China. Both companies have to decide how much to adapt their menus to local tastes.

4. Wal-Mart faced challenges in using the same strategies in Mexico as it did in the United States. When the company opened a supercenter in Monterrey in 1993, it was criticized for charging 15–20 percent more than the Wal-Mart in Laredo, Texas, two hours by car to the north. The company also lacked leverage with Mexican vendors that gave it an advantage in the United States. Distribution systems were different in Mexico, where thousands of suppliers shipped directly to stores rather than to retailer warehouses. Wal-Mart also faced ambivalent preferences for U.S. goods. The Mexican news media warned about shoddy foreign goods, and some consumers were moved by the spirit of Mexican nationalism to purchase domestically produced goods. Differences in Mexican lifestyles also meant that the model of a large store with thousands of products did not immediately transfer to Mexico.

6. McDonald's mini-restaurants cost 30 percent less to build in 1991, but could handle 96 percent of the volume of a full-sized restaurant. This is an example of a decision based on incremental costs and revenues. The lower costs of these smaller units also opened up market niches in small towns and other areas that could not support traditional restaurants.

Application Questions

2. McDonald's responded to the changing economic conditions in China that included increased incomes, urbanization, and use of automobiles. This led to the development of its strategy of emphasizing the drive-through as a major engine of growth. The company had to develop relationships with Chinese governmental authorities and had to consider how local customs and preferences affected its menu offerings. Wal-Mart faced similar challenges in Mexico, particularly in terms of lifestyle differences and the adaptation of its distribution strategies to the Mexican economy. Both companies faced competition from other multinational corporations and from local firms.

4. McDonald's has focused on changing tastes and preferences by developing more healthy alternatives on its menus. It developed Happy Meals and in-store playgrounds to appeal to children. The company has tried to improve the quality of its service by hiring mystery shoppers to evaluate service, cleanliness, and food quality. McDonald's has developed different menus and restaurant designs in various countries around the world.

Glossary

Absolute price level: A measure of the overall level of prices in the economy using various indices to measure the prices of all goods and services.

Accounting profit: The difference between total revenue and total cost where cost includes only the explicit costs of production.

Adjusted R^2 statistic: The coefficient of determination adjusted for the number of degrees of freedom in the estimating equation.

Advertising elasticity of demand: The percentage change in the quantity demanded of a good relative to the percentage change in advertising dollars spent on that good, all other factors held constant.

Aggregate demand–aggregate supply equilibrium: The equilibrium level of real income and output and the price level in the economy that occurs at the intersection of the aggregate demand and supply curves.

Aggregate demand curve: The curve that shows alternative combinations of the price level (P) and real income (Y) that result in simultaneous equilibrium in both the real goods and the money markets.

Aggregate expenditure: The sum of personal consumption, investment, government, and net export spending on the total amount of real output produced in an economy in a given period of time, which equals the income generated from producing and selling that output.

Aggregate expenditure function: The relationship between aggregate expenditure and income, holding all other variables constant.

Aggregate production function: The function that shows the quantity and quality of resources used in production, the efficiency with which resources are used, and the existing production technology for the entire economy.

Aggregate supply curve: The curve that shows the price level at which firms in the economy are willing to produce different levels of real goods and services and the resulting level of real income.

Antitrust laws: Legislation, beginning with the Sherman Act of 1890, that attempts to limit the market power of firms and to regulate how firms use their market power to compete with each other.

Arc price elasticity of demand: A measurement of the price elasticity of demand where the base quantity or price is calculated as the average value of the starting and ending quantities or prices.

Automatic stabilizers: Features of the U.S. federal government expenditure and taxation programs that tend to automatically slow the economy during times of high economic activity and boost the economy during periods of recession.

Autonomous consumption expenditures: Consumption expenditures that are determined by factors other than the level of real income in the economy.

Average fixed cost: The total fixed cost per unit of output.

Average product: The amount of output per unit of variable input.

Average revenue: Total revenue per unit of output. Average revenue equals the price of the product by definition.

Average revenue function: The functional relationship that shows the revenue per unit of output received by the producer at different levels of output.

Average total cost: The total cost per unit of output, which also equals average fixed cost plus average variable cost.

Average variable cost: The total variable cost per unit of output.

Balance of payments (BP) accounting system: A comprehensive measure of all economic activity between a country and the rest of the world.

Balance of payments issues: Issues related to the relative value of different countries' currencies and the flow of goods, services, and financial assets among countries.

Balance of trade: The relationship between a country's export and import spending, which can be positive if there is a trade surplus (exports exceed imports) or negative if there is a trade deficit (imports exceed exports).

Barriers to entry: Structural, legal, or regulatory characteristics of a firm and its market that keep other firms from easily producing the same or similar products at the same cost.

Barter system: A system in which goods and services are exchanged directly without a common unit of account.

Beige Book: A publication of the Federal Reserve System that includes information on current economic conditions gathered from the Federal Reserve banks' staff and interviews with business contacts, economists, market experts, and other sources.

Best practices: The production techniques adopted by the firms with the highest levels of productivity.

Budget surplus/deficit: The relationship between federal government revenue and expenditure with a surplus indicating revenue greater than expenditure and a deficit indicating revenue less than expenditure.

Bundling: Selling multiple products as a bundle where the price of the bundle is less than the sum of the prices of the individual products or where the bundle reduces the dispersion in willingness to pay.

Business cycles: The periodic increases and decreases in overall economic activity reflected in production, employment, profits, and prices.

Business fixed investment: Spending on the structures, equipment, and software that provide the industrial capacity to produce goods and services for all sectors of the economy.

Capacity utilization rates ($CURs$): The ratio of production to capacity calculated monthly for the manufacturing, mining, and electric and gas utilities industries and used as an indicator of business investment spending on structures and equipment.

Capital flows: The buying and selling of existing real and financial assets among countries.

Capital inflow (k_i): Borrowing from another country that occurs when the country has a trade deficit and its citizens sell real and financial assets to foreigners.

Capital-intensive method of production: A production process that uses large amounts of capital equipment relative to the other inputs to produce the firm's output.

Capital outflow (k_o): A lending of a country's savings that occurs when the country has a trade surplus and its citizens purchase real and financial assets from abroad.

Cartel: An organization of firms that agree to coordinate their behavior regarding pricing and output decisions in order to maximize profits for the organization.

Change in demand: The change in quantity purchased when one or more of the demand shifters change, pictured as a shift of the entire demand curve.

Change in quantity demanded: The change in quantity consumers purchase when the price of the good changes, all other factors held constant, pictured as a movement along a given demand curve.

Change in quantity supplied: The change in amount of a good supplied when the price of the good changes, all other factors held constant, pictured as a movement along a given supply curve.

Change in supply: The change in the amount of a good supplied when one or more of the supply shifters change, pictured as a shift of the entire supply curve.

Changes in business inventories: Changes in the amount of goods produced but not sold in a given year.

Circular flow model: The macroeconomic model that portrays the level of economic activity as a flow of expenditures from consumers to firms or producers, as consumers purchase goods and services produced by these firms. This flow then returns to consumers as income received from the production process.

Coefficient of determination (R^2): A measure of how the overall estimating equation fits the data, which shows the fraction of the variation in the dependent variable that is explained statistically by the variables included in the equation.

Coincident indicators: Economic variables, including employment, income, and business production statistics, that tend to move in tandem with the overall phases of the business cycle.

Compensation of employees: The wages and salaries and the fringe benefits paid by employers to employees.

Complementary goods: Two goods, X and Y, are complementary if an increase in the price of good Y causes consumers to *decrease* their demand for good X or if a decrease in the price of good Y causes consumers to *increase* their demand for good X.

Concentration ratios: A measure of market power that focuses on the share of the market held by the X largest firms, where X typically equals four, six, or eight.

Confidence interval: The range of values in which we can be confident that the true coefficient actually lies with a given degree of probability, usually 95 percent.

Conjoint analysis: An approach to analyzing consumer behavior that asks consumers to rank and choose among different product attributes, including price, to reveal their valuation of these characteristics.

Consumer Confidence Index (CCI): An index, based on a mail survey of 5,000 households conducted by the Conference Board, that measures households' perceptions of general business conditions, available jobs in the households' local area, and expected personal family income in the coming six months.

Consumer Price Index (CPI): A measure of the combined price consumers pay for a fixed market basket of goods and services in a given period relative to the combined price of an identical basket of goods and services in a base period.

Consumer Sentiment Index (CSI): An index, based on a telephone survey of 500 households conducted by the University of Michigan, that measures households' attitudes regarding expected business conditions, personal financial conditions, and consumer confidence about purchasing furniture and major household appliances.

Consumer surplus: The difference between the total amount of money consumers are willing to pay for a product rather than do without and the amount they actually have to pay when a single price is charged for all units of the product.

Consumption function: The fundamental relationship in macroeconomics that assumes that household consumption spending depends primarily on the level of disposable income (net of taxes) in the economy, all other variables held constant.

Contractionary monetary policy: Federal Reserve policy to decrease the rate of growth of real GDP by decreasing the amount of bank reserves in the system and raising the federal funds and other interest rates.

Cooperative oligopoly models: Models of interdependent oligopoly behavior that assume that firms explicitly or implicitly cooperate with each other to achieve outcomes that benefit all the firms.

Core rate of inflation: A measure of absolute price changes that excludes changes in energy and food prices.

Corporate profits: The excess of revenues over costs for the incorporated business sector of the economy.

Cost function: A mathematical or graphic expression that shows the relationship between the cost of production and the level of output, all other factors held constant.

Cross-price elasticity of demand: The percentage change in the quantity demanded of a given good, X, relative to the percentage change in the price of good Y, all other factors held constant.

Cross-sectional data: Data collected on a sample of individuals with different characteristics at a specific point in time.

Crowding out: The decrease in consumption and investment interest-related spending that occurs when the interest rate rises as government spending increases.

Currency appreciation: One currency can be exchanged for more units of another currency or the value of R increases.

Currency depreciation: One currency can be exchanged for fewer units of another currency or the value of R decreases.

Currency exchange rate: The rate at which one nation's currency can be exchanged for that of another, which is determined in foreign exchange markets.

Current account: A measure of the current flows of goods, services, investment income, and unilateral transfers between a country and the rest of the world.

Deflation: A sustained decrease in the price level over time.

Degrees of freedom: The number of observations (n) minus the number of estimated coefficients (k) in a regression equation.

Demand: The functional relationship between the price of a good or service and the quantity demanded by consumers in a given time period, *all else held constant.*

Demand curve: The graphical relationship between the price of a good and the quantity consumers demand, with all other factors influencing demand held constant.

Demand deposits: Another name for checking accounts or checkable deposits, one of the major components of the M1 measure of the money supply.

Demand elasticity: A quantitative measurement (coefficient) showing the percentage change in the quantity demanded of a particular product relative to the percentage change in any one of the variables included in the demand function for that product.

Demand shifters: The variables in a demand function that are held constant when defining a given demand curve, but that would shift the demand curve if their values changed.

Depository institutions: Institutions that accept deposits from individuals and organizations, against which depositors can write checks on demand for their market transactions and that use these deposits to make loans.

Direct consumer surveys: An approach to analyzing consumer behavior that relies on directly asking consumers questions about their response to prices, price changes, or price differentials.

Discount rate: The interest rate the Federal Reserve charges banks who borrow reserves at the Fed's discount window.

Discouraged workers: Persons 16 years of age and over who are not currently seeking work because they believe that jobs in their area or line of work are unavailable or that they would not qualify for existing job openings.

Discretionary expenditures: Federal government expenditures for programs whose funds are authorized and appropriated by Congress and signed by the president, where explicit decisions are made on the size of the programs.

Diseconomies of scale: Incurring higher unit costs of production by adopting a larger scale of production, represented by the upward sloping portion of a long-run average cost curve.

Disposable income: Personal household income after all taxes have been paid.

Dominant strategy: A strategy that results in the best outcome or highest payoff to a given player no matter what action or choice the other player makes.

Durable goods: Commodities that typically last three or more years, such as automobiles, furniture, and household appliances.

Earnings or income approach: Measuring overall economic activity by adding the earnings or income generated by selling the output produced in the economy.

Economic profit: The difference between total revenue and total cost where cost includes both the explicit and any implicit costs of production.

Economies of scale: Achieving lower unit costs of production by adopting a larger scale of production, represented by the downward sloping portion of a long-run average cost curve.

Elastic demand: The percentage change in quantity demanded by consumers is greater than the percentage change in price and $|e_p| > 1$.

Employed: Persons 16 years of age and over who, in the survey week, did any work as an employee; worked in their own business, profession, or farm; or worked without pay at least 15 hours in a family business or farm.

Equilibrium level of income and output: The level of income or, equivalently, the aggregate output where the desired spending by all sectors of the economy just equals the value of the aggregate output produced and the income received from that production.

Equilibrium point for the perfectly competitive firm: The point where price equals average total cost because the firm earns zero economic profit at this point. Economic profit incorporates all implicit costs of production, including a normal rate of return on the firm's investment.

Equilibrium price: The price that actually exists in the market or toward which the market is moving where the quantity demanded by consumers equals the quantity supplied by producers.

Equilibrium quantity (Q_E): The quantity of a good, determined by the equilibrium price, where the amount of output that consumers demand is equal to the amount that producers want to supply.

Expansion: The rising phase of a business cycle, in which the direction of a series of economic indicators turns upward.

Expansionary monetary policy: Federal Reserve policy to increase the rate of growth of real GDP by increasing the amount of bank reserves in the system and lowering the federal funds and other interest rates.

Expenditure or output approach: Measuring overall economic activity by adding the expenditure on the output produced in the economy.

Expert opinion: An approach to analyzing consumer behavior that relies on developing a consensus of opinion among sales personnel, dealers, distributors, marketing consultants, and trade association members.

Explicit cost: A cost that is reflected in a payment to another individual, such as a wage paid to a worker, that is recorded in a firm's bookkeeping or accounting system.

Export spending (X): The total amount of spending on goods and services currently produced in one country and sold abroad to residents of other countries in a given period of time.

Federal Deposit Insurance Corporation (FDIC): The government regulatory institution that supervises the activities of depository institutions in the United States and provides depositors with accounts up to a certain amount (currently $250,000) with a guarantee that they will receive their funds even in the event of a bank failure.

Federal funds market: The private financial market where banks borrow and loan reserves to meet the minimum reserve requirements.

Federal funds rate: The interest rate that commercial banks charge each other for loans of reserves to meet their minimum reserve requirements.

Federal Open Market Committee (FOMC): The Federal Reserve body that has the primary responsibility for conducting monetary policy.

Federal Reserve System (Fed): The central bank in the United States that implements monetary policy and helps regulate and operate the country's financial system.

Final goods and services: Goods and services that are sold to their end-users.

Financial account: A measure of the change in the stock of real assets (buildings, property, etc.) and financial assets (bank deposits, securities, etc.) held by a country's residents in foreign countries and by foreigners in the given country.

First-degree price discrimination: A pricing strategy under which firms with market power are able to charge individuals the maximum amount they are willing to pay for each unit of the product.

Fiscal policy: Changes in taxes and spending by the executive and legislative branches of a country's national government that can be used to either stimulate or restrain the economy.

Fixed exchange rate system: A system in which the central banks of various countries intervene in the foreign exchange market to maintain or stabilize currency exchange rates.

Fixed input: An input whose quantity a manager cannot change during a given period of time.

Flexible exchange rate system: A system in which currency exchange rates are determined strictly by the forces of demand for and supply of the currencies and there is no intervention by any country's central bank in order to influence the level of exchange rates.

Fractional reserve system: A banking system in which banks are required to keep only a fraction of their deposits as reserves.

F-statistic: An alternative measure of goodness of fit of an estimating equation that can be used to test for the joint influence of all the independent variables in the equation.

Functional relationship: A relationship between variables, usually expressed in an equation using symbols for the variables, where the value of one variable, the independent variable, determines the value of the other, the dependent variable.

Game theory: A set of mathematical tools for analyzing situations in which players make various strategic moves and have different outcomes or payoffs associated with those moves.

GDP deflator: A measure of price changes in the economy that compares the price of each year's output of goods and services to the price of that same output in a base year.

Gold standard: A fixed rate system in which central banks agree to buy and sell gold to keep exchange rates at a given level.

Government consumption expenditures and gross investment (G): The total amount of spending by federal, state, and local governments on consumption outlays for goods and services, depreciation charges for existing structures and equipment, and investment capital outlays for newly acquired structures and equipment in a given period of time.

Gross domestic product (GDP): The comprehensive measure of the total market value of all currently produced final goods and services within a country in a given period of time by domestic and foreign-supplied resources.

Gross private domestic investment spending (I): The total amount of spending on nonresidential structures, equipment, software, residential structures, and business inventories in a given period of time.

Group pricing: Another name for third-degree price discrimination, in which different prices are charged to different groups of customers based on their underlying price elasticity of demand.

Herfindahl-Hirschman Index (HHI): A measure of market power that is defined as the sum of the squares of the market share of each firm in an industry.

Historical cost: The amount of money a firm paid for an input when it was purchased, which for machines and capital equipment could have occurred many years in the past.

Horizontal summation of individual demand curves: The process of deriving a market demand curve by adding the quantity demanded by each individual at every price to determine the market demand at every price.

Horizontal summation of marginal cost curves: For every level of marginal cost, add the amount of output produced by each firm to determine the overall level of output produced at each level of marginal cost.

Imperfect competition: Market structures of monopolistic competition, oligopoly, and monopoly, in which firms have some degree of market power.

Implicit cost: A cost that represents the value of using a resource that is not explicitly paid out and is often difficult to measure because it is typically not recorded in a firm's accounting system.

Import spending (M): The total amount of spending on goods and services currently produced in other countries and sold to residents of a given country in a given period of time.

Imputed value: An estimated value for nonmarket transactions, such as the rental value of owner-occupied housing, included in GDP.

Income elasticity of demand: The percentage change in the quantity demanded of a given good, X, relative to a percentage change in consumer income, assuming all other factors constant.

Increasing marginal returns: The results in that region of the marginal product curve where the curve is positive and increasing, so that total product increases at an increasing rate.

Individual demand function: The function that shows, in symbolic or mathematical terms, the variables that influence the quantity demanded of a particular product by an individual consumer.

Individual supply function: The function that shows, in symbolic or mathematical terms, the variables that influence the quantity supplied of a particular product by an individual producer.

Induced consumption expenditures: Consumption expenditures that result from changes in the level of real income in the economy.

Industry concentration: A measure of how many firms produce the total output of an industry. The more concentrated the industry, the fewer the firms operating in that industry.

Inelastic demand: The percentage change in quantity demanded by consumers is less than the percentage change in price and $|e_P| < 1$.

Inferior good: A good for which consumers will have a smaller demand as their incomes increase, all else held constant, and a greater demand if their incomes decrease, other factors held constant.

Inflation: A sustained increase in the price level over time.

Injections: Any supplement to consumer spending that increases domestic aggregate output and income.

Input substitution: The degree to which a firm can substitute one input for another in a production process.

Inputs: The factors of production, such as land, labor, capital, raw materials, and entrepreneurship, that are used to produce the outputs, or final goods and services, that are bought and sold in a market economy.

Interest-related expenditure (IRE) function: The function that shows the inverse relationship between planned consumption and investment spending and the real interest rate, all else held constant.

Intermediate goods and services: Goods and services that are used in the production of other goods and services.

International Monetary Fund (IMF): An international financial organization created at the Bretton Woods conference in 1944 that helps coordinate international financial flows and can arrange short-term loans between countries.

Investment spending function: The functional relationship between investment spending and income, holding all other variables that influence investment spending constant.

Joint profit maximization: A strategy that maximizes profits for a cartel, but that may create incentives for individual members to cheat.

Keynesian model: A model of the aggregate economy, based on ideas developed by John Maynard Keynes, with a horizontal short-run aggregate supply curve in which all changes in aggregate demand result in changes in real output and income.

Kinked demand curve model: An oligopoly model based on two demand curves that assumes that other firms will not match a firm's price increases, but will match its price decreases.

Labor force: Those individuals 16 years of age and over who are working in a job or actively seeking employment.

Labor-intensive method of production: A production process that uses large amounts of labor relative to the other inputs to produce the firm's output.

Lagging indicators: Economic variables, including measures of inflation and unemployment, labor costs, and consumer and business debt and credit levels, that turn down after the beginning of a recession and turn up after a recovery has begun.

Law of diminishing marginal returns or law of the diminishing marginal product: The phenomenon illustrated by that region of the marginal product curve where the curve is positive, but decreasing, so that total product is increasing at a decreasing rate.

Leading indicators: Economic variables, such as manufacturing, employment, monetary, and consumer expectation statistics, that generally turn down before a recession begins and turn back up before a recovery starts.

Leakages: Any uses of current income for purposes other than purchasing currently produced domestic goods and services.

Lean production: An approach to production pioneered by Toyota Motor Corporation, in which firms streamline the production process through strategies such as strict scheduling and small-batch production with low-cost flexible machines.

Learning by doing: The drop in unit costs as total cumulative production increases because workers become more efficient as they repeat their assigned tasks.

Lerner Index: A measure of market power that focuses on the difference between a firm's product price and its marginal cost of production.

Limit pricing: A policy of charging a price lower than the profit-maximizing price to keep other firms from entering the market.

Linear demand function: A mathematical demand function graphed as a straight-line demand curve in which all the terms are either added or subtracted and no terms have exponents other than 1.

Linear supply function: A mathematical supply function, which graphs as a straight-line supply curve, in which all terms are either added or subtracted and no terms have exponents other than 1.

Liquidity: The ability of a financial asset to be used to immediately make market transactions.

Lock-in and switching costs: A form of market power for a firm in which consumers become locked into purchasing certain types or brands of products because they would incur substantial costs if they switched to other products.

Long-run aggregate supply curve: A vertical aggregate supply curve that defines the level of full employment or potential output based on a given amount of resources, efficiency, and technology in the economy.

Long-run average cost (*LRAC*): The minimum average or unit cost of producing any level of output *when all inputs are variable*.

Long-run production function: A production function showing the relationship between a flow of inputs and the resulting flow of output, where all inputs are variable.

Luxury: A good with an income elasticity greater than 1, where the expenditure on the good increases more than proportionately with changes in income.

Macroeconomics: The branch of economics that focuses on the overall level of economic activity, changes in the price level, and the amount of unemployment by analyzing group or aggregate behavior in different sectors of the economy.

Managed float: A fixed rate system in which central banks buy and sell foreign currency to maintain exchange rates at a given level.

Managerial economics: Microeconomics applied to business decision making.

Marginal benefit: The valuation that a consumer places on each additional unit of a product, which is measured by the price of that product.

Marginal cost: The additional cost of producing an additional unit of output, which equals the change in total cost or the change in total variable cost as output changes.

Marginal product: The additional output produced with an additional unit of variable input.

Marginal propensity to consume (*MPC*): The additional consumption spending generated by an additional amount of real income, assumed to take a value less than 1.

Marginal propensity to save (*MPS*): The additional household saving generated by an additional amount of real income, which equals $1 - MPC$.

Marginal revenue: The additional revenue that a firm takes in from selling an additional unit of output or the change in total revenue divided by the change in output.

Marginal revenue function: The functional relationship that shows the additional revenue a producer receives by selling an additional unit of output at different levels of output.

Marginal revenue for the perfectly competitive firm: The marginal revenue curve for the perfectly competitive firm is horizontal because the firm can sell all units of output at the market price, given the assumption of a perfectly elastic demand curve. Price equals marginal revenue for the perfectly competitive firm.

Market demand function: The function that shows, in symbolic or mathematical terms, the variables that influence the quantity demanded of a particular product by all consumers in the market and that is thus affected by the number of consumers in the market.

Market power: The ability of a firm to influence the prices of its products and develop other competitive strategies that enable it to earn large profits over longer periods of time.

Markets: The institutions and mechanisms used for the buying and selling of goods and services. The four major types of markets in microeconomic analysis are perfect competition, monopolistic competition, oligopoly, and monopoly.

Market supply function: The function that shows, in symbolic or mathematical terms, the variables that influence the quantity supplied of a particular product by all producers in the market and that is thus affected by the number of producers in the market.

Markup pricing: Calculating the price of a product by determining the average cost of producing the product and then setting the price a given percentage above that cost.

Microeconomics: The branch of economics that analyzes the decisions that individual consumers, firms, and industries make as they produce, buy, and sell goods and services.

Minimum efficient scale (*MES*): That scale of operation at which the long-run average cost curve stops declining or at which economies of scale are exhausted.

Mixed economy: An economy that has both a private (household and firm) sector and a public (government) sector.

Monetary base: Currency plus reserves (both required and excess), a variable controlled by central bank policy.

Monetary policies: Policies adopted by a country's central bank that influence the money supply, interest rates, and the amount of funds available for loans, which, in turn, influence consumer and business spending.

Money: The stock of financial assets that can easily be used to make market transactions and that serves as a medium of exchange, a unit of account, and a store of value.

Money multiplier: The money multiplier, mm—which is usually smaller than the simple deposit multiplier, d—reflects individuals' decisions to hold some of their assets in cash rather than deposit them in a checking account and banks' decisions to hold excess reserves.

Money supply: Currency plus checkable accounts or demand deposits (M1).

Monopolistic competition: A market structure characterized by a large number of small firms that have some market power as a result of producing differentiated products. This market power can be competed away over time.

Monopoly: A market structure characterized by a single firm producing a product with no close substitutes.

Multiple regression analysis: A statistical technique used to estimate the relationship between a dependent variable and an independent variable, *holding constant the effects of all other independent variables*.

Multiplier: The multiple change in income and output that results from a change in autonomous expenditure.

Nash equilibrium: A set of strategies from which all players are choosing their best strategy, given the actions of the other players.

National income: Income that is generated from the sale of the goods and services that are produced in the economy and that is paid to the individuals and businesses who supply the inputs or factors of production.

National income accounting system: A system of accounts developed for each country, based on the circular flow, whose purpose is to measure the level of economic activity in that country.

National Income and Product Accounts: The U.S. national income accounting system, operated by the Bureau of Economic Analysis (BEA) in the U.S. Department of Commerce.

Natural rate of unemployment: The minimum level of unemployment that can be achieved with current institutions without causing inflation to accelerate.

Necessity: A good with an income elasticity between 0 and 1, where the expenditure on the good increases less than proportionately with changes in income.

Negative (inverse) relationship: A relationship between two variables, graphed as a downward sloping line, where an increase in the value of one variable causes a decrease in the value of the other variable.

Negative marginal returns: The results in that region of the marginal product curve where the curve is negative and decreasing, so that total product is decreasing.

Net capital flow ($K_N = k_i - k_o$): The difference between capital inflows and outflows, which must match the trade balance, or export spending minus import spending.

Net export expenditure: The difference between export spending on domestically produced goods and services by individuals in other countries and import spending on foreign-produced goods and services by domestic residents in a given period of time.

Net export spending (F): The total amount of spending on exports (X) minus the total amount of spending on imports (M) or ($F = X - M$) in a given period of time.

Net interest: The interest private businesses pay to households for lending money to the firms minus the interest businesses receive plus interest earned from foreigners.

Net investment income: The difference between the interest income or receipts earned on investments in the rest of the world by the residents of a given country and the payments to foreigners on investments they have made in the given country.

Network externalities: A barrier to entry that exists because the value of a product to consumers depends on the number of consumers using the product.

Nominal exchange rate: The value at which one currency can be exchanged for another, or R.

Nominal GDP: The value of currently produced final goods and services measured in current year prices.

Nominal interest rate: The real interest rate plus the expected rate of inflation, which may differ substantially from the real interest rate during periods of inflation.

Nominal money supply (M_S): The money supply (M1), controlled by the Federal Reserve, which is defined in dollar terms.

Nominal terms: Measuring expenditures and income with the price level allowed to vary, so that changes in these values represent changes in the actual amount of goods, services, and income; changes in the price level; or a combination of both factors.

Noncooperative oligopoly models: Models of interdependent oligopoly behavior that assume that firms pursue profit-maximizing strategies based on assumptions about rivals' behavior and the impact of this behavior on the given firm's strategies.

Nondiscretionary expenditures: Federal government expenditures, for programs such as unemployment compensation, that increase or decrease simply as a result of the number of individuals eligible for the spending programs.

Nondurable goods: Commodities that last less than three years and may be consumed very quickly, such as food, clothing, and gasoline.

Normal good: A good for which consumers will have a greater demand as their incomes increase, all else held constant, and a smaller demand if their incomes decrease, other factors held constant.

Oligopoly: A market structure characterized by competition among a small number of large firms that have market power, but that must take their rivals' actions into account when developing their own competitive strategies.

Open economy: An economy that has both domestic and foreign sectors.

Open market operations: The major tool of Fed monetary policy that involves the buying and selling of government securities on the open market in order to change the money supply and influence interest rates.

Opportunity cost: The economic measure of cost that reflects the use of resources in one activity, such as a production process by one firm, in terms of the opportunities forgone in undertaking the next best alternative activity.

Outputs: The final goods and services produced and sold by firms in a market economy.

Panel data: Cross-sectional data observed at several points in time.

Perfect competition: A market structure characterized by a large number of firms in an industry, an undifferentiated product, ease of entry into the market, and complete information available to participants.

Perfectly inelastic demand: Zero elasticity of demand, illustrated by a vertical demand curve, where there is no change in quantity demanded for any change in price.

Perfectly (or infinitely) elastic demand: Infinite elasticity of demand, illustrated by a horizontal demand curve, where the quantity demanded would vary tremendously if there were any changes in price.

Personal consumption expenditures (C): The total amount of spending by households on durable goods, nondurable goods, and services in a given period of time.

Personal income: Income received by households that forms the basis for personal consumption expenditures.

Personalized pricing: Another name for first-degree price discrimination, in which the strategy is to determine how much each individual customer is willing to pay for the product and to charge him or her accordingly.

Point price elasticity of demand: A measurement of the price elasticity of demand calculated at a point on the demand curve using infinitesimal changes in prices and quantities.

Positive (direct) relationship: A relationship between two variables, graphed as an upward sloping line, where an increase in the value of one variable causes an increase in the value of the other variable.

Potential GDP: The maximum amount of GDP that can be produced at any point in time, which depends on the size of the labor force, the number of structures and the amount of equipment in the economy, and the state of technology.

Predatory pricing: A strategy of lowering prices below cost to drive firms out of the industry and scare off potential entrants.

Price-cost margin (PCM): The relationship between price and costs for an industry, calculated by subtracting the total payroll and the cost of materials from the value of shipments and then dividing the results by the value of the shipments. The approach ignores taxes, corporate overhead, advertising and marketing, research, and interest expenses.

Price discrimination: The practice of charging different prices to various groups of customers that are not based on differences in the costs of production.

Price elasticity of demand (e_P): The percentage change in the quantity demanded of a given good, X, relative to a percentage change in its own price, all other factors assumed constant.

Price experiments: An approach to analyzing consumer behavior in which consumer reaction to different prices is analyzed in a laboratory situation or a test market environment.

Price leadership: An oligopoly strategy in which one firm in the industry institutes price increases and waits to see if they are followed by rival firms.

Prices: The amounts of money that are charged for goods and services in a market economy. Prices act as signals that influence the behavior of both consumers and producers of these goods and services.

Price-setter: A firm in imperfect competition that faces a downward sloping demand curve and must set the profit-maximizing price to charge for its product.

Price-taker: A characteristic of a perfectly competitive market in which the firm cannot influence the price of its product, but can sell any amount of its output at the price established by the market.

Prime rate: The interest rate that banks charge on loans to their best customers.

Producer Price Index (PPI): A measure of the prices firms pay for crude materials; intermediate materials, supplies, and components; and finished goods.

Production function: The relationship between a flow of inputs and the resulting flow of outputs in a production process during a given period of time.

Profit: The difference between the total revenue a firm receives from the sale of its output and the total cost of producing that output.

Profit maximization: The assumed goal of firms, which is to develop strategies to earn the largest amount of profit possible. This can be accomplished by focusing on revenues, costs, or both.

Profit-maximizing rule: To maximize profits, a firm should produce the level of output where marginal revenue equals marginal cost.

Progressive tax system: An income tax system where higher tax rates are applied to increased amounts of income.

Promotional pricing: Using coupons and sales to lower the price of the product for those customers willing to incur the costs of using these devices as opposed to lowering the price of the product for all customers.

Proprietors' income: The income of unincorporated businesses, such as medical practices, law firms, small farms, and retail stores.

Real exchange rate: The nominal exchange rate times the ratio of the domestic price level to the foreign price level.

Real GDP: The value of currently produced final goods and services measured in constant prices, or nominal GDP adjusted for price level changes.

Real interest rate: The nominal interest rate adjusted for expected inflation, which is the rate that influences firms' investment decisions.

Real money demand: The demand for money in real terms, which is a function of the real interest rate and the level of real income.

Real money supply (M_S/P): The nominal money supply divided by the price level, which expresses the money supply in terms of real goods and services and which influences behavior.

Real terms: Measuring expenditures and income with the price level held constant, so that any changes in these values represent changes in the actual amount of goods, services, and income.

Recession: The falling phase of a business cycle, in which the direction of a series of economic indicators turns downward.

Relative prices: The price of one good in relation to the price of another, similar good, which is the way prices are defined in microeconomics.

Rental income: The income households receive from the rental of their property.

Reserve assets: Assets, including foreign currencies and gold certificates, that central banks use to maintain exchange rates between countries at a given level or in a predetermined range.

Reserve requirement: Required reserves kept in banks' vaults or as deposits at the Federal Reserve divided by demand deposits or the fraction of deposits banks are required to keep as reserves.

Residential fixed investment: Spending on newly constructed housing units, major alterations of and replacements to existing structures, and brokers' commissions.

Revenue or T-account: An accounting statement that shows expense-generating items on the left-hand or debit side and income-generating items on the right-hand or credit side.

Saving (S): The amount of disposable income that households do *not* spend on the consumption of goods and services.

Second-degree price discrimination: A pricing strategy under which firms with market power charge different prices for different blocks of output.

Services: Noncommodity items, such as utilities, public transportation, private education, medical care, and recreation.

Short-run aggregate supply curve: An aggregate supply curve that is either horizontal or upward sloping, depending on whether the absolute price level increases as firms produce more output.

Short-run average total cost ($SATC$): The cost per unit of output for a firm of a given size or scale of operation.

Short-run cost function: A cost function for a short-run production process in which there is at least one fixed input of production.

Short-run production function: A production process that uses at least one fixed input.

Shutdown point for the perfectly competitive firm: The price, which equals a firm's minimum average variable cost, below which it is more profitable for the perfectly competitive firm to shut down than to continue to produce.

Simple deposit multiplier: The amount by which the money supply can be increased in a fractional reserve banking system, which equals $(1/rr)$, where rr is the reserve requirement.

Simple regression analysis: A form of regression analysis that analyzes the relationship between one dependent and one independent variable.

Stagflation: Higher prices and price increases (inflation) combined with lower real output and income (stagnation), resulting from a major increase in input prices in the economy.

Standard error: A measure of the precision of an estimated regression analysis coefficient that shows how much the coefficient would vary in regressions from different samples.

Statistical discrepancy (SD): The imbalance between the capital and current accounts in the balance of payments statement or between payments and receipts in the revenue or T-account that arises from inefficient data collection.

Sterilized intervention: Actions taken by a country's central bank to prevent balance of payments policies from influencing the country's domestic money supply.

Strategic entry deterrence: Strategic policies pursued by a firm that prevent other firms from entering the market.

Substitute goods: Two goods, X and Y, are substitutes if an increase in the price of good Y causes consumers to *increase* their demand for good X or if a decrease in the price of good Y causes consumers to *decrease* their demand for good X.

Supply: The functional relationship between the price of a good or service and the quantity supplied by producers in a given time period, *all else held constant.*

Supply curve: The graphical relationship between the price of a good and the quantity supplied, with all other factors influencing supply held constant.

Supply curve for the perfectly competitive firm: The portion of a firm's marginal cost curve that lies above the minimum average variable cost.

Supply curve for the perfectly competitive industry: The curve that shows the output produced by all perfectly competitive firms in the industry at different prices.

Supply shifters: The other variables in a supply function that are held constant when defining a given supply curve, but that would cause that supply curve to shift if their values changed.

Tacit collusion: Coordinated behavior among oligopoly firms that is achieved without a formal agreement.

Targeted marketing: Selling that centers on defining different market segments or groups of buyers for particular products based on the demographic, psychological, and behavioral characteristics of the individuals.

Technical factors: Other influences on the commercial banking system's reserves that are unrelated to Fed monetary policy.

Test marketing: An approach to analyzing consumer behavior that involves analyzing consumer response to products in real or simulated markets.

Third-degree price discrimination: A pricing strategy under which firms with market power separate markets according to the price elasticity of demand and charge a higher price (relative to cost) in the market with the more inelastic demand.

Time-series data: Data collected on the same observational unit at a number of points in time.

Total benefit: The total amount of money consumers are willing to pay for a product rather than go without the product.

Total cost: The sum of the total fixed cost plus the total variable cost.

Total fixed cost: The total cost of using the fixed input, which remains constant regardless of the amount of output produced.

Total product: The total quantity of output produced with given quantities of fixed and variable inputs.

Total revenue: The amount of money received by a producer for the sale of its product, calculated as the price per unit times the quantity sold.

Total revenue function: The functional relationship that shows the total revenue (price times quantity) received by a producer as a function of the level of output.

Total variable cost: The total cost of using the variable input, which increases as more output is produced.

Trade balance: The relationship between a country's exports and imports, which may be either positive (exports exceed imports) or negative (imports exceed exports).

Trade deficit: Occurs when a country's import spending exceeds the spending on its exports.

Trade surplus: Occurs when a country's export spending exceeds the spending on its imports.

Trade-weighted dollar: An index of the weighted exchange value of the U.S. dollar versus the currencies of a broad group of major U.S. trading partners.

Transfer payments: Payments that represent the transfer of income among individuals in the economy, but do not reflect the production of new goods and services.

t-test: A test based on the size of the ratio of the estimated regression coefficient to its standard error that is used to determine the statistical significance of the coefficient.

Two-part pricing: Charging consumers a fixed fee for the right to purchase a product and then a variable fee that is a function of the number of units purchased.

Underground economy: Economic transactions that cannot be easily measured because they are not reported on income tax returns or other government economic surveys.

Unemployed: Persons 16 years of age and over who do not currently have a job, but who are actively seeking employment.

Unilateral transfers: Flows of goods, services, and financial assets, such as foreign aid, from one country to another in which nothing of significant economic value is received in return.

Unitary elasticity (or unit elastic): The percentage change in quantity demanded is exactly equal to the percentage change in price and $|e_P| = 1$.

Unplanned inventory decrease: An unexpected decrease in inventories that occurs when desired aggregate expenditure exceeds the level of output currently produced.

Unplanned inventory increase: An unexpected increase in inventories that occurs when desired aggregate expenditure is insufficient to purchase the level of output currently produced.

Value-added approach: A process of calculating the value of the final output in an economy by summing the value added in each stage of production (i.e., raw materials to semifinished goods to final products).

Variable input: An input whose quantity a manager can change during a given period of time.

Versioning: Offering different versions of a product to different groups of customers at various prices, with the versions designed to meet the needs of the specific groups.

World Bank: An international financial organization created at the Bretton Woods conference in 1944 that helps developing countries obtain low-interest loans.

X-inefficiency: Inefficiency that may result in firms with market power that have fewer incentives to minimize the costs of production than more competitive firms.

Index